The
SERVICE
QUALITY
Handbook

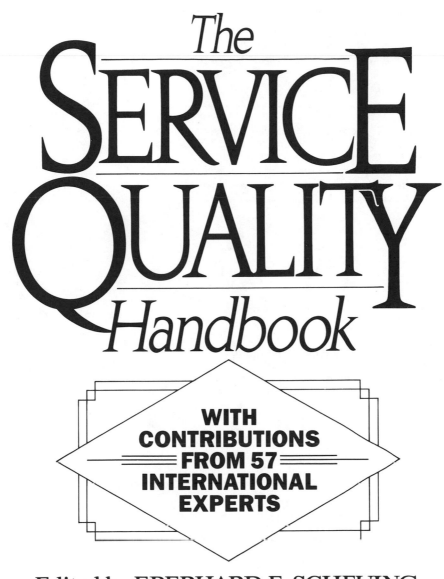

**WITH
CONTRIBUTIONS
FROM 57
INTERNATIONAL
EXPERTS**

Edited by EBERHARD E. SCHEUING
and WILLIAM F. CHRISTOPHER

American Management Association

New York • Atlanta • Boston • Chicago • Kansas City • San Francisco • Washington, D.C.
Brussels • Mexico City • Tokyo • Toronto

This book is available at a special
discount when ordered in bulk quantities.
For information, contact Special Sales Department,
AMACOM, a division of American Management Association,
135 West 50th Street, New York, NY 10020.

This publication is designed to provide accurate and authoritative
information in regard to the subject matter covered. It is sold with the
understanding that the publisher is not engaged in rendering legal,
accounting, or other professional service. If legal advice or other expert
assistance is required, the services of a competent professional person
should be sought.

Library of Congress Cataloging-in-Publication Data

The Service quality handbook / Eberhard E. Scheuing and William F.
    Christopher, editors ; with contributions from 57 international
    experts.
            p.   cm.
        Includes bibliographical references and index.
        ISBN (invalid) 0-8144-0119-6
        1. Customer service—Quality control—Handbooks, manuals, etc.
    2. Total quality management—Handbooks, manuals, etc.   I. Scheuing,
    Eberhard E. (Eberhard Eugen), 1939–   .   II. Christopher, William F.
    III. American Management Association.
    HF5415.5.S467   1993
    658.8'12—dc20   93-26614
                                                                        CIP

Printing number

10   9   8   7   6   5   4   3   2   1

Contents

Preface   vii

PART I
The Evolution of the Service Quality Movement   1

1. Service Quality vs. Manufacturing Quality: Five Myths Exploded—*A. Blanton Godfrey and Edward G. Kammerer*   3
2. Quality Comes to Service—*Christian Grönroos*   17
3. The Baldrige Award and Service Quality—*Curt W. Reimann*   25
4. The Impact of the Baldrige Award—*W. Kent Sterett and Dale C. Durkee*   39

PART II
Creating the Quality Vision   53

5. Service Quality as Strategy—*Paul Kahn*   55
6. Service Quality Principles—*D. Otis Wolkins*   69
7. Service Within: Middle Managers as Service Leaders—*Karl Albrecht*   77
8. Working Hard and Working Smart With Organized Labor—*Paul A. Allaire*   88
9. Quality Improvement Through Strategic Alliances—*David D. Auld and Betty A. Conway*   95

PART III
Creating the Service Quality Framework   109

10. Creating a Service Quality Culture—*Kathryn Troy and Lawrence Schein*   111

11. Creating Service Climates for Service Quality—*Benjamin Schneider and Beth Chung*   124
12. Introducing Change Into a Large Organization: A Partial Success—*Stephen G. Leahey*   134
13. Service Mapping: Gaining a Concrete Perspective on Service System Design—*Jane Kingman-Brundage*   148
14. Creating a World-Class Service Quality Management System—*William Hensler and Kateri Brunell*   164

PART IV
Deploying Service Quality   **175**

15. A Dynamic Process Model of Service Quality Assessment— *William Boulding and Richard Staelin*   177
16. Leaders Listen!—*Stew Leonard, Jr.*   195
17. Putting the Service Profit Chain to Work—*Leonard A. Schlesinger and Roger H. Hallowell*   205
18. Implementing Quality for Performance Improvement— *Edward J. Kane*   219

PART V
The Role of Employees in Service Quality   **231**

19. Selecting and Developing the Right People to Sustain a Competitive Advantage—*Antonio T. Rivera*   233
20. Motivating Employees Through TLC—*Roger J. Dow*   248
21. Empowering Employees—*M. Ven Venkatesan*   259
22. Leveraging Employee Suggestions—*Michael T. Fraga*   267

PART VI
Implementing Service Quality   **277**

23. Building Power Into Quality Education—*Nancy J. Burzon*   279
24. Achieving Personal Quality—*Norma M. Rossi*   294
25. Partnership Teams—*Robert S. Rider*   302
26. Staff Training Delivers Quality Service at Tokyo's Imperial Hotel—*M. Ignatius Cronin III*   312

PART VII
Delivering Service Quality   329

27. The Role of Service Design in Achieving Quality—*Bo
    Edvardsson*   331
28. Fail-Safing Services—*Richard B. Chase and Douglas M. Stewart*   347
29. Managing the Evidence of Service—*Mary Jo Bitner*   358
30. Purchasing and Service Quality—*Douglas P. Brusa and
    Eberhard E. Scheuing*   371

PART VIII
Measuring Service Quality   379

31. Benchmarking Practices and Processes—*Robert C. Camp and
    John E. Kelsch*   381
32. Measuring Customer Satisfaction—*Lawrence A. Crosby*   389
33. Using the Critical Incident Technique in Measuring and
    Managing Service Quality—*Bernd Stauss*   408
34. Performance Measurement—*Alfred C. Sylvain*   428

PART IX
Reinforcing Service Quality   445

35. Sunburst Farms: Leaders Through Alignment in Flower
    Distribution—*Paula Anderson-Findley, Abraham Gutman, and
    Abe Wynperle*   447
36. Customer Service and Service Quality—*George L. Mueller and
    Don E. Bedwell*   458
37. The Art of Service Recovery: Fixing Broken Customers—And
    Keeping Them on Your Side—*Ron Zemke*   463
38. Using Service Guarantees—*Christopher W. L. Hart*   477
39. Recognition, Gratitude, and Celebration—*Patrick L. Townsend
    and Joan E. Gebhardt*   488

PART X
Managing Quality in Government Services   497

40. TQM: An Integrative Methodology for Doing "More With
    Less" in Public Service—*B. Terence Harwick and Marty Russell*   499

41. Quality in Public Services: The IRS Quality Journey—*Joel
    Parfitt*   514

Index   529

About the Editors   537

About the Contributors   539

Preface

During the past decade, service organizations around the world have been discovering the value and power of quality. Defined as understanding and meeting customer requirements, quality acts as a unifying force, driving and streamlining organizations and processes to focus on delivering consistent value to customers. It is also a powerful force that reshapes attitudes and actions toward creating customer satisfaction and loyalty and thus lasting competitive advantage in a turbulent environment of vigorous global competition.

Leaders in service businesses, manufacturing companies, government agencies, and nonprofit organizations realize that they must instill and practice service quality throughout their organizations to survive and grow. Service quality is the strategic imperative that must penetrate everything an organization is and does because it satisfies customers, improves work processes, increases productivity, reduces costs, and enhances profitability.

To assist service leaders in this transformation process, we are proud to present in this handbook a valuable, comprehensive, state-of-the-art resource of world-class service quality strategies, tools, and practices. A unique international team of authors presents cutting-edge insights, experiences, and guidelines of immense practical value and proven impact. This talent pool of fifty-seven world-class experts from three continents includes thought leaders and executives from industry, government, business services, and academia to present a multifaceted picture of the fascinating opportunities inherent in service quality leadership.

The Service Quality Handbook is the most comprehensive book ever published on the critical issues of service quality. It is designed to serve as a practical resource and reference for leaders in any organization anywhere in the world who are responsible for achieving competitive advantage and superior performance in their organizations. Applicable to quality efforts in both service and manufacturing companies as well as in the private and public sectors, the *Service Quality Handbook* presents the views and experiences of a broad array of pioneers and organizations from around the world.

The *Handbook* is organized into ten parts:

Part I describes how quality management has come to services and examines the usefulness and impact of the Baldrige Award for service companies, after exploding some myths about the differences between service and manufacturing quality.

Part II highlights service quality as strategy and a set of principles that guide action in dealing with internal and external constituencies.

Part III discusses organizational issues involved in creating the framework for service quality in the form of culture, climate, and system. It reports on the challenges of introducing change into a large organization and outlines the use of service mapping in service system design.

Part IV presents a set of tools that can be used to obtain input and feedback from customers and to fine-tune the system for performance improvement. It also contains a thought-provoking chapter on how to put the service profit chain to work.

Part V emphasizes the crucial role of employees in service quality. Service quality begins with selecting the right people and motivating them through caring attention to their personal needs. Employees are a tremendous source of suggestions for improvement and should be empowered to do what is right for the customer.

Part VI carries this theme further by analyzing the importance and methods of quality training and education. It is rounded out by chapters on how to achieve personal quality and work successfully in self-managed teams.

Part VII delves into the issue of how to design quality into services and fail-safe them. It also features guidelines for managing the evidence of service and looks into the role of the purchasing function in delivering service quality.

Part VIII reviews powerful methods for measuring service quality, ranging from processes and programs to specific techniques. The results can then be used to improve performance.

Part IX presents approaches to reinforcing service quality, which include the art of preplanned recovery from service failures. Other chapters deal with the role of customer service and service guarantees in achieving service quality. Further contributions present the impact of strategic alliances and recognition, gratitude, and celebration on maintaining the quality momentum.

Last, but not least, Part X demonstrates the impressive progress that has been made in applying quality management methods in public services.

As editors, we are deeply indebted to the fifty-seven international authors who generously contributed their time and talent to sharing time-tested techniques and pioneering experiences with our readers. Many of them are personal friends, living in a number of different countries and working in a variety of professional settings. What brought us all together is a spirit of dedication to the service quality cause that is manifested in such forums as the International Service Quality Association, the biennial Quality in Services (QUIS) Conferences, and research efforts supported and/or conducted by such nonprofit organizations as the Marketing Science Institute in Cambridge, Massachusetts, The Conference Board in New York, the First Interstate Center for Services Marketing in Tempe, Arizona, and the Service Research Center in Karlstad, Sweden. All of us truly care about enhancing the quality of life for both employees and customers of organizations everywhere. We all have caught quality passion. It is our sincere hope that you, the reader, will join us after reading and applying the contributions in this *Handbook.*

As we reflect on the genesis of this *Handbook,* we are filled with gratitude for the patient support that our wives, Carol Scheuing and Gloria Christopher, have given us during the many months that it took to complete this journey. We are also most grateful to Andrea Pedolsky, our acquisitions editor, and Richard Gatjens, our associate editor, for their enthusiasm and quiet professionalism in this exciting project.

Enjoy the *Handbook* and put it to good use! And let us know how we can make it even better next time.

Eberhard E. Scheuing
Tivoli, New York
William F. Christopher
Stamford, Connecticut

PART I

THE EVOLUTION OF THE SERVICE QUALITY MOVEMENT

1

Service Quality vs. Manufacturing Quality: Five Myths Exploded

A. Blanton Godfrey and Edward G. Kammerer, Juran Institute, Inc.

Why are there separate books on manufacturing quality management and on service quality management? Are these two types of quality management so different? Are the processes, tools, and methods used for managing service quality truly different from the processes, tools, and methods used for managing manufacturing quality?

The answer is a resounding no—in theory. The same management processes and the same basic concepts, tools, and methods apply to managing both manufacturing and service quality. But the answer is also a resounding yes—in practice. For the most part, service companies are years behind manufacturing companies in the application of quality concepts, tools, and methods. There are notable exceptions, of course, and we cite some. This lag in application notwithstanding, we feel strongly that the approaches used in managing quality in the manufacturing sector are both applicable and applied in service industries.

Quality management has a long and rich history in manufacturing. In some countries, product specifications and requirements, inspections to these written specifications, and systems of rewards and punishments go back thousands of years. In this century, particularly since the 1950s, global competition has forced many manufacturing companies to develop quality management approaches that continuously eliminate waste, improve customer satisfaction, and involve every member of the organization in these improving processes, efficiencies, and customer-supplier relationships. The lessons learned by these manufacturing companies offer a quick start in managing quality in other types of organizations, especially service companies.

Note: Our thanks to Dr. A. C. Endres, Juran Institute, for a key observation that greatly improved this chapter.

The Five Myths About Service Quality

There have been many myths perpetuated about service quality. Some are sustained by well-meaning people in service companies who have just begun to manage service quality and think their meager efforts are truly all there is. Some are created by people who have made initial, half-hearted attempts to measure service quality and have failed.

Other service-quality myths originate with people who have only a superficial knowledge of the processes, basic concepts, and tools and methods for managing manufacturing quality and therefore, in their blissful ignorance, think that every way they discover to manage service quality is different and new. Still other myths arise from people who think that managing manufacturing quality means nothing more than conforming to specifications or offering a product with zero defects. Some even believe that managing manufacturing quality means basically just inspection. Unfortunately, the published material on manufacturing quality management, both historical and recent, is full of descriptions that help support these myths.

Myth 1: The Way to Manage Service Quality Is Different From the Way to Manage Manufacturing Quality

This may be the easiest myth to explode. All we have to do is examine the goals of Total Quality Management, the management processes, infrastructure, and foundations for managing quality. In doing so, we find no differences between managing service quality and managing manufacturing quality.

SIMILAR TOTAL QUALITY MANAGEMENT RESULTS

The universal goals of Total Quality Management (TQM) are lower costs, higher revenues, empowered employees, and delighted customers (see Figure 1-1). These goals need almost no explanation.

Since the late 1980s, with increasing "world class" competition, we have moved away from the amateurish belief that quality just means conforming to specifications and reducing the costs of poor quality. We know now that quality also means satisfying, even delighting, customers, and exceeding their needs, wants, and expectations. Quality means having the right features, the correct documentation, error-free invoices, on-time delivery, friendly and accurate technical support, *and* no failures either on receipt of the goods and services or during their use. Higher quality may also mean premium prices or higher market share leading to increased revenues.

Figure 1-1.   Goals of Total Quality Management.

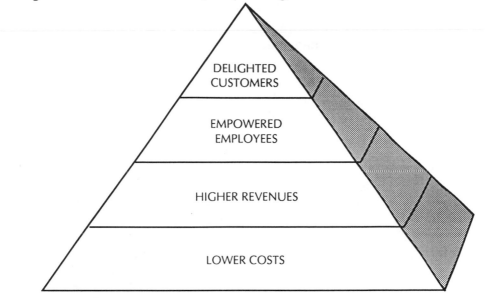

Source: Copyright 1991 Juran Institute, Inc.

Delighted customers are customers who buy over and over again, advertise your goods and services for you, and who check you first when they are going to buy anything else to see if you also offer those goods or services. We cannot delight customers just by giving them a product that works or by quickly repairing their plumbing. We must also manage all the processes surrounding the basic product or service. We must also manage the business processes (order taking, distribution, new product and service development, billing, information) as well as the supplier relationships, support systems, and employee interactions with both internal and external customers.

A few years ago a leading U.S. manufacturing company conducted a thorough study on customer satisfaction. It found that for the most part, customers were well satisfied with product quality and reliability. But they were not satisfied with order taking, product support, software quality, information quality and documentation, distribution, and billing.

A customer-satisfaction study by a leading railroad showed that users of transportation services were more concerned with administrative effectiveness than with such traditional issues as transit time. In short, customers were not happy with the way billing errors were handled, shipments were traced, or complex contracts were administered.

One major transportation company found that it was losing business even though it had the lowest price and best service. Why? Proposals were late getting to customers. Its customers had changed their own processes dramatically in the preceding years. One of these changes— just-in-time inventory management—had tightened the supply chain. The old two week to one month response time to a price request was no longer acceptable.

Analysis of the proposal process showed that the company's system for preparing proposals was extremely complex. It had fifty-eight separate steps and nineteen handoffs. A quality-improvement team using the same process improvement methods widely used in manufacturing companies redesigned the process. The new way had 50 percent fewer steps and a response time of forty-eight hours.

Thus, whether the product is an appliance or a service, the principles of TQM apply and the desired results are the same.

EMPOWERED EMPLOYEES IN BOTH MANUFACTURING AND SERVICE COMPANIES

In the manufacturing sector, it is widely acknowledged that empowered employees are a means for achieving lower costs, higher revenues, and happy customers; as such, they are a major goal of TQM. Of course, Total Quality Management requires a permanent change in the way a company manages itself. The goal is not only to solve the problems of today but to create an organization that can solve, or even avoid, the problems of tomorrow.

Thus, the concept of empowered employees embraces many new ideas. Empowered employees have self-control. They have the means to measure the quality of their work, interpret the measurements, compare them to goals, and take action when the process is not effective. But the concept of empowered employees goes far beyond self-control. These employees also know how to change the process and improve performance—increasing both the effectiveness and the efficiency of the process.

They also understand how to plan for quality. They understand who their customers are, what their customers need, want, and expect; how to design new goods and services to meet these needs; how to develop the necessary work processes; how to create and use the necessary quality measurements; and how to continuously improve these processes. Many manufacturing companies have been empowering their employees for years, with great TQM effect.

In a service company, empowered employees can have the same impact as in a manufacturing company. For instance, a major U.S. railroad had chronic poor service results in picking up and delivering cars to customers. The service times were erratic, crews could not keep to schedules, car pick-ups and deliveries were often missed completely, and crews could not respond to last-minute changes.

This problem was given to a quality-improvement team including switching crew members and other employees. The team quickly found that these matters were quality-planning problems, and it followed a quality-planning process to develop a new means for picking up and delivering cars. In doing so, the team interviewed customers to determine their needs, worked with crew members to develop a feasible schedule, and established work rules that allowed for action to be taken when last-minute changes occurred.

These changes put the employees in a state of self-control. They understood what was expected of them. They knew how well they were performing. With new rules, they could react to changes in customer needs. The results of the new process were impressive:

1. Service failures disappeared.
2. Safety incidents fell from nine to one per month.
3. Customer satisfaction reached its highest levels ever.
4. There was a significant drop in absenteeism.
5. The company saved over $100,000 per month.

In summary, empowered employees—whether in a manufacturing or a service company—understand and use daily the three basic processes for managing quality: quality planning, quality control, and quality improvement. These processes are a key to Total Quality Management.

IDENTICAL BASIC QUALITY MANAGEMENT PROCESSES

Total Quality Management consists of three basic management elements: foundation, infrastructure, and processes. These are essential in managing service quality as well as manufacturing quality (see Figure 1-2). At Juran Institute, a leading teaching and consulting institution, we define the processes as quality improvement, quality planning, and quality control—the Juran Trilogy (Figure 1-3). These are the fundamental management processes used by self-directed work teams. They are also the building blocks for systemic thinking, or the true "learning organization." The Juran Trilogy applies at every level of every organization—service and manufacturing alike.

There is far more to achieving Total Quality Management than just understanding these processes, though. A company must build the necessary infrastructure to support its quality management efforts. This infrastructure consists of several key pieces (see Figure 1-4). The first, and one of the most important, is a quality assurance system. Best defined by ISO Standard 9004—the Guidelines for Quality Management and Quality Systems promulgated by the International Standards Organization—the quality assurance system is the piece of TQM infrastruc-

Figure 1-2. Total Quality Management.

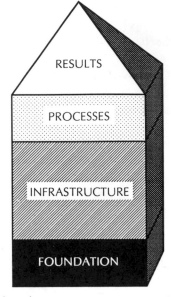

ture most often mistaken by service quality practitioners as applying only to manufacturing quality management.

The other elements of the infrastructure are also important. There must be strong relationships with both suppliers and customers. There must be organization-wide information systems that support all quality management activities. There must be the necessary measurements. And there must be ongoing education and training support for the entire organization.

Whether a company is supplying a product or a service, quality output relies on quality supply. For example, the fastest-growing mode of transportation today is intermodalism, the combination of several modes of transportation in moving particular shipments. Its high quality of service is the direct result of the joint effort of several transportation companies. If the joint effort fails, the service fails, since none of the players can compensate for inconsistent service by any other link in the transportation chain.

A company must have a solid foundation upon which to build the quality infrastructure. The three components of this foundation are strategic quality management, leadership, and customer focus (see Figure 1-5). Strategic quality management involves making quality the strategic imperative of a firm that penetrates the entire organization and guides every action. This requires executive leadership that models the importance of quality and "walks the talk." The entire effort will be for

Figure 1-3. The Juran Trilogy of Processes.

Source: Copyright 1991 Juran Institute, Inc.

naught, though, unless it is clearly focused on understanding and satisfying customer requirements.

Myth 2: Service Quality Is "50,000 Moments of Truth a Day."

Years ago, Jan Carlzon, CEO of SAS, one of the world's leading airlines, wrote a charming book describing the journey SAS had taken toward service quality management. Unfortunately, many people read only the title, or their memories are so weak that they remember only a few cleverly worded phrases, like "50,000 moments of truth a day."

Too many people have interpreted managing service quality as no more than managing those 50,000 personal contacts with the customer each day. This has led to those infamous service-quality "smile schools" and the "have a nice day" approach to quality.

Managing service quality is far more than pleasant person-to-person relationships. For example, a manager rushes to pack for a critical business trip, assembling clothes, papers, and materials needed for the trip, and notes for her presentation to the president the morning prior to the trip. On the way to work, she stops at the bank for the cash she needs for the trip. The ATM flashes its all too familiar message, "Out of Service."

She quickly detours several miles out of her way to another bank, but for some reason it limits her to one hundred dollars, far too little even for cab fares. She rushes to work, quickly finishes her presentation to the president, and hurries to another branch of her bank only five miles from work. Its ATM isn't working either, but the bank is open so she rushes inside to find three lines of four to five people each.

For once in her life, she appears to have picked the right line, since it moves quickly to the point where only one person is in front of her.

Figure 1-4.   TQM infrastructure.

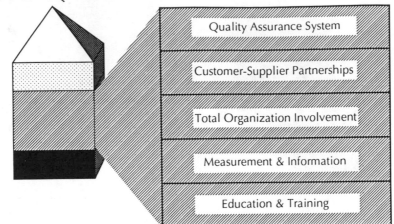

Source: Copyright 1991 Juran Institute, Inc.

Unfortunately, this person is there because of an error in his account—a deposit has not been correctly entered. Finally, after ten long minutes with two vice-presidents and the president getting in the act to straighten out the "computer error," the manager's turn comes.

The teller smiles sweetly, greets her by name, and starts asking about her family. He finally cashes her check, tries to tell her about a special on CDs, and wishes her a "nice day" on her way to an almost-missed flight. The manager is ecstatic about her bank's outstanding service quality—right? Would you be?

Just as manufacturing quality is far more than a pleasant salesperson who sells the customer a new car, service quality is far more than the care given the customer as one part of a complex service process. Dr. Kanecko, a leading Japanese consultant on service quality and a former top executive in a Japanese shopping center complex, has explained the service quality management process quite clearly. According to Kanecko, the management of any organization must define the market and business strategy, which includes identifying the target customers—their wants, needs, and expectations. Management then develops the systems and processes that are to be used by the organization to meet those needs. Figure 1-6 outlines the roles of quality management.

The work force operates within the system to provide quality service. It also has clear goals and objectives, the means to measure performance, and ways to adjust performance within the system. The work force and management work together to continuously improve the systems and processes, both to remove faults and to create even higher levels of performance.

Today, in many companies, workers are also part of quality planning

Figure 1-5. TQM foundation.

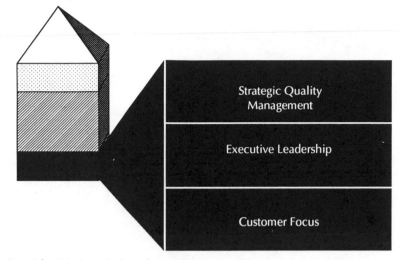

teams that develop new systems and processes used by the organization to meet customer needs.

Much service quality is provided without person-to-person contact. Every day, AT&T has over 125 million "moments of truth." Each time a customer picks up the telephone to place a long-distance call, a $40 billion investment in technology stands ready to support the call. For instance, a dial tone is given in less than three seconds, signaling that the switch is ready to receive the customer's commands. As the customer dials, the digits are collected and analyzed. Switches and transmission facilities across the country (or the world) are activated to find a path for the call. Analog signals are processed to digital signals, then sent at the speed of light, reprocessed to analog signals, and delivered to the receiving party.

The customer's perception of quality is based on set-up efficiency and accuracy, lack of transmission noise, no cut-offs, and accurate billing at the end of the month. Only when operator services are needed—a rather rare event in the United States—do other aspects of service quality management come into play. Thus, almost all the determinants of telecommunication service quality are in place long before the customer uses the service.

For many years, customer service in the railroad industry was a function of the complaint department. Its function was to listen to customer problems and give updates on what to expect. Sometimes, the department made an attempt to expedite car movement. Today, it is recognized that a late shipment is the result of poor planning and a

Figure 1-6.   Quality management roles.

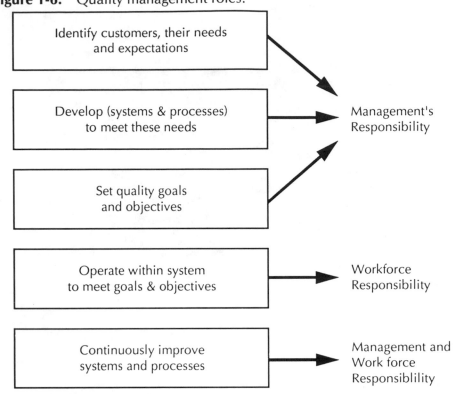

series of events that started early in the process. The only way of ensuring on-time delivery is to avoid upstream delays and errors.

Thus, quality management is a total organizational goal—and much more than customer interfaces, even if they number 50,000.

Myth 3: It Is Harder to Measure Service Quality Than Manufacturing Quality

This myth must have been started by someone who never tried to develop a quality measurement system. The truth is that all quality measurement is hard. Indeed, good quality measurements are what distinguish world-class companies from "wannabes."

A simple example illustrates the point. Some years ago, AT&T Bell Laboratories scientists and engineers were developing the transatlantic cable TAT 8. This was a revolutionary design, the first undersea light fiber system. Lasers in underwater repeater cases are a critical part of the system. For the system to meet its reliability objectives, the lasers need to have a mean time to failure (MTTF) of over twenty-five years.

The problem was to develop a measurement that would accurately predict the MTTF. Testing a large quantity of lasers for twenty-five years to see if half of them were still working at the end of this period was not a feasible solution. A team of two Ph.D. reliability experts and two Ph.D. physicists attacked the problem. After three years of research, tests, and experiments, they developed a measurement to accurately predict laser reliability based on a two-year accelerated life test.

There are few areas of service quality measurement where adequate effort and talent could not develop a reliable measurement. This applies equally to service and manufacturing quality improvement efforts. Indeed, the steps involved in deciding what and how to measure quality are identical for service and manufacturing companies. Stories about manufacturing tests that measure the wrong variable are well known. The same often occurs in service industries.

For example, customers had complained to a transportation company that equipment supply was not adequate to meet their needs. The company found that much of its equipment was unserviceable, so a new emphasis was placed on equipment maintenance. Internal measurements showed that the problem was soon solved: Equipment availability levels had never been higher. However, customers were still complaining.

Deeper analysis showed that the type of equipment customers needed was different from the equipment being repaired and made available. The equipment in high demand never came in for repair; therefore, it was often in unacceptable condition. The company had been using as a measure of customer satisfaction the amount of dollars spent on repair. But customers were interested in the availability of specific types of equipment. The measurements chosen thus proved to be far off the mark in determining true customer satisfaction.

There is a fundamental reason why service quality appears harder to measure than manufacturing quality. For the most part, manufacturing companies have a long history of quality management. Competitive pressures, a more scientific approach to management, long experience in industrial engineering process design, and more sophisticated quality cost systems have led to a wealth of quality measurements and an extensive and solid literature base about quality management. Indeed, manufacturing companies rarely have to invent new product quality measures. They are able to beg, borrow, or steal most of the measures they need. Only in the newer areas of quality management, such as managing business process quality, are manufacturing companies struggling to find new quality measures.

Ironically, these new areas of quality management are exactly those where manufacturing and service companies are most alike. They include information quality, invoice quality, distribution quality, technical support service quality, and most internal supplier-customer relation-ships. Many service companies are working hard to develop measure-ments in these areas of quality management that are common between manufacturing and service companies and common across service com-panies while they are also trying to develop quality measurements for the unique aspects of their particular businesses. Manufacturing compa-nies may thus be able to benefit from the insights gained by their service sector counterparts.

Myth 4: Service Quality Is Determined During Real-Time Interactions

It is difficult to imagine how this myth originated. Even if we exclude all government services, telecommunications services (at least some of these are provided on the customer's premises), banking and other financial services, transportation services, and health care services, this belief is still not true.

Rather, service quality, like manufacturing quality, is determined early in the quality process and far in advance of real-time.

For an airline customer to experience good service quality, much more is needed than a polite pilot or friendly flight attendant. On-time arrivals depend far more on the supporting systems than on the pilots' efforts to leave on time. Customer in-flight satisfaction depends as much on seat design (and maintenance), working lights and sound system, and at least partially edible food as it does on flight-attendant perform-ance. And, of course, customer satisfaction depends most on safe arrival.

No matter how well trained airline employees are, their efforts at customer service cannot make up for archaic computer systems that create long check-in lines, ticketing errors, and seat assignment mistakes. No amount of pilot effort is going to overcome delays caused by worn-out planes, chaotic maintenance procedures, and poorly designed sup-port systems for food, fuel, and baggage.

Conversely, even extremely well-trained service personnel find the smile and courteous response wear thin as angry passengers confront them with system-caused problems.

One of America's leading railroads found in a critical service corridor that its on-time delivery performance was averaging 60 percent. Custom-ers expect much better performance and significant market share was going to the railroad's competition. A quality team was assigned the project of solving this problem. It found that shipments left on schedule 95 percent of the time, but on-time arrival was only 60 percent. The team's analysis proved that delays early in the process could not be made up downstream. Leaving earlier would not solve the problem. Shipments sometimes even arrived early, also causing customer dissatisfaction.

Consistent service was the requirement. The team followed the quality improvement process used in many manufacturing companies. It:

1. Developed a clear problem statement
2. Mapped the process
3. Collected data
4. Hypothesized the causes
5. Identified the root cause
6. Created and tested remedies
7. Changed the process
8. Established new controls

The results were impressive. On-time delivery increased to 95 percent. Customer satisfaction improved markedly, and the railroad regained market share. But these improvements all depended on upstream improvements to ensure quality service later in the process.

Myth 5: Service Companies Are All Alike

By separating manufacturing quality management from service quality management, we imply that service companies are different from manufacturing companies, but that service companies are all alike.

Nothing could be farther from the truth.

What we call the service sector includes a broad array of industries, from fast-food restaurants to lawyers' offices, from government agencies to telecommunications companies, and from transportation companies to barber shops. In fact, many service companies have more in common with certain manufacturing companies than they do with other service companies.

Telecommunications, for example, is similar in some ways to high-tech manufacturing. Many service companies produce "things" using production processes similar to those used by manufacturing companies. Insurance companies produce policies; hospitals produce X-rays, lab test results, and bills; restaurants produce meals. Some well-run three-star kitchens work at production schedules with a precision and efficiency that would startle some manufacturing managers.

Summary

Businesses have far more to learn from each other in quality management than they have differences. The basic quality management processes are the same for service and manufacturing companies, the concepts are the same, the tools and methods are the same.

Two major developments of the 1980s have proved this. The first was the National Demonstration Project in Health Care Quality Improvement. In this project, twenty-one leading health-care organizations tried to apply the techniques used by manufacturing companies to delivering health care. Their success and the subsequent adoption of these ideas and methods show how well they can work in service industries.

The second major event was the creation of the Malcolm Baldrige National Quality Award and the widespread acceptance of its criteria as a de facto total quality management standard by manufacturing and service companies alike. We have but to review each of the ninety-nine questions in the Baldrige Award application to understand that the principles of quality management apply equally to both service and manufacturing companies.

References

Berwick, Donald M., A. Blanton Godfrey, and Jane Roessner. *Curing Health Care: New Strategies for Quality Improvement.* San Francisco: Jossey-Bass, 1991.

Carlzon, Jan. *Moments of Truth.* Cambridge, Mass.: Ballinger Publishing Company, 1987.

Juran, J. M. *Juran on Leadership for Quality: An Executive Handbook.* New York: Free Press, 1989.

2

Quality Comes to Service

Christian Grönroos, Swedish School of Economics, Helsinki, Finland

Quality came to the service literature at the beginning of the 1980s. This was actually quite extraordinary because the emerging research into services at that time was very much marketing-oriented. And in the traditional marketing models, there are no quality concepts or quality management models. The management literature did not include quality models either. Instead, quality was treated more or less as a given variable. Today, engineers and operations people talk about quality, and researchers from these areas are interested in quality models. In the marketing literature, quality is still considered a given variable and, to quote Evert Gummesson of Stockholm University, "treated as a black box." Services marketing is the remarkable exception.

The interest in service quality among researchers and practitioners alike has to a high degree come from research into services marketing. Hence, one cannot understand why and how quality came to services without considering the characteristics of services and the nature of services marketing.

The Nature of Services Marketing

In traditional marketing models, which are geared predominantly to the demands of consumer packaged goods, the well-known marketing mix is the core of marketing. The marketing mix is a set of variables that is manipulated by the marketer in order to make customers buy a given product. Product is one of those marketing mix variables. The product variable is thought of as a physical good. The marketer may decide upon the depth and width of the product range, on packaging, and even on accompanying services, but the quality of the product is not within the scope of the marketer. Marketing does have an indirect impact on quality, though, because the quality of a given product may be based on market research data provided by the marketing people. In the organizational hierarchy, marketing is often separated into a department of its own. As a function, marketing comes in between production and consumption without any real interfaces with these functions; no interfaces between production and consumption are taken into account, either.

Services are different, however. Although there are very few pure services, and very few pure goods, there are a number of characteristics that apply better to services than to goods. Such characteristics are the *intangibility* of most services, the *inseparability* of vital parts of the consumption and production of a service, the fact that services are *processes*, and the fact that the customers often to some extent *take part in these processes as a production resource*. Hence, unlike traditional marketing models, a services marketing model has to be based on the fact that the production (and delivery) process and the consumption process overlap, as is illustrated in Figure 2-1.

The interface between production and consumption may be broad and may extend over a long period of time, as in restaurants or on an inclusive tour; or it may be limited and quickly passing, as in making an operator-assisted phone call. It may involve interactions between the customer and service employees—so-called contact personnel—or between the customer and a machine or automated system—as when using an ATM. This interface is called a buyer-seller interaction or the service encounter. Regardless of the content of the interface, what happens in the simultaneous part of the production and consumption processes is always of critical importance to the customer's perception of the service. If the service encounter is perceived negatively, the customer is often less than pleased, although most of the efforts to produce the service are beyond the line of visibility from the customer's point of view and may have been properly taken care of.

Thus, marketing researchers realized that the service encounter is

Figure 2-1.   The nature of services marketing.

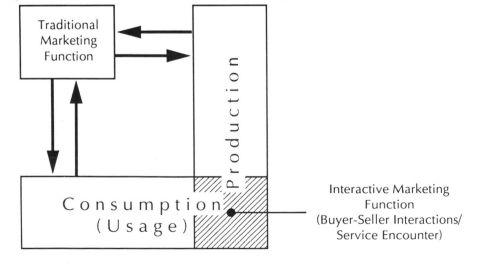

of critical importance to the development of an enduring customer relationship. If the service encounter is perceived favorably, the customer will probably return. On the other hand, if the customer is not satisfied, he will look for other solutions to his problems, even if the traditional marketing activities of the company—such as advertising, sales promotion, and often even pricing—are managed effectively and aggressively. As Figure 2-1 indicates, the service encounter becomes a second marketing function alongside the traditional marketing mix. In the service literature, the term *interactive marketing* describes the marketing aspect of the service encounter.

Hence, how customers perceive the service encounter—or in other words, how customers perceive the *quality* of the service delivered in the service encounter—has a crucial marketing impact. According to their very nature, services are processes in which the customer in most cases gets involved. If the processes are perceived to function well, this has a positive impact on the perception of the quality of the service, and vice-versa. Thus, from a marketing point of view, having a good marketing impact on customers requires good quality of the service.

It is, therefore, logical to state that marketing—especially the interactive marketing dimension—and the quality of services are two sides of the same coin. Marketing depends on the quality of the service rendered. This is why marketing researchers realized that understanding service quality is imperative to developing successful services marketing models. And, therefore, efforts to understand how customers perceive the quality of services and how to manage service quality became integral parts of research into the marketing of services.

Perceived Service Quality: Expectations and Experiences

In the early 1980s, Total Quality Management (TQM) and similar approaches to quality management were not very developed yet, and they were largely geared to goods manufacturing. As services did not seem to resemble physical goods, a service quality concept was developed virtually from scratch. Instead of using quality concepts from manufacturing, services marketing researchers developed a service quality concept based on models from consumer behavior. This, of course, was a field that they knew better, and since the manufacturing-oriented concepts and models of quality did not seem to fit services, this seemed a logical way to proceed.

To understand why service quality developed the way it did, one has to realize that it is not based on the way operations people, service engineers, or service designers think, but on the mindset of marketers.

And according to the marketing concept, customers should come first. Therefore, the customer became the focal point for the development of service quality.

Service quality development has from the beginning been based on the notion that it is what customers perceive as quality that is important, not what designers or operations people feel is good or bad quality. According to some models of consumer behavior, the customer's post-purchase perception of a product is a function of his pre-purchase expectations. This notion was the foundation of the so-called confirmation/disconfirmation concept of service quality, which up until today has been the generally used service quality concept. The customer's quality perception depends on the degree to which quality expectations are confirmed or disconfirmed by experience. The author of this chapter introduced the Perceived Service Quality model in 1982. According to this model, the quality of a service, *as perceived by the customer*, is the result of a comparison between the expectations of the customer and his real-life experiences (see Figure 2-2). If the experiences exceed the expectations, the perceived quality is positive. If the experiences do not reach the level of expectations, the perceived quality is low.

Conceptually, this confirmation/disconfirmation concept has an important impact on people's thinking about quality. It implies that quality is not an objective phenomenon that can be engineered beforehand. But with proper preparation prior to the service encounter, good quality may be achieved. Customers perceive quality in a subjective manner, and, depending on the level of expectations, the same level of quality, as measured in some objective sense, will be perceived in a different way. Thus, what is good quality for one person may be less acceptable for

Figure 2-2.   The perceived service quality model.

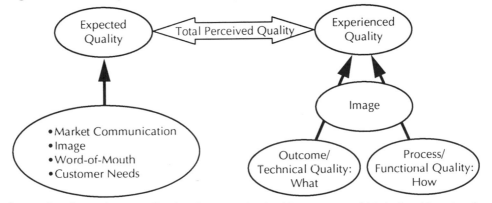

Source: Based on a figure in Christian Grönroos, *Service Management and Marketing: Managing the Moments of Truth in Service Competition.* (Lexington, Mass.: Free Press, Lexington Books, 1990), p. 41.

another. The concept also points out another link between service quality and marketing that marketers and quality managers tend to neglect: Marketing, especially the traditional parts of the marketing mix such as advertising and selling, is to a large extent a matter of expectations management. Advertising and selling partly determine the level of customer expectations. If expectations are raised too high—owing to an advertising campaign, for example—the quality of a given service may be disappointing, if only because the customers had unrealistic expectations.

The oval at the left-hand side of Figure 2-2 indicates that market-communication activities, such as advertising and selling, together with word-of-mouth communication, the image perception, and the needs of the customer influence the level of expectations. Marketers should learn from this not to overpromise. Studies of how service quality is perceived typically show that delivering on promises is an important facet of perceived service quality.

The confirmation/disconfirmation concept has pinpointed several important issues in service quality management, and it has been the foundation for most of the model building within the service quality field during the 1980s—for example, the well-known Gap Analysis and SERVQUAL models by V. A. Zeithaml, A. Parasuraman, and L. L. Berry. However, when one starts to measure service quality, this concept may have some inherent problems, which have been discussed by a growing number of researchers especially in recent years.

Perceived Service Quality—Outcome and Process

Another important aspect of service quality pointed out by the Perceived Service Quality model is the distinction between the *outcome* (what the customer gets) and the *process* (how the process and service encounter are perceived)—see the right-hand side of Figure 2-2. Again, the focus on customer behavior made early service quality researchers aware that the customer's quality perception not only relates to the outcome of the service production and delivery process but, to the extent that he or she is involved in it, also has an impact on the perceived service quality. In the original Perceived Service Quality model, the outcome dimension is called *technical quality*, since it refers to what the customer gets as a technical solution to his or her problem, as a result of the service production and delivery process. Conversely, the process dimension is called *functional quality* because it depends on how the process itself functions. Other terms, such as *interaction quality* and *physical quality*, have been used for these two distinct aspects of quality.

When introducing the Perceived Service Quality model, this author postulated that, as long as the outcome, or the technical quality, is acceptable, the process dimension, or functional quality, frequently may be more critical to the customer's overall quality perception. Since then, research in Europe and North America—for example, research related to the SERVQUAL model—has demonstrated that this indeed is the case.

Another aspect of perceived quality shown in Figure 2-2 is the image—either corporate or local or both—of the service firm. The image may play the role of a filter. If the image of the firm is good in the customer's mind, problems may at least to some extent be excused. But if problems continue to occur, the image will eventually suffer. And if the image is bad, quality problems are easily perceived to be worse than they really are.

Current Trends in Service Quality

Lately, the validity of the confirmation/disconfirmation concept has been questioned by some researchers. These doubts seem to be based on problems in developing a proper means of measuring service quality. As a conceptual model describing the many facets of how service quality is perceived, the Perceived Service Quality model is probably valid. In its basic form, the model is static, however, while quality perception is a dynamic process. Obviously, one has to take this fact into account when measuring quality.

Some of the critics of the confirmation/disconfirmation concept state, for example, the following:

▲ If expectations are measured at the same time as the experience is measured, the results are biased by the experience, and this is not according to the model.

▲ If expectations are measured prior to the service experience, these expectations may not be comparable after the experience. In other words, the customer's experience with a service encounter may change his expectations. These altered expectations are the scale against which the experience should be weighed if one is to determine the customer's true quality perception.

▲ Measuring expectations is not a sound method because service experiences are, in fact, perceptions of reality. Inherent in these perceptions are any prior expectations.

In addition, some marketers say that if the perceived service quality is low because the experience is below expectations, marketing must communicate to customers that the service is not as good as they believe or that the service encounter will not function as well as they expect—something that is totally absurd. However, these critics are unaware of the concept of *demarketing*, which is applicable in such situations. Marketing should not only raise expectations but also set expectations at an appropriate level, even if this requires making customers expect less or something different.

When measuring perceived service quality, one encounters the problems of how to confirm or disconfirm whether and to what extent expectations are met by experiences. One suggestion is that it is enough to measure customer experiences of service quality as providing a close approximation of perceived service quality. There are, in fact, some studies that support this view. Theoretically, as the third critical point indicated earlier shows, this may indeed be a valid way of measuring perceived quality.

Conclusions

Interest in service quality emerged among marketing researchers. Probably because of this, the importance of quality to customers was quickly realized. The models that were developed were geared to the notion that customers decide what is good or bad quality, and thus the concept of perceived service quality was introduced. A similar development has taken place within the manufacturing sector. Today, it is no longer meaningful to draw a sharp line between service and manufacturing industries. Quality models and quality management approaches that are developed within one or the other industry are cross-fertilizing, helping all business people understand the quality implications in a mix of goods and services.

References

Brown, S. W., E. Gummesson, B. Edvardsson, and B. O. Gustavsson, eds. *Quality in Services—Multidisciplinary and Multinational Perspectives*. Lexington, Mass.: Free Press, Lexington Books, 1990. This book includes a large number of articles on various aspects of service quality. It is based on academic research and real cases presented at the first special conference series on service quality, or QUIS (Quality in Services). The first conference was held in Sweden in 1988 and the second in the United States in 1990.

Grönroos, C. *Service Management and Marketing: Managing the Moments of Truth in Service Competition*. Lexington, Mass.: Free Press, Lexington Books, 1990. In this book, two chapters are devoted to service-quality models and to quality management. The Perceived Service Quality model is developed and illustrated. Throughout the book the relationship between service quality and various subareas of managing a service business is discussed.

Gummesson, E. *Quality Management in Service Organizations*. New York: ISQA, 1993. In this publication the author discusses the various concepts and models of service quality that have been developed since the early 1980s, and he synthesizes the international research information in this area.

Zeithaml, V. A., A. Parasuraman, and L. L. Berry. *Delivering Quality Service: Balancing Customer Perceptions and Expectations*. New York: Free Press, 1990. In this book the SERVQUAL model of describing and measuring service quality and the Gap Analysis framework are developed and discussed in detail.

3

The Baldrige Award and Service Quality

Curt W. Reimann, National Institute of Standards and Technology

The Malcolm Baldrige National Quality Award (the Award) was created by the Congress of the United States through Public Law 100-107 and signed into law by President Reagan on August 20, 1987. The Award annually recognizes U.S. companies that excel in quality management and quality achievement. All manufacturing companies and service companies, large and small, are eligible.

The Award was established to promote:

- Awareness of quality and its importance to national competitiveness
- Understanding of the requirements for quality excellence
- Sharing of information on successful quality strategies and on the benefits derived from implementation of these strategies

Award Criteria

The Malcolm Baldrige National Quality Award Criteria are the basis for both making awards and providing feedback to applicants. In addition, they help elevate quality standards and expectations; facilitate communication and sharing between and within organizations of all types based upon common understanding of key quality requirements; and serve as a working tool for planning, training, assessment, and other uses. The Award Criteria are directed toward two results-oriented goals: to project key requirements for delivering ever-improving value to customers while maximizing the overall effectiveness and productivity of the delivering organization. To achieve these results-oriented goals, the Criteria are built upon a set of values that together address and integrate the overall customer and company performance requirements.

Core Values and Concepts

The Award Criteria are built upon ten core values and concepts:

1. Customer-Driven Quality
2. Leadership
3. Continuous Improvement
4. Employee Participation and Development
5. Fast Response
6. Design Quality and Prevention
7. Long-Range Outlook
8. Management by Fact
9. Partnership Development
10. Corporate Responsibility and Citizenship

These core values and concepts are described in the Malcolm Baldrige National Quality Award Criteria booklet.

CRITERIA FRAMEWORK

The core values and concepts are embodied in seven categories:

1.0   Leadership
2.0   Information and Analysis
3.0   Strategic Quality Planning
4.0   Human Resource Development and Management
5.0   Management of Process Quality
6.0   Quality and Operational Results
7.0   Customer Focus and Satisfaction

The framework connecting and integrating the categories is shown in Figure 3-1.

The framework has four basic elements:

1. *Driver*—Senior executive leadership creates the values, goals, and systems, and guides the sustained pursuit of quality and performance objectives.
2. *System*—System comprises the set of well-defined and well-designed processes for meeting the company's quality and performance requirements.
3. *Measures of progress*—Measures of progress provide a results-oriented basis for channeling actions to delivering ever-improving customer value and company performance.

Figure 3-1. Baldrige Award Criteria framework.

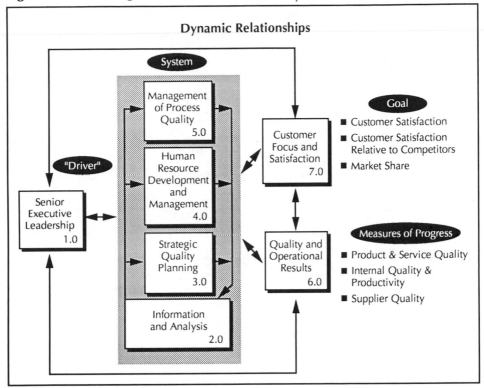

4. *Goal*—The basic aim of the quality process is the delivery of ever-improving value to customers.

The seven categories shown in Figure 3-1 are further subdivided into twenty-eight examination items. Item descriptors are given in Figure 3-2. Each Item focuses on a major element of an effective quality system. All information submitted by applicants is in response to the specific requirements given within these Items.

The Pivotal Role of the Quality and Operational Results Category

The Quality and Operational Results Category (6.0) plays a central role in the Award Criteria. This category provides a focus and purpose for all quality system actions. In addition, it represents the bridge between the quality system and the customer. Through this focus, the dual purpose of quality—superior value of offerings as viewed by the customer and the marketplace; and superior company performance as determined

Figure 3-2.   Baldrige Award examination items.

1.0   Leadership

    1.1   Senior Executive Leadership
    1.2   Management for Quality
    1.3   Public Responsibility

2.0   Information and Analysis

    2.1   Scope and Management of Quality and Performance Data and Information
    2.2   Competitive Comparisons and Benchmarks
    2.3   Analysis and Uses of Company-Level Data

3.0   Strategic Quality Planning

    3.1   Strategic Quality and Company Performance Planning Process
    3.2   Quality and Performance Plans

4.0   Human Resource Development and Management

    4.1   Human Resource Management
    4.2   Employee Involvement
    4.3   Employee Education and Training
    4.4   Employee Performance and Recognition
    4.5   Employee Well-Being and Morale

5.0   Management of Process Quality

    5.1   Design and Introduction of Quality Products and Services
    5.2   Process Management—Product and Service Production and Delivery Processes
    5.3   Process Management—Business Processes and Support Services
    5.4   Supplier Quality
    5.5   Quality Assessment

6.0   Quality and Operational Results

    6.1   Product and Service Quality Results
    6.2   Company Operational Results
    6.3   Business Process and Support Service Results
    6.4   Supplier Quality Results

7.0   Customer Focus and Satisfaction

    7.1   Customer Relationship Management
    7.2   Commitment to Customers
    7.3   Customer Satisfaction Determination
    7.4   Customer Satisfaction Results
    7.5   Customer Satisfaction Comparison
    7.6   Future Requirements and Expectations of Customers

through productivity and effectiveness indicators—is maintained. The other major purpose of Category 6.0 is to provide key information (measures of progress) for evaluation and improvement of quality system processes and practices.

The Quality and Operational Results Category probes four areas:

6.1 *Product and Service Quality Results.* This item calls for reporting quality levels and improvements for key product and service attributes— attributes that truly matter to the customer and in the marketplace. These attributes are derived from customer-related Items ("listening posts"), which make up Category 7.0. If the attributes have been properly selected, improvements should show a strong positive correlation with customer and marketplace improvement indicators, captured in Items 7.4 and 7.5. The correlation between quality and customer indicators is a critical management tool. It focuses management on key attributes, based upon the nature of the company's business. In addition, the correlation may reveal emerging or changing market segments, or reflect the changing importance of attributes.

6.2 *Company Operational Results.* This Item calls for reporting performance and improvements in operational quality and productivity of the company. Paralleling Item 6.1, which focuses on attributes that matter to the customer, Item 6.2 focuses on attributes that best reflect overall company performance. Such attributes are of two types: (1) generic—common to all companies, and (2) business- or company-specific. Generic attributes include cycle time, internal quality, and other factors that relate to productivity, as reflected in use of labor, materials, energy, capital, and assets. Indicators of productivity, cycle time, or internal quality should reflect overall company performance. Business- or company-specific effectiveness indicators vary greatly and may include rates of invention, environmental quality, export levels, new markets, and percentage of sales from recently introduced products or services.

6.3 *Business Process and Support Service Results.* This Item calls for reporting performance and improvements in quality, productivity, and effectiveness of the business processes and services that support the principal product and service production activities. This demonstrates how support units of the company link up with and contribute to overall improvement in quality (reported in Item 6.1) and overall improvement in company operational performance (reported in Item 6.2). This Item is thus a useful device in aligning support activities with the company's overall principal quality, productivity, and business objectives. Through this item, special requirements—which differ from work unit to work unit, and which define work-unit effectiveness—can be set, tracked, and linked to one another.

6.4 *Supplier Quality Results.* This item calls for reporting quality levels and improvements in key indicators of supplier quality. The term *supplier* refers to external providers of products and services upstream and/or downstream from the company. The focus should be on the most critical quality attributes from the buyer's point of view. Trends and levels of quality should reflect results by whatever means they occur—via improvements by suppliers within the supply base, through changes in selection of suppliers, or both.

Key Characteristics of the Award Criteria

1. *The Criteria are directed toward producing results.* The core values outlined here reflect the dual-result goal of the Criteria. These results are a composite of key performance areas summarized as follows:

- Customer satisfaction
- Customer satisfaction relative to competitors
- Market share
- Customer-related improvement indicators such as complaint reduction and customer retention
- Responsiveness and cycle time
- Product and service quality
- Internal quality, productivity, waste reduction, and asset utilization
- Company-specific effectiveness indicators such as new markets, new technology, and new products
- Supplier quality and supplier development
- Environmental quality, occupational safety and health, and regulatory compliance
- Employee development, well-being, and satisfaction
- Contributions to national and community well-being

Assessment of these results is based on one or more of three factors: (1) improvement trends; (2) current levels, and (3) benchmarks, evaluations, and other comparisons that establish levels and trends relative to the performance of others, especially appropriately selected leaders.

2. *The Criteria are nonprescriptive.* The Criteria represent an integrated set of requirements incorporating the ten core values. However, they do not prescribe how these values are to be implemented in a particular company. Specifically, they do not prescribe:

- Company organization
- Quality organization, if any (the seven Categories do not necessarily correspond to departments or company units)

▴ Specific quality techniques
▴ Type of quality system
▴ Method of quality system implementation
▴ Technologies to be used

The Criteria are nonprescriptive because organizations, techniques, and technologies vary greatly among businesses, depending on business size, type, and other factors. Also, by focusing on requirements, companies are encouraged to develop unique, creative, or adaptive overall approaches to achieving the goals.

3. *The Criteria link process to results.* The Award Criteria focus on the linkages between processes and results. Integration is achieved through many direct and indirect relationships and linkages among the requirements. In addition, many parts of the Criteria call for aggregation and assessment of unit-level and company-level performance, thus encouraging an integrated view of all activities.

4. *The Criteria are part of a diagnostic system.* The Criteria and scoring system form a two-part diagnostic system. The Criteria focus on requirements; the scoring system focuses on the factors that should be used in assessing strengths and areas for improvements. Together, they direct attention to activities that contribute to reaching the goals and results.

5. *The Criteria are comprehensive.* The requirements contained in the Criteria cover all operations, processes, and work units of a company. In addition, the Criteria support business strategy and business decisions and pertain to all transactions, including those related to fulfilling public responsibilities, such as meeting all key environmental requirements.

6. *The Criteria include key learning cycles.* The arrows in Figure 3-1 denote linkage and dynamic relationships and feedback among the framework elements. The primary dynamic characteristic of the Criteria is their inclusion of cycles of continuous improvement. These cycles of learning, adaptation, and improvement are explicit and implicit in every part of the Criteria. The cycles have four stages:

a. Planning, design of processes, selection of indicators, deployment of requirements
b. Execution of plans
c. Assessment of progress, taking into account internal and external indicators
d. Revision of plans, taking into account progress, learning, and new information

7. *The Criteria emphasize quality system alignment.* The Criteria call for improvement cycles to occur at all levels and in all parts of the company.

To ensure that improvement cycles carried out in different parts of the organization do not operate at counterpurposes, overall aims need to be consistent or aligned. Alignment in the Award Criteria is achieved via interconnecting and mutually reinforcing key indicators, derived from overall company requirements. The latter relate directly to delivery of customer value, improvement of organizational performance, or both. The key indicators are intended to channel activities toward agreed-upon goals. At the same time, they avoid detailed procedural prescriptions and unnecessary centralization of process management. Key indicators thus provide a basis for deploying customer and company performance requirements to all work units. Such alignment ensures consistency while at the same time challenging work units to consider new approaches to superior performance.

The Award Criteria and Quality-Related Corporate Issues

The Award Criteria are linked to a number of corporate efforts, which are discussed below.

Incremental and Breakthrough Improvement

Nonprescriptive, results-oriented Criteria and key indicators focus management's attention on what needs to be improved. This approach helps ensure that improvements throughout the organization contribute to the organization's overall purpose. In addition to supporting creativity in approach and organization, the results-oriented Criteria and key indicators encourage breakthrough thinking—openness to the possibility of major improvements as well as incremental ones. However, if key indicators are tied too directly to existing work methods, processes, and organizations, breakthrough thinking may be discouraged. For this reason, analyses of operations, processes, and progress should focus on the selection and value of the indicators themselves. This helps ensure that indicator selection does not unwittingly stifle creativity and prevent beneficial changes.

Benchmarks may also stimulate breakthrough thinking. Benchmarks offer the opportunity to achieve significant improvements based on adoption or adaptation of current best practice. In addition, they encourage creativity through exposure to alternative approaches and results. Also, benchmarks represent a clear challenge to "beat the best," thus encouraging major improvements rather than incremental refinements of existing approaches. As with key indicators, benchmark selection is critical. For this reason, benchmarks should be reviewed periodically for appropriateness.

Financial Performance

The Award Criteria address financial performance via three major avenues: (1) emphasis on quality factors and management actions that lead to better market performance, market share gain, and customer retention; (2) emphasis on improved productivity, asset utilization, and lower overall operating costs; and (3) support for business strategy development and decisions.

The focus on superior offerings and lower costs of operation means that the principal route to improved financial performance is by channeling activities toward producing superior overall value. Delivering superior value—an important part of any business strategy—also supports other business strategies such as pricing. For example, superior value offers the possibility of charging price premiums or competing via lower prices, which may enhance market share and asset utilization.

A business strategy usually addresses factors in addition to quality and value—for example, market niche, strategic partnerships, facilities location, diversification, acquisition, export development, research, technology leadership, and rapid product turnover. A basic premise behind the Award Criteria is that quality principles support the development and evaluation of business decisions and strategies, even though many factors other than product and service quality must be considered.

Potential Applications of the Award Criteria to business decisions and strategies include:

1. Quality management of the information used in business decisions and strategy—scope, validity, and analysis
2. Quality requirements of niches, new businesses, export target markets
3. Quality status of acquisitions—key benchmarks
4. Analysis of factors—societal, regulatory, economic, competitive, and risk—that may bear upon the success or failure of strategy
5. Development of scenarios built around possible outcomes of strategy or decisions including risks of failure, probable consequences of failure, and management of failure
6. Lessons learned from previous strategy developments, within the company or through research

The Award Criteria and evaluation system take into account market share, customer retention, customer satisfaction, productivity, asset utilization, and other factors that affect financial performance. However, they do not call for aggregate financial information such as quarterly or annual profits to be supplied in applications for Awards. This exclusion is made for several technical, fairness, and procedural reasons.

First, short-term profits may be affected by such factors as accounting practices, business decisions, write-offs, dividends, and investments. Some industries historically have higher profit levels than others. Also, the time interval between quality improvement and overall financial performance improvement depends upon many factors. This interval would not likely be the same from industry to industry or even for companies in the same industry.

Second, the Award Criteria address performance relative to rigorous, customer-oriented, company performance criteria. Though improved quality should improve a company's financial performance, its financial performance depends also on the quality performance of competitors, which the Award process cannot measure directly. The inclusion of aggregate financial indicators in evaluations would thus place at a disadvantage many applicants in the most competitive businesses.

Lastly, financial performance depends upon many external factors, such as local, national, and international economic conditions and business cycles. Such conditions and cycles do not have the same impact on all companies.

Invention, Innovation, and Creativity

Invention, innovation, and creativity—discovery, novel changes to existing practices or products, and imaginative approaches—are important aspects of delivering ever-improving value to customers and maximizing productivity. While the state of technology may play a key role in corporate involvement in research leading to discovery, innovation and creativity are crucial features in company competitiveness and can be applied to products, processes, services, human resource development, and overall quality systems. The Award Criteria encourage invention, innovation, and creativity in all aspects of company decisions and in all work areas. For example:

- ▲ Nonprescriptive criteria, supported by benchmarks and indicators, encourage creativity and breakthrough thinking as they channel activities toward purpose, not toward following procedures.
- ▲ Customer-driven quality places major emphasis on the "positive side of quality," which stresses enhancement, new services, and customer relationship management. Success with the positive side of quality depends heavily on creativity—usually more so than steps to reduce errors and defects, which tend to rely on well-defined quality improvement techniques.

- Human resource management stresses employee involvement, development, and recognition, and encourages creative approaches to improving employee effectiveness, empowerment, and contributions.
- Continuous improvement and cycles of learning are integral parts of the activities of all work groups. This requires analysis and problem solving throughout a company.
- Strong emphasis on cycle time reduction in all operations encourages companies to analyze work paths, work organization, and the value-added contribution of all process steps, thus fostering change, innovation, and creative thinking.
- Strong emphasis on cycle time and design encourages rapid introduction of new products and services, including those based on new concepts emerging from research.
- Quality and quality improvement requirements are deployed to all work units, including research, development, and other groups with responsibility for addressing future requirements. For such groups, measures and indicators are expected to reflect quality, productivity, and effectiveness appropriate to the exploratory nature of their activities.
- Focusing on the future requirements of customers, customer segments, and customers of competitors encourages companies to think in terms of attributes and, hence, find innovative and creative ways to serve needs.

Service Quality

Much has been said about the different natures of services and manufactured goods. Most comparisons seeking to emphasize differences focus on customer contact ("moments of truth") service experiences, distinguishing such experiences from hard goods. The distinctions relate mainly to the importance of and unpredictability of human factors and to the intangibility of services. Based on such comparisons, some analysts then argue that separate Award Criteria should be created for services.

A single set of criteria is used because the Award addresses basic quality system *requirements*, not the specific methods for meeting these requirements. Each of the twenty-eight Items spells out several requirements that are equally valid for service and manufacturing organizations. Accordingly, all applicants for the Baldrige Award must address the same set of basic requirements. However, applicants need not (and usually do not) address them in the same way. Information in the application must be sufficient to show that there are well-defined *systems* and *processes* that produce results of the type described earlier. A key requirement is that these systems and processes show continuous improvement in an *appropriately selected* set of results indicators. The ability to demonstrate improvement across such a wide range of results indicators is valid evidence of a strategy for addressing overall organizational performance. That is, the company's strategy does not seek to trade off gains in one key results area for losses in another. Strategies yielding improvements in all key results areas are regarded as worthy of emulation.

The single set of criteria for manufacturing and service organizations thus implies neither sameness in customers nor standardized behaviors in service providers. It does not imply that mere conformity or defect reduction are the only aims or the principal aims of quality improvement in a service organization.

From the point of view of service quality, there are two especially important aspects of the Baldrige Criteria: (1) customer-driven quality and (2) customer relationship management. These are described in detail below.

Customer-Driven Quality

Quality is judged by the customer. All product and service attributes that contribute value to the customer and lead to customer satisfaction and preference must be addressed appropriately in quality systems. Value, satisfaction, and preference may be influenced by many factors during the customer's purchase, ownership, and service experiences. This includes the relationship between the company and its customers—the trust and confidence in products and services—that leads to loyalty and preference.

This customer-driven quality concept includes not only the product and service attributes that meet basic requirements, but also those that enhance and differentiate them from competitive offerings. Such enhancement and differentiation may include new offerings as well as unique product-product, service-service, or product-service combinations. It may also include enhancement or differentiation based on special relationships and/or responsiveness.

Customer-driven quality is thus a strategic concept. It is directed toward market share gain and customer retention. It demands constant sensitivity to emerging customer and market requirements, and measurement of the key factors that drive customer satisfaction. It also demands awareness of developments in technology, and rapid and flexible response to customer and market requirements. Such requirements extend well beyond defect and error reduction, merely meeting specifications, or reducing complaints. Nevertheless, defect and error reduction and elimination of causes of dissatisfaction contribute significantly to the customer's view of quality, and are thus also important parts of customer-driven quality. In addition, the company's approach to recovering from defects and errors is crucial to improving its quality and strengthening its relationships with customers.

Figure 3-3. 7.2 Customer Relationship Management.

Describe how the company provides effective management of its relationships with its customers and uses information gained from customers to improve customer relationship management strategies and practices.

AREAS TO ADDRESS

a. how the company determines the most important factors in maintaining and building relationships with customers and develops strategies and plans to address them. Describe these factors and how the strategies take into account fulfillment of basic customer needs in the relationship; opportunities to enhance the relationships; provision of information to customers to ensure the proper setting of expectations regarding products, services, and relationships; and roles of all customer-contact employees, their technology needs, and their logistic support.

b. how the company provides information and easy access to enable customers to seek assistance, to comment, and to complain. Describe types of contact and how easy access is maintained for each type.

c. follow-up with customers on products, services, and recent transactions to help build relationships and to seek feedback for improvement.

d. how service standards that define reliability, responsiveness, and effectiveness of customer-contact employees' interactions with customers are set. Describe how standards requirements are deployed to other company units that support customer-contact employees, how the overall performance of the service standards system is monitored, and how it is improved using customer information.

e. how the company ensures that formal and informal complaints and feedback received by all company units are aggregated for overall evaluation and use throughout the company. Describe how the company ensures that complaints and problems are resolved promptly and effectively.

f. how the following are addressed for customer-contact employees: 1) selection factors; 2) career path; 3) special training to include knowledge of products and services, listening to customers, soliciting comments from customers, how to anticipate and handle problems of failures ("recovery"), skills in customer retention, and how to manage expectations; 4) empowerment and decision making; 5) attitude and morale determination; 6) recognition and reward; and 7) attrition.

g. how the company evaluates and improves its customer relationship management practices. Describe key indicators used in evaluations lead to improvements, such as in strategy, training, technology, and service standards.

With customer-driven quality, organizations need to determine the key attributes of products and services and the relative importance of these attributes to their customers (or customer segments). Thus, product and service "dimensions" are treated equally from a conceptual point of view. However, it is important to emphasize that equal treatment of product and service dimensions does not imply identical or even similar design or delivery process characteristics. Product and service designs need to take into account the specific characteristics of each key dimension as well as the performance requirements associated with each dimension.

Customer Relationship Management

Customer relationship management is a central issue in the Baldrige Award Criteria. It is the most heavily weighted "process" Item and includes the most detail. Because of its importance, this item is presented in Figure 3-3.

Conclusion

The requirements described in this chapter show that the Award Criteria are extremely sensitive to service and relationship issues. Accordingly, much attention is devoted to a wide range of "frontline" requirements—those that relate to the direct interface between the company and its customers. Clearly, the requirements are not confined to matters of technical quality dimensions. The Award Criteria stress that applicants address perceived quality and technical quality, and that strategies be based on the critical quality dimensions—from the customer's point of view.

4

The Impact of the Baldrige Award

W. Kent Sterett and Dale C. Durkee, Southern Pacific Transportation Company

It has been half a decade since the first Malcolm Baldrige National Quality Awards (the Award) for excellence in quality management were presented. It seems appropriate to reflect on the Award, as it, too, is subject to the process of continuous improvement that it so diligently honors. To identify the Award's impact on service quality, we asked, What's going right? Are expectations being met? What's the pace of progress? Do others value the process? What's the fallout? And is the process being replicated for those not yet included in its scope?

The Award

The Award was created after congressional hearings resulted in the enactment of Public Law 100-107, signed on August 20, 1987. The Award program led to the creation of a new public-private partnership. Principal financial support for the program comes from the private sector through the Foundation for the Malcolm Baldrige National Quality Award, established in 1988.

The Findings and Purposes Section of the law states, in part, that a "national quality award program of this kind in the United States would help improve quality, productivity and competitive position" by:

▴ Helping to stimulate American companies to improve quality and productivity for the pride of recognition while obtaining a competitive edge through increased profits.

> After winning the Award in 1992, Horst Schulze, president and chief operating officer of The Ritz-Carlton Hotel Company, stated that "our commitment to continuously improve is stronger than ever. Since we are all empowered to provide the most reliable and consistent products and services in the industry, we will become more efficient than ever before."

It is clear from this statement that the National Quality Award is not an endpoint for the Ritz-Carlton; rather, it's a fresh charge of competitive energy, as intended.

▲ Recognizing the achievements of those companies that improve the quality of their goods and services and providing an example to others.

Fred Smith, chairman of Federal Express, remarked, "It has been a great honor indeed to be the first service company winner of the MBNQA and it has inspired us to redouble our TQM efforts, expand our own benchmarking process to learn how to bring every aspect of our company up to world class standards and continue to work with our customers, who are in effect our business partners, to help them develop world class products and services.

These partnerships, both with suppliers and customers, enable us to be the premier express transportation company in the world and through the utilization of the Total Quality Management process we can continue to improve both our and our customers' business results."

Again, we hear values expressed that are in accord with the Award's design.

▲ Establishing guidelines and criteria that can be used by business, industrial, governmental, and other organizations in evaluating their own quality improvement efforts.

On a broad organizational basis, we discovered a unique application as described by Rob Davis, AT&T Universal Card's quality vice president, when he observed that "Universal Card used the Baldrige as a template as management began to build the organization and develop its strategic plan."

In a more classic application as was envisioned for the Award, Mary Ann Horwath of Texas Instruments explained, "One of the nice things about the MBNQA criteria is the way it helps you prioritize your improvements based on the weighted scores. . . . The application-writing phase is crucial and should not be avoided or skipped. We learned a tremendous amount about ourselves during that time."

Mary's use of the Award hits the nail on the head for what the Award promotes!

▲ Providing specific guidance for other American organizations that wish to learn how to manage for high quality by making available detailed information on how winning organizations were able to change their cultures and achieve eminence.

> In both small and large companies, we are hearing the desired kinds of statements. "We've visited Milliken and Disney, and Xerox has been here. We've benchmarked Spiegel's— and all of that is Baldrige inspired," said Guy Schoenecker, president and chief quality officer at Business Incentives, an Award applicant.
>
> "Our people now think in terms of processes, and you'll see approach/deployment/results as a discipline in our business plan. The battles we had over our application helped change the culture. It did a lot to open this company up. Also, there hasn't been a de-emphasis on quality because of the current recession. That's another positive change," said Dan Whelan of Ford Motor Company.

From the comments, it is evident that the intended reinforcing actions are taking place and having the desired impact for the applicants. But what about the companies that do not apply?

Criteria Distribution

When we look at the numbers, we can conclude that the process is working. The Award is generating a large amount of interest, making available detailed information, and fostering changes in business practices for improved quality. Those inquiring about the Award go beyond the eligible groups defined to include governments, nonprofit organizations, and academicians. One indicator of interest in TQM practices is that since 1988, 667,000 copies of the Award Criteria booklet have been requested. At this rate, the booklet will soon rival some bestsellers in the number of copies distributed.

Responsibility for the Award process has been assigned to the Department of Commerce. The National Institute of Standards and Technology (NIST), an agency of the Department's Technology Administration, manages the Award program. NIST has allowed photocopying of the Criteria, and many organizations have taken the opportunity to further distribute the materials to employees and vendors, in many cases with print runs in the thousands. Every conceivable type of company, a multitude of communities, and a list of foreign countries that reads like the United Nations have requested and received the Criteria. It is clear that hundreds of thousands of people are being exposed to the tools and techniques highlighted in the Criteria.

There has been national and international interest in the Award Criteria far beyond those intending to apply. A comparison of Criteria request data and applications data shows that the Baldrige is not an Award race; rather, with fewer than 1 application for every 2,000 Criteria booklets requested we have a massive learning process that goes far beyond the Award itself.

Who Is Using the Criteria?

By looking at formal applications for the Award, we see balanced participation in the three eligible categories: small business, service, and manufacturing (see Figure 4-1). These data support the Award goal of sharing among and within organizations of all types, the key quality requirements and techniques for rapid improvement.

There is close competition among many good candidates, as evidenced by the number of site visits examiners make prior to the final selections. These visits are sound evidence of the increasing level of implementation broadly shared in many organizations. The numbers also reflect the rapidly maturing understanding of the importance and techniques of quality management in the service and small business industries. It is encouraging to note that the percentage of small companies applying during the 1988 to 1992 period has increased from 18 to 48 percent.

Further evidence of the Award's positive influence are the achieve-

Figure 4-1. Applications for National Quality Award.

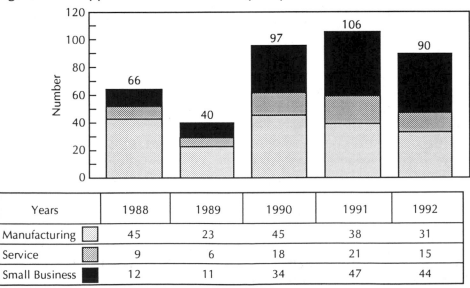

Years	1988	1989	1990	1991	1992
Manufacturing	45	23	45	38	31
Service	9	6	18	21	15
Small Business	12	11	34	47	44

ments being made in each of the Award categories. There are more winners in an environment of increasingly tougher standards as the understanding of what works grows each year and is reflected in the annual fine-tuning of the Award Criteria.

Beyond the Process

The extended impact of the Award process is most impressive. There is serious learning going on about quality and its management. Organizations are endeavoring to learn more about quality using the Criteria as a guide.

Focused on the Award are an increasing number of examiners (including nine judges) who, in turn, transfer quality knowledge to those with whom they interact on a day-to-day basis. In 1992, there were 148 experienced examiners and 118 newly trained examiners. They are selected to represent as broad a base of industry types as possible and are senior people in their organizations. The multiplier effect of this group is difficult to quantify, but obviously is high. An especially strong multiplier are the academics, who influence a large stream of students.

Even when we consider that there is generally only one examiner per organization, there are hundreds of organizations that now have an in-house expert directly involved in the organization's implementation efforts.

Spreading the Word

The Award-winning companies are helped in sharing their experiences and advice for improving management of quality. Be it through public news media, professional associations, or other interested stakeholders, the experiences are being studied by many organizations. For example, one of the high-level exchanges facilitated by the Conference Board is the Quest for Excellence Conference. In this two-and-one-half-day conference, held nationally and regionally, CEOs and other key individuals from each of the past year's winning companies offer a presentation and respond to participants regarding each of the Criteria categories. High-level leaders network with their counterparts, view the winning company's displays, and learn how to better manage quality. Attendance in 1988 was 421; by 1992 it had grown to a cumulative total of 7,063.

What Is the Fallout?

The Malcolm Baldrige National Quality Award competition has provided information and education in Total Quality Management for managers and professionals and other employees throughout industry, government, and nonprofit institutions. All learn from the Award Criteria, the experience of applying for the Award, and from the publicized experiences of the Award winners. The impact and influence has been wide-ranging.

Additional Quality Awards

Ruth Haines of the Federal Quality Institute estimates that over half of U.S. government offices and agencies have or are in the process of implementing quality management practices. Although for many this effort is just beginning, most were about two years into implementation by the fall of 1992. This is a large-scale effort. According to an article in the Spring 1992 *National Productivity Review*, "The federal government is turning to quality because it is too important to be championed only by private-sector leaders. The federal government is the nation's biggest employer and its biggest customer. With three million civilian and two million military employees, it is bigger than the first seventeen of the Fortune 500 companies combined."

Government isn't just reporting on quality, it is using it! Two awards have been designed for quality, and they follow the Baldrige Award in both process and scoring, tailored to fit the government environment. The Presidential Award for Quality and the Quality Improvement Prototype Award have been presented to selected federal groups since 1988.

Likewise, the Department of Defense's top command has been in attendance at quality workshops with the Juran Institute and others. According to Lieutenant-General Vernon J. Kondra, at a recent Juran Institute quality conference, "Never have so many people and supplies been moved farther and faster than in Operation Desert Shield/Desert Storm . . . the tools of Total Quality Management helped to ensure its success."

A positive movement is also underway at the state level, where the National Governors Association is monitoring and facilitating the establishment of State Quality Awards. Many states are using the Baldrige Award process and criteria as a model for their awards. At this writing, over half of the states have an awards program in place or are in the process of establishing one (see Figure 4-2). Specifically, twenty-two states have awards, and of these, seventeen are modeled after the National Quality Award. An additional nine states report that they are about to implement quality awards, all inspired by the National Quality Award. Two excellent models of reinforcement—yet different in their approach—are Minnesota's Council of Quality, which grants awards and financial payments; and Wisconsin's Quality Network, which focuses on learning and information sharing without awards or financial payments.

Figure 4-2. State Quality Awards.

States Using the Malcolm Baldrige National Quality Award as a Model for Their Award Programs

Alabama	Massachusetts	New Mexico
Arizona	Michigan	New York
Colorado	Minnesota	North Carolina
Connecticut	Missouri	Rhode Island
Florida	Nevada	Tennessee
Maine	New Jersey	

States With Own Award Framework

Delaware	Pennsylvania	Wyoming
Maryland	Virginia	

States Planning, But Award Not Implemented

California	Indiana	Ohio
Georgia	Kentucky	Oregon
Hawaii	Montana	Utah

States With No Reported Award Action

Alaska	Mississippi	South Dakota
Arkansas	Nebraska	Texas
Idaho	New Hampshire	Vermont
Illinois	North Dakota	Washington
Iowa	Oklahoma	West Virginia
Kansas	South Carolina	Wisconsin
Louisiana		

Professional Associations

A list of professional associations with an emphasis on quality would be lengthy. For our purposes, we focus on the American Society for Quality Control (ASQC), the association directly involved in the administration of the National Quality Award.* ASQC's total membership has more than doubled since the first National Awards, standing at 113,000 in 1992.

In 1991, a service division was formed for the membership with interests specific to that sector. As of October 1992, new members were

*American Society for Quality Control, P.O. Box 3005, Milwaukee, Wisconsin 53201-3005.

signing up at an average of over 200 per month, according to Kateri
Brunell, ASQC Service Industry Division's membership chairman.
"We've already reached 3,821 members and with at least 70 percent of
the total U.S. employee base working in a service capacity there's no
near-term end in sight for our growth."

Applications in Other Fields

In 1991, the outcome of a national demonstration project (NDP) on
quality improvement in health care was published. With an eight-month
time limit on the project, the focus was on using technical methods to
solve specific problems. However, the study concluded: "The evidence
of the NDP is . . . that quality improvement, far from being a diversion,
leads directly to greater efficiency and cost reduction. . . . Far from being
an interesting, but tangential, activity, there is reason to believe that
quality is likely to become an important basis for competing in health
care over the next decade." Major hospital systems such as Hospital
Corporation of America are aggressively implementing quality processes
in their hospitals nationwide.

Likewise, some creative and interesting new partnerships are developing between business and education. Major universities are involved
with companies such as Xerox, Ford, Eastman Kodak, Shell Chemical,
Allied-Signal, and IBM. The companies are helping academicians build
Total Quality Management (TQM) into their curricula. At the heart of
this is a recognition of the National Quality Award Criteria as a model
for Total Quality Management. For example, excellent TQM programs
are offered by University of Chicago, Columbia University, Fordham
University, University of Illinois, University of Maryland, MIT, University
of Miami, University of New Mexico, Oregon State University, and
University of Tennessee. Look for this list to grow rapidly in the 1990s.

Most of these joint company-university TQM programs have been
offered at the graduate level. However, there is an accelerating trend
toward teaching quality techniques on the undergraduate, vocational,
and K–12 levels. This extension of learning is being speeded by specific
quality skills materials offered to educators on interactive media by major
suppliers such as Jostens Learning Corporation. In addition, universities
are working with community colleges to upgrade and add higher-level
competencies in quality and engineering education. Funding for this
comes from the National Science Foundation, with thirty-two universities
involved.

Community colleges are forming consortia to meet the geographic
training needs of multi-location companies and also for sharing curricula.
In turn, colleges and businesses are working together to obtain federal

and state grants from sources such as NIST and the Economic Development Network (EDNET).

Speedy Information Exchange

The National Science Foundation has established electronic data systems with universities to speed information sharing and transfer knowledge. The American Association for Quality and Higher Education has established a database system with over 200 business and engineering schools participating. The Northern Center for Quality Excellence at Fort Collins, Colorado, was formed by companies in the area to extend quality training between and beyond their organizations to other companies and the community. Among the contributing organizations are Hewlett-Packard, Kodak, Teledyne/Water Pik, and Anheuser-Busch.

Regional TQM cooperatives are being established across America. There are thirty-three companies participating in the Center for Quality Management in New England. Five companies in the Northwest have formed Partnerships for Competitiveness with the help of the American Electronics Association, and the association is planning for more in the future. The U.S. Chamber of Commerce is sponsoring a satellite seminar series on quality learning, targeted to small business operators. And Houston's American Productivity and Quality Center is establishing a computerized international benchmarking clearinghouse and bulletin-board service for information sharing.

In short, there is a flood of ideas crossing organizational boundaries and helping form new relationships for improving quality.

A Review of Performance

We thought it might be interesting to look at performance in relation to Baldrige Award winners. Obviously, the United States has yet to develop the historical validation that the thirty-year track record of winners of the Japanese Deming Prize provides. It is encouraging, though, to see that Deming Prize winners have consistently improved or maintained a level of business performance above the industry average.

The Conference Board, a New York business research group, and PIMS Associates, a subsidiary of the Strategic Planning Institute in Cambridge, Massachusetts, have both reported positive results from studies of the impact quality management can have. Other studies, such as those by Arthur D. Little and Rath and Strong Inc., however, have not been as encouraging.

Congressman Donald Ritter, with the endorsement of twenty-nine other members of Congress, asked the General Accounting Office (GAO) to determine the impact of Total Quality Management practices on the performance of selected U.S. companies. The findings are summarized as: "Achieving high levels of quality has become an increasingly important element in competitive success."

The General Accounting Office was able to define a clear model of Total Quality Management, as shown in Figure 4-3. And in another encouraging sign, this first GAO report on twenty high-scoring applicants for the Award is GAO's all-time bestseller, with more than 60,000 copies distributed worldwide.

Happily, corporate quality programs seem to be achieving their primary aim. As reported in a survey of logistics professionals done by Cleveland Consulting Associates: When asked to indicate the results perceived from quality improvement efforts, 74 percent of respondents cited increased customer satisfaction in their top three ranking results, and 39 percent ranked it number one (see Figure 4-4).

Also, improved internal productivity was a major benefit. Over 42 percent of respondents ranked it in the top three, although just 7 percent called it the top benefit. In general, external quality awards were not major aims for the respondents' programs. While 20 percent of the

Figure 4-3. GAO Total Quality Management model.

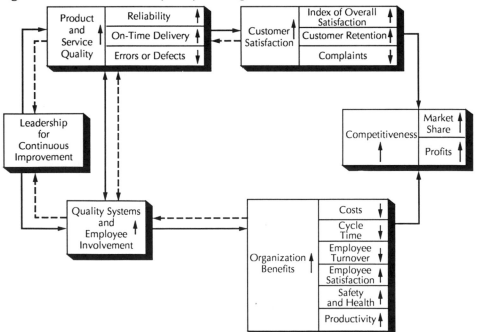

Note: The solid line shows the direction of the total quality processes to improve competitiveness. The dotted line shows the information feedback necessary for continuous improvement. The arrows in the boxes show the expected direction of the performance indicators.

Figure 4-4. Results of quality improvement efforts.

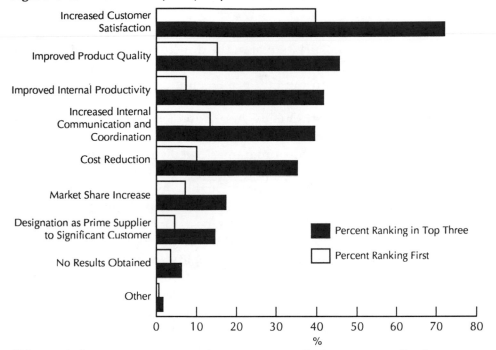

What results has your company seen from corporate quality improvement efforts?

companies noted that they were working toward the prestigious Malcolm Baldrige Award, the majority were not working toward any award. In contrast, quality education programs are underway in many businesses where they involve a large percentage of the work force.

According to the 1992 Electronic Business survey, U.S. commitment to quality is growing, not shrinking. Executives said they increased spending on quality-related training from 2.1 percent of revenues in 1991 to 3.9 percent in 1992. The percentage of companies who give quality training to upper management increased from 66 percent in 1991 to 90 percent in 1992, and the number that give training to top executives increased from 56 percent to 83 percent. The percentage of companies using quality improvement measurement tools rose from 40 percent to 76 percent.

Of seventy companies polled in the Electronic Business survey, 91 percent said their quality improved versus their competitors; 73 percent said their industry segment improved versus the foreign competition. And no company had scrapped its TQM program. Bear in mind that the 1991 National Quality Award winners came from this industry group, where quality is being valued for its contribution to business performance.

International Impact

Quality awards similar to the Baldrige Award are being given in Mexico, Australia, and Canada. Curt Reimann, the director of the Baldrige Award program at NIST, has communicated with people in Sweden, Spain, Colombia, Argentina, and the European Community about our national program. In addition, quality experts from several European countries have created the European Quality Award, which uses criteria inspired by the National Award Criteria. Reimann recently helped Mexico and Sweden set up Baldrige-style programs. Swedish authorities say they handed out more copies of the criteria in the first ten weeks than Reimann's office did in the National Quality Award's first year. "We looked at various supplier awards, ISO 9000, the Deming prize, and many others, but the Baldrige was the best tool for quality improvement," says Johnny Lindström, president of the Swedish Institute for Quality, which administers the Swedish Quality Award.

The Malcolm Baldrige National Quality Award reinforces service quality on an international level more by indirect influence than direct application. There will be other awards, keeping in mind that each country has unique values. These awards may include businesses in international services, health care, and education as well as government agencies and volunteer organizations. There may be other criteria and different scoring. Yet what the National Quality Award has created is an approach and a process that can be replicated easily and that meets society's needs for learning, talking about work quality, and serving others better in this world.

Conclusion

Although an action considered by many companies, the practice of requiring suppliers to apply for the National Quality Award—as both Motorola and certain units of IBM have done—has not spread. Curt Reimann recognizes that the multiplier potential of this practice is yet to be realized: "For a decade or more, a lot of people have beaten up on the government, business leaders, trade associations, and professional associations. They've asked, 'Why don't you do something about this mess? Why do you sit there and let other nations eat our lunch?' Well, here we are, making companies more competitive, working with them to define the elements of competitiveness, and alerting a lot of organizations to what they need to do to help the national effort."

Dr. Robert Blake, of Scientific Methods Inc. and a long-time organization development and change consultant, has stated: "I see quality as a cultural norm that must be owned and committed to by all work associates. To the extent that the actions triggered by the Baldrige Award bring about the commitment to solve problems, cause associates to work comfortably with the truth (rejecting—and not hiding behind—casual explanations), and cause leaders to take on the ownership and responsibility . . . it will be a positive force for improving quality."

There are now hundreds of thousands of individuals learning how to achieve quality. There are thousands of organizations committed to delivering quality and learning to manage for quality. And there are thousands of practitioners—individuals dedicated to advancing quality, helping organizations implement quality practices for competitive advantage and the common good.

We feel that the National Quality Award has helped American business reach the point of critical mass, that point where the momentum begins to carry us forward. We have a broad base of understanding, a large number of trained individuals and groups, committed executive leadership, and focused consumer attention. We are now part of a global quality revolution.

Are we seeing real value in the pursuit of quality? The answer comes across loud and clear, from a host of major companies: Corning, Digital Equipment, Eastman Kodak, Florida Power and Light, Ford Motor Company, General Motors, Globe Metallurgical, Goodyear Tire and Rubber, GTE Corporation, Hoechst Celanese, IBM, L. L. Bean, Milliken & Co., Motorola, Paul Revere Insurance Group, Seagate Technology, Timken Company, USAA Insurance, Westinghouse Electric, and Xerox Corporation. And we can add the U.S. Government and its agencies such as the Department of Defense, the Internal Revenue Service, and the Federal Reserve Banking System.

As these major organizations turn to their suppliers and request, demand, or even require quality evidence in order to do business, we will see the rush of change. There will be standards and certifications such as in ISO 9000. And there will be cultural changes guided by continuous reviews of conditions for excellence, including the Malcolm Baldrige National Quality Award Criteria.

References

"Award Criteria." Malcolm Baldrige National Quality Award. Washington, D.C.: General Accounting Office, 1993.

Berwick, Donald M. et al. *Curing Health Care: A Report on the National Demonstration Project on Quality Improvement in Health Care.* 1st ed. San Francisco: Jossey-Bass, 1991.

Blake, Robert, Scientific Methods Inc. Telephone interview with Dale Durkee on observations about quality and the Malcolm Baldrige National Quality Award, October 27, 1992.

Brunell, Kateri, American Society for Quality Control; vice-chairman, Services Industries; ASQC Service Industries Division and Qualtec Quality Services, Inc., consultant. Telephone interview with Dale Durkee, October 27, 1992.

Burrows, Peter. "Forget the Nitpicks! The Baldrige is Working." *Electronic Business* 18, no. 13 (Oct. 1992), pp. 34–38.

———. "TQM Reality Check: It Works, But It's Not Cheap or Easy." *Electronic Business* 18, no. 13 (Oct. 1992), pp. 47–52.

United States General Accounting Office. *Survey of Quality Management of Federal Organizations*, GAO/GGD 939BR. Washington, D.C.: General Accounting Office, 1992.

George, Stephen. *The Baldrige Quality System (The Do-It-Yourself Way to Transform Your Business)*. New York: John Wiley & Sons, 1992.

Haines, Ruth, Federal Quality Institute. Telephone interview with Dale Durkee, November 2, 1992.

Horwath, Mary Ann, Quality Training Administrator, Materials & Controls Group, Texas Instruments. *Juran IMPRO Conference*, p. 3C–8, Atlanta 1991.

Jorgensen, Barbara. "Industry to B Schools: Sharpen Up on TQM or Else," *Electronic Business* 18, no. 13 (Oct. 1992), pp. 85–90.

Kano, Noriaki et al. *The TQC Activity of Deming Prize Recipients and Its Economic Impact*, 21st Annual Meeting of Japanese Society for Quality Control, Tokyo, Japan, April 1982.

Kondra, Lieutenant-General Vernon J., Military Airlift Command, Operation Desert Shield. *Juran IMPRO Conference*, p. 1.9, Atlanta 1991.

Mendelowitz, Allan I. et al. *Management Practices—U.S. Companies Improve Performance Through Quality Efforts*. Report to the Honorable Donald Ritter, House of Representatives, May 1991. GAO/NSIAD-91-190. Washington, D.C.: General Accounting Office. A free copy of the report may be ordered by calling (202) 275-6241. Alternatively, it may be ordered by writing to the U.S. General Accounting Office, P.O. Box 6015, Gaithersburg, MD 20877.

Parent, Robert, The Conference Board. Telephone interview with Dale Durkee, October 27, 1992.

Port, O. et al. "Special Report—Quality." *Business Week*, November 30, 1992, pp. 66–75.

Read, William F. *The State of Quality in Logistics: A Survey of Logistics Professionals*. Cleveland: Cleveland Consulting Associates, 1991, p. 17.

Schulze, Horst, President and COO, Ritz-Carlton Hotel Co. News release, Atlanta, Georgia, October 14, 1992.

Whiting, R. "AT&T Started a Quality Bonfire to Learn How to Put it Out." *Electronic Business* 18, no. 13 (Oct. 1992), pp. 95–102.

Wood, Patricia B. "How Quality Government is Being Achieved." *National Productivity Review*, Spring 1992, pp. 257–264.

PART II

CREATING THE QUALITY VISION

5

Service Quality as Strategy

Paul Kahn, President, AT&T Universal Card Services

A saturated marketplace in a mature industry dominated by large, well-established players doesn't often turn corporate planners into venture capitalists, particularly when their traditional business is in an entirely different field. At first glance, the successful entry of AT&T into the credit card field seems serendipitous. Closer inspection reveals a careful plan that took full advantage of the weaknesses of an industry relying on "business as usual."

AT&T's Universal Card Services (UCS) has broken convention with a vengeance, bringing a telecommunications and computer-oriented corporation into the forefront of the "bank card" business. UCS has created an enormous opportunity for both bottom-line return on investment and overall enhancement of the AT&T brand image by focusing tightly on a single strategic element: service quality.

How effective has the effort been? UCS's first-year numbers indicate that a service quality commitment resonated strongly with potential customers. It took only 78 days for the new enterprise to gain its first million accounts. By 120 days, UCS had cracked the top ten rankings. At the end of its first year, UCS numbered more than 8.5 million customers and employed more than 2,000 associates occupying seven buildings in four states. In addition, AT&T's Universal Card Services was a 1992 Malcolm Baldrige National Quality Award service industry winner.

Today, two years after its entry, the AT&T Universal Card is second in terms of accounts and cardholders in the U.S. credit card industry. It recently won its ten millionth customer account and is profitable well ahead of schedule. Significantly, in 1991, Equitrend, a major national quality rating service, ranked UCS fourth in consumer satisfaction, behind Lexus, BMW, and Mercedes, and ahead of Acura. The next credit card in the rankings was forty-second.

That kind of explosive growth in a long-established industry rarely happens, and when it does, it is normally the result of a breakthrough technology or product that leapfrogs existing competitors. That is exactly what has happened here, in a service industry, but it has not been driven by advanced technology. Leading-edge telecommunications and computing resources are certainly present, but the real breakthrough has been one of corporate attitude.

AT&T set customer delight at the foundation of everything designed into the new enterprise, and then used the detailed template provided by the Malcolm Baldrige National Quality Awards criteria as a design point for operations. In doing so, the ground rules defining the bank card industry were radically rewritten, with service quality jumping to the forefront as a competitive advantage and product differentiator.

Existing industry players have had to reconsider their competitive strategies. AT&T's rapid, profitable expansion—a business worth over $5 billion in receivables that continues to grow at a remarkable 7 percent a month—has attracted other major entrants into the field. Both General Motors and General Electric have announced credit card offers of their own that seek to make use of and expand their existing, huge customer bases. It seems unlikely that they will remain the only new competitors.

The strategic key that AT&T's Universal Card sees as central to its continued growth is its obsession with service quality that leads to customer delight. Success in a restructured industry will hinge on the degree to which that competitive edge can be maintained.

Protecting the Core Business

AT&T's initial interest in creating UCS reflected ongoing corporate concern about the state of its traditional core business—long-distance telecommunications. Since AT&T's breakup in 1984, the corporation's focus has been, understandably, directed toward anticipating and responding to competitive pressure from other carriers against that customer base.

The idea that a corporate-branded credit card including calling card functions could be a strong auxiliary avenue to keep, attract, and recapture long-distance customers was intriguing. While it entailed substantial investment and some risk, the business proposal saw the AT&T Universal Card becoming profitable after four years of operation and stressed that the AT&T brand reinforcement function was the primary goal. Most appealing was the entry strategy AT&T had developed. The corporation's planners were convinced that there was a gaping window of opportunity for a major new player to rewrite the ground rules in the credit card industry.

Opening a Window of Opportunity

The existing credit card industry was under very little pressure to make service quality an integral part of day-to-day operations. While some competitors did give it emphasis, it was not perceived as a critical factor in the industry. Front-line positions answering customer calls and responding to written inquiries were treated as entry-level, high-turnover slots. Minimal wages, training, and attention to the customer service component of the credit card business were the industry norm.

We brought in a core development staff, drawn half from the credit card industry and half from AT&T, that was keenly aware of changes we wanted to make in creating UCS. Our experience was that customer delight was anything but typical. Billing problems, disputed claims, card replacements, and virtually any other customer interaction routinely stretched out into weeks or even months of frustration. The UCS management team felt that putting our prime emphasis on meeting and exceeding customer needs would not only succeed, it would lead the industry into a new era.

That message found ready acceptance at AT&T because the basic service quality emphasis was already strongly embedded in its corporate culture. Within AT&T, there's a deeply appreciated tradition of customer service that extends back a century. The enduring image of the small-town telephone operator of early twentieth-century America as the hub of local life, called whenever there was a problem because she could be depended on to find the right person to answer it, is part of the AT&T self-image.

We set out to create a corps of customer-oriented Universal Card telephone associates and support associates who embraced service quality with an almost messianic fervor. UCS was determined to recreate the potent image of the helpful AT&T telephone operator in a new environment, buttressed by the most powerful high-tech tools. AT&T's core competencies in telecommunications and computing technology could be effectively mated with the cultural core competency that embraced service quality as a goal.

Taking a "Green Field" Approach

AT&T's analysis of the opportunity led to the development of the service quality strategy as the key to the business plan. We had a rare chance to exploit the "green field" advantage that came from starting from scratch, without an entrenched base of existing procedure and mindset.

Our team decided to use the Baldrige guidelines as the blueprint for the new business operation. We reasoned that the quality approach used so successfully by previous Baldrige winners to turn around faltering enterprises could also be employed guiding a startup's design.

The goal was to create a total service quality corporate culture at UCS, creating an esprit de corps that would make delivery of extremely ambitious service goals possible. Team quality, defined in terms of customer delight, continuously measured using the Baldrige standards as a guide, became the center point of each employee's work day.

UCS carefully structured its business, considering everything from an employee-friendly physical working environment to compensation strategies, to support that goal. At UCS, there is a marked emphasis on front-line employees as the key deliverers of service quality.

Among nonmanagement workers, the premier subset of employees are telephone associates providing customer assistance, and they are paid accordingly. The skills of phone associates operating during the graveyard shift, when complex international calls are routine as a consequence of a twenty-four-hour, seven-day world-wide availability policy, are particularly appreciated, by both customers and UCS.

The Consumer Advocate Strategy

A key part of AT&T's strategy was to embrace a proactive consumer advocacy philosophy. Put another way, we felt very strongly that there was room in this business to give something back to the customer. This strategy was driven by two goals: achieving a competitive advantage that created a significant and visible differentiator from its established competition; and building an efficient new business that met the Baldrige standards.

The AT&T Universal Card immediately gained public recognition from its decision to link interest rates to the prime rate and to waive annual fees—moves which addressed consumer dissatisfaction with the industry as a whole. "Free for Life" and variable interest rates were key factors in the AT&T Universal Card's immediate consumer acceptance.

The "Delight the Customer" philosophy guiding UCS's operations also led to the conscious decision to take an active role as customer advocate whenever a card member had a dispute concerning a transaction involving the AT&T Universal card. Customer service personnel are trained and encouraged to act as card-member advocates in all disputes, sending out letters from AT&T seeking favorable settlements of disputed charges and/or personally calling anyone from store clerk to senior management in order to quickly resolve the problem.

Successful interventions that result in delighted customers are sought-after accomplishments for UCS customer service staff, and are rewarded with both official recognition and informal respect from co-workers. The most noteworthy successes are incorporated into a growing body of corporate legend and get retold with relish by everyone from executives to front-line phone associates.

Working With Suppliers

UCS took a leadership position in a widely visible effort to reform the credit bureau reporting industry as a natural result of its pro-consumer stand and because of a need to meet its internal quality expectations. Since service quality is the most potent force directing UCS's measurements and operational goals, consumer advocacy and internal quality initiatives regularly coincide.

When UCS began operations, it found that one out of every ten credit-worthy applicants was rejected because of inaccurate information reported by credit bureaus. UCS pressured the credit industry to open its records to consumer review and correction. AT&T is working closely with the leading bureaus to help them establish and operate robust quality programs based on the Baldrige template. It also has trained its phone associates, in association with the bureaus, to act as effective mediators when consumers have questions or differences regarding the credit information about them.

The improvement in credit reporting has been dramatic. UCS currently measures report accuracy that is 250 percent better than when it began business in the summer of 1991. UCS routinely forges similar close bonds with its other suppliers in order to assure its ability to meet Baldrige standards in the delivery of service quality.

Employee Recognition and Performance

Service quality and financial goals are inseparable in UCS's vision, and comprehensive internal communications programs, awards, and recognition structures are key elements in its delivery strategy. Figure 5-1 shows UCS's management practices.

Unique to the UCS strategy is a compensation structure, colloquially called "a piece of the pie," that provides direct monetary tie-ins for each management and nonmanagement employee to achieve the daily team quality goals. These service-quality goals are based on both internal and external customer needs. More than 100 daily internal quality measurements are taken throughout UCS that keep close track of critical service quality elements, such as the average speed of answer (ASA) and the telephone abandon rate. Figure 5-2 is an example of the measurement process.

Since a measurement focus is such a strong part of UCS's business design, we looked for a way to ensure that people throughout the business paid close attention to the information we generated. We posted the daily quality results all around the buildings, on both TV monitors

Figure 5-1. Management practices and mechanisms to promote employee involvement.

Practice	Participation	Feedback Mechanism
Your Ideas . . . Your Universe (UCS suggestion program)	I/G*	Acknowledgment of receipt of employee suggestion within 24 hours; written acceptance decision; monetary awards/recognition
Ask Fred	I/G	Within 1 week, executive vice president (EVP) of Customer Services responds to improvement opportunity
Employee opinion survey	I	Results communicated in special issue of *UNIverse* and Business Team organizational meetings; volunteers participate in follow-up activities (employee action teams, focus groups)
Meeting of the Minds	I	Small groups of employees meet with a Business Team member to discuss improvement opportunities
TLC Leadership Committee	I	Continuous improvement of TLC programs; monthly programs; quarterly challenges; results posted on bulletin boards; wellness publications
Quarterly UCS-wide meetings	I/G	Business Team question and answer sessions at all locations
Quarterly Lakeside Chats	I/G	Question and answer session with EVP of Customer Services
Quality Awareness Week	I/G	Recognition for commitment to quality via sharing rallies, employee publications, and public recognition
Recognition programs	I/G	Peer recognition; awards
Contributions to employee publications	I/G	Employee bylines; certificates of appreciation
Improvement teams	G	Semi-annual sharing rallies; quarterly recognition breakfasts
Excellence Award program	G	Daily results; financial incentive awards

I = individual, G = group

Source: Copyright 1992 AT&T.

Figure 5-2. Product and service production and delivery measurement process.

Processes Measured	Types of Measures	Frequency of Measure	Subset of Process Measures
Customer Inquiry Management			
18 process measures covering: telephone inquiry, claims, correspondence, settlement retrieval, company hand-offs, labeled envelopes, customer letters, and telephone disputes	Accuracy, timeliness, courtesy	20–100 daily depending on measure	Telephone inquiry, correspondence
call management	Abandoned, ASA	100%	Telephone inquiry
Application Processing			
24 process measures covering: application processing, correspondence, telephones, support, fraud transactions, and inbound and outbound collection calls	Accuracy, timeliness, courtesy	40–80 daily depending on measure	Application processing, telephone inquiry, correspondence
call management	Abandoned, ASA	100%	Telephone inquiry
Payment Processing			
9 process measures covering: address changes, exception payments, and payments	Accuracy, timeliness	100–450 daily depending on measure	Payment processing, address changes

Source: Copyright 1992 AT&T.

and paper. Having everyone's daily compensation bonus riding on those results gives a strong reason to improve the numbers. The strategy works very effectively.

In addition to daily incentives, UCS regularly uses a broad range of individual and team awards as a means of employee recognition. These range from informal Polaroid snapshots of teams and team members tacked to department walls to major company recognitions. Employee involvement in feedback vehicles is also robust. UCS's employee suggestion program is used by more than 55 percent of its associates. The annualized rate of suggestions per employee is currently over five per year—thirty times the banking industry average. Employees get a direct percentage share in the dollar benefits of accepted suggestions.

An Information-Hungry Environment

Once UCS created an operating framework centered on the delivery of superior service quality, its motto DELIGHT THE CUSTOMER propelled the direct customer-UCS interface into a dominant position, affecting planning, equipment investment, and personnel policies.

The 70,000 or more customer calls a day that can pour into UCS's Jacksonville, Florida, headquarters demand a major company focus on technology to provide immediate, accurate service responses. UCS is halfway through the implementation of a major Strategic Systems Plan that calls for substantial capital investment in the development of a secure, integrated enterprise-wide database instantly accessible by specifically authorized management and customer service personnel. At this time, each customer account contains more than 1,000 elements detailing its entire life cycle. Needed information can be rapidly called up by customer service personnel in an icon-based Windows environment.

There are four key customer listening posts that feed information into the enterprise so it can drive improved service quality:

1. Customer expectation and needs research
2. Performance research
3. Direct customer feedback
4. Process management

The communications loop driving the UCS customer service strategic response is shown in Figure 5-3.

Institutionalized Employee Learning

Each new customer service associate at UCS receives four weeks of specialized training at Universal Card University (see Figure 5-4). This is job-specific coursework that acclimates new employees to the technical demands of the job—how to use the work stations efficiently and answer inquiries—and acculturates them into the service quality, delight-the-customer environment of UCS. Employees are empowered to take any

Figure 5-3. Customer relationship management strategies.

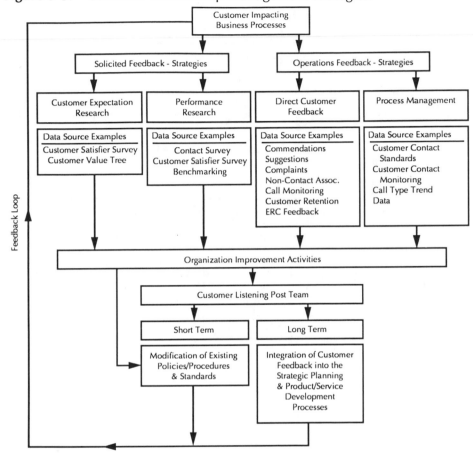

actions needed to rapidly resolve customer problems without consulting managers or rule books—and they are expected to use their initiative. Trainers are responsible for their students' quality results for thirty days after graduation, at which point there is a follow-up evaluation for each student.

Continued training and education is encouraged on an individual basis and encompasses personal development areas such as wellness programs and on-site college courses along with career-based skills development and quality methodologies. All employees are encouraged to continually broaden their skills and knowledge as part of the team response to increasingly demanding quality goals. In line with this, UCS also provides complete tuition reimbursement for any undergraduate or graduate coursework, job-related or not.

Figure 5-4.   Universal card university.

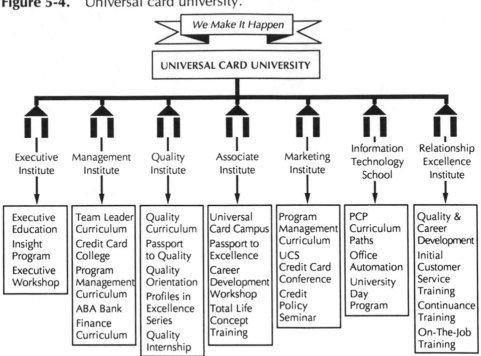

Source: Copyright 1992 AT&T.

Going Beyond Efficiency

UCS is structured as a lean, efficient operation. Calling-load forecasts are broken down into fifteen-minute intervals, and customer service personnel are called in on a just-in-time basis to ensure that precisely the right number of personnel is available at any given time. Customer service personnel are extremely productive. Nearly 90 percent of each phone associate's total on-the-job work time is spent actually responding to customer calls.

While efficient operations are an important part of a customer service strategy, even greater emphasis is given to employee efforts that go beyond that carefully calibrated structure. Central to UCS's service quality mind-set is the recognition and celebration of extraordinary individual actions that have resulted in customer delight. The guiding maxim is QUALITY IS IMPORTANT, EFFICIENCY IS IMPORTANT, BUT IF A CUSTOMER IS IN TROUBLE, DROP EVERYTHING AND HELP. The results of this philosophy are a rapidly growing number of success stories that motivate the UCS work force, reinforce a powerful product and brand image, and build word-of-mouth promotion of the Universal Card.

Outstanding employee initiative is feted. For example, there's the time a phone associate received a collect call from a stranded tourist in Paris, whose card had been "eaten by the ATM" on a Saturday afternoon. The card member was broke, scheduled to leave the next day, and desperate. While the customer stayed by the phone, the UCS associate called the U.S. embassy, arranged for a limousine that would carry the traveler to the one bank still open in the city, and authorized an emergency cash advance.

Other "trophy" stories—the wandering Alzheimer's patient found for a distraught husband by placing a hold on the card and arranging twenty-four-hour notification of any activity; the cardholder whose dispute with a hotel was championed and not only received dropped charges but a free weekend's stay—are impossible to miss after even brief exposure to the UCS work force. The narratives form an integral part of the pride in service quality delivery that has been designed into the business.

Consideration for All Potential Customers—Even Marginal Ones

The long-term service quality strategy adopted by UCS is not confined to its most attractive customer subsets. In keeping with the consumer advocacy focus that runs throughout its operations, UCS puts substantial effort into its relationships with two groups of people usually given short shrift by most businesses: denied applicants and delinquent accounts.

Each person who applies for an AT&T Universal Card and is turned down receives a detailed description of the specific reasons why they were denied. In addition, disappointed applicants are given a telephone number they can call if they have questions. Thousands of calls to this number are answered by UCS employees every week, an expense accepted as part of a service strategy designed to win customer and AT&T brand loyalty.

Existing customers who have let their accounts descend into the nether world of delinquency also benefit from the service quality focus at UCS. Collections are known internally as customer assistance, and operate under the slogan, MAKE 'EM HAPPY, MAKE 'EM PAY.

In sharp contrast to the traditional aggressive, intimidating collections posture commonly employed, UCS personnel have as their prime goal keeping the account. Collections works closely with customers, explaining what they are doing at each step of the collections process, and working to find ways to assist in payment. Follow-up surveys ask successfully dunned customers to rate UCS's handling of the collection process and to offer suggestions on how it could be improved. A remarkable eight out of ten respondents say that they would recommend Universal Card to a friend as a result of their experience.

Coping With Success

The startling speed with which Universal Card has become a leading player in the bank card industry has caused AT&T to rethink parts of its strategy. The commitment to service quality remains undiminished, but the role of the Universal Card product has been expanded.

Originally designed to buttress AT&T's core business of long-distance calling, the Universal Card has succeeded beyond expectations. In 1991, calling-card revenues for Universal Card members grew 40 percent. The offering has forged more than 16 million direct AT&T consumer relationships and has grown a business currently valued at nearly $2 billion.

Universal Card's ability to contribute to the overall AT&T brand image has also been extremely successful:

- 1992 Malcolm Baldrige winner
- Best Product of 1990—*Business Week*
- *Fortune* Magazine—Hot Product of the Year
- *USA Today*—One of the Year's Hottest Products
- The Year's Top Marketing Idea by *Advertising Age*
- The Top Banking Innovation by *American Banker*
- The Edison Award (Best New Idea) from the American Management Association
- The Compass Award for Service Excellence from the American Marketing Association

Figure 5-5. Improvement of process standards.

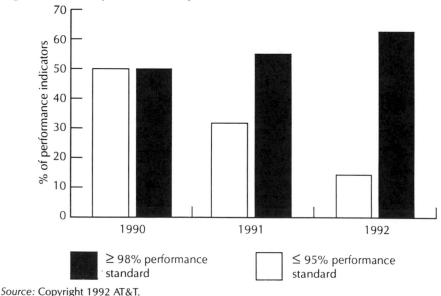

Source: Copyright 1992 AT&T.

▲ Gold and Bronze Effies for customer advertising and communications from the American Marketing Association
▲ The Echo Award from the Direct Marketing Association
▲ The AT&T Chairman's Quality Award/Gold Improvement Award

A strong, institutionalized focus on measurement and continuous quality improvement is central to UCS strategic plans. During 1991, for example, more than a dozen key quality indicators were raised from a 95 percent goal to 100 percent. See Figure 5-5 for a summary of results. Universal Card's explosive growth has made it more than an auxiliary source of brand identification and core business reinforcement. It is a rapidly growing profit center for AT&T, significantly ahead of schedule.

Employee Motivation

In the service quality strategy that UCS is depending on to continue its growth, a potential obstacle is the growing need to attract and retain a

Figure 5-6. Employee action and opinion results.

Employee Opinion Survey	(% of Favorable Responses)						
	Annual	Monthly				Benchmarks*	
	1991	Oct 91	Nov 91	Dec 91	Jan 92	National* Norm	Financial* Services Norm
Management Leadership	55	79	75	77	75	47	57
Teamwork	65	79	81	79	77	68	72
Job Satisfaction	68	80	82	75	83	70	70
Corporate Values	N/A	88	75	83	82	NA	NA
Empowerment	61	80	60	86	87	NA	NA

Adverse Indicators			
Employee Attrition	1990	1991	Benchmark†
UCS Total	9.7%	10.1%	
Manager	8.7%	9.0%	14%
Associate	10.1%	10.5%	23%
Customer-contact associates	10.2%	10.7%	23%
Absenteeism Rate		1991	Benchmark*
Managers	N/A	1.3%	1.3%
Associates	N/A	2.2%	1.9%

Source: International Survey Research—Fortune 500 companies that do surveys.
†Source: Saratoga Institute for HR Research—financial services companies.
Source: Copyright 1992 AT&T.

quality work force. At the present time, UCS uses a detailed screening process to sift through potential employees and hires only one in ten. A determined attempt to create an attractive employee environment is part of the UCS strategy to ensure that ample numbers of qualified applicants are available and remain with the company.

In addition to the cultural emphasis on employee education and empowerment described earlier, UCS pays careful attention to the employee's overall needs. Among other actions, the company sponsors a wide range of day-care initiatives and provides a fully staffed and equipped twenty-four-hour health club on-site that is free to employees and their spouses. UCS is a major sponsor of culture and the arts in the communities surrounding its offices, and actively encourages employee involvement in nonwork activities.

Improved employee satisfaction is one of the primary areas targeted by UCS as critical to providing service quality. Employee satisfaction, measured by monthly and annual opinion surveys, provides an aggressive company-wide focus on employee satisfaction with positive results (see Figure 5-6).

Maintaining a "Delight the Customer" strategy is the challenge that UCS sees as key to continued growth. Market entrants like GE and GM are entering the competition for accounts, and existing bank card issuers are adopting similar campaigns to stem their loss of market share. AT&T's Universal Card has built up remarkable momentum with its Baldrige-designed focus on service quality, and it continues to invest heavily in people and in the cultural commitment to deliver that service quality.

6

Service Quality Principles

D. Otis Wolkins, GTE Corporation

During the early 1980s, GTE's senior management team began focusing on quality as a critical business issue. There was clear evidence from other industries that being a quality leader provided a competitive edge. Conversely, it was clear that companies that failed to meet customers' quality needs and expectations could see their market shares erode rapidly or could even go out of business.

The lessons of poor quality being taught by the electronics, automobile, motorcycle, and other consumer goods industries were not lost on GTE. Senior management began to question the company's efforts to assure quality and to consider how well existing practices would serve the company in coming years, which almost certainly would be ones of fierce global competition.

To find out how well GTE compared with other companies, GTE's chairman and CEO launched a corporate-wide benchmarking program called BEST. The data produced by the BEST program made it clear that GTE had a lot of work to do if it expected to be a global leader in all its businesses. Many "gaps" in quality performance were identified, adding up to a total picture of a company that, while not in a crisis, certainly had great room for improvement. These quality gaps became the driving force for GTE's quality strategy, and closing these gaps became the objective of all GTE employees.

The BEST program not only produced competitive benchmark data but also provided some insights into how other companies were pursuing quality. Armed with this information, GTE senior management began to address company-wide quality improvement in 1985, with three major initiatives. These initiatives became the seeds of GTE's quality strategy, which has been aggressively implemented throughout the company.

The initiatives were (1) to define quality for the corporation from a customer perspective; (2) to establish a quality policy demanding leadership in all markets served; and (3) to create the office of vice-president–quality services to oversee and assist implementation.

Since 1985, GTE's emphasis on quality has increased steadily throughout the company, and has become a driving force in all decision making. Further, the past seven years have provided great insight into the requirements for successfully implementing a quality strategy in a large service corporation.

Six Quality Principles

Creating a management style and environment for a service company that is conducive to quality improvement requires adherence to certain principles. These principles have been tested over time by organizations now considered quality leaders. These principles are applicable to manufacturing organizations, but they take on added significance for service organizations, which are not so readily geared to such "hard" techniques of quality improvement as Statistical Process Control and Design of Experiments.

These principles are absolutely critical to establishing and maintaining the proper environment for quality improvement that will enlist the support of suppliers, employees, and customers. They provide a mechanism for continuously evaluating the present situation and taking actions necessary to stay on course in what is now normally referred to as a strategy of continuous improvement. Adherence to these principles helps ensure that quality is seen as a business strategy to gain or maintain competitive advantage, and not just a program.

Implicit in these principles is an unmistakable emphasis on the company's attitude toward quality as stated in its vision or mission statement. This statement should carry a clear message on the importance of high-quality products or services. Further, the company's strategic plan should explicitly outline the various strategies that will be pursued to achieve or advance toward realizing the vision.

The company must be able to show its customers, employees, and suppliers that quality is an essential part of its operating philosophy. The clearer this message, the easier it will be to communicate it throughout the company and to the outside world.

Leadership

Definition and implementation of the company's quality strategy must be seen as a senior management initiative. The top officers of the company must take the lead in driving the company to increasingly higher levels of quality performance. Without this executive leadership, quality efforts will be largely confined to small advances in pockets of the organization, with very little impact on the overall business.

The idea that leadership is essential to quality improvement has been around for a long time. Management commitment to quality is so often stated that it has become trivial—so common an idea that little thought goes into setting forth management actions that prove the commitment. This gap can create a cynical response by employees. They quickly realize and understand this "quality gap" between words and actions, even though their response and enthusiasm for senior management's quality strategy influences the success of all quality improvement initiatives. The greater the gap, the more disappointing the results. Conversely, eliminating this gap results in high levels of employee involvement and commitment. Closing this quality gap, then, is essential to long-term success.

Education

All company personnel—from senior managers to entry-level employees—must be educated on the subject of quality. Senior managers must be "quality smart" if they are to be seen as leaders of the quality strategy. Only with a solid understanding of quality-improvement techniques can managers fully understand their roles in building and sustaining an environment that fosters employee commitment. Furthermore, managers must understand quality principles and techniques in order to review progress and recommend changes to the strategy, as required by competitive forces or changing customer expectations.

Three key areas must be addressed in order to educate senior managers. The first is the concept of quality as a business strategy vs. quality as simply a methodology to achieve low defect rates. All too often, companies view quality as nothing more than a way to achieve a low-cost position; it is clear, however, that the positive impact of quality on revenue growth can also affect a company's profit position.

Without high-quality products and services, a company cannot expect to maintain or gain market share. On the other hand, becoming a leader in quality can often aid a company in gaining market share at the expense of its competition, and these increased sales can result in increased profitability. It is also true that the market leader in quality can frequently command a premium price for its products and services, and this, too, can favorably impact the bottom line. A comprehensive quality strategy, therefore, must incorporate actions and programs to address both the cost and revenue sides of the business equation.

The second element of executive education is to understand the full range of tools and techniques available today to implement the quality strategy once it is clearly defined. This does not mean, however, that the executive must master the complex mathematics of Statistical Process Control or become intimate with the fine details of other statistical tools. But understanding how these tools can be applied to process improvement is necessary to assess whether or not the organization is pursuing the correct path.

The third, and perhaps most important, issue of executive education is the role of the executive in implementing the quality strategy. Many executives do not understand that their part extends beyond merely stating the company's commitment and then delegating responsibility to someone else. They must understand that their commitment and involvement in the quality strategy is critical to each employee.

Providing effective quality education to the company's executives will almost certainly change their behavior, allowing them to put quality prominently on the corporate agenda.

Without clear top-management understanding of these three areas, quality often takes a secondary role in the company's decision processes. Short-term financial performance becomes more important than long-term business success, and the "quality gap" grows increasingly wider.

Education helps not only in the formulation of an executive-led quality strategy, but also to outline the major programs to be developed or implemented in support of the company's vision. During the education experience, the executive team can begin to formulate a strategy that is correct for the organization, its competitive situations, and the marketplace. The result usually is a custom-tailored quality strategy and process that is unique to each company—an approach that employees can view as their own, rather than a program forced on them by outsiders.

Planning

The strategic planning process must encompass the quality measures and objectives to be used in tracking the company's success in achieving its vision. The strategic plan must become more than a statement of the present and future expectations for net income, return on investment, and other financial measures. It must also encompass the company's vision with respect to quality and provide a clear linkage between financial performance and quality objectives.

Financial performance and quality performance must never be separated in the operational philosophy of the company. The strategic plan sets the stage for these elements to work together to the same end, rather than being at odds with each other. While education provides the basis for understanding the relationship between quality and profit, the strategic plan provides the real measures and objectives of that relationship.

Quality measurements must be based on customer perceptions of a product or service, and any other measure of company performance must support these customer perceptions. It is common today to find many measures that are not based on customer perceptions but are instead measures of quality that drive internal operations. While these may be significant and necessary to monitor the company's manufacturing or service processes, they cannot be the primary measures of quality performance. Only customers can determine whether or not the company's products and services meet their requirements and expectations.

Customer perceptions can and must be measured. It is also useful to relate these perceptions to the competition. This not only lets a company know how its efforts are going, but it keeps an eye on how well the competition is doing. Significant improvement in performance does not guarantee anything in the marketplace if the competition's efforts achieve greater gains in the eyes of the customers. Quality measurements based on customer perceptions obviously are subject to change, and this requires a measurement-definition process that keeps up with customer expectations. Nevertheless, whatever method is used to measure customer perceptions and satisfaction, it must give more than a snapshot of the status quo. The measurement system must provide early warning signs of any shifts in customers' evaluations of the company's performance.

Anticipating new customer requirements and expectations often requires marketing processes different from what currently exists. Staying on the leading edge of customer perceptions clearly is a senior management responsibility.

Review

The review process is the single most effective tool that management can employ to change organizational behavior. While the strategic planning process lays out objectives and a measurement system, the review process provides the mechanism for ensuring constant attention to achieving objectives. The review process encompasses many different forums for ascertaining present and future performance. Weekly department meetings, monthly operations reviews, and regular reports to the company's board of directors are the most common ways to apprise management.

It is common for the review process—especially the monthly operations review—to concentrate entirely on the month's financial performance: revenues, net income, return on investment, and so on. If month after month, year after year, senior management only reviews financial statistics, it sends a clear message that to succeed requires only meeting the budget. Any actions designed to help improve the health of the business in the long term, but resulting in a poor report at this month's operations review, will be forsaken.

If, however, reports and discussion of quality performance have a prominent place on the review agenda, then a completely different message is sent: Meeting the company's quality objectives is an important factor in the overall performance of the business. In fact, the linkage between high quality and low cost becomes obvious when quality and financial performance are examined together during an operations review.

Management's unending attention to reviewing quality will eventually lead to all employees' being sensitive to quality performance. No single individual or department would want to be the reason for a poor report to senior management. Good reports foster pride while poor results always generate a great deal of activity to correct deficiencies.

Communications

The speed with which the quality strategy is implemented throughout the organization is a direct function of the company's communications processes. Communications must reach three different audiences, each with different expectations of what constitutes good communication.

The first and perhaps most important audience is the employees. Employee communications must emphasize quality objectives, as stated in the strategic plan, as well as the company's present status with respect to these objectives. A critical point here is that employees know the company's mission, goals, and objectives. Without this knowledge, they will be unable to identify with and comprehend communications that report on performance. Employees want and deserve credible performance reports. This requires a communication process that educates all employees on company plans and objectives.

Very often, senior management is reluctant to share the details of a strategic plan with employees for fear that this information will be misunderstood or perhaps fall into the wrong hands. If this is the prevailing philosophy, the employees will inevitably take this as an issue of trust, or rather, mistrust. Employees will never sign on to a program in a climate where management and employees are on opposite sides of a "trust gap." Furthermore, employees cannot be expected to put out maximum effort in their daily work while being kept ignorant of overall company strategy. The key to ensuring that employees are operating at their full potential, in accord with company goals, is to develop a communications strategy that enlists their support and understanding of the company's direction.

The second audience is customers—the end users of a company's products and services. Some quality improvement activities are readily and instantly recognized by customers, but many are not so easily seen. It is possible to achieve major quality improvement in a company's operations, yet have no significant impact on customer perceptions. Perception often lags reality when dealing with customers; this requires a communications process that keeps customers informed of improved service levels.

These communications can take many forms, from informative inserts in monthly invoices to full-scale forums at which customers discuss key service issues with company executives. The best forms of communication provide a mechanism for getting customer input regarding the perceived results of quality efforts. But whatever forms are used, the intent is to make customers aware that services have been improved. Comprehensive communications ensure that any lag between perception and reality is minimized.

Finally, communications must reach out to other company stakeholders; including suppliers, shareholders, and security analysts. Public recognition of a company as earnestly pursuing quality as a strategic weapon in an increasingly competitive marketplace can go a long way toward helping the company achieve its objectives.

This last audience must be reached by more than just advertising. Advertising can, and certainly should, have a place in the communications process—but only a small part, at that. For example, quality issues can be addressed by the company's managers in public conferences sponsored by various organizations that speak to business issues. Many of these conferences over the last few years have been dedicated to quality, but conferences on other topics can also provide a platform. In short, there are many ways to get the company's attitude toward quality into the public media, so every appropriate means should be pursued.

It is often said that communications is one of the hardest things to do well in business, especially for large organizations. Colleges and universities offer courses and curricula on this subject. Specialists in communications are used more and more by the business world to maximize communications opportunities. But the fact that effective communications is difficult does not relieve senior management from developing an effective communications strategy. While experts in this area can be helpful, it nonetheless remains a leadership issue.

Rewards and Recognition

Rewards and recognition are the reinforcing mechanisms for ensuring that quality leadership processes become institutionalized within the company. Employees want to be recognized for high quality performance. They see a lack of connection between good work and recognition as evidence that management doesn't really care. The quality gap widens and achieving improved quality becomes elusive.

The subject of rewards and recognition is complex. It deals with the root causes of why people do what they do—human behavior—and so constructing a rewards and recognition process requires a great deal of thought. Management must consider employee expectations, competitive forces, and the character of the business (growth, profitability, investment risk). What works for one company may not work for another. A custom-made rewards and recognition process is a virtual requirement.

Nevertheless, there are certain characteristics of a successful rewards program that can be used to evaluate an existing plan or establish a new one. The most useful tool for understanding the reward environment is the employee opinion survey. Questions that address employee feelings can give management the knowledge to correct any problems that exist.

Rewarding good results produces lasting change, promotes employee pride, and inspires high morale. Penalizing poor results may produce improvements in the short term, but will eventually lead to behavior that impedes high-quality performance. "Driving out fear," as it is commonly called, is so obvious a management philosophy that it doesn't require elaboration. Suffice it to say that, while many companies profess this philosophy, some do not have the elementary human resource systems to support the concept.

Processes that give immediate reward and recognition for desired results are most effective. The longer the time between the achievement and the recognition or reward, the weaker the connection between them. If the time is very long—one year, for example—confusion will almost certainly result.

Often, incentives and bonus plans are given out only on the basis of "meeting the bottom line." An effective quality strategy must change this so that quality performance becomes an equal partner with other business objectives, in the incentive system as well.

Summary

There is nothing unique about developing and implementing a quality strategy. Simply stated, quality improvement involves the fundamental, time-tested techniques that top management applies to all other aspects of business. Business objectives must be defined, implementation processes must be developed, and management systems must ensure that the entire organization is working to achieve its objectives. The key to success is leadership—the first principle of quality improvement.

By its very nature, leadership is a process, a pursuit that never ends. Quality becomes an integral part of the leadership process when it is supported by education, planning, review, communications, and rewards and recognition—the remaining five principles of quality improvement. When these principles are applied effectively, quality improvement takes on a long-term dimension that eventually influences all aspects of the business. By vigorously integrating these principles into its management philosophy and systems, an organization will not only improve customer satisfaction but realize the rewards of sustained growth, reduced costs, and increased profitability.

7

Service Within: Middle Managers as Service Leaders

Karl Albrecht, Chairman, The TQS Group

The most frequently quoted statement from the book *Service America! Doing Business in the New Economy* is:

> IF YOU'RE NOT SERVING THE CUSTOMER,
> YOUR JOB IS TO SERVE SOMEBODY WHO IS.[1]

This means that everybody in the organization has customers, either external "paying" customers or internal "working" customers. Those who never see the paying customers nevertheless have customers of their own—namely, the other people and departments in the organization who depend on them.

Internal Service

The concept of internal service is one of the most exciting and compelling ideas of the service management paradigm. It has the potential for animating an organization, for aligning internal departments and groups toward a common purpose, and for concentrating energy on the ultimate objective of delivering superior customer value.

The internal service concept supersedes the old notion that there are two kinds of people in the organization—that is, "customer service" people and everybody else. This old concept leads to a number of unhealthy attitudes that work against the objective of offering superior customer value. The existence of a "customer service" department, for example, can easily tempt those in other departments to feel that someone else is looking after the customers, and so they don't have to worry about them. By implication, anyone who is not in "customer service" has other, more important things to do.

[1]Karl Albrecht and Ron Zemke (Homewood, Ill.: Dow Jones-Irwin, 1985).

This often leads to a pronounced form of introverted thinking. People in some departments see themselves as doing the work of their own department, rather than contributing to the ultimate value delivered to the customer. They preoccupy themselves with their own tasks, procedures, problems, and priorities. In the extreme, departments may exist as virtually independent fiefdoms, each defending its own way of life and answerable to no higher purpose than its own survival and territorial protection.

Indeed, some organizations are literally at war with themselves. Interdepartmental competition, feuding, and backbiting can divert precious energy from the issues of quality and customer value. This ultimately penalizes the front-line departments trying to create a high-quality customer interface. As a consequence, customers experience an inferior service product.

However, the internal service concept can reverse the effects of years of interdepartmental conflict by helping all units in the organization think in customer-value terms. When unit leaders adopt the customer-value focus, they compete less and cooperate more. They begin to grasp the reality of their interdependence and see the real possibility of competitive synergy for the organization as a whole.

Ideally, each internal department operates like a customer-focused business, much as it would if it were a company in and of itself, and its customers were free to buy its services from competitors. Indeed, some companies operate in exactly that way. The internal service unit has to demonstrate that it delivers value to its internal customers equal to or better than that obtainable in the free market. This entrepreneurial focus makes customer value the ultimate measure of a unit's success.

Applying this concept, however, can be a challenging proposition. Years of habit, tradition, and introverted thinking create formidable resistance. Making the internal service approach work requires that middle managers learn to act less like bureaucrats and more like service leaders. Service leadership is crucial, offering great opportunities for developing truly competitive, customer-focused cultures in a business organization.

The unit or department leader must begin to think like a corporate leader. He or she must view the unit in terms of its contribution to its customers, not merely in terms of how it carries out its activities. Just as a company's leaders must understand the company's customers, create a vision and mission for the organization, and lead the way toward its accomplishment, so the unit leader must do the same. This requires careful thinking, skillful decision making, and strong personal leadership to help the people in the unit focus their energies on customer value.

Five Action Steps to Service Leadership

Service leadership involves five basic steps:

1. Identifying and understanding the unit's customers
2. Defining the service mission of the unit
3. Educating the people in the unit about customer value
4. Aligning or realigning the unit's systems toward customer value
5. Setting up a system for quality measurement and customer feedback

These five steps constitute the basic Total Quality Service (TQS) process, applied at the unit level.

Identifying and Understanding the Unit's Customers

There are certain common symptoms of a lack of customer-value focus in an organization, which show up as antagonistic behavior. Units that should treat one another as customers actually view these internal customers as enemies. The most common atrocities perpetrated by one unit against another are known as the "seven sins of internal service."

The Seven Sins of Internal Service

1. *The Black Hole*—Things seem to go in but nothing ever seems to come out. Requests for information, advice, pleas for special assistance, requests to expedite processes—all seem to go unheeded. The department operates on its own self-motivated priorities, and virtually ignores special requests from anybody except senior management or somebody else who can put on the heat.

2. *The Bounce-Back*—The department seems to make a hobby of rejecting requests for service on procedural grounds. "You didn't fill in line 24 of the standard Service Request Form." Or "We are returning your request without action because you failed to provide a budget number." Instead of calling up the customer department to get the missing information, they self-righteously reject the request and throw it back at the requesting department.

3. *Edicts*—The department seems to enjoy making declarations of what it will or won't do in the future. "Effective today, this department will no longer process budget requests unless they are accompanied by a written justification, signed by the unit supervisor." The message is "This is how it's going to be; you can take it or leave it."

4. *The Gotcha*—The department has a functional responsibility that puts it in a position of surveillance over others. In such cases, it may get

carried away with its policing roles, and take sadistic pleasure in catching people in other departments making mistakes or violating the rules. Internal audit, legal, and affirmative action departments often assume this role distortion and adversarial mentality.

5. *No-ism*—Some departments tend to be "yes departments" while others are "no departments." A "no department" is one that enjoys exercising its veto power. The folks there like to say no more often than they say yes. Instead of a can-do attitude, they have a "no, you can't" attitude. They are always telling their customers why something can't be done instead of looking for ways to meet legitimate needs.

6. *The Papermill*—The department likes to bury you in paperwork every time you try to get something done. They've got forms and special requests for everything you can think of. They've long since forgotten how to discuss a problem over the phone and take immediate action. Now everything has to be submitted on the standard form, in triplicate, with fifteen signatures, before they'll even decide whether to say yes or no.

7. *Turfism*—There's a jealous preoccupation with one's assigned area of responsibility, to the exclusion of common sense and compromise in the name of getting results. A turfist department is always poised for attack, just in case others get the idea that they can do something on their own or take unilateral action. All departments must look after their missions, of course, but it is not uncommon to see a turfist department head ignoring the needs of the customers and then jumping on them for trying to fulfill those needs themselves.

HOW TO BEGIN

To assess an organization's internal service orientation, one should examine the various departments' attitudes toward one another. Which departments have earned reputations as sinful operations in the eyes of their customers? Which ones make a point of avoiding any sins against their customers, and finding ways to add value to what they offer? Each unit leader can make an honest and objective appraisal of his or her unit's reputation in the eyes of its customers. This can be the starting point for creating a new focus on cooperation and customer value.

Another key part of understanding the organizational customer is to conduct some customer research. This involves going directly to the unit's customers, such as the managers or employees of departments that depend on its services. The customer focus group meeting, for example, is a simple but powerful method for discovering fundamental viewpoints, needs, attitudes, and wants of internal customers. This can be an informal discussion, led by a skilled moderator, to give customers a chance to express their needs in their own words. The manager of the serving unit may serve as the moderator or use a disinterested third party to serve in that role.

In the focus group method, the moderator explores various aspects of customer needs while an assistant records the ideas, opinions, judgments, and suggestions offered. Later, the unit manager and the team review the input and develop a *customer value model*, which is a list of the most important elements of value desired by the customers. These may include fairly obvious factors such as a cooperative attitude, speed of response to requests, flexibility in solving problems, and minimum paperwork. The research might also turn up some unexpected value factors such as willingness to educate the customer, giving the customer a greater voice in deciding how things get done, and delivering results in a form compatible with the customer's work processes.

Defining the Service Mission of the Unit

With the customer value model in hand, combined with a good understanding of the views and desires of the customer, the unit manager then formulates a *service mission* for the group. This mission statement should express who the customers are, as defined by their specific needs, what unique value the unit provides, and the special approach the unit takes to delivering that value. The unique value refers to the ultimate benefit in the customer's world—that is, what does the service enable the customer to do, or do better?

Educating the People in the Unit About Customer Value

The third step, once the unit manager understands the customer and has formulated a mission statement, is to *share the mission and its key ideas of customer value* with everyone in the unit. This can be an informal process for a small unit, or an intensive process of training and communication for a large group. The manager must make the task of communicating the customer-value message a never-ending one. This message must be refreshed and reinforced every day, in both words and behavior. All leaders in the organization have the responsibility of helping employees keep their minds focused on customer value, both internal and external, as the means for ensuring the organization's survival and success.

Aligning or Realigning the Unit's Systems Toward Customer Value

Next is a review of the systems used by the unit to deliver value to its customers. The leader and the key people in the unit should review all

work methods, procedures, policies, physical systems, information systems, and customer communications media from the standpoint of
customer friendliness. This also is a never-ending process that should
include everyone in the group. Employees who apply the processes
every day have a valuable perspective on the problems and pitfalls
involved. They also are likely to understand the impact of those processes on the customers.

Quality action teams are also a useful method for rethinking and
redesigning organizational systems and processes to make them more
effective. Small groups of interested and committed employees, given
the needed information and some useful quality-analysis tools, can often
identify significant improvement opportunities.

All members of the unit should be continuously seeking new and
better ways to work, trying to simplify and streamline the operation.
They should be trying to eliminate useless activities and refocus resources on creating value. And they should be eliminating unneeded
paperwork, making sure that critical information is available to those
who need it.

Setting up a System for Quality Measurement and Customer Feedback

The final step in the customer-focus process is building a system for
continuous assessment, measurement, and feedback. The unit's leaders should
be continuously assessing the quality of the service package, from both
the customer's point of view and in terms of organizational efficiency.
They need to use quality measurements carefully and positively, rather
than bureaucratically. And they need to set up an ongoing system for
gathering customer feedback and making that information available to
all employees so they know how well they are performing.

Customer feedback is extremely important. Although most managers instinctively shrink from the prospect of listening to their customers
complain, they and their units can benefit enormously from encouraging
customers to give feedback. Not all the feedback will be negative, and
much of it will be helpful in prioritizing improvements in the unit's
processes. When there is a request for customer feedback, the question
really asks "Will you teach us how to be a better service organization?"
The more customers believe the feedback is desired, the more information they will give, and the more valuable that information will be.

Applying the Five-Step Model

These five steps provide a basic and useful model for leadership, especially at the middle management level. If skillfully applied, this approach

can create an extraordinary sense of mutuality, alignment, and common purpose. However, the real challenge goes beyond applying the model to any one or all of the business units. The real challenge is for managers to become leaders. They must learn to provide more to their employees than just "management."

In the words of Professor Warren Bennis, noted authority on leadership,

TODAY'S EMPLOYEE IS
OVERMANAGED AND UNDERLED.

We are moving into an era in which personal leadership will be more important than management or administration. Leadership skills will be critical for creating the kind of organizational culture that enables people to deliver superior value to the customers and at the same time makes the organization economically successful. Quality commitment on the part of employees must be earned by managers of the organization, and it takes leadership to earn that commitment.

Formal Authority and Earned Authority

What makes for a great leader? What qualities, skills, or special capabilities have the great leaders in history possessed? What made people follow them? What makes some people successful in politics, in the military, in public life, or in corporate management, while so many others try and fail? In short, what does it take to get people to put you in charge and keep you there?

The great "movers and shakers" of history have been people who knew how to influence others. They understood people, they understood themselves, and they knew how to use the tools of authority. Not all of them were well-rounded, and not all of them were sane. But all of them knew how to be in charge. They knew how to shape the people and situations that fortune had handed them.

There are two kinds of authority you can use in accomplishing things through people:

1. *Formal authority*—Authority associated with your formal rank within an organization; what you are "legally" entitled to do; the ability to make decisions, allocate resources, hire, fire, promote, demote, reward, discipline, and tell people what to do.
2. *Earned authority*—The authority you as an individual have in the eyes, hearts, and minds of the people who look to you for leadership; this earned authority comes only through the personal relationships you are able to build, which makes people see

you as someone who can help them achieve what they want in their lives.

The ideal way to influence events, of course, is to have both formal authority and earned authority in good measure. However, managers with little or no formal authority can still be very effective if they have high earned authority. In fact, there are situations in which a person with no formal authority and high earned authority has greater influence over others than a person with only high formal authority. We all know executives, managers or supervisors who have not earned the respect, trust, and allegiance of those who work for them.

Earned authority depends solely on the individual and his or her ability to win people to the cause. Although an organization can issue a measure of formal authority or rank, it cannot help the manager earn authority from others. Formal authority is part of the manager's or leader's formal organizational role, while earned authority is part of the personal relationships between the individual and others.

To Lead Is to Serve

One of the Latin titles used to refer to the Pope is *servus servorum*, which means "the servant of servants." This title carries over to anyone in a leadership role, whether it involves formal authority or not. The role of the leader is to lead by *enabling* others, not by trying to drive them.

In today's world, corporate leaders are called upon to provide a new kind of leadership: service leadership. Gone are the days when a simple command-and-control style would work. The old "kick-in-the-rear" military style has outlived its time; it does not fit contemporary social values and is no longer effective. People need and expect positive personal relationships with their leaders—relationships that help them focus their energies, work at their best, surpass their expectations of themselves, and experience satisfaction with their accomplishments.

What is service leadership? It is the capacity to lead with a service focus—service to those who benefit from the planned accomplishments, and service to those who work to achieve the objectives. It means working with a spirit and a set of values that emphasize contributing something worthwhile. It means enabling or helping others accomplish something worthy, not just being in charge.

The service leader is willing to put empowerment above personal power, contribution above ego satisfaction, and the needs of the team above his or her own needs for credit and acclaim.

Albert Schweitzer, the famous physician and humanitarian, said:

THERE IS NO HIGHER RELIGION
THAN SERVING OTHERS.

The Six Dimensions of Service Leadership

As Figure 7-1 shows, a service leader is highly effective in six major dimensions of accomplishment in working with others:

1. *Vision & Values*. To be great visionaries, service leaders have to be able to see the big picture, understand what's happening, and decide where the unit needs to go. They are the ones who provide the vision, spell out the group's purpose and contribution, and develop a strategy for accomplishing it. They also take a personal stand for the values that lie behind the vision. They must know who they are, what they stand for, and what they believe to be right. And they must make these values real and compelling for others.

2. *Direction*. The job of leaders is to help people get things done. They turn the strategic vision into reality or, as it is sometimes said, they must transform great thoughts into crude deeds. Leaders set the overall direction for the team by choosing what's most important to accomplish, by formulating goals to accomplish it, by setting priorities that keep everyone's mind on the goals, and by helping everyone understand the plan.

3. *Persuasion*. It's not enough to have a clear vision and a sense of direction, although those are critical elements of effective leadership. Leaders must also be able to get others to see, understand, and believe

Figure 7-1. The six dimensions of service leadership.

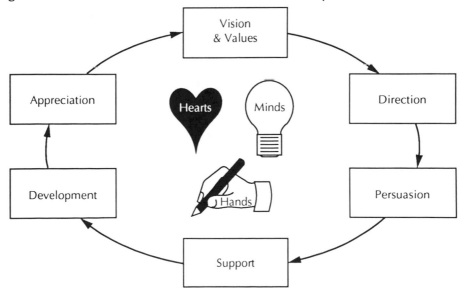

Source: Copyright 1992 Karl Albrecht, The TQS Group.

in the vision. Warren Bennis calls this leadership skill the ability to "enroll others in your vision."

Effective leaders use their formal authority effectively—not heavy-handedly, but not timidly either. They are comfortably and effectively in charge. They project self-confidence in dealing with others and communicate clearly and with impact.

4. *Support.* Effective leaders are there to help when people need help. They help by keeping employees' minds focused on the true priorities and maintaining a positive frame of mind about the work. They make sure that the unit operates well as a team, has the necessary resources to accomplish its mission, and has effective systems and methods to work productively. A critical part of their role as supporter is making effective decisions. They need to have the skills to think logically and analytically. They need a good command of essential facts and figures. And they must be able to approach problems systematically as well as creatively.

Leaders create a climate that fosters innovation and creativity. They make sure that team members know they are authorized to think; after all, companies want them to look for better ways to get things done.

In their support role, leaders organize people so well that they all know where they fit and what they have to do. Leaders put the right people into the right roles and help them work synergistically.

5. *Development.* Service leaders have the ability to help people develop their capabilities and express their potential, both individually and collectively. People don't thrive when they're stuck in dead-end jobs, doing the same old things over and over. Everyone needs to be challenged at times, to take on new things, and to learn new skills. Effective leaders see to it that people have a chance to grow. They have an idea of each person's skills and capabilities, developmental needs, and desires for learning and personal advancement. They occasionally discuss with each person his or her needs and desires to understand what is needed to help them develop.

One of the most important things a leader does is expect high performance from every person on the team. Some people are better at some things than others, and others have more experience in some areas, but leaders should expect everyone to work effectively and make a contribution.

6. *Appreciation.* This is letting people know you care for and care about them. Leaders have a special relationship with those they lead. Once workers accept a leader as the person to whom they will look for guidance and support, they want to know that their efforts and achievements will be recognized and acknowledged.

A great leader inspires people and helps them feel good about what they're doing. Keep in mind this observation made by William James, one of the founders of modern psychology:

THE DEEPEST CRAVING IN HUMAN BEINGS
IS THE NEED TO BE APPRECIATED.

All of us want respect and recognition, no matter how sophisticated, educated, or mature we are. Appreciation is the basic nourishment of the human soul. Great leaders know that and act on it every day.

Great leaders capture our loyalty, not by the way they make us feel about them, but by the way they make us feel about ourselves. They help us surpass ourselves, and then they help us feel good about what we've accomplished.

Service Within—The Imperative

The imperative is for *service within*. It is the need for managers to see themselves as service leaders, to give of themselves, create a sense of meaning, and help others buy into that meaning. Service within requires creating an environment in which people can strive, succeed, fail, learn, grow, and thrive. By adopting a customer-focused view of the unit's mission, and by learning and applying the practices of the service leader, any manager can transform his or her organization into a truly customer-committed entrepreneurial business-within-a-business—one that delivers superior value for the customer and contributes to the economic success of the organization as a whole.

8

Working Hard and Working Smart With Organized Labor

Paul A. Allaire, Chairman and CEO, Xerox Corporation

Successful labor-relations managers know that bullying—"Give me concessions or layoffs are the alternative"—doesn't work, especially in the long run, when what you need to achieve is a spirit of cooperation and productivity. Both sides want to work hard and work smart at the bargaining table. But the secret of successful negotiations is to talk to each other before you get to the table; that creates a foundation of trust on which sound negotiations and solid contracts are built.

It must be a given that unionized companies can't survive in the marketplace of the 1990s without the full commitment of their employees and the unions to the long-term prosperity of the company. Similarly, management must accept and encourage broader roles for union participation in shaping company goals.

People work most effectively with management that listens to them, respects them, encourages them, provides positive reinforcement, and offers guidance. Employees work most productively when they have relevant information about their jobs, know their department's goals, understand the state of the organization, and are encouraged to help share in its future.

People support what they create, so employees should have input in decisions that affect how their work is accomplished. And management should organize work in order to promote a team effort and meet individuals' needs for self-respect and personal improvement and development.

It may be a cliché in management overtures to organized labor each time seats are taken at the table, but employees really are a company's most valuable resource. Imagination, ingenuity, and creativity are widely distributed through every work force, as are dedication and the desire to contribute. Fostering that foundation of trust is key. Workers need to feel that they are being told the truth about the company's economic condition, while management needs to admit it doesn't have all the answers and feel that the negotiators on the other side of the table believe in the company and have more than higher wages on their minds.

The First Steps Toward Total Quality

Through the 1960s and well into the 1970s, the Xerox Corporation enjoyed a huge advantage in the document processing market—then confined almost exclusively to copiers—largely protected through its patented reprographic process. During those years, relations between the company and the union—the Amalgamated Clothing and Textile Workers Union (ACTWU)—were relatively peaceful, although there was one strike and some occasional job actions. The management-union relationship was typical of many companies at the time, using the traditional forms of dispute resolution: collective bargaining and the grievance procedure.

The extensive patents enjoyed by Xerox effectively kept competition to a minimum. The demand for convenient, plain-paper copying was enormous, while efforts to manage the explosive growth made cost control far less important than today. The company was free to offset inefficiencies by increasing prices. In the process, Xerox was losing sight of the customer.

By 1980, with many patents expired, Xerox faced tremendous competition from Japanese and European competitors, not to mention IBM and Kodak in this country. Xerox saw its market share cut in half and its revenues flatten.

Hoping it was correctly interpreting the warning signs, Xerox took a series of steps, not the least of which was turning to its workers for help through genuine employee involvement. In 1982, what was then known as the Corporate Management Committee concluded that Xerox needed to implement a total quality process if the company was to remain competitive in the global market. The committee realized that quality is a very powerful vehicle for change. Proof of this was evident in the experience of the Japanese, where quality principles have been applied since the early 1950s.

Thus, it became apparent that for a quality strategy to succeed at Xerox, the highest levels of management would have to lead the implementation and act as examples for the rest of the corporation. In 1983, twenty-five senior executives from around the world, working as a team, designed Leadership Through Quality, developing a policy that quality would be the basic business principle for Xerox and that quality improvement would be the job of every Xerox employee (see Figure 8-1).

Fundamental to the quality process is communication with workers, and this bit of Xerox history, with more to come, helps focus on our

Figure 8-1.   Xerox's policy for quality.

Leadership Through Quality

The Xerox Quality Policy

"Xerox Is A Quality Company. Quality Is *The* Basic Business Principle For Xerox. Quality Means Providing Our External And Internal Customers With Innovative Products And Services That Fully Satisfy Their Requirements. Quality Improvement Is The Job Of Every Xerox Employee."

---

relationship with our 4,000-member union. The communications segment of the quality effort is designed to keep Xerox workers informed of the objectives and priorities of the company in general and their work groups in particular, and of how they are doing in meeting those priorities.

The quality process at Xerox could not work without the support of the ACTWU, which appreciates the important role union workers have played in the success of Xerox. Further, it is understood that quality improvement is a continuous process. Every time Xerox improves, so does its competition, and, in addition, customer expectations increase. The result is a never-ending spiral of increased competition and customer expectations.

Union and Management Partnership Building

When Local 14A of the ACTWU and Xerox entered into collective bargaining in 1980, the company was grappling with shrinking market share but had not yet shifted its business strategy in response. Both sides agreed to experiment with what was then termed a quality-of-work-life (QWL) effort, focused on the creation of shop-floor problem-solving groups comparable to quality circles.

The QWL proposal was made by management and initially drew skepticism from the union. The union agreed to proceed only after assurances that oversight would be joint, that QWL would be more than a short-lived program, and that it would be kept separate from the management structure, the union structure, and the collective-bargaining relationship. Problem-solving groups were given strict guidelines about issues that were permissible and those that were off-limits.

The off-limits issues included salaries, grievances, the contract itself, benefits, company policy, working hours, breaks, overtime, and discipline. Permissible areas included product quality, work safety, savings in materials and costs, improvements in process, improvements in tools and equipment, and the elimination of waste of materials and supplies.

Within the first eighteen months, more than 90 problem-solving groups were established in the four main plants. After two years, about 25 percent of the 4,000 workers had volunteered for QWL training and participated in a problem-solving group. In the next six months, there were more than 150 such groups, tackling such issues as improving the quality of manufactured parts, developing training for new technology, eliminating chemical fumes, reducing paperwork, reducing downtime, eliminating oil spills, organizing tool storage, redesigning floor layout for greater efficiency, and improving communications across all departments. About 20 percent of the successful proposals included estimates of cost savings, which totaled almost half a million dollars.

Naturally, there were some barriers that sprang up. There was high turnover in many of the groups, not only because of job moves but because of layoffs in 1981 and 1982. Those layoffs, although an accepted part of the collective-bargaining relationship, served to "undercut attempts to emphasize the commonality of interests between labor and management," as a 1988 study of the relationship by the Massachusetts Institute of Technology put it. The amount of time it took for the groups to come up with and implement solutions—sometimes a year or more—was another problem.

At one point, in 1983, when the union learned that management was subcontracting some sheet metal work, it informed management that it could no longer cooperate in the QWL effort. As a result, the subcontracting was stopped; but more than that, management agreed not to make such unilateral decisions in the future.

That same year, in settling a three-year contract, Xerox agreed to a moratorium on layoffs of ACTWU members for the term of the contract. That same contract had no wage increase in the first year and changes in co-pay provisions for health benefits. But another provision—this one illustrative of the two-way street in collective bargaining—called for a restrictive "no fault" absenteeism program, permitting a limited number of instances for employees' missing work, regardless of the reason. Absenteeism dropped, but it put employees with good records at a greater risk than they would otherwise have been in the event of illness or other events beyond their control. As that became evident, it was seen as contrary to the union and management emphasis on participation and cooperation. That, in turn, led to a decline in volunteers for problem-solving groups. Three years later, when a new contract was negotiated, the policy was modified and made less restrictive regarding events beyond a worker's control.

The development of the Leadership Through Quality commitment that permeates Xerox today paralleled these labor-related developments. Indeed, the quality program effectively serves as the basis for negotiations today.

The most recent Xerox–ACTWU contract (ratified in 1992) demonstrates that commitment; the groundwork for rational, productive talks was begun nearly two years before the real talks began. The chief issue for the company was the creation of "focus factories"—those which produce a single product line with the goal of reducing work-in-progress inventory and materials on hand. But that required moving workers around while giving them more responsibility. To do that, ACTWU cooperation was necessary.

Gary Bonadonna, assistant manager of the ACTWU's Rochester Joint Board, and Joe Laymon, director of Xerox Corporate Industrial Relations, traveled extensively on benchmarking missions, trying to find out what worked and what didn't work at locations in the United States and Europe. As a result, redesigned factories now allow Xerox to build some of its low-volume copiers less expensively, lessening the likelihood that the work would be sent overseas.

Another key to smoother negotiations was a reduction in the size of negotiation teams. The company's team has shrunk from forty-one to seven; the union's from forty-three to fourteen. Efforts were made to eliminate those who had had significant clashes with the union in the past. Further, the negotiating schedule was changed. Talks took place only during traditional business hours—a move designed to keep negotiators better rested and mistakes to a minimum.

Members of the company's team took refresher quality courses, boning up on listening better, offering positive feedback, and avoiding assumptions. Union negotiators found they, too, were drawing on their quality training.

The foundation of trust is essential to a commitment to quality, so both sides avoided the temptation to cloak priorities within other demands. An atmosphere of distrust violates a cornerstone of Leadership Through Quality that advocates building quality into a product rather than looking for faults after it's made.

For the union, job security was the No. 1 issue. It got this assurance after give-and-take negotiations over shift differentials, a Christmas shutdown, and a move to save administrative costs by shifting from weekly to biweekly pay.

Meeting Everyone's Interests

Employment security is probably the key concept for reducing, and even eliminating, tensions between competitiveness and human values, as we have learned in our work with the Collective Bargaining Forum. Not only does the concept lead to greater acceptance of new technology, it enhances the motivation and competitiveness of the work force.

Top management must be committed to promoting job security as a policy objective and as a corporate value. It requires the same importance and level of attention customarily given product development and marketing. The union must be able to believe management when it says that permanent layoffs will only be used as a last resort and not a threat hanging over negotiations. When layoffs are required, a sincere effort to help those who are losing their jobs is imperative.

Similarly, there must be an honest commitment to employee training, retraining, and development, not only to ensure that workers are prepared for jobs of the future but to prepare them for changing markets and technologies. These goals should be shared by labor and management. Management should take pains to ensure that employees have input in the design and application of new technology and in the planning and development of new systems for allocating tasks.

I am happy to note that the Compact for Change drafted by the Collective Bargaining Forum in 1991 outlines concepts that have been used by Xerox for some time. One is the "joint exploration of the experiences here and abroad of unions and management moving into successful relationships." This facilitates the initiation of new efforts to adopt the more constructive and effective experiences of others. Further, the compact recommends, "efforts should be undertaken to think through new concepts which would have the potential of improving relationships between the parties."

In the 1988 MIT case study of Xerox and the ACTWU, researchers concluded that "the combined set of social and performance indicators suggest that, in general, the interests of the employees, the union and the firm are indeed all being met. . . . This is not to say that there have not been important conflicts within and across these collectivities, nor is it to say there will not continue to be conflicts in the future. Rather, it suggests that it is possible to have such conflicts and still achieve joint gains."

Corporate America should take note that the same study found that "the very existence of a union . . . proved critical in sustaining and diffusing many innovations, particularly when there was managerial turnover." The ACTWU has a tradition of attention to the competitive situation of the companies that employ its members. At the same time, the local representing Xerox workers was able to innovate without fanning tensions within the international union.

In any union-management relationship there will always be competing interests. Those interests can make collective bargaining difficult, but with the right commitments to the right goals, settlement is always within reach. Everyone has ideas about how their work can be done more effectively. In most cases, people are willing and eager to share their thoughts and take part in developing solutions to business problems. The people closest to problems often have the best solutions, but that nearly limitless source of knowledge and creativity can be tapped only through employee involvement.

9

Quality Improvement Through Strategic Alliances

David D. Auld and Betty A. Conway, Baxter Healthcare Corporation

Baxter Healthcare Corporation, a manufacturer and distributor of medical and healthcare products, has recognized that improving, expanding, and enhancing the services that it provides to its customers is as valuable to its customers as are its product offerings.

By working jointly with our customers and sharing our unique strengths in manufacturing, distribution, systems, and consulting, we can add compelling value to our customer relationship. For example, through a joint effort, a hospital was able to reduce processing time in its ordering, receiving, and accounts payable departments, moving from sixty-four hours per month to six hours. In another hospital, expanded distribution and warehousing services allowed a hospital to close down a 30,000-square-foot warehouse, resulting in over $500,000 in annual savings. Providing consulting support on blood-transfusion processes in a third hospital resulted in over $20,000 in annual savings in testing and processing costs.

Our chairman and CEO, Vernon Loucks, has described what Baxter will look like five years from now: "Baxter will be the most important single source of product and service that a hospital relies on. We will be an asset to them, not only in terms of the products we sell, but in terms of the services we provide in making them a stronger economic entity, focusing on how to get their costs optimized." Over the last several years, Baxter has developed an innovative and proactive service strategy that supports Loucks' vision. It involves a well-planned and strategically positioned marketing and service effort that results in market differentiation and long-lasting relationships with our customers.

Key to the success of this strategy is a commitment to quality and continuous improvement. The utilization of quality techniques breaks down barriers and assures sustainable process improvement. Understanding the principles of teamwork, employee involvement, and effective communication establishes the framework for the service strategy. And a commitment to continuous improvement assures customers that we will be continually looking for better ways to serve them and improve our ability to meet their ever-changing requirements.

Customer Service—Beyond the Product

Improving service to the customer has been a popular topic in the last few years. In the past, particularly in businesses that provide a tangible product or a well-defined service, the primary focus has been on assuring product quality, expanding product lines, developing new products, and marketing and selling the product at a profitable price. However, few businesses today have a monopoly on any product. Free-market competition demands that businesses differentiate themselves in ways other than just by the product they sell.

The services provided to a customer in conjunction with a product or independently of the product have become recognized as highly differentiable processes. The goal becomes, therefore, to *improve and differentiate ourselves in the market based on the services we offer.*

Baxter has a very large product line—approximately 120,000 items can be purchased from our thirty-six product and service divisions. But to the customer, all of the divisions are part of Baxter Healthcare Corporation, and our representatives must present a united front to our customers. All product lines must be represented and services planned and provided in a consistent and integrated way. This is one of the purposes of Baxter's Corporate Program.

Baxter's Corporate Program

Baxter's Corporate Program emphasizes strategic alliances with our healthcare customers. The program was developed by Terrance J. Mulligan, corporate vice-president of sales and marketing. The primary objective of the corporate program is to develop long-term, mutually beneficial relationships with selected customers based on providing value and managing the relationship to satisfy the unique requirements of the customer.

From a service perspective, these alliances allow Baxter to focus customized service-improvement efforts on those customers who have made a long-term commitment to us. The additional value we can provide becomes a powerful incentive to become a Corporate customer. Additionally, the relationships that are developed and the knowledge that is gained help us identify ways to improve our processes for the benefit of all our customers.

Key Features of the Program

One of the key features of the Corporate Program is a focus on dealing one-on-one with the customer by strategically aligning all levels of our organization with the customer's organization. In this manner, we are better able to communicate with our customers and maintain a focus that enables us to better understand and meet their requirements. Figure 9-1 shows how this approach applies to a customer hospital. Applying quality improvement techniques to these one-on-one relationships helps Baxter and the hospital identify both product and service improvement opportunities, and allows those most directly involved in the area to analyze and implement sustainable improvements.

Another key feature of the program is to provide Baxter's internal resources to the customer. Baxter is recognized for having unique strengths in manufacturing, distribution, systems, and quality management. Allocation of these resources to address a hospital-defined issue or need results in measurable benefits to both the hospital and Baxter.

Benefits to Baxter

The Corporate Program develops profitable business growth in all Corporate accounts. The benefits can be measured in several ways:

Figure 9-1. Baxter Corporate Program.

PENETRATION (IN COMPARISON TO NON–CORPORATE PROGRAM ACCOUNTS)

Baxter divisions provide approximately 120,000 different products, which represent about 60 to 70 percent of hospital supply needs. Sales penetration is a measure of the extent to which a customer is using Baxter products; the more sales dollars per bed, the more penetrated the account. Figures on sales dollars per bed in 1991 revealed that customers in the Corporate Program bought twice as much per bed in comparison to non–Corporate Program accounts (see Figure 9-2).

GROWTH IN SALES (IN COMPARISON TO NON–CORPORATE PROGRAM ACCOUNTS)

Again, in comparison to non–Corporate Program accounts, sales growth in 1991 was 8 percent higher. In accounts where consulting services had been provided through the Corporate Program, the growth was 13 percent higher (see Figure 9-3).

CUSTOMER RETENTION

Less quantifiable is the issue of customer retention. Several of our customers have indicated to us that, because of the value-added services and customization which we have provided, they would consider other vendors only if they could do the same thing. Recently, one customer was asked to change to a different vendor by a buying group of which he was a member. He refused and we retained business that we would have otherwise lost.

Benefits to the Customer

Specific consulting projects wherein Baxter consultants work with the customer to analyze data and make recommendations for savings oppor-

Figure 9-2. Comparison of sales penetration.

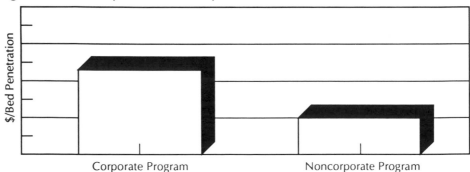

Figure 9-3. Comparison of sales growth.

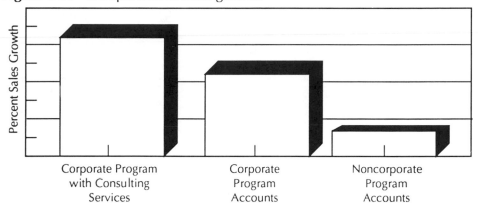

tunities yielded an average of $486,750 annual value for the Corporate customer in 1991.

Customized service improvements have yielded reductions in inventory and labor savings in numerous hospitals while simultaneously providing benefits to Baxter (see Figure 9-4). Assistance in the implementation of a Total Quality Management process has provided several hospitals with a long-lasting benefit. Baxter provides its own internal expertise, materials, and our Quality Leadership Process to assist hospitals in the implementation of a sustainable TQM process.

Other consulting advice provides knowledge that may not be readily available to customers to help them solve specific problems, explore alternatives, or make operational or administrative decisions.

The Quality Leadership Process

Essential to the success of all of these services is the integration and utilization of Baxter's internal Total Quality Management (TQM) process, which we call the Quality Leadership Process (QLP). QLP is Baxter's internal process for implementing and sustaining a commitment to quality and continuous improvement.

Officially implemented in 1985, the program has had successes and failures that have provided the experience necessary to help others. In addition, the majority of our employees have been trained in the tools and techniques of quality improvement, which help them in problem solving and process improvement when working with our customers.

The basic concepts of the Quality Leadership Process are grouped into three areas:

Figure 9-4. Examples of distribution system improvements.

	Hospital A	Hospital B
Fill Rate Improvement*	94% - 99+%	93% - 99+%
Delivery Improvement	2 deliveries/wk to 1 delivery every 2 wks	3 deliveries/wk to 1 delivery/wk
Receiving Time Improvement	12 hours to 1 hour	18 hours to 3 hours
Payment to Baxter (Days Sales Outstanding)	70 days to 7 days	87 days to 30 days
Sales Impact for Baxter	Retention of business	40% Increase in sales

*% of order line items received in first shipment

A Business Commitment to Quality

The first area builds the framework for understanding, creating, and measuring quality. Quality is defined as "understanding our customer's requirements and providing the processes that consistently meet those requirements." Product quality is achieved primarily through process control and prevention, not detection and inspection. Service quality emphasizes reliability, responsiveness, and flexibility.

Often, in joint meetings with customers, basic requirements for a service are not understood. Many quality problems are resolved simply by defining requirements and outlining a process for meeting these requirements to which both customer and supplier agree.

Total Employee Involvement and Teamwork

This is the "human" element of quality. Improving communication and trust between internal and external customers and suppliers is one of the major goals of the QLP. Barriers that typically prevent us from openly and objectively assessing performance, understanding requirements, and working together are broken down by a mutual commitment to quality.

For instance, in a joint team meeting with a customer to discuss improvements in their receiving processes, we introduced the person responsible for packing and shipping their deliveries. This hospital and

Baxter have now established an ongoing dialogue between receiving personnel and shipping people to continually assess and improve quality. Communication links have been formed that better serve the customer as well as create ownership and job satisfaction for our employees.

Providing opportunities for all employees to meet with their customers, to work jointly on process improvements, and to receive appropriate feedback and recognition for their ideas and team participation is essential in establishing a commitment to quality at all levels of the organization.

Continuous Improvement

The third area shifts the QLP from a "program" to a "process." Quality is not a destination; it is a never-ending journey. The achievement of short-term goals and objectives are just stepping stones along the way. Changing technology, changing requirements, and aggressive competitors require that an organization have processes in place to focus on continuous improvement. Services that delight customers today may become expected services tomorrow.

For instance, the electronic data interchange ordering system we set up several years ago is no longer a competitive differentiator. In fact, our competitors installed similar systems and improved the concept to offer even more advantages to our customers. As occurred with our ordering system, we are required to be continually innovating and improving our products and services to maintain a leading edge.

Quality Improvement Through Strategic Alliances

Baxter's Corporate Program is based on the concepts of the Quality Leadership Process. Value is provided to the customer through process improvements that reduce overall costs and through customized services and sharing of experience and expertise that is of tangible value to the customer. In exchange, the customer commits to a long-term relationship and to an increased purchasing commitment to Baxter.

A strategic alliance may involve a major shift in the typical buyer-seller relationship. The new interaction is based on fundamental quality management concepts—requirements definition, employee involvement and teamwork, process improvement and innovation, and elimination of rework and correction.

The Fourth Principle for Transformation

The concept of integrating quality management with buyer-seller relationships is not new. A recognized quality expert, Dr. W. Edwards

Deming, has some very clear thoughts on this subject. Dr. Deming is credited by many for the success achieved by Japanese industry. In the early 1950s, many of his ideas were not well received in the United States. But today, many of his "Principles for Transformation" are well understood and have been put into practice.

One of the most frequently quoted of Deming's principles is his Fourth Principle for Transformation, which states: "End the practice of awarding business on the basis of price tag. More important than price . . . is continual improvement of quality, which can be achieved only on a long-term relationship of loyalty and trust."

But Deming also states that "this close-knit, dependent relationship between customer and supplier presumably provides the supplier with ample rewards for achievement. The penalty for failure, however, is devastating."[1] The need, therefore, for a well-planned, strongly controlled strategic alliance approach is apparent. Without clear objectives, and an organization capable of meeting the expectations of an alliance customer, the loss of the contract may be minor compared to the loss of trust and the disillusionment that may accompany it.

Making It Happen

As Dr. Deming recognized, if suppliers have a strong relationship with their primary customers, they are more informed and thus better able to improve their products and services. By forming alliances with customers, suppliers gain a better understanding of their business from the customer's perspective. Based on this knowledge, suppliers can make improvements that better meet the needs of customers, often at less cost.

But how does a supplier develop and maintain this relationship and achieve the expectations that have been agreed upon? Establishing a framework for this new relationship is essential. Our experience at Baxter indicates that building this framework involves the following steps:

1. *Establish a continuing dialogue.* To begin building the relationship, a forum for the exchange of ideas and information must be created. Adversarial relationships and fault-finding are replaced by an attitude of "How can we improve?" The dialogue focuses on understanding requirements, identifying improvement opportunities, and developing an action plan for achieving the desired results.

The benefits of this dialogue are often immediate and astounding. Small and large opportunities are identified and all participants begin to view each other as partners in improving the quality of their interlinked processes.

2. *Create a structure for the relationship.* As in all improvement activities, committing resources to work on joint teams and to implement

change is essential. Who will participate, how often they will meet, what is expected of the team—these basics must be established and monitored by management. Creating a structure establishes accountability and responsibility as well as creates a more productive environment in which to discuss and analyze improvement opportunities.

3. *Collect data and measure improvement.* Key indicators of performance must be determined and methods for data collection agreed upon. Evaluation and assessment of quality and improvement progress requires that all improvement efforts start with baseline data. The use of quantitative techniques assures that the most important opportunities are identified, and that facts rather than opinions and guesses steer the improvement efforts.

Quantitative evidence and testimonials of the benefits derived from joint efforts help promote the value of the alliance and allow assessment of whether expectations and requirements are being met.

4. *Utilize quality improvement methodology.* Proven quality improvement methods and techniques provide a common language and a process for problem solving and improvement. These tools have been useful in removing emotion and helping the team focus on the process rather than the people and the issues involved.

Process flow diagramming is one such essential tool. Cause-and-effect (fishbone) diagrams provide an excellent brainstorming mechanism that ensures all potential sources of a problem are considered. Since people's resistance to change may be a problem, a Forcefield diagram (barrier analysis) often yields insight into major environmental issues (see Figure 9-5).

Improvement methods encourage and facilitate teamwork, allowing creative involvement of all members of the team. Because of the discipline involved, the analysis is more thorough and decisions are more effective and sustainable.

5. *Involve and empower people.* As customers and suppliers learn about each other's operations, they must go beyond the traditional relationships and establish contact with other important players in each organization. Process improvement must involve all participants in the process. These people have the best ideas for improvement, know how the process really functions, and will be responsible for making the changes happen. Key to their involvement, however, is the concept of empowerment. Within the scope of their job, they should be empowered to make decisions and take actions to continually improve the process to meet the needs of customers.

Creating and Adding Value

The alliance strategy through the Corporate Program focuses on providing improved services, both in conjunction with the product being sold

Figure 9-5. Forcefield diagram—stockless Just-In-Time program.

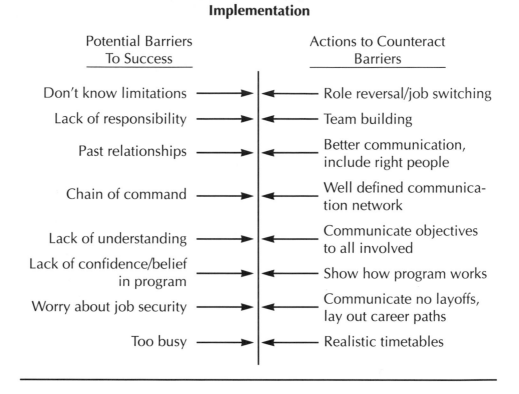

Successful ValueLink Implementation

Potential Barriers To Success	Actions to Counteract Barriers
Don't know limitations	Role reversal/job switching
Lack of responsibility	Team building
Past relationships	Better communication, include right people
Chain of command	Well defined communication network
Lack of understanding	Communicate objectives to all involved
Lack of confidence/belief in program	Show how program works
Worry about job security	Communicate no layoffs, lay out career paths
Too busy	Realistic timetables

and independent of our product as a value-added service. Following are examples of the service improvements that have been implemented as part of our strategic alliances with customers.

ORDERING PROCESS IMPROVEMENTS

Hospital and Baxter joint teams working on improving the ordering process and reducing inventories have developed lists of major products the hospital orders from us on a regular basis. By establishing these *core lists* and determining approximate order volumes, we can better forecast our inventory and provide almost 100 percent assurance of being able to fill their orders. This enables the customer to take safety stock inventory out of its system and establish a more reliable supply process.

The ordering process can also be streamlined. If both parties know the products involved, all that is needed on the order is the quantity required. The transmission of the order can be done through electronic data interchange (EDI), which significantly reduces the order placement time for both Baxter and the customer.

As we have worked closer with customers, we have provided them with information about their ordering patterns—products, number of orders, timing of orders, number of emergency orders—which has helped them make improvements in their purchasing operations. Customers also have provided us with information with which we can assess and improve our picking and packing, delivery, and invoicing.

Jointly, we have better defined the requirements for the processes involved in ordering, delivery, and invoicing. By better understanding each other's processes and requirements, not only have we seen significant reductions in the number of errors but also significant improvements in the customer-supplier relationship. Trust and loyalty are not an issue when continuous improvements are experienced by both parties.

DELIVERY ENHANCEMENTS

Our ordering process transmits the purchase order in the form of a picking and packing list to the local distribution center. The traditional focus is to correctly pick, pack, and ship the product requested. Service to the customer is directed at making sure the correct product in the correct quantity is delivered at the scheduled time.

But we have found that delivery offers many other service opportunities of value to the customer. For instance, joint improvement teams have reviewed the way Baxter products are packed and labeled, and how pallets are configured. They also have reviewed the processes for unloading, receiving, sorting, and storing at the hospital dock. By analyzing the process, collecting data, and implementing process changes, significant improvements have been realized. For example, product deliveries can be customized with hospital labeling, and pallets can be configured to match the hospital's storage and distribution needs, which saves the hospital significant time and labor at little cost to Baxter.

The receiving paperwork and invoicing process can also be improved to better meet the unique needs of the customer. Joint improvement teams have investigated the causes of invoice and pricing discrepancies, analyzed the process, and implemented changes that have helped streamline or automate the billing and payables process. The results have significantly decreased bill payment times as well as reduced the manual labor involved in auditing and correcting invoices.

One outcome of several joint improvement efforts has been to decrease significantly the number of errors made both by Baxter and the hospital. Participation by people directly involved in the process has increased ownership and pride in their work. The focus on quality has also pointed out that errors usually result from how the process is designed and are not the fault of the people involved.

Additionally, there has been a strong focus on establishing backup procedures for systems or processes to ensure a continual supply of products. Particularly when inventories have been reduced in the hospital, the customer is even more dependent on our responsiveness; in a hospital, lack of critical supplies can be a matter of life or death.

SPECIALIZED LOGISTICAL SERVICES

Baxter has formed several strategic alliances with hospitals to perform a service we call ValueLink. This logistical service, developed as a result of customer suggestions, is now a stand-alone division within Baxter. The division provides customized delivery services that go beyond the services typically provided by our distribution centers.

The ValueLink staff works closely with the hospital to implement improvements that directly affect the logistic and inventory processes within the hospital. Through improvements in ordering and distributing supplies, significant savings can be realized in the hospital regarding inventory, labor, and storage space. In addition, the supply process becomes more reliable and customer needs are better met. See Figure 9-6 for examples of ValueLink savings.

VALUE-ADDED SERVICES

Most Baxter divisions provide services that go beyond those provided in conjunction with the product. These are part of our strategic planning to address a hospital-defined issue or need. Value-added services result in measurable benefits to both the hospital and Baxter.

These value-added services represent expertise or resources that

Figure 9-6. ValueLink case histories.

	Hospital A	Hospital B	Hospital C
Number of beds	400	1,100	950
One time savings			
Inventory reduction	$580,000	$650,000	$1,300,000
Annual savings			
Inventory holding cost	$116,000	$117,000	$300,000
Labor	325,000	275,000	610,000
Total	$441,000	$392,000	$910,000
Space freed up	54,000 sq. ft.	30,000 sq. ft.	11,000 sq. ft.
Fill rate	99% +	99% +	99% +

Baxter has in place and involve little incremental cost to Baxter. From a value standpoint, their contribution is one of relationship-building and providing direct benefits to our customers.

1. *Corporate Consulting Group.* The Corporate Consulting Group provides a broad spectrum of services designed to enhance the operational effectiveness and efficiency of our customers. The key element of their approach is an objective assessment of a hospital's operational performance. Data-driven analysis pinpoints areas for improvement as well as areas of strength. Fact-based techniques support the development of solutions and prioritization of areas of opportunity.

2. *Quality Leadership Process.* The Quality Leadership Process is Baxter's approach to teaching and incorporating a Total Quality Management philosophy into daily operations. Sharing our experience, materials, and structured approach is a service offered by the QLP consulting group, with the goal of transferring our expertise to the customer's organization and developing the hospital's self-sufficiency.

3. *Executive perspectives.* Many Baxter executives and managers have developed strong consulting abilities as a result of their experience and are able to share their knowledge and assist customers in making improvements in specific areas of the hospital (see Figure 9-7).

ACCESS PROGRAM

Through the ACCESS program, Baxter can offer additional products, systems, and services that reach beyond the traditional scope of Baxter products and services. By associating with other leading corporations,

Figure 9-7. Executive perspectives.

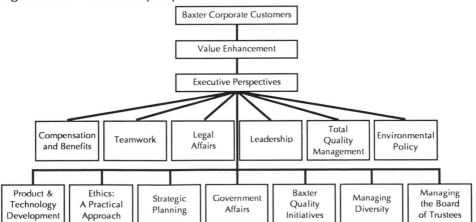

we are able to address specific needs and offer strategic solutions to corporate customers. For example, the companies we associate with can provide resources for meeting challenges in the areas of hospital information systems, hospital food services, and medical waste management. Our alliances with these companies allow them access to the healthcare market while providing us with a more comprehensive capability to address customer needs.

Summary

Our internal goals and strategies cannot ignore the financial crisis in American healthcare today. Our goals must support and relate to those of hospitals—that is, to cost-effectively meet customers' (patients, physicians, community) needs. Baxter's Corporate Program and Value-Added Service strategies are based on a commitment to quality and continuous improvement to best meet the needs of our customers, now and in the future.

NOTE

1. W. Edwards Deming, *Out of the Crisis* (Cambridge, Mass.: Massachusetts Institute of Technology, 1982).

REFERENCES

Berry, Leonard L., and A. Parasuraman. *Marketing Services: Competing Through Quality.* New York: Free Press, 1991.

Blumberg, Donald F. *Managing Service as a Strategic Profit Center.* New York: McGraw-Hill, 1991.

Grönroos, Christian. *Service Management and Marketing: Managing the Moments of Truth in Service Competition.* Lexington, Mass.: Lexington Books, 1990.

Hanan, Mack, and P. Karp. *Competing on Value.* New York: AMACOM, 1991.

Schonberger, Richard J. *Building a Chain of Customers: Linking Business Functions to Create a World Class Company.* New York: Free Press, 1990.

Zemke, Ron, and Chip R. Bell. *Service Wisdom: Creating and Maintaining the Customer Service Edge.* Minneapolis: Lakewood Books, 1990.

PART III

CREATING THE SERVICE QUALITY FRAMEWORK

10

Creating a Service Quality Culture

Kathryn Troy and Lawrence Schein, The Conference Board

In its work on organizational change, The Conference Board has identified the commonly shared values of managers and workers as the core element of corporate culture. These values set forth both the basic beliefs as to what is significant in the life of the company and expectations governing the behavior of employees. Typically, these values have to do with the importance of people in the company, the style of management, the relationships with customers, standards of performance, tolerance of nonconformity, and the nature of reward and punishment—definitions that all companies need to work out. These definitions and interpretations and their resulting behaviors vary among companies and industries, and create considerable diversity in business practice.

Any significant change in corporate culture involves a fundamental reinterpretation or redefinition of critical values. The movement toward Total Quality Management (TQM) is associated with new thinking about competitiveness, relationships with customers and suppliers, and interaction between managers and workers. Different perceptions emerge as to waste and errors, and to the way work is performed. There is dissatisfaction with the status quo, and the corporate culture becomes refocused on the marketplace. The changed culture stresses such values as customer primacy, total commitment, unacceptability of error, employee empowerment, and participative management as well as the management, measurement, and systematic improvement of processes.

As Leonard Berry and others have noted, there are unique properties of services not shared by manufacturing processes, such as intangibility, perishability, great variation in labor content, and inseparability of production and consumption. This leads culturally to an emphasis on exhaustive knowledge of the customer and on the values of timeliness, responsiveness, accuracy, and empathy. Quality practitioners in services tend to stress the many details of service delivery and customer transactions, whereas manufacturing executives tend to concentrate on the "vital few" factors that are the principal causes of output variations.

To measure the strength of a corporation's quality culture is to measure the extent to which the system, structure, strategy, staffing, and skills of the organization support the central values. If a quality culture permeates the business, then most if not all of the supporting elements will reflect the values of customer focus, process management, and continuous improvement. Hard evidence of the fit between culture and behavior is scarce. A great deal of information is anecdotal or based on a case study approach. In its own research program, the Board has employed a quantitative approach that seeks to establish the prevalence of practices supportive of a quality culture in *Fortune* 1000 companies with a TQM process.

The two surveys whose findings are summarized below deal with employee involvement and empowerment—human resource dimensions of quality culture. The support systems examined include training and education, communications, teamwork, and recognition and reward. In contrasting manufacturing and service companies, the surveys document the relative recency of TQM in the service sector and observe some differences in training, learning, involvement, and recognition.

Winning Employee Commitment

Research findings and discussions with executives experienced in Total Quality Management suggest that there is a TQM maturation process. Experts estimate that it takes eight to ten years to fully implement TQM. And data from Conference Board studies suggest that companies require at least three to four years to engender "buy in" among employees (see Figure 10-1 for a profile of study participants). In launching TQM, manufacturers had a two-year lead on service companies. Thus, when discussing differences in practices between the two sectors, it is important to realize that some variations are as much a function of the maturation of the TQM process as of cultural dissimilarity. The service sector's lag time may be a boon, since these companies have had the opportunity to learn from the mistakes of TQM pioneers. Survey results suggest that they are ahead of manufacturers in implementing some of the practices that help win employee commitment to quality.

Progress Toward Implementing TQM

Leadership is the sine qua non of the quality process. Experts stress that TQM must be initiated and driven from the top of the organization. Executives surveyed reported that periodic quality review meetings with top management can be vital to success. Says a banking executive whose company has such meetings weekly, "People put their time where their

Figure 10-1. Profile of study participants.

In 1991 and 1992, two Conference Board reports examined Human Resources practices among large companies with a TQM process. The first study was an overview of practices firms use to promote employee "buy-in" to the quality process. The second focused on non-cash recognition. Respondents were primarily senior quality executives and were drawn from the universe of the 1,000 largest U.S. firms, based on financial size.

Industry Sector	Buy-in Respondents (N = 158)	Non-cash Respondents (N = 96)
Manufacturing	63%	65%
Service	37%	35%
Number of Employees		
under 5,000	28%	29%
5,000 to 15,000	31	29
15,000 to 30,000	19	16
30,000 or more	22	25
Companies with Total Quality Management in place for 5 years or more		
Manufacturing	50%	48%
Service	30	30

priorities are, so this sends a loud and clear message about the importance of quality." Over 60 percent of service companies queried can count on high levels of support among top management, compared to about 50 percent of manufacturers. And service organizations are slightly ahead of manufacturers in receiving strong support from senior and middle managers as well (see Figure 10-2(a)).

However, a different picture emerges when the service industry is broken into two segments—financial services and other services (utilities, retailers, transportation, and others). Financial-service companies report much greater difficulty in garnering support for TQM at all levels of the organization. And they are the least likely of all industry groups to win high levels of support from middle managers (see Figure 10-2(b)). When asked to assess their company's progress toward involving employees in TQM, executives in financial service organizations were also the least likely to report high levels of satisfaction. Surprisingly, the start of TQM in financial services predates that in other services—twice as

Figure 10-2. Support for TQM in service organizations.

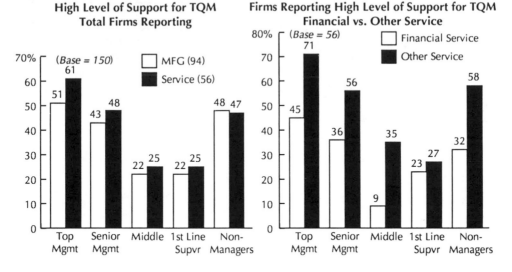

many financial service companies (over 40 percent of those queried) instituted TQM prior to 1985. It is probable that the tradition-bound culture of this industry is slowing progress toward the attitudinal and behavioral changes needed for TQM to thrive.

Perhaps hobbled by this resistance, financial-service executives rate their companies further from the goal of world-class quality than do their counterparts in manufacturing and other services. Using past winners of the Malcolm Baldrige National Quality Award to mark 90 to 100 percent of the way to world class, respondents were asked to assess where their company stood. Roughly a third of the manufacturers and nearly 30 percent of nonfinancial service executives judged their companies "almost there" (at least three-quarters of the way to the goal). This was true for only 17 percent of financial service companies.

Enabling Employees

Early in the TQM process, companies must help employees understand why change is needed, communicate what new attitudes are required, and train them in the requisite skills. Manufacturers and service companies follow similar patterns in the techniques used to roll out TQM. Eight out of ten companies sponsor special meetings with top management, print articles in company periodicals, distribute management letters, and mount audio-video presentations. Nearly half produce special brochures or other publications. Many of the same techniques are used by both sectors to maintain the quality message. However, the strategy in financial service companies places more stress on company-wide rallies and articles in company publications that are targeted to managers than is the case with other industry groups. Financial service companies appear to be confronting a change-resistant culture by focusing on management behavior and using quality celebrations to build enthusiasm.

Initially, quality training is likely to focus on awareness and attitudinal and behavioral change. Then, as the quality process takes hold, the emphasis shifts to skills development. Team building, process management, statistics, and tools of quality measurement are among the skills stressed. Service companies lag behind manufacturers in the use of quality training (see Figure 10-3) and in the number of hours of training offered to non-managers. Although 40 percent of manufacturers offer more than fifteen hours of training per non-management employee each year, this is true for less than 20 percent of service companies. Some of this difference may be explained by the more recent implementation of quality in service companies. Moreover, workers involved in product development may require more technical training in the use of quality tools than do those in service delivery. And finally, high turnover in entry-level jobs in service companies may make management reluctant to invest in training for some non-managerial employees.

Sparking Employee Involvement

Quality practitioners see teams as a highly valuable implementation tool. Short-term teams, such as task forces or quality circles, are beneficial because they involve people at all levels and give tangible results quickly.

Figure 10-3. Techniques for involving employees in TQM (% using techniques).

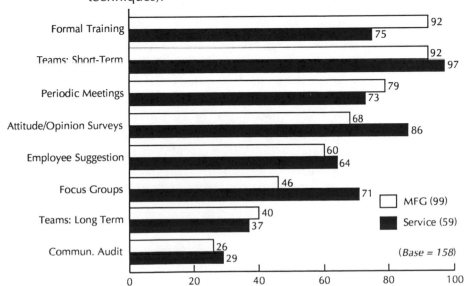

These groups may meet over a brief time span to investigate issues, solve specific problems, or make recommendations. Such teams are impermanent and may be disbanded or reconstituted as needs change. Members of long-term teams not only make recommendations but have the power to implement solutions. According to one practitioner, "short-term teams were useful in the beginning to learn to solve the easier problems; then we expanded to self-managed work groups for long-term benefits."

Nonfinancial service companies and manufacturers are equally likely to use both types of teams, although use of short-term teams is slightly more pronounced in services (see Figure 10-3). Again, financial service companies lag behind other industries in implementing long-term teams; only 30 percent have them, compared to 40 percent of companies in other industries. Overall, service companies trail manufacturing companies in the scope of their team effort. For example, manufacturers involve half of their senior managers and a third of their non-management employees in short-term teams, compared to about 20 percent of each group among service companies. The differences are even greater with long-term teams. As services take on tougher process improvement challenges, more extensive team participation and longer-lived, self-managing teams are likely to move to the top of the quality agenda.

Use of employee feedback devices, coupled with appropriate action, demonstrates to employees that management listens and takes their opinions seriously, practitioners say. Service companies are much more likely to use employee surveys and focus groups than are manufacturers, and about equally likely to devise employee suggestion programs and conduct communications audits (Figure 10-3). Focus groups can be linked to the service culture—"we get feedback regarding service quality and ideas for improving services," said a study participant.

Walking the Talk

Teams, surveys, focus groups, and other feedback devices enhance bottom-up information flow, and employee attention is also directed upward to scrutinize management behavior. Do those at the top recognize and reward quality achievement, or is the system still reinforcing pre-TQM behavior patterns? To demonstrate that the company's managers are "walking the talk," companies develop a portfolio of incentives tied to quality. These include performance appraisal, compensation, and promotion as well as formal and informal recognition and award programs.

RECOGNITION

Showing appreciation for a job well done can be as informal as a supervisor's spontaneous thank-you for an employee suggestion or as formal as an annual Awards Day celebration at which plaques and certificates for exemplary individuals and teams are presented by the CEO. One way to ensure that managers pay sufficient attention to recognition is to build it into the management development program. Service companies have a slight edge over manufacturers in adopting this practice, although they are likely to rely on internal courses, while manufacturers may use company orientation programs, visits to other companies, and mentoring activities as well. Another way to underscore the importance of recognition is to use the company awards program as a self-assessment tool for teams or company divisions and units. Although the incidence of this practice tends to grow as the TQM process matures, service companies responding to the Conference Board study were more likely to use awards for self-assessment than were manufacturers, especially those of consumer goods.

Quality awards programs may be targeted to individuals, teams, or company units. At least half the manufacturers surveyed favored non-cash awards for individuals, while the same proportion of service companies used a combination of cash and noncash. When recognizing teams, noncash awards predominate in both sectors, but service companies lag manufacturers in creating a team awards program—about 60 percent of service companies recognize teams, compared to 90 percent of manufacturers. Unit and plant-wide awards programs are still evolving in both sectors, but service companies are somewhat more likely to add a cash element to their program (see Figure 10-4). One clue to the differences between the sectors may lie in sources of information chosen during the design of the program. Service companies are more likely to depend on internal employee surveys and to seek the help of an outside consultant than are manufacturers. When evaluating the program after it is in place, both sectors make heavy use of surveys, but service companies are also strong users of focus groups.

Research suggests that companies institute quality recognition with a noncash awards program and choose to add a cash program or component later, if at all. Although service companies adopted TQM more recently than did manufacturers, they have a similar number of awards programs—one cash and two noncash awards. Typically, surveyed companies recognized about 10 percent of managers and 17 percent of non-managers with noncash awards. However, financial service companies recognized a slightly lower proportion of managers, while giving awards to 25 percent of non-managers.

Top management and immediate supervisors are most likely to be the recognition givers. In service companies, customers are more often involved in recognition than in manufacturing, and in financial service companies peer recognition is more prevalent than in other sectors (see Figure 10-5). Like manufacturers, service companies place high priority

Figure 10-4.   Service awards programs.

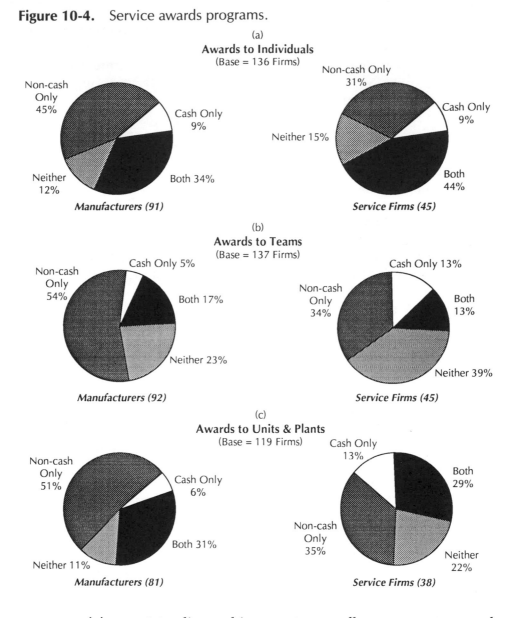

(a)
Awards to Individuals
(Base = 136 Firms)

Non-cash Only 45%
Cash Only 9%
Neither 12%
Both 34%

Manufacturers (91)

Non-cash Only 31%
Cash Only 9%
Neither 15%
Both 44%

Service Firms (45)

(b)
Awards to Teams
(Base = 137 Firms)

Non-cash Only 54%
Cash Only 5%
Both 17%
Neither 23%

Manufacturers (92)

Cash Only 13%
Non-cash Only 34%
Both 13%
Neither 39%

Service Firms (45)

(c)
Awards to Units & Plants
(Base = 119 Firms)

Non-cash Only 51%
Cash Only 6%
Neither 11%
Both 31%

Manufacturers (81)

Cash Only 13%
Both 29%
Non-cash Only 35%
Neither 22%

Service Firms (38)

on recognizing outstanding achievement as well as on system and process improvement, such as a reduction in the number of non-conformances in a process or implementation of a prevention system. Service companies are more likely than manufacturers to give awards for quality leadership (see Figure 10-6). At First National Bank of Chicago, those winning leadership awards must demonstrate that they "do the right things; do the right things right; and do the right things right the first time."

Budgets for noncash awards are higher in nonfinancial services,

Figure 10-5. Selection of award recipients.

	Number of Companies	Senior Management	Supervisor	Other Executives	Peers	Subordinates	Customers	Other
Manufacturing:								
Durable Goods	37	73%	70%	46%	57%	30%	19%	22%
Nondurable Goods	25	68	88	68	64	44	44	8
Total Manufacturing	62	71	74	55	60	35	29	16
Service:								
Financial Services	19	63	74	58	84	42	53	10
Other Services	15	68	73	47	60	53	53	33
Total Services	34	65	73	53	73	42	53	21
Total (All Companies)	96	69	74	54	65	40	37	18

Figure 10-6. Award-eligible activities.

	Manufacturing (N = 62)			Service (N = 34)		
Award-Eligible Activities	Total	Durables	Nondurables	Total	Financial	Other
Outstanding Achievement . . .	79%	84%	72%	73%	79%	67%
System/Process Improvements .	79	81	76	56	63	47
Completion of Quality-Related Activities	71	81	56	44	37	53
Innovation	60	62	56	53	68	33
Employee Suggestions	48	43	56	53	68	33
Performance Based on Defined Goals	52	49	56	44	53	33
Leadership	45	43	48	56	74	33
Problem-Solving Skills	52	62	36	38	53	20
Certification as Instructor	24	22	28	15	10	20
Mentoring/Teaching/ Facilitating	26	27	24	15	10	20

averaging about $150,000 annually, compared to $40,000 for financial service companies and $50,000 for all sectors. However, manufacturers make a broader array of activities eligible for awards and use a greater variety of awards than service companies (see Figures 10-6 and 10-7).

PERFORMANCE APPRAISAL, COMPENSATION, PROMOTION

Practitioners surveyed say that compensation linked to quality is the most powerful incentive to quality commitment among top management. This appears to be true throughout the TQM life cycle. In contrast, ceremonies and symbolic awards are highly effective with non-managers

Figure 10-7. Most frequent elements of a formal recognition program.

	All Companies (N = 96)	Manufacturing (N = 62)	Service (N = 34)
Company Recognition (Bulletin Board, Employee Publication, etc.)	62%	66%	56%
Personal Letters/Notes of Commendation	38	37	41
Symbolic Awards:			
Plaques/Medallions	63	69	53
Certificates	55	60	47
Jewelry or Other Mementos	33	32	35
Company Banquets and Ceremonies	59	66	47
Other Special Occasions	33	39	23
Face-to-Face Interaction With CEO	41	40	41

at all stages of TQM implementation. These noncash incentives grow in importance with top managers as the TQM process matures. Ties to compensation become more effective with middle managers after TQM is in place for a few years and have an impact with non-managers over the long term.

Performance must be appraised before it can be rewarded. Service companies are more likely than manufacturers to link quality achievement to performance appraisal and to do so for both managers and non-managers. They lag behind manufacturers in tying compensation to quality, but are more likely than manufacturers to include both managers and non-managers. Whatever the industry sector, less than half of surveyed companies tie quality to opportunities for promotion. However, of those companies rating themselves closest to world class, based on the Baldrige Award Criteria, half tie quality to promotion for managers and one-fourth make the link for non-managers. This benchmark poses a challenge to the 60 percent of service companies and 55 percent of manufacturers that have yet to connect quality achievement to promotion (see Figure 10-8).

Implications for the Service Quality Culture

Data from both surveys indicate that differences between the manufacturing and service sectors may be due primarily to a differential rate of maturation in the quality process. Service industries in the United States have not, as a rule, faced as serious competitive pressures from abroad as have many sectors of manufacturing. Also, service companies have

Figure 10-8. Quality achievement linked to performance measurement.

	All Companies (127)	Manufacturing (85)	Service (42)
Linked to:			
Performance Appraisal	74%	75%	86%
Managers & Non-managers	46	43	64
Managers Only	27	32	21
None	26	25	14
Compensation	59	62	50
Managers & Non-managers	27	25	31
Managers Only	31	38	19
None	41	38	50
Promotion	45	46	41
Managers & Non-managers	20	18	17
Managers Only	24	28	24
None	55	54	59

needed more time to develop measures for processes that are less tangible than production processes. As services become more competitive, and as service companies become increasingly sophisticated in anticipating and measuring changing customer expectations, the gap is likely to narrow.

The data at hand, though limited, do suggest some difficulties. Service industries appear to have bought into employee involvement to a lesser extent than manufacturing. Less formal training is provided, particularly in the case of non-managerial employees. The high labor turnover and lower wages in many service jobs are contributing factors. But an additional factor may be that customer-sensitivity training involving attentiveness, empathy, and responsiveness may be harder to accomplish than teaching the intellectual skills required for problem solving and reduction of variation in machine processes.

Senior quality executives in all industries agree that the team is the principal organizational vehicle for continuous quality improvement and for deploying TQM throughout an organization. Yet among the companies studied, service companies involve fewer managers and non-managers in team efforts and also reward teams for quality achievement to a considerably lesser extent than do manufacturing companies.

The lowest commitment to the values of empowerment is shown by the financial services sector. There is less support for TQM in all echelons and less satisfaction with the rate of progress in involving employees in

TQM when compared to nonfinancial services and manufacturing. When these findings were reported at a recent quality conference, an executive for a large insurance company remarked, "you've described my traditional and conservative industry to a Tee."

Ironically, the financial institutions in the study have had longer experience with TQM than the utilities, transportation companies, and other nonfinancial companies. It is possible that deregulation, restructuring, and downsizing in an industry historically noted for long-term employment security have contributed to slower acceptance of TQM, particularly among middle managers.

More congruence between cultural ideal and actual practice seems apparent in the nonfinancial sector whose support of TQM is strong, most notably among upper management. Also, satisfaction with progress toward employee involvement with TQM is higher among nonfinancial respondents than in the other industry sectors.

Possibly because of intense and detailed customer focus, service companies appear readier to use listening and sensing devices to learn what internal customers think, including employee attitude surveys and focus groups. Also, customers are more involved as award-givers in the quality recognition programs of service companies.

Although growth in the U.S. labor force is slowing, companies seem inclined to continue to reduce their ranks through layoffs, early retirement, and attrition. This has created a pool of managers and workers who are older, fairly well educated, and highly experienced. Service companies may be able to shortcut some of their training and team development activities by tapping into a labor market whose job motivation and strong values of organizational commitment may link well with the demands of a service quality culture.

Two recommendations flow from the Conference Board research. One is that larger service samples are needed to better represent and perhaps better differentiate the several segments of the service industry. The second is that other dimensions of quality culture and their support systems need to be addressed by the survey method, including leadership, participative management, process measurement, and continuous improvement.

REFERENCES

Conference Board. *Human Resource Briefing* 8, no. 10 (October 1992).
Peters, Barbara H., and Jim L. Peters, eds. *Total Quality Management*. Report no. 963. New York: Conference Board, 1991.
———. *Maintaining the Total Quality Advantage*. Report no. 979. New York: Conference Board, 1991.

Schein, Lawrence. *A Manager's Guide to Corporate Culture.* Report no. 926. New York: Conference Board, 1989.

———. *The Road to Total Quality: Views of Industry Experts.* Research bulletin no. 239. New York: Conference Board, 1990.

Troy, Kathryn. *Quality Training: What Top Companies Have Learned.* Report no. 959. New York: Conference Board, 1991.

———. *Employee Buy-In to Total Quality.* Report no. 974. New York: Conference Board, 1991.

———. *Recognizing Quality Achievement: Noncash Award Programs.* Report no. 1008. New York: Conference Board, 1992.

Zeithaml, Valarie A., A. Parasuraman, and Leonard L. Berry. *Delivering Quality Service: Balancing Customer Perceptions and Expectations.* New York: Free Press, 1990.

11

Creating Service Climates for Service Quality

Benjamin Schneider and Beth Chung, University of Maryland at College Park

As Charles Darwin believed, survival is of the fittest. Remaining the "fittest" requires adaptation to changing environmental conditions, and adaptation occurs best when all the parts of a system are integrated. In the case of living organisms, all parts of the organism (e.g., genes, organs, and limbs) work together to change in order to survive. Organizations are complex living organisms, too, and are subject to the same rules of survival. Organizational survival is dependent on the integration of all subsystems making up the organization. And this integration requires a common focus of energy.

While all organizations need to adapt in order to survive and prosper, service organizations *must* adapt. Service organizations exist as a function of their customers; service quality, then, is the primary survival strategy. To achieve service quality, there needs to be a climate for service. Thus the focus of this chapter is on establishing the relationship between a climate for service and service quality. This climate for service, we propose, leads to service quality if applied throughout an organization. In other words, a service climate can lead to service quality if service is the strategic focus of all subsystems in the organization. We present an overview of the general literature on climate with respect to strategic issues, then we discuss the service construct, showing how services differ from goods and how the differences affect the design of a service climate. We follow with a section on how a service climate can lead to service quality when there is multisystemic coordination.

Organizational Climate

Climate refers to how an organization "feels"—more specifically, to the perceptions of organization members about how resources, energies, and competencies are focused and/or what is considered important.

These global perceptions are based on conditions people experience: events, practices, procedures, and the behaviors they see rewarded, supported, and expected. An organizational climate is created by thousands of experiences and perceptions that are organized by its members into themes. We group these events, practices, and procedures and call them "routines," while the actions that are rewarded, supported, and expected are "behaviors." Thus, routines and behaviors send messages about what is important; these messages are organized into themes; and themes make up the climate of an organization.

The climate is a thematic summary perception of routines and behaviors that connote a particular goal or orientation for an organization. Employees use the climate to guide their current and future actions. Thus, in creating or changing climate, an organization must have a strategic focus. For example, in creating a service climate, the company must identify all the routines and behaviors related to service quality. Only then can their status in the organization be assessed and an attempt be made to change the way they function. One way to assess a particular strategic climate is to review employee perceptions of the routines and behaviors expected by the organization.[1] This identifies the extent to which the strategic focus is indeed present and where it is lacking.

The Service Construct: Introduction and Overview

In the period since 1983, it has become clear that service organizations need to be managed differently from the way organizations producing goods are managed.[2] This is because services differ from goods on three continua:[3]

1. *Tangibility-intangibility continuum.* Products are tangible and can be physically possessed, while services are experiences and perceptions. Intangibility is the major defining attribute of services but not the only one.

2. *Simultaneity continuum.* Many services are produced and consumed simultaneously. This makes them difficult to inventory for future use and also makes quality identical with delivery. The delivery creates the experience.[4]

3. *Customer participation continuum.* Customers participate actively to differing degrees in the production of many services they receive. For example, customers use ATMs, give information to physicians, and clear their tables at fast-food restaurants. In this way, customers can be viewed as "partial employees."

These three continua have implications for the design and management of a service organization, and thus are important considerations for creating a service climate.

For example, a company must consider the employees that deliver the service. These employees have been conceptualized as boundary spanners,[5] in that they link an organization with the environment in which it operates.[6]

These boundary-spanning employees function as information processors and external representatives of the organization.[7] In service encounters, they serve two unique functions: (1) they work together with customers in the creation of many services, since services are typically produced and consumed simultaneously; and (2) their behavior shapes customers' service evaluations.[8] Thus, service employees are in an optimal position to gather information about when and how often the organization succeeds or fails to meet the needs of the customer.

In fact, research has shown that there is a psychological closeness between boundary-spanning employees and customers. One study found strong relationships between the quality of service employees thought customers received and the quality of service customers said they received. Its results further showed that when employees reported that service quality is rewarded and supported in a bank branch (i.e., a service climate existed), customers reported having received superior service.[9]

A follow-up study indicated that a company's human resources practices are reflected in the quality of service its customers report. The underlying assumption is that, if employees are treated as valuable resources, then they will in turn treat customers as valuable assets.[10]

The specific human resources dimensions explored in this study, as reported by employees, include:

1. *Supervision.* "Supervisors I work with use the rewards they have to let people know when they have done a fine job."
2. *New employee socialization.* "People coming on the job get special training that helps them get started."
3. *Work facilitation.* "Conditions on my job do not permit people to reach their work goals" (reversed-scored).
4. *Organizational career facilitation.* "The organization provides information and counseling about my career."
5. *Organizational status.* "People outside the organization think the people who work here are high-caliber."

Each of these human resources dimensions was significantly correlated with customer reports of the quality of service.

There have been several additional studies showing that employees' attitudes significantly correlate with customers' perceptions of quality of the service.[11] Together, these research efforts demonstrate that to create a service climate that leads to service quality, both internal and external marketing are necessary. The service quality concept cannot be communicated only to customers; it must also be communicated to employees through the routines and behaviors that characterize an organization. This is especially true because of the unique aspects of service organizations that lead to the psychological closeness between service employees and their customers. If the service concept is evident to employees, then it will also be evident to customers.

It has been suggested that changing a single aspect of an organization almost never results in a substantial change in performance.[12] For example, the effects of a service quality program are not likely to be realized if the strategies employed are not applied simultaneously to all subsystems of an organization through all of the organization's routines and behaviors. It is not enough to have a new mission statement, slogan, and newsletter. Instead, a service climate must be evident in tangible ways—deeds that demonstrate to employees that new service routines and behaviors are valued and important. Further, management cannot just target a single level or facet of an organization. Rather, it must consider, assess, and change the multiple levels and subsystems of an organization, influencing not only individual behaviors and attitudes, but also group norms and interactions, as well as organizational structures and strategies. Changing or creating a climate for service requires changes at all levels throughout an organization.

Organizations as Open Systems

Various authors have proposed that organizations are open systems.[13] This way of thinking arose from the systems approach of a theoretical biologist, Ludwig von Bertalanffy. The systems approach states that organizations, like living organisms, are open to their environment and must achieve an appropriate relationship with that environment if they are to survive.

There are a number of key issues on which the open-systems approach usually focuses. First, there is the emphasis on the environment in which the organization exists. Classical management theorists often viewed the organization as a closed system, paying no attention to the outside environment. The open-systems view, however, has changed all this, suggesting that we must always take the larger environment into account. Thus attention has been focused on understanding the immediate *task environment*, defined by the organization's direct interactions with customers, competitors, suppliers, and government agencies, as well as the broader contextual, or general environment. This thinking stresses the importance of sensing changes in the task and contextual environments, of bridging and managing critical boundaries and areas of interdependence, and of developing appropriate strategic responses to cope with changes in the environment. Much of a service organization is in constant contact with its environment. This is especially true for lower-level employees who, in contrast to manufacturing organizations, are in constant contact with customers.[14]

A second focus of the open-systems approach is that an organization is viewed as a set of interrelated subsystems. Organizational subsystems are like organs in the body, which are whole systems within themselves, but also interdependent. The subsystems come together to form a whole that is more than the sum of its parts. Similarly, organizations are made up of individuals who work in groups or departments that, in turn, belong to organizational divisions. When we define the organization as a system composed of subsystems, the strategic focus of all subsystems is on service, and the organization will have a service climate throughout.

A third focus of the open-systems perspective is the congruencies among the subsystems. The goal is to identify and eliminate dysfunctions. In essence, this focus stresses the importance of integration and coordination among the parts. For example, if the sensory neurons in our hands did not communicate information to the brain, and the brain did not integrate this information with prior knowledge, then we would never know if our hands were burned. It is the integration and congruence of different subsystems that leads to the successful adoption of an organizational climate or vision. Service quality cannot be achieved if a service climate is not fostered in all subsystems.

The Human Resources Subsystem

Successfully creating a service climate that fosters service quality depends on the extent to which the service vision is communicated and implemented in all subsystems of an organization. We discuss the human resources subsystem of organizations in detail because it is the core of the routines and behaviors that communicate a service climate to employees. The elements of the human resources subsystem include:

- Socialization
- Selection
- Training
- Reward systems
- Performance appraisals
- Decision making

Socialization

Socialization refers to the process by which one is taught and learns the ropes of a particular organizational role.[15] Newcomers are taught and learn which behaviors and perspectives are customary and desirable in the work setting. A service climate is best taught by role models who demonstrate desired behaviors. Second, it is important to build on a newcomer's prior identity during socialization, so as to convey to employees that they are important and that the organization values their talents and prior experience. This is crucial because we need to select people who are service-oriented and build on these characteristics.

Selection

Selection processes are important because the people in the organization ultimately determine what it is like and can become. Organizations are functions of the kinds of people they contain, and these people, in turn, are functions of an attraction-selection-attrition cycle.[16] Service organizations should attract, hire, and retain people who are service-oriented. Service-oriented individuals enjoy interpersonal contact, and are friendly, understanding, responsive, dependable, and polite. They create and maintain the kind of climate that produces service excellence.

Training

Another necessary route to creating a service climate is through training and development. It is not enough to train the employees who deliver service to end-user consumers. *All* levels of the organization need to be trained with a service focus. Subordinates are not likely to be service-oriented if their supervisors are not; similarly, supervisors are not likely to be service-oriented if top management is not. Due to direct customer contact, front-line workers often develop an excellent understanding of their customers' service needs. One study found that warehouse workers at a national distributor were more accurate than managers in predicting customers' opinions about service.[17]

The possible content of training programs in the service sector can be roughly divided into three categories: (1) technical job skills, (2) interpersonal or customer relationship skills, and (3) cultural values and norms. Historically, there has been a tendency for service companies to concentrate on technical skills (e.g., teaching maids how to make beds). But evidence from excellent service providers suggests that training in all three categories, on a continuing basis, is needed to achieve and maintain service excellence. Companies such as Disney and American Express teach new employees not only about their jobs but also about the organization and its culture, citing heroes, stories, and slogans. So, who gets trained in what subjects are important issues in creating a service climate.

Reward Systems

Reward systems are one of the strongest communicators of desired behaviors.[18] It follows, then, that if an organization seeks to be an excellent service provider, it should employ rewards to facilitate that end. All too often, though, organizations fail to get desired behaviors from their employees because they reward other-than-desired behaviors. For instance, management may want to achieve greater courtesy from employees but instead rewards how quickly they answer the phone or how many customers they talk to. In addition, management often takes a narrow view of the rewards that can be given. They mostly think of such rewards as financial bonuses or promotion and ignore recognition or praise, as well as perks like compensation time or theater tickets. All of these facets of a reward system communicate to employees that a service orientation is desired and appreciated.

Performance Appraisal

Often associated with reward systems, performance appraisal carries more weight when it is tied to organizational rewards. Representing another indicator of organizational norms and goals, it communicates to employees the importance of certain behaviors. Companies that wish to promote service quality should emphasize quality, not only quantity, in their appraisals. Further, the items on the appraisal form should be specific and behaviorally anchored. They should relate to parts of the job that are relevant to service quality. One team of researchers has identified ten dimensions of service quality, including courtesy, responsiveness, and reliability, which can be used to establish criteria of effectiveness against which employees can be appraised.[19] These are the same criteria that external customers use in assessing the effectiveness of a service organization.

Decision Making

Research has demonstrated that employees know how customers feel about the service quality they receive.[20] This suggests that perhaps employees should be consulted in decisions pertaining to service quality. They often have creative ideas for the design and implementation of new services, changes in service delivery, and new internal procedures and equipment. A consultative decision making style in service organizations can produce many benefits including higher morale and pride, a sense of ownership and trust, acceptance of a new policy, and a more accurate and complete picture of the issues to be considered. In this way, decision making becomes an environment-sensing endeavor that benefits both the organization and the employees involved.

Routines and behaviors are the facets of a human resources subsystem that can create a climate for service. Consistency in these facets sends a coherent message to employees regarding the importance of quality service. Service quality is not created by top management or by machines, but by service workers. To achieve service quality, a company must consider both external and internal service quality. To the extent that marketing, finance, operations, and other functions also promote a service climate, the total organization will enjoy a service climate and deliver service excellence.

Summary

We have emphasized that service organizations need to have a service climate in order to achieve excellent service quality. Because service organizations are different from manufacturing organizations, there are often no explicit quality checks. Rather, the direct supervision of the delivery process requires the indirect supervision provided by a service climate. This service climate, in turn, is composed of all the routines and behaviors of an organization that communicate to employees what is desired and valued. Only by consistent application of the service focus to all aspects of the organization, across systems and subsystems, however, can that service climate be created and maintained. Like a living organism, a company depends on the coordination and integration of all parts of the system to ensure its adaptation and survival. A wise woman once said that if the left hand doesn't know what the right hand is doing, both may not be doing anything.

NOTES

1. B. Schneider, "The Climate for Service: An Application of the Climate Construct," in B. Schneider, ed., *Organizational Climate and Culture* (San Francisco: Jossey-Bass, 1990).
2. D. E. Bowen and B. Schneider, "Services Marketing and Management: Implications for Organizational Behavior," *Research in Organizational Behavior* 10 (1988), pp. 43–80; W. H. Davidow and B. Uttal, *Total Customer Service: The Ultimate Weapon* (New York: Harper & Row, 1989); A. Parasuraman, V. A. Zeithaml, and L. L. Berry, "A Conceptual Model of Service Quality and Its Implications for Future Research," *Journal of Marketing* 49 (1985), pp. 41–50.

3. Bowen and Schneider, "Services Marketing and Management."

4. L. L. Berry, "Services Marketing Is Different," *Business*, May–June 1980, pp. 24–29.

5. H. E. Alderich and D. Herker, "Boundary-Spanning Roles and Organizational Structure," *Academy of Management Review* 2 (1977), pp. 217–230; D. E. Bowen and B. Schneider, "Boundary-Spanning Role Employees and the Service Encounter: Some Guidelines for Management and Research," in J. A. Czepiel, M. R. Soloman, and C. Surprenant, eds., *The Service Encounter* (Lexington, Mass.: Lexington Books, 1985).

6. J. E. G. Bateson, *Managing Services Marketing: Text and Readings* (Chicago: Dryden, 1989).

7. Alderich and Herker, "Boundary-Spanning Roles and Organizational Structure."

8. Bowen and Schneider, "Boundary-Spanning Role Employees."

9. B. Schneider, R. A. Guzzo, and A. P. Brief, "Climate for Productivity Improvement," in W. K. Hodson, ed., *Maynard's Industrial Engineering Handbook* (New York: McGraw-Hill, 1991).

10. B. Schneider and D. E. Bowen, "Employee and Customer Perceptions of Service in Banks: Replication and Extension," *Journal of Applied Psychology* 70 (1985), pp. 423–433.

11. C. A. Paradise-Tornow, "Management Effectiveness, Service Quality, and Organizational Performance in Banks," *Human Resource Planning* 14 (1991), pp. 129–140; W. W. Tornow and J. W. Wiley, "Service Quality and Management Practices: A Look at Employee Attitudes, Customer Satisfaction, and Bottom-Line Consequences," *Human Resources Planning* 14 (1991), pp. 105–116; D. Ulrich, R. Halbrook, D. Meder, M. Stuchlik, and S. Thorpe, "Employee and Customer Attachment: Synergies for Competitive Advantage," *Human Resource Planning* 14 (1991), pp. 89–104; J. W. Wiley, "Customer Satisfaction and Employee Opinions: A Supportive Work Environment and its Financial Cost," *Human Resource Planning* 14 (1991), pp. 117–128.

12. B. Schneider and K. J. Klein, *What Is Enough? A Systems Perspective on Individual-Organizational Performance Linkages*. Unpublished manuscript, Department of Psychology, University of Maryland, College Park; B. Schneider, R. A. Guzzo, and A. P. Brief, "Climate for Productivity Improvement," in W. K. Hodson, ed., *Maynard's Industrial Engineering Handbook* (New York: McGraw-Hill, 1991).

13. D. Katz and R. L. Kahn, *The Social Psychology of Organizations* (New York: Wiley, 1978); G. Morgan, *Images of Organization* (Beverly Hills, Calif.: Sage, 1986).

14. Morgan, *Images of Organization*.

15. J. Van Maanen and E. H. Schein, "Toward a Theory of Organizational Socialization," in B. Staw and L. Cummings, eds., *Research in Organizational Behavior* 1 (1979), pp. 209–264.

16. B. Schneider, "The People Make the Place," *Personnel Psychology* 40 (1987), pp. 437–453.

17. S. A. Gunnarson, *Some Organizational Correlates of Employees' Agreement With*

Customers' Perceptions of Service Quality. Unpublished M. A. thesis, Department of Psychology, University of Maryland, College Park.

18. S. Kerr, "Some Characteristics and Consequences of Organizational Reward," in F. D. Schoorman and B. Schneider, eds., *Facilitating Work Effectiveness: Concepts and Procedures* (Lexington, Mass.: Lexington Books, 1988). Also S. Kerr, "On the Folly of Rewarding A While Hoping for B," *Academy of Management Journal* 18 (1975), pp. 769–783.

19. Parasuraman, Zeithaml, and Berry, "A Conceptual Model."

20. Schneider and Bowen, "Employee and Customer Perceptions"; B. Schneider, J. J. Parkington, and V. M. Buxton, "Employee and Customer Perceptions of Service in Banks," *Administrative Science Quarterly* 25 (1980), pp. 252–267.

12

Introducing Change Into a Large Organization: A Partial Success

Stephen G. Leahey, President, Canadian Quality Management Centre

Much of the material we read on Total Quality Management (TQM) characterizes the human and financial results as unqualified improvements. But these results are often based on impressions and unreliable documentation. As experienced "change masters" can attest, few if any major interventions to effect a substantial cultural shift proceed smoothly.

Since anything short of a large improvement is regarded as a failure, change practitioners must ensure the success of their programs. So they avoid reporting examples of solid, honest results—the type that are invariably messy and involve a healthy mix of the good and the bad. Change efforts are often based on the positive results of a single pilot project. Those acting on these limited outputs are unaware of the many unsuccessful endeavors of their predecessors and are left to make similar mistakes and produce similar results.

This chapter attempts to move one small step toward correcting this situation by tracing a cultural change process in a Canadian company with over 55,000 employees. This report demonstrates the unevenness with which organizations adapt to fundamental shifts in the way they do business. At the time of the change process, the companies typically report the results as being very successful. Only with hindsight can it usually be determined that they were only a partial success.

Background

As managers, we constantly hear about new approaches to management that are supposed to make organizations more efficient or productive. In the mid-1980s, this author was placed in charge of a major productivity-improvement effort in a large Canadian company. Before it was finished, management had directly changed the lives of some 20,000 employees, and indirectly those of another 30,000.

We began the work with the enthusiasm and confidence that came with the knowledge of where the company needed to go and how best to get there. For us, it was obvious that by empowering employees and letting them establish team objectives aimed at satisfying their clients, the company would experience a substantial boost in productivity, gain a reputation for providing quality service, and be a much better place to work.

We had been steeped in the literature of involvement and believed the stories about remarkable improvements that seasoned managers, both public and private, attributed to their quality philosophy: the ninety-day process that was compressed to five, the defect-free products, the industrial plant that did not break down, and the courier organization for which "99 percent on time" is not good enough.

Our silent mantra was that all but a few cynics and cranks would agree with the goal of humanizing the company while improving its operational dimension. We were to learn, however, that bringing change to a large, multi-functional organization—with its processes, organization, attitudes, objectives, and way of life—was neither casual, automatic, nor easy.

The Beginnings

Experienced change agents know that altering an organization is difficult, and that a decision to head down the quality management road represents a major commitment. Though it is a decision to be taken with great care, this is seldom the case. In reality, upper management decides that something needs to be done to "fix" a productivity or quality problem, and quickly pulls together some resources before going back to its "regular" work. A variation occurs when middle management, discouraged by a stream of failures and seeking refuge from authoritative directives, initiates the change process itself with the tacit agreement of the company's executives. Such was the case with our endeavor.

The Productivity* Council

As a result of the 1981–82 recession, the company had established a Productivity Council composed primarily of functional vice-presidents drawn from corporate staff groups. The objective of the council was to generate ideas to improve the effectiveness of the organization and then to hand them over to the line groups. The council met regularly for

*In our initial efforts, the operative word was *productivity*. However, because of its negative associations with headcount, cost-reduction efforts, and efficiency measures, it was dropped, with *quality* substituted.

eighteen months without satisfactorily identifying a single project that could have a noticeable impact on productivity. Hundreds of ideas were sifted through, including more than 300 provided by a select group of junior managers established for that purpose.

There were several reasons for the council's failure. To have a significant impact, the innovation would have to be large in scope. This in turn required one of several things to occur:

1. A substantive change in the company's strategy, an alternative not compatible with senior executive desire to maintain long-sanctioned organizational structures.
2. A large impact on a particular functional department like operations, but ideas were met with robust opposition as either having been tried or being impractical because of timing and/or resource requirements.
3. An intradepartmental approach for which there were no obvious champions.

At heart, the executives wanted to find that mythical painless improvement that would gain the ready support of the organization without the need to initiate and orchestrate broad-based changes.

With pressure mounting to produce, the council prepared and sent a letter to the responsible executive vice-president, laying out a plan to effect cultural change in keeping with what we now know as Total Quality Management. The letter pointed out that such a transformation would take five to six years to fully implement. The reply, with a copy to all council members, was swift in coming: "If your recommendations were meant to be provocative, then by God, they succeeded in provoking me. I want ideas that will have a six-month payback and I want them soon."

Cowered by this executive impatience and anxious to prove their mettle, the council members scoured all possibilities, culminating in a two-day retreat under the aegis of a professional facilitator. Fourteen slides of ideas were generated and their impacts tallied. They ranged from administrative changes through travel policies to new tools for the craft people. The total potential for cost savings was less than $25 million on a budget close to $4 billion! We were left with one of two options: admit failure or confront the executive on the need for cultural change as the only promising idea. All of this was to be done while salvaging the perception that the council had thoughtfully discharged its responsibilities.

A meeting was held with the executive vice-president, in a "one for all" tone. Our proposal was that the company establish a productivity department to whom the council would report. The mission of the new organization would be to implement TQM over time. The alternative was to disband the council and discontinue further efforts. Faced with what passed as an ultimatum, the executive concurred and agreed to support the initiative.

Moving Away From a Tayloristic Environment

Before 1982, the company's productivity program was primarily concerned with efficiency considerations. In terms of the productivity equation—output divided by input—the focus was on managing input. Since approximately half of the company's input expenses were employee-related, the emphasis of the productivity-improvement program was on managing headcount. Standards for work units were developed through time and motion studies, and applied throughout the blue-collar (BC) work area. Given the requirements of industrial engineering techniques for repetition, standard methods, and defined outputs, very little was done to measure the white-collar (WC) workers. For these activities, budgets were used to effect cost containment.

In reviewing these efforts, the council felt that the traditional focus on Taylorism and the scientific method had been exhausted. Moreover, since most of these efforts had been concentrated on the blue-collar area, we felt that the white-collar area presented the greatest potential. Adding impetus was the knowledge that our WC employee expenditures had risen from 20 percent of total personnel costs in 1975 to 40 percent in 1982, and were expected to continue their sharp climb. The question was how to go about the task. Jobs were not routine, and we were often unsure of the outputs. Even when outputs were known, the outcomes were often more valuable. For example, when a salesperson spends the majority of his or her time developing a sales approach—perhaps a presentation—the output is the presentation and the outcome is the sale. Which is the most important? Historically, we had found that outcomes were difficult to measure. As a result, our WC programs were based on relative priorities. That is, people were asked to develop a priority list and to drop the least important—a simplistic system of control.

Council Initiatives

To effect what the council saw as a broad-based cultural change, a vice-president of productivity* was appointed and given responsibility for overseeing several groups, some only tangentially involved with this mission; this was done, as in most organizations, for load-balancing purposes.

*The title was later changed to vice-president, quality.

To understand the various approaches to productivity and quality that were available, select groups of council members spent time researching existing methods and learning what other companies were doing. We visited seven companies and made extensive use of the research done by the American Productivity and Quality Center.

Through the vice-president, internal consultants were made available to departments who initiated change processes. A wide-ranging, integrated program was put in place, consisting of the following:

▲ A three-day off-site course for vice-presidents to acquaint them with the concepts of the new culture and the types of results they might expect. One of the themes pushed most ardently was that upper management's role was not so much to make decisions as it was to ensure that good decisions were made.
▲ The establishment of a reward system for suggestions, overseen by a dedicated staff of five people. The purpose, among others, was to demonstrate to management that employees everywhere had good and useful ideas that could benefit the organization.
▲ The preparation of a quarterly newspaper whose purpose was to promote the new culture and the opportunities, objectives, and benefits of our productivity and quality program, as well as the exchange of successful ideas.
▲ The participation of sixteen departments in experiments to improve performance, covering all dimensions of the company's operations and ranging in size from 20 to 200 employees. Their purpose was to try one of two quality and productivity improvement processes, and to document the resulting successes and failures. This would provide the basis for further advances.
▲ Monthly meetings of the council to review progress, to launch new pilots, to identify roadblocks, and to continue the solicitation and maintenance of upper management's support.

The Pilot Districts

In deciding how best to approach the task of implementing the framework for the pilot programs, we experimented with two well-known models: the American Productivity and Quality Center's IMPACT program and Tarkenton's six-step methodology. After a thorough evaluation, we concluded that neither approach was complete. The IMPACT method overemphasized quality of work life and could lead to employee expectations inconsistent with the desired outcomes. The Tarkenton approach reinforced many of the strict measurement principles we were attempting to deemphasize. Out of these considerations, we evolved the EQUIPE concept.

The EQUIPE Concept

EQUIPE stands for *E*xcellence through *QU*ality, *I*nitiative, and *P*articipation of *E*veryone. The process was founded on two beliefs: first, that employees want to contribute but need to be equipped with tools, techniques, and methodologies to enhance their analysis and presentation skills; second, that working in teams enhances the range of options considered and eases the buy-in, and therefore implementation. Thus, the term had significance in both French and English since *équipe* is the French word for "team." An overview of EQUIPE appears in Figure 12-1.

EQUIPE became the basic means for implementing our quality thrust. A highly participative and structured process, its principal objective was to help employees gain a clear understanding of customer requirements and identify opportunities to improve service. As Figure 12-1 shows, EQUIPE's target was quality defined as conformance to customer expectations, whether the customer is external or internal.

The first steps in the program involved creating an awareness of the importance of quality, establishing who the customer was, and determining what the customer's needs were. The five key components of the EQUIPE program are shown in the center of Figure 12-1.

Figure 12-1.   The EQUIPE process.

Customer Analysis and Organization Direction

Once the importance of quality had been raised and accepted, participants defined their environment in terms of their customers and their business direction. Questions that were raised included the following:

- ▲ Whom did the organization serve? Who were its customers or users?
- ▲ What were the customers' or users' needs?
- ▲ What were the products and services the organization produced to satisfy customer and user needs?

Out of these meetings, each team was also expected to develop the core purpose of the unit and a vision of the future.

For many, this exercise proved to be traumatic. Staff groups had a particularly difficult time identifying their customers. Consider the case of a budget group. Whom do they really serve? Some people were very sure of the customers they served but were at odds with others in their group. Several employees of the methods department saw their role as supporting the product designers by providing the methods needed for delivery. Others felt that they supported the line groups in delivering products to the "real" customers. A fundamental requirement of maximizing effort is to score on the same goal. At the conclusion of this stage, groups were required to identify those few critical areas where success had to be achieved to accomplish the organization's mission.

The Group Performance Index

Measurement is the "hard-wired" communications system. Our efforts confirmed the truism that people do what is measured. We also discovered that the communications power of measurement went beyond guiding people's efforts and elucidated the mission and critical success factors. Our early efforts to establish departmental missions or goals often resulted in one or two paragraphs that became published, sometimes on cards or plaques. The essence was lost in faulty prose. The EQUIPE process overcame this problem by demanding that measures be articulated for the mission.

Teams were then asked to develop their own indicators to support and track progress toward the desired outcomes. The approach often was a Group Performance Matrix, which developed a family of indicators and combined them into a comprehensive matrix to produce a single number.

The Performance Index was a major departure from the pre-1982 measurement systems. This index measured team, not individual, performance and was based on progress toward a goal, a numerical scoring system, and weighing factors. In addition, instead of an imposed standard, a participative approach was used in developing the index. An example of the Group Performance Matrix, with some indicators for a personnel department, is illustrated in Figure 12-2.

For example, for a number, ratio, or fraction to be included as an indicator, it had to meet certain criteria:

1. Be easily identifiable
2. Use readily available data
3. Measure service performed rather than simply counting activities (measure outcomes rather than outputs)
4. Be developed with a purpose in mind (focus on facets that contribute to the achievement of the organization's mission)
5. Be simple to understand
6. Account for inflation if the indicator was a monetary one

Examples of indicators that reflected our company's mission and priorities included a customer satisfaction index, employee turnover, the ratio of rework hours to total hours, the ratio of hours expended to documents completed, and the percentage of out-of-service complaints fixed within twenty-four hours.

Figure 12-2.   Group performance matrix.

ORGANIZATION: PERSONNEL (example)

Indicators	Performance	Range of Scores											Score	Weight	Value
		0	1	2	3	4	5	6	7	8	9	10			
No. Staff Recruited / No. Staff Interviewed	30	10	15	20	25	30	35	40	45	50	55	60	4	20	80
No. Interviews / No. Interviewers	11	6	7	8	10	12	14	16	18	20	22	24	3	20	60
Employee Turnover / Total Employees	19	20	19.5	19	18.5	18	17.5	17	16.5	16	15.5	15	2	25	50
No. Staff Recruited / No. Vacancies Filled	33	40	37	34	31	28	25	22	19	16	13	10	2	25	50
Actual Expense / Expense Budget	110	124	121	118	115	112	109	106	103	100	97	94	4	10	40

Target Index = 300   Performance Index = 280

Benefits of the EQUIPE Process

The councils believed that discussing specific topics and reaching agreement were the most beneficial aspects of the EQUIPE process. The real value came from focusing people's efforts on the jobs they needed to do and on clarifying the goals and mission of their organization in terms of its customers. Observing this process in action for two years, we became convinced that people wanted to do a good job and the real trick was to get them involved in the process. Communication was the key to managing WC people and linking their efforts to what was in the best interests of the company.

While the major contribution of the process was to enhance the performance of knowledge workers, we nonetheless found that it could be used with equal success to promote the performance of line functions. Whereas measures relevant to the organization's mission could be developed for WC workers, efficiency, quality of service, and other appropriate measures could be combined into an index for line groups.

The perceived success of the initial sixteen pilot programs was such that the methodology was picked up and used widely throughout the company, to the point where the council estimated that upwards of 10,000 people were directly involved in some way or another and another 10,000 were indirectly involved. During the three-year period of intensive activity, the aggregate level of total factor productivity for the company as a whole registered a gain of approximately 6.7 percent—one of the highest in its history. This success was achieved without laying off any employees.

At the unit level, results were equally encouraging. With the introduction of EQUIPE, the previous system of using efficiency measurements was abandoned, replaced by performance targets and trends. Surveys conducted in both staff and line departments uncovered many tangible and intangible benefits, including:

- Reduced grievances, sometimes by over 50 percent
- Reduced absenteeism
- Improved understanding of department missions
- Reduced operating expenses
- Increased customer focus
- Elimination of unnecessary paperwork, forms, and reports
- Improved efficiency, timeliness, teamwork, employee involvement, and use of technology

Wider-Ranging Benefits and Conclusions

In addition, several findings began to be accepted by the council as a result of monitoring the various teams over the course of the three years.

▲ *Employee involvement cannot work without participatory management.* It is not appropriate to demand behaviors that we are not prepared to model.

▲ *There must be explicit understanding that no employee will lose his or her job as a result of improvements undertaken.* This does not mean just a commitment to employment or job security, but more important, it signifies the company's dedication to a market expansion philosophy that best protects jobs.

▲ *The process can succeed only if introduced in a structured manner.* This is one of the main features of EQUIPE.

▲ *Management must be willing to respond to employee proposals.* EQUIPE allowed employees to improve the quality of their operations. This led to many suggestions for change that, if ignored or overanalyzed by management, could reduce the motivational effect of the system.

▲ *The status quo will invariably be challenged.* This leads to discomfort, particularly for managers and employees who have spent years in cost-based management systems.

▲ *The process is time-consuming.* It takes time to change tradition and develop a new corporate culture.

▲ *Organizations must show patience for results to appear.* Most of the work involves defining a mission, generating consensus, and developing the process. For this reason, overly aggressive use of measurement techniques should be avoided.

A large measure of our success with pilot teams could be attributed to our decision to develop internal change agents. Staff members in the vice-president's organization were trained to act as consultants for project leaders in all kinds of organizational matters. They were available on a full-time basis to meet with pilot leaders and their staffs, to do research with their people, and then to feed this research back to the managers so that they could see what they were doing and how it was affecting their internal operations. From the council's vantage point, this put gifted and trusted individuals at the disposal of pilot managers and eased the movement of insights and changes.

Long-Term Failures

The positive results of the council's efforts were described by company executives when called upon to speak on the subject of TQM, involvement management, and the like. Regrettably, the story does not end there. With the return of good financial results, the attention of executive officers turned elsewhere and support for continuing the council's work was slowly withdrawn. Many officers began to lapse into old-style management modes, demands on employees bypassed the team concept and returned to an onus on individual and dictated outcomes, and the most promising practitioners of the new culture often were reassigned to tasks where they could no longer take a leadership role.

Much to the chagrin of the council, when we attempted to reengage the executives, we found they often had not understood the changes being brought forth and were in a poor position to articulate them to others. For example, the president consistently mistook the concept of TQM to mean an extension of the company's stress on a wide array of quality-of-service indices. Similarly, the senior vice-president of personnel was unable to articulate the concepts behind the new culture and regarded the council and its work as a direct threat to long-established personnel policies. And one of the most influential executive vice-presidents refused to believe or understand that one could improve quality and contain costs simultaneously.

The council and its projects continued on for some time, but without executive attention and nourishment it became progressively ineffectual, until it was ultimately disbanded. The vice-president for quality was retitled as vice-president for strategy and his responsibilities realigned accordingly. The internal consultants were passed on to the senior vice-president for personnel, who disbanded the group shortly thereafter as a cost-cutting measure.

Much contemporary writing in the field of management, in both theory and practice, is devoted to the subject of change. A casual observer might therefore conclude that people in organizations are eager, willing, and able to embrace new procedures and concepts, and to install the functional and structural reorganizations that change entails. As our failure to achieve substantive change attests, this is not the case. With hindsight, we see that there were many important complex organizational and historical issues that swirled around the council's efforts, posing insurmountable barriers against total and long-lasting change.

Credibility

When the change was not too complex and our authority was without challenge, the attitude of many of our pilot units was to sweep any opposition under the rug and proceed to accomplish things. While this had immense short-term advantages, we left behind many dissatisfied senior managers, whose resentment against the substantial changes underway continued to grow. Consequently, one could always find an influential group to argue against the change taking place, regardless of the results.

Participatory Management

From the beginning, the council worked to sell the executives and managers on the advantages of participative management. We told them that it would increase employee motivation and result in improved satisfaction and productivity, which turned out to be true. However, we had not alerted them to the drawbacks of participation. Participatory management is neither a traditional nor a "natural" way for leaders to behave, nor is it the way decisions are made in most organizations. In the first months, countless hours were wasted in trivial group decisions while at the same time legitimate sources of expertise were ignored in the spirit of full participation. In the end, this inability to combine participation with leadership tried the patience of many senior managers, who began to make unilateral decisions, often counter to those the EQUIPE teams had decided for themselves.

Involvement and Support From the Top

Major change efforts need the continued involvement and support of top management. The senior officers of our company lacked the in-depth knowledge, evidence, and role models that would allow them to be consistent in their follow-up support. The pilot units took on the image of a council crusade, which left many people in doubt of its motives and validity. It gave the impression that the process lacked sincerity, purpose, and commitment.

A period of sustained priority for work restructuring is important in achieving the critical mass to supplant the existing management paradigm. When the initial pilot units were launched, there was a high sense of urgency about improving employee relations and productivity. But with improved competitiveness, the sense of urgency receded, causing it to lose some of its validity.

Pilot Projects as Poor Models for Change

When organizations engage in experimental work restructuring, there is an underlying assumption that if the innovation is effective it will be adopted by other units. Most of us expect that an effective new organizational pattern will be recommended by superiors and emulated by peers. Our experience showed, however, that this is not necessarily true. Even if the pilot project remains viable over time, it may be ineffective for diffusion because it lacks either visibility or credibility. This may occur because the outcomes are seen to reflect the behavior of specific leaders in the experiment; or there may be particular characteristics inherent in the pilot project, such as work mix, a favorable union climate, modern equipment, or closeness to suppliers or markets, that don't apply to other situations. Also, higher management can fail to communicate the diffusion policy by being too conceptual or by stating the desired work structures too operationally.

Union Opposition

While most of our pilot units were exclusively in the white collar, non-union domain, some five or six required involvement of a union. While members, and often their union stewards, were supportive, the union leadership was at best ambivalent and at worst hostile.

Departmental Barriers

Diffusion efforts were frustrated by existing organizational routines that limited local autonomy. In our case, we launched our pilot projects while maintaining many of our traditional human resources policies on pay, review, promotion, and structure. Innovative teams felt harassed by staff groups, who for their part became irritated and impatient with demands for self-sufficiency and exemption from uniform company policies. These tensions were glossed over during the early months, but gathered momentum over time.

Threatened Obsolescence

A new structure of the work environment requires new roles and new skills, while others become obsolete. This process generates negative dynamics relative to the change. One such dynamic was the impact on middle managers. Their positions in the pilot units often were decreased and sometimes eliminated. When retained, they were changed in ways that required new attitudes and greater interpersonal, coaching, and group skills. Without formal training and counseling, this proved to be an insurmountable challenge for many.

Other Shortcomings

It is of little import that the project had a grand design and that all the changes fitted together to meet the final objective. The main point is that far too much was attempted. We did not have the time to oversee all the changes, nor did we have the energy to nurture them all. We did not have the power to push them all, and we did not have the insight to involve everyone who should have been involved.

Conclusion

In reality, culture change—in contrast to other types of change—must be modeled by those with influence—namely, senior managers. Inevitably, there will be a need for change to meet the dynamic environment that is our future. Most models are theoretical and untried rather than empirical. This, combined with other negative experiences, suggests that senior management must be the first to try new technologies and, when convinced of their value, recommend them to subordinates. In this way, the organization is saved the apparent inconsistency in purpose and the constant waste of effort in trying technologies to which there will be no real commitment. In the end, attempting change from the bottom up is doomed when one considers the resources and time needed to gain converts. Only senior management can provide these. In our case, conversion of fewer than twenty senior officers would have been more important than converting 50,000 employees or 900 or so middle managers.

Without active participation by senior management, total quality can never be more than a partial success. Expectations of achieving "significant results quickly, within weeks" are serious inhibitors to change. Total Quality Management is not a program that can be installed easily. It takes time, patience, considerable effort, and above all, support. We must avoid talk of "quick hits" and "grabbing low-hanging fruit." These certainly sound admirable, and surely are action-oriented. But what is really being said? Do those words project the conviction that Total Quality Management will bring results—or the need for results to maintain conviction? Local process teams are capable of figuring out how to reduce things like cycle time. The hard part is listening to their recommendations. However, once it is clear that senior management is behind change, the barriers are suddenly no longer insurmountable.

It is an ancient Chinese perception that, given time, the wheels of circumstance will return to the same place. In the early 1990s, the company has found itself in a similar financial and competitive situation as it did at the start of the 1980s. There is, however, a major difference. Many current executive officers were once either council members or closely aligned with it. With the experience of the previous decade, they are determined to do things differently.

Senior management is leading the move to TQM. They are taking the time to learn, practice, and internalize the new paradigms so that they will not only be able to recommend Total Quality but coach others. Seen in a philosophical light, perhaps the council's greatest legacy was the preparation of this new generation of senior officers.

13

Service Mapping: Gaining a Concrete Perspective on Service System Design

Jane Kingman-Brundage, Kingman-Brundage, Inc.

The practice of service design is complicated by the service characteristics of intangibility, simultaneous production and consumption, and the ever-present possibility that the consumer will participate actively as co-producer. A *service* can be described as a system or "a group of interrelated elements forming a collective entity" that is open to the consumer rather than closed, as is the traditional assembly line.[1] *Service design* can be viewed as (1) the design articulation of a service concept for providing value to the user; and (2) the construction of a system and process by which the service is rendered or value is transmitted.[2] Reliability, responsiveness, assurance, empathy, and tangibles are factors of service quality identified through research conducted under the auspices of the Marketing Science Institute.[3] Other researchers have distinguished value-adding service elements from nonvalue-adding service overhead.[4] George Robson, program manager at General Electric Aircraft Engines, distinguished service elements that add value in customers' eyes from elements that add technical value to the process but are nonetheless invisible to customers.[5]

Richard Normann, a founding principal of The Service Management Group in Paris, calls for "holistic thinking in designing service systems, the ability to think in terms of wholes and of the integration of structure and process [that] is indispensable to the creation of effective service systems."[6] Other authors define service system design as the "iterative act of defining and refining an initial service concept, reaching a master design [that] involves repeating the cycle of definition, analysis, and synthesis many times."[7] Service blueprinting and service mapping are proposed as fundamental techniques of service system design.

I would like to recognize the contribution of Barbara Zuppinger, Vice-President Training Services, Ontario Training Corporation, Toronto, Ontario, Canada, for making it possible to use the SkillsLink example.

The purpose of this chapter is twofold. The first goal is to show the role of service mapping in making service ideas visible and in building quality into the design of new service systems. However, achievement of this first goal demands pursuit of a second, loftier, goal—namely, to demonstrate how service mapping helps one view a service system as an integrated whole, thus giving form to what has been described as the service paradigm or the internal logic of an emerging service model.[8] [9] The usefulness of service mapping for spotlighting the dynamic complexity of a proposed service system is explored first, then service mapping is applied to an example.

Origins of Service Mapping

Developing a service map of a proposed new service may be compared to assembling a 2,000-piece puzzle when someone has thrown away the box top. During the past five or six years, a picture of service system design has slowly come into view. It is composed of generic structural elements that may be the underpinnings of all successful service systems.

Four pieces of the service design puzzle can be better understood by looking at the evolution of service mapping. In 1985, I created a service blueprint for Weight Watchers, using Shostack's line of visibility. Weight Watchers is a pure service. I learned that I had to show not only manual work steps but behavioral events as well. Before 1985, only industrial engineers were developing service blueprints. In many organizations, industrial engineers still draw blueprints, or process maps. However, at Weight Watchers, I learned that there are dimensions to a work process that go beyond the simple performance of work steps. These dimensions refer to *effectiveness*, which is psychological in nature and systemic in scope, rather than merely *efficiency*, which is the domain of industrial engineers.

At about this time, I became acquainted with the service quality research conducted by Parsu Parasuraman, Valarie Zeithaml, and Leonard Berry. The SERVQUAL factors made it possible to interpret patterns in work steps recorded on service maps. As the researchers released increasing evidence that the SERVQUAL factors are stable across industry lines, it became clear that many of the patterns and connections found on service maps are operationalizations of these factors. This discovery is important because it suggests that the SERVQUAL factors can be operational criteria for designing quality directly into service processes. The SERVQUAL researchers also introduced me to the concept of *customer expectations*, which set a baseline for service quality in terms of customer satisfaction.

In 1989, another significant piece of the service design puzzle surfaced. The PIMS studies conducted by Robert Buzzell and Bradley Gale include the deceptively simple observation that repeat business is the key to long-term profitability. To understand the significance of this observation, I should mention here that my training in flowcharting techniques is grounded in instructional technology rather than industrial engineering. Hence my professional paradigm includes systems thinking. By *systems thinking* I do not mean detail complexity, or situations characterized by many variables that can be analyzed in a linear fashion. I mean something quite different.

In 1991, Peter Senge of MIT characterized systems thinking as *dynamic complexity*, or situations where connections between cause and effect are subtle, and where the effects of interventions made over time are not readily apparent. Defining a system as "a set of variables that influence one another," Senge asserted that the practice of systems thinking starts with the concept of feedback, which shows how actions can reinforce or counteract (balance) each other. The concept of feedback is important for service system design because it fosters an ability to identify cause-and-effect relationships latent in ordinary work steps. For example, the PIMS studies suggest that repeat service users provide higher profit margins than do first-time service users. The obvious business goal is customer retention. The design problem is how to build a loyal customer base. The design solution is found by examining the dynamic complexity of a service system. Dynamic complexity has two elements—feedback and structure—that are discussed in turn.

Feedback

Service companies usually use a linear cause-and-effect chain to describe the components of a service process (see Figure 13-1). A service system, however, is different. Service characteristics—intangibility, simultaneous production and consumption, and the customer as co-producer—complicate service dynamics. Consequently, a service system may be understood dynamically as a series of instrumental interactions, or goal-directed give-and-take activities.[10] These interactions are demonstrated by adding the customer's point of view to the linear chain (see Figure 13-2).

Figure 13-1. Linear service chain.

ADVERTISING → SALES → SERVICE PERFORMANCE → CUSTOMER SATISFACTION

Figure 13-2.   Interactive service chain.

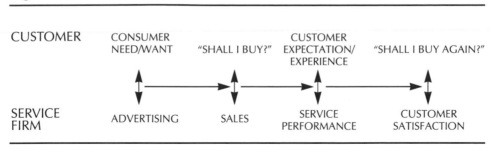

Notice that two customer decision points punctuate the service chain. The first question, "Shall I buy?" is the culmination of sales activity, and the second question, "Shall I buy *again?*" operationalizes customer satisfaction. Clearly the repeat buying question is not necessarily the last link in a service chain; a customer's positive answer represents the beginning of a new service experience, which initiates a new revenue stream, while a negative answer is the last link in the chain and cuts off future revenue. A technique is needed for showing how these customer decisions affect the service process.

Senge developed the following system diagram to illustrate a reinforcing feedback process wherein *actions snowball* (see Figure 13-3). The diagram assumes the sale of a good product. A service system can be understood as a reinforcing feedback process. Figure 13-4 shows the dynamic complexity inherent in a service system. Indeed, dynamic complexity is the heart of service mapping.

The service concept specifies values to be provided for targeted consumers. It functions like the North Star, orienting the entire service organization, just as the North Star orients a ship's crew in the Northern Hemisphere. The service concept is communicated via a core of advertising and promotion that stimulate consumer interest. Sales activity fosters positive response to the initial purchase decision, and generates customer expectations. Customer experience yields varying levels of customer satisfaction to the extent that customer experience matches, falls short of, or exceeds customer expectations. Satisfied customers spread positive word-of-mouth that can increase sales levels; dissatisfied customers spread negative word-of-mouth that can depress sales levels. A program of customer retention is thus designed to mitigate customer dissatisfaction.

Examination of the dynamic complexity of a service system suggests that the goal of service system design is the *creation of a service experience that customers want to repeat.* The ideal service system is often characterized as an "integrated whole" perceived by customers as seamless. The

Figure 13-3.   System diagram.

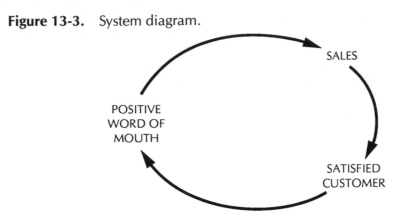

Figure 13-4.   Service system diagram.

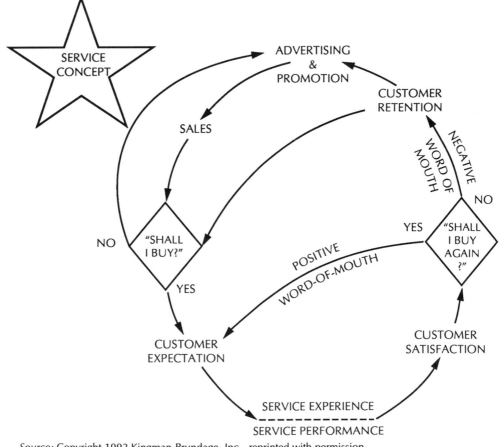

Source: Copyright 1992 Kingman-Brundage, Inc., reprinted with permission.

methodological question is, then, How is an integrated whole developed?

The service map records the dynamic complexity inherent in a service system. In Figure 13-4, the broken line between Service Experience and Service Performance represents the top line of a generic service map (Figure 13-5). Termed the *line of interaction*, this line may be compared to the net in a tennis game. Customer and frontline service personnel rally, or interact, back and forth across a line of interaction that spans a multitude of functions—sales, order taking, operations, billing. The solid line is the *line of visibility*. Everything above this line of visibility is visible to the customer; everything below is hidden from customer view. The majority of production processes are invisible; to customers, only the final outcome is visible.

The lower broken line is a *line of internal interaction* separating support functions from the primary service process. Internal customer relationships and functional handoffs characterize the line of internal interaction. Finally, a solid *line of implementation* separates management and reporting functions from the actual service process. Audit reports are feedback mechanisms that gauge both the efficiency and the effectiveness of the service process. Management uses audits to evaluate performance of the service system overall. Management then performs its own functions: refining strategy, allocating resources, and coordinating functions.

Although a system diagram lays out the dynamics of a service system, it does not show how service elements work together to create service value. When the dynamic features of a service system are imposed on the service map format (as in Figure 13-5), however, customer, frontline, and support activities are spotlighted in a way that demonstrates important cause-and-effect relationships, even when cause and effect are located in disparate parts of the system. For example, advertising that creates positive customer expectations out of line with actual service capability will have a negative effect on the service experience, as frontline employees attempt to realign customer expectations to fit "what we can *really* do." By juxtaposing operating issues against the two critical customer buying decisions, the service map answers the question, How does what we do affect our customers?

Structure

Service mapping enables the design team to understand the dynamic complexity inherent in a service system, and thus recognize types of structures that recur. In the same vein as social psychologists D. Katz and R. L. Kahn, Senge observes that human behavior forms patterns that are structural in nature.[11] Repetitive behavior arises when people in

Figure 13-5. Universal service system.

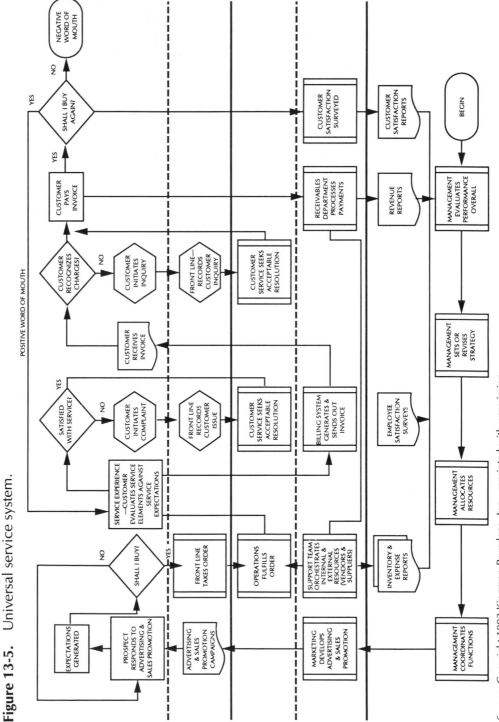

the same environment attempt to solve similar problems or achieve similar goals. To the extent that employees are trying to solve similar problems or achieve similar goals—render the service concept—employee behavior is repetitive, and hence structural. Similarly, consumer behavior is also largely repetitive and structural to the extent that targeted consumers attempt to solve similar problems or achieve similar goals—for example, to realize their expectations about a service.

The ability to recognize patterns in existing work steps, or to arrange patterns in proposed work sequences, is aided by reference to the SERVQUAL factors, which provide a generic picture of behavior valued by customers. Figure 13-6 locates the SERVQUAL factors on the service map. *Tangibles* includes everything the customer apprehends via the five senses—sight, sound, touch, taste, even smell—and are to be found in the customer zone. Acknowledged as the single most important service factor, the issue of *reliability*—or the ability to get it right the first time— permeates the service organization, including frontline, back office, and support teams. The last three SERVQUAL factors—*responsiveness, assurance*, and *empathy*—characterize frontline service activities: responsiveness is the willingness and ability to provide prompt service; assurance is the competence and courtesy needed to foster customer confidence; and empathy is having a caring attitude toward the customer that includes the flexibility needed to resolve service issues. These three factors characterize internal customer relationships as well.

The SERVQUAL factors may be used as criteria of service quality. As design criteria, they help managers see the work process imaginatively— that is, they are especially useful for anticipating cause-and-effect relationships and for spotlighting work steps expected to add customer and/ or technical value. These capabilities are illustrated in the following example.

Figure 13-6.   SERVQUAL factors by primary service zone.

Customer Zone	• Tangibles
Front Line Zone	• Responsiveness • Assurance • Empathy • Reliability
Support Zone	• Reliability

Source: Copyright 1992 Kingman-Brundage, Inc., reprinted with permission.

Example of a Service System

The search for a suitable example of service mapping was complicated by the fact that most managements regard the processes documented on service maps as highly confidential, even proprietary. The Ontario Training Corporation (OTC) of Canada agreed to allow their SkillsLink service maps to be used to illustrate the service design process.

This section explores how service mapping facilitates the service system design process at both structural or technical and process levels. Technically, service maps help the design team perform three functions: first, to define and depict the service concept; second, to map the proposed service process; and third, to audit the proposed service process. At the process level, service mapping is a valuable communications device. By revealing underlying professional assumptions, service maps facilitate communication up and down the management chain and laterally across departmental boundaries and functional specialties. By orienting the design team to the customer's point of view, service mapping fosters the growth of a shared understanding of the service concept and development of a common language for discussing it.

Defining and Depicting the Service Concept

Theoretically, the service concept is the point of departure for service system design. An effective service concept specifies the values intended for customers by answering the question, What value elements must characterize the actual or anticipated service process in order to attract first-time customers and increase the likelihood that first-timers will buy again? Effective service system design identifies and builds into the service system the value-adding elements that foster a desire to buy not just once, but again and again.

The SkillsLink course information service began with a modest idea: training decisions made simple. In order to promote training effectiveness in the province of Ontario, OTC purchased training directory software for customization to the needs of the Ontario business community. OTC proposed to populate the directory database with information about training courses available in Ontario and to offer the information on a subscription basis to the training departments of provincial business organizations. Data obtained from usage tracking reports would be used, not only to create customer invoices, but as a feedback device for identifying search strategies that require refinement and training needs not filled by available courses.

This verbal description of the service concept requires the reader or listener to mentally integrate various service elements. However, a simple sketch of the service concept shows how parts of the proposed service system relate to each other (see Figure 13-7). Service maps make service ideas visible. Verbal descriptions of service process steps and sequences imply patterns and connections that service maps make explicit.

Mapping the Proposed Service Process

A service process is constructed from a sequence of work steps. Design of even the most complex service system reduces it to an arrangement of steps and sequences. To customize the directory to fit market needs, focus groups were held to introduce the directory and to learn what training managers needed and wanted from it. Participants rated accessibility, defined as "ease of use," as the single most important feature. Based on this market feedback, the software was customized to meet the needs of the Ontario business community.

The SkillsLink development plan called for hiring technical special-

Figure 13-7. SkillsLink service sketch.

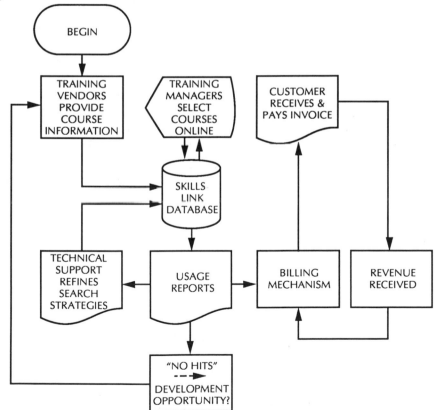

Source: Copyright 1992 Kingman-Brundage, Inc., reprinted with permission.

ists to populate the database with course information obtained from training vendors and then for retraining the technicians to serve as customer service representatives. Unfortunately, during the time required to populate the database (approximately eight months), the technicians developed both an affinity for the needs of the training vendors upon whom they depended for course information and a subtle skepticism regarding the needs of the end user.

With the launch date four months away, the project manager chose to develop a SkillsLink service map (Figure 13-8) to obtain a picture of the SkillsLink service in its entirety and to see SkillsLink from the customer's point of view. She felt that a holistic view of SkillsLink was needed to shift the focus of project team members from their inward preoccupation with the vendor database outward toward the service needs of the end user, the Ontario business community.

Examination of the structure underlying the SkillsLink service system shows how customer expectations, initial buying decision, customer satisfaction, and repeat buying decision punctuate the proposed service experience, which is depicted as a sequence of instrumental interactions. Service mapping forces the service design team to anticipate how "what we plan to do" will affect both internal and external customers.

At a process level, effective service systems require a collaborative effort, and service system design is itself a team activity. A day-long work session was attended by all functional specialists. The design team was introduced to the SERVQUAL factors as a way of orienting people to the customer's point of view. The consultant played the customer role, using information gained from market research. SkillsLink team members walked through the SkillsLink process from anticipated advertising through initial installation to ongoing subscriber usage. Using team input, the consultant sketched a preliminary service map.

Service system design requires the contributions of professionals representing a minimum of four or five major functional specialties. Professionals totally immersed in the requirements of their specialties are hard-pressed to see a service in its entirety, to identify system-wide issues, or to consider the service process from the customer's perspective. Service mapping spotlights these biases through disciplined examination of a proposed service process *from the customer's point of view.*

As the process flow takes shape, team members begin to view the service system as an integrated whole. They learn how different parts of the service work together on behalf of the external customer. Functional specialists see how "what I do" fits into the service scheme. In this way, the quality of handoffs across functional and departmental lines is improved, and a shared understanding of the service concept is fostered.

But even seeing the service system as an integrated whole is not enough. Because each specialist brings his or her own professional

Figure 13-8. Concept SkillsLink service map.

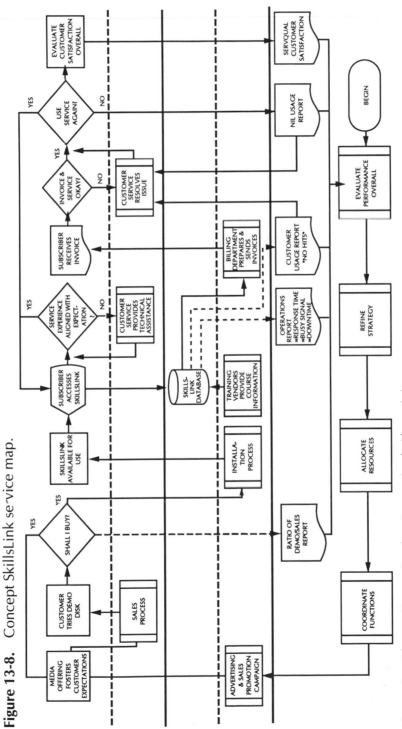

Source: Copyright 1992 Kingman-Brundage, Inc., reprinted with permission.

worldview to the map, each quite literally "sees" different issues: systems specialists see software and hardware connections; human resources managers see job descriptions and performance reviews; marketing managers see advertising copy, promotional campaigns, and fulfillment packages; purchasing managers see equipment orders; billing managers see invoices, and so on. Consequently, for quality to be designed into a service system, there must be a common language for discussing functional issues. In my experience, specialists trained in the SERVQUAL factors learn to describe the merit of their contribution in terms of value delivered to the external customer. SERVQUAL factors thus operate as a common language for describing various technical inputs.

To build value into the system, each work step was analyzed for the presence of a SERVQUAL factor. For example, sales, installation, technical assistance, and customer service (billing) processes were tested against a set of criteria composed of SERVQUAL factors, which were operationalized as answers were developed to the following questions:

1. How does this workstep contribute to service *reliability*?
2. What could go wrong, and what is the recovery tactic?
3. What are the respective roles of employee and system in demonstrating *responsiveness* and *empathy* at this work step?
4. What *tangible* evidence of service quality does the customer receive via the five senses?
5. How can employee *competence* and *courtesy (assurance)* instill customer confidence?"

Auditing the Proposed Service Process

Qualitative and quantitative prelaunch audits were undertaken. Qualitative audits are conducted by walking through the service system with customer, technical, and employee perspectives.

The customer perspective is audited by asking, What is the customer trying to do, and why? How is our service process expected to affect the customer? What service factors do we anticipate will add value in the customer's eyes? SkillsLink market research provided the raw customer data that, through service mapping, could be incorporated into a customer logic represented as a sequence of instrumental interactions. Service maps allowed the SkillsLink design team to build quality into the service design by using the SERVQUAL factors to predict service elements expected to add value in customer eyes. Training of frontline personnel assured that service performance would exhibit quality factors known to be valued by customers. Training of the support team ensured they knew how "what we do" contributes value to customer experience.

The technical perspective was audited by asking, How do we know the service process will work right the first time? What are our recovery strategies? How can we increase the efficiency of service elements that add technical value to the process? The technical audit surfaced team members' underlying assumptions. For example, the mapping process uncovered the assumption, held by SkillsLink's technical specialists, that the customer would be able to provide the correct baud rate (bits per second required for modem transmission) for their computer. SkillsLink is usually ordered by a training or financial manager. Discussion clarified that it was unrealistic to assume these managers would know the baud rate.

The SkillsLink project manager knew from the market research that accessibility was the customer's primary value and from service mapping sessions that an inaccurate baud rate would jeopardize reliable installation. Based on these facts, she made the decision to invest in a programming solution. Hidden in the installation diskette is a subprogram that allows a SkillsLink technician to walk the customer through a procedure to alter the baud rate, thus ensuring reliable recovery from a potential service failure. Interestingly, a competitor withdrew a comparable on-line training directory over this point. Unwilling to make the programming investment and unable to provide reliable service, the competitor chose to leave the market. By uncovering a major potential fail point, the service map allowed project management to make a decision based on facts rather than on an educated guess or outright hunch.

The employee perspective was audited by asking, What is the employee trying to do, and why? How do we expect employees to feel performing the service? How does the service system foster employee commitment to providing quality service experiences for customers? Difficulties involved in asking employees to perform first a technical, then a customer service function must not be underestimated. Service mapping accompanied by SERVQUAL training enabled employees to shift their allegiance from training vendors or suppliers to training managers or end users. Moreover, elements of the service system are operational variables that influence employee behavior, and they can be arranged—and changed—to achieve desired results. For example, the subprogram that allows the technical specialist to change a baud rate enhances technician competence and hence instills customer confidence. Had the subprogram not been created, an erroneous baud rate would have meant frustration for both technician and SkillsLink customer. No amount of personal responsiveness or empathy on the technician's part could have compensated for the lack of technical capability.

At a quantitative level, service maps facilitate identification of measurement points that provide feedback on how well SkillsLink functions as a system. As a rule, each decision point in a service map is a potential measurement point. For example, the ratio of demonstration disks to sales report tracks positive response to the initial buying decision. At the other end, the nil usage report tracks subscribers who are not using SkillsLink. Customer service consults the nil usage report in a follow-up program that involves contacting inactive subscribers and exploring reasons for their inactivity. The customer usage report monitors the database; the report includes "no hits" data that show when a search strategy has failed. "No hits" data are used by technicians to improve search strategies and by customer service representatives in a program of customer education designed to increase usage.

Conclusion

Service mapping is a design tool useful for helping managers think holistically about service system design. Technically, service maps help the design team (1) define and depict the service concept; (2) map the proposed service system; and (3) audit the proposed service process. As a process tool, service mapping reveals the underlying assumptions that accompany professional perspectives. By concretely orienting the design team to the customer's point of view, service mapping facilitates development of a shared understanding and common language for implementing the service concept. Service mapping thus fosters the ability of managers to build elements of service quality directly into the design of new service systems.

NOTES

1. James A. Fitzsimmons and Robert S. Sullivan, *Service Operations Management* (New York: McGraw-Hill, 1982).
2. Bo Edvardsson, "Service Design—A Powerful Tool in Quality Improvement." Working paper, University of Karlstad, Sweden, 1991-09-06.
3. A. Parasuraman, Valarie A. Zeithaml, and Leonard L. Berry, "A Conceptual Model of Service Quality and Its Implications for Future Research," *Journal of Marketing* (Fall 1985), pp. 41–50.
4. Leonard A. Schlesinger and James L. Heskett, "The Service-Driven Service Company," *Harvard Business Review* 65, No. 5 (September–October 1991), pp. 71–81.
5. George D. Robson, *Continuous Process Improvement* (New York: Free Press, 1991).
6. R. Normann, *Service Management: Strategy and Leadership in Service Businesses* (New York: Wiley & Sons, 1984).
7. G. Lynn Shostack and Jane Kingman-Brundage, "How to Design a Service,"

in Carole A. Congram, ed., *The AMA Handbook of Marketing for the Service Industries* (New York: AMACOM, 1991), pp. 243–262.

8. Evert Gummesson, *Quality Management in Service Organizations—Interpretation of the Service Quality Phenomenon and a Synthesis of International Research.* Research report no. 1 (New York: International Service Quality Association, 1993).

9. Schlesinger and Heskett, "Service-Driven Service Company."

10. Jane Kingman-Brundage, "The ABC's of Service System Blueprinting," in Mary Jo Bitner and Lawrence A. Crosby, eds., *Designing a Winning Service Strategy* (Chicago: American Marketing Association, 1989), pp. 30–33.

11. Peter M. Senge, *The Fifth Discipline: The Art and Practice of the Learning Organization* (New York: Doubleday/Currency, 1990).

REFERENCES

Buzzell, Robert D. and Bradley T. Gale. *The PIMS Principles.* New York: Free Press, 1989.

Gummesson, Evert, and Jane Kingman-Brundage. "Service Design and Quality: Applying Service Blueprinting and Service Mapping to Railroad Services." In P. Kunst and J. Lemmink, eds., *Quality Management in Services.* Maastricht, Netherlands: VanGorcum and Company, 1992.

Katz, D., and R. L. Kahn. *The Social Psychology of Organizations,* 2nd ed. New York: Wiley & Sons, 1978.

Kingman-Brundage, Jane. "Technology, Design and Service Quality." *International Journal of Service Industry Management* 2 (1991), pp. 47–59.

Shostack, G. Lynn. "Designing Services That Deliver." *Harvard Business Review* 62, no. 1 (January–February 1984), pp. 133–139.

14

Creating a World-Class Service Quality Management System

William Hensler and Kateri Brunell, Qualtec Quality Services, Inc.

As the twenty-first century approaches, an increasing number of employees in the most advanced countries are working in the service sector, and that trend is expected to continue. Yet so far the major gains in quality and productivity have been realized largely in the manufacturing sector, particularly on the factory floor. But similar gains must be achieved in the service arena if the standard of living in industrialized countries is to be maintained or improved.

As customers experience improved product quality and better service from global competitors, they apply higher expectations to all services. This holds true whether they deal with a service business or a support area within a traditional manufacturing concern. Improving service quality is no longer an option. It has become a requirement for staying in business. Therefore, service companies must adopt a world-class approach to management even if they compete only in local markets.

What is a world-class service quality management system? Several theoretical frameworks have emerged since the mid-1980s. The Malcolm Baldrige Award (the Award) guidelines in the United States and the ISO 9004-2 standard in the European Community are two examples. By design, these standards are not prescriptive. The Deming Prize criteria that have evolved in Japan since 1951 are even less directive. The latter's criteria are subject to interpretation by counselors from the Union of Japanese Scientists and Engineers (JUSE) who perform the audits.

None of these standards or criteria, however, really answer the following questions:

1. What does a world-class service quality management system look like?
2. What changes must be made for a company to become a world-class service provider?
3. Once the changes have been made, how can a company know when it has reached world-class status?

This chapter describes the approach developed by a U.S. electric utility (Florida Power & Light Company) over an eight-year period. Its efforts to implement a world-class Total Quality Management (TQM) system culminated in its becoming the first organization outside of Japan to win the Deming Prize, and one of only a handful of service companies, in Japan or elsewhere, to receive the Prize. The approach has been refined since 1989 through application by more than 100 other service companies worldwide. Thus, the management system described in this article is compatible with many of the quality standards emerging all around the world, including the Award criteria in the United States and the ISO 9004-2 standard in Europe.

Principles of TQM

Implementing a world-class service quality management system requires some fundamental changes in an organization's culture and value system. In general, there are four principles that must be internalized if world-class quality is to take hold, namely customer satisfaction, respect for people, management by fact, and continuous improvement.

▴ *Customer Satisfaction.* A company must change its attitude toward the customer and in many cases broaden its definition of a *customer*. Quality no longer means conformance to a set of specifications. Now it is defined by the customer. Customer expectations extend far beyond fair treatment and freedom from defective products and services. Customer demands must be satisfied in many other areas as well, including price, safety, and timeliness. Therefore, everything the company does must be organized to satisfy the customer.

Quality equates with the value the service provider adds to the customer's business or quality of life. The higher the value, the greater the customer satisfaction. Value and satisfaction are also based on customer perceptions, not entirely on objective measures of quality. Thus, measurement of customer satisfaction is not as clear-cut for a service as it is for a physical product, so service quality measurement is one of an organization's greatest challenges.

In addition to external customers, world-class service companies embrace the concept of internal customer-supplier relationships. They realize that the quality delivered to the external customer by frontline employees directly depends on the quality of support the frontline receives from the rest of the organization, especially management.

▴ *Respect for people.* World-class service companies realize that all employees, regardless of organizational level or position, have a desire to contribute. They all have unique talents and creativity, and the organization's most valuable resource is this pool of talent. There is an emphasis on teamwork because these companies believe that "together everyone achieves more."

However, true respect for people goes far beyond treating people well and giving some an opportunity to participate on problem-solving teams. It requires that the management system be consciously configured to provide opportunities for people at all levels to be involved in a meaningful way in the organization's success.

▲ *Management by fact.* World-class quality calls for a reorientation toward management by fact. This means decisions are based on data rather than gut feel. There are two major aspects of TQM that highlight the management by fact principle. The first is *prioritization*, the concept that improvement cannot be made in all areas at the same time owing to limited resources. Using data to stratify a situation allows management, teams, and sometimes even individuals to focus on the vital few instead of the trivial many areas where the greatest improvement can be gained from the least amount of effort.

The second is *variation*, or the variability of human performance. It has long been recognized that variation is inherent in everything, including natural phenomena, human interactions, and organizational systems. Statistical data provide a picture of the variability that is a natural part of any organizational system. They can indicate how stable (in control) the system is, and whether or not it is capable of meeting customer needs. When managers understand the nature of variation in their organization and gain control of it, they are better able to predict the results of their actions.

Since service quality is so heavily influenced by customer perceptions and frontline employee performance, it may not be possible or desirable to drive out all variation in a service process. Nevertheless, management by fact is a very important factor.

▲ *Continuous improvement.* A world-class service quality management system incorporates an operating philosophy of continuous improvement. To be successful, a company must follow a systematic process for achieving continuous improvement. This plan-do-check-act (PDCA) cycle is a never-ending spiral of movement: planning, implementing the plan, checking on the results of the plan, taking corrective measures, or otherwise acting on the results. In Japan, continuous improvement is referred to as *kaizen*. Whatever the label, in a world-class environment the best companies realize that to stand still is to regress. The current situation is never "good enough." Everyone must be dedicated to this never-ending pursuit of improvement. The PDCA concept is embodied in all three parts of the management framework discussed in the next section.

The Service Quality Management System Framework

A world-class service quality management system consists of three components (see Figure 14-1).

- ▲ *Policy management* involves strategic quality planning and encompasses the organizational system as a whole. It is the major responsibility of top management to initiate the process and ensure that the corporate resources are correctly focused.
- ▲ *Process management* deals with the continuous improvement of cross-functional, horizontal business processes, as well as improving the many local, repetitive processes necessary to provide goods and services to the customer.
- ▲ *Quality teams* focus on improvement opportunities at all levels in the company. Through teams, employees can have an opportunity to become involved in improvement activities.

In a world-class TQM environment, all three components of the triangle are in place, interacting with one another synergistically.

Figure 14-1. Components of a world-class service quality management system.

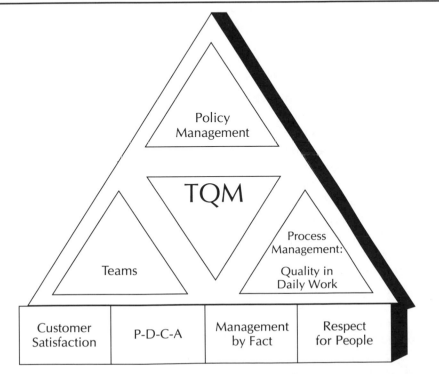

Policy Management

The keystone of a world-class service quality management system is policy management, or a strategic quality planning system. Business writer Peter Drucker once described the difference between efficiency and effectiveness as "doing things right" versus "doing the right things." Policy management is the means for ensuring an organization is doing the right things. Organizational effectiveness is augmented because the corporate direction is driven by customer needs and trends in the business environment.

The Japanese use the analogy of a quiver of arrows to illustrate the benefit of policy management, or what they call *Hoshin Kanri*. A company without a strategic quality planning process driven from the top is like a quiver of arrows dumped out onto the ground. The arrows are scattered and pointing in every direction. Likewise, a company's energies may be scattered and objectives may conflict with one another. Policy management is akin to drawing the arrows out of the quiver one by one, and arranging them so that all the vectors are in alignment. Every part of the company is pointed in the same direction.

How does one go about this? The first action a company must take is to involve the president or CEO and his or her direct reports. They meet routinely to guide the improvement activities and are frequently referred to as the quality council. This council guides the implementation of the process, which involves the following three phrases:

1. Establishing policy
2. Deploying policy
3. Implementing and reviewing policy

In the policy establishment phase, the quality council begins by writing the mission statement and formulating a vision for the organization. Its *mission* is an organization's essential reason for being, its unique identity. The *vision*, on the other hand, is a description of the organization's most desirable future state and a declaration of what the organization needs to care about most in order to reach that future. A vision statement has been described as "a dramatic picture of the future that has the power to motivate and inspire."[1]

Once the quality council sets the mission and vision, it then analyzes the *voice of the customer*. This is based on detailed research data related to customer requirements. These requirements are then translated into quality elements, or the broad organizational activities and processes that are necessary to meet customer requirements. This activity allows an organization to identify the internal processes or activities that have the largest impact on customer satisfaction.

The quality council also reviews data related to the business environment and key stakeholders, who are referred to as the *voice of the business*. It assesses the current situation as well as results from the previous year's plan or strategic initiatives currently under way.

Although the mission and vision influence the choice of policy, the twin voices of the customer and the business should have the most impact on policy selection. The customer and business analysis should highlight the factors most in need of improvement, or the *critical success factors*. These critical success factors, when grouped into broad categories, are used to formulate a limited number of breakthrough objectives that will propel the company toward its vision.

However, breakthrough objectives tend to be too general to be actionable. Therefore, the next step in the establishment of policy is for the quality council to provide more specific focus by translating the breakthrough objectives into a number of priority activities. Each member of the quality council normally assumes responsibility for one or more of the priority activities and becomes the coordinating executive. As such, he or she is responsible for ensuring that improvement activities throughout the company are coordinated for cross-functional progress.

The quality council deploys the policy by analyzing data related to the priority activity, establishing an indicator or metric, and setting a target for improvement. Through stratification, it also identifies, organization-wide, the major contributors to achieving the target. Targets and means that are acceptable to each contributing area are negotiated through an iterative process.

The means to achieve the targets are a collection of improvement projects with associated cost-benefit analyses. The final task in deploying policy is to select the mix of projects that will allow for the most improvement given the resources available. Figure 14-2 summarizes the policy formation process.

Policy deployment should be traceable from the organizational target down to the lowest organizational level along a single reporting line. The graphic representation of the target deployment for a priority activity is called a flag system. Each flag in the system should represent a sponsor, an indicator that contributes to the whole, a target, and an action plan identifying the means to achieve the target. An example of a flag system is shown in Figure 14-3.

Once the improvement projects have been selected, individuals and quality teams implement them throughout the year. Management remains active by reviewing frequently the results of the improvement efforts, as well as the execution of the policy management process itself. It checks to see if the indicators are on track. Are they where we thought they would be at this point in the year? If they are not on track, why? Do we need to do something differently? Was the improvement estima-

Figure 14-2.   Policy formation process.

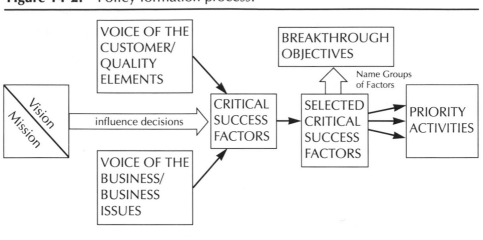

tion unrealistic? Or was the implementation ineffective? By periodically reviewing both the process and the results upstream, management can take the appropriate corrective action early enough to ensure that targets will be met at the end of the year.

Depending on the organization's size, there may be several different levels of reviews. For example:

1. The CEO reviews progress on corporate indicators with the coordinating executives (quality council).
2. Coordinating executives review progress on priority activity indicators with key functional contributors.
3. Local management reviews progress on negotiated targets within their areas of responsibility.

Quality Teams

The second component of a world-class service quality management system are quality teams. These teams support policy management by working on improvement projects related to priority activities.

Quality teams can also provide an opportunity for groups of employees to identify and solve problems within their work areas, mainly in support of existing processes. Usually, these teams use a multistep, systematic problem-solving approach that incorporates the seven statistical tools of quality: checksheet, Pareto chart, cause-and-effect diagram, scatter diagram, histogram, control chart, and graphs.

Teams can also be formed to tackle more strategic, cross-functional issues related to designing new services and processes or redesigning

Figure 14-3. Example of a flag system.

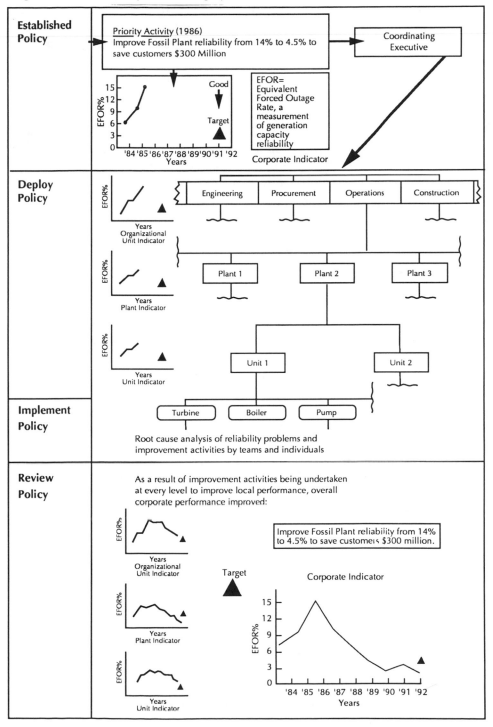

existing ones. A methodology such as Quality Function Deployment (QFD) has been effective in a small but growing number of instances where design quality or a preventive approach was critical. QFD teams use the seven new quality control tools, particularly matrix diagrams, when completing design projects.

Teams may also be formed to benchmark competitors and to incorporate best-in-class practices into the organization's processes to effect improvements.

Ideally, these team efforts would surface as a result of policy management. But a full-scale policy management system does not have to be in place for a company to derive some benefits from quality team activities. All of the team methodologies involve employees in improving the workplace, and enable them to work with others in a shared-responsibility environment and to learn new data-gathering, analysis, and communication skills.

Process Management

The third component of a world-class service quality management system is process management, or quality in daily work. Process management supports policy management by providing tools to deal with the day-to-day relationships among functions. It is also a useful technique for locking in the gains achieved from breakthrough activities and then adding incremental improvements to those gains.

Process management facilitates problem-solving activities. Problem areas or themes are often identified when a process is documented. In addition, establishing and monitoring a control system can highlight persistent problem areas to be worked on. For example, a process could be unstable or unpredictable. A control system can help a company determine, statistically, how much variation in a given process is normal and when an abnormal deviation occurs. This special cause is then investigated and eliminated.

Once a process is stable, a control system can also be used to improve its capability of producing an output that will meet customer needs. Activities directed toward improving process capability can also be tracked statistically.

Integration and Implementation

The service quality management system presented in this chapter provides a logical framework for integrating many of the other TQM or service quality tools and techniques currently being practiced. Some of these include:

▴ Employee suggestion programs
▴ Employee surveys
▴ Customer-satisfaction monitoring practices, such as surveys, mystery shoppers, and measuring defections
▴ Customer-retention programs
▴ Service recovery processes
▴ Service guarantees
▴ Error modes or failure modes and effects analysis (EMEA or FMEA)
▴ Total productive maintenance
▴ Supplier quality improvement programs

The selection of specific tools depends upon the type of organization. The main point is that tools and techniques, used in isolation without the rationale of a Total Quality Management system, will only afford limited results. A world-class service quality management system must have a strong framework in place. The proper mix of methods needs to be chosen, and employees must be trained extensively on the tools. In addition, reward and recognition systems are required to reinforce the new behaviors.

In terms of implementation, quality initiatives in service companies have varied widely, and with some justification. Each organization's circumstances are unique; another company's management models and practices cannot merely be superimposed without some modification. But based on the experience of organizations that have implemented TQM, two areas are critical:

▴ *Detailed implementation planning*. The sequence for implementation must be based on an assessment of corporate needs, and a detailed plan must be developed, approved, and progress monitored by the quality council. This plan should map the implementation and identify associated costs, as well as specify pilot areas, training schedules, participants, and indicators to measure implementation progress.

▴ *Top management commitment*. The ultimate success of a TQM effort is dependent on the executive team's long-term commitment to the process. Their commitment is important for approval of resources to implement the plan, ongoing communication of the TQM vision and purpose to the entire organization, rewarding and recognizing successes, and remaining active during implementation through frequent reviews.

Conclusion

As the global service economy grows, the contours of the world-class service quality management system can be expected to change. Customer expectations will continue to rise, giving momentum to new standards. New players, companies, or countries will emerge with variations on the service quality theme.

Notes

1. John L. Hudiburg, *Winning With Quality: The FPL Story* (White Plains, N.Y.: Quality Resources, 1991).

References

Akao, Yoji, trans. *Hoshin Kanri: Policy Deployment for Successful TQM.* Cambridge, Mass.: Productivity Press, 1991.

Brown, Stephen W. et al. *Service Quality: Multidisciplinary and Multinational Perspectives.* Lexington, Mass.: Lexington Books, 1991.

Deming, W. Edwards. *Out of the Crisis.* Cambridge, Mass.: MIT Center for Advanced Engineering Study, 1991.

Drucker, Peter. *Management Tasks, Responsibilities, Practices.* New York: Harper & Row, 1974.

Hudiburg, John J. *Winning With Quality: The FPL Story.* White Plains, N.Y.: Quality Resources, 1991.

ISO 9004-2 First Edition. Geneva, Switzerland: International Organization for Standardization, 1991.

Malcolm Baldrige Award Guidelines. Gaithersburg, Md.: U.S. Department of Commerce, National Institute of Standards and Technology, 1992.

Quinn, James Brian. *Intelligent Enterprise.* New York: Free Press, 1992.

Quality Council Workshop Manual. North Palm Beach, Fla.: Qualtec Quality Services, Inc., 1992.

Steering Committee Workshop Manual. North Palm Beach, Fla.: Qualtec Quality Services, Inc., 1992.

PART IV

DEPLOYING SERVICE QUALITY

15

A Dynamic Process Model of Service Quality Assessment

William Boulding and Richard Staelin, Duke University

Since the early 1980s, the concept of *quality* has become a corporate gospel. The popular press worries about U.S. industry being able to match the quality of foreign competitors; CEOs exhort their organizations to "think quality"; and company advertisements attempt to link the corporate name with a quality image. Despite all this emphasis on quality, it is not at all clear that everyone is talking about the same thing. For many, quality is the absence of things gone wrong and is measured by looking at the production process. This is not surprising, given the fact that early leaders in the quality movement relied heavily on statistical quality control and were concerned with production procedures and reducing defects. Thus, quality was defined in terms of measures associated with internal operations (e.g., defects per thousand). However, companies have begun to realize that internally generated measures of quality often do not match customer perceptions of quality. More important, they know that it is customer, not management, perceptions that ultimately count in the marketplace. Consequently, new measures of quality based on customer perceptions began to emerge. Customer satisfaction and the voice of the customer became a new thrust of the quality movement.[*]

This movement from internal measures to customer perceptions also occurred in service industries. One of the first examples of this shift (and the work that seems to have become the industry standard) was put forth by Parasuraman, Zeithaml, and Berry.[1] Known as Gap Analysis or the Gaps model, it defines service quality in terms of the gap between a customer's expectations of what the service should provide and the customer's perceptions of what the service actually provides; it assumes that the smaller the gap, the higher the quality of the service. The Gaps

---

*As one indicator of this attention to customer perceptions, a recent survey conducted by *Inside Research*, a publication for research industry executives, estimated that in 1991 companies in the United States spent $100 million on customer satisfaction programs, up 26 percent from 1990. These programs involved the collection and/or analysis of information regarding the delivery of a product or service from the customer's point of view.

that the smaller the gap, the higher the quality of the service. The Gaps model has a number of distinctive characteristics. First, its concept of service quality refers to a *cumulative* measure of the overall quality level of a company's service delivery system. This is in contrast to the customer-satisfaction construct, which refers to a *particular* transaction. Second, the implication of this definition is that quality can be improved by either increasing perceptions or lowering expectations. Third, the conceptualization is static in that it implicitly assumes that expectations are not affected by a specific service encounter, allowing one to measure expectations and perceptions contemporaneously in determining the service quality gap.

In this chapter, we build upon the Gaps model by centering attention on (1) the cumulative construct, overall quality level of a company's service delivery system, and (2) the expectations and perceptions of the customer. However, we depart from the Gaps model in that we explicitly acknowledge the fact that perceptions and expectations dynamically change over time and can be influenced not only by service contacts but also by such factors as word-of-mouth, competitive actions, and a company's communications. Probably most important, we no longer define service quality in terms of a gap, but instead relate it directly to the customer's current perceptions of the service.

Specifically, we report on an individual-level process model of service quality developed and tested elsewhere that traces the way customers form and update their perceptions and expectations of service quality, and identifies the consequences of these perceptions for behavioral intention variables that affect the strategic health of the company.[2,3] At the core of this model is the concept that individual current perceptions of the service quality of a company just after a service contact are a blend of (1) his or her prior expectations of what *will* and *should* transpire during the contact and (2) the actual delivered service that transpires during the service encounter. The benefit of this model is that it allows us to address, among others, the following questions:

1. What is the best way to measure the perceived service quality of an organization? Is it the gap between expectations and perceptions, or some other measure?
2. How should a company monitor its service quality level? Should this monitoring involve only internal observations on the service (e.g., number of smiles, length of lines) or concentrate on customer measures? If the latter, what are the constructs (e.g., perceptions, expectations, satisfaction) that a company should monitor?
3. What factors influence a company's service quality level? Can a company influence these factors in ways other than by providing

excellent service? What is the impact of competitive actions on a company's perceived quality level?

4. How do customer perceptions of service quality influence future behavior with the company (e.g., repeat business, favorable word-of-mouth)?

This chapter first presents our conceptual model of how a customer's expectations influence his or her perceptions of the service quality of a company and how these expectations and perceptions are updated over time. We next summarize our empirical findings from two very different studies, one a controlled laboratory experiment and the other a field study concerning customer perceptions and expectations of an actual service. These findings give credence to the robustness of our model. We then discuss how one can estimate the influences prior expectations and the actual service encounter have on a person's perceptions of service quality where expectations and perceptions data are obtained from an attitudinal survey conducted *after* the service encounter. Finally, we discuss the managerial implications of our process model.

Model Development

Since our model has many of the same contructs found in prior models of customer satisfaction/dissatisfaction (CS/D) and service quality, we briefly review the dominant concepts in these two literatures before presenting our view of how customers form and update their perceptions of the overall service quality of a company. One concept found in both literatures is customer expectations. Interestingly, these literatures do not agree on how to operationalize the measure of this construct. The CS/D literature normally defines expectations in terms of *predictions* of future events,[4] while the service quality literature usually uses *normative* expectations.

A second concept used in both literatures is the disconfirmation of expectations paradigm.[5] This paradigm holds that a customer's expectations going into an event act as an anchor against which the customer measures the subsequent company performance.[6] In the CS/D literature, satisfaction is determined by the difference between prior expectations and actual performance, with greater differences leading to less satisfaction. Similarly, in the service quality literature, service quality is defined in terms of a difference. However, it assumes expectations are unchanged by the service. Consequently, it uses contemporaneous expectations, and not prior expectations, as the standard. Also, instead of using actual performance in calculating the difference, the service quality literature uses perceived performance. More succinctly, service quality is measured by the difference between *contemporaneous* expectations and *perceptions* of actual performance. Our model also includes expectations, perceptions, and actual performance. However, instead of centering our attention on the difference between actual performance (or perceptions of actual service) and expectations, we assume that prior expectations directly influence the way people perceive their actual service encounter, and that these perceptions determine people's assessment of quality. Said differently, we treat expectations as antecedents to perceptions, which in turn are the impetus for a person's overall assessment of service quality. We next present our concept of how customers form and update their perceptions of service quality. To facilitate the description of our model, we segment it into three components. The first describes how customers form and update their expectations, the second is concerned with the formation of perceptions, and the third is involved with how these perceptions affect future actions of the customer.

The Process Generating Expectations

We start our discussion with the observation that customers think about services in terms of *j* distinct dimensions.[7] For example, people might differentiate services along the dimensions of responsiveness and tangibility. We define customer expectations as their pretrial beliefs about the service on a particular dimension. Although we do not explicitly state how these pretrial beliefs are formed, we point to the fact that customers normally have many sources of information to help them form these expectations. These sources include word-of-mouth, prior experience with the service or the service of a competing company, and the company's communications to the customer via such actions as pricing and advertising.

We next assume that customers have two types of expectations. Consistent with the CS/D literature we postulate that customers have expectations about what *will* happen in their next service encounter with a company. We refer to these predictive expectations as *will expectations*. We also postulate that customers form expectations about what *should* happen. These expectations, which measure what customers feel they deserve, are referred to as *should expectations* and are close in spirit to the "what ought to happen" expectations proposed by Tse and Wilton.[8] It should be noted, however, that these normative expectations are different from the ideal or desired standard now being proposed in the service quality literature.[9] The former expectations are likely to change over time as customers receive new information about competitive services or are told what they should expect via the company's communications. In contrast, desired and ideal expectations are more akin to an absolute standard and thus are less likely to be related to what is reasonable or feasible or what the service provider tells the customer to expect.

Finally, we explicitly acknowledge that both *will* and *should expectations* can change over time. We center our attention on three points of time between two service encounters occurring at times $t-1$ and t. We refer to these three points of time as point A (just after the service encounter at time $t-1$), point B (just prior to the next service encounter which occurs at time t), and point C (just after the service encounter occurring at time t). We let expectations at point B be different from those at point A—the difference being due to the fact that the customer receives new information such as word-of-mouth or a company's communications during the period from A to B. We denote this new information affecting the *will expectations* with the vector ΔX_t. Finally, we let expectations at point C differ from point B; in this case the difference is due to the customer's most recent encounter with the actual service. We denote this actual service as AS_t.

We formalize our model of expectations for these three points of time as follows. Define the ith customer's *will expectations* for the jth unique dimension of the service at time t (i.e., just after experiencing the service) to be WE_{ijt}. Then the expectations at point of time A (e.g., at time $t-1$) are WE_{ijt-1}. Next assume customers update their *will expectations* whenever they receive relevant new information. We represent this updating process as $WE_{ijt-1} + \delta_{1jt}(\Delta X_{it})$, where δ_{1jt} is a vector of weighting factors. Finally, we hypothesize that a customer's expectations of what will happen after contact with the company's delivery system is a weighted average of (1) the person's expectations going into the service encounter and (2) the actual service encounter. Mathematically, we represent this belief as follows:

$$WE_{ijt} = \alpha_{jt}(WE_{ijt-1} + \delta_{1jt}(\Delta X_{it})) + (1 - \alpha_{jt})AS_{ijt}, \qquad (1)$$

where the scalar α_{jt} is restricted to lie between zero and one. Conceptually, the first term represents the customer's prior expectations, including all the new external information that modifies customer expectations, while the second term represents the actual service contact that is composed of a number of objective factors—for example, length of the line and the number of thank you's—that define the actual service delivered.

Two features should be noted from equation 1. First, the equation represents a Bayesian-like updating process whereby a customer enters into the service encounter with a prior expectation ($WE_{ijt-1} + \delta_{1jt}(\Delta X_{it})$), experiences a new service encounter (AS_{ijt}), and develops a posterior prediction of future service (WE_{ijt}) based on these two inputs. Second, the sum of the weights on the prior expectation (α_{jt}) and the actual service $(1 - \alpha_{jt})$ are constrained to equal unity. This ensures that when a person experiences a service encounter equal to his or her prior expectations, the updated expectation remains unchanged.

The process by which *should expectations* are modified from the point in time A to the point in time B is similar to that set forth above. We acknowledge that new information such as a company price change, its communications about how it plans to alter service from previous levels, and the customer's exposure to unanticipated levels of competitive service could alter the customer's *should expectations*. An example of the latter might be a customer modifying his or her *should expectations* for the Infiniti car after learning that Lexus (a competitive car manufacturer) has instituted a policy of replacing a Lexus car if a customer is unhappy with the paint job of the original automobile. We represent this updating of *should expectations* mathematically as follows. First, we define the i_{th} customer's *should expectation* at time $t - 1$ to be SE_{ijt-1}. Also, we represent the new information affecting person i's *should expectations* during the period from $t - 1$ to just prior to the service encounter at time t by the vector ΔZ_{it}. Then, the i_{th} customer's *should expectation* for the j_{th} dimension at point B (i.e., just prior to the service encounter) is the person's expectation at time $t - 1$ updated by the new information, i.e., $SE_{ijt-1} + \delta_{2jt} (\Delta Z_{it})$, where δ_{2jt} is a vector of weights.

A customer's *should expectations* can also be modified if the customer experiences an unanticipated level of service with the company's delivery system. For example, the customer who received the new car from Lexus after complaining about the paint job might alter his or her *should expectation* for Lexus based on this unanticipated service experience. We represent this shift in expectations by postulating that the more the company's actual delivered service exceeds the customer's prior *should expectation*, the more the customer will increase his or her future *should expectation* for that company. This is quantified as follows:

$$SE_{ijt} = SE_{ijt-1} + \delta_{2jt} (\Delta Z_{it}) + \beta_{jt} \cdot K_{ijt} AS_{ijt}$$
$$\text{where } K_{ijt} = 1 \text{ if } AS_{ijt} > (SE_{ijt-1} + \delta_{2jt} \Delta Z_{it}). \qquad (2)$$

In words, a person's past *should expectations* are shifted up or down by new information as denoted by ΔZ_{it}, and are shifted up if what is actually delivered exceeds the person's beliefs about what should be delivered.

Equations 1 and 2 implicitly assume that *will expectations* and *should expectations* are unique constructs. Ultimately, this is an empirical question. An important aspect of our empirical work, using a variety of methods and different service settings, is that we demonstrate that these two sets of expectations exist and are used by consumers to form perceptions of quality.

The Process That Generates Perceptions

Our concept of how customers form their perceptions of the overall service quality level of a company's delivery system differs from the disconfirmation formulation most often found in the CS/D literature[10] and the gaps formulation found in the service quality literature.[11] The basic idea behind our formulation is that a person's perceptions of the service quality of a company are influenced not only by the most recent contact but also by the belief structure that the person brings to the service encounter, where the belief structure is captured by the person's *will expectations* and *should expectations*. Interestingly, as we show soon, the implications from this formulation are compatible with the transaction-specific implications derived from the CS/D literature. Thus, in our model, a satisfying (dissatisfying) experience leads to increases (decreases) in perceptions of the overall service quality level of the company. However, our model differs from a satisfaction model in that satisfaction with this transaction does not necessarily imply the customer has a good perception of the company's service quality level, since this latter construct also depends on prior transactions and information. In this way, our model integrates the transaction-specific satisfaction construct found in the CS/D literature into the cumulative framework found in the service quality literature.

More formally, let PS_{ijt} be the i_{th} person's perceptions of the service quality level of dimension j at time t—that is, just after exposure to the service. We postulate that PS_{ijt} is influenced not only by customer i's actual service contact AS_{it}, but also by the person's belief structure just before the service contact—this belief being captured by the person's *will expectations*—$WE_{ijt-1} + \delta_{1jt} (\Delta X_{it})$—and *should expectations*—$SE_{ijt-1} + \delta_{2jt} (\Delta Z_{it})$. By including these two expectations, we explicitly acknowledge that perceptual biases occur when individuals evaluate "hard to judge" stimuli. In this way, our model allows two customers experiencing the identical service to have different perceptions of the service quality if they have different sets of prior expectations.

We model the individual effects of a person's belief structure as follows. Since *will expectations* represent a person's belief about what the service provider will provide, we postulate that this belief positively influences a person's perceptions. Thus, all else being equal, the person entering into the service contact who believes a service will provide a higher quality will also perceive the service to be at a higher level after contact with the service compared to the person who has lower prior *will expectations*. Conversely, *should expectations* are postulated to have a negative influence on perceptions, the logic being that *should expectations* reflect a person's degree of criticalness. Thus, all else being equal, the higher the person's *should expectations* for a given service, the less favorable the persons' perceptions of the service's level of quality. Said differently, we hypothesize a positive bias associated with a person's prior *will expectations* and negative bias for prior *should expectations*. Finally, we believe the actual service should have a positive influence on perceptions. These ideas can be presented mathematically as follows:

$$P_{ijt} = \alpha_{jt} \, (WE_{ijt\text{-}1} + \delta_{1jt} \, (\Delta X_{it})) + (1 - \alpha_{jt}) \, AS_{ijt} + \gamma_{jt}(SE_{ijt\text{-}1} + \delta_{2jt}(\Delta Z_{it})) \qquad (3)$$

where γ_{jt} is an updating parameter reflecting the influence of the *should expectations* on perceptions, and is postulated to be less than zero.

Equation 3 has a number of interesting characteristics. First, it reflects the assumption that customers blend their prior *will expectations* with the service contact experience in a manner identical to that used to form the new *will expectations*. Second, it explicitly acknowledges the positive influence of prior *will expectations* and the actual service contact on perceptions and the negative impact of *should expectations*. Third, by replacing the first two terms in equation 3 with equation 1, the resulting equation makes explicit the difference between a person's current perceptions of service and the individual's expectations of what will happen in the future. Specifically, while current *will expectations* only measure a person's best prediction of likely future service, current perceptions of the quality level also reflect a person's belief structure of what should happen.

Equation 3 also can be used to reconcile the apparent difference between the transaction-specific emphasis found in the CS/D literature and the emphasis on cumulative perceptions found in the service quality literature. To do this, first assume two individuals experience an identical service contact. Let us also assume that there is only one dimension of service quality ($j = 1$) and that the actual service rated a 10. Further, let each of these individuals have identical prior belief structures about what should happen, but different *will expectations*, with person L having a lower *will expectation* of 8 and person H having a higher *will expectation* of 12. Which of these individuals will find this service contact more satisfying? Which person will perceive the service quality level to be the highest? Will this service contact increase or decrease each individual's expectations of what will happen in the future? The answers come from equations 1 and 3 and the definition of satisfaction—that is, satisfaction is determined by the difference between performance and expected performance. Thus, person L with the lower prior *will expectations* will have a more satisfactory experience than person H. However, person L will perceive the overall service quality level to be lower than person H since this person has lower prior expectations going into the contact. More important, since person L had a satisfactory experience, he or she will show an increase in expectations while person H will show a decrease in his or her expectations of future service. Thus, our model allows for transaction-specific satisfaction influencing perceptions, while acknowledging that perceptions are more than the customer's satisfaction with the last service encounter.

Finally, note that equation 3 has the pleasing characteristic of having increases in the company's actual service quality level lead to higher customer perceptions even if *will expectations* of what the company will provide also increase. This is in contrast to a model that measures service quality as the gap between perceived performance and *will expectations*. In the latter case, commensurate increases in perceptions and expectations would not translate into any overall increase in assessment of service quality.

Overall Assessment of Quality

Until now, most of our attention has centered on the j dimensions of service quality and not the customer's overall assessment of the company's service quality level. We next turn our attention to this overall construct. We follow the lead of prior research that suggests that customers' assessments of quality are composed of their assessments of a number of different quality dimensions.[12] Analogous to the multiattribute attitude formation work, we define the ith customer's overall perception of the firm's service quality at time t (denoted OSQ_{it}) to be:

$$OSQ_{it} = \sum_{j=1}^{J} \phi_j \, PS_{ijt} \qquad (4a)$$

where ϕ_j is the weighting factor for the perceptions pertaining to dimension j. This definition differs from the prevailing model of service quality, the Gaps model, in a number of ways. First, the Gaps model has no temporal sequencing. Thus, overall quality is represented by their Gap 5, which consists of contemporaneous perceptions minus contemporaneous *should expectations*. (Since the Gaps model is static, expectations prior to the service contact are implicitly assumed to equal those after the service.) Second, actual service implicitly enters their model via Gaps 1–4, since these gaps contain, among other things, information about the actual service. Mathematically, their conceptualization is captured by the following expression:

$$OSQ_{it} = \sum_{j=1}^{J} \phi_j \, (PS_{ijt} - SE_{ijt}) \qquad (4b)$$

Comparison of equations 4a and 4b makes clear a major difference between our formulation and the Gaps model. Although both formulations postulate a positive influence of perceptions of the individual dimensions of quality on the customer's overall assessment of service quality, the latter also postulates an equally negative influence of *should expectations*. In contrast, our formulation postulates that once one measures perceptions, *should* and *will expectations* have no additional effect on a customer's assessment of overall service quality level. (We discuss these differences when we present our empirical results.)

The final component of our model is the link between the overall assessment of quality and intended actions such as favorable word-of-mouth and repeated use of the service. It is our strong belief that favorable assessment of the service quality of a company leads to customer behaviors that are beneficial to the strategic health of the company. We capture this belief with the following equation:

$$BI_m = \lambda_m \, OSQ_{it},\tag{5}$$

where $\lambda_m > 0$, and BI_m is the ith person's behavioral intention for action m at time t.

Study Summary

The preceding discussion provides a framework for managers to evaluate the quality of their service delivery system. It emphasizes that perceptions of quality are influenced not only by the customers experiencing the objective aspects of the service, but also by the customers' prior expectations, which in turn are influenced by competitive and company actions, and word-of-mouth. Thus, companies interested in understanding and managing customer perceptions need to track not only perceptions but also *should* and *will expectations*. In addition, they need to understand the factors that influence these expectations.

The question then becomes, how robust is our model? Fortunately, our structural model as specified in equations 1, 2, 3, 4a, and 5 generates a number of testable hypotheses involving how expectations influence perceptions, how perceptions of the service-quality dimensions affect overall perceptions of service quality level, how this overall assessment affects future actions of the customer, and the ability of this dynamic model to outperform the static Gaps model with respect to predicting overall quality assessments. Moreover, by acknowledging that the updating parameters α, γ, and β can vary by person and change over time, our model speaks to a wide range of service encounter situations. For example, we would expect customers involved in assessing a service with hard-to-evaluate attributes to place more weight on cues or signals to form quality perceptions. These cues work through expectations, and thus imply greater absolute values for α and γ. Similarly, customers who have considerable prior experience with a service should place less emphasis on the last service contact in coming up with their perceptions. Thus, in monitoring customers over time, we would expect the absolute values of their parameters α and γ to increase.

In order to test these and other hypotheses, we conducted two very different studies. The first was a laboratory study where ninety-six subjects were asked to evaluate a hotel's service quality based upon two simulated stays at the hotel.* Prior to these experiences, the subjects were provided information intended to manipulate their *will* and *should* *expectations*. For example, some subjects received information that led to high *should expectations* while others received information that led to medium *should expectations*. *Will expectations* were similarly manipulated. Subjects were then provided with two service encounters—one designed to be positive, the other less so. Measures were taken for the customer's *will* and *should expectations* prior to the first service contact as well as after each of the two contacts. In addition, measures of overall perceived service quality and behavioral intentions were obtained after the service contacts. In order to simplify the task for the subjects, the measures were concerned with a unidimensional concept of service. This is equivalent to assuming $j = 1$. Also, we did not provide any additional information after forming expectations. Thus, we did not test the effects of ΔX and ΔZ since both were zero in our experiment. These data allowed us to estimate equations 1, 2, 3, and 5 for two different time periods. (Estimation of equations 4a and 4b was precluded since we did not obtain the j component measures of expectations and perceptions. We were able, however, to estimate these two equations and thus do a model test in a second study, which we describe next.)

Our second study was conducted in a field setting and involved measuring the expectations, perceptions, and behavioral intentions of 177 customers of an educational service.† In all, thirty-six questions were asked for *will* and *should expectations* and perceptions. These questions were designed to tap the five dimensions of service quality specified in the SERVQUAL instrument.[13] In addition, each customer was asked to give his or her assessment of overall service quality of the organization and his or her intended behavior with respect to six actions important to the strategic health of the institution (e.g., recommend the school to a

*For more details about this study see Boulding et al., "Dynamic Process Model" and Ajay Kalra, "An Empirical Validation and a Transaction Level Investigation of an Expectations-Based Process Model of Service Quality," Ph.D. dissertation, Duke University, 1992.

†For more details about this study see Boulding et al. "Conceptualizing and Testing."

friend, contribute money after graduation). As with almost all field studies on quality, these measures were taken at one point in time—that is, no longitudinal measures were obtained. Such data allow direct estimation of equations 4a, 4b, and 5, but preclude direct estimation of equations 1, 2, and 3. Interestingly, we can still estimate the parameters α and γ found in equations 1 and 3. We discuss this procedure more fully in the following section.

Results—Study 1

The experimental data allowed us to conduct a series of planned contrasts (e.g., holding fixed both prior *should expectations* and the actual service delivered, what is the effect of varying the level of prior *will expectations?*) in order to test various aspects of our model. These data led us to the following conclusions:

1. That we were able to successfully manipulate initial *will* and *should expectations*.
2. Holding fixed initial *should expectations* and actual service, higher initial *will expectations* led to higher future *will expectations*, higher perceptions of service quality, and higher behavioral intentions.
3. Holding fixed *will expectations* and actual service, higher initial *should expectations* led to lower perceptions of service quality and lower behavioral intentions.
4. Holding fixed initial *will* and *should expectations*, better service led to higher future will expectations, higher perceptions of service, and higher behavioral intentions.
5. *Should expectations* at time t equaled *should expectations* at $t-1$ unless the actual service exceeded initial *should expectations*.

These data were also used to estimate the specific coefficients in equations 1, 2, 3, and 5 for two different time periods—that is, $t=1$ and $t=2$. The obtained results were as follows:

$$\alpha_1 = .38, \ \alpha_2 = .55, \ \beta_1 = .13; \ \beta_2 = .12;$$
$$\gamma_1 = -.11; \ \gamma_2 = -.21, \ \lambda_1 = .91; \ \lambda_2 = .98.$$

All the coefficients were statistically significant at the .01 level. These results led us to the following conclusions:

1. From the results concerning α_1 and α_2, we see that current *will expectations* are a positive blend of initial *will expectations* and the actual service. Moreover, since $\alpha_2 > \alpha_1$, we note that as a person gains more exposure to the service, the person's prior expecta-

tions have a greater effect and the actual service encounter has less of an effect in terms of updating *will expectations* and perceptions of service quality.

2. From the results concerning γ_1 and γ_2, we see that a person's *should expectations* have a negative influence on perceptions. Moreover, this influence appears to increase over time.

3. As hypothesized, individuals update their *should expectations* after a service encounter only when the service encounter provides them with a pleasant surprise—that is, the actual service exceeds their prior *should expectations*.

4. From the results concerning λ, we see that perceptions of quality strongly influence behavioral intentions and the strength of this relationship seems to be increasing over time.

Results—Study 2

In addition to providing additional evidence concerning the validity of our model, study 2 also allowed us to compare the veracity of equations 4a and 4b, and to explicate a research methodology that allows a company to estimate two key parameters of our model—α and γ—using data collected from a single point in time. This method is exceptionally important in that it enables a manager to infer the impact of the company's delivered service without actually measuring the service.

Model Estimation

Given space limitations, we do not develop the actual method used to estimate the two parameters of our dynamic model using data collected at one point in time.[14] The basic concept, however, is quite straightforward and relies on two major assumptions.

- The model as specified in equations 1, 2, and 3 is, in fact, correct.
- There are multiple measures for each individual on each of the j dimensions of service quality and each question taps the specific dimension being measured.

The actual estimation equations are as follows:

$$(PS_{ijnt} - PS_{ij \cdot t}) = \left(\frac{\alpha_{jt} + \gamma_{jt}}{\alpha_{jt}} \right) (WE_{ijnt} - WE_{ij \cdot t}) + \epsilon_{6it} \qquad (6)$$

$$(PS_{ijnt} - PS_{ij \cdot t}) = (\alpha_{jt} + \gamma_{jt})(SE_{ijnt} - SE_{ij \cdot t}) + \epsilon_{7it} \qquad (7)$$

where PS_{ijnt}, WE_{ijnt}, and SE_{ijnt} are the nth measure of the jth dimension for the appropriate construct and the $\cdot$ notation indicates the mean for the ith individual on the jth dimension. In words, equations 6 and 7 state that for each individual there is a relationship between how that person responds to the nth perception question tapping dimension j relative to his or her mean response, and how the same person responds to the analogous *will* and *should expectations* question relative to the respective mean response. These equations result in within-individual analyses. Thus, having multiple (repeated) measures allows one to control for all individual-specific factors that remain unchanged at time t. In study 2, this included the actual service delivered to a given individual, the individual's "history," and characteristics, including a person's proclivity to use a specific portion of the response scale, and any new information received prior to time t. As a result, equations 6 and 7 no longer contain any unobserved variables, enabling consistent estimation of two coefficients: (1) $(\alpha_{jt} + \gamma_{jt})/(\alpha_{jt})$, and (2) $(\alpha_{jt} + \gamma_{jt})$. From these two coefficients we can fully identify the two key structural parameters found in equations 1 and 3.

We used the study 2 data and equations 4a, 4b, 5, 6, and 7 to derive the following conclusions:

1. As expected, given study 1 results, we found using equations 6 and 7 that *will expectations* positively and *should expectations* negatively influenced perceptions of quality. Also, from equation 5 we found overall perceptions of quality strongly influenced behavioral intentions.
2. By comparing the statistical significance of equations 4a and 4b with a more general model that captures both equations, we found strong empirical support for our model relative to the Gaps model.
3. From equation 4a, we found reliability was the primary driver of overall perceptions of quality.
4. Finally, we noted from equations 6 and 7 that one can successfully estimate parameters from our dynamic model using data taken from one point in time.

Conclusions

This model has been tested using data derived from two very different studies, the first a longitudinal laboratory experiment, the second a field study using questionnaire data collected at one point in time. In both cases, the results were strongly compatible with all aspects of the process model.

We find this convergence of results encouraging. The model appears robust to different analytic approaches, different data collection methods, and different service settings. The formulation also provides a number of insights into how companies can best increase customer perceptions of overall service quality. But our most important managerial insights relate to the role of expectations. The prevailing model of service quality defines perceived service quality as the gap between expectations and perceptions, and does not differentiate among types of expectations. This leads to the strategic implication that companies can either try to increase perceptions or lower expectations in their quest to increase overall service quality. Our empirical results are incompatible with both a one-dimensional view of expectations and the Gap model of service quality. First, we find that service quality is directly influenced only by perceptions. Second, increasing customer expectations of what a company will provide during future service encounters actually leads to higher perceptions of quality after the customer is exposed to the actual service, all else being equal. From this we infer that companies should manage customers' predictive expectations upward rather than downward if they want to increase customers' perceptions of overall service quality. In addition, our results strongly support the premise that customers' expectations of what a company should deliver during a service encounter decrease their ultimate perceptions of the actual service delivered, all else being equal. Therefore, improved assessments of service quality can result when customer expectations of what a company should deliver are managed downward.

The issue of managerial importance then becomes how to manage both types of expectations. Ideally, one would want to increase customers' *will expectations*, however managing *should expectations* is more ambiguous. For example, one never wants to take actions that increase *should expectations* beyond the level a company can deliver. However, one would like to increase *should expectations* if this occurs via service delivery that exceeds prior *should expectations*. In this case, the *should expectations* will not exceed the company's ability to deliver service. Moreover, note that such an action probably will also cause the consumer's *should expectations* for a competitive company to increase. Assuming the competitor cannot deliver to this new level of demanded service, a company can raise customers' *should expectations* and improve its standing relative to its competition. Thus, our model is compatible with the idea that a key to competitive success lies in setting new industry standards.

We can unambiguously conclude that the best way to manage both sets of expectations is to deliver the best possible service. Managers should not worry about the phenomenon of rising expectations as long as their companies are causing these rising expectations. Beyond this we can say little as to how to best manage expectations. However, we can see a clear need for better understanding of the antecedents of *will* and *should expectations.*

A second point with important managerial relevance is that we present a method of estimating the two key parameters from our dynamic model using survey data from customers taken at only one point in time. Because this approach does not require measuring the actual service provided or prior expectations, it provides managers with an easily implementable method for estimating our model. However, we caution the reader that the estimation technique requires (1) multiple measures of perceptions and expectations, (2) measures within a dimension to have an identical influence on that dimension, and (3) that managers segment the customers so as to reflect the possible differences in the updating parameters if they believe customers have much different levels of prior experience.

In sum, our research activities have led us to the following conclusions:

1. Our conceptual model closely approximates how consumers' expectations and perceptions evolve over time.
2. Companies must understand, and manage, two different kinds of expectations held by their customers as well as their delivered service.
3. Although perceptions of quality are formed in a dynamic process, managers can measure and track this process using data collected at one point in time.

Notes

1. A Parasuraman, V. A. Zeithaml, and L. L. Berry, "SERVQUAL: A Multiple-Item Scale for Measuring Consumer Perceptions of Service Quality," *Journal of Retailing* 64 (Spring 1988), pp. 12–40.
2. William Boulding, Richard Staelin, Ajay Kalra, and Valarie Zeithaml, *Conceptualizing and Testing a Dyanmic Process Model of Service Quality*, working paper (Cambridge, Mass.: Marketing Science Institute, 1992).
3. William Boulding, Ajay Kalra, Richard Staelin, and Valarie Zeithaml, "A Dynamic Process Model of Service Quality: From Expectations to Behavioral Intentions," *Journal of Marketing Research* 30 (February 1993).
4. John A. Miller, "Studying Satisfaction, Modifying Models, Eliciting Expectations, Posing Problems, and Making Meaningful Measurements," in *Conceptualization and Measurement of Consumer Satisfaction and Dissatisfaction*, H. Keith Hunt, ed. (Bloomington, Ind.: School of Business, Indiana University, 1977), pp. 72–91; Mary C. Gilly, "Complaining Consumers: Their Satisfaction With Organizational Response," in *New Dimensions of Consumer Satisfaction and Complaining Behavior*, Ralph L. Day and H. Keith Hunt, eds.

(Bloomington, Ind.: School of Business, Indiana University, 1979), pp. 99–107; John E. Swan and Frederick I. Trawick, "Satisfaction Related to Predictive vs. Desired Expectations: A Field Study," in *New Findings on Consumer Satisfaction and Complaining*, Ralph L. Day and H. Keith Hunt, eds. (Bloomington, Ind.: School of Business, Indiana University, 1980), pp. 15–22; Mary C. Gilly, William L. Cron, and Thomas E. Barry, "The Expectation-Performance Comparison Process: An Investigation of Expectation Types," in *International Fare in Consumer Satisfaction and Complaining Behavior*, Ralph L. Day and H. Keith Hunt, eds. (Bloomington, Ind.: School of Business, Indiana University, 1983), pp. 10–16; Ved Prakash, "Validity and Reliability of the Confirmation of Expectations Paradigm as a Determinant of Consumer Satisfaction," *Journal of the Academy of Marketing Science* 12 (Fall 1984), pp. 63–76.

5. Richard L. Oliver, "Effect of Expectation and Disconfirmation on Post-Exposure Product Evaluation: An Alternative Interpretation," *Journal of Applied Psychology* 62 (April 1977), pp. 480–486.

6. Ralph L. Day, "Towards a Process Model of Consumer Satisfaction," in *Conceptualization and Measurement of Consumer Satisfaction and Dissatisfaction*, H. Keith Hunt, ed. (Cambridge, Mass.: Marketing Science Institute, 1977), pp. 153–183; Gilbert A. Churchill, Jr., "A Paradigm for Developing Better Measures of Marketing Constructs," *Journal of Marketing Research* 11 (August 1979), pp. 254–260; William D. Bearden and Jesse E. Teel, "Selected Determinants of Customer Satisfaction and Complaint Reports," *Journal of Marketing Research* 20 (November 1983), pp. 21–28; Robert B. Woodruff, Ernest R. Cadotte, and Roger L. Jenkins, "Modeling Consumer Satisfaction Processes Using Experience-Based Norms," *Journal of Marketing Research* 20 (August 1983), pp. 296–304.

7. A. Parasuraman, "A Cognitive Model of the Antecedents and Consequences of Satisfaction Decisions," *Journal of Marketing Research* 17 (November 1980), pp. 460–469; A. Parasuraman, Valarie A. Zeithaml, and Leonard L. Berry, "A Conceptual Model of Service Quality and Its Implications for Future Research," *Journal of Marketing* 49 (Fall 1985), pp. 41–50.

8. David K. Tse and Peter C. Wilton, "Models of Consumer Satisfaction Formation: An Extension, *Journal of Marketing Research* 25 (May 1988), pp. 204–212.,

9. Valarie A. Zeithaml, Leonard L. Berry, and A. Parasuraman, "The Nature and Determinants of Customer Expectations of Service," working paper (Cambridge, Mass.: Marketing Science Institute, 1991).

10. Oliver, "Effect of Expectation."

11. Parasuraman et al., "Conceptual Model."

12. E. Scott Maynes, "The Concept and Measurement of Product Quality," *Household Production and Consumption* 40, no. 5 (1976), pp. 529–559; Chr. Hjorth-Anderson, "The Concept of Quality and the Efficiency of Markets for Consumer Products," *Journal of Consumer Research* 11, no. 2 (1984), pp. 708–718; Morris B. Holbrook and Kim P. Corfman, "Quality and Value in the Consumption Experience: Phaedrus Rides Again," in *Perceived Quality*,

J. Jacoby and J. Olson, eds. (Lexington, Mass.: Lexington Books, 1985), pp. 31–57; Parasuraman et al., "Conceptual Model"; David A. Garvin, "Competing on the Eight Dimensions of Quality," *Harvard Business Review* 65 (November-December 1987), pp. 101–109; Valarie A. Zeithaml, "Consumer Perceptions of Price, Quality, and Value: A Means-End Model and Synthesis of Evidence," *Journal of Marketing* 52 (July 1988), pp. 2–22.

13. A. Parasuraman, V. A. Zeithaml, and L. L. Berry, "SERVQUAL: A Multiple-Item Scale for Measuring Consumer Perceptions of Service Quality," *Journal of Retailing* 64 (Spring 1988), pp. 12–40.

14. Boulding et al., "Dynamic Process Model."

16

Leaders Listen!

Stew Leonard, Jr., Stew Leonard's

When Stew Leonard's dairy store had been open only a couple of weeks, my dad was standing at the front door, proud as punch, greeting his customers just like the maître d' of a restaurant. Suddenly, a half-gallon of eggnog was thrust into his hands by the most upset woman he had ever met. "Taste this," she said. "It doesn't taste right."

"My eggnog from my new dream dairy? Impossible!" He took a quick sip—and uttered words he would soon regret. "You're wrong! It might be a little too spicy, but it's ok," he said. "Watch, I'll prove it to you." Then he handed the carton to his store manager, Barry Belardinelli. "Doesn't this taste fine to you?" he asked. Barry smelled it and tasted it, and naturally agreed with him.

"See?" he said to the woman. By now, other customers had stopped to listen, so to convince them as well he added the clincher: "Besides, it can't be bad. We've sold over 200 cartons of this batch of eggnog so far this week, and you're the only one who has complained."

The veins bulged in her neck. "It's bad," she said again. "And I want my money back."

Obviously, he was talking to a closed mind. Eggnog was selling at 95 cents a half-gallon. So he reached into his pocket and handed her a dollar. But instead of thanking him and being grateful, she turned on her heels and bolted out the door. The last words he heard her yell were, "I'm never coming back to this store again." And she even forgot to give him the nickel change from his dollar!

Humiliated and embarrassed, he turned to Barry. "I don't understand what she's so mad about. After all, I gave her the money back, didn't I?" Barry shrugged, being as dumbfounded as my dad was, and with all the curious customers now drifted off, both went back to work.

But he couldn't get the incident out of his mind. That night at home, he continued to relive it, hearing over and over again the customer's parting shot: "I'm never coming back to this store again." Everything he had in the world was tied up in his new dairy store. If customers stopped coming back, not only would he be out of business, he could see my mom and the kids all standing in a row watching the furniture being carried out of our house.

As usual, he turned to Mom for help.

Telling her the story, he was astonished to see that she was getting mad at him, too. When he finished, she exploded. "Don't you realize you insulted her?" She said. "You not only told her she was wrong, you as much as called her a liar! That's exactly what a lot of the managers of other stores do too—insult us when we complain."

For the second time that day, he was dumbfounded. Mom is usually a pretty calm person and he hadn't seen her get this upset in a long time. Yet here she was furious at him and all the other store managers for trying to defend their stores. "You know," she went on, calming down a little. "You're lucky. At least your customer cared enough to complain. Most of the time, I dread the experience so much that I don't even bother. I just go to a different store."

She didn't add, "How could you be so stupid?" But she might as well have because that's the way he felt. The truth was, his ego had been bruised when the woman complained. He had devoted everything to this store, both financially and emotionally. He had also refused to compromise on quality. Now he had a customer telling him that he had compromised quality.

Well, someone was wrong here—my dad! The fact was, after an investigation, he discovered that she had been right. We had goofed. A new spice had been used that was twice as concentrated and half the quantity should have been used in the recipe. So the complaining customer wasn't his enemy, she was his friend. She helped discover a problem.

The more he thought about it, the more fully he understood that in business the customer who complains actually gives you a great gift: the opportunity to improve. From that day forward, he decided, no customer in the store would ever be wrong again. Or to put it another way, the customer was always going to be right. It wasn't a new idea. John Wanamaker had built his Philadelphia department store into the largest department store in the world on this premise—more than one hundred years ago! With this simple principle a century later, Stew Leonard's became the world's largest dairy store.

The business has grown from one store with seven employees to two stores with combined sales of over $175 million and over 1,300 team members. Most of this growth has come from listening to the 200,000 customers who come through our doors each week.

Listening to Customers

I grew up in this business and have learned how important it is to listen. Just before the exit of our store is a suggestion box. The area is large enough for three or four people to stop and write down their comments. There's a bigger-than-life picture of my smiling dad asking the question, "What do you like, what don't you like? I'd love to know." Since our customers have to shop at our competitors (we carry only 900 different products versus 24,000 different products at a normal supermarket), they know if we're meeting competitive levels of quality, service, and value.

We read and type up these suggestions every day before 10 A.M. There are over 100 suggestions a day, and they're distributed to the managers and handed out in our cafeteria. We want everyone to read the suggestions. We count and categorize these comments into compliments, ideas, and complaints (see Figure 16-1).

Customer Ideas

Of the ideas we receive in the store, about half are product suggestions and recommendations for improving store operations. For example, customers write notes about adding products like low-fat cheeses, exotic vegetables, skinless chicken, and more recyclable packaging.

All customers get a response, usually a letter. It's possible for us to react to about one-third of all notes—we make the change or fix the problem. Obviously, we're unable to react to every note, but we do look for trends. This is a great way to listen every day. In fact, some of the ideas we've been given are priceless. Here are some notes that came in duing one week:

- ▲ "We would love to see you add a quality rye bread to your bakery. My neighbors agree!" Great idea! We immediately experimented and sales are fantastic!
- ▲ "Get rid of those hand dryers in your rest rooms. It takes forever

Figure 16-1. Listening to our customers.

	Why Captured	How	Data Quality
Customer Suggestions	Evaluate perception of service and product quality	Suggestion box	Suggestion box reviewed daily
Customer Attitudes	Evaluate perception of service and product quality	In-store surveys, telephone surveys, focus groups	Cross-comparison of data

to dry my hands. Where's the paper?" We thought about this, but some customers throw paper on the floor, which then brings notes like "the rest rooms are messy." We decided to keep the dryers, add paper towels, and beef up our rest room inspections. Everyone is happy.

▲ "Your new Stew Leonard vegetarian chili is fantastic, but a bit too spicy." We recorded six notes like this one. We backed off on the spices—a little.

Also, we listen to customers when something good happens. "Tom, in your meat department, was very helpful on a day when your veal truck broke down. He called me at home to tell me the truck had finally arrived!" We made Tom one of our Heroes of the Week. Hero of the Week is one of our ways of recognizing a team member who has shown specific outstanding customer service. One of management's main functions is to celebrate performance, and we do it with vigor!

One day, a customer dropped the following story in our suggestion box: "I love your corn muffins, but I only eat the tops and throw the bottoms away. I know this may sound crazy, but could I only buy the tops?" Zita, the manager of our bakery, tried the idea. It was simple. Instead of using the regular muffin pans, she used a flat pan and made the corn muffins very thin. She cut and packaged them and put up a sign in the store, "A customer idea—Corn Muffin tops $2.59 a package." Guess what became our best-selling muffin? Sales of corn muffin tops jumped to 2,000 packages a week!

These notes provide feedback on customers' present needs, their expectations, and future requirements. For instance, we noticed an increased frequency of requests for Chinese food at our hot salad bar. Anticipating a trend, we responded, resulting in $20,000 in sales volume per week in this hot food item alone. But not all notes can be acted on. For instance, "Could you provide valet parking?" Nice idea, but too costly. Another, "I love your half-gallon of milk at such a great price, but there is only my husband and me at home. Can't you sell quarts?" Our store is a volume business and we promote only the best-sellers. The half-gallon is the most popular.

Customer Complaints

One of Stew Leonard's favorite sayings is, "Customers who complain are our best friends because they give us the opportunity to improve." This saying is posted prominently in the store. Customer complaints represent valuable inputs for improving customer service. All complaints are studied, evaluated, and acted upon. At the weekly managers' meeting, the complaints and actions taken to resolve the complaints are discussed.

The customer service manager reports on product returns that may be indicative of a problem, as well as any other complaints received by the department during the week.

Within twenty-four hours of receiving a complaint, the customer service department, a department manager, or upper management responds to the customer. Most complaints are relatively minor, but all are taken very seriously. Product-oriented complaints ("my flower died after two days") can be handled by a single phone call or letter (with a refund, of course). When the complaint is about the quality of a product, it is routed to the department manager for further investigation. Complaints on customer service are also sent to the appropriate department manager for review and corrective action. About 99 percent of all complaints can be resolved on the first contact with the customer.

Some complaints involve store operations. For example, we had been receiving many customer complaints about the noise from our internal paging system. Most of the phone calls were for our managers and buyers who are out on the store floor with our customers. One day we were visiting Harry's Farmers Market in Atlanta, Georgia, and noticed that he equipped his managers with walkie-talkies. BINGO! We bought the walkie-talkies, issued them to our managers, and our complaints about noisy store paging have disappeared.

Complaints, when indicated, are forwarded to a department to determine the root cause. This practice has resulted in improvements in many areas throughout the organization. For example, in 1989 several complaints indicated dissatisfaction with the normal one- to two-week turn-around-time required to certify a courtesy-card credit application. When the problem was researched, we determined that more sophisticated credit systems were available. The final outcome: we purchased an automated system, and today the customer's new courtesy card is in the mail in less than twenty-four hours from the time application is made (see Figure 16-2).

In the bakery department, several complaints on the texture and taste of our oat bran muffins led to recipe testing and a new, better-tasting, better-selling muffin. After a complaint has been handled at the store, I randomly follow up and ask the customer if he or she is satisfied.

Figure 16-2. Response time on courtesy card applications.

	1988	1989	1990	1991
Time to Respond	8 Days	5 Days	2 Days	8 Hours

This ensures that our standards of customer service are kept high. The successful resolution of these one-on-one "moments of truth" helps assure continued improvement and growth.

Recurring or frequent complaints are highlighted at the weekly managers' meeting and assigned to a team for further evaluation. Based on the team's findings, further corrective action is taken. For instance, on some weekends, the phone rang more than twice before being answered because of greater activity at the customer service desk. Additional personnel were added in customer service for the weekend just to answer the phones. The complaints disappeared.

Customer Focus Groups

Customer notes are cross-checked in focus groups, and reviewed in communication meetings with team members. Indeed, Stew Leonard's is a leader in the use of customer focus groups to determine customer satisfaction and to seek information for improvement. I usually conduct the focus groups, along with several members of management.

Twice a month, we gather fifteen customers for a meeting at our stores. We use our customer lists to get some of these participants, and I personally ask other customers on the floor if they would like to attend. The purpose of these meetings is to ask "How are we doing?" We want to know what Stew Leonard's can do to improve. All department managers attend the meeting.

Stew Leonard's limited selection serves us well. However, it forces our customers to shop at other stores. Consequently, they see what our competitors are doing more often then we do, and this feeds the ideas and suggestions at these focus group meetings. For example, one lady recently said, "I stopped buying my cold cuts from your deli."

"Why?" we asked.

"They are sliced too thick!" Other customers agreed (funny thing that this paralleled a slowing growth in our deli meats): "My kids like them thin-sliced!" One customer exclaimed, "Thin-sliced tastes better on a sandwich." "Yeah, it tastes more like a deli sandwich," another customer said.

"Great idea," I said. Our deli manager, Bill Hollis, responded, "We have a hard time slicing them thin because they shred and don't stack neatly."

"Who cares?" replied a customer. "Who wants cold cuts neatly stacked anyway?" That day, Bill tried slicing and shredding the cold cuts. Sales shot up 40 percent!

Another group complained about the fish. "It's packaged," said a customer. "I never buy my fish packaged in a foam boat with plastic wrap. I buy my fish off the crushed ice. It's fresher that way!" As Tom Peters has always said, "A customer's perception is all that matters!" We tried fish on ice and sales zoomed 200 percent.

One time, a customer asked, "Have you tried to go shopping with your kids on a rainy day? The carts are always wet and so is the baby seat! How about some paper towels at the front entrance on rainy days?" Superb idea. Every time it rains, a sign goes up, along with a paper towel holder. It reads, "A great customer idea: Paper towels to wipe off your cart." Recognition like this encourages customers to keep the ideas coming!

Learning From Feedback

Over 100 phone calls are made monthly by team members, managers, and executives to customers on a random basis, inquiring how they like the store, the products, and the service. For example, we phoned over 300 customers to follow up on how they liked the holiday gift baskets they ordered. A whopping 96 percent loved the cookies, and one customer asked, "I love the cookie tins, fresh fruit, and gift baskets I buy in the store during the holiday. How about putting a sign up offering to mail these for us?" We tried her idea. A gift catalog developed and we now do over $1 million per year in holiday gifts. We keep calling customers and asking, "What do you think of our gifts?" New ideas generate, we react, and steady growth continues.

Data for improvement are also obtained through management's review of case studies on customer satisfaction, obtained from regional colleges and universities. An informal information exchange is encouraged between the academic community and Stew Leonard's. Visitors from Harvard, University of Connecticut, Yale, Boston University, New York University, Columbia, the Culinary Institute of America, and local schools are given a tour and an opportunity to meet with management. In turn, student reports on customer satisfaction are shared with Stew Leonard's. Customer surveys are conducted by students and sometimes our own team members, which are then reviewed by management, and acted upon. The result is a win-win-win situation: The customer wins through improved products or services, the team member wins through education, and Stew Leonard's wins through improved sales!

Serving Customers Better

Our vast communications network assures immediate assistance to customers. There are telephones in every department and at every cash register, and all department managers and team leaders carry walkie-talkies. Cashiers often will call departments to bring up items for customers that they forgot or missed. It's not unusual for a customer to ask a question and via the walkie-talkie, the answer comes back immediately.

The process for determining product likability is through active listening and observation, both internal and external. Many times, a customer will be stopped by management in the store and asked about a product, "Why did you buy the 2 percent fat content milk?" Or, and more importantly, "Why didn't you buy the 2 percent fat content milk?"

Strong emphasis is placed on visiting our competition and other retail markets to help us improve both products and services. For instance, a visit to Tiangus (a large ethnic supermarket in southern California) revealed an extensive fresh-squeezed juice section. Armed with the knowledge that Stew Leonard's customers were increasingly health-conscious, the concept was introduced with outstanding success. Close monitoring through in-store product demonstrations allows us to evaluate the product's acceptance and make changes to meet customer expectations. Once the fresh-squeezed orange juice was introduced and sampled, customers wanted it sweeter. Even though it was more expensive, we blended oranges from Florida and California and ended up with a top-quality fresh-squeezed orange juice!

Putting Quality Service First

Stew Leonard's uses customer-related data to assess costs and planning strategies and to find the most efficient and cost-effective way to develop new projects. Customer preferences are detailed in the data coming from the cash register. This activity continuously reshapes the 900 or so items offered for sale.

Further evaluation is provided through close scrutiny of the daily production report, weekly product activity reports (hit list and current week), and the green sheet. The hit list prints the bottom-fifty selling products company-wide, which will either be remarked or discontinued. The current week report ranks the movement of each product in a specific department and compares it to the prior week. The green sheet prints customer count per week by department. These reports allow us to immediately see our customers' acceptance or rejection of products.

Stew Leonard's is continuously evaluating and improving its processes for determining customer requirements. This is done through tracking product sales, department reports, and customer feedback. We introduce many new and seasonal products on a trial basis. If customer acceptance is high, it validates the process. Likewise, personal experience with the products often leads to improvement. One day, I was digging through our refrigerator and found some Heinz ketchup. "Where's the Stew Leonard's ketchup?" I asked my wife. "The kids like Heinz better!" she said. My own kids like Heinz better? Back to the drawing board. We reformulated our Stew Leonard's ketchup, sampled it in the store, and sales increased! She now buys Stew Leonard's ketchup!

I went to a friend's house for dinner. In his refrigerator were all sorts of new high-energy, sports-type drinks, but none of our Stew Leonard's fruit punch. "Why?" I asked. "The kids are drinking this at school because it gives them more energy." We reformulated our fruit punch line to include "all natural sugars" like fructose and relaunched it as a Stew's sports drink. Now we have our own sports drink and sales have been fantastic!

Though the goal is always to create high customer satisfaction, the cost of achieving this is not rigorously tracked. Return on expenditures in this area is not the utmost concern, as perhaps is the case with other companies. For example, Stew Leonard's pays over $20,000 per year to repair automobiles that have been damaged in our parking lot owing to run-away grocery carts. No analysis is done to determine if this investment in customer satisfaction directly benefits the store.

Working With Suppliers

We visit suppliers frequently, and always ask them to teach us about what they do. Then we do a lot of listening. It is easy for us to become isolated in our retail environment and fail to see our suppliers' viewpoint. Indeed, though our suppliers have different views, our goals ultimately are the same.

On a recent trip to our orange juice supplier in Florida, from whom we buy about 10,000 gallons a week, we asked about grapefruit juice because so many of our customers were requesting it to be fresh-squeezed, like our orange juice. We found that grapefruit juice volume is only about 25 percent of orange juice, and that is not enough to justify a full tanker. The supplier told us that it would supply us with grapefruit juice in 300-gallon containers, however, and we could piggy-back these containers on refrigerated trucks of produce that come up from Florida several times a week. Now our customers not only get the freshest produce from Florida but fresh grapefruit juice as well.

Listening to the Experts

Lots of my phone calls are to local product and equipment suppliers, attorneys, accountants, advertising people, or local and state officials.

When I hear a receptionist or secretary with an impersonal this-is-my-hundredth-call-today-voice, I introduce myself and ask her if she shops at our store. Usually, a few minutes of conversation develop, and then I get transferred to the person I'm calling. These conversations do two things: (1) they allow me to listen for possible good ideas, and (2) customers know that Stew Leonard's cares and is a company that listens.

Most shoppers are with family or friends, and so they talk like crazy on the store floor, whether in our store or at a competitor's. I like to pretend I'm shopping, but I'm really eavesdropping to hear some straight-from-the-horse's-mouth comments. For instance, a new chain store opened in our town recently, and on opening day I was there, walking the aisles. I also go into the Stew Leonard's parking lot and ask customers what they just thought of the store. It's raw data from a small sample, but every type of listening helps find useful ideas.

My father received the Entrepreneur Award from President Reagan in 1986. He's also sat around and "talked shop" with people like Sam Walton, Frank Perdue, Tom Monaghan (Domino's Pizza), and Paul Newman (salad dressing). There is one thing that all successful business leaders seem to have in common, and that's the ability to listen. Watching my father build his business has taught me a valuable lesson: Leaders listen. Ultimately, Stew Leonard's aim is to be a world-class listener.

17

Putting the Service Profit Chain to Work

Leonard A. Schlesinger and Roger H. Hallowell, Harvard Business School

The service profit chain shown in Figure 17-1 illustrates an empirically proven, simple set of relationships that many organizations have found to be the key to profit through enhanced customer retention. The chain shows that satisfied and fulfilled employees provide better service, which then better satisfies customers. The greater customer satisfaction—and the profit it generates through repurchases—in turn adds to employee satisfaction.

The service profit chain is driven by customer and employee satisfaction, its leverage points. Satisfaction is derived from a self-reinforcing cycle supported by individual service delivery and human resources strategies. While these are powerful management tools in their own right, the chain's strength lies not in its underlying individual strategies, but in the manner in which these strategies support and reinforce each other. In short, the sum is greater than the parts.

The Links in the Profit Service Chain

To understand the service profit chain better, we provide an analysis of the components and their relationships. Note that the chain has no real beginning or end. The limitations of a two-dimensional format, however, require that a point be chosen, so we begin with profit.

▸ *Profit link to customer retention.* The magnitude of the relationship between profit and customer retention has just begun to be understood by academics and service providers. A recent study by consultant Frederick Reichheld and Harvard professor W. Earl Sasser[1] illustrates the increase in profits in a variety of industries from customer retention over time. By reducing by 5 percent the number of customers who defect, a company can increase profit (customer value) by between 25 and 85

Figure 17-1.   The service profit chain.

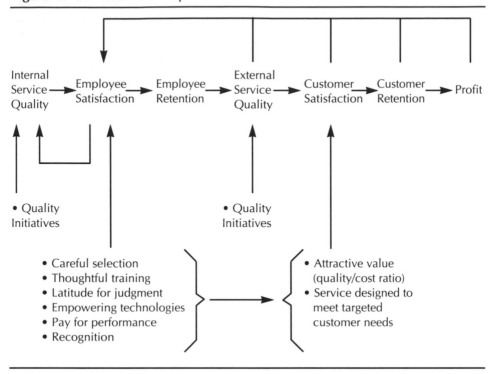

Source: Questions the Service Profit Chain Raises for Management, unpublished manuscript.

percent (profit varies based on the industry). The study shows the sources of this additional profit to be, in order of magnitude for the fifth year in the life of a customer relationship: increased purchases, reduced operating costs, profit from referrals, and profit from price premiums.

A service organization can profit from this knowledge by establishing the value of its customers and determining how that value changes over time. Given that information, the relationship of customer retention to profit becomes clear. The organization can determine the value of preventing service problems from occurring and the cost of recovering from those problems that are not prevented. Appropriate efforts can then be made to improve employee and customer satisfaction, the service profit chain's leverage points.

▲ *Customer retention link to customer satisfaction.* The relationship between customer retention and customer satisfaction is intuitive. Simply put, satisfied customers return to repurchase. Given the high degree of customer-perceived risk in a service encounter, a customer who has been satisfied by one service provider may actively seek out that service again. In short, by providing superior service, an organization can enhance the customer's switching costs. Switching costs are the sum of the customer's fear of the unknown and the certainty of satisfaction from an organization providing superior service.

▲ *Customer satisfaction link to external service quality and service delivery strategy.* While external service quality is integral to customer satisfaction, it is not the only necessary element. A service must also be designed to meet the needs of its targeted customers and provide attractive value, defined as quality for cost. A specialty store might sell the finest down jackets, providing the highest level of service at very competitive prices, and still not satisfy customers if it is located in the tropics. Similarly, no number of peripheral amenities or degree of personal attention will make a hotel successful at a luxury rate unless the rooms have comfortable beds.

There are two leverage points in delivering external service quality: employee retention, driven by employee satisfaction, which is in turn driven by human resources strategies; and the service delivery strategy, providing value to a focused customer base. Organizations successfully following the service profit chain model integrate these strategies, enabling them to reinforce one another.

▲ *External service quality link to employee retention.* Many service organizations are plagued by extraordinarily high frontline service-provider turnover. Rates of 200 percent for entry-level jobs and 50 percent for unit-management positions are not uncommon in some industries. The results and causes are that (1) organizations are reluctant to provide adequate training for these workers; (2) organizations opt to pay the lowest wage possible (effective minimum wage) because they have little invested in service providers, who in turn have little invested in the organization; and (3) organizations systematically deskill jobs, making them tedious and repetitious.

These service providers have neither the skills nor the inclination to provide good service. They lack adequate training to solve customer problems. They are detached from their work environment, having (personal or financial) relationships with neither the company nor its customers. They are unhappy with their jobs. The organizations are unhappy about employee performance. Customers are unhappy with the service organizations provide. This situation is detailed and graphically illustrated by what Schlesinger and Heskett refer to as the Cycle of Failure (see Figure 17-2).[2]

▲ *Employee retention link to employee satisfaction.* This point is empirically proven and intuitively obvious in job markets with any fluidity. Behind the statement, however, is the difficult question of how to enhance employee satisfaction. A combination of specific human resources strategies and their integration with an organization's service delivery strategy may be the answer.

Figure 17-2. The cycle of failure.

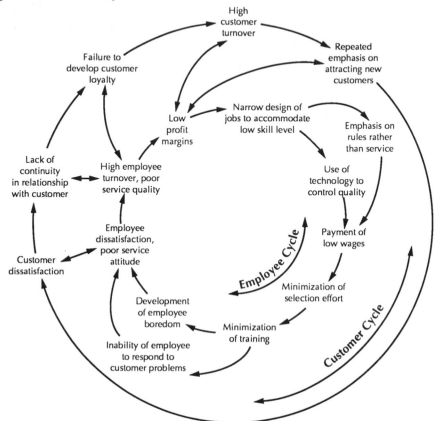

Source: Schlesinger and Heskett, "Breaking the Cycle of Failure in Services," *Sloan Management Review,*
Spring 1991.

▴ *Employee satisfaction link to internal service quality.* The quality of
service provided by individuals and operations within an organization is
its internal service quality. It has a clear effect on employee satisfaction.
Who hasn't been angered and frustrated by the poor performance of an
internal function, whether individual, machine, or department? Who
would not rather have directed the energy that went into dealing with
that anger, frustration, and effort to have work performed properly into
a more productive process? By improving internal service quality, an
organization can improve employee satisfaction.

The Service Profit Chain's Leverage Points

Consistently delivering satisfaction to employees and customers is possible only by breaking the cycle of failure. This cycle is the plight in

which many service companies find themselves, with no employee selection, poor training, deskilled jobs, and high turnover. This in turn leads to delivery of poor service quality to customers, who fail to repurchase, which then depresses profit.

We discuss five organizations that have broken the cycle of failure and initiated the service profit chain by integrating specific human resources strategies with their service delivery strategies. The components of the strategies include knowledge of customer needs and desires, and focus on them; enfranchisement; providing appropriate tools (including technology); careful training and development; redesign of service delivery systems; and a new role for middle management. These organizations are: Au Bon Pain (a French baker and café chain), Fairfield Inn (Marriott's economy, limited-service hotel chain), Nordstrom (a chain of fashion-goods department stores), ServiceMaster (a management services company supervising food service and janitorial workers), and Taco Bell (a chain of Mexican fast-food restaurants).

Focus on Customer Needs and Desires

It should not be necessary to point out that focusing on customer needs is the sine qua non of sustained business success. This fact is, nonetheless, often overlooked as the element around which all component strategies must be built. Knowledge of customer needs and desires is at the core of an organization. From it stems an understanding of the company's true economics and the basis for the service delivery strategy.

At Nordstrom, the service delivery strategy is a combination of location, depth of inventory, pay-for-performance compensation, and "lack of rules" for salespeople. All four are examples of how Nordstrom has identified what its customers want. Referring to the small fleet of mopeds used by salespeople to deliver panty hose to office buildings near one store, one of the Nordstroms commented that "If we had rules, we'd definitely have one against that."

Au Bon Pain determined that developing repeat business was the key to its success, so pleasing the repeat customer became the company's focus. Recognizing that day-to-day operating decisions were best left to individuals at the local operations, with the authority to make decisions and a personal stake in the outcome, Au Bon Pain management enfranchised its management to better please its repeat customers.

Fairfield Inn's focus is on providing the best economy, limited service (ELS) room to "road warriors" (traveling salespeople). Every aspect of the organization—location of each inn, room design (a desk large enough to work at), selection of staff (Fairfield Inn has been known to interview over 500 people for the thirteen housekeeper positions at one inn), incentive compensation of housekeepers and desk clerks, and a computer system capable of tracking individual employee performance—is designed to aid in the delivery of quality service.

One of ServiceMaster's largest divisions manage the janitorial staff of some hospitals, schools, and factories. ServiceMaster's goals (its focus) are (1) "to honor God in all we do" and (2) "to help people develop." The way ServiceMaster treats its staff on a day-to-day basis is a reflection of these goals. Employees have an opportunity to grow in their jobs and beyond, assisted by ServiceMaster's training and development programs. That personal growth results in improved quality and efficiency, which ultimately helps ServiceMaster's growth, so it can affect the lives of more frontline service providers, helping more people to develop.

Taco Bell's focus is on delivering value to the customer. Value is defined as FACT (Fast, Accurate order, Clean, Temperature—hot food hot, cold food cold) at below market prices. FACT was established as a result of Taco Bell's customer study. The organization identified the restaurant general manager as the leverage point in this delivery process. Thus, every one of the seven major new programs implemented at Taco Bell from 1989 to 1991—which are largely responsible for its financial success—either supports the manager in delivering FACT or delivers it to the customer directly.

Enfranchisement

A term with a new meaning derived from the words *empower* and *franchise, enfranchisement* describes a combination of a pay-for-performance compensation program and the empowerment of service providers. For a company to gain full benefit of either concept, the two must be combined. An empowered employee with no incentive frustrates an organization; an employee given incentives but lacking authority to make decisions frustrates him- or herself.

Nordstrom provides a good example of enfranchisement. The average salesperson at Nordstrom earns an above-market wage based on his or her sales per hour. The variable component of compensation is significant. Achievement of targets is mandatory as management induces turnover to weed out the unproductive. These are the primary elements of the pay-for-performance program.

Empowerment occurs through a no-rules strategy. Nordstrom expects its salespeople to use common sense; with that exception, they are told to do what is necessary to satisfy the customer. This includes courtesies not ordinarily found at other stores, such as calling other branches in search of an item in a particular size, or occasionally delivering packages needed by a customer right away. Less frequently, it may involve accepting a return on an item not purchased in the store; as one Nordstrom salesperson put it, "so that the customer has no reason to go back to that other store."

The relationship between compensation and empowerment is clear at Nordstrom. Because salespeople have a high commission component to their total compensation, they want to sell. The fact that there are no rules enables them to better meet the needs of their customers. Enfranchisement has aligned the interests of salespeople with those of customers and of the corporation. Customers' needs are met, salespeople earn above-market salaries, and the corporation makes above-average profits. It is win-win-win, which is the essence of the service profit chain.

The Tools to Succeed and Excel

No human resources strategy can optimize performance unless individuals are given the tools they need to do the best job they can. Those same tools can enhance the integration of human resources and service delivery strategies. In this context, tools can be thought of as anything that improves the chances of success or reduces the effort necessary to complete a task. This broad definition is critical in understanding the interlocking nature of the tools, human resources strategies, and the service delivery strategy.

At Nordstrom, a close relationship exists among service delivery, human resources strategy, and tools. Part of Nordstrom's service delivery strategy is to have deep inventory so that customers can both find what they want and not be frustrated by finding something they like but that is not "right for them." This is part of what Nordstrom defines as good service. But depth of inventory can also be considered a tool for salespeople. It enables them to satisfy the customers, and satisfaction brings those customers back, generating higher commissions for salespeople. Thus from the salesperson's perspective, deep inventory is a tool to earn more.

Another example of a tool to coordinate the service delivery and human resources strategies is Fairfield Inn's Scorecard. This is the video display that approximately 50 percent of guests opt to use at checkout to rate the hotel's quality. There are four questions, and scores are tied to the guest's room (thus the housekeeper) and the desk clerks responsible for checkin and checkout. In the economy inn sector, these are the key contacts the guest has with the hotel. Thus, compensation for housekeepers and desk clerks is tied to the number of "excellent" responses they receive on Scorecard.

Scorecard serves as a tool enabling pay-for-performance for jobs for which performance was previously considered impossible to measure. This in turn makes it possible to attract a better caliber of housekeeper—one who is confident that he or she will do well under a pay-for-performance compensation plan—and to retain that better housekeeper longer. The situation benefits the housekeepers, desk clerks, and management. It supports and integrates both the human resources strategy and the service delivery strategy.

Recruitment and Selection of Frontline Service Providers

An organization cannot have a service delivery strategy that will deliver consistently superior service without addressing the issue of who will provide that service—the frontline service providers. Automation has not yet and is not soon expected to become sophisticated enough to displace frontline service providers. As a result, managers must recognize these individuals as key to creating satisfied customers who will return to buy again. Yet if frontline people leave at turnover rates of 50 to 200 percent per year, how can they, in a cost-effective manner, be trained to provide quality service? Clearly they cannot.

Taco Bell provides an excellent example of careful selection. Its program has focused on store management, with applicants screened using a life-themes indicators test to reveal what values are important to them compared to values held by successful store managers. While there is added expense associated with the development and delivery of such a test, Taco Bell believes the results are well worth the effort. It regularly finds "better fit" candidates, and turnover among unit-level management has been reduced by 50 percent since the introduction of this program.

Recruitment has been handled successfully in a less scientific way as well. Service profit chain companies agree that the most effective recruiting is via word-of-mouth, or referrals from current employees. Employees tend to have friends with values similar to their own, so in this way these candidates are pre-screened. In addition, current employees of successful organizations are winners and their friends want to associate with winners. This has an effect on both whom employees recommend for a position and the behavior of those individuals once they join the organization.

Training and Development

Empirical evidence suggests that organizations that treat training and development as an end rather than a means devote the resources and attention necessary to maximize their benefits. The link between training and development and integrated service delivery and human resources strategies can be understood by considering the following three principles:

1. The extent and mix of training and development are a direct function of the frequency, length, and complexity of interaction between a customer and a service worker.

2. Training and development (both task-specific and general, continuing education) act as drivers for broader job definitions. Broader job definitions prevent individuals from becoming limited to repetitive and boring jobs.*
3. Training and development (specifically of a general, continuing education nature) improves the quality of employees' lives, which in turn improves the quality of employees. As the quality of employees improves, the quality of the workplace improves, which has an immediate and tangible effect on the quality of service provided to customers.

Taco Bell focused its customer-satisfaction efforts on frontline management in its restaurants. The training for these managers supports the first principle. Frequency, length, and complexity of interaction with customers are the variables used in determining the extent and mix of training. As the focal point for customer satisfaction, restaurant managers are responsible for every aspect of contact with the customer. Thus it is reasonable to consider any contact the customer has with Taco Bell as a contact with the store manager.

Frequency of contact depends on frequency of visits. From Taco Bell's perspective, the more the better. Length of contact depends on the type of visit (short for drive-through or take-out, longer for a customer who eats in the restaurant). The typical duration lasts twenty to twenty-five minutes and complexity initially appears to be low. How difficult is it to greet a customer, take an order, make change, or even solve a customer's problem at a Taco Bell? In fact, these are only the tip of the iceberg. Since the managers are responsible for any contact between Taco Bell and the customer, anything that affects a customer's experience is within their province. That includes operation of all equipment, maintenance of the premises, assembly of food, and most difficult to influence and/or control, the attitudes of the crew.

By increasing the quantity of training for restaurant managers and significantly changing its focus through a radical shift in content, Taco Bell now teaches trainees product fundamentals in a restaurant. In addition, the in-restaurant training provides good role models in terms of interpersonal dynamics. There is also a classroom segment, described by Taco Bell as follows:

> Introduces Taco Bell's management philosophy, values and concepts. The eight management skills used to get results are the focus of the course: Administrative, leadership, interper-

---

*This is in addition to the efficiencies traditionally associated with manufacturing environments created through increased labor flexibility.

sonal, communication, personal adaptability, personal motivation, occupational/technical knowledge, cognitive.

This type of training is not specific to running a restaurant, and applies to managing almost any operation. It is consistent with the third principle of training and development—that broad-based training improves employees and effectively raises the caliber of people working at and attracted to the organization, and thus improves the quality of work performed by the organization.

But perhaps the best example is ServiceMaster, where the organization's second goal is "to help people develop." CEO William Pollard refers to this as an end objective, in contrast to means objectives such as providing excellent service and growing profitability. Training and development has never had a better ally.

Research on ServiceMaster indicates that it actively uses all three principles in its training and development. For example, regarding the first principle, ServiceMaster trains the individuals it manages who clean patients' rooms in hospitals. Many organizations view this type of cleaning as a menial task, requiring little if any training. ServiceMaster, however, recognizes that individuals who are given the appropriate tools, the knowledge of how to use them, and an understanding of the purpose of their task are more efficient and produce higher quality work.

The training occurs in two forms. First is a task-specific session in which, among other skills, hospital room cleaners are taught Service-Master's famous *S* stroke for mopping a floor. The *S* stroke does a better job of cleaning by pulling the dirt off the floor and out of the room (in contrast to just swishing it around) and is easier on the back of the person mopping.

Second is training that recognizes that both patients and room cleaners need human contact. Patients generally want to say hello to the person they see daily (or more often) cleaning their room. ServiceMaster knows that it will reinforce the self-esteem of the room cleaner if he or she is able to communicate with the person for whom the task is being performed. Because many of ServiceMaster's employees do not speak English or are not acculturated, the company offers an English-as-a-second-language program and trains its room cleaners in the basics of communication. This training is so deeply ingrained that the last step in the eight-step process used to clean a hospital room is to ask the patient if there is anything in the room that still needs to be cleaned.

ServiceMaster also uses training as a driver for broader job design. The company has a goal of hiring 20 percent of its new managers from its own ranks. To do this, it must offer cross-training and other programs to expand individuals' skills and ability to solve problems. ServiceMaster acknowledges the role continuing education can play in helping individuals improve themselves. Guest speakers such as physicians explain the importance of housekeeping in the hospital. Bankers provide information on loans and wills. Practical information to help entry-level service workers is provided in an attempt to help them improve their lives. Thus, the effect on their lives and the quality of their work may be small on average, but the many small improvements ultimately allow ServiceMaster to provide better quality service at competitive prices.* Its training and development programs have made ServiceMaster one of the most consistently profitable service companies in the country, with a return on equity of over 35 percent for the last ten years.

Both Taco Bell and ServiceMaster are examples of companies that use training and development to integrate human resources and service delivery strategies. Training and development are regarded as a key part of the development of a superior work force, integral to a service company's development of a competitive advantage.

The Redesign of Service Delivery Systems

Redesigning a company's service delivery systems makes integration of human resources and service delivery strategies possible.

An organization often begins its life with a tightly coordinated service delivery system. Over time, however, gradual changes occur in the environment in which the organization operates. The organization responds by making adjustments to its service delivery system, adding components to deal with new problems and opportunities, and layering small change upon small change. After a period of time—often related to the rate of change in the industry and its environment—the organization finds itself bogged down in bureaucracy. Explanations such as "but we've always done it that way" are heard as systems take on a life of their own, obscuring the original service delivery system and its purpose.

Only by taking a "clean slate" approach and redesigning the service delivery system—often to meet the needs for which the original system was designed—can this situation be corrected. Incremental changes and bottom-up approaches cannot provide the type of jarring change necessary to free an organization, its systems, processes, procedures, and constituents from its less-than-optimal service delivery system.

For example, after testing its new value menu (reduced prices), Taco Bell recognized that it could significantly increase sales by lowering prices systemically. While volume increases alone would not compensate for the associated loss in margin, senior management believed savings in

---

*It is worth noting that, from a competitive standpoint, the tangible tools ServiceMaster provides are considerably easier to duplicate than is ServiceMaster's attitude toward training and development.

administrative costs and better use of assets through higher volume and reduced investment could more than compensate for the margin lost due to lower prices. It undertook to redesign the service delivery system to: (1) produce higher volume at lower cost, (2) improve quality and consistency, and (3) simplify and reduce the management of the processes. Their primary vehicles were programs called K-minus and SOS.

K-minus stands for Kitchen-minus and refers to Taco Bell's redesign of their restaurant kitchen, from a cook-and-assembly operation to simply an assembly operation. The nature of Taco Bell's product (with slight reformulation) allowed it to be prepared offsite and shipped ready to warm and assemble. This removed hours of labor in the form of chopping, dicing, stirring, and frying, with most of this labor shifted to a central commissary. The effect of the change was to invert the restaurant's configuration from 70:30 kitchen : seating to 70:30 seating: kitchen. This increased eat-in capacity while also reducing the investment in a Taco Bell restaurant by 30 percent. Most significant, it eliminated a major management headache and enabled restaurant managers and crew to focus on satisfying customers. Removing the kitchen was not a new concept, but it had never been done in a fast-food chain of Taco Bell's size. The move was based on a recognition that what customers want is value, and that they don't care where the food is cooked.

At the same time K-minus was introduced, Taco Bell began SOS, or speed of service. This program introduced a staging mechanism to hold assembled food in inventory until purchased and delivered to a customer. Though SOS was essentially a copy of programs McDonald's, Burger King, and other fast-food chains had been using for years, it countered a fundamental Taco Bell principle, which was that the customer would cheerfully wait as long as it took to receive a just-assembled taco. The problem was, no one at Taco Bell had asked the customer. Until Taco Bell commissioned the SMART study to understand customer preferences, the old truth had been the law.

SMART (Simple Multi-Attribute Regression Technique) was a conjoint analysis of customer preferences. It revealed that customers valued speed considerably more than they valued just-made food. So, in response, SOS delivered that speed, reducing the average total wait by 71 percent to 30 seconds. Equally important, SOS increased peak hour transaction capacity by 54 percent. Thus the program had a significant effect on both quality (wait time) and return on assets.

The K-minus and SOS programs marked the redesign of the service delivery system at Taco Bell. It could not have been done without radically changing what previously existed. Taco Bell attempted to incrementally change its kitchen setup during the mid-1980s, but the results were only small improvements that eventually made the company competitive with its rivals. Only the radical K-minus and SOS programs instituted at the end of that decade succeeded in helping Taco Bell gain an advantage over its competitors. The redesign of a service delivery system paved the way for integration of the human resources and service delivery strategies. Enfranchisement and training would have had a less significant impact on profit had the restaurant general manager been focused on preparation of food instead of crew development, customer satisfaction, and business building, as he or she now is.

The New Role of Middle Management

Middle management plays a critical part in the integration of human resources and service delivery strategies. Middle managers tend to resist change, as do most people, when that change decreases their authority and control. As organizations move from command and control systems to enfranchised environments, middle managers find themselves less needed. Ultimately, they may become obsolete. In the meantime, if the human resources and service delivery strategies of organizations are to be integrated, middle managers must not obstruct change. Instead, they should adopt a new role, characterized as *unit support*.

There is no doubt that the role of the service profit chain organizations' middle managers will change. Taco Bell and Au Bon Pain middle managers now focus on providing support for restaurant management, such as helping with business building, acting as advisers on employee matters, and working to develop and train restaurant management. They sometimes earn less than the restaurant managers they supervise. They also serve as the individuals who terminate franchise relationships. Thus, they still have a monitoring role, but now it is focused on restaurant success in meeting specific goals. At Taco Bell, this has been simplified with the availability of individual-unit operating results. These are provided on a daily basis to middle management through TACO (Total Automation of Company Operations), a system of computers located in each unit linked to middle management and corporate headquarters. The new enfranchised role of the restaurant manager and availability of current data have allowed Taco Bell to increase its number of units per middle manager from six to twenty-five, eliminating approximately 38 percent in total overhead costs. Much of this money has been reallocated to improved service and food quality—areas valued by customers.

Conclusion

The connection between customer retention and profit has been demonstrated empirically, while the relationship between customer satisfaction and customer retention is intuitively obvious. The service profit chain shows the relationship of employee satisfaction to customer retention, and provides a model of how a human resource strategy and a service delivery strategy can help generate employee satisfaction. As service organizations review their strategic and operating options, they may wish to consider the relationships illustrated in the service profit chain and apply them in improving their operations.

Notes

1. Frederick F. Reichheld and W. Earl Sasser, "Zero Defections: Quality Comes to Services," *Harvard Business Review* 68, no. 5 (September–October, 1990).
2. Leonard A. Schlesinger and James L. Heskett, "Breaking the Cycle of Failure in Services," *Sloan Management Review,* Spring 1991.

18

Implementing Quality for Performance Improvement

Edward J. Kane, The Dun & Bradstreet Corporation

There has been a multitude of efforts by organizations launched under the labels Total Quality, Business Process Improvement, Business Reengineering, and in earlier days, Industrial Engineering, Systems Analysis, and Organizational Development. These efforts have too often simultaneously led to inspiration and frustration and therefore confusion. There are two causes of the confusion:

- Company associates see the effort as hype, new labels for old pressures, or even worse, a euphemism for cost cutting and layoffs.
- Middle and senior managers who, at the end of the day, are responsible for performance, often fail to see the connection between this new thing (whatever it is called) and performance improvement.

What has occurred broadly is a record of mixed success, largely because the designers of a total quality effort often fail to make the critical connection to performance improvement.

We should be clear, therefore, at the outset that we are attempting to create a high-performance organization. The objective is to get results. And this is done, not through magic methodology, but by basing the effort on key principles and then dedicating ourselves to their implementation. Whatever approach is taken, it must be internalized and suit the culture and style of the organization. The new focus should become "the way we get our jobs done," as opposed to some secondary agenda for which no one has time.

This chapter attempts to provide some of the principles and key elements that help create a base for improved performance.

Key Principles in Building the Performance Culture

Too many companies today are dysfunctional. Key people agree generally as to business priorities but in actuality other priorities govern decisions and daily activities, which prevent progress. Also, vital information takes too long to obtain or never penetrates the organization, hence it is not used effectively. Everyone agrees on the need for change, but fights it in the processes each controls. Associates feel they have little ability to affect the way work is done. And there is minimal cooperation between departments and functions.

Two principles upon which to base a new organizational design and help attack these issues are:

1. *The business organization is a* system *that exists to achieve specific purposes.* A system can be defined as a harmonious arrangement of interacting parts forming a unified whole. Therefore, it is the whole that counts, not the parts. The organization must think in terms of total optimization to achieve its purpose.

2. *The business organization is a* living *organism depending on people both inside and outside its boundaries for success.* Corollaries to these principles are:

   a. Cross-functional views and interactions are vital to achievement.
   b. Organizational systems must have boundaries, goals for achievement, inputs, processes for transformation, outputs, and feedback.
   c. Everything outside the organization's boundaries that it influences or is influenced by is its environment. The organization must define and interface with the relevant factors in this environment.
   d. For optimal goal realization, people working within the system must adopt the vision of the organization, participate in its design and accomplishment, and share in the rewards.

Evolution of a Total Quality System

Figure 18-1 shows how most companies evolve their total quality effort, beginning with a period of awareness and gradually building to an advanced stage of redesign of the organization's critical business processes. Let's look briefly at the five stages.

1. *Awareness.* Usually, an organization embarks on a major effort to educate its management team and all associates on quality principles

Figure 18-1.   Stages of total quality effort.

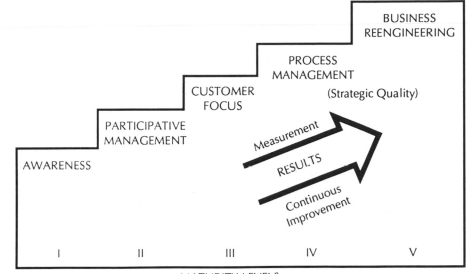

and the need for continuous improvement in all areas of the business. A focus on the customer is usually proclaimed, with attempts to define who the customers are and how their "requirements" might be better satisfied.

Normally, this stage is typified by learning problem-solving techniques and by measuring activity (e.g., number of class days, number of problem-solving teams).

2. *Participative management.* The second stage adds a realization that the new culture must try to abandon management by control. It attempts to place improvement activity in the hands of the people actually doing the work. Where this is the true objective, rather than simply an attempt to change employee perception, it can be effective. It is also difficult for most organizations to effect and requires both time and commitment.

3. *Customer focus.* While awareness of the customer emerged in stage 1, a more definitive and disciplined attempt usually follows. This starts with defining each of the internal and external customers served by the particular work flow under examination. It continues by exploring effective ways to understand needs and expectations, and determine how these can be converted to highly satisfactory products and services.

This stage is typified by formal customer surveys, focus groups, advisory panels, and product boards.

4. *Process management.* There are several versions of process management approaches, all serving to discretely identify priority business processes, evaluate their effectiveness, and redesign them to improve

performance. Figure 18-2 shows the methodology in its simplest form as used by Dun & Bradstreet Software. In this approach, great emphasis is placed on implementation, since it is the only thing that affects performance.

5. *Business reengineering.* Figure 18-1 depicts stages 4 and 5 as the beginning of strategic quality management because they are similar in approach, both seeking to embed quality principles into the organization's strategy and management systems. There are differences as well, however, which we explore next.

Typical Performance Improvement Approaches

Whether or not a company has been evolving a total quality or similar effort, it has probably been trying to achieve some kind of improvement in performance usually through isolated or disconnected means. Some of these are:

1. *Cost reduction.* Normally, cost-reduction efforts occur in combination with a financial crisis. Creative ideas such as budget cuts, outsourcing, downsizing, and internal best practices sharing are explored and/or implemented.

The issue in most cost-reduction efforts is that they deal with efficiency only, are short-term oriented, and result in no fundamental changes. As a result, the costs return and are again dealt with at the next crisis.

Figure 18-2. Process management methodology.

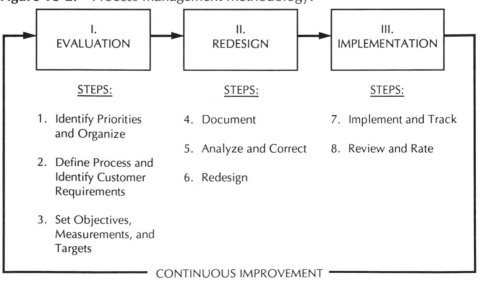

2. *Organizational restructuring*. Many companies use changes in reporting relationships or remissioning to shake up the organization. Delayering, increasing spans of control, centralizing or decentralizing, and workplace redesign are typical. Often they are used in conjunction with cost-reduction measures.

3. *Work or process redesign*. Attempts to change the way work is done are essential if any lasting effect is to be achieved. At its simplest level, task or activity elimination or simplification of procedures may be utilized. These attempts will take on greater meaning if incorporated with strategic change in conjunction with process management and business reengineering.

4. *Continuous improvement*. At one level, this can be considered as instituting incremental or tuning changes to existing procedures and activity. It takes on larger implications when incorporated into a total quality effort to employ breakthrough strategies.

Holistic Approaches to Performance Improvement

Let us look closer at three specific methods currently in vogue that target major fundamental change. Two have already been referenced—process management and business reengineering. The third is change management. These three methods—usually communicated separately—have much more in common than they have differences and should be used in conjunction for maximum effectiveness. The methodology selected must focus the training and provide a road map for action. It is helpful, particularly initially, to concentrate on the steps to be taken. The methodology also reinforces the key principles embodied in the cultural change.

The common elements of these methods are indicated in Figure 18-3. As shown, both change management and business reengineering commonly result in structural change. Since change is the objective, the organizational structure is normally dramatically affected. Process management, by virtue of its cross-functional approach, does not rely on structural change.

Change management and process management seek to drive continuous improvement. Business reengineering, as positioned by most consultants, is project-oriented with no clear ownership for continuous change.

Process management and business reengineering share the fundamental common elements of redesign and often radical change of work processes. Change management concerns itself with getting the organization properly conditioned for major change. It is not helpful in designing content.

Figure 18-3. Combining approaches for total quality.

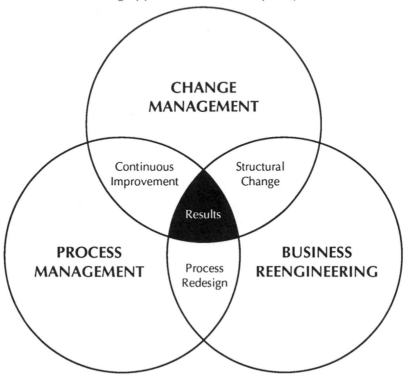

A Comparison of Process Management and Business Reengineering

Neither process management nor business reengineering are explored in detail here.* Both have similar aims: to redesign, even reinvent business processes so that they are simplified and made more effective and efficient. The purpose of both is to radically upgrade the organization's performance, and some of the critical components are:

▲ Setting stretch objectives
▲ Encouraging the breaking of old rules
▲ Eliminating sequential procedural steps
▲ Innovating new approaches and redesigning
▲ Simplifying work
▲ Moving decision making to the work site
▲ Using information technology as an enabler

*For a description of process management, see *Closing the Quality Gap* by Alexander Hiam (Prentice Hall, 1992), Chapter 14; for a description of business reengineering, see "Reengineering Work: Don't Automate, Obliterate," by Michael Hammer, *Harvard Business Review*, July/August 1990.

As for differences, there are only two of significance. First, process management, while incorporating information technology, advises that it be considered after the process is redesigned. This is to prevent automation of obsolete or faulty procedures and to encourage innovation. Business reengineering supports this view, but introduces upfront consideration of information technology as important. By so doing, innovation will be assisted and more challenging goals will be established. This occurs because the designers are more knowledgeable as to what is possible.

The other difference relates to the fact that business reengineering is project-oriented. In contrast, process management views continous improvement as a primary value. It therefore seeks to establish clear executive ownership of each priority process. It also incorporates a strong link to the strategic plan and business definition, and provides for ongoing tracking and results measurement. Process management employs the concept of repetitive recycling through the methodology to achieve significant incremental benefit beyond the initial breakthrough. It uses competitive benchmarking to the challenge to reach world-class status. Figures 18-4 and 18-5 summarize the key similarities and differences.

Figure 18-4. Maximizing performance.

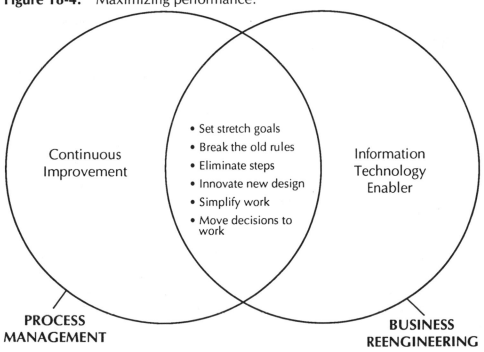

Figure 18-5.   Continuous improvement.

- Ongoing Customer Focus
- Link to Strategic Planning
- Ownership/Accountability
- Objectives/Measurements/Targets
- Competitive Benchmarking

Change Management

Change management is more of a concept than a methodology. It is critical in preparing the organization to accept and enlist in the implementation of the redesign. Before discussing the specific factors that govern change management, however, let us look first at what motivates an organization to change.

Motivation for significant change falls into three general categories. The largest group—possibly representing 65 to 75 percent of change masters—is motivated by desperation. They have most likely experienced one or multiple cases of cost escalation, competitive losses, customer dissatisfaction, market integration, broken business processes, and/or financial losses.

The second group—possibly 20 to 25 percent—are those who through foresight look to improved performance for new opportunity, to delight rather than simply satisfy customers, or seek to be the cost leaders or product differentiators in their industry.

The smallest group—estimated at 5 to 10 percent—are those who drive for cultural renewal. They see change as a major theme and a value in itself, and are focused on continuous improvement.

Let me quickly add there is nothing wrong in being motivated by crises. If we find our reality populated by losses and unhappy customers, we must take action. But if we survive such firestorms or learn from the experience of others, we realize the great benefit of anticipating and preventing negative occurrences.

And so the objective should be to migrate as quickly as possible from desperation to foresight and renewal. However a company is motivated to stimulate change, it must seek ways to gain the wholehearted support of the organization. To understand this challenge, consider the factors that enable change or inhibit change. If the organization wishes to raise its odds of success, it should nurture the enablers and exorcise the inhibitors. The balance at time of initiation will largely determine the timeframe required for implementation.

Enablers

- Committed top manager with vision
- Communicated need for change throughout the organization
- Senior managers motivated to be involved
- Effective, well-understood criteria to measure performance and the process to support it
- System for internal and external feedback
- Trust within the organization

Inhibitors

- Knowledge or expertise gap
- Stop-go practices
- Short-term focus only
- Belief in obsolete systems
- Incentives based on financial results

Despite best intentions, good efforts sometimes go awry. Some of the most common reasons for failure are:

1. *Inadequate application of resources.* Major change cannot be effected by "doing it on the sly." It requires commitment and a realistic business case.

2. *Ineffective or unrealistic assessment of existing processes.* A tie to strategic planning is essential to ensure that the capabilities and limitations of key processes are understood in light of future direction.

3. *Timidity in redesign and inability to think outside the box.* The people who created and manage existing procedures are often too close to see the potential for dramatic change.

4. *Underestimation of what it takes to implement.* Beyond resources, considerable communication, training, incentive, and measurement revision will be required.

These items are critical success factors that must be understood and agreed on by senior management at the outset of any performance-improvement effort. There are times when outside resources can bring new ideas and contribute realistic assessments of requirements to this process.

A Framework for Implementation

We have explored and compared three separate approaches to implement change and improve business performance. Rather than position these

Figure 18-6.   Key elements of an integrated approach.

- Develop a vision of success.
- Benchmark competitive processes.
- Select breakthrough goals.
- Establish clear ownership for results.
- Ensure measurements are established for each objective.
- Take a cross-functional approach to improvement.
- Organize around process outputs and critical value-added components.
- Make decisions where the work is done.
- Capture and verify information once at the source. Make it available where most needed.
- Use information technology to store, transmit, and modify.
- Conduct ongoing analysis and continuous improvement.

Figure 18-7.   The customer focus framework.

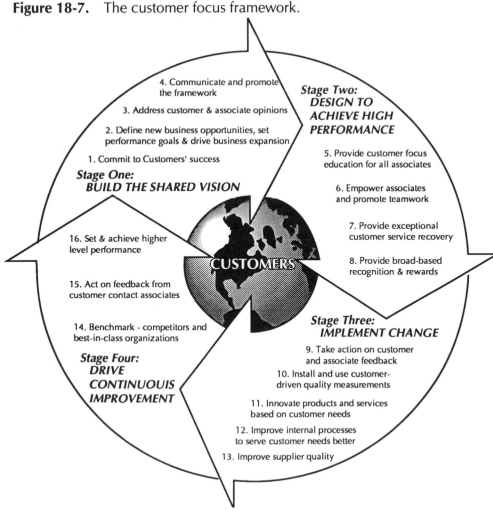

as potential choices, an approach embracing all three is recommended. Since internalization by each company is required, a melding of key elements is appropriate at any rate. While it is best for each organization to develop its own approach, here are two models as a start. Figure 18-6 lists the elements of the three approaches integrated.

Figure 18-7 represents a recent effort by the Dun & Bradstreet Corporation, called the Customer Focus Framework. The effort integrated previously disconnected efforts by various business units, focused on total quality, process management, business reengineering, and customer focus. The framework brings together ideas from all the units so they may be shared with resulting synergy. It serves also to promote the one-company feeling by describing the four stages of performance improvement used by all units.

1. Build the shared vision
2. Design for high performance
3. Implement the change
4. Drive continuous improvement

The next level of detail provides for sixteen activities that assist in carrying out the four stages. The framework gives direction to the effort but is not overly prescriptive as to how it is to be accomplished. Each unit determines how and on what schedule the changes will be implemented.

There are many other examples of successful total quality efforts. Key to that success is an organization and senior management that are clear in direction and focus from the outset.

PART V

THE ROLE OF EMPLOYEES IN SERVICE QUALITY

19

Selecting and Developing the Right People to Sustain a Competitive Advantage

Antonio T. Rivera, USAA

In an industry that has often been characterized by indifference to its customers, the United Services Automobile Association (USAA) has an enviable reputation for quality products and service. This reputation reflects its record and is consistent across its full range of insurance, investment, and banking services, which has resulted in phenomenal growth for USAA. At the end of 1991, USAA owned and managed over $20.7 billion in assets. USAA is currently the nation's fifth largest insurer of automobiles (up from sixteenth in 1968), the fifth largest insurer of homes, and the forty-third largest life insurer. The USAA Federal Savings Bank is the third largest MasterCard provider in terms of sales volume. Standard financial ratings agencies give USAA products top marks, and consumer groups and surveys place USAA at or near the top in service. This reputation and documented solid performance is a tribute to the leadership of USAA's current chairman and chief executive officer, Retired Air Force Brigadier General Robert F. McDermott and the talent, innovation, and commitment to excellence of USAA's 14,000 employees.

USAA was founded June 20, 1922, in San Antonio, Texas, by a group of army officers who were experiencing difficulty in obtaining automobile insurance because of the transient nature of their occupation. These officers formed a member-owned reciprocal insurance association, insuring each other and sharing in the association's profits and losses. Originally limited to army officers, USAA's membership gradually expanded and is now open to all active duty, retired, or separated military officers and members of their families. Today, USAA's membership totals over 2.2 million.

USAA's Corporate Culture

It should be no surprise that USAA's corporate culture reflects the values and professional ethics of its membership—duty, honor, and country. The concepts of service, mutual trust, integrity, quality, and respect are the expectations of the membership. McDermott focused these expectations and institutionalized them in USAA's statements of mission, creed, and philosophy. Each of these components builds on the other, and they form the central guidance for all USAA plans, operations, and training. The golden rule of, "Do unto others as you would have others do unto you" underlies USAA's corporate culture. Most important of all is service. As McDermott has said on numerous occasions, "If you put service first, growth, profitability, and everything else will follow."

McDermott introduced the concept and use of Key Result Areas (KRAs) to USAA in 1970. The KRAs incorporated into the first USAA long-range business plan were service, financial strength, profitability, and growth. Over time, USAA added new KRAs and modified existing ones to reflect changing management concerns. They now include service, financial strength, product value, resources, growth, and public outreach. In spite of some changes, service has always remained the No. 1 KRA.

In the support environment, service is key to a successful program. Employees or "internal customers" receive the same quality service as USAA provides to all its members. The concept of service to internal customers that permeates all areas of USAA's staff is spelled out in the Human Resources Department's Belief and Commitment Statement shown in Figure 19-1. This statement clearly demonstrates how USAA's corporate culture and service ethic have affected how we treat our employees in a very positive way. The employees know this and work hard to make things right for our customers and each other.

USAA's Recognition of the Value of Employees

USAA understands that its employees are at the core of its continued progress, success, and good reputation and is committed to maintaining a professional and motivated work force. To this end, USAA places special emphasis on the initial acquisition and development of employees. It fosters the concept of teamwork in accomplishing company goals, encourages the positive attitude that continuous quality improvement is everyone's job, and provides an outstanding work environment that is both pleasing and conducive to productivity. Today, USAA's national reputation as an enlightened employer attracts talented workers. The net result of everything is a high retention rate and low absentee rates.

Figure 19-1. USAA personnel creed.

HUMAN RESOURCES
OUR BELIEF AND COMMITMENT

- We PLEDGE ourselves to the highest STANDARDS of ETHICS and PERSONAL INTEGRITY.

- Our commitment is to USAA & ITS MEMBERS.

- We take PERSONAL PRIDE in producing QUALITY SERVICE AND PRODUCTS.

- We share CONCERN FOR PEOPLE, their dignity and self worth as individuals.

- We will TREAT ALL EMPLOYEES FAIRLY regardless of race, creed, sex, age or national origin.

- We will strive to improve the QUALITY OF WORKLIFE for all.

- If we COMMIT A WRONG, WE WILL MAKE IT RIGHT.

- We will PROVIDE OPPORTUNITIES FOR CAREER GROWTH of individuals.

- We encourage CHANGE, to "DO IT BETTER."

- We have a CIVIC OBLIGATION to the communities in which we work and live.

- We PLEDGE ourselves to TEAMWORK, OPEN COMMUNICATION, ACTIVE INVOLVEMENT.

USAA's Definition of a Quality Employee

To ensure that USAA will continue to attract and retain quality employees, the home office and field employment areas of the company look for applicants who:

1. Meet the job specifications, or have the capacity and capability to successfully complete entry-level training
2. Are educated
3. Have records of past success or achievement
4. Have demonstrated initiative or get-up-and-go attributes
5. Possess solid reasoning ability
6. Have experience in related fields
7. Have excellent communication and interpersonal skills
8. Possess a professional image and cultural fit
9. Have an ability, desire, and will to succeed

Finding employees who meet USAA's definition is not an easy task, but it is the top priority for USAA's employment and placement functions. USAA's reputation for caring for its employees has helped attract, train, and retain quality employees. Selecting such high-caliber employees, in turn, helps USAA continue to be a place where good things happen and others desire to join. The conceptual model that USAA follows in its acquisition process is depicted in Figure 19-2. The USAA Personnel Acquisition Process focuses on the selection of high-quality individual employees, with the net result being a productive, talented, and culturally diverse work force.

Where Quality Hiring Begins

The selection of quality employees begins with a job candidate's visit to USAA's home office or field employment facilities. These modern, well-appointed facilities are easily accessible and contain ample free parking. The professional atmosphere and surroundings help motivate potential employees to want to be part of USAA. Unlike some companies, USAA has an open-door philosophy and accepts applications for employment with USAA rather than for specific, time-oriented positions. This affords the job candidate multiple opportunities for employment and provides the employment functions with more flexibility in filling positions.

USAA enjoys an enviable reputation as the employer of choice in the San Antonio area. In 1991, USAA ended the year with 30,341

Figure 19-2.   The USAA personnel acquisition process.

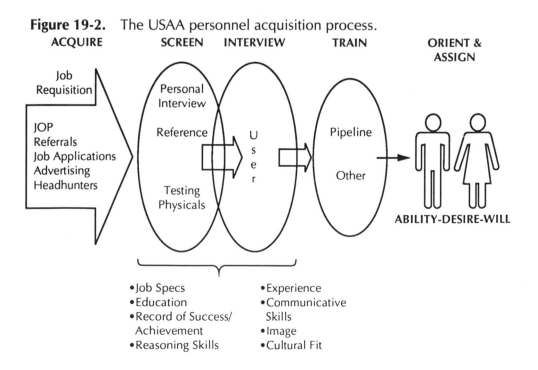

applications or résumés on file. During this same period 820 external applicants were hired. The resultant applicant-to-hire ratio of 37:1 provided USAA with an outstanding pool of candidates.

As prospective employees enter the employment facilities, a receptionist provides an application instruction sheet, the application for employment, and a supplement to the employment application. Additionally, the prospective employees must complete the supplement to the employment application, which requires writing one or two paragraphs describing their career goals. In addition to learning about the individual's motivation and career aspirations, the supplement provides a sample of the person's writing ability—a skill that is of particular importance to USAA.

After applicants have completed these documents, they receive a face-to-face interview with a screening interviewer. This screening interviewer reviews the individual's completed application and, by using a structured interview guide, obtains additional information from the person. This interview is an essential element of USAA's selection process because the results determine the initial classification of the individual by relevant occupational code(s). It also establishes the person's initial employability index. (A description of this unique process follows later.) The screening interview also determines whether the applicant should be scheduled for testing.

USAA's Employment Testing Program

Currently, USAA's employment testing program consists of two modules: an automated, self-grading typing test that is administered on a personal computer; and industry-based job-specific, cognitive abilities tests. The latter tests make up the Job Effectiveness Prediction System (JEPS), which the Life Office Management Association (LOMA) developed and validated for the insurance industry. The screening interviewer determines which candidates take which tests, if any.

The typing-test software consists of several typing applications—for example, speed and statistical typing tests. Candidates are offered two three-minute practice exercises before taking the five-minute timed typing test. The results provide a printout of the actual typing sample with all errors indicated in bold-face type, the gross words per minute (WPM) typed, and the number of errors. Candidates have two attempts to qualify. If they do not qualify on the second attempt, they may not retest for thirty days.

The JEPS is ideally suited to assess the cognitive abilities of entry-level clerical and technical or professional jobs. A total of eleven separate JEPS test booklets are available to users. These measure the following:

two levels of numerical ability; one level each of mathematical skill, spelling, language usage; two levels of reading comprehension, and one level each of verbal comprehension, filing, coding and converting, and comparing and checking.

The basis of JEPS, as with any selection testing program, is job analysis. USAA obtains critical performance area data from a representative sample of job incumbents and supervisors who complete JEPS job description questionnaires. LOMA analyzes the optical character readable answer forms for USAA and identifies the JEPS test booklets most predictive of the job's critical performance areas. These booklets are combined into test batteries that may consist of as few as three test booklets or as many as five.

To compile the Predicted Performance Score (PPS) for an individual, that person's test booklet raw scores (the number of correct answers) are multiplied by the weights for each of the booklets and totaled. Use of a constant converts the score to a standard score, or T-score. The PPS is then compared to conversion tables to determine how the applicant compares against nationwide norms and with employees having six months' experience, and estimates probability of success on the job. JEPS data sheets are subsequently made available to placement specialists and selecting supervisors as an additional tool to aid them in the selection process. At this time, USAA loads test results onto the Applicant Tracking System/Test Data Base (ATS/TDB).

USAA's Employability Index (EI) Program

As mentioned previously, the screening interviewers at the employment facilities use the interview to establish each applicant's Employability Index, or EI. The EI is a tool for identifying quality individuals from among the thousands of individuals who are on file in USAA's ATS/TDB. The EI is a screening process that was developed, validated, and tested by USAA in 1990 and deployed company-wide in 1991. The EI provides a common focus for all screening interviewers to use in evaluating the potential of external applicants in five key employment areas: work performance capability, work attitude, interpersonal skills, oral communication, and written communication. The interviewers assess the applicant's job potential based on their critical review of the application and supplement, and structured questioning conducted during the initial screening interview. The interviewers assign a numerical rating of 1 to 7 ranging from "very limited potential at this time" to "high potential at this time" to each component of the EI. The EI information can be retrieved later by placement specialists who are staffing job requisitions and used, along with other relevant information, to help them identify the best qualified external job candidates for referral to selecting supervisors.

After the screening interviewers complete EI rating forms, they send the forms to the support staff, along with the application and supplement for data entry into the ATS/TDB. USAA retains copies of all of the documents and JEPS test score data for six months. Employment managers continuously review the EI ratings assigned by each screening interviewer to assess their objectivity and consistency. This process and periodic training sessions ensure the reliability of this screening tool.

USAA's Employment and Placement Process

Home office and field office employment and placement staffs recruit and hire applicants who meet established criteria for education and/or experience and who demonstrate acceptable aptitude for selected jobs and also handle the internal placement of employees through the Job Opportunity Program (JOP), all in consonance with USAA's obligation as an equal opportunity employer.

It is USAA's policy to fill jobs with the best available candidate by allowing selecting supervisors to consider both internal and external candidates. Employment and placement staffs screen both external and internal candidates concurrently and provide the selecting supervisor with a list of the best qualified candidates.

The JOP enables employees to apply for jobs for which they are qualified, and affords them the opportunity to move upward to more challenging positions or to change career fields. Nonmanagerial job vacancies are posted daily on bulletin boards throughout USAA. Employees applying for JOP vacancies undergo a similar selection, testing, and interview process as applicants with the exception of the Employability Index.

The JOP process starts when a selecting supervisor generates an employee requisition form. When employment and placement staffs receive this form, it is assigned to a placement specialist. At USAA, placement specialists work closely with selecting supervisors to ensure their complete understanding of customer needs. This personal touch has paid handsome dividends for the employment function by demonstrating concern for serving internal customers and helping placement specialists establish staffing priorities.

Upon notice of the placement specialist assignment, the support staff enters the requisition into the ATS/TDB, which generates a draft JOP posting that reflects the job title, description of typical duties, required and preferred backgrounds, the selecting supervisor, and placement specialist who is staffing the job. If the placement specialist approves the draft JOP posting, it is posted for a week on all USAA bulletin boards.

Employees indicate their interest in applying for a job by completing the JOP program request form, which is available near each JOP board. Employees must complete the form by a designated date and must meet specific eligibility requirements spelled out in the USAA Personnel Policies Manual.

At the end of the posting period, the staffing team assembles the files of the employees who have posted for the position and provides them to the placement specialist. The placement specialist reviews the files of all candidates, evaluates their qualifications and records, and interviews candidates who meet the required criteria for the position. The placement specialist then determines those who qualify and releases those who do not, and then refers the qualified individuals to the selecting supervisor. Candidates who are not referred receive an explanation and career counseling for self-development purposes.

Upon making a selection choice, the supervisor notifies the placement specialist, the selectee, and the candidates who were not selected. The placement specialist updates the disposition of the job requisition in the ATS/TDB and sends it to Human Resources Records Management. This office updates the automated human resources management system and microfilms the requisition for inclusion in the employee's records.

At the same time the internal hiring process is occurring, the assigned placement specialist searches the ATS/TDB for external individuals who meet the requirements for the position. This includes the required Employability Index. In combination, these tools assist the placement specialist in narrowing the pool of applicants to manageable limits for further evaluation. During this process, the placement specialist is empowered to change the EI scores on any of the dimensions based upon this second assessment, and these changes become the new EI scores of record in the ATS/TDB. Next, the placement specialist reviews the applications and supplements, résumés, test results (if applicable), and further reduces the list of candidates for scheduling of placement interviews. The support staff contacts the applicants and arranges the appointments.

Based on the results of these interviews, the placement specialist identifies the finalists for referral to the selecting supervisor. Concurrently, the placement specialist requests background checks, investigative reports, or motor vehicle records checks (if applicable) on these individuals. Based upon the results of these checks and the physical examinations and drug tests, the candidates are cleared for referral.

If the selecting supervisor chooses an external job candidate, the selecting supervisor does not notify the selectee. Rather, the placement specialist handles the notification, which insulates the company against possible misrepresentation of information to the candidate and reduces USAA's risk of possible exposure to litigation. Once a hiring salary is established, the placement specialist confirms it in a written job-offer letter. If the external hire lives outside of the local area and is eligible for relocation at USAA's expense, details of the relocation package and entitlements are also provided along with the job-offer letter.

USAA's New Employee Orientation

USAA's employment and placement functions also conduct the new employee orientation program. This one and one-half day program is a new employee's first exposure to USAA's corporate culture, quality principles, and member service focus. To reinforce this critical foundation, all new employees receive a copy of the Corporate Culture Manual along with the Employee Handbook. The manual describes USAA, its history, and tradition of service and serves as a reminder of the quality values that are USAA's heritage.

Special Search and Development Programs

At the conclusion of the new employee orientation, all new member-contact employees enter a full-time formal training class. These classes typically involve policy service, claims, or sales training. Because quality and service are such strong USAA cultural values, these concepts are woven into every course, and it is made abundantly clear that quality is everyone's job. To keep everyone focused on quality, a customer relations education function specializing in the presentation of quality-related courses and material ranging from managing extraordinary service to coaching and facilitation training courses was recently established. One of its major responsibilities is to conduct "Professional Development Days" for several of the operating divisions. Here, member-contact employees meet with their senior management for a "how goes it" session, share success stories in serving members, discuss service techniques, review cross-selling of products, and identify approaches to better meet members' needs. These highly motivational sessions are extremely successful in reinforcing quality service values in these employees who "are USAA" each and every time they interact with members.

All training at USAA is the responsibility of the Training and Development (T&D) Department, which provides high-quality, customized employee training. Its focus is to develop fully trained employees who are ready to provide USAA's renowned service both technically and professionally. Organizationally, T&D stands at the same level as Human Resources and has a large staff of professional, experienced instructors and trainers. USAA enjoys an employee-to-trainer ratio of 46:1. In 1991, T&D conducted 770,635 hours of formal, in-house training—an average of 57.9 hours annually per employee. The average for U.S. industry (Department of Labor Statistics) is 35 hours annually per employee.

USAA's Executive Placement Function

This unit is responsible for all actions associated with USAA's Executive Management Group (EMG). The EMG consists of executive directors and all officer positions in the company. This unit receives and responds to employment inquiries received directly from individuals and referrals that come from senior management or executive search firms. It maintains relationships with designated executive search firms, administers the annual organizational review program (internal succession planning), and maintains the EMG employee records. Because of the extreme sensitivity associated with staffing positions at these levels, the support staff members must maintain strict confidentiality at all times while carrying out their critically important job responsibilities. This staff enjoys considerable empowerment, however, necessary to be responsive to these senior managers' needs.

USAA's Recruiting Program

The company's targeted college and university recruiting efforts focus on identifying college graduates for hard-to-fill jobs. These typically are associated with accounting, actuarial, and information systems disciplines. Currently, USAA is affiliated with twelve colleges and universities primarily located in Texas and the south-central United States. Recruiting teams travel to these campuses twice each year. This arrangement has worked especially well in assessing not only the technical skills of prospective applicants but also their cultural fit with the company. Recently, videos depicting USAA's corporate culture and work environment were developed to supplement the recruiting program. Following these trips, selected candidates are invited to San Antonio or field offices for further assessment and exploratory or placement interviews. Additionally, USAA also participates in numerous job fairs and career-day orientation programs in the San Antonio and field office areas. These recruiting efforts have been highly successful in identifying entry-level women and minority candidates who possess the skills and potential for a career with USAA.

Specialized Development Programs

In addition to supporting primary recruiting and hiring functions, Human Resources professionals work in partnership with the Property and Casualty Division claims staff to develop two unique claims management development programs: the Claims Management Intern Program (CMIP) and the Program to Identify and Recognize Mid-Managers and Executives (PRIME). Both of these programs are designed to provide for an anticipated expansion of mid-level managers in claims.

USAA's Hiring Quality Assurance

Employment and placement functions continually evaluate work processes to be more responsive to internal customers. One of the primary tools that staffing teams use to determine customer satisfaction is a staffing evaluation form. Each selecting supervisor receives one within one week after the job requisition has been filled. It applies to both internal (JOP) and external hires. The selecting supervisor returns completed forms to employment and placement senior managers for evaluation. After review, the forms are sent to staffing team managers for review and discussion with the appropriate placement specialist or support staff. For purposes of tracking performance, staffing managers rely on the overall evaluation scale of 1 to 5 that ranges from "Did not meet expectations" to "Exceeded expectations." Based on past experience, home office staffing teams agreed to use an overall rating of 4 as their goal for 1991 (up from 3.5 the previous year). Happily, the teams exceeded this goal and achieved overall evaluation averages of 4.25 (Property and Casualty) and 4.26 (Corporate and Subsidiaries). In addition to this primary source of feedback, other customer-satisfaction surveys are used to assess the effectiveness of the employment centers, new employee orientation programs, and moving services provided to relocating employees. Another survey evaluates all phases of the hiring process.

Staffing managers and placement specialists receive valuable feedback on how the system is working by visiting supervisors, attending meetings, participating in working groups, and conducting house calls. For example, the vice-president of personnel operations frequently visits employment and placement activities and asks job candidates if their expectations are being met and what they would change. Suggestions for change are shared with the managers and in numerous cases they have been adopted. The result has been continuous quality improvement.

Other Quality Hiring Initiatives

Because the selection process is critically important and exposes the company to potential risks of litigation, USAA has taken extra measures to emphasize the importance of this function. It recently developed a Selection Interview and Employee Orientation Guide for managers that was published and distributed to all managers and supervisors in the company. This guide serves as a primer on the subjects of effective employee selection, interviewing guidelines, and unit-level orientation. The guide will be updated periodically to ensure its currency with legal developments and changing policies and procedures.

Beginning in 1990, in partnership with the Training and Development Department, the executive director of employment and placement now presents a four-hour block on the subject of personnel selection and placement in its Management I course. This is particularly important because Management I is mandatory for all newly appointed managers or candidates identified for these positions. This hands-on course covers USAA's policies and procedures for recruiting and hiring qualified candidates, and shows how to conduct effective selection interviews. One such practical exercise deals with lawful and unlawful questions, and includes an explanation of the rationale for each response. This hard-hitting, focused information has drawn favorable response from the new managers who have completed Management I.

Additionally, staffing managers randomly sit in on the interviews being conducted by their placement specialists to evaluate their effectiveness and to offer suggestions for improvement, where appropriate. This mentoring approach has been well received by the placement specialists and has generally improved the quality of placement interviews. Recently, home office employment and placement employees formed a quality circle representing every function within the organization. One of the first projects undertaken by the circle was to document the existing work processes of each function. The results illustrated numerous opportunities for work-flow improvements, and many of the suggested process improvements have been successfully implemented.

In 1988, USAA established an employee referral bonus. This program paid bonuses to employees in cases where the employment and placement functions would have had to pay hefty agency fees or increase advertising to staff hard-to-fill positions. Current bonuses range from $250 to $500, depending upon the position and location experiencing a hiring difficulty. When USAA hires the referral, the recommending employee receives the bonus three months after the new employee's hire date. The program has been exceptionally successful. Since its inception, USAA has paid 310 bonuses totaling $188,000. One of the primary benefits of the program is the discretion and selectivity employees exercise in recommending someone for employment in their company. This goes a long way toward ensuring the quality of USAA's employees because no one wants to recommend a failure. Clearly, this is a key by-product of the corporate culture and employees' commitment to excellence.

Attracting future quality employees goes beyond normal hiring procedures. USAA has numerous programs to help youths get better education and to stay in school. While these are the primary purposes, the students at all levels tend to think of USAA as a great place to work. Many youths learn about USAA through the USAA mentor and summer hire programs. Others are exposed to USAA through USAA support of magnet schools and Junior Achievement programs. College scholarships sponsored by USAA are also available to highly qualified students as well as internship programs. All of these programs provide USAA employees as positive role models for personal and professional development. The long-term result is many talented students who decide to join USAA as they begin their careers.

Indicators of USAA's Quality Employees

USAA's commitment to the best interests of its quality employees perhaps is best illustrated by reviewing the company's very low absenteeism and turnover rates. Sick leave is the measure of absenteeism that the company uses as a leading indicator of employee morale. USAA calculates this rate by dividing the total number of work hours available into the total number of sick leave hours taken. Absenteeism rates for the past five years are reflected below:

1987	2.4%
1988	2.1
1989	1.8
1990	1.9
1991	2.0

Another key indicator of interest to USAA is its employee turnover rate. For purposes of monitoring and reporting, an overall rate reflecting both voluntary and involuntary losses is used. This annualized rate is determined by dividing the number of total losses by the average number of employees at the end of each reporting year. USAA's turnover rates for the past five years are shown below:

1987	9.5%
1988	8.1
1989	8.5
1990	7.0
1991	7.2

USSA's benchmark is the most recently conducted survey of absenteeism and turnover that was conducted by the Life Office Management Association (LOMA). In this survey, USAA's absenteeism rate at the end of 1991 was 2.0 percent, which compared favorably against the LOMA average rate of 2.5 percent for companies with 2,000 employees or more. With respect to turnover rate, USAA again compared favorably with LOMA's data. The company ended 1991 with a termination rate of 7.2 percent compared with LOMA's average rate of 12.5 percent for companies reporting 2,000 employees or greater.

USAA's Belief in People

By many measures, USAA is a great place to work. It has an excellent reputation in the insurance and financial services community. This reputation began in 1922 and has steadily gained in stature based on hard work and responsive quality service to the members. Its culture is rich in historical legacy and an established values system anchored in the twin principles of quality member service and concerned commitment to the best interests of each employee.

Continuous opportunities are available for education, training, recognition, and advancement. Because of USAA's commitment to people, it keeps the working environment beautiful, safe, and pleasant. And USAA maintains a friendly climate of mutual respect. Management at all levels believes in open communication, and keeps employees informed of plans and goals on a continuing basis. Employees have the right and are encouraged to verbally express their opinions, suggestions, or complaints without recrimination.

Recognizing that USAA's past success can be attributed to outstanding employees, its future success depends on continually building a superior work force. The involvement and empowerment of trained and highly motivated employees who believe in "doing the right things right" and serving the member as their top priority is critical. The Human Resources Department continues to work closely at USAA with everyone who helps to keep our work force a world-class group of employees. The Human Resources motto of "Serving the employee to serve the member" captures the pride and commitment that it demonstrates every day at USAA. Our "profit" is the applause we get from meeting our customers' needs and knowing that we are ensuring USAA will continue to be a high-quality company in the future.

References

Life Office Management Association (LOMA). "1990 Human Resources Practices: Absenteeism and Turnover Survey." Atlanta, May 1990.

USAA Corporate Quality, USAA Property and Casualty Division, Malcolm Baldrige National Quality Award Subdivision. San Antonio, April 1990.

USAA Employment & Placement. "Selection Interview and Employee Orientation Guide for Managers." San Antonio, January 1992.

USAA Employee Services. "USAA Employee Handbook." San Antonio, January 1992.

———. "USAA Personnel Policies Manual." San Antonio, February 1992.

USAA Strategic Plans & Analysis. "Strategic Planning Guidance Document, 1992–1996." San Antonio, June 1991.

20

Motivating Employees Through TLC

Roger J. Dow, Marriott Corporation

If you take care of your people, they will take care of your customers and your business will take care of itself.
J. Willard Marriott, Sr., Founder, Marriott Corporation

In 1927, J. Willard Marriott, Sr., opened a nine-seat root beer stand in Washington, D.C. Little did he know that this small business would grow to be an $8 billion global lodging and management services company employing over 210,000 associates. The company was built on the philosophy of providing quality food, service, and value in a clean surrounding with a strong culture toward treating employees (whom we now refer to as associates) fairly and as partners in business. These simple, yet extraordinarily important values have been the cornerstone of Marriott's spectacular growth. Basically, our philosophy toward the treatment of our people has been the key to our success.

Over the years, our management systems and capabilities have become very sophisticated. We've come a long way from the nine-seat root beer stand in the decor and design of our 750 worldwide hotels and resorts. These properties have beautiful furnishings, decor, and amenities. Yet when we receive complimentary letters from satisfied customers, they never refer to our soaring atriums or marble and brass; rather, they refer to an associate who took the time to cater to their specific needs. No matter what your business, service, or product, its success ultimately depends on how well your employees interact with your customers. Through the years, whenever we have drifted from Bill Marriott's philosophy regarding people, we have found ourselves getting into trouble, and had to bring ourselves back to our founding principles and culture.

Business has gone through a transition from agriculture to assembly-line manufacturing to today's service and technology marketplace. In the past, businesses succeeded with a view that employees were hired hands, and a centralized, control-oriented, hierarchical management structure worked extremely well when employees' hands were far more valuable than their minds. In today's fast-paced global marketplace, the truly successful organizations will be those that are able to involve and capture the creativity and enthusiasm of their employees. This can take place only in organizations where employees are treated well, their needs are met, and they are able to clearly see opportunity in their relationship with the organization.

The successful organization is able to build a strong relationship with its employees by focusing on the following areas: fairness and freedom, training and development, compensation, recognition, involvement, and opportunity. The relationship is based on the attitude that a business only has two *appreciating assets*: its employees and its customers. In this chapter, we focus on how Marriott and some other successful organizations have been able to build on the value of their appreciating employee asset, which has led to their business success.

At Marriott, we quantitatively link employee satisfaction to customer satisfaction. We dedicate a great deal of time to and put much emphasis on understanding customer satisfaction and associate (employee) satisfaction. This is done through formal surveys, focus groups, and quantitative and qualitative research on an ongoing basis. When we looked at the relationship between dissatisfaction among customer and associate groups, we discovered that those business units where customers are most satisfied are staffed by associates with the highest satisfaction levels. Therefore, it is clear that treating your employees with tender loving care (TLC) is not only the right thing to do but is critical to business success.

Let's take a look at each of the areas management must focus on to treat employees with tender loving care (TLC) and have a thriving, growing operation.

Fairness and Freedom

At Marriott, we have a Guarantee of Fair Treatment for all our associates (see Figure 20-1). It outlines the principles we believe in and assures our associates that they will be fairly treated and have the right to voice their opinion. This is especially important when a company asks its employees to take risks to satisfy customers, as opposed to merely quoting rules, regulations, and policy. Situations are changing constantly, especially for frontline employees, and they must know that they have the freedom to act on behalf of the customer, which is for the overall good of the company.

In a recent *Inc.* magazine article, Herb Kelleher, co-founder and CEO

Figure 20-1.   Marriott Corporation guarantee of fair treatment.

Marriott Corporation policy provides that every associate, regardless of position, be treated with respect and in a fair and just manner at all times. In keeping with this long-established policy, all persons will be considered for employment, promotion or training on the basis of qualifications without regard to race, color, creed, sex, national origin, disability or veteran status.

We recognize that, being human, mistakes may be made in spite of our best efforts. We want to correct such mistakes as soon as they happen. The only way we can do this is to know of your problems and complaints. **NO MEMBER OF MANAGEMENT IS TOO BUSY TO HEAR THE PROBLEMS OR COMPLAINTS OF ANY ASSOCIATE.**

If you have a problem or complaint, this is what you should do:

Step 1—TELL YOUR IMMEDIATE SUPERVISOR. During this discussion, feel free to share your honest feelings and concerns. Your supervisor will listen in a friendly, courteous manner because it is his/her desire to understand and aid in solving problems which arise in your work. Generally, you and your supervisor will be able to resolve your problems.

Step 2—If you do not get your problem straightened out with your supervisor, see your manager or department head. He/She will obtain all the facts and work to settle your problem in a fair and equitable manner. If you still are not satisfied, he/she will arrange for you to see your General Manager or Director of Human Resources.

Step 3—Your General Manager or Director of Human Resources will confer with you and all others involved to carefully review the facts and circumstances. If, after a thorough discussion of the matter, you still feel the problem has not been resolved to your satisfaction, the entire matter will be referred to your Regional Director of Human Resources.

NOTE: Your problem may be such that you prefer to discuss it directly with your General Manager, Director of Human Resources, or a representative of the Hotel Division Employee Relations staff. Always feel free to do so. It is the policy of Marriott Corporation that all associate suggestions and complaints shall be given full consideration. There will be no discrimination or recrimination against any associate because he/she presents a complaint or problem.

J. W. Marriott, Jr.
Chairman, President and
Chief Executive Officer

of Southwest Air Lines, stated that companies must consider whether promises made to the customer are fair to the employees, and must recognize their capability of delivering on them: "When we started out, we had to come up with promotions that were colorful and made good stories to get the media coverage we couldn't afford. But one of the big risks with marketing is creating expectations that cannot be fulfilled. . . . We have turned down many promotions because they imposed too great a burden on our people. The staff can't provide good Customer Service if they are distracted by some new guarantee, and you've got to remember that advertising is a message to your people as well as the outside world."[1] Treating employees with TLC is about never making promises to customers that your employees can't deliver on. Your advertising and marketing messages must convey respect for your employees.

AT&T Universal Card has recently won the Malcolm Baldrige National Quality Award. The company has been built around treating its employees fairly and understanding their needs. According to *USA Today*, Universal Card Services goes to great lengths to take care of employees' needs. AT&T certifies local day-care providers and helps find qualified care for mildly ill children of employees. Its credit union provides car loans at 6.75 percent versus the national rate of 9.6 percent. The company health club is free to employees and their families. When asked whether this health club lowers insurance costs, Peter Gallagher of AT&T Universal Card Services replied, "I suppose it does, but it's good for them, they enjoy it and we'd give it to them even if it didn't lower cost."[2] Treating employees well has a big payoff since AT&T Universal Card's turnover of service representatives is only 8 percent versus a 40 to 50 percent industry average.

Armand Shapiro, CEO of the highly successful Garden Ridge Pottery, has built his company around the stated philosophy of "being nice" to its customers, employees, and suppliers. When workers compensation costs were projected to increase to $1.2 million, Armand asked his employees what he should do. They came up with a program whereby they would work together to reduce these costs and share in the savings to the company. This resulted in Garden Ridge's leaving the workers compensation system and compiling an excellent safety record at substantially lower cost and greater compensation for the company's highly motivated employees.[3]

When Paul Revere Insurance Group decided to exit the group medical business, 120 jobs or 7 percent of the home office staff were impacted. About 60 of these jobs were eliminated. According to Bob Lea, vice president of human resources and quality, the situation was stated fairly and honestly *in person* by the company's president to the employees involved. The employees were then given the opportunity to decide fairly how to handle this, which resulted in no employee's being forced out of the company. A few employees opted to leave the organization and pursue other opportunities. The company provided support services and retraining to enable the remaining people to find other positions within Paul Revere, which resulted in 80 of the 120 people being redeployed. This has created a spirit within Paul Revere Insurance Group that employee groups can take the initiative to eliminate jobs and find other opportunities within the organization. This has enabled the company to make great strides in eliminating bureaucracy and work duplication.[4]

Training and Development

One of the most important things an organization can do for its employees is to train them and provide them with a development plan. Not only is it important for the employee but it is critical to the success of the business and is a major factor in achieving customer satisfaction. During difficult times many businesses make the erroneous decision that they can save money by eliminating or cutting back on training. When this occurs, employees feel they are in dead-end positions, and a job becomes just a job and not a career commitment. When an organization allows poorly trained employees to interact with its customers, it is putting both its customers and its employees at risk. This lack of training results in increased turnover, which is far more costly to the business than the training itself.

At Marriott, our training is constant, both formal and informal. Each of our associates goes through an orientation program that focuses on sharing the Marriott values, culture, and philosophy. Following orientation, the employee receives job-specific training conducted by management and by peers.

It is our stated goal to provide each Marriott associate with forty hours of training per year. Each discipline has developed its own curriculum, augmented by more general courses developed by Marriott's Corporate Training Department. For example, in the area of sales and marketing, we have five formal one-week training programs that range from the basics of selling to the complexity of running a sales and marketing department. Each associate has a personal development plan that focuses on the training skills needed to advance to the next position. Training is a critical part of our career development program.

If you spend time at companies that are leaders in their fields, you will see that they have a very strong commitment to the training and development of their employees. Many organizations, such as McDonald's, GE, Kodak, and Apple Computers have their own "universities" with dedicated teaching staffs. Similar to Marriott, Malcolm Baldrige Award winner Milliken & Company has a formal course catalog that is published for its employees, listing literally hundreds of available development courses. These courses teach everything from Dale Carnegie to computer programming skills. The employees are free to choose courses that they and their supervisor believe will be of benefit to them and their career.

In a recent discussion, Tom Malone, president of Milliken & Company, shared his thoughts on the importance of peer training. Tom stated that the most effective learning takes place when employees learn from one another. It has been his observation that

> our people's eyes tend to glaze over when senior management attempts to tell them how to implement programs. For example, we failed miserably when we tried to duplicate the plant safety success of one of the leading companies in the world. Our senior managers repeatedly visited the plant and then shared their learning with our people. No matter how hard we tried, our competitor still had a safety record which was ten times better than our very good record. We finally sent the employees from one of our plants to observe our competitor's safety program on a first-hand basis. They returned and quickly implemented what they had observed with great success at their plant. We have since replicated this process at all of our other plants. It is very clear that *peer training* through sharing of success stories is successful and also helps build relationships within an organization. This results in higher associate satisfaction, teamwork, and reduced turnover.[5]

Many companies model their training programs on successful businesses outside their industry. Mid-Columbia Medical Center of The Dalles, Oregon, is one of the nation's most progressive health-care providers, with its entire program focused on some very simple values: to treat patients with respect; to recognize the importance of families, friends, and volunteers in the healing process; to be honest about providing patients access to information about their illness and treatment alternatives; to offer choices; to provide the opportunity for participation; to inform patients that they can trust each other; and to keep no secrets. According to President Mark Scott,

> We provide our people with more than forty hours a year of formal training based on organizational philosophy—to treat patients and families in a very personalized, humanized, and demystified environment—and values, plus their specific jobs. Our employees must be part of the healing process in their

attitude and behavior. Therefore, we have taught them that they are "on stage" when it comes to dealing with our patients and their families. We have found the best training to take place at Disney and Ritz-Carlton Hotels. Our senior management has spent a great deal of time with these organizations to learn what training methods work for them and have applied them at Mid-Columbia.[6]

As stated earlier, our employees are one of our two appreciating assets. It makes good sense to build the value of this asset through an ongoing training and development program. This is an important part of treating your employees with TLC and will pay great dividends.

Compensation

With over 210,000 employees, Marriott is the tenth largest employer in the United States and is a nonunion organization. A key factor in our employees' not seeing the need to organize has been our approach to compensation. We spend a great deal of time doing compensation studies within the industry and in similar businesses to be sure that our compensation program is fair and equitable. Each of our employees' compensation is reviewed on an annual basis. Our management compensation is tightly tied to specific performance goals as well as customer-satisfaction measures. We have found that it is very important to have a compensation program that is flexible, goal-oriented, and clearly understood by the associates.

At fast-growing Rosenbluth International, compensation is used to build employee loyalty and morale, and give them a competitive advantage. According to Kathy Veit, vice-president for quality and organization development, the company recently implemented a compensation program that provided its reservations associates with much higher compensation based on increased accuracy, service, and customer satisfaction. This new program resulted in 95 percent of the people in the reservations department making more money, with the average increase amounting to 32 percent. The company was able to achieve accuracy of 99.6 percent and reduced operating costs 4 percent in the process. Rosenbluth International also experienced increased productivity and quality according to customer surveys. Kathy stated, "You can't improve service without the commitment of your people and your compensation program is a key ingredient in gaining their commitment."[7]

Robert Manschot, president and CEO of Rural/Metro Corporation, the Scottsdale-based provider of privatized fire and ambulance emergency services, also found that compensation was an important factor in his company's success. He needed to halt the turnover of both customers and employees in order for the company to survive, so Manschot has made a priority of increasing employee compensation, tying it to training skills and retention of customers. The results have been dramatic, and Rural/Metro is now among the nation's largest private emergency services companies, with a fleet of over 400 vehicles and over 2,000 employees serving nearly 6 million people in five states. Rural/Metro also recently announced an initial public offering of common stock, which is now traded on the NASDAQ National Market System under the symbol RURL.[8]

Compensation clearly is a determining factor in the overall satisfaction of employees. A fair compensation program tied to specific goals as well as training and development is a necessary ingredient in any employee TLC program.

Recognition

Recognition appears to be the fuel that drives most successful employee TLC programs. At Marriott, we have found recognition to be extraordinarily important in building morale and teamwork, and in retaining the best people. Our recognition programs vary substantially from hotel to hotel, with the common element of celebrating those things most important to the success of our business. We have the standard Associate of the Month programs, but we find that more sporadic, ongoing recognitions are more effective. For example, we are constantly posting letters from satisfied customers in the employee work areas. Tom Chase, general manager of the Marriott City Center in Minneapolis, has one of the highest customer and employee satisfaction ratings in our company. Every week Tom sends at least ten letters to employees' homes regarding outstanding things they have done for customers. The impact is special when the employee receives a letter at home, which is often read with the family regarding his or her outstanding performance. This type of recognition costs Tom only 29 cents in postage but goes a long way toward celebrating achievements.

All Marriott managers are strongly encouraged to have constant recognition programs at their business units to reward employees for doing a great job. Most of these programs are nonmonetary and range from letters of commendation, certificates, and plaques to complimentary dinners.

In summarizing how AT&T Universal Card won the Malcolm Baldrige National Quality Award, *USA Today* stated that the company bases its success on the following simple philosophy: "Rather than punishing employees who do something wrong, AT&T rewards people for doing things right."[9] This attitude of constant recognition and reward for the right behavior has resulted in extraordinary growth, customer satisfaction, and employee retention.

Likewise, Tom Malone at Milliken & Company says the company's great success has been achieved by creating a "Super Bowl atmosphere for excitement and recognition." Tom stated that no other factor has had as much of an impact in building success than encouraging creativity and excellence among the employees. He correlates Milliken's recognition program to having "fans in the stands." Tom states rhetorically, "I doubt many athletes would excel or give their utmost if there were no fans in the stands to cheer them on!"[10]

Involvement

In the introduction to their book *In Search of Excellence*, business writers Tom Peters and Bob Waterman state that everyone has a need to "be a conforming member of a winning team and to be a star in his own right,"[11] which certainly applies to the concept of recognition and involvement. In an effective organization, employees must feel involved and that their input is valued. Once again, successful organizations have strong employee involvement and empowerment programs. These companies truly value the skills and capabilities of their people and do the best to maximize them.

At Marriott, we recently totally reengineered our hotel check-in process. This was done through the extensive involvement of our customers and our employees, and by benchmarking other organizations. It was amazing to see the solutions that employees offered for problems that had existed for many years. All our major breakthroughs have come from asking people *doing the job* about how we could make a particular process better. It is important to give people ownership and the freedom to carry out their responsibilities. When I asked a bellman at our San Antonio Marriott what he liked about Marriott versus a competing chain he had worked for, he replied, "The managers let us do what we gotta do!" This sums up the importance of having employees involved with their jobs to the point of ownership and acting with the best interests of the organization and its customers at heart.

RE/MAX International, a large real estate brokerage organization, was concerned with negative field reports involving shipping and receiving of promotional materials from their distribution center. RE/MAX has a very large network of agents throughout the U.S. and Canada, so the timeliness and accuracy of orders for these materials was very important. Under the direction of Robert Fisher, president, a study was initiated to determine the solution. A project team was organized involving and utilizing all essential levels of input, including the agents and the employees who actually took and filled the orders. The process was revamped where necessary, and in just a few months, of all orders received, 95 percent were being shipped within twenty-four hours and 10 percent within forty-eight hours.[12]

Milliken & Company achieves continuous improvement as a result of the input of its employees. Tom Malone has stated that most employee suggestion programs fail because employees feel that management does not really care about their ideas. At Milliken they instituted a 24/72 Suggestion Program, with the numbers referring to the twenty-four-hours acknowledgement period for employee suggestions and seventy-two-hour notification of response to the suggestion. When the company implemented the 24/72 Suggestion Program, employee suggestions sky-rocketed, in both number and value.[13]

Jack Welch, CEO of General Electric, summed up his thoughts on employee involvement in a recent *Newsweek* interview:

> We believe right to our toes that we've got to engage every mind in this place. They've got to feel good about being here. They've got to feel their contributions are respected. That doesn't mean our standards aren't higher than ever in terms of productivity; we just happen to think [this] is the right way to do it. Breaking down boundaries, taking away hierarchy. The idea is to liberate people.[14]

The Ritz-Carlton Hotel Company recently won the Malcolm Baldrige National Quality Award. President Horst Schulze attributed a great deal of the company's success to employees' feeling involved in the running of their particular departments. According to Schulze, an important ingredient in involvement is to have respect for your employees and their judgment. He tells of instances of where a housekeeper feels empowered to order a new washing machine if the one they are using cannot be repaired, or of the desk clerk who has the latitude to adjust guests' bills on the spot. The involved employee is one who is truly a partner in the success of the business.[15]

Opportunity

If you treat your employees with TLC, you truly show them that you care about their personal growth by providing future opportunities for them. Good people are attracted to organizations where they clearly see a great deal of opportunity for growth if they excel at their jobs. At Marriott, our associates are able to look around and see many colleagues who have advanced to positions of greater responsibility through the years. Fifty percent of our managers started out as hourly employees. On the other hand, when people are associated with organizations that don't demonstrate opportunity for growth and advancement, they quickly become disinterested, which results in a loss of morale and customer satisfaction as well as costly turnover and a decline in business.

Summary

It has been said that people don't care how much you know about them until they know how much you care about them. Treating your employees with TLC is not only the right thing to do but a major factor in business success. Those organizations that truly care about their employees find that employees in turn truly care about the business and its customers. A well-balanced employee TLC program includes the following elements: fairness and freedom, training and development, compensation, recognition, involvement, and opportunity. The organizations that succeed in the future will be those that have built strong, interdependent relationships with their employees.

Notes

1. "Beware the Impossible Guarantee," *Inc.* magazine (November 1992), p. 30.
2. "Universal Success: AT&T Card Aimed High From Start," *USA Today* (October 15, 1992). Copyright 1992, USA TODAY. Used with permission.
3. Interview with author.
4. Interview with author.
5. Interview with author.
6. Interview with author.
7. Interview with author.
8. Interview with author.
9. "Universal Success: AT&T Card Aimed High From Start," *USA Today* (October 15, 1992). Copyright 1992, USA TODAY. Used with permission.
10. Interview with author.
11. *In Search of Excellence* (New York: HarperCollins, 1982).
12. Interview with author.
13. Interview with author.
14. "He Brought GE to Life," *Newsweek* (November 30, 1992), pp. 62–63.
15. Interview with author.

21

Empowering Employees

M. Ven Venkatesan, University of Rhode Island

As we approach the twenty-first century, American industries are experiencing rapid changes. The focus has shifted to attaining continuous quality improvement and sustaining such quality gains. Most of the quality improvements in the manufacturing industries have been achieved through technological changes and downsizing of the organizations. The concept of Total Quality Management (TQM) has become the password for success in the new, challenging global competitive arena.

There is a quiet revolution taking place in service industries as well. While many service industries have implemented automation and other technological changes, their ability to use downsizing to increase productivity is limited owing to the very nature of their business. Instead, in competitive service markets, companies search for ways to become less bureaucratic and more responsive to the needs of their customers. The companies expect high levels of performance from their employees, not just adherence to bureaucratic rules and procedures. This focus on service quality has led to changes in management thinking. There has been a major reordering of power relationships. The best-managed service companies are beginning to empower their employees in order to achieve high levels of service quality.

This chapter presents the concept of empowerment in the context of the service industries. It outlines the reasons for empowerment and provides guidelines for successful implementation of employee empowerment.

The Nature of a Service Business

The need for employee empowerment can be better understood if one looks at the distinctive characteristics of quality service. One characteristic is the need for simultaneous production and consumption of services. A service's perceived value or quality is created at the point of contact between the customer and the frontline employee. Contact personnel are in a position to provide superb service or not, depending on their degree of adherence to bureaucratic rules and procedures. Therefore, the perceived performance of frontline employees becomes the overriding factor in customer perceptions of the service experience.

A large number of services require customization and are not amenable to an "industrialization" of service delivery by technological means. Customization can take place only at the point of service delivery. To the customer, the most important person is the frontline employee, who acts alone or as part of a team to demonstrate organizational effectiveness in providing the required customization. To harness the energy of these frontline employees, there must be a new organizational arrangement and culture.

Service performance affects all levels of organizations since service companies have both external and internal customers. In the marketing literature, internal marketing is advocated as a way of inculcating a service culture in employees. Some authors have even suggested that employees be treated as "partial customers." These concepts do not go far enough, however. Radical changes in the present management style and corporate culture are needed if the level of service quality is to be enhanced. Thus, the concept of empowerment appears well suited to service employees. Indeed, the need for empowerment has been recognized by those designing new work cultures for service industries seeking a competitive advantage.

The Nature of Empowerment

Douglas MacGregor stated in the 1960s in his Theory Y that most people will grow and achieve, and will assume responsibility, if given an opportunity to do excellent work. Marvin Weisbord believes that managers are caught between the old paradigm of autocratic management and the new paradigm.[1] He further states that the forces of technology and democratic values will lead the way toward a lessened bureaucracy and revamp present organizational designs. In his view, the old model of the expert manager solving the problems from the top is rapidly being replaced by the new model of everyone in an organization improving the whole system. *Dignity, meaning,* and *community* will become the watchwords of the workplace. Already, organizations that are empowering their employees are amazed at the transformations taking place in terms of creativity, productivity, and receptivity to change.

In service industries, the key to service quality is people management, owing to the simultaneity of service production and consumption. The prevalent notion in the manufacturing industries is that people are variable costs and therefore these costs can be reduced. This perspective is inappropriate for service companies with their high customization, however. Service contact personnel are the principal resource for delivery of the company's services. To achieve pride and quality of service, management must look at how the service performance is designed and how the organization is structured. It is especially in this context that the concept of empowerment is gaining increased recognition.

There is a fundamental difference between a manufacturing organization's and a service organization's quest for quality. The objective of a manufacturing process is to minimize the variability of goods produced on the production line; therefore, there are limits to employee empowerment. In contrast, the goal of a service organization in providing customization and quality service is to maximize the variability—that is, to provide the greatest customization possible in order to differentiate itself from its competitors. The vision of quality service means exceeding customer expectations by enhancing the perceived performance of contact personnel. The goal should be to do whatever is needed to meet and exceed customer expectations for quality service.

What is *empowerment*? Most dictionaries define the word as "the giving of official authority or legal power." David Bowen and Edward Lawler note the humanistic flavor in the definition of empowerment.[2] After reviewing the management literature on empowerment, Jay Conger and Rabindra Kanungo conclude that most conceptualizations of empowerment involve participative management techniques.[3] In their view, empowerment should not be seen as a new term for participatory management, incentive management, or delegation. Rather, it means that employees are included in decisions that affect their performance. Conger and Kanungo offer their definition of *empowerment* as

> a process of enhancing feelings of self-efficacy among organizational members through the identification of conditions that foster powerlessness and through their removal by both formal organizational practices and informal techniques of providing efficacy information.[4]

In this context, *self-efficacy* means the expectation of individuals that their effort will bring in a desired level of performance for the organization, and that this performance will produce the desired outcome for the organization. Empowerment is thus a motivational concept or a state of mind that enables employee accomplishments through a strong sense of personal freedom and responsibility.

While there is no universal agreement on the meaning of empowerment, it is recognized that it is not the *giving* of power to subordinates by management—or what management is going to *do* for its employees, or resource sharing—but that it is an internal event: something that employees decide to do for themselves, with management providing the enabling conditions. In this view, employees are resources and partners in the enterprise; work is not just a job that needs to be completed; and management's role shifts from one of delegation to one of supporting, coaching, and teaching. Essentially, empowerment means the freedom to respond to the needs and expectations of one's customers in whichever manner one sees fit.

Empowerment is not spread by its espousal by management. It can be spread only by employee actions. Empowerment entails the freedom to respond to the needs and expectations of an organization's internal and external customers, in a manner that meets the best interests of the customers and the service company. One of the executives taking part in a symposium of the Conference Board observed that empowerment is extraordinarily difficult to communicate because, essentially, the job of an empowered employee is to break the rules.[5] Therefore, it must be a personal initiative.

Constant quality improvement in service performance cannot be imposed on contact personnel. It has to come from the individual. The only way employees can adopt constant improvement of their performance as a way of life is for them to be empowered.[6] Thus empowerment is not a result—not a management program-of-the-month. It is a value aimed at providing quality service to customers. This implies that a service organization must take a long-term perspective, since employee empowerment involves transforming a controlling culture into an enabling one.

Empowerment may well be peculiarly suited for service organizations in a quest to create and sustain an organizational culture that enhances employee performance to achieve service quality goals. Benjamin Schneider believes that an organization and its culture are a function of the kind of people that the organization attracts.[7] The individuals who seek jobs in service organizations appear to be different, in that they view themselves as people-oriented. Thus, this self-selection helps the organization in training for empowerment. The broader societal context also is conducive to employee empowerment since as a society we value individual freedom, dignity, and self-governance. Employee empowerment basically instills these values throughout an organization.

Benefits of Empowerment

There is considerable anecdotal evidence of the benefits of empowerment in service industries,[8] but no well-evidenced research findings are available. The chairman and chief executive officer of KPMG Peat Marwick stated that the company's Constant Improvement Program really took off and became successful when it empowered its employees.[9] NYNEX indicated that it has embraced the concept of employee empowerment and is implementing the empowerment process throughout its organization.[10] Glowing accounts of employee empowerment come from the president of Semco[11] and the CEO of Johnsonville Foods.[12]

For instance, Semco made drastic changes in its practice of management based on three fundamental values: democracy, profit sharing, and information. The company insisted on making decisions collegially, and many decisions were made on the basis of company-wide votes. The company gave its employees control over their lives, including factory workers, and let them set their own schedules. It also eliminated time clocks, abolished manuals, rules, and regulations, and even did away with dress codes. In short, employees were treated as responsible adults. The reported results were astounding. Within one year sales doubled, inventories fell from 136 to 46 days, and quality improved from a one-third rejection rate to less than 1 percent. The division's productivity in terms of dollar amounts per year per employee jumped from $14,200 to $37,500 in four years. Their market share went up from 54 to 62 percent.[13]

In the case of Johnsonville Foods, initially the CEO found that employees took no responsibility for their work, as management made all the decisions. The goal, as articulated by the CEO, was to create, instead of a traditional organizational chart with lines and boxes, a group of "individuals who knew the common goal, took turns leading and adjusted their structure to the task at hand." Each individual was to be responsible for his or her own performance. "The goal was not so much a state of shared responsibility as an environment where people insist on being responsible." The CEO did not order the change, but managed the change. Employees managed themselves, but the management managed the context and allocated the resources. The company's performance exceeded expectations in terms of sales, margins, quality, and productivity.[14]

What are the likely benefits to an organization that empowers its service employees? First, it achieves performance that is right for the customer and exceeds the customer's expectations. The job of the empowered employee changes to creative rule breaking and employees are no longer obedient slaves to bureaucratic rules and procedures. They have control over the means and methods of service performance and the quality of their output increases.

Second, employees feel that they are challenged, trusted, and listened to. They derive dignity, community, and meaning from their empowerment.

Third, empowered employees are great sources of information, since they are on the front lines and have intimate knowledge of the attitudes and preferences of customers. Their experiences provide valuable marketing research input for the company about customer preferences and ideas for new services.

Finally, employee empowerment is positively related to overall employee job satisfaction, as has been found in a recent study by James Pailin.[15]

The Implementation of Empowerment

At Johnsonville Foods, the CEO recognized that the company's management style kept employees from assuming responsibility. Managers had created expectations that they were in charge of solving problems and that employees were motivated to carry out the solutions. Even when the employees were allowed to make decisions, they were viewed as not having made the *right* decisions—namely, the decisions that the management would have made. The managers learned to be better coaches, provided resources, and shared information. They realized that there was no end to this change and that it was a continuing process.

Semco also faced formidable obstacles: size, hierarchy, lack of motivation, and ignorance. The biggest obstacles were the hierarchy and the inability and unwillingness of managers to share their power. Breaking down the hierarchical barriers, empowering employees, implementing a profit-sharing program, and providing complete information on all aspects of the company helped them turn the corner.

How do you implement a program of employee empowerment? Companies are learning by trial and error how to empower their employees. David Bowen and Edward Lawler point out that empowering service employees is less well understood, but they indicated what the process needs to accomplish.[16] In their view, employees are empowered if they

1. Get information about organizational performance
2. Are rewarded for contributing to organizational performance
3. Have the knowledge and skills to understand and contribute to organizational performance
4. Have the power to make decisions that influence organizational direction and performance

Bowen and Lawler identify three approaches or levels of empowering employees: suggestion involvement, job involvement, and high involvement. In addition, they provide guidelines for the conditions under which employee empowerment processes should be implemented:

1. The service is differentiated, customized, and personalized.
2. Long-term relationships are to be managed.

3. Service involves nonroutine and complex performance requirements.
4. Managers believe deeply in empowering service employees.

The following steps should be followed in empowering employees in service organizations:[17]

1. Formulate a vision of the company to provide focus for its efforts.
2. Translate this focus into a simple-to-understand inspirational statement, such as "world-class service quality."
3. Diagnose the conditions that impede employee empowerment, such as supervisor reluctance, bureaucratic rules and procedures, hierarchy, and/or company policies.
4. Commit to the program by implementing employee-empowering strategies such as coaching, training, feedback, and a reward system.
5. Enhance self-efficacy of individuals by providing information and encouragement, as well as opportunities for collaboration and self-determination.

Employee empowerment is a long-term process that should be viewed as a long-term strategy. It evolves. As someone observed, selling employee empowerment to management is like selling revolution to the ruling class. Empowering employees to change helps them focus their energies on the unfettered performance of their tasks. Empowered change takes a long time, since it is a process and not a destination. Many of the companies embarking on this journey realize that it will take years to have fully empowered employees in their productive workplaces. Empowered employees will make this change happen.

Employees have to progress from dependence to independence to interdependence. In the performance of service activities, they have to act both individually and in teams. Employee empowerment needs to encourage independence as well as interdependence, since "interdependence is a choice only independent people can make."[18] There are many obstacles to overcome, such as the urge to hold on to old habits of decision making at the top, and old structures. Therefore, the vital task of service management is to create a learning climate rather than provide solutions. As Weisbord has observed: "The game has changed from telling people what to do or doing it yourself to managing boundaries and helping others gain skills."[19] The service organization can be taught to provide quality performance through its employees if they are truly empowered to do so.

Notes

1. Marvin R. Weisbord, *Productive Work Places* (San Francisco: Jossey-Bass, 1987).
2. David E. Bowen and Edward E. Lawler III, "The Empowerment of Service Workers: What, Why, How and When," *Sloan Management Review* 33 (1992), p. 32.
3. Jay R. Conger and Rabindra N. Kanungo, "The Empowerment Process: Integrating Theory and Practice," *Academy of Management Review* 13 (1988), pp. 251–252.
4. Ibid.
5. 75th Symposium Series. *Leadership and Empowerment for Total Quality* (New York: The Conference Board, 1992).
6. William C. Byham, *Zapp: The Lightning of Empowerment* (New York: Ballantine Books, 1988).
7. Benjamin Schneider, "The People Make the Place." Presidential Address, Society for Industrial and Organizational Psychology, American Psychological Association Annual Convention, Los Angeles, August 1985.
8. James A. Belasco, *Teaching the Elephant to Dance* (New York: Plume, 1991).
9. Jon C. Madonna, "A Service Company Measures, Monitors and Improves Quality," report number 992. In *Leadership and Empowerment for Total Quality* (New York: The Conference Board, 1992).
10. "An Essay on Empowerment." In *On Quality: The NYNEX Magazine Dedicated to the Spirit of Excellence*, 1990.
11. Ricardo Semler, "Managing Without Managers," *Harvard Business Review* 89 (1989), pp. 76–84.
12. Ralph Stayer, "How I Learned to Let My Workers Lead," *Harvard Business Review* 68 (1990), pp. 66–83.
13. Semler, "Managing Without Managers."
14. Stayer, "How I Learned to Let My Workers Lead."
15. James Pailin, "Empowerment: Increasing Customer Satisfaction With Service Encounters." Paper presented at the Frontiers in Services Conference, Center for Services Marketing, Vanderbilt University, September 24–26, 1992.
16. Bowen and Lawler, "Empowerment of Service Workers."
17. Conger and Kanungo, "The Empowerment Process," pp. 471–482.
18. Stephen R. Covey, *The Seven Habits of Highly Effective People* (New York: Fireside, 1990).
19. Weisbord, *Productive Workplaces*.

22

Leveraging Employee Suggestions

Michael T. Fraga, Florida Power & Light Company

Florida Power and Light (FPL) is the fourth largest electric utility in the United States, serving about half the state of Florida with a population of more than 6 million people. With assets of well over $13 billion and annual revenues over $5 billion, FPL is one of the fastest growing utilities in the United States. Six of the ten fastest growing metropolitan areas in the country are located within our service territory. We anticipate adding anywhere from 80,000 to 100,000 new customers every year through the 1990s. By the year 2000 we expect to have more than 4 million rate-paying customers.

One of FPL's most successful programs is its Bright Ideas suggestion system. It has achieved some dramatic results. In three and a half years, more than 50 percent of our employees have submitted more than 60,000 suggestions significantly contributing to the improvement of work processes, customer satisfaction, and dollar savings.

Response to a Changing Environment

External changes were occurring in FPL's business and corporate environment in the 1980s. There was mounting support in government to deregulate the electric utility industry, and customer confidence was declining. Competition for customers was increasing in the form of co-generation (potential customers generating their own electricity) and lower rates from neighboring utilities. There was also uncertainty about nuclear energy's future, and few significant technological advances were to be expected.

In 1982, FPL began a quality-improvement process with the formation of quality-improvement teams and substantial training in the use of quality tools, which provided a structured environment for employees to work together to solve problems. The implementation of a total quality process and continuous improvement ultimately led to the company's receiving the prestigious Japanese Deming Prize in 1989. Employee involvement in trying to solve work problems also placed greater emphasis on revitalizing FPL's suggestion program.

FPL's Suggestion Program

FPL's original suggestion program was centralized within the corporate human resources office. All suggestions were sent to the suggestion office for processing and routing to the appropriate evaluator. The suggestor remained anonymous, since many ideas applied to improvements outside the employee's work area.

Accepted suggestions received a $50 cash award and were eligible for semiannual review by the suggestion committee for a major award of up to $1,000. But we had no process for implementation, and in some instances, awards were made prior to implementation or without actually being implemented. As a result, it took too long to evaluate suggestions, and many suggestions impacted large areas of the company. There were a low number of suggestions per year and the participation rate was declining as indicated in Figure 22-1.

Several attempts were made to revitalize the existing program. In 1985, a team of employees visited Kansai Electric in Japan. The team studied Kansai's program, making recommendations to analyze FPL's current suggestion system and to develop a new program with the following objectives:

- Increase participation and implementation rates
- Promote employee-supervisor communications
- Decrease processing time
- Improve the quality of products and services

In 1986, a suggestion office task team developed a program similar to the Japanese model. This model was piloted in three areas of the company, with limited success in participation. The committee's recommendation was to form another cross-functional team to analyze the pilot results. In 1987, the Bright Ideas task team was formed with strong upper-management commitment. This team consisted of management-level personnel and representatives from the suggestion office. The team studied other companies with successful programs. The following chart represents a comparison to programs in other companies, including another U.S. electric company having the best electric utility suggestion program at that time. FPL's goal for 1988 was benchmarked against this U.S. electric company (see Figure 22-2).

A survey was given to FPL employees to determine their requirements for a successful suggestion program. Their response is summarized as follows:

1. Local management recognition was needed.
2. Implementation of ideas was more important than awards.

Figure 22-1. Participation rate for suggestion program.

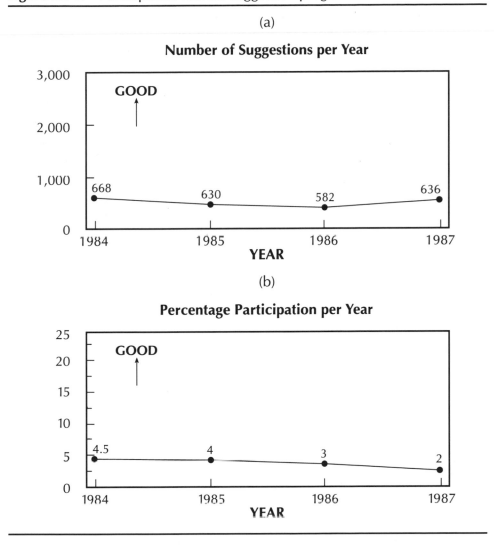

(a)

Number of Suggestions per Year

(b)

Percentage Participation per Year

3. Employee awareness of the program needed to be strengthened.
4. Quick feedback on suggestions was necessary.

Based on the employee survey, information received from other successful programs, and team input, the Bright Ideas task team made the following recommendations:

1. Train employees in the process.
2. Increase program visibility and promote the program quarterly.
3. Focus on participation and results.

Figure 22-2. Comparison of results: employee suggestion programs.

COMPARISON TO OTHER COMPANIES – 1987				
COMPANY	FPL	U.S. ELECTRIC COMPANY	U.S. MANUFACTURING COMPANY	JAPANESE ELECTRIC COMPANY
EMPLOYEES	15,000	30,000	2,300	25,000
SUGGESTIONS RECEIVED/YEAR	600	11,500	5,600	51,000
PARTICIPATION RATE	2% ALL EMPLOYEES	23% ALL EMPLOYEES	95% HOURLY EMPLOYEES	80% HOURLY EMPLOYEES
ADOPTION RATE	12%	39%	48%	36%
AVERAGE TIME TO PROCESS (DAYS)	144	60	62	20–60

4. Decentralize evaluation and tracking.
5. Include the supervisor in the award and recognition process.
6. Give awards only after implementation.
7. Provide merchandise for recognition and awards.
8. Establish a target of no more than 48 days to complete processing.

The decentralization would have employees submit ideas directly to their supervisor for evaluation, the supervisor would give the award to the employee, and local coordinators would track suggestions.

During their study of Japanese programs, FPL's task team members also considered the Japanese *kaizen* philosophy, which involves everyone and focuses on incremental improvements within each individual's work area. The results of this philosophy are on-the-spot improvements in morale and self-development.

The Bright Ideas System

The Bright Ideas suggestion system began as a pilot program in March of 1988, in five locations within the FPL system. To obtain a good cross-section of the company, a staff group, two district offices, employees at a fossil plant, and those at a nuclear plant were chosen to participate. For five months, these groups were monitored with selected individuals participating in a focus group to obtain feedback on the results. This feedback was reviewed by the task team and action was taken where appropriate.

The results of the pilot included demonstrating a commitment to the new program, generating participation, and heightening employee awareness.

Other comments from the pilot group provided FPL with the opportunity to hear what the participants wanted in their program. They noted that there was no process to track suggestions; the evaluation process was too complex; too much technical terminology was used; and too much emphasis was placed on tangible savings. The task team recommended the development of an on-line decentralized computer tracking system. The existing tracking system was centralized in the suggestion office and had very limited capabilities. As a result, the Bright Ideas Tracking System (BITS) was developed. BITS evolved from a basic system to a flexible user-friendly system that tracks suggestions, provides various audit and statistical reports, searches for suggestions by key words, and identifies tracking coordinators within the program. Initially, when an implemented suggestion was received, the points awarded on the evaluation form were entered in the system by the suggestion office. This feature would later be decentralized with only verification of award points made by the suggestion office prior to transmitting the data to FPL's merchandise vendor.

Revisions to the suggestion submittal and routing form and the suggestion point evaluation form are results of lessons learned by evaluators and suggestors. Forms were revised to make them simpler and to focus on effects and economic benefits.

The recognition and awards program for adopted suggestions is a point-based system connected to a merchandise catalog. Participants can accumulate points for a specific item in the catalog as an incentive to submit additional suggestions. Associated payroll taxes for the awards are paid by FPL.

Several enhancements to the awards program have been implemented based on participant feedback. One is the addition of a travel option from the awards vendor, and our most recent change was a gift certificate program that included several retail outlets and FPL's corporate travel consultants.

In August 1988, the Bright Ideas Suggestion System was introduced company-wide to an assembled network of Bright Ideas coordinators. These representatives from various FPL management units participated in Train the Trainers classes. They were given basic training in the employee suggestor process and additional training for the supervisor or evaluator. They returned to their business units and introduced the program to their employees. Coordinators were also responsible for tracking the suggestions and communicating policy guidelines to FPL's 15,000 employees.

The suggestion office has the responsibility for monitoring the progress of the program, developing corporate promotion campaigns, and communicating with employees through corporate publications. Each participant in the program is sent a small gift in appreciation for his or her submittal of a suggestion. Local promotions throughout the company are also supported by the suggestion office.

Initial Results of the Program

The goal of the program for the first year was to create awareness and employee involvement. The corporate goal of 12.5 percent participation was established, using one-half of the benchmarked company's 1987 actual participation rate of 23 percent. We met and exceeded that goal for 1988, and established a more aggressive goal for 1989 of 30 percent participation. The results for 1989 were phenomenal. By June, the corporate goal had been revised to 50 percent and year-end results were 52 percent participation and more than 25,000 suggestions.

This success, however, did not come without problems and lessons learned. We discovered that there was a need to develop a more comprehensive training program and tracking system. In late 1989, resources were acquired to develop training materials and revise the suggestion submittal and evaluation forms. A more comprehensive training program was introduced in April 1990, again using the Train the Trainer concept. Training materials included a simplified employee user guide, revised forms, a tracking system user guide, and a fifteen-minute videotape depicting the evolution of two actual suggestions from the many thousands that had been received.

The objective of this training was to improve, through development and education, the quality of suggestions being submitted. Quality would be measured by the adoption rate, and in 1989 the average adoption rate was 57 percent. The employee user guide included guidelines for implementation to be used by the suggestor and the evaluator.

Guidelines are designed to ensure that a suggestion:

- Benefits an internal or external customer
- Falls outside of any previously assigned task
- Is within FPL's control
- Does not duplicate a suggestion in progress
- Is not already being considered by management for action
- Does not impact on the type or level of employee benefits, collective bargaining negotiations, or agreements

- Is not a routine item, such as correcting spelling mistakes in procedures or maintenance repairs
- Does not diminish the existing quality or safety of products or services
- Has a complete reason for improvement
- Has a workable solution for improvement

The success of this training became evident as the implementation rate began to increase and an average of 69 percent was realized by year-

Figure 22-3. National implementation rate.

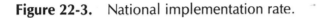

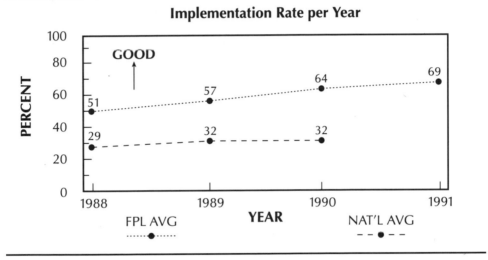

Source: National Association of Suggestion Systems.

Figure 22-4. Results of Bright Ideas system.

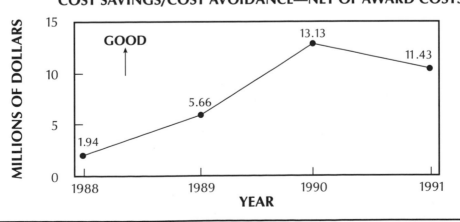

Figure 22-5.   Participation in company suggestion program.

(a)

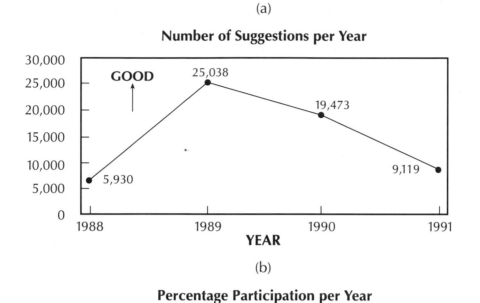

(b)

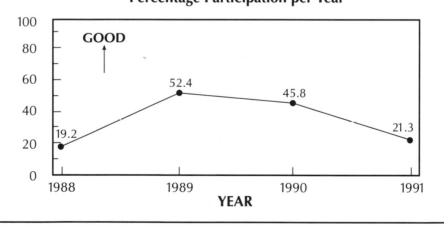

end 1991. Implementation rates continue to remain high and are well above the national average, as shown in Figure 22-3.

Effects and Economic Benefits

The Bright Ideas system has now reached the mature stage, where we are seeing the economic benefits of leveraging employee suggestions. As shown in Figure 22-4, the Bright Ideas system has achieved significant economic results for FPL. Although the number of suggestions and the employee participation level reached its peak in the year we won the Deming Prize (1989), and has since declined, we are now seeing the benefits of a mature program: a high implementation rate with high cost savings. The declines in the number of suggestions and the level of employee participation were not unexpected. During 1989, we had an intense employee suggestion promotion campaign leading up to the examination for the Deming Prize. Our employees were searching for and submitting suggestions for the smallest improvement idea, most of which are now implemented (see Figure 22-5).

As training and education of employees continues to focus on the development of quality ideas, the benefits to FPL will continue to increase. In 1992, the focus of the Bright Ideas system was to look for better, faster, more cost-effective ways to streamline work processes through innovation and creativity.

As competition grows in the electric utility industry, the Bright Ideas system will become more important in order for FPL to provide cost-effective products and services, continuous improvement, and greater customer satisfaction.

PART VI

IMPLEMENTING SERVICE QUALITY

23

Building Power Into Quality Education

Nancy J. Burzon, GTE Corporation

Quality education has played a major role in every documented study of a successful quality-improvement effort. It is also probable that quality education has played a major role in the quality-improvement efforts of companies that have failed to reach the levels of performance they targeted. What marks the difference between optimal and suboptimal results? How can you ensure that the quality education you provide employees will have a positive impact on the company's results?

This chapter outlines content elements for high-impact quality education that are appropriate at the frontline, management, and executive levels of an organization. It also provides an example of how these elements have been applied in practice. Finally, it concludes by identifying five critical success factors in implementing quality education.

The Top of the Inverted Pyramid

The discipline of quality in service owes much to Jan Carlzon, president and CEO of Scandinavian Airlines (SAS), for the concept of the inverted heart or pyramid organizational structure, which he described in his 1987 book *Moments of Truth*. That concept visually describes the importance of customers, and the frontline employees who serve them directly, to the ultimate success of a business enterprise. Visually turning the organization upside down and aligning corporate resources to the new priorities was radical thinking at the time. Using this new structural paradigm (see Figure 23-1), Jan Carlzon recreated SAS into an airline with value-added travel services targeted to business travelers who were served by empowered frontline employees.

This service quality strategy created unique value for particular customers who make buying decisions based on scheduling frequency, convenience, and comfort, not price alone. Carlzon was able to turn around a money-losing company and create a competitive advantage

Figure 23-1. Inverted organizational pyramid.

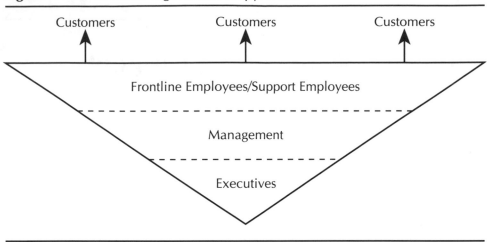

that led to world-class quality and industry-leading profitability in the mid-1980s.

While many executives have conceived brilliant competitive strategies, few are able to implement them with the degree of success achieved by Jan Carlzon. Though there are always many interdependent factors contributing to success, the key ingredient in Carlzon's formula was the shared focus and commitment of his employees who understood the concept. With the application of knowledge, skill, and effective work processes, they translated the strategy into a personal level of accountability, making customer satisfaction a reality.

The ultimate aim of quality education is to provide employees with an understanding of management's business and market goals, familiarity with the strategies designed to achieve those goals, and the knowledge and skills to implement these strategies successfully. In designing a high-impact approach to quality education, your starting point is an understanding of what knowledge and skills frontline employees need in order to serve your customers' interests in relation to the products or services you offer. You want to create a culture and work climate for employees that is in harmony with what you offer to the marketplace. Employees at all levels who support the company's front line are a part of that culture. If they are somehow excluded, or develop a culture that is at variance with the front line, their effectiveness in supporting the front line is diminished.

Case studies that document successful quality-improvement initiatives always stress the need for commitment at the top, which refers to the traditional pyramid structure of an organization. Quality education, to have an impact, needs to begin with a committed senior management team. However, I see senior management at the bottom of the pyramid, as in Jan Carlzon's model. Furthermore, to be powerful and to have high impact, the quality education effort must be designed to serve the needs of the customer. Before starting, you must determine what information, knowledge, skill, and tool combination is required to support the quality requirements of customers at every level and step of the value-added chain that delivers products and services to the customer.

Implications of this concept are numerous. First, appropriate quality education varies with the organization and with job classifications within the organization. Forcing a uniform training program on all employees, regardless of position, does not make sense. However, there are some components of the training that must be the same for all employees to ensure that they seek common goals and have a common basis for communication. Executives have the responsibility for defining those goals, so their training must come first.

Quality Education for Executives

When the Malcolm Baldrige National Quality Award (the Award) criteria were developed in 1988, they delineated broad responsibilities for senior management teams who aspired to world-class quality standards in their organizations. Those responsibilities have continued to evolve and are described in the 1992 Core Values and Concepts of the Award, as follows:

Customer-Driven Quality

Quality is judged by the customer. All product and service attributes that contribute value to the customer and lead to customer satisfaction and preference must be addressed appropriately in quality systems. . . . Customer-driven quality is thus a strategic concept. It is directed toward market share gain and customer retention. It demands constant sensitivity to emerging customer and market requirements, and measurement of the factors that drive customer satisfaction. . . .

Leadership

A company's senior leaders must create clear and visible quality values and high expectations. Reinforcement of the values and expectations requires their substantial personal commitment and involvement. The leaders must take part in the creation of strategies, systems, and methods for achieving excellence. The systems and methods need to guide all activities and decisions of the company and encourage participation and creativity by all employees. Through their regular personal involvement in visible activities, such as planning, review of company quality performance, and recognizing employees for quality achievement, the senior leaders serve as role models reinforcing the values and encouraging leadership in all levels of management.

Continuous Improvement

Achieving the highest levels of quality and competitiveness requires a well-defined and well-executed approach to continuous improvement. Such improvement needs to be part of all operations and of all work unit activities of a company. . . .

Long-Range Outlook

Achieving quality and market leadership requires a future orientation and long-term commitments to customers, employees, stockholders, and suppliers. Strategies, plans, and resource allocations need to reflect these commitments and address training, employee development, supplier development, technology evolution, and other factors that bear upon quality. . . .

Management by Fact

Meeting quality and performance goals of the company requires that process management be based upon reliable information, data, and analysis. . . .

Partnership Development

Companies should seek to build internal and external partnerships, serving mutual and larger community interests. . . .

Public Responsibility

A company's requirements and quality system objectives should address areas of corporate citizenship and responsibility. These include business ethics, public health and safety, environment, and sharing of quality-related information in the company's business and geographic communities. . . .

If a company's quality system is to address these responsibilities and others outlined in the Award criteria, the quality education provided at the senior management or executive level needs to be strategic in nature and broad in scope. It should facilitate and have as an output the development of a long-term, comprehensive quality management plan for the organization that can be shared with all employees. The quality management plan should communicate such elements as:

- Company vision
- Management values
- Business objectives
- Market and quality strategies
- Employee standards of performance
- Rewards for excellent performance
- Support resources available to employees

If this step is fulfilled, senior management will have accomplished one of its primary responsibilities: providing a clear sense of direction to guide the work efforts of all employees.

The second responsibility of senior management is to ensure that the work processes that deliver products and services to customers make sense and do not erect barriers for employees in fulfilling their responsibilities to customers. The responsibility for process management and continuous improvement is also prescribed in the Award values concerning design quality, prevention, and fast response.

Understanding the philosophy and methodology of process management is a critical skill required by senior management. While this management strategy is founded on engineering principles, it has only recently found its way into general management curricula and therefore may not reside in the skill set of many senior managers.

A third, and perhaps most difficult, responsibility of senior management in effecting a culture change is to act as role models for behaviors appropriate in the new culture. Defining those new behaviors is another component of quality education at this level of management. This is a soft side of management that is not as easy to teach or learn. In order to be effective, it first requires an acknowledgment of management practices and beliefs that are operational in the current environment and which are not in harmony with the desired environment. Next, it requires a definition of new performance expectations. Last, it demands a change in behavior and, ultimately, a belief that is visible to others and can serve to change the behavior of others. The ultimate success of a quality management plan is how well management has been able to gain the attention, support, and commitment of employees throughout the organization. Assuming that a commitment to quality management is a change of direction, at least to some degree, from the past, employees will watch senior management's behavior for their direction far more than they will listen to their words!

Quality Education for Management Employees

Middle management has a key role to play in a major change effort, such as quality. First, middle managers must translate the broad vision and objectives for the overall organization into an actionable vision for their part of the organization. They need to be able to describe how their function contributes to and supports the overall vision. Further, they need to understand and describe how failure to meet their functional objectives will affect the overall success of the organization. To accomplish this, they need to have a broader understanding of the business. They need to think of the organization as a system of interrelated components that must work together smoothly and easily to meet the requirements of the end customer. They must understand how the business works, much like an auto mechanic must understand how the total automobile works in order to maintain an optimal level of performance. Without this broad understanding, it becomes easy to say "Quality—it's not my job!" and believe that it's true.

Second, they will be responsible for developing shorter-term (one to two years), tactical work plans for reaching the broader long-term objectives. This builds upon the need for overall knowledge of the business, but adds to that a requirement to work together across functions or departments to develop interim performance objectives that are internally integrated and aligned. For the organization to move toward its vision, the tactical plans must be viewed in terms of the priorities for resource allocation and the sequencing of plans. (Some things cannot be initiated until other plans are completed, while other plans can proceed in parallel.)

Third, managers are responsible for communicating their functions' responsibilities to the employees who will accomplish the work and interact with customers. They, too, are role models, but employees view them in a way different from executives. Employees have come to view executives in a more formal, ritualistic role. In large, geographically dispersed organizations, the opportunities to see senior managers are typically scheduled well in advance, and are highly planned and orchestrated events. Senior managers may elect to take an action that is highly visible and make a decision that is in marked contrast to one which would have been made in the past, in order to dramatically demonstrate the new order. In contrast, exposure to middle managers needs to be much more frequent and routine. The behavior of middle managers becomes the reality check for what is really important.

Middle managers can therefore be a make-or-break group in an organization's culture change effort. In a series of interviews conducted in 1991 with GTE senior executives about the effectiveness of their quality-improvement initiatives over the previous five-year period, many cited middle managers as barriers to effective quality management systems. As the interviewer discussed with the senior managers the specific actions they had taken to improve quality in their organization, it became clear that the special needs of middle managers had not been fully considered when designing the original training effort. The focus had been on senior managers, who had to formulate new directions for their organization in order to sustain competitive advantage, and frontline employees, who had to do the work in a new way and satisfy new customer requirements. With perfect hindsight, we saw that we had failed to take into account that middle managers had to perform in a new way as well, and might not have the skills and knowledge to perform these new tasks.

When planning quality education for middle managers, what should be the content? In consideration of the role played by middle managers, the following components should form the basic common requirements of a training approach:

1. Knowledge of the organization's strategic business plan. Special emphasis should be placed on the marketing, quality, and technology strategies that support the plan. This group of employees needs to know the competitive challenges and the risks to the plan in order to take appropriate actions.
2. Skill in process management techniques for continuous improvement of major work processes that they "touch" in their daily work. They should be actively involved as team members on standing process management and improvement efforts that impact their function.
3. Familiarity with the key system technologies in their business and industry, and an understanding of how those technologies are likely to evolve in the future.
4. Skill in utilizing fact-based problem-solving methodologies. A consistent way of communicating problems and the analytical approach taken to resolve them with others in the organization who are affected by the outcome is essential.
5. Effective team leadership skills.
6. Skill in coaching employees and providing timely and specific feedback on performance.

Differences in quality education are due to the level of proficiency needed in the productivity-enhancing technologies for their business function and maintaining up-to-date skills and knowledge unique to the functional position. Many would argue that these are not quality education programs, and in the traditional view of quality education, that is true. However, you cannot achieve quality results when employees have not yet completed the basic training needed to do the job they are occupying. I have observed specific instances of employees working with obsolete training manuals and other situations where we have asked employees to dramatically improve their productivity with tools that do not have the potential to deliver what is needed. To try to implement traditional quality training within a work environment marked by significant hurdles to implementation is counterproductive. Quality education must be viewed in an integrated way with the rest of the job knowledge and skills required to do a specific job.

Quality Education for Frontline Employees

Frontline employees are those who do the work of the organization: They fulfill the vision of the organization as it relates to the marketplace. This group includes all those employees who directly serve the customer; those employees who design, make, and deliver the products and/or services offered; and those employees who provide support services to their colleagues who directly interact with the external customer. As noted, not all of these employees interact directly with the external customer, but they do have an impact on the customer's perception of the quality of the products or services of the organization.

As a result of the highly visible role that they play, frontline employees have tended to be the focal point of quality-improvement initiatives over the years. There is an increasing body of evidence that suggests excellent frontline employees can in fact compensate for poor quality in the internal processes and systems of an organization. They can mask many of the problems through superior handling of the customer interaction. However, this does not create a sustainable competitive advantage. Over time, the high costs of poor quality will negatively impact on the organization's profitability.

At a very basic level, what we as managers expect of frontline employees is that they represent or be the embodiment of the values of the organization. With the role of quality increasingly being one of a competitive table stake rather than a competitive advantage, there is a real need for a clear understanding of what constitutes quality relative to the products and services offered. The knowledge and skills required by frontline employees vary with the job classification, but within that framework, there are some common elements:

1. *Strategic alignment*. The unique strategies for customer satisfaction that have been selected for the organization need to be well understood by those employees primarily serving the customer. Additionally, the

employees need to understand how their area of responsibility fits into the broader picture of the organization.

2. *Clarity on management's expectations for performance.* Specific, measurable standards of performance should be in place for frontline employees. Whenever possible, these standards should be included in a performance tracking system that can be monitored by the performer so that corrective action can be taken at the performer level.

3. *Customer requirements relative to the employee's role in product or service development and delivery.* Depending on their particular task in the value-added chain, employees may be part of either needs assessment (sales personnel) or needs satisfaction (product or service design). They must be thoroughly versed in the advantages their product or service provides to the user and how it compares to competitive alternatives. This information helps employees position the product or service appropriately and also alerts them to deviations from the intended design, which could potentially lead to competitive disadvantage.

4. *Proficiency with productivity-enhancing technologies.* We have said earlier that it is management's responsibility to ensure that employees have the best tools for their trade. In addition, employees must be proficient at operating the support systems.

5. *Proficiency with job skills.* Employees need to be up-to-date with current products and services, current procedures, and internal processes that affect their task of serving the customer. In the rapidly changing environment of the past decade, this has been and will continue to be a challenge.

6. *Communication skills.* Excellent listening and communication skills are essential to interact effectively with customers and other employees. This skill development is a major component of quality education for frontline employees.

7. *Problem-solving skills.* The responsibilities of frontline employees frequently involve problem-solving. After all, if everything were perfect, many of the opportunities to contact a customer would not exist. Employees should understand the limits or constraints on their authority to satisfy a customer. Within those boundaries, employees should be empowered to take appropriate action. They should also recognize the difference between individual situations and systemic problems. Systemic problems require a different approach to problem-solving and a different set of constraints.

The common elements of the quality education curriculum are summarized in Figure 23-2.

Figure 23-2. Common curricula and results for quality education.

	Elements	Expected Outputs
Executives:	• Strategic quality management • Process management • Human performance management • Leadership/role-model behavior	• Organization-wide quality management plan • Commitment of necessary resources • Well-designed work processes • Role model behavior
Managers:	• Quality management plan • Process management techniques • Understanding key system technologies • Fact-based problem-solving methodologies • Team leadership skills • Coaching, counseling skills	• Translate, integrate, demonstrate the new requirements of the quality plan • Well-managed work processes • Role model behavior • Continuous improvement
Frontline Employees:	• Strategic alignment • Individual performance standards • Customer requirements relative to performer's task • Skills at operating support systems • Skills at performing job tasks • Skills at fact-based problem solving • Skills at communication	• Implement the quality plan to deliver results • Continuous improvement of work process • Customer satisfaction • Employee satisfaction

Case Study: GTE Automotive and Miniature Lighting*

Automotive and Miniature Lighting, located in Hillsboro, New Hampshire, is a division of the global GTE Electrical Products Group, which is headquartered in Danvers, Massachusetts. The division manufactures incandescent and halogen miniature lighting products, components, and assemblies. It is a leader in the highly competitive global automotive lighting market as well as a number of highly specialized lighting markets. Domestic OEM (original equipment manufacturer) customers

*Developed for a GTE Quality Case Study in 1992, for internal training purposes.

include General Motors, Ford Motor Company, and Chrysler Corporation. The international OEM market consists of Japanese- and Korean-owned automotive manufacturing facilities in North America; international auto OEMs exporting vehicles to North America and producing for local markets; and internationally owned automotive lighting companies in North America, Japan, Korea, and Europe. Competitors for this business include General Electric, Wagner, Osram, Philips, Ford Plastic Parts and Trim Division, Inland Fisher Guide, North American Lighting, and Stanley. The division employs over 1,500 people at its two plants.

Total Quality Demands in the Automotive Industry

Involvement in the automotive industry has set the tone for quality at GTE Automotive and Miniature Lighting. Quality emphasis and competition from Japan are passed on directly to the division as a supplier to the automotive industry. Not only do customer requirements for responsiveness and product specifications set the pace for change, but customers are very visible in the plant and interact with employees.

Quality Manager Don Fuller stresses that the number of customer surveys is "beyond numerous. Customers visit our factories to confirm that we are doing what we say we are doing. Almost on a monthly basis, teams will spend two to five days going over our systems to make sure they meet their expectations." Fuller elaborates on the division's philosophy, "Never let a customer walk for any reason. It doesn't matter if it appears unreasonable. A customer is a customer. We don't differentiate. The customers are not just king, they are God."

Planning and Implementation

The Total Quality Council (TQC), formed in 1988, is responsible for the majority of the total quality planning. It consists of the general manager and staff—the directors of Human Resources, Engineering, Marketing and Sales, the operations controller, and two plant managers. The TQC has monthly day-long meetings to review quality performance, identify areas that require attention, and sustain the continuous quality-planning process. The Council's first action was to articulate a quality definition and requirements so that they could be communicated to all employees. They defined the following mission:

> Sustain a leadership role in the automotive and miniature lighting industries by providing the highest quality light sources and lighting systems at competitive prices.

Supporting this mission were five overall objectives:

1. Pursue leadership in quality, cost, and technology.
2. Grow market share.
3. Provide profits for continued investment and stockholder return.
4. Provide a safe, professional work environment for employees.
5. Be a good corporate citizen.

The strategy to implement the total quality concept throughout the organization has three main components:

▴ Apply project-by-project concept of continuous improvement to all functions and processes.
▴ Maintain a corporate culture in which all employees recognize internal and external customers and continually improve the way they do their jobs to better satisfy customer needs.
▴ Eliminate reasons for any customer to buy from our competitors.

Long-term (five-year) quality goals were quantified and integrated into the strategic plan and operational plans for each year of the planning horizon. The actions taken by the TQC to gain organizational commitment included communications, training, and role-modeling management's commitment.

▴ *Communications.* A Total Quality Card was distributed to all employees in early 1990. It summarized the mission, objectives, strategies, and long-term goals in a format that could be carried easily as a constant reminder. Additionally, quality is a key topic at plant-wide meetings held monthly by the plant manager, the plant newspaper features total quality articles, and bulletin boards are found in every department displaying relevant performance measures and status of progress.

▴ *Training.* In 1988, the senior management team attended a course entitled "Quality: The Competitive Edge," which focused on quality strategy development at the business-unit level and on gaining organization-wide commitment to the implementation of the quality strategy. This course served as a catalyst for much of the quality planning at this division. In 1989, management decided to create what it considers a world-class training program to address the specific training needs of all employees within the organization.

Human Resources Manager Doug Allen believes that the internal training commitment was extremely important. He described the development process:

The staff sat down with all of our management personnel and we asked, "What do you need to do your job better? What do you need to help the organization make progress toward these types of goals? What type of information do you need, what type of guidance?" And they gave us a lot of feedback. From that feedback we developed approximately thirty two-hour total quality training modules that covered a wide range of topics. We put together a training course that represented approximately sixty hours of training and then we taught all of it in 1990 [see Figure 23-3]. Our philosophy is that if we want to get across a point and get acceptance, we'd better be the ones saying it and we'd better be the ones acting it and doing it. And it was valuable for us to go through that process as well. The general manager and his staff demonstrated their commitment to quality to direct reports by preparing training programs on their own time. They had to learn before they could teach. The effort on their part was absolutely critical. They did not delegate as others had in the past.

Figure 23-3. GTE quality training program.

**GTE Automotive and Miniature Lighting
Total Quality Managerial Training Modules**

Quality leadership	Who are your customers?
Quality gurus (Deming, Juran, Crosby)	Supplier quality
Kaizen	How to be a good customer
Change leadership	Project by project management
Process management	Killer gap projects
Department head values	Closing killer gaps
Quality communication	Selling the solution
Listening skills	Taking 100% responsibility
Human performance management	Systematic problem solving
Management styles	Making SPC work for you
Teamwork	Spare parts & preventive maintenance
Conflict resolution	Lessons learned
Confrontation skills	Safety—our first concern
Confrontation skills II	Coaching and motivation
Conducting performance appraisals	

Total Quality Frontline Employee Modules

What is total quality?	Process management
Taking 100% responsibility	Who is your customer?
Teamwork	Systematic problem solving

Following the managerial training, the participants were asked to identify what modules should be taken to all frontline employees. They selected five modules for total rollout.

Quality education is viewed as an ongoing process. The 1991 training effort focused on increasing job and skill flexibility among employees. There are currently fifty-three job classifications of which thirty-nine are active. The goal is to consolidate skills and reduce the number of job classifications to ten.

Management Commitment and Employee Involvement

The size of the facility and the work force at Automotive Miniature Lighting permits management to be a visible force on a daily basis. Management has, over the years, learned to use this accessibility to advantage with the employees. The change began in the early 1980s, when a new general manager was appointed. The new manager came out of a financial discipline, and the local reaction at the time was that he was going to ruin everything. As Plant Manager Rick Dolan relates,

> He was a real surprise. Because of his lack of technical knowledge, he was inquisitive and asked lots of questions. He really liked his job. He forced the issue of customer satisfaction. He never asked about financial variances at the end of the month. He was relentless on satisfying the customer. I think he discovered it by listening. For the first time, a manager did not come into a job with a lot of preconceived ideas. He was really involved with our wellness program. He became a runner and participated in various activities. It became another medium for contact with employees. He was really visible on the shop floor.

This accessibility is not limited to the GM—it pervades the Hillsboro environment. Demonstrating what is expected of employees is exhibited in such diverse ways as attention to housekeeping details, safety, use of personal names when addressing employees, and attention and concern for employees' personal lives. Doug Allen explained that the division's goal to provide a safe, professional work environment for employees "goes beyond a clean environment in which they are not going to get hurt to one in which they can grow."

As is the trend in manufacturing, quality as defined by the customer has expanded beyond product conformance to specification and product reliability to encompass service dimensions like meeting customer needs and partnering for the future. Employees are expected to be involved in the operation. Employees have been trained in teamwork—what it means and how to be a team member. Some employees receive training to be team leaders and/or facilitators. Teams are cross-functional, utilizing skills and knowledge at varying levels of experience from different areas of the plant. Employees are involved with vendors and with customers. Employees are afforded the opportunity to visit customer locations and to participate in meetings dealing with quality issues and opportunities.

Conclusion

What are the elements of a quality education program that mark the difference between optimal and suboptimal performance? Five lessons were learned from our implementation experience at GTE, and these are keys to building power into quality education.

First, make certain that quality education is expressly linked to the accomplishment of high-priority business objectives. When employees are working on important issues and making a contribution to business success, they apply themselves to learning new methods and skills that can help them accomplish their objectives. The learning process becomes a facilitator for results rather than extra work.

Second, consider quality education in its broadest context. It is counterproductive to whip up enthusiasm for quality when employees lack the necessary tools, training, and other resources to do the level of work expected. World-class companies ensure that the total work environment is supportive of excellence.

Third, the personal commitment and involvement of management cannot be overemphasized. The single most powerful ingredient of GTE's quality education was the willingness and commitment of executives at the business-unit level to teach business strategy and quality management methods to their employees. This gave them an opportunity to exert visible leadership for quality in a very different setting from the daily work environment. Further, it set a high expectation for results.

Fourth, the desired behaviors developed through training need to be reinforced on the job in a variety of ways before they become skills practiced on a daily basis. Reinforcement is secured when the recognition, reward, and performance appraisal systems are aligned; the communications channels continuously emphasize quality and highlight success stories; and the compensation system balances the achievement of quality results with financial results and other key objectives.

Finally, it is important to design the training, and continuously measure the effectiveness of the training, in terms of its impact on customers. The fundamental purpose of education and training is to enable employees to serve customers better.

References

Carlzon, Jan. *Moments of Truth*. Cambridge, Mass.: Ballinger, 1987.
"1992 Award Criteria," Malcolm Baldrige National Quality Award, pp. 2–3.

24

Achieving Personal Quality

Norma M. Rossi, Metropolitan Life Insurance Company

Metropolitan Life Insurance Company (MetLife) is a large, complex company offering insurance and other financial services to a wide spectrum of customers. This chapter tells MetLife's story in its journey toward service excellence, focusing particularly on one program devoted to the service excellence of individual employees.

Elements in MetLife's Quality Journey

MetLife started its formal total quality effort in 1984. We researched what some of the top companies were doing, talked to quality experts, and arrived at certain conclusions.

First, you have to understand and fulfill customer expectations. You must engage in customer dialogue, using surveys, focus groups, and other proactive techniques to find out what your customers want. Next, you need the involvement and commitment of all levels of management so that managers and supervisors use the results of customer dialogue to guide their decision making. They must support their commitment to quality not merely with their words but also with their deeds, by modeling, rewarding, and nurturing the appropriate behavior.

Another important aspect is problem solving by multifunctional work groups. This is particularly important if you have the traditional type of organization that tends to be bureaucratic, with poor communication between units. In such an organization, the view tends to be by internal function, defined by a series of units and subunits, rather than from the customer's perspective. Each unit sets its own standards, which may appear reasonable at first glance, but the sum total of their efforts may not meet customer expectations. So, particularly at the beginning of a search for service excellence, you need multifunctional work groups that look at transactions from the *customer's* point of view, not the organization's.

Finally, there is the aspect of focusing on the continuous improvement of your systems and procedures—what we at MetLife call "raising the bar." If you are already meeting your current standards and doing it consistently, change the standards. Make them more challenging so you can reach increasing levels of effectiveness.

It is also important to remember that all the factors mentioned here—management commitment, problem solving by cross-functional teams, focus on continuous improvement—must point you back to that first element, which is understanding and fulfilling customer expectations. Otherwise, you can still have dissatisfied customers because your organization's efforts are not focusing on those elements of your service that are most important to them.

Quality improvement is a process just like any other in a company, and ought to be subjected to the same standard of continuous improvement. Since 1984, we have continued to seek out new knowledge and to use it to enhance our process, and to introduce new tools and techniques into the way we manage and work at MetLife.

One of these tools is the subject of this chapter. It focuses on the *personal* aspect of service quality—that is, the role of the individual in delivering quality service to customers.

The Achieving Personal Quality Program

An important event in the development of MetLife's quality improvement process occurred in 1985, when we discovered the service quality research conducted by Leonard Berry, Parsu Parasuraman, and Valarie Zeithaml.[1] This research has been underway since 1983, and the results of the first three research phases are presented in their book *Delivering Quality Service*. The book contains an in-depth description of the characteristics of services; how they differ from products; how customers evaluate services; how you can measure quality from the customer's point of view; and some of the actions managers can take to improve service quality.

MetLife's Achieving Personal Quality program is derived from their concepts and gets to the heart of what makes services unique—the characteristics that also make quality of services a difficult matter to ensure.

The inherent nature of services presents special challenges to organizations that wish to measure and then improve the quality of their services. And just how, exactly, do customers judge quality in the service sector? The research revealed that customers evaluate a service by comparing their expectations to their perceptions of actual performance. Customers have expectations about two aspects of the service: process and outcome.

Process is how you treat the customer; *outcome* is the actual end result—what you deliver to the customer. For some types of services, process can be not just as important but even more important than outcome. This is especially true for those services whose outcome cannot be judged by the customer until significant time has passed.

These insights into the nature of service quality led us to the conclusion that to win market acceptability as compared to our competitors, we had to first concentrate on the outcome aspects of service. This is another way of saying that the core of service quality is an organization's ability to keep its promises, to be reliable, and to provide service to customers that they judge to be timely and accurate.

However, organizations that seek to exceed their customers' expectations in order to enhance their quality image should take advantage of the best opportunity for doing so: during service delivery. It is during delivery that customers directly experience the service skills of an organization's employees. It is during delivery that organizations are best able to enhance the service core of reliability in ways that will distinguish them as high-quality providers of service.

Put directly, how you treat the customer (the process aspect of service quality) is what distinguishes you from your competitor. It has to do with an organization's willingness to respond to customers, the ability to treat them as a name as opposed to a number, and the ability to create trust and confidence in the relationship with customers. None of these abilities is possible without the commitment and skills of individual service providers.

It was this conclusion that led MetLife to develop a program aimed at the personal aspects of quality customer service, the Achieving Personal Quality program. We wanted more than just "smile" training, the typical courtesy training given to customer contact employees. Our starting point was our own research with both internal and external customers. Using focus groups we asked customers to describe critical incidents of good service and bad service. We were looking for universal "wish lists" for a service interaction, irrespective of the type of service being provided. Out of the many stories recorded, we identified a finite number of behaviors and grouped them into categories that we call the six attributes of personal quality:

1. *Treat customers as you like to be treated when you are a customer.* This category or attribute recognizes that we are not islands unto ourselves. Rather, we all benefit from each other's progress. It recognizes a fundamental law of human nature: that others treat us as we treat them. There is a natural tendency to reciprocate. If we treat others in a careless, condescending, or cruel manner, we are likely to get the same treatment in return. If we treat others in a courteous way, we increase the chances of getting the same behavior in return.

Some specific behaviors underlying this attribute are:

- Asking customers and co-workers how to be helpful to them without being asked.
- Listening to the concerns of others, offering support, and with-holding criticism.
- Sharing credit for success.

2. *Take personal responsibility to see that customers' needs are met.* Some of the behaviors in this category include:

- Setting clear goals and objectives when addressing job tasks.
- Seeing that action is taken by someone to solve a problem, instead of saying "that's not my job."
- Following through on commitments, which builds trust.

People who lack this attribute tend to focus on what others should do or how they have been handicapped, overlooked, underrated, unap-preciated, and held back. Because they see themselves as victims, they are less action-oriented. They wait for the lucky break or expect someone else to take care of their problems—but their wait is likely to be in vain.

3. *Constantly seek to improve by learning as much as possible about the job to improve service to customers.* Excellent service providers are always reading, learning, asking questions, looking for a way to improve them-selves, their team, their company. They know that they will never get to the end of their journey, and they plan to enjoy every step along the way.

Specific behaviors in this category are:

- Asking for and being open to feedback and suggestions from customers and co-workers.
- Not being afraid to admit not knowing how to do something or being embarrassed to seek help.
- Reading constantly to expand job knowledge.

4. *Share knowledge, skills, and time with others, offering help and assis-tance to customers and co-workers.* People who exhibit this attribute are good team players. The most valuable team members recognize that part of their job is to help others succeed. Sharing with others increases everyone's ability to contribute. Individuals who are willing to share can help create a team.

Service providers exhibit these behaviors that underlie this attribute:

- Sharing information gathered and lessons learned.
- Recognizing the contributions of others.
- Treating co-workers as equals and genuine team members.
- Worrying less about who does the work or gets the credit, and more about satisfying customers.

5. *Have a positive outlook and be persistent in meeting customer expectations.* Why is it that some people have the ability to see the positive in the most adverse conditions? Perhaps it is because those who remain positive have a philosophy that helps them ride through the rough periods. Perhaps it is because they have confidence in their own ability to turn the tide on their current problems. One thing is for certain— everyone would rather work with someone who maintains a positive outlook.

Being persistent and having a positive outlook includes:

- Taking prompt action and not procrastinating.
- Rarely complaining; instead, attacking obstacles and accepting challenges as opportunities.
- Being enthusiastic about work and focusing on good outcomes.
- Finding new ways to approach a task.
- Working hard to solve customer problems.

6. *Communicate effectively in dealings with customers and fellow employees.* Individual service providers never serve customers entirely by themselves. Our customers are served best when we all communicate and deal effectively with each other. People who provide high-quality service are excellent at managing relationships. The core skills of managing these relationships are the skills of communication: speaking effectively, writing well, and listening carefully to what your customers are saying. This last skill—listening—is especially important since it is the one that is most often neglected.

Behaviors associated with this category include:

- Asking questions, especially open-ended ones that allow others to share openly.
- Making statements of concern and understanding for other people's point of view.
- Listening carefully and then rephrasing what other people have said to show true understanding.
- Speaking clearly, concisely, and using language that is easily understood by others.
- Avoiding jargon.

Using Self-Mastery to Change Behavior

There's nothing very surprising about the six attributes of personal quality. In fact, as we moved ahead into the development phase, we had no argument from anyone about their validity to personal experience. Their real power with MetLife people was based on the fact that this information was coming directly from our customers, not from on high or any other part of MetLife management.

The question then becomes: If we accept these six attributes as at the heart of customer service, why don't our customers always receive this kind of treatment? In other words, while it's easy to *identify* what customers want, it's not so easy to *do* what customers want.

Why? Because these attributes focus on human behaviors, and another word for human behavior is habit. It's much easier to fall into bad habits than it is to fall into good habits. So the first objective of the Achieving Personal Quality program was to make these attributes the model of the way to treat customers at MetLife. The second objective of the program was designing a training and communication program that would help employees develop good habits.

Developing good habits implies a personal process of change, one that affects the way an individual interacts with customers and co-workers. This process of change involves willingness and discipline—in other words, self-mastery. It means that a person must overcome ineffective ways of functioning and substitute good habits—good customer service behaviors.

Our training included a self-directed performance management process that can be used to improve or enhance behavior in the area of the six attributes. It can also be applied to any personal goals employees want to change. The process consists of a series of steps that lead to mastery of a new or changed behavior.

At the core of the performance management process is the idea of a positive vision—what it is that a person wants to be. This is then broken down into specific goals, pinpointing the behaviors that will lead to that positive vision. For example, a runner who dreams of completing a marathon race sets a goal based on greater endurance. One of the behaviors the runner pinpoints to increase endurance is correct pacing.

Identifying activators—things that get a person started and serve as cues to help fall into "good" habits—is the next step. A common example of an activator is the "To Do" list; personal models are another type of activator. The runner might identify marathon winners and study their techniques, for example.

The next step is to have a tracking system to know if a person is making progress—a way to evaluate results. The runner should keep an accurate count of how many miles were run each day, and write the results in a notebook, thus creating a simple tracking system that measures progress over time. When the tracking system shows success, a reward helps reinforce the changes taking place.

Finally, since this is a journey without end, a person must continually evaluate progress. As one goal is achieved, there must be a look forward to the next goal. After all, performance management is a cycle, and going through a cycle only once doesn't get you very far!

Elements of the Program

We wanted MetLife people to be able to apply the attributes of personal quality to various types of situations. At the same time, we recognized we were touching on some very personal issues. So we developed a series of videotapes to spread the personal quality message. The videos have three common elements. Each begins with a succession of external customers talking about a particular attribute and what it means to them. The series also includes service providers—some MetLife people—talking about what it means to practice this attribute.

The other major elements of each video include segments discussing self-mastery, and episodes featuring the Personal Time Players. The Personal Time Players are fictitious members of a customer service unit in an imaginary company. While they try their best to do a good job for their customers, they've adopted more bad habits than good. Over time, they start to apply the six attributes to their work. In this way, the episodes are the basis for discussions on how individuals can deliver better service to customers in a nonthreatening way.

Along with the videotapes there are a number of supporting materials, including an employee handbook that summarizes the material on performance management that appears on each tape; and a personal development journal that features written exercises to encourage people to work on their own, applying the attributes of personal quality to both work-related and nonwork-related objectives. During each video segment, employees are requested to concentrate on one attribute—how well the Personal Time Players practice it and how it can be applied in their own personal work environments at MetLife.

Finally, employees felt strongly that the best way to get the most benefit from the Achieving Personal Quality program was by participating in discussion groups. Thus, the program also provides a discussion leader's guide and trained employees to be discussion leaders. In this way, small groups of employees—ten or so—can meet with a discussion leader, look at the tapes, engage in some exercises, and discuss what the six attributes mean in terms of their own work situations.

Summary

In conclusion, MetLife's quality efforts have focused on both people and processes. In our efforts toward continuous improvement we have translated what we've learned from the latest service quality research. One of those efforts focuses attention on personal quality, the interactions with customers which are often called "moments of truth."

The critical role played by an individual service provider in a MetLife "moment of truth" was described in the video used to introduce the Achieving Personal Quality program to all employees.

> At some point today, for some customer somewhere, whether internal or external, YOU will be MetLife, and our entire reputation as a company will be in your individual hands. In that moment, you will make an impression. The impression will either be good or it will be bad, and you will speak more loudly than all our community involvement, all our advertising, and all our public relations put together.

In essence it's the process of service delivery that sets a service provider apart from its competition. By making our employees aware of how customers want to be treated, by improving their interactions with customers, by encouraging them to practice the personal quality attributes, MetLife believes that it can achieve and sustain a competitive advantage.

Notes

1. Valarie A. Zeithaml, A. Parasuraman, and Leonard L. Berry, *Delivering Quality Service: Balancing Customer Perceptions and Expectations* (New York: Free Press, 1990).

25

Partnership Teams

Robert S. Rider, in collaboration with the Employee Involvement and Communications Group at Corning Incorporated

It seems that every organization is jumping on the bandwagon of self-managed teams, high-performance work systems, and empowerment programs. Yet many fail. What are self-managed teams and what are their benefits? The objectives in this chapter are to understand self-managed teams and to analyze the key elements for progress in an organization as they relate to self-managed teams.

During the past twenty-five years with Corning, I have seen many changes, yet none has been as significant as the movement toward improved utilization of employee skills and competencies, and the empowerment of each person to implement positive change. My experiences have included both manufacturing management and involvement in high-performance work systems in administrative customer-service areas. The following information on self-managed teams was compiled by the Employee Involvement and Communications Group at Corning Incorporated, drawing on its extensive experience and progress during the past several years.

The Potential Benefits of Self-Managed Work Teams

Often there is confusion regarding what constitutes a self-managed team. The proper label must fit your organization and corporate culture, and therefore is usually best derived from the organization's actions, roles, and responsibilities.

Simply put, however, a self-managed team is a group of people who have complete responsibility for a product, service, or process. The team meets regularly; works effectively without supervision, and identifies, analyzes, and makes improvements. Team members are empowered to manage their own training to improve their skills, set their own work schedules, establish objectives and measures, communicate performance to management and peer groups, and give individual performance reviews.[1]

Self-managed teams can thrive in both manufacturing and staff or administrative areas. However, most organizations better understand linear processes like manufacturing (raw materials, added-value labor steps, quality evaluation, product delivery), and therefore self-managed teams usually appear first in this environment. But when an organization understands that administrative activities have some similar processes, then a self-managed team approach can succeed here also. Examples of administrative processes that create products and/or services are budgeting, order entry, contract pricing and negotiations, product development, equipment documentation, forecasting, scheduling, employee communications, and medical and pension benefits.

Once it becomes obvious that all work within an organization is a process or a group of processes, self-managed teams can be successful in improving quality, service, and productivity by focusing on nonvalue-added elements.

Unfortunately, though many organizations see the clear benefits to self-managed teams, they simply assign teams and expect improvement. When success comes, it is mostly a matter of luck. Without a total *partnership* environment, self-managed teams usually result in pain, not progress.

Instituting self-managed work teams involves organizational and cultural changes based upon a commitment to total quality and customer satisfaction. This type of organizational change means rethinking the ways people organize their work and the ways they work together. It means redesigning the organization to be more productive and more responsive to customer requirements. It also means listening to, involving, and empowering the people who do the work—the people who are closest to and know the most about the work. It means that all employees share in the success and financial prosperity of the business. These organizational and cultural changes must be built on a foundation of mutual trust and respect.[2]

Why all the stress today on self-managed teams? Many success stories show their significant benefits for both employees and the organization. But most important, the competitors are doing it, and if you don't, you will lose!

Common sense tells you that better utilization of the skills and experience of people who actually do the work will maximize the success of an organization. Management's role in most cases is to create this environment for employee teamwork and then get out of the way!

Partnership—A Process for Self-Managed Teams

To effect lasting, beneficial change in an organization, there must be a spirit of partnership among the employees, for the ultimate greater satisfaction of customer needs. Partnership was not designed to make employees happier, though job enrichment is a by-product. The goal of partnership is to deliver error-free products and services on time, and to meet customer requirements 100 percent of the time.[3]

Overall, partnership organizations are showing 25 to 50 percent gains in both quality measurements and productivity. Further, they are experiencing increased flexibility for change, a higher quality of work life for employees, and greater employment stability.

Partnership is the relationship and interaction between two or more groups in attaining a common goal through full utilization of talents, experiences, and available resources. Figure 25-1 shows a continuum outlining the levels of participation. Most successful organizations today are moving rapidly from the control end of the spectrum to the participative end.

There are six common characteristics of partnership:[4]

1. *Clear vision, goals, and overall business plan.* Everyone in an organization needs to understand where the company is headed and what the overall game plan is if they are to help make it happen.

2. *Shared information.* This includes all aspects of the business, including customers, suppliers, competitors; cost, prices, market conditions; and current efforts and future plans. The key is to build a common database in the organization so that everyone can make good decisions, work well with customers, and perform day-to-day work in an informed manner. This means sharing a great deal of information, at all levels in the organization, on an ongoing basis.

3. *Processes designed to fit systems and people resources.* One major step in the partnership process is often referred to as sociotechnical redesign. It involves having the people who do the work analyze and document the technical system (the steps they go through to produce their product

Figure 25-1. The partnership spectrum.

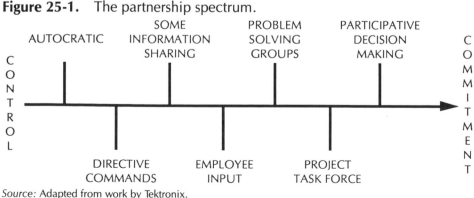

Source: Adapted from work by Tektronix.

or service), eliminate nonvalue steps, and determine a better way to do it. It also involves analyzing and documenting the social system (the way people work together to get the work done).

4. *Self-managed, customer-focused work groups*. People frequently equate partnership with teams. Self-managed teams are indeed one very important element. They are often an outgrowth of designing work processes to fully satisfy customer requirements. The basic idea is to bring the right people together to improve processes, make decisions, and improve results.

5. *Continuous improvement of people and processes*. A journey of growth and development, partnership requires ongoing focus, analysis, and training to support continuous individual, team, and organizational improvement.

6. *"Whole" organization approach*. Partnership is for all parts of the organization, not just manufacturing. It acknowledges that organizations are made up of systems, and these systems must support a common direction.

The Seven Steps in the Partnership Process

The following is a model for the partnership process using self-managed teams. Although in theory the steps appear to be sequential and static, in practice they are iterative and dynamic (see Figure 25-2). There is no single right way to reach partnership with self-managed teams, but the model represents what is the most common and successful approach, based on the experiences of a number of organizations.[5]

Step 1: Develop Strategy and Leadership

Top leadership assesses the business need for change; becomes educated on various approaches to change, including partnership; determines scope and actions for the change, which include determining the need for consulting resources; and establishes the overall strategy, which includes early involvement and support by union leadership, where appropriate. Key actions are to:

▴ Educate top leadership on partnership. Suggest readings, site visits, and key workshops. Also discuss pros and cons of this type of change effort.

▴ Tie partnership to business strategy by assessing business needs for partnership, determining how partnerships support business goals, and determining the tie to corporate partnership mission and goals.

Figure 25-2.   Seven steps of the partnership process.

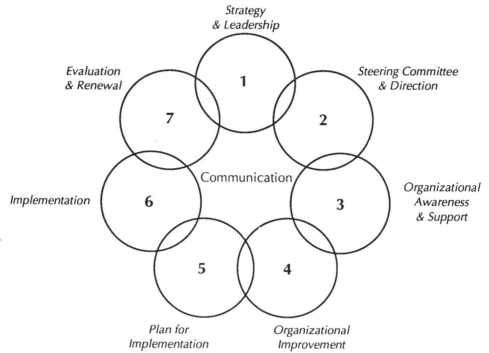

- Identify the major strengths of and barriers to achieving partnership.
- Establish a strategy for early involvement and support by union leadership.
- Define the initial scope and actions for change.
- Determine the need for consulting resources and internal support.
- Establish success and measurement criteria.
- Begin development of leadership to support the effort.

Step 2: Appoint Steering Committee and Determine Direction

The steering committee, which is developed from a cross section of the organization, becomes educated about the business, establishes its role, and develops the vision or mission for the organization to determine the scope and boundaries of the change effort. Key actions are to:

- Establish the steering committee to handle the following functions: identify barriers and opportunities; begin strengthening union-management relationships; educate key stakeholders on partnership, union, and management leadership; and jointly establish selection criteria for steering committee members.

▲ Complete the initial tasks, including role and responsibilities of the steering committee, review business strategy plans and organizational climate, and provide leadership to ensure plans are consistent with the mission and goals.

▲ Determine the scope and boundaries of the change effort by identifying available resources, pinpointing areas of potential increased involvement, integrating gain-sharing, tying the effort to other units or corporate activities, and to mission and strategic goals, including quality performance.

▲ Develop a communications and involvement strategy, including a plan for the changing role of leadership and how to directly involve leaders in the process.

Step 3: Build Organizational Awareness and Support

The support and involvement of all employees are gained by sharing all business information including customer needs, business conditions and strategy, reasons for change, what partnership and self-managed teams are and aren't. Key actions are to:

▲ Build a common database of understanding across the organization about the business and partnership, including customer information, business strategy, what partnership is, and a plan for the organization.

▲ Develop an ongoing communications and awareness plan with key stakeholders in the organization, including support groups, customers, suppliers, union leadership, and supervision.

▲ Use multiple approaches for communication, awareness, and involvement. Include training, communication meetings, newsletters, and site visits.

▲ Determine how you will assess people support and understanding of the change effort on an ongoing basis.

Step 4: Begin Organization Improvement

The steering committee commissions self-managed teams consisting of people closest to the work. These teams assess the environment, analyze the technical and social systems, and develop recommendations to review with all appropriate stakeholders. Key actions are to:

▲ Establish self-managed teams that determine member selection method and criteria, provide training and resources, offer skills development as a working team, understand the change process, define communication and data gathering, and set their success criteria.

▲ Assess the unit environment.

▲ Conduct process analyses of both technical systems and social systems.

▲ Develop improvement recommendations, and ensure involvement of support groups and fit with other efforts in supporting systems.

▲ Review the recommendations with appropriate stakeholders, including unit leadership, steering committee, and business leadership.

Step 5: Plan for Implementation

Implementation plans are developed to move work groups toward increasing levels of self-management teams, develop success criteria in the form of measures, address resource requirements, determine skill development needs for all employees, and outline the changes needed for support systems. Key actions are to:

▲ Determine who is responsible for an implementation plan.

▲ Develop a project plan with milestones by defining change requirements for technical systems and social systems, and documenting and securing needed resources.

▲ Define the needed skills to support the design.

▲ Determine the training and development requirements and develop the plan.

▲ Ensure specific implementation plans are made regarding supporting systems, including compensation systems, selection process, job configuration, career development and planning, accounting, information systems, and communications.

▲ Define and align success criteria and measures with the work design. Include proposing recommended adjustments to gain-sharing plans based upon implementations, ensure that the teams have goals, and identify leadership behavior required to support this change.

▲ Develop a plan for continuous improvement.

Step 6: Implement the Plan

Changes in work process, equipment, and people utilization take place, including changing support systems, providing training and development, and determining methods of performance feedback. Key actions are to:

- ▴ Communicate the improvement plan and success criteria to all key stakeholders.
- ▴ Implement improvements in work process, equipment, and people utilization.
- ▴ Implement changes required in supporting systems.
- ▴ Customize and further detail the design by each self-managed work team.
- ▴ Provide training and development for all levels including basic skills, technical skills, team skills, business skills, and leadership skills.
- ▴ Facilitate the transition of increasing responsibility and authority to the self-managed teams.
- ▴ Jointly establish and communicate goals and measures (unit, team, individual).
- ▴ Determine methods of performance feedback and tracking.
- ▴ Recognize and reward as appropriate.

Step 7: Provide Evaluation and Renewal

The organization ensures that there are plans for continuous improvements for both people and processes, and evaluates their progress in creating a total organizational change. Key actions are to:

- ▴ Review progress vis-à-vis change plan.
- ▴ Revise change plan as needed.
- ▴ Celebrate accomplishments.
- ▴ Provide for ongoing individual and team development.
- ▴ Work toward continuous improvement of the process.
- ▴ Evaluate and revisit support and resources needed.
- ▴ Establish the vision for the next generation of partnership.

Working With Self-Managed Teams

Managers placed in the new role of coach for a self-managed team are often confused as to procedures. Here are some tips on coaching in a self-managed team environment.[6]

▲ Let the work team know that you're there if they need you. The group needs to have a clear idea of purpose, goals, and authority, as well as a sense of responsibility and how it relates to the company as a whole. Team members also need a clear understanding of your role as coach. A good coach helps the players learn the game and practice as a team before playing in the major leagues. If a group gets off target, step in and lead it back.

▲ Let the group know that you support the concept of partnership and trust them, and that you will work with them to make needed change. Letting go is difficult, but you must let employees learn, grow, and make mistakes. Most employees are conditioned to act in ways that please managers. For them to trust the concept of increasing employee involvement, they must see your commitment to the partnership on a daily basis.

▲ Facilitate the team's ability to communicate. Don't attempt to censor them. As manager, you're responsible for making sure the team can give and receive all information necessary to do the job. Support an open, accepting environment where team members speak up without fear of reprisal.

▲ Learn to be a resource provider, to help identify needs, and help meet them. Don't blame ignorance when things go wrong. As coach you need to be sure the group has the knowledge to meet customer requirements. If it has trouble understanding something or lacks knowledge in a particular area, identify the needs and make suggestions for resources that might be helpful.

▲ Ask the group to reevaluate decisions you are certain will have negative consequences. Present additional information; don't tell the group, "This just isn't going to work," overriding a major group decision. Your role as a coach is to train team players to trust their instincts and apply their experience and knowledge to solve problems, not police their decisions.

▲ Ask to be kept informed of the group's goals and progress. Don't expect to attend and participate in every meeting. Sooner or later, the group won't need you as much. Don't let the team rely on your coaching to the point where it looks to you before making a decision. A group with responsibility but with no authority becomes resentful and frustrated.

▲ Continually seek to learn and reinforce partnership principles for yourself. Don't slip into old ways of management. Just as employees have been conditioned to obey company authority, managers have learned to act with authority, making all key decisions, assigning tasks, and interpreting policy.

Summary

Self-managed teams are a way for an organization to utilize the skills and talents of the entire work force. Many organizations have derived significant benefits from self-managed teams in regard to quality, services, productivity, and customer satisfaction. Teams are a key element in creating an overall partnership environment and ensuring continuous quality improvement. This chapter reviewed the steps for implementation of a partnership process, as well as offered tips on managing a successful partnership environment.

Notes

1. R. Harper and A. Harper, *Succeeding as a Self-Directed Work Team* (MW Corporation, 1989), Chap. 2.
2. Corning Incorporated, *Corning Partnership Process*, December 1991.
3. N. E. Garrity, "People, Partnership, and Productivity," *Quality Publication* IV (1991), p. 18.
4. Corning Incorporated, *Six Characteristics of a Partnership Environment*, December 1991.
5. Corning, *Partnership Process*.
6. Corning Incorporated, *Face to Face*, July 1991.

26

Staff Training Delivers Quality Service at Tokyo's Imperial Hotel

M. Ignatius Cronin III, Imperial Hotel, Tokyo

At Tokyo's 103-year-old Imperial Hotel, the objective is for every guest to feel thoroughly satisfied with the hotel's services, facilities, and cuisine on every visit. To ensure this superior level of guest satisfaction, and to continually refine key services in line with changing market expectations, all employees receive carefully orchestrated, ongoing training and are involved in the Imperial's Total Quality Control action program. Its key elements include:

- ▲ Personnel development
- ▲ Capability development
- ▲ Guest critiques
- ▲ Service improvement committee
- ▲ Zero complaints movement
- ▲ Patron increase

Personnel Development

Personnel development focuses on staff in the different divisions of the company, centering on improving performance within the context of each staff member's specific duties. Nonetheless, training programs vary widely according to the needs and responsibilities of each division. The following outlines the current training systems used by the Rooms Division as an example. The Rooms Division consists of the front office, which is further divided into the front desk, front desk information, tour and group office, and bellmen's office; the rooms reservations department; and the housekeeping department, which is further divided into the housekeepers' office and the laundry facility offices.

The Rooms Division training program offers training for all members of the division as a group as well as individualized training for each member. A training committee composed of division staff administers the divisionwide program.

Divisionwide Training

A Workplace Exchange Program rotates all Rooms Division personnel to other departments and sections of the Rooms Division, where each participant is briefed in detail on the job he or she is to observe over a given period. The trainee then actually performs the work he or she has been monitoring. The results of this practical exposure to and actual experience with the various operational systems and workloads within the division deepen the trainees' understanding of the purposes and characteristics of each position and its function. This training has been very effective in enhancing work orchestration and streamlining intrasection and intradepartment cooperation.

The divisionwide program also includes work-specific English-language capability improvement classes and training stints in other divisions of the hotel whose operations are linked with those of the Rooms Division.

Individual Staff Training

Job-specific training takes place in each department and section within the Rooms Division according to the demands and characteristics of each individual position. Each person in the Rooms Division also makes his or her own personal inspection of the division's primary commodity, the hotel's guest rooms. The points to be inspected vary according to the specific department or section to which the "inspector" belongs, with a view towards refining related operational systems.

It is crucial that each member of the Rooms Division knows the product, and how it functions and is used, in minute detail, so these inspections include actually staying in and using the guest rooms overnight the same way a paying guest would. Rooms Division staff have made numerous important discoveries during their test stays and have subsequently been able to suggest improvements in amenities, layout, furnishings and appointments, lighting, hardware, and guest-room-related services since the initiation of this program.

Rooms Division personnel also need to be aware of what competing hotels in Tokyo offer their guests in terms of accommodations and related services. Toward this end, they use test stays at the Imperial's major competitors in Tokyo.

Front desk information staff and bellmen also take their research outside the hotel so that they can secure up-to-date information to furnish to their guests. Front desk information personnel are requested to take all the major organized sightseeing tours and to visit the city's major business districts and facilities, as well as the main entertainment and shopping spots, trendy areas, and events of interest to both foreign and Japanese guests. This enables them to secure firsthand experience with and information about each, including access and transportation problems. Data are compiled by each staff member after such an excursion, and they serve as a basis from which to brief or assist Imperial guests.

Bellmen actually visit the various facilities at Narita and Haneda airports to study the facilities and transportation systems and how these will be used by guests, and to keep abreast of actual conditions that might allow for improved guest support with the various transportation options. They also study how baggage is handled and processed at the airport, and how it is loaded and transported with the guest to the hotel from the airport. This ensures better guest service.

Each department and section within the Rooms Division also requires each staff member to inspect and test the major facilities and services within the hotel, including restaurants, tenant services, the post office, and the maintenance department. They also observe training programs at other departments outside their own division. This familiarity with the diverse aspects of the total hotel operations is very conducive to a more efficient, consistent performance on the job.

In the reservations office, cross-job training takes place within each section, so that work can be fine-tuned for maximum speed, accuracy, and effectiveness.

The Rooms Division training programs are carried out in addition to preliminary job-specific training conducted for newly transferred personnel.

Capability Development

One of the major programs designed to ensure that guests receive the finest in professional services is the Capability Development Program. It consists of the following subprograms.

Increasing Occupational Ability and Knowledge

This is done through on-the-job training, individual department-sponsored off-the-job training, and domestic and overseas study and inspection tours.

On-the-job training systems take full advantage of the Japanese practice of regular personnel rotation. When an employee is transferred to a new department, as almost all Imperial staff are on a regular basis, he or she assumes a sort of apprentice status, following superiors within the department as they perform their various duties, one supervisor at a time. The new employee is encouraged and expected to ask questions and take complete notes. After a while, the roles are reversed, and the apprentice attends to his or her duties followed by the superior, until he or she is able to perform them satisfactorily.

A new member of the front desk staff, for example, will stand behind an experienced employee as guests are greeted and checked in, noting the entire procedure, including what is said, and following the handling of all the paperwork and documentation involved in each different circumstance. He or she listens as the senior staff member answers questions or meets requests from the guests, and notes the diverse methods used in problem solving.

After the new member has had time to be exposed to a representative set of circumstances typical of the workload in that specific department or section, he or she actually performs the work with the superior standing in back of the new member checking the performance and serving as a safety device if the novice is about to make an error. The senior staff member later instructs the novice about various points in the performance that need improvement or attention, and this continues until the senior member is totally confident that the novice has learned enough about his or her duties to handle them independently.

Typically, new employees are rotated to all major departments within the hotel to give them a well-balanced, multifaceted professional education that provides them with a highly practical broad base of working knowledge that greatly enhances their efficiency level in whatever future duties they may be assigned during their careers with the hotel.

Off-the-job training is organized by each individual department in the hotel, under the direction of the personnel office. Emphasis is placed on departments in which work is specialized, such as the Restaurant Division, where chefs, although rotated to different kitchens, remain specialists of a highly defined nature. Restaurant Division training is divided into several programs adjusted to the participating employees' length of service and their future positions. The programs cover highly specialized subjects such as classical and contemporary French cuisine, oenology, table settings, kitchen systems, restaurant layout, general gastronomy, and serving techniques, including such things as tableside presentations for dishes requiring decoupage or flambée methods. Personnel are frequently sent to sample, test, or inspect similar luxury-class hotels in Europe, North America, and Japan as well as leading or newly opened dining establishments of note at home or abroad.

Imperial staff inspecting other leading hotels and restaurants or new hotels and dining establishments take note of service approaches, menus, dishes, cutlery and appointments, accommodation qualities, and operational characteristics that may be applied to their work at the Imperial. When the Imperial opens a new dining facility, for example, staff are routinely sent to leading-edge restaurants, both inside Japan and abroad, to glean new ideas and innovations. When the hotel decided to upgrade its existing coffee house into a higher-caliber dining facility featuring California- and Pacific Coast-type dishes, it sent ten staff members from its restaurant department, kitchens, chefs' department, and planning department, including a managing director, to California to dine at and monitor the latest and most successful California-style restaurants: their methods of operation, menu choices, interior designs, wine lists, service styles, and graphic designs.

The Rooms Division sends staff to the top luxury hotels in Southeast Asia (where many of the highest-ranking luxury hotels are located) to inspect the various guest-room-related services and front-of-the-house operational systems. The groups include, for example, housekeepers on the Imperial staff, who have a chance to be on the receiving end of service in these luxury hotels, allowing them to refine the services they provide to their guests when on duty at the Imperial. Housekeepers are also sent to the best hotels in North America (e.g., The Waldorf-Astoria) and Europe for the same purpose, sometimes on long-term exchange programs, giving them valuable exposure to diverse national or regional customs, styles, and preferences, experience that they can later draw on when called for, depending on the nationality of the given guest at the Imperial.

To increase their knowledge of wines, Imperial sommeliers, accompanied by senior hotel waiters, take part in inspection and study tours to California and Europe every three years, visiting and studying at famous wineries, to broaden their professional knowledge of wines.

Imperial restaurant personnel are also requested to report on any new dishes they may encounter outside the Imperial that they feel may be worth noting for future use or adaptation at an Imperial outlet.

The Imperial regularly hosts two- to three-week-long international food festivals at which famous chefs from the theme country are invited to take charge of one of the hotel kitchens and produce authentic dishes from their homeland. While the presence of these top chefs and the chance to observe their art in progress are in themselves highly valuable learning experiences, before these events are held, chefs and kitchen staff from the Imperial often visit the theme country to sample representative dishes with the chefs to be invited to Tokyo. This familiarizes them with the ingredients, preparatory methods, tastes, and local atmosphere and styles of service.

Imperial restaurant staff also include their own outlets among their inspection activities, dining exactly as a patron might, so that they have the correct perspective from which to assess and offer refinements of their own hotel's ambiance, food, presentational styles, and caliber of service.

Individual staff from selected departments within the Imperial also stay in any major new hotel in Tokyo shortly after it has opened, checking and recording the quality and style of service and the new hotel's various facilities, including guest rooms, public spaces, dining outlets, banquet spaces, recreational facilities, and executive services.

Service Manners Training

The second major segment of the Capability Development Program focuses on the etiquette and psychology of guest contact and attitudes of service. The service manners training program is obligatory for *all* personnel working at the Imperial Hotel, regardless of department or position. This includes all personnel who, from the viewpoint of the guest, work as part of the total hotel operations, even if they are actually employees of tenant restaurants or shops, short-term contract workers, parking lot attendants, limousine drivers, maintenance staff, or temporary banquet staff.

The program can vary in focus and length depending on the position of the trainee, but the basic mandatory training is designed to equip all staff with the minimum level of etiquette prescribed by the management, covering the areas of personal appearance, use of deferential language, service attitudes, general behavior, and proper telephone manners. The program is ongoing throughout the year, administered by the personnel department in accordance with varying staff requirements. The basic course takes one full day.

The morning is spent videotaping each participant during a partially improvised 1.5-minute-long speech delivered before the other participants. The purpose of this exercise is to demonstrate to the trainee how he or she appears to others, such as guests. The classes average twenty trainees. The format for the videotaped speech includes standard greeting, self-introduction with full name and post, mention of the trainee's speech theme, the actual contents, a repeat of the speaker's name, and concluding greetings, which constitute appreciation for listening. The videotape is then analyzed by the instructor point by point. Posture is checked. The trainee's proper eye contact with the audience is checked, as is the position of his or her hands and feet. The hotel believes that, out of respect for the guest being addressed, hands should be folded in front of the speaker and feet should be in the position of the letter V, with slight variations for men and women. Next, clothing is studied for cleanliness, neatness, style, and appropriateness for the given time, place, and occasion. Personal idiosyncrasies or unflattering mannerisms are pointed out and corrected. How staff should appear to hotel guests is stressed and demonstrated, with emphasis placed on cleanliness, a sense of understated elegance, and good taste.

Next, guest psychology is discussed, and six main points to remember are introduced.

1. Imperial Hotel patrons, given the rank and reputation of the hotel, expect to be considered your most important priority, the center of your attention.
2. Guests do not want to suffer losses of any kind while in the hotel.
3. Guests expect to be received in a warm, welcoming fashion.
4. A guest does not want to be extended a level of treatment that is in any way inferior to that provided to other guests of the hotel.
5. Guests wish to experience an appropriate feeling of prestige or superiority, purely by virtue of their using what is commonly evaluated as a deluxe enterprise.
6. Guests enjoy feeling possessive about the hotel's facilities and services, and expect exclusive attention.

Examples of each point above are given, and standards of attention and treatment are analyzed by the instructor, who stresses that the desired behavioral traits when attending to guests' needs are kindness and consideration; speediness and timeliness, expressed not just through actions but—for example, when guests must wait for some reason—through eye contact, gesture, and language; and efficiency and accuracy, supported by the taking of notes when necessary and by teamwork.

The instructor goes next to basic principles governing body language and movements. Detailed explanations and demonstrations of pleasing movements are given, covering eight main points:

1. Facial expressions, appearance, and posture when standing
2. Movements and posture used when welcoming and receiving guests, such as when bowing or shaking hands
3. Pleasing, attractive ways of talking and carriage
4. Proper positions when seated
5. How and when to bow
6. Correct postures and hand motions when receiving or handing over objects
7. Pleasing hand motions and body language when giving directions
8. Proper posture, carriage, and courtesy when escorting guests within the hotel premises

Since the bow is used regardless of the national origin of Imperial guests, the traditional Japanese fashion of bowing is also demonstrated and practiced. Bows are executed to all guests when called for by local custom. A bow of welcome involves a 15° angle, a bow of gratitude is 30°, and a bow of apology is a full 45° from the normal straight standing position.

The remainder of the service manners training program concentrates on the complexities of the honorifics in the Japanese language and their appropriate hotel industry applications. Some twenty-five common daily expressions are practiced in their politest forms. The parallel English-language equivalents of these phrases are taught separately in the hotel's ongoing English-language training classes. A request or an order taken from a guest in English is acknowledged in English, for example, with a "very well, sir" or a "very good, madam" rather than with an "okay" or a "sure." Students are also taught that "one moment, sir" is preferable to "just a second, please." Advanced students are instructed in more complex phraseology, such as that required in explaining sensitive matters related to billing or problems related to specific house rules or local customs.

Training According to Corporate Rank

The third major segment of the Capability Development Program focuses on ongoing training of middle-management-level and new and junior-level personnel according to rank within the organization.

The goal of this program is to instill in each participant a proper understanding of his or her position within the organization and what is expected of him or her in that position, to help ensure that the specific duties involved are completely and effectively accomplished, thus strengthening the total operation. This ongoing training is divided into seven distinct programs according to rank or position.

CORRESPONDENCE TRAINING FOR NEW EMPLOYEES PRIOR TO ACTUAL EMPLOYMENT

Recruits scheduled to join the hotel upon graduation from a university, junior college, or high school are mailed materials for study several months before the day they actually begin work. The materials include a complete history of the Imperial Hotel since its founding by Japanese aristocracy in 1890; the Japanese- and English-language brochures; an outline of the company's basic operations and corporate structure; restaurant brochures; training program summaries and schedules; applications for hotel staff English-language testing and classes; basic guidelines on personal hygiene, dress codes, and appearance; and an outline of work ethics and manners expected of all employees. Recruits are asked to be thoroughly familiar with the contents of all materials before they begin work.

NEW RECRUIT TRAINING

This training takes place the first two weeks after beginning employment and develops an awareness of the new roles in society the recruits are expected to play, as opposed to the lifestyles they adopted during student life. Instructors try to instill into trainees a sense of their responsibility as Imperial Hotel personnel, inasmuch as they will represent the hotel to guests and patrons, and to others outside the hotel, once they begin their professional life. Discussions are encouraged on the subject of the essence of service and its importance both to guests and staff and to society at large. Each participant is encouraged to consider how he or she can best fulfill the duties of an employee for the sake of superior service.

BRUSH-UP TRAINING FOR JUNIOR EMPLOYEES

Six months after they have begun work, new employees take a second orientation seminar organized and administered by the personnel office. This gives them a chance to voice their opinions and personal feelings about their duties, their workloads, the workplace, their fellow employees and superiors, and the organization as a whole. While the hotel strives to implant specific ideals at the time of recruitment and initial orientation, it has found that many new employees become somewhat disillusioned or have been influenced in a negative way by other employees with more seniority. Some demonstrate feelings of disappointment with what they had anticipated would be a more glamorous or interesting working environment, despite the duty rotation system by which their specific responsibilities change regularly.

Complaints are discussed, and procedures for solving problems are reviewed. Attitudes and approaches to the performance of each participant's duties are corrected by the personnel department staff in charge of the seminars. The recent employee is also taught how to treat and lead the group of new employees who will join the hotel after another six months have passed, their first "juniors," to whom they are asked to serve as role models.

TRAINING PROGRAM FOR NEWLY APPOINTED CHIEFS

Some fifty people each year are appointed to the post of *kakaricho*, or section chief. This program centers on just what is expected of them. It lasts two full days, during which participants are also given lectures by independent professional personnel development specialists. Topics discussed include procedures for maintaining the service standards expected at top international hotels and the role the chief plays in executing these procedures. The chief performs a key role in providing service to guests, since he or she is in actual control of a specific function of the hotel operations and is responsible for supervising that function from start to finish.

Brush-Up Training for Recently Appointed Chiefs

A full day is devoted to brush-up training for recently appointed chiefs six months after they have been appointed. A check is conducted to measure the chief's effectiveness in administering his or her duties in accordance with the principles and procedures set forth during the initial training for the position, and any gaps between theory and actual practice are corrected. Many new section chiefs understand the operational guidelines taught during their initial chiefs' training but cannot put them into practice, so this program gives them a chance to analyze alternatives or more effective modes of administering their operations.

Training for Newly Appointed Supervisors

Each year some thirty middle-level employees are promoted to the rank of *kanrishoku*, or supervisor, and each is given intensive, specialized training prior to assuming the post. Trainees are made to recognize exactly what is expected of them in their new supervisory posts in order to execute general administrative policies and strategies, including the management of personnel matters in their own departments and labor union issues.

Brush-Up Training for Recently Appointed Supervisors

Brush-up training is done six months after the supervisor has assumed the position, with an interval of three weeks between the first and second days of this two-day program. On the first day, the supervisor reviews his or her goals with seniors, discussing how he or she was or was not able to realize them, and the reasons. During the following three-week interval, the supervisor is asked to be particularly conscious of those goals he or she has yet to reach, and to make every possible attempt to realize them or to put a specific plan of action into effect. On the second day, after the three weeks have passed, the supervisor reports on progress toward each specific aim and analyzes in detail what he or she could or could not carry out, and why. Finally, the supervisor devises a strategy to enhance effectiveness further and is requested to put it into actual practice.

Specific Occupational Training

The Imperial Hotel actively offers to the participating employee a variety of outside training and study programs depending on the specialized needs and his or her specific field of work within the hotel. These programs, administered by independent educational organizations, include the following:

- Management Strategy Decision Making
- Secretarial Ability Development
- Computer Technology
- Financial Management
- Human Resources Strategies
- Personnel Evaluation Techniques
- Labor Management
- Creative Planning
- Marketing
- Negotiating Strategies
- Hotel-Related Equipment Operator Qualifications
- Food Hygiene
- Presentation Know-How
- Schedule Management
- Troubleshooting
- Leadership Quality Development
- New Enterprise Development

Guest Critiques

The Imperial's guest critique forms, referred to as blue letters for both the color of the paper they are printed on and the effect they often have upon the hotel staff who handle them, do not use an item-by-item format. A short message from the general manager at the top of an empty page specifically requests "criticism, not commendation," inducing the writer to recall those parts of the experience he or she was dissatisfied with.

When a blue letter is received, it is opened immediately by the general manager, or by the next in command in his absence. If the sender is still in the hotel and the contents are a complaint, action is taken on the spot to rectify the situation, and a letter of apology is composed and delivered to the guest's room, often by a senior staff member who takes a gift of some kind to the guest and offers personal apologies on behalf of the hotel.

If the sender has already departed, a letter is composed and signed by the general manager, expressing apologies and, when needed, giving an explanation of why a particular service, amenity, or facility is provided in the way it is.

Each and every blue letter of complaint is forwarded to the department head involved, with an order from the general manager for an immediate, detailed explanation. A typical case might be a complaint regarding service in a restaurant. The blue letter is opened and read by the general manager, who routes it to the vice-president, who is also in charge of overseeing all sales and marketing. From there it is sent to the managing director directly under the vice-president, and from there to the head of the marketing department, and next to the manager of the planning section of the marketing department. The planning department manager then routes the letter to a junior staff member, who distributes copies to all departments involved, including, in the case of a restaurant complaint, the restaurant division, the sales division, and the kitchens and guest relations division. A copy of the letter is also sent to the duty manager, who serves as head concierge, with additional copies going to individual staff members in each department who may be involved with the specific complaint or suggestion.

Complaints are recorded and records maintained at each related department. These are reviewed, for the purpose of refining or correcting the areas of service involved, on a monthly, six-month, and annual basis. In the case of a serious complaint, an exhaustive report is submitted to top management by the managers of the departments concerned.

The blue letters are an extremely valuable means of measuring guest preferences and expectations, which in turn reflect trends and emerging standards within the hotel industry as a whole. For example, in Japan smoking has traditionally been silently tolerated by the nonsmoking population, whereas North Americans and Europeans have increasingly found it unhealthy and objectionable. No-smoking floors and no-smoking areas in the hotel's restaurants today are a direct result of foreign guests' criticism of the earlier lack of such facilities, expressed through blue letters. The Imperial was the first major hotel in Japan to initiate no-smoking areas. Preferences for specific exercise equipment, guest-room-use office and communications technologies, low-calorie and vegetarian foods, fitness facility hours, and multilingual video information facilities are other examples of consumer feedback received at the Imperial, representing demands by international travelers.

Another Imperial facility created in response to guest critiques is the enlarged Executive Services Center, the largest such hotel facility in Japan, equipped with a full range of advanced office systems and private computerized work stations. Nearby are a lounge for early-arriving and late-departing guests, complete with showers and ironing facilities; a soundproof music practice room for visiting musicians; a meeting room for VIPs designed with security in mind; and a child-care center.

Blue letters also allow the hotel to confirm positive guest evaluations of services, cuisine, and facilities, and in many cases provide encouragement to staff members whose performances have pleased guests to such an extent that they wish to inform the management of their satisfaction.

Service Improvement Committee

The Imperial's Service Improvement Committee is made up of the managers of all major departments within the hotel. Some twenty department managers are involved. The Service Improvement Committee meets monthly to discuss problems within each department, report on newly adopted operational procedures and measures designed to refine or streamline services, propose and discuss means of interdepartmental cooperation, exchange ideas, keep abreast of developments in other departments, and offer suggestions.

Since the hotel performs best through synchronized, coordinated efforts, this meeting provides department managers with a forum for strengthening interdepartmental strategies aimed at increasing sales through an improved, more rationally structured product.

Zero Complaints

The Zero Complaints movement focuses on instilling in each employee an awareness of the hotelier's elementary philosophy of assuring each guest of the highest possible level of satisfaction. The slogan "Zero Complaints" was introduced by a senior executive for use on posters and back-of-the-house communications designed to enhance personnel performance and morale. The slogan functions as a sort of service industry keyword, reminding employees that a lack of complaints from guests and patrons is a basic ideal each employee must embrace in the performance of his or her duties.

Patron Increase

Patron increase *(kokyakuzukuri)* is one of the functions of the marketing department at the Imperial Hotel. It primarily involves promotional activity in support of two frequent-guest clubs, the Hibiya Club and the Imperial Club International. The Hibiya Club is made up of frequent users, both foreign and Japanese, living inside Japan, while Imperial Club International members are frequent guests living overseas.

Guest histories are maintained on members of both clubs; these include preferred room type and rate; average length of stay; dining preferences; personal data; any specific requests, such as for extra length beds, minibar stock, Main Building or Tower Building and other location-related preferences; and any pertinent data provided by the guest on allergies, condition of health, or, in some cases, flower preferences.

Hibiya Club guests are granted a range of privileges, from priority reservations, express check-in and checkout, and priority laundry services to special arrangements at the hotel's restaurants, at the limousine desk, and at wedding facilities within the hotel. The hotel also organizes special events just for Hibiya Club members, including deluxe tours to Europe. They are also sent the Hibiya Magazine, created specifically for members, with news of events and offerings at the hotel. A questionnaire is mailed to all members every year in order to evaluate club services, solicit member feedback on past stays or on restaurant usage, and measure how the various benefits and advantages of club membership suit member needs.

Hibiya Club members also receive the Japanese-language in-house magazine, published quarterly, and other direct mail announcements. They are also invited to make use of the Clubroom, a members-only lounge on the fifth floor of the hotel's Main Building, adjacent to the Executive Services Center.

Imperial Club International members are extended privileges and benefits similar to those extended to Hibiya Club members. Membership is by invitation, and offers guaranteed reservations, express check-in and check-out, late check-out privileges, complimentary fitness facility usage, and other advantages. The hotel maintains ongoing contact with members through mailings and its English-language in-house magazine, *The Imperial*.

Guaranteed reservations for the member's preferred type of accommodation are a strong aspect of both clubs, since during busy peak seasons occupancies jump and it often becomes almost impossible to secure accommodations in central Tokyo without substantial lead time. Guest loyalty is fostered in this way.

Hibiya Club members qualify for special services and deferential arrangements when holding weddings at the hotel, which increases banquet facility patronage. At major hotels throughout Japan, banquet, restaurant, and miscellaneous sales revenues account for some 60 to 70 percent of total annual revenue, with guest-room revenue generally in the area of 30 percent. Thus, promotion of banquet sales is a crucial segment of hotel marketing in Japan.

Employee Case History

To illustrate how intensive, ongoing training, through experience on the job and through specific training programs, assures Imperial guests of high-quality service, a summary of the activities and positions of a typical hotel employee are presented.

Yukiko Saito joined the Imperial Hotel after graduation from International Christian University in Tokyo, and after completing a battery of tests and interviews conducted by the hotel. Since the Imperial Hotel, like most Japanese corporations, considers employees long-term human resources, Ms. Saito's résumé and background as well as her test and interview scores were studied thoroughly before she was accepted as a new recruit. Interviews are conducted during the summer prior to graduation. After she accepted the hotel's offer of employment, for six months Ms. Saito received packets of information on the hotel industry, the Imperial Hotel, and her upcoming training courses. She went through the usual general training for all new employees upon beginning her job. This was followed immediately by learning stints in the housekeeping department, as a waitress, in the banquet department office, and finally as staff at the front desk, for a period of six months. In each post, she was instructed individually by a veteran member of the department staff, with emphasis on the know-how accumulated by the hotel over the past ten decades.

Six months after she began, she underwent the standard follow-up training for new employees, followed by a three-and-a-half-year term in the planning and publicity office, where—partly as a result of her fluency in English, which she had achieved before joining the hotel—she was put in charge of the English and Japanese versions of the in-house magazine, produced under her supervision by a subcontractor publisher.

This post greatly increased Ms. Saito's professional knowledge of the hotel industry and of the Imperial Hotel. She researched articles for the in-house magazines on a veteran Imperial housekeeper, Chief Attendant Toshiko Takeya, who was the hotel's first woman employee and served in the housekeeping department for over sixty years, ending her career in her late seventies with a decoration from H.I.M. The Emperor. Ms. Takeya's seniority and experience led to her being posted to attend to the hotel's VIP guests, members of international royalty, heads of state, celebrities, and business leaders. Ms. Saito spent days watching Ms. Takeya perform her duties and read Ms. Takeya's published autobiography devoted to her decades at the Imperial. She learned firsthand how Ms. Takeya put into practice the philosophy of being continually useful to guests while anticipating their needs in advance, as well as the countless intricacies and protocol involved in looking after VIPs.

Ms. Saito also researched an article on another veteran Imperial staff member, Kimi Hayashi, who served as a waitress for over forty years and as a trainer for employees newly posted to the hotel restaurants. Ms. Saito recalls learning from Ms. Hayashi a world of information about food, dining styles, and restaurant operations, as well as the lengthy history of the hotel's restaurant operations. She learned, for example, of Ms. Hayashi's detailed notes on the preferences and dislikes of her patrons over the years, and her philosophy of being demanding and strict with her fellow workers and subordinates and, most of all, with herself.

After her stint with the Planning and Publicity Office, Ms. Saito was sent to train at a deluxe hotel in Germany, where she remained for over two years. There she was exposed to the classic European style of hospitality and the traditional professionalism of European hotel managers in receiving their guests, which she felt was higher than that of Japanese hoteliers. She trained at the German hotel's front desk and concierge desk during her tenure in Europe and gained a great deal of practical experience from the German staff she supported in these posts and was impressed by their zeal. She also learned that the Imperial Hotel was well known throughout Europe, and by virtue of her coming from the Imperial, she was given a high level of freedom in fulfilling her various duties. She realized as well that she had a responsibility as an Imperial employee to live up to the accompanying expectations.

Upon her return to Tokyo, Ms. Saito was assigned a position in a department established to set up an enhanced guest relations office, which began operations a year later, in 1990, on the occasion of the centennial anniversary of the founding of the hotel, and to which she was subsequently assigned as a chief. She had been with the hotel for seven years, but nonetheless she underwent the prescribed training given to all staff in new positions, followed by a secondary training program for that post six months later. Two years later she was promoted to assistant manager of the guest relations office.

During her years in guest relations, Ms. Saito worked hand in hand with veteran staff members, each of whom had had years of experience in attending to guests. Her duties brought her into daily contact with the Imperial's most mature and finest personnel, from the duty managers who supervise the guest relations desk and the doorman to the chief telephone operators and protocol officers, who work closely with Japan's Ministry of Foreign Affairs and various embassies on formal arrangements for visiting dignitaries and distinguished guests of the Japanese government. She also had the chance to attend to the needs of VIP guests herself upon their arrival, and to deal with the detailed logistics of their stays through departure. Through direct exposure to a variety of the hotel's guests, she also had an excellent opportunity to learn about their opinions and evaluation of her department's various services, and how these could be improved or refined.

Ms. Saito was recently transferred to the planning section of a new Imperial Hotel subsidiary, based inside the Tokyo hotel, that will operate a group of small hotels in major subcenters in greater Tokyo.

Conclusion

The Imperial's various service improvement programs and multilevel training systems are an ongoing and integral part of its total operations that have a direct bearing on its administrative efficiency and consequently on the standard of service provided to guests.

The hotel is fortunate to have access to a labor force that has been, for the most part, thoroughly educated, both formally and informally, in a cultural context where tradition confers great value on consideration of others in the group and where forbearance, diligence, and obedience, along with generally unquestioning loyalty, are exalted virtues of the highest social order.

PART VII

DELIVERING SERVICE QUALITY

27

The Role of Service Design in Achieving Quality

Bo Edvardsson, University of Karlstad, Sweden

Fundamental elements in modern quality thinking are prevention, Zero Defects, and quality by design.[1] Quality by design means that quality should be built into a product at the development and design stages. Quality defects are often recurrent and are caused by wrongly designed production processes and delivery systems. According to Joseph Juran, 92 percent of the quality defects in manufacturing companies can be attributed to faults in the system.[2] In the service sector, it is estimated that system-related quality defects account for 70–80 percent of quality problems.

The development of new services is often not a well-organized process. My experience with Swedish companies is consistent with that of Scheuing's, who says that new services "often come about as the result of intuition, personal fancy or inspiration, availability of capacity, or competitive action. Rarely are new product ideas subjected to careful, thorough scrutiny."[3] However, some service companies, such as Marriott with its Courtyard concept and Merrill Lynch with its Cash Management Account, have successfully developed formal structures to drive, direct, and control their new service activities.

The ability to design services in a systematic way is far less developed than the ability to design goods. Manufacturing companies have for many years used well-established methods for the construction of goods and the design of manufacturing processes and production systems.[4] These concepts, approaches, and models are based on the production logic of industrialized society and therefore stress technical solutions and tangible product benefits. They do not to any great extent take service characteristics into consideration. Therefore, we need to build conceptual models suitable for services and service production.

The purpose of this chapter is to discuss the role of service development and service design in achieving quality, with the emphasis being placed on the latter, and to present a descriptive model for both the outcome of service design and the service design process. The frame of reference is based on current research on service management with an emphasis on quality. The model is based on empirical studies in Swedish service companies, mainly Swedish Telecom.

Characteristics of Services and Quality: Implications for Service Design

The concept of a service can be defined in various ways. In ISO 9004-2, it is defined as follows: "The result generated by activities at the interface between the supplier and the customer, and by supplier internal activities, to meet customer needs."[5]

Service is not a uniform concept. There are great differences, for instance, between professional consulting, telecommunications, hotel services, transportation, and cleaning services. Despite these differences, however, services and the conditions under which they are produced display certain general characteristics. One of these characteristics is that the customer often participates in a direct and active way in the production process as co-producer by carrying out parts of the service. A telephone call presupposes that the customer dials the telephone number and knows how to operate the equipment. The same is true for telefax services. A "quality" haircut requires that the customer be physically present at the barber shop and communicate wishes concerning style. In medical services, it is imperative that the patient explain his or her condition to the doctor and understand and follow the doctor's orders. With the customer as co-producer, quality control becomes more complicated. Customer-adapted service processes and sound training of customers in their role as co-producers are therefore important aspects of new service development.

Services are largely intangible and are therefore difficult for the performer to explain and the customer to assess. This places special demands on the marketing of a service so that accurate rather than unrealistic expectations are built up in the purchaser's mind. All too frequently, this principle is ignored.

Since quality can be defined as meeting customer expectations, services must be designed in such a way that service providers actually live up to these expectations. This means that it is not sufficient to create a design that generates the service; one must also keep in mind the kind of marketing communication that is needed to generate appropriate expectations. Thus, marketing design should be an integral part of the service design process.

Many services are closely tied to the employees of the service company. Since consumers often assess a service on the basis of the knowledge, motivation, and actions displayed by the staff, one could say that the people delivering the service *are* in essence the service. It is therefore important to define the service offer in terms of quality and customer value throughout the organization. If a company's goals—its business concept, its targeted customers, and their needs, demands, and expectations—have not been clarified and understood by all employees, quality will be very difficult to achieve.

A service is composed of various value-bearing elements, sometimes referred to as core service and support services. The value and quality of the service depend on how the customer perceives it in its totality. The service package often includes a number of components delivered by other service producers. For example, airlines may engage taxi companies for air-taxi services. The airline company must make sure, in the design stage, that these support services, too, provide the right quality. If this is not done, customer dissatisfaction will be turned against the company delivering the core service—in this case the airline.

In many service companies, the lack of precise and accepted definitions of quality creates problems in the design of new services. However, it is not easy to understand and define quality. The concept of quality is defined in ISO 9004-2 (E) as: "The totality of features and characteristics of a product or service that bear on its ability to satisfy stated or implied needs."[6] A common definition of service quality is that the service should correspond to the customer's expectations and fulfill his or her needs and requirements. Other interested parties such as employees and company owners should also be involved in discussions on quality from the outset. To be able to offer the right service quality, one must satisfy these two groups as well.

Quality means fulfilling customer, employee, and shareholder needs and expectations. It is vital to have a good understanding of how these are formed so that the expectations of these potentially conflicting groups can be balanced. We should also keep in mind that needs and expectations are not fixed and cannot be expressed by a number. Instead, they can be described, from the service provider's point of view, in terms of tolerance zones delineated by the acceptable and desired levels of service.[7] The nature of these tolerance zones is an important point of departure when developing quality services.

Service Design—Definition and a Model for the Service Construct

To the extent that managers use the concept of service design, it is often ill-defined. In the recently presented standard—ISO 9004-2 (E), *Quality Management and Quality System Elements, Guidelines for Services*—a clear description is given of what is meant by "designing a service." The ISO standard will probably be of great importance for standardized services, such as those offered by telephone companies. Thus, Swedish Telecom has already made a policy decision to adopt this standard. Below is a summary of ISO's description and definition of service design.

> The process of designing a service involves converting the service brief into specifications for both the service and its delivery and control, while reflecting the organization's options (i.e., aims, policies, and costs).
>
> Service specifications define the service to be provided, whereas the service delivery specification defines the means and methods used to deliver the service. The quality control specification defines the procedures for evaluating and checking on features of the service delivery.
>
> Design activities for the service specification, the service delivery specification, and quality control specification are interdependent and interact throughout the design process. Flow charts are useful in depicting all the activities and their relationships and interdependence. The principles of quality control should be applied to the design process itself.[8]

By "service brief," one means the customer needs that the service is to fulfill, the expectations that are to be met by the service-producing organization, and the service that is to be designed to meet customer expectations. "This brief defines the customers' needs and the related service organization's capabilities as a set of requirements and instructions that form the basis for the design of a service." Consumer needs must be clearly defined and accurately described when designing the new service in order to determine the demands they will place on the producing organization.

The ISO description is similar to the service concept, which I have introduced and used in my research. ISO does not explicitly regard the consumer as being involved in the service process. This is a sign that it is the logic of industrial production, not that of service production, that has been the guiding principle for the ISO service standard.

A Conceptual Model of the Outcome of the Service Design Process

Defining a service construct as the outcome of a service design process, I present three subconcepts to explain it: the service concept, the servuction system, and the servuction process.

The Service Concept

The *service concept* is a detailed description of a service offering that matches the chosen customers' needs and expectations (see Figure 27-1).

Figure 27-1.   Model of the service concept.

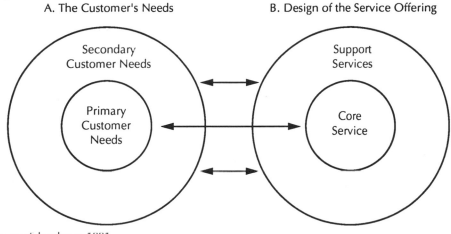

A. The Customer's Needs   B. Design of the Service Offering

Source: Edvardsson, 1991.

I make a distinction between intended and realized service offerings. The former is service in theory, or the intended outcome of the service process, while the latter is service in action, or the actual outcome of the service process. In franchise-based service companies, such as McDonald's, the service concept is spelled out in detail. When McDonald's was established in Sweden, it took about one year before a Swedish supplier was able to meet the specifications for McDonald's cucumbers. The service concept defines the requirements of the process that is to produce the service, and of the system that provides the resources for the activities to be carried out.

We can distinguish between primary and secondary customer needs. Primary needs are those that are determined by a basic need—for instance, to take a trip. This can be done in several ways: by taxi, train, airplane, or car. If the choice is to travel by air, a number of other questions arise, such as how to order the ticket, how to get to the airport, and how to get from the airport to the destination. Such needs are functions or results of the chosen service and can be called secondary. Different choices would have triggered other secondary needs.

In order to satisfy these secondary needs, a range of additional services are required. These can be called *support services*. Examples of support services are airport taxis, airport buses, and contracts between airlines and travel bureaus that make it possible to book several services at the same time. It is even possible to have the tickets sent to one's home, in which case the post office also contributes a support service.

A satisfied customer has had both primary and secondary needs met. My studies show that unspoken expectations about the fulfillment of secondary needs are common. A good-quality service contains a relevant set of support services of the right quality as well. What separates successful service companies from their less successful competitors is often the extent and quality of support services.

Some of the secondary needs are implied. The customer takes it for granted that a number of support services will be available to provide reasonable satisfaction of secondary needs. Before designing the service, it is therefore necessary to identify and understand these unspoken needs, wishes, and expectations. This requires dialogue with potential customers.

The terms *needs*, *wishes*, and *expectations* must be clarified. A need is basic—for example, hunger. Different people wish to have their needs met in different ways. A wish is directed towards a specific product or service—for example, seafood or meat, at home or at a restaurant. Expectations are tied to a specific service by a certain service provider—for example, lobster at Fisherman's Wharf. Expectations emanate from the customer's needs and wishes but are also influenced by the company's image or reputation in the market, the customer's previous experiences with the service company, and the way in which the company markets itself.

Unlike customers' rather stable basic needs, wishes and expectations are constantly changing. It has become obvious that what is difficult but also vital when developing new service concepts is understanding the dynamic and subjective elements in people's needs, wishes, and expectations. This calls for a meaningful dialogue with competent and perceptive customers to make it easy for them to articulate what they want and thereby clearly define the value-bearing activities.

Such a customer-active approach is preferable when designing and testing new service concepts. Direct and active customer cooperation is becoming more and more important in the development of high-technology products as well as in the automobile industry. Maintaining customer dialogue should be even more natural and valuable in the development of services. Thus, organizing customer dialogue is an essential task for the service designer.

Services are often part of a larger system that includes other services, existing and/or new. In order to achieve the right quality and high productivity, such system features should also be taken into consideration. It could be useful to describe this situation as a modular system in which service atoms form service molecules which in turn make up a service package or a service offer.

Merrill Lynch's Cash Management Account (CMA), launched in 1977, is viewed as one of the most revolutionary financial service concepts in decades. "CMA rocketed the industry into the age of one-stop shopping. . . . CMA combines most of the major financial services you need in one convenient place."[9] For the first time, a Wall Street company had sought to tie a standard, marginable brokerage account to a money market fund and then grant customers access to that account via either a Visa debit card or traditional checks.

Ramada Hotels has developed a hotel concept based on standardization. Its hotel rooms are designed, equipped, and furnished identically all over the world. The advantage is that a business traveler feels at home regardless of where he or she is.

In the early 1980s, Marriott designed a new hotel concept for travelers who were not satisfied with existing hotels. Two segments were identified: business travelers and pleasure travelers. Management faced a critical question: What types of hotel facilities and services should Marriott design and offer to attract these travelers away from the competitive facilities they were currently using? Marriott developed the Courtyard concept on the basis of careful analysis of customer needs and wants. In order to meet management's profit and growth objectives, it was essential:

- To assure that the new hotel offered consumers the best value for their money
- To minimize "cannibalization" of Marriott's other hotel offerings
- To establish a market position that offered the company a substantial competitive advantage

THE SERVUCTION SYSTEM

In order to realize the service concept and produce outcomes of service processes in accordance with the concept, specific resources are needed. These must be organized in a logical way and form a system. Merrill Lynch's Cash Management Account is very much dependent on a new computer system. One vital part is the sweep function, the automatic investment of idle cash in a money market fund. Other components of the system are the employees handling the CMA and the customer using the CMA services.

Marriott's Courtyard concept was based on a careful market analysis that formed the basis for designing the service system. It included the following features:

- Hotel size: Small (125 rooms) two-story hotels.
- Corridor/view: Outside stairs and walkways to all rooms. Restricted view. People walking outside window.
- Pool location: Not in courtyard.

Some of the specific attributes Marriott selected for inclusion were amenities such as shampoo and soap, in-room kitchen facilities, and "limo" to airport.

In order to stress that production, delivery, and consumption of services are not separable but overlapping activities in which the customer participates, the concept of "servuction" is used.[10] The term is derived from the words "service" and "production." Service activities take place within the framework of a system, which is called the servuction system.

In this model, the components—better expressed as resources—of the servuction system are employees, customers, organizational structure, and the physical/technical environment. Examples of the latter are telephone services, including switchboards, computers, and other technical systems used by both seller and buyer. These have certain characteristics and provide some of the resources for the servuction process.

Employees are often regarded as a service company's key success factor. I agree. Studies show that customers' perception of service quality to a large extent depends on how they evaluate the employees' knowledge and commitment. For many customers, the individual employee is in essence the service. If we accept this perspective, we ought to consider employees as more than a resource; they are an essential ingredient in the service. The abstract service becomes concrete in the encounter with the individual employee—"the moment of truth." It is in the interaction between the employee and the customer—"the process of truth"—that the service comes about.

If we focus on the employees as not just one resource among others but the critical and decisive bearers of good service quality, it becomes natural to adapt the technical systems, routines, and other resources to human logic or to the way people actually function. Consequently, when designing a new service, we should not only specify requirements with regard to systems and processes; we also need to find out how individuals and groups of people can best contribute to the work. We should consider employees' special needs, demands, and wishes, not just those of the customers. Competent, motivated, and committed employees will do a much better job than those who lack the competence that the tasks and the customers require.

Knowledge and experience alone—without motivation and enthusiasm—have proved to be insufficient for good performance. Motivation is created by work content and good relationships between colleagues, with superiors, and with customers. If a company succeeds in formulating attractive tasks and providing a stimulating, rewarding work environment, employee turnover will decrease significantly. High staff turnover is a big problem in many companies, and it is both expensive and negative from a quality point of view.

Since employees are often the decisive element in customers' perception of quality, and since their salaries make up the bulk of a service company's expenditures, their ideas must be considered when designing services. The servuction system thus becomes a sociotechnical system focusing on the staff. Satisfied employees are more likely to produce the right services and thus contribute to higher productivity.

Recruitment, training, development, and phasing out of personnel are not always carried out in a systematic and professional manner. The selection of new employees and their training and education ought to be an integral part of the design of new services. Furthermore, analysis of work content and job design as well as agreement on a reward system are important but often neglected factors.

Naturally, the customers should play a key role. The servuction system should be designed to enable the customer not only to participate but to play an active role in the process. Pedagogical servuction systems, featuring customer training, are crucial in this context.

Potential customers should be present when new services are designed and existing ones redesigned to ensure that their interaction with various parts of the servuction system will lead to the right level of quality. This was the case when Marriott's Courtyard concept and Merrill Lynch's Cash Management Account were developed.

Services are interactions, and service quality is to a large extent the result of different interactions: interaction between customers; interaction between customers and staff; the customer's interaction with the physical environment, including equipment, furniture, computer systems, and the premises; and the customer's interaction with the organization, for example in routines and opening hours.

The physical environment—technical systems, premises, and equipment—sends out clear signals about quality. This is true, for example, for the location of a hotel, the design of the building, the layout of the lobby, and the way the rooms are furnished. The structure of the organization, distribution of responsibility and authority, planning and information systems, cooperation between different departments, administrative procedures, and accessibility also have definite effects on quality. Examples are routines for checking in and booking different support services such as the sauna or solarium. Administrative routines are also important, for example how informative and easy to understand the bill is. These organizational aspects must also be included in the service design process.

The servuction system forms part of a larger system, the service management system, which comprises the target group, or the customers toward whom the business is directed, as well as the service concept and the organizational culture and image (see Figure 27-2). Image refers to the perception external customers have of the service company and its individual services. Organizational culture refers to the norms and values that characterize the service company with regard to management and decision style, behavior, and attitude.

Figure 27-2. Service management system.

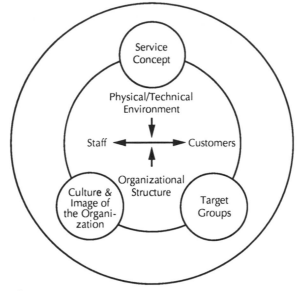

Source: Edvardsson & Gustavsson, 1990.

THE SERVUCTION PROCESS

The servuction process refers to the chains (or streams) of activities that are necessary if the service is to take place. Certain links in the chain are more problematic or critical than others. These should receive special attention in designing services if the right quality is to be achieved.

For a service to match the service concept in all respects, the process, including the microprocesses that generate the right service offering, must be chiseled out in detail. Quality and productivity must be built in from the beginning by designing the "right" servuction process. The term *service chain* may be used instead.

It is necessary that all departments of an organization as well as customers participate in the design of the servuction process. However, there is an obvious risk that each department or function will optimize its own processes and not take into account the whole and the interfunctional dependencies that exist in all organizations. It is a vital management task in service design to create an understanding of the service as a whole and of the interdependencies among departments, functions, and professional groups that are involved with the service.

During the process, various resources of the servuction system are utilized. The system denotes the structure, the unchangeable elements, the prerequisites regarding resources. The process, which consists of activities, should produce the desired service with the right quality. This process should be designed in such a way that the service company's potential and that of its employees are optimized and its limitations are handled in the best way possible. Many new services are to a greater or lesser degree dependent upon the conditions in an existing system. This means that in designing new services, employees with a good knowledge of the servuction system's potential and limits must be included not only in the general process but also in its details.

Unfortunately, it is not uncommon to find that a system has built-in, recurring defects that cause serious problems in the process. In some cases, the system actually hinders the process. Consequently, the service chain must be designed together with the servuction system, starting with the potential and limitations of the latter. If the servuction system needs to be redesigned, the implications this will have for other parts of the system and the company's financial situation should always be considered.

A Four-Phase Model for the Systematic Design of Quality Service

In the previous section, the outcome of the service design process was described with the help of three concepts: the service concept, the servuction system, and the servuction process. In this section, a model of how to work systematically when designing quality services is introduced. The service design process can be viewed as a combination of simultaneous and sequential activities. Scholars have presented a number of models for developing new services. Donnelly et al. define six stages: strategic guidelines, exploration, screening, comprehensive analysis, development and testing, and introduction.[11] Scheuing suggests a normative model of new service evolution with fifteen steps: formulation of new service objectives and strategy, idea generation, idea screening, concept development, concept testing, business analysis, project authorization, service design and testing, process and system design and testing, marketing program design and testing, personnel training, product testing and pilot run, test marketing, full-scale launch, and postlaunch review.[12]

Based on my research, a model of the service design process consisting of four main phases is suggested: idea evaluation and concept development, customer and competitor analysis as a basis for concept evaluation and specification, design of the servuction system, and detailed design of the servuction process. The four phases of the service design process are outlined below.

Idea Evaluation and Concept Development

New service ideas can be internally or externally generated. Customers are often the most important external source of new service ideas.[13] Such ideas should be evaluated systematically and critically by the management, and, in my opinion, demanding and competent customers should be included in this evaluation process more often than is the case today. However, some service companies, such as Citibank and Swedish Telecom, have learned to utilize customer input in a systematic way in the evaluation process. Market aspects should be considered through an analysis of customer needs and of the value the service will bring, the competitive situation, and the size and growth potential of the market. In addition to this, the technical possibilities of realizing the service at the right level of quality are analyzed. A preliminary description and evaluation of the service concept and a commercial evaluation concerning revenue and costs are carried out.

People with knowledge and experience in this particular field, both employees of the service company and key customers, should participate in the evaluation process. The purpose is to decide if it is feasible and profitable to proceed, and to identify key factors that will affect the quality of the service and its value for potential customers.

The concept is also tested against other services and examined from a technical and economic point of view. As a basis for the economic evaluation, a cost analysis is conducted and a value-based price is set.

Employees, suppliers, and customers evaluate the new service idea together. Based on their input, management decides whether or not to proceed. It must consider how the new idea ties in with company goals, how well consumers' primary and secondary needs can be met, the relative advantage for the customer, and the competition in the market. Taking both primary and secondary needs into account, the core service as well as the support services are specified. How well does the new service fit in with the company's current range of services? A central question in this analysis is to what extent the current servuction system can be used.

Customer and Competitor Analysis for Concept Evaluation and Specification

At this point, a more comprehensive analysis of consumer needs, wishes, and expectations is carried out. This calls for up-to-date information from and about potential customers. A thorough analysis of competitors and other businesses with similar services is also helpful. The process of designing a service includes detailed description and analysis of consumer needs and expectations, detailed analysis of competing services, detailed analysis of the core and support services in relation to consumers' needs and expectations, and a commercial (revenue and cost) evaluation of the service concept.

Design of the Servuction System

The service concept places certain demands on the servuction system. Its resources must be used in such a way that the right service is produced. The design of the servuction system and the servuction process must go hand in hand.

The components of the servuction system are the staff of the service company, the customers, the organizational structure, and the physical environment. The design of a servuction system includes specification of resources based on the service concept, thorough evaluation of the resources in the existing servuction system, and a detailed description of the design of the new servuction system.

Detailed Design of the Servuction Process

At this stage, those activities that are to be utilized to produce the service are specified. Critical areas in the process must be considered. The role of the customer is clarified. Detailed flowcharts of how the service is to be produced are made. Alternative servuction processes are tested. It is possible to use computer-based simulation techniques. The development of the servuction process should result in a detailed description of this process with regard to activities, equipment, critical points, and line of visibility (what the customer is allowed to see). Furthermore, costs are calculated in detail, and a value-based price is determined; ideas on how to guide customer expectations are discussed; marketing communications are prepared; and instruments for measuring quality and for follow-up are decided on. Franchise based companies such as McDonald's and Tuff Cote in Europe have detailed process descriptions to assure high and even quality.

Closing Comments

The notion of service design has been received with great interest by practitioners in Sweden. My ongoing research on service design in major service organizations has generated some tentative results. First, practitioners see the generic differences between the task of developing physical products and that of developing services. Second, service providers feel the need for a more systematic way of developing new services. This should shorten lead times when launching new services and reduce failure rates, which will result in higher productivity. Third, service providers often express the problem of controlling the new service development process from a holistic point of view. In contrast, technical systems and solutions seem to determine the design process. Softer aspects, such as customer needs and behavior, become secondary.

My overriding theme has been that service design is the best route to lasting results in achieving quality in service operations. I have suggested that successful service design may be achieved by designing the service concept in conjunction with the servuction process and system.

Notes

1. Philip B. Crosby, *The Eternally Successful Organization* (New York: Plume, 1988); J. M. Juran, *Juran on Quality by Design: The New Steps for Planning Quality Into Goods and Services* (New York: Free Press, 1992).
2. Juran, *Juran on Quality*.
3. Eberhard Scheuing, *New Product Management* (Columbus, Ohio: Merrill, 1989), p. 366.
4. Bo Edvardsson, "Tjänstekonstruktion." Paper presented at the conference Kvalitet i kommuner och landsting, Gothenburg, Sweden, September 1991 (in Swedish).
5. ISO 9004-2, *Quality Management and Quality Systems Element—Part 2: Guidelines for Services.* ISO, 1991.
6. Ibid.
7. A. Parasuraman, L. L. Berry, and V. A. Zeithaml, "Understanding Customer Expectations of Service," *Sloan Management Review* 39 (Spring 1991).
8. ISO 9004-2, *Quality Management*.
9. E. S. Perelman, "The Story of CMA," *The Journal of Financial Service Strategy* 3 (April 1984), p. 21.
10. P. Eiglier and E. Langeard, *Servuction. Les Marketing des Services* (Paris: Wiley, 1987).
11. J. H. Donnelly, L. L. Berry, and T. W. Thompson, *Marketing Financial Services* (Homewood, Ill.: Dow Jones-Irwin, 1985), p. 147.
12. Eberhard Scheuing, *New Product Management*, p. 371.
13. E. V. Hippel, "A Customer-Active Paradigm for Industrial Product Idea Generation." *Industrial Innovation, Technology, Policy, Diffusion*, edited by M. J. Baker (London: Macmillan, 1979).

References

Buzzell, S. D., and B. T. Gale. *The PIMS Principles: Linking Strategy to Performance.* New York: Free Press, 1987.

Chase, Richard. "Service Quality and the Service Delivery System: A Diagnostic Framework." The QUIS-symposium, CTF, University of Karlstad, 1988.

Conti, T. "Process Management and Quality Function Deployment." *Quality Progress* 22, No. 12 (1989).

Crosby, P. B. *The Eternally Successful Organization.* New York: Plume, 1988.

Donnelly, J. H., L. L. Berry, and T. W. Thompson. *Marketing Financial Services.* Homewood, Ill.: Dow Jones-Irwin, 1985.

Edvardsson, B. *Company Strategies for Research and Development.* Institute for Economics and Statistics, SLU, Uppsala. Diss, 1981 (in Swedish).

————. "Service Quality in Customer Relationships: A Study of Critical Incidents in Mechanical Engineering Companies." *The Service Industries Journal* (1988).

————. "Management Consulting: Towards a Successful Relationship." *International Journal of Service Industry Management* (1990).

————. "Tjänstekonstruktion." Paper presented at the conference Kvalitet i kommuner och landsting, Gothenburg, Sweden, September 1991 (in Swedish).

Edvardsson, B., and B. O. Gustavsson. *Problem Detection in Service Management Systems—A Consistency Approach in Quality Improvement.* Working paper 90:13, CTF, University of Karlstad.

Edvardsson, B., and B. Thomasson. *Kvalitetsutveckling—ett managementperspektiv.* Lund: Studentlitteratur, 1991 (in Swedish).

Eiglier, P., and E. Langeard. *Servuction. Les Marketing des Services.* Paris: Wiley, 1987.

Ferguson, I. "Process Design." *Total Quality Management* (April 1990).

Gummesson, Evert. "Att utveckla servicekvalitet eller Varför finns det inga servicekonstruktörer?" In *Management i tjänstesamhället*, edited by B. Edvardsson and E. Gummesson. Lund: Liber, 1988 (in Swedish).

————. *Service Quality—A Holistic View.* Research report 90:8, CTF, University of Karlstad, 1990a.

————. "Service Design—The First Step Towards Service Quality." *Total Quality Management* (April 1990b).

Gupta, Y., and G. Torkzadeh. "Redesigning Bank Service Systems for Effective Marketing." *Long Range Planning* (1988).

Hippel, E. V. "A Customer-active Paradigm for Industrial Product Idea Generation." In *Industrial Innovation, Technology, Policy, Diffusion*, edited by M. J. Baker. London: Macmillan, 1979.

Hosick, W. *The Use of Blueprinting to Achieve Quality in Service.* Working paper, 1990.

ISO 9004-2, *Quality Management and Quality Systems Element—Part 2: Guidelines for Services.* ISO, 1991.

Juran, J. M. *Juran on Quality by Design: The New Steps for Planning Quality into Goods and Services.* New York: Free Press, 1992.

Larsson, R., and D. Bowen. "Organization and Customer: Managing Design and Coordination of Services." *Academy of Management Review* (1989).

Luchs, R. "Successful Businesses Compete on Quality—Not Costs." *Long Range Planning* 19 (1986).

Parasuraman, A., L. L. Berry, and V. A. Zeithaml. "Understanding Customer Expectations of Service." *Sloan Management Review* 39 (1991).

Perelman, E. S. "The Story of CMA. " *The Journal of Financial Service Strategy* 3
    (1984).
Scheuing, E. *New Product Management*. Columbus: Merrill, 1989a.
Scheuing, E., and E. M. Johnson. "Proposed Model for New Service Develop-
    ment." *The Journal of Services Marketing* 3 (1989b).
Shostack, G. L. "Designing Services that Deliver." *Harvard Business Review*
    (January–February 1984).
———. "Service Positioning Through Structural Change." *Journal of Marketing*
    51 (1987).

28

Fail-Safing Services

Richard B. Chase and Douglas M. Stewart,
University of Southern California

The service quality movement has borrowed many things from manufacturing Total Quality Management (TQM), particularly statistical methods, but it has overlooked one approach that can fundamentally alter the way we plan and execute quality management in services. That approach is *fail-safing*. Fail-safing, quite simply, is designing into a process certain features to prevent mistakes from becoming defects. It is different from the statistical process control approaches to quality in that it is concerned not with tracking errors but with eliminating them. Here we describe the basic theory underlying fail-safing in manufacturing, then propose a framework by which fail-safing can be systematically applied to services.

The fact that perfect quality is attainable from systems that are not being monitored and controlled by statistical control techniques (such as control charts) was brought to the fore by the late Shigeo Shingo, the engineering genius who created many of the features of the Toyota Just-In-Time system (JIT). Shingo argued that statistical quality control methods do not prevent defects. Although they tell us probabilistically when a defect can be expected to occur, they are after the fact. He contended that the way to prevent defects from coming out at the end of a process was to introduce fail-safe controls within the process.

Although one can find examples of fail-safing in services (indeed, we will provide several), we know of no service company that has adopted Shingo's philosophy in its quality programs. If one has, it is probably in the service analog of the factory—the back office—where materials rather than people are being processed. For Shingo's ideas to be used throughout the service delivery process, they must be recast to include various forms of customer interaction, be they in the front office, in the field, or over the phone. To do this requires addressing the technical elements of fail-safing and then linking them to the nature of service quality.

A Shingo Primer

In order to apply Shingo's methods to service quality, it is necessary to first understand the technical elements of fail-safing and how they relate to statistical methods. Statistics is a set of mathematical tools used to leverage the power of a small number of carefully chosen observations in order to infer population characteristics. Statistics can be a very powerful assessment tool for problem diagnosis, capability analysis, and experimental design. However, statistical sampling, being primarily a monitoring tool used to target corrective action efforts, is not capable of providing the proactive control over the process necessary to achieve zero defects. To justify this statement, we must first address the question: "Why do we perform inspections?"

The purpose of inspection should be to let us know when something in the process has gone wrong and needs to be fixed. Once this information is known, the source is located and the problem corrected. Shingo refers to this as informative inspection.[1] If the cause is "special," such as a broken tool, it will continue to create defects until it is fixed; therefore, the information feedback should occur as quickly as possible.

Although inspection serves an important need, historically it has involved an additional, separate function, making the inspection of a large volume of items very expensive. To save on costs, statistical sampling schemes have been developed that signal when there is a high probability of a problem with a special cause in the process. These sampling procedures are the essence of statistical process control (SPC). What is lost in this sampling process is immediate feedback and the ability to detect and correct defects that arise from common cause variation.

Since SPC samples are taken periodically over time, any special causes that arise during the interval will not be detected until the next sample is taken. If a special cause produces defects, these defects will continue to be produced undetected during this time. This may not be a great problem in batch production, but in just-in-time production or services, where those defects will be fed directly to the next stage (or, worse still, to the customer), this shortcoming becomes critical.

Fortunately, 100 percent inspection need not be an expensive process. The manner in which it is performed can greatly reduce costs and increase the rate of informative feedback. Shingo provides three 100 percent inspection methods and a family of inspection and prevention devices to provide this cost reduction. By eliminating or automating the mind-numbing job of the inspector, these methods can also reduce the possibility of inspector errors, which are commonly cited as another justification for the use of sampling.

Inspection Methods

Shingo classifies his inspection methods as *successive checking, self-checking*, and *source inspection*. A successive check is made at the beginning of the next processing step. Since the producer is notified immediately, production of defects due to special causes is limited to the work-in-process inventory between the two stages. If the inspection is moved back to the end of the current step through self-checking, only one defect will be produced before detection. A defect that is discovered at the end of a production step is the result of an underlying error in that step. For example, machine-based errors could include broken tools, missing or improperly aligned materials, or misadjustment. A human error might involve a forgotten step or a mistake in processing. By moving the inspection further back to check for the error at the source, defects can be prevented from ever occurring.[2]

Poka-Yoke

Utilizing the existing employees as inspectors can help reduce costs; however, much of the gain will be lost if these employees' jobs are made more difficult. To prevent this, it is necessary to make the act of inspection automatic and fast. Shingo accomplishes this with *poka-yoke* devices[3]—inexpensive procedures or automatic inspection devices that perform or facilitate one or more of the inspection methods mentioned above. These devices are usually developed by the workers and are generally simple and inexpensive. Common examples include jigs that will not allow parts to be incorrectly inserted, sensors to detect broken tools, and counters to ensure that the correct number of tasks were performed. The introduction of poka-yoke devices with the above inspection methods makes 100 percent inspection feasible and extremely effective in preventing defects.[4]

Shingo's approach (which also includes his single minute exchange of die [SMED] procedures) is now widely used in manufacturing, and there is evidence that Japanese firms are moving toward this approach to reduce defect levels below those normally obtainable through SPC. Shingo notes that Toyota Motor's production machines are equipped with an average of twelve fail-safe devices each.[5] Japan is not alone in recognizing the benefits of Shingo's ideas. In 1988, a Shingo Prize for Excellence in Manufacturing was established to recognize the growing number of U.S. firms enacting SMED and Zero (Defects) Quality Control in their operations.

Transferring Shingo's Concepts to Services

The essence of a service is the encounter between customer and server. To fail-safe a service, therefore, one must fail-safe the actions of each party, along with whatever supporting technology is employed. This is in contrast to manufacturing, where just the producer's actions (and equipment) must be fail-safed.

There are three aspects of the customer's involvement in the service that must be monitored to prevent customer errors that lead to defects: the *preparation for the encounter*, the *encounter* itself, and the *resolution of the encounter*. In fact, research done by TARP, a Washington, D.C.–based service research firm, indicates that one-third of all customer complaints are caused by the customers themselves.[6] Customers can make errors in preparation, such as failing to bring the necessary materials, failing to understand their role in the transaction, and failing to engage the correct service. During the encounter, the customer may fail to remember steps in the service process, fail to follow the system flow, fail to specify desires sufficiently, or merely fail to follow instructions. From a service improvement standpoint, customers can also be encouraged to signal service failures, learn from the experience, adjust expectations appropriately, and execute appropriate postencounter actions during the resolution of the encounter. In manufacturing, the customer does not directly interact with the production process, and his or her actions are generally ignored.

Obviously, inspection efforts cannot be focused entirely on the customer. The service provider must also monitor its own operations, just as the manufacturing producer does. The difference for services is that in addition to monitoring the *task*, or mechanics of the process, the service provider must monitor the *treatment* of the customers and the *tangible* or physical elements involved in the service. Task quality involves, among other things, doing the requested work correctly, in the correct order, and at the correct time. Maintaining the tangible aspects of service quality involves ensuring that errors such as dirty waiting rooms, unclear bills, annoying noise, unpleasant odors, harsh or inadequate lighting, or uncomfortable temperatures are corrected before they are discovered by a customer. The treatment quality is, however, a function of the interpersonal interaction between the customer and the provider. This is dependent on actions such as acknowledging the customer, listening to the customer, and reacting to the customer in an appropriate fashion, in order to provide what is perceived as courteous and professional service.

Service Fail-Safe Classification

Figure 28-1 presents a fail-safe classification scheme for services. It adds Shingo's manufacturing classification to the service quality dimensions discussed above.

Figure 28-1. Fail-safe classification scheme.

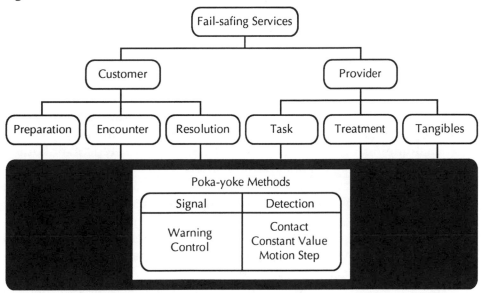

There are two ways in which a poka-yoke can signal a problem: through a passive warning or through an active control. Warning methods are merely lights or buzzers that call attention to the problem, and hence may be overlooked. Control methods prevent a warning from being ignored by stopping the production process until the error is corrected.[7]

Under Shingo's classification system, poka-yoke devices can have three means of detecting errors: contact methods, constant value methods, and motion step methods. These are the methods by which the poka-yoke identifies the problem; they can be used with either type of signaling. They translate roughly into identification by characteristics (by weight, dimension, or shape), by deviation from constant values (by counters, part kits, or critical condition sensors), and by deviation from process steps (systems that stop the process if a necessary step is omitted).[8]

Contact Methods

In manufacturing, contact setting functions rely on physical or electronic contact with the product to ensure that it is oriented correctly, that it is the correct part, or that it is of the proper dimensions. Common devices are jigs or notched parts that allow insertion in only one orientation; limit switches, photoelectric devices, or proximity sensors to ensure that a part is fully inserted into a machine, that all parts have been inserted, or that the correct tool is installed; and guides on conveyors that allow only correctly oriented or sized parts to pass.

Poka-yoke devices using contact methods abound in services and are used to prevent customer errors as well as provider errors. A prime example is found in many bus, train, and air terminals: Armrests are put on the seats to prevent people from sleeping on them and detracting from the tangibles of the facility. Chains that are used to configure lines in service facilities ensure that customers follow the flow and are served in an equitable fashion. Automatic flush toilets overcome another common customer error, and ensure that the service facility is maintained. At theme parks, height bars are often used to prevent guests who are too large or too small from boarding an attraction. Other prevalent contact methods are bells at store doors to signal the arrival of a customer and line length sensors to signal that a new register should be opened. Mirrors can be a visual contact warning device when they are placed in areas that allow service providers to periodically check personal appearance, a tangible aspect of the service.[9]

At the 300-seat Cove Restaurant in Deerfield Beach, Florida, there's often a forty-five-minute wait for a table. But silent pagers allow customers to roam the marina surrounding the restaurant without fear of losing their table call. These small devices vibrate when activated from the master seating control board at the host stand. Many restaurants use silent pagers to alert wait staff that food is ready, but the Cove Restaurant and the Texana Grill chain in Antioch, Tennessee, are among the first to use the technology to assist customers. "The pagers work beautifully for us," says Paul Hines, manager at the Cove. "We used to waste so much time searching for guests when their table was ready. Now we just buzz them and they know to come on up." Customers are less anxious about waits as well, he adds. "They know they can roam around, have a drink at our outside bar, and not worry about missing their table call. The wait time is much more relaxed." The Cove's system, which cost close to $5,000, has forty-eight pagers, and the host takes keys, a license, or a valet ticket in exchange for each pager.[10]

Constant Value Methods

Constant value methods involve some counting or measuring scheme in which a correct magnitude or setting must be present for production to proceed. In manufacturing these devices are normally counting devices or sensors (e.g., to measure temperature, pressure, or torque) set to some prespecified level and connected to the production machinery. An example of this is found on a welding machine; if the machine has not made the necessary number of spot welds, the clamp holding the part will refuse to disengage.[11] Part kits or automatic dispensers are also used to ensure that the correct number of parts are used, since if any parts remain, something has been forgotten. Constant value methods can also take the form of procedures, such as putting all necessary materials onto a layout mat so that nothing is omitted.

Hospitals are prominent users of constant value poka-yoke devices because of the potentially high cost of service failure. In the operating room, gauze is prepackaged in fixed numbers, and all instruments required for an operation come on a tray with indentations for each item. Before closing, all gauze is counted and the presence of all instruments is verified to ensure that nothing has been left inside the patient that would have to be removed later. The medication at many hospitals is prepackaged for each patient according to the doctors' prescribed dosage. As the nurse makes his or her rounds, he or she will use up the medication on the cart. Any medication remaining at the end of the round must be reconciled with changes ordered by the doctors. All of the items for some common procedures, such as catheter installation, come in kits. Any unused items remaining in the kit signal an improper installation.

Constant value methods are useful in more mundane services as well. McDonald's french fry scooper is a commonly seen example; it ensures that the task of putting the "just right" amount of fries in each package is done correctly.[12] Child care centers use things such as outlines on the floors and walls to show where toys are to be placed at the end of play time, the resolution stage in the children's encounter. In addition, check lists abound in many operations. A fast food restaurant identified friendliness as a desired treatment factor that they wanted to emphasize. Instead of telling the employees to smile all the time, they provided a mental check list of times when a smile was important, such as when greeting the customer, taking the order, informing the customer about the dessert special, and giving the customer change.[13]

Motion Step Methods

Motion step methods involve devices that require the completion of one step in the process before another can be completed. In manufacturing, these can take the form of switches in part bins that control shutters on other part bins. This prevents a part from being removed until the previously needed part has been taken. Kanban cards or sensing devices that can identify products are used to control access to parts, allowing only the correct parts to be mounted. Devices are also used to stop the product flow until a particular machine or tool has been activated, ensuring that the operation of concern was conducted.

In services, motion step methods are particularly useful in correcting or preventing customer errors. Airline lavatory doors are equipped with locks that must be used in order to activate the lights; this also activates the occupied sign and prevents embarrassing service failures.

A motion step method is employed by a cable TV company in trouble-shooting over the phone. A common mistake made by customers who report reception problems is that they have inadvertently changed the channel setting on their TV. However, if the repairperson asks if the customer is on the correct channel, he or she will often feel embarrassed or automatically say "yes." The poka-yoke used by the company to avoid these reactions is to instruct the customer to "turn the channel selector from channel 3 (the correct setting) to channel 5, and then back to 3." This ensures that the check is performed and that low-tech customers do not feel inept.[14]

At Sewell Cadillac's service department, color-coded tags are placed on top of newly arriving cars to identify which cars belong to a specific service adviser. The service adviser can then look out across the sea of cars to see which one should be dealt with next.[15]

Another motion step procedure is found in a service flyer for DEC. A simple flowchart is provided, and the decisions needed to arrive at the correct service contact telephone number are dependent on the customer's equipment model, installed equipment, and warranty classification. Because the customer must determine this information before calling, DEC is able to obtain all of the information necessary to quickly dispatch an appropriate service technician.

Fail-safing to ensure customer feedback in the resolution stage can also be obtained by inserting a necessary feedback step, such as the return of a guest comment card, before an incentive step, such as presentation of a small gift from the hotel.

Implementing Fail-Safing

Implementation of Shingo's methods in a service environment would logically begin at the design or start-up stage, when all obvious trouble spots are fail-safed. Later, during the course of normal operation, as unexpected defects arise, they could be fail-safed in a continuous improvement manner. The actual fail-safing process involves three steps.

First, it is necessary to understand the process flow. A good tool for this is a service blueprint, which traces the processing steps and the information flow between the customer and the server. The information flow includes such things as the directions the customer receives, the service request placed by the customer, and the nature of customer feedback. Between the customer and the server can be drawn a line of visibility, as suggested by Shostack[16] and shown in Figure 28-2. It is on

Figure 28-2. Fail-safing a typical automotive service operation.

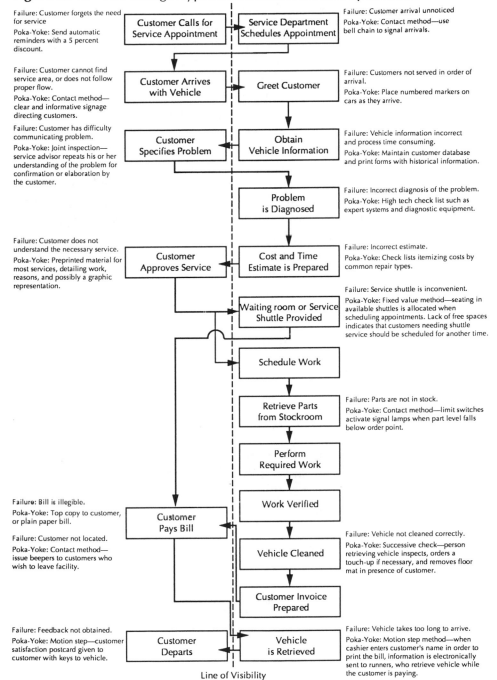

Failure: Customer forgets the need for service
Poka-Yoke: Send automatic reminders with a 5 percent discount.

Customer Calls for Service Appointment

Service Department Schedules Appointment

Failure: Customer arrival unnoticed
Poka-Yoke: Contact method—use bell chain to signal arrivals.

Failure: Customer cannot find service area, or does not follow proper flow.
Poka-Yoke: Contact method—clear and informative signage directing customers.

Customer Arrives with Vehicle

Greet Customer

Failure: Customers not served in order of arrival.
Poka-Yoke: Place numbered markers on cars as they arrive.

Failure: Customer has difficulty communicating problem.
Poka-Yoke: Joint inspection—service advisor repeats his or her understanding of the problem for confirmation or elaboration by the customer.

Customer Specifies Problem

Obtain Vehicle Information

Failure: Vehicle information incorrect and process time consuming.
Poka-Yoke: Maintain customer database and print forms with historical information.

Problem is Diagnosed

Failure: Incorrect diagnosis of the problem.
Poka-Yoke: High tech check list such as expert systems and diagnostic equipment.

Failure: Customer does not understand the necessary service.
Poka-Yoke: Preprinted material for most services, detailing work, reasons, and possibly a graphic representation.

Customer Approves Service

Cost and Time Estimate is Prepared

Failure: Incorrect estimate.
Poka-Yoke: Check lists itemizing costs by common repair types.

Waiting room or Service Shuttle Provided

Failure: Service shuttle is inconvenient.
Poka-Yoke: Fixed value method—seating in available shuttles is allocated when scheduling appointments. Lack of free spaces indicates that customers needing shuttle service should be scheduled for another time.

Schedule Work

Retrieve Parts from Stockroom

Failure: Parts are not in stock.
Poka-Yoke: Contact method—limit switches activate signal lamps when part level falls below order point.

Perform Required Work

Failure: Bill is illegible.
Poka-Yoke: Top copy to customer, or plain paper bill.

Work Verified

Customer Pays Bill

Failure: Customer not located.
Poka-Yoke: Contact method—issue beepers to customers who wish to leave facility.

Vehicle Cleaned

Failure: Vehicle not cleaned correctly.
Poka-Yoke: Successive check—person retrieving vehicle inspects, orders a touch-up if necessary, and removes floor mat in presence of customer.

Customer Invoice Prepared

Failure: Feedback not obtained.
Poka-Yoke: Motion step—customer satisfaction postcard given to customer with keys to vehicle.

Customer Departs

Vehicle is Retrieved

Failure: Vehicle takes too long to arrive.
Poka-Yoke: Motion step method—when cashier enters customer's name in order to print the bill, information is electronically sent to runners, who retrieve vehicle while the customer is paying.

Line of Visibility

this line that the search for errors begins. Defects can occur any time information, materials, or people pass across this line.

The next step is to find chronic defects and determine where they have been occurring. By following the service map backwards through the process, the original source of the defect can be located. It should be noted, however, that this could involve crossing the line of visibility several times before the source is located.

The final step is to set up a fail-safing system to block each mistake from turning into a defect. Joseph Juran terms this step "error cause removal." This may call for source inspection, self-inspection, or sequential checks as defined earlier; or it may call for what we would term "joint inspection" involving both customer and server, which will occur only in a service encounter. An example of joint inspection involves repeating the order back to the customer to ensure that the correct information was accessed, exchanged, and understood.

As in manufacturing, a multitude of fail-safes will often be needed to ensure quality in services. Hiroyuki Hirano, of the JIT Management Company, has found that a 60 percent rule works well for implementing potential fail-safes. If you think there is a better than even chance that a particular fail-safe will work, try it. If it doesn't work, you will probably learn enough from your effort to design another that will.[17]

Conclusion

While fail-safing seems most appropriate for standardized services, it can also be applied to customized services such as those provided by professional service firms. Although a firm may provide a broad menu of services, the processes are typically the same. "Custom" services often have many operations that are continually repeated, such as common filings of wills, contracts, and powers of attorney in law firms or common specifications for building pipes, sprinkler systems, and landscaping in engineering consulting firms. Our advice is to manage the exceptions, but fail-safe the common steps.

Fail-safing techniques have been very successful in manufacturing, and it is now time to incorporate them to their fullest extent in services as well. The key benefits of fail-safing are that it gives a focus for service quality efforts that is simple and nonthreatening and, most importantly, provides an immediate improvement in quality.

Notes

1. Shigeo Shingo, *Zero Quality Control: Source Inspection and the Poka-Yoke System*, trans. Andrew P. Dillon (Cambridge: Productivity Press, 1986), p. 58.

2. Ibid., pp. 67–92.
3. From the Japanese *yokeru*, "to avoid" and *poka*, "inadvertent errors."
4. Shingo, *Zero Quality Control*, p. 52. Matsushita Electric achieved six months with zero defects in 1977. During this period, they processed over 30,000 items per month.
5. Alan G. Robinson and Dean M. Schroeder, "The Limited Role of Statistical Quality Control in a Zero Defect Environment" (to appear in *Production and Inventory Management Journal*).
6. Kristin Anderson and Ron Zemke, *Delivering Knock Your Socks Off Service* (New York: AMACOM, 1991), pp. 39–40.
7. Shingo, *Zero Quality Control*, pp. 99–100.
8. Nikkan Kogyo Shimbun, Ltd./Factory Magazine, *Poka-Yoke: Improving Product Quality by Preventing Defects* (Cambridge: Productivity Press, 1988), p. 17.
9. Theodore Levitt, "Production-Line Approach to Service," *Harvard Business Review* (September–October 1972).
10. Jeffrey Edelson, "The Food Service Industry: Examples in Products and Services," (USC EMBA Failsafe Project Report, June 1989), p. 4.
11. Shingo, *Zero Quality Control*, p. 186.
12. Levitt, "Production-Line Approach."
13. Fred Luthans and Tim Davis, "Applying Behavioral Management Techniques in Service Organizations," *Service Management Effectiveness* (San Francisco: Jossey-Bass, 1990), p. 194.
14. Anderson and Zemke, *Delivering Knock Your Socks Off Service*, pp. 59–60.
15. Carl Sewell and Paul B. Brown, *Customers for Life* (New York: Doubleday, 1990), p. 63.
16. G. Lynn Shostack, "Designing Services that Deliver," *Harvard Business Review* (January–February 1984).
17. Nikkan Kogyo Shimbun, Ltd./Factory Magazine, *Poka-Yoke*, p. 24.

29

Managing the Evidence of Service

Mary Jo Bitner, Arizona State University

When a company offers an intangible service, how do consumers choose it, evaluate it, and assess its quality? On what evidence is an intangible service judged? For example, how do consumers choose between two different dentists, and how do they judge whether they are satisfied with the services of a particular car repair business? Research and theory suggest that customers rely on a variety of cues or surrogate indicators of service to choose among alternatives and judge quality.

Intangibility and Service Evidence

The primary characteristic that distinguishes goods from services is the relative intangibility of most services. While a manufactured good can be seen, felt, and touched, most services cannot be, and therefore they must be experienced by consumers before they can be evaluated. Clearly, tangibility exists along a continuum, and all products exhibit some tangible as well as intangible qualities.[1] However, services *tend* to be more intangible, while goods *tend* to be more tangible. It has been suggested that because of their intangibility, it is more difficult for consumers to evaluate services prior to purchase, to compare different service alternatives, and to judge the quality of service even after it has been experienced.[2]

Research suggests that customers rely on the tangible evidence of service, or perhaps surrogate indicators of service, when they are unable to judge the actual quality of service. For example, one study suggested that first impressions of a firm's reception area design will influence consumers' overall impressions of the firm.[3] Another study showed that travel customers' beliefs about and satisfaction with a travel agent were influenced by whether the travel agent's office was organized or disorganized.[4] And another study showed that airline customers were likely to perceive an airline as having lower safety standards if there were coffee stains on its tray tables. Research on service quality across a variety of service industries suggests that above and beyond the basic reliability of service, consumers rely on cues such as employee responsiveness, empathy, assurance, and tangibles to assess quality.[5]

Clearly, the reception area decor, the travel agent's desk (organized vs. disorganized), the coffee stains on the tray table, and the empathy of a service provider can and may be totally independent of the objective quality of service. That is, the disorganized travel agent *may* in reality have an outstanding record of reliable service and provide better quality overall than competitors. However, customers are likely to rely on cues like office clutter in the absence of other criteria on which to choose or judge a service. The process or operational flow of activities by which the service is delivered is also critical in forming perceptions of the service.

Figure 29-1 depicts the three major categories of service evidence as experienced by the customer: people, process, and physical evidence. Together, these elements constitute what is referred to here as the "evidence of service." All three elements, or a subset, are present in every encounter a customer has with a service firm.

People

All of the human actors involved in the delivery of a service provide cues to the customer regarding the nature of the service itself. This includes the employees of the service firm and other customers in the service environment. How these people are dressed, their personal appearance, and their attitudes and behaviors all influence the customer's perceptions

Figure 29-1. The evidence of service.

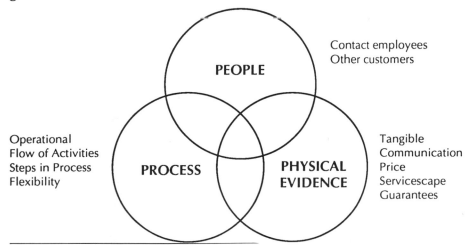

of the service. The service provider or contact person can be very important. In fact, for some services, such as consulting, counseling, teaching, and other professional relationship-based services, the provider *is* the service. In other cases, the contact person may play what appears to be a relatively small part in service delivery, for instance, a telephone installer, an airline baggage handler, or a hotel bellperson. Yet research suggests that even these providers may be the focal point of service encounters that can prove to be critical for the firm.[6]

Other customers can also influence perceptions of the service. Prior to purchase, a person may use other customers as a cue to the type of service being offered and the market segment. For example, before entering a restaurant, a potential customer may peer through the window to see whether he or she "fits" with the other customers already in the restaurant. The decision to go in or not is partially determined by the other customers and the evidence they provide regarding the type of restaurant and market segment. Frequently, the service experience itself is influenced by other customers, since in many instances, for example, in classrooms, hospitals, retail stores, airplanes, and restaurants, customers experience the service together. The experience of one customer may easily influence the experiences of many others. Sometimes, the needs of one customer may even conflict with the needs of another.[7]

Process

The actual steps the customer experiences, or the operational flow of service, will also provide him or her with evidence on which to judge the service. Some service operations are very complex, requiring the customer to follow a complicated and extensive series of actions to complete the process. Highly bureaucratized services frequently follow this pattern, and the logic of the steps involved often escapes the customer. Another distinguishing characteristic of the process that can provide evidence to the customer is whether the service follows a production-line/standardized approach or whether the process is an empowered/customized one.[8] None of these characteristics of the process are inherently better or worse than others. Rather, the point here is that these process characteristics are another form of evidence used by the consumer to judge service. For example, two successful airline companies, Southwest (U.S. airline) and SAS (Scandinavian airline), follow extremely different process models. Southwest is a no-frills (no food, no assigned seats), no exceptions, low-priced airline that offers frequent, relatively short-length, domestic flights in the United States. All of the evidence they provide (from their price, to their people, to the standardized process they follow) is consistent with their vision and market position. SAS, on the other hand, focuses on the business traveler and is concerned with meeting individual traveler needs. Thus, its process is highly customized to the individual, and employees are empowered to provide nonstandard service when needed. Both airlines have been very successful, and in both cases the evidence of service that is showcased in their operational process is highly compatible with the firm's goals and the needs of the identified market segment.

Physical Evidence

The physical evidence of service includes tangible representations of the service such as advertising and other forms of communication, including billing statements, letters, and business cards; service guarantees; price; and the physical environment in which the service is delivered and the customer and the firm's employees interact.[9] When consumers have little on which to judge the actual quality of service, they will rely on these cues, just as they rely on the cues provided by the people and the service process. Physical evidence cues provide excellent opportunities for the firm to send consistent and strong messages regarding the firm's purpose, the intended market segments, and the nature of the service.

In many service industries, the service setting, or "servicescape," provides a particularly prominent representation of physical evidence. The servicescape is defined as the "built environment, or the human-made, physical surroundings of the service."[10] The servicescape plays a variety of roles with respect to both the customers and the employees of the service firm. For example, the servicescape serves as a "package" for the service offering in a way not unlike that of a product's package. Product packages are designed to portray a particular image to the consumer as well as evoke a particular sensory or emotional reaction.[11] In a service setting, the servicescape does the same thing through the interaction of many complex stimuli. The service package can also convey the values of the organization and the ideals it hopes to achieve.

The physical surroundings may also serve to differentiate a firm from its competitors and signal who the intended market segment is. In strolling through any large shopping mall, one quickly notes the environmental distinctions between clothing stores catering to the youth market and those aimed at older market segments. Even without examining the merchandise, a shopper instinctively knows that neon signs, bright lights, and loud music signal a youth market segment. Similarly, legal clinics and legal chain operations intended for price-sensitive, middle-income persons can effectively use their physical environments to distinguish themselves from large, corporate law firms. By keeping furnishings relatively simple and functional, the legal clinics signal both intended market segment and price level to potential customers, and simultaneously differentiate themselves from the large firms.

A final role of the servicescape is that of facilitating the individual and interdependent actions of persons in the environment, namely the customers and employees. How the environment is designed enhances or inhibits the efficient flow of activities in the servicescape. A well-designed, functional facility can make the service a pleasure to experience from the customer's point of view and a pleasure to perform from the employee's viewpoint. On the other hand, poor and inefficient design may frustrate both the employee and the customer as they seek to carry out their respective plans. Similarly, the servicescape can encourage and nurture certain social behaviors between and among customers and employees. For example, Benihana restaurants and Club Med facilities show how servicescapes can be designed to enhance employee/customer and customer/customer interactions. On the other hand, airport waiting areas and university classrooms are notorious for discouraging interpersonal interaction through the way they are designed and laid out.

Identifying the Evidence

Service evidence will communicate to the consumer, whether the messages sent are intended or unintentional, planned or accidental. This section of the chapter proposes a way of thinking about service evidence that can enhance the strategic value of all three types of evidence cues.

Mapping the Service

The three categories of service evidence—people, process and physical evidence—may be more or less important for a particular service firm or industry.[12] Thus, a first step in determining evidence strategy would be to identify the relevant forms of evidence presented to the customer in a given context. Service mapping, or blueprinting, provides a useful tool to begin assessing and identifying evidence opportunities.[13]

A service map visually displays the service by simultaneously depicting the process of service delivery, the roles of customers and employees, and the visible elements of the service. The service map provides an excellent starting point for isolating evidence opportunities. Figures 29-2 and 29-3 show service maps for two different services: express mail and an overnight hotel stay. (The blueprints are deliberately kept very simple, showing only the most basic steps involved in the process. Complex diagrams could be developed for each and every step, and the internal processes could be much more fully developed, if desired.) The horizontal lines of the blueprint separate (1) the actions of the customer from those of the contact person, and (2) those contact

Figure 29-2. Express mail delivery service.

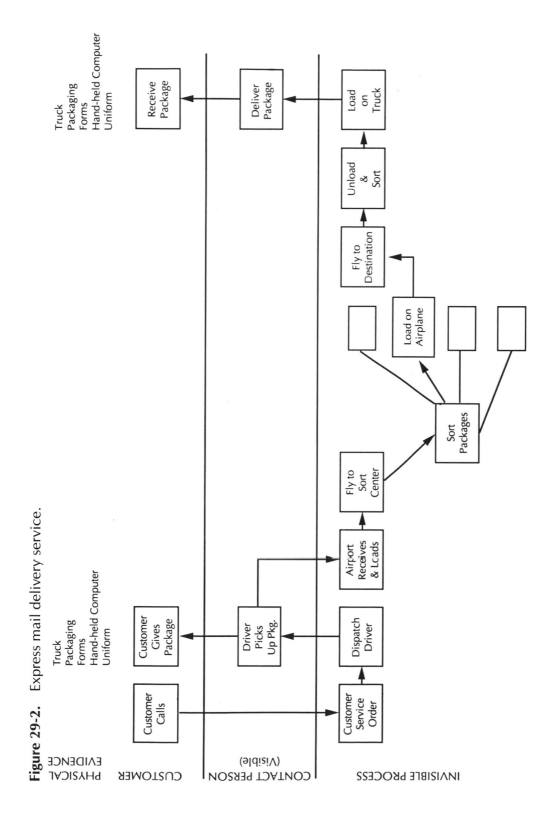

PHYSICAL EVIDENCE

Truck
Packaging
Forms
Hand-held Computer
Uniform

Truck
Packaging
Forms
Hand-held Computer
Uniform

CUSTOMER

Customer Calls

Customer Gives Package

Receive Package

CONTACT PERSON (Visible)

Driver Picks Up Pkg.

Deliver Package

INVISIBLE PROCESS

Customer Service Order

Dispatch Driver

Airport Receives & Loads

Fly to Sort Center

Sort Packages

Load on Airplane

Fly to Destination

Unload & Sort

Load on Truck

Figure 29-3. Overnight hotel stay.

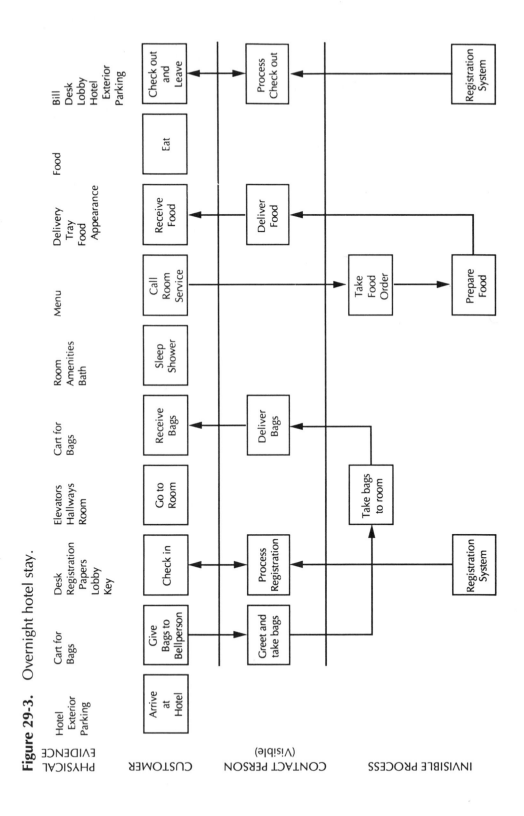

person steps that are visible from the invisible process steps. A service map may be read horizontally from left to right to understand the actions or steps that must be performed by either the customer or the contact employees of the firm, or it may be read vertically to understand the structural relationships that exist to support the actions of the customers and employees.

For example, in reading the express mail blueprint, the customer actions are simply three: phone call, turn over package, receive package (a different customer). The visible contact employee actions are minimal as well: pick up package, deliver package. A significant number of complex steps and procedures must occur behind the line of visibility, however, to ensure that these two actions can be performed accurately and reliably. In fact, customers are usually fascinated to see the complexities of the express mail process, and Federal Express frequently invites its customers to tour its sorting and delivery facilities in order to further make tangible this seemingly simple service.

Evidence Opportunities

The maps presented in Figures 29-2 and 29-3 help in visualizing the three types of evidence and provide a common ground for beginning to assess and identify evidence opportunities. For example, the complexity of the *process* and the actual steps involved from the customer's point of view are clearly evident reading horizontally across the top section of the blueprint. From the customer's point of view, the process of staying overnight at a hotel is more complex and interactive than the process of using an express mail service. The *people* who interact with the customer are also clearly identifiable by reading across the line of interaction and noting each crossover point where there is an interaction with an employee of the firm, whether or not the customer sees that employee (i.e., whether there is a face-to-face interaction or a phone conversation). There are many more points of human interaction in the hotel example than in the express mail example. In both cases, it is clear from the blueprint exactly who the customer interacts with and at what steps in the process. Each of these interaction points is a potential opportunity for providing service evidence. The *physical evidence* of service, while not typically shown on a blueprint, can easily be added, as it has been in Figures 29-2 and 29-3. This was done by analyzing each step in the process (from the customer's point of view) and adding relevant evidence that the customer would evaluate at that step.

The two case examples will be described in a bit more detail to illustrate the uses of the blueprints.

Express Mail

In examining the express mail map in Figure 29-2, it is clear that from the customer's point of view there are only three points at which evidence of the service is provided: when the phone call is made, when the package is picked up, and when the package is delivered. The visible evidence at each of these points of interaction is depicted on the blueprint and can be analyzed for its consistency and ability to communicate clearly the firm's image and purpose. In the specific case of Federal Express, the employee's uniform, the forms and packaging used to transmit the package, the truck driven by the employee, and the hand-held computer carried by the employee are the "tangible evidence" of the service. In this case, the servicescape does not play a role with respect to the customer, since the customer would not routinely see the airplane, the sorting facility, and the customer service center where much of the actual service delivery process is carried out. From the customer's point of view, the *process* is simple (three steps) and relatively standardized, the *people* that perform the service are the phone order taker and the delivery people, and the *physical evidence* is composed of the document package, the transmittal forms, the truck, and the hand-held computer. The complex process that occurs behind the line of visibility is of little interest or concern to the customer.

Once the evidence of service has been identified through the mapping approach, then opportunities for change can be evaluated. Is enough evidence of service provided so that the customer *knows* that the service has actually been performed? Is the evidence compatible and consistent? Does the evidence communicate the desired image? Does the evidence fit the needs and preferences of the target market?

Overnight Hotel Stay

In the case of the overnight hotel stay depicted in Figure 29-3, it is clear that the customer is more actively involved in the service than he or she is in the express mail service just described. Even in this simple overnight hotel stay, the customer performs a number of actions in experiencing the service. The guest must first check in, then go to the hotel room, where a variety of steps take place (receiving bags, sleeping, showering, eating breakfast, etc.), and finally check out. Imagine how much more complex this process *could* be and how many more interactions might occur if the service map depicted a week-long vacation at the hotel, or even a three-day business conference. From the service map it is also clear (by reading across the line of interaction) whom the guest interacts with and thus the *people* who provide evidence of service to the customer. Several interactions occur with a variety of hotel employees, including the bellperson, the front desk clerk, the food service order desk, and the food delivery person. Each of the points of interaction is an evidence opportunity. In addition, the servicescape plays a *major* role in service delivery. The hotel facility itself is critical in communicating the image of the hotel company, in providing satisfaction for the guest through the manner in which the hotel room is designed and maintained, and in facilitating the actions and interactions of both the guest and the employees of the hotel. In the hotel case, the *process* is relatively complex (although again somewhat standardized), the *people* providing service evidence are a variety of front-line employees as well as other guests in the hotel, and the *physical evidence* includes everything from the guest registration form to the design of the lobby and room, to the uniforms worn by front-line employees.

Again, as with the express mail case, once the points of evidence are identified through mapping, opportunities for change can be assessed. Given the importance and complexity of the servicescape in the hotel industry, special attention will be focused on the facility design from the perspective of *both* employees and customers.

Guidelines for Evidence Strategy

Given the relative intangibility of most services, the strategy for managing the evidence of service is critical. And customers will react to the company's evidence whether or not an evidence strategy exists. That is, the tangible evidence of service will communicate to customers, whether or not its power to do so is recognized and planned. The following guidelines capture the essence of a plan for evidence strategy.

Recognize the Strategic Impact of Evidence

Before an evidence strategy can be effective, it must be linked clearly to the company's overall goals and vision. Thus the first step is to know what those goals are and to determine how the evidence strategy can support them. At a minimum, the basic service concept, the target markets (both internal and external), and the firm's broad vision of its future must be identified.

Map the Evidence of Service

The next step is to map the service. Everyone should be able to *see* the service process and the existing elements of evidence. An effective way to depict service evidence is through the service map. While service maps clearly have multiple purposes,[14] they can be particularly useful in visually capturing evidence opportunities. People, process, and physical evidence can be seen in the service map. From the map, one can read the actions involved in service delivery, the complexity of the process, the points of human interaction that provide evidence opportunities, and the tangible representations present at each step. Employees, customers, and managers can all be involved in constructing the service map, which will then give them common ground for moving ahead to identify opportunities.

Clarify Roles of the Servicescape

Sometimes the servicescape has no role in service delivery from the customer's point of view. This is essentially the case with express mail, where the customer rarely sees the actual facilities where service is provided. However, in many cases, such as hotels and health care, the servicescape plays multiple roles with respect to both customer and employee actions and attitudes.[15] Clarifying the roles played by the servicescape in a particular situation will aid in identifying opportunities and deciding just who needs to be consulted in making facility design decisions.

Assess and Identify Evidence Opportunities

Once the current forms of evidence and the roles of the servicescape are understood, then possible changes and improvements can be identified. One question to ask is: Are there missed opportunities to provide service evidence? For example, the service map of an insurance or utility service may show that little if any evidence of service is ever provided to the customer. A strategy might then be developed to provide more evidence of service to show the customer exactly what he or she is paying for. Or it may be discovered that the evidence provided is sending inconsistent messages that don't serve to enhance the firm's image or goals. For example, a restaurant might find that its high price cue is not consistent with the design of the restaurant, which suggests "family dining" to its intended market segment. Another set of questions to address concerns whether the current evidence of service suits the needs and preferences of the target market. And, finally, does the evidence strategy take into account the needs (sometimes incompatible) of both customers and employees? This question is particularly relevant in making decisions regarding the servicescape.[16]

Be Prepared to Update and Modernize the Evidence

Some aspects of the evidence, particularly the servicescape, require frequent or at least periodic updating and modernizing. Even if the vision of the company doesn't change, time itself takes a toll on physical evidence, necessitating change and modernization. Organizations clearly understand this when it comes to advertising strategy, but sometimes other elements of physical evidence can be overlooked.

Conclusion

In presenting itself to the consumer, a service firm is concerned with communicating a desired image, with sending consistent and compatible messages through all forms of evidence, and with providing the type of service evidence the target customers want and can understand. Frequently, however, evidence decisions are made over time and by various functions within the organization. For example, decisions regarding employee uniforms may be made by the human resources area, servicescape design decisions may be made by the facilities management group, process design decisions are most frequently made by operations managers, and advertising and pricing decisions may be made by the marketing department. Thus, it is not surprising that the evidence of service may at times be less than consistent. Service mapping, or blueprinting, is presented here as a valuable tool for communicating within the firm, identifying existing service evidence, and providing a springboard for changing or providing new forms of evidence.

Notes

1. G. Lynn Shostack, "Breaking Free From Product Marketing," *Journal of Marketing* 41 (April 1977), pp. 73–80.
2. Valarie A. Zeithaml, "How Consumer Evaluation Processes Differ Between Goods and Services," in *Marketing of Services*, James H. Donnelly and William R. George, eds. (Chicago: American Marketing Association, 1981), pp. 186–190.
3. Suzyn Ornstein, "First Impressions of the Symbolic Meanings Connoted by Reception Area Design," *Environment and Behavior* 24, no. 1 (January 1992), pp. 85–110.
4. Mary Jo Bitner, "Evaluating Service Encounters: The Effects of Physical Surroundings and Employee Responses," *Journal of Marketing* (January 1990), pp. 71–84.
5. A. Parasuraman, Valarie A. Zeithaml, and Leonard L. Berry, "SERVQUAL: A Multiple-Item Scale for Measuring Consumer Perceptions of Service Quality," *Journal of Retailing* 64, no. 1 (1988), pp. 12–40.
6. Mary Jo Bitner, Bernard H. Booms, and Mary Stanfield Tetreault, "The Service Encounter: Diagnosing Favorable and Unfavorable Incidents," *Journal of Marketing* 54, no. 1 (January 1990), pp. 71–84.

7. Boas Shamir, "Between Service and Servility: Role Conflict in Subordinate Service Roles," *Human Relations* 33, no. 10 (1980), pp. 741–756; Charles L. Martin and Charles A. Pranter, "Compatibility Management: Customer-to-Customer Relationships in Service Environments," *Journal of Services Marketing* 3, no. 3 (Summer 1989), pp. 5–15.

8. David E. Bowen and Edward E. Lawler III, "The Empowerment of Service Workers: What, Why, How, and When," *Sloan Management Review* 33, no. 3 (Spring 1992), pp. 31–39.

9. Leonard L. Berry and A. Parasuraman, *Marketing Services* (New York: The Free Press, 1991), Chapter 6.

10. Mary Jo Bitner, "Servicescapes: The Impact of Physical Surroundings on Customers and Employees," *Journal of Marketing* 56, no. 2 (April 1992), pp. 57–71.

11. Michael R. Solomon, "Packaging the Service Provider," *Services Industries Journal* 5, no. 1 (1985), pp. 64–71.

12. Stephen J. Grove, Raymond P. Fisk, and Mary Jo Bitner, "Dramatizing the Service Experience: A Managerial Approach," in *Advances in Services Marketing and Management: Research and Practice, Vol. 1*, Teresa A. Swartz, David E. Bowen, and Stephen W. Brown, eds. (Greenwich, Conn.: JAI Press, Inc., 1992).

13. G. Lynn Shostack, "Designing Services That Deliver," *Harvard Business Review* 62 (January-February 1984), pp. 133–139; G. Lynn Shostack, "Service Positioning Through Structural Change," *Journal of Marketing* 51 (January 1989), pp. 34–43; Jane Kingman-Brundage, "The ABC's of Service System Blueprinting," in *Designing a Winning Service Strategy*, Mary Jo Bitner and Lawrence A. Crosby, eds. (Chicago: American Marketing Association 1989), pp. 30–33.

14. Kingman-Brundage, "The ABC's of Service."

15. Bitner, "Servicescapes."

16. Ibid.

30

Purchasing and Service Quality

Douglas P. Brusa, Lamont-Doherty Geological Observatory,
and Eberhard E. Scheuing, St. John's University

Within an organization, the purchasing function provides the critical link to an organization's external sources of goods and services. In the value chain extending from the organization's external suppliers to its external customers, the quality of the inputs received from suppliers vitally affects the quality of the outputs delivered to customers. Purchasing professionals thus play an essential role in their organizations' quality processes by assuming responsibility for the quality of external inputs as well as the quality of their own performance in serving their internal customers.

More than half of an organization's revenue stream typically flows back out in the form of payments for externally acquired goods and services. Purchasers must make sure that this money is well spent. Accordingly, they are often held to the Golden Rule of Purchasing:

To Acquire Needed Goods and Services

▲ Of the right quality
▲ In the right quantity
▲ At the right price
▲ At the right time
▲ From the right source

The right quality is the quality that does the job—not more, not less. For purchasers, this means meeting the requirements of both external and internal customers. These requirements go beyond meeting specifications and include such other factors as timeliness, accuracy, responsiveness, and communication. Purchasers must endeavor to understand the full range and complexity of their customers' requirements, communicate them to suppliers, and manage the suppliers' performance against them.

Purchasing's Role in Quality Management

If quality means meeting customer requirements, purchasing must begin this journey by identifying its customers. At first blush, it seems easy to determine who purchasing's customers are. After all, are they not the internal user departments that forward requisitions that prompt purchasing to issue purchase orders?

The actual dynamics of the situation are considerably more complex than that. Multiple players from several functions are usually involved in the group decision-making process that can be referred to as a "buying center." Quality can be achieved only if their individual and collective requirements are fully understood and prioritized. This requires an open dialogue and careful analysis in a cross-functional setting.

Once purchasing has reached a comfort level with regard to its understanding of customer requirements, its job is to communicate these requirements to the chosen suppliers. Traditionally these suppliers have made only half-hearted efforts to meet customer requirements. This limited responsiveness was due to the fact that purchasers placed only individual orders with them and thus gave them little incentive to excel. They had to compete with a multitude of alternative sources, received only part of an organization's business, and were continually being squeezed for further price concessions.

The fallacy of this transaction-oriented multiple sourcing approach has become painfully evident in recent years. Its short-sighted obsession with reducing first-in cost has been detrimental to the achievement of quality in purchased goods and services. It resulted in suppliers being preoccupied with meeting dates and cost targets rather than quality targets. Enlightened organizations have consequently been trimming their supplier bases in an effort to foster closer, longer-term working relationships. This difficult process has been paying off. Organizations that have decided to partner with selected suppliers have found these suppliers considerably more attentive to stated requirements.

Ideally, this communication process will far transcend written exchanges. Face-to-face communications, mutual site visits, and broad-based interactions are essential to an open, fruitful dialogue concerning quality. Purchasing needs to be the driver and owner of this powerful process. Long-term mutual commitment is at the heart of supplier-customer linkages that are less vulnerable to competitive underpricing because they are based on trust, openness, and joint effort toward continuous improvement of quality and cost.

Where these prior steps have been properly taken, purchasers find it relatively easy to manage actual supplier performance to meet customer requirements. Suppliers who fully understand customer requirements will be able and motivated to diagnose and correct their own shortcomings. Thus purchasers will be able to cooperate closely with them in identifying the root causes of potential and actual quality problems and preventing their future occurrence.

Purchasing Quality vs. Quality of Purchasing

Although it is essential that an organization's purchasing function obtain quality inputs from outside sources, rendering quality service to the internal constituencies is just as important. Dissatisfaction of internal customers is still all too common. Why do they perceive inadequate performance by purchasing? And what can and should purchasers do about it?

Inasmuch as purchasers are not only intermediaries but also drivers and process owners in interactions with external suppliers, they are pivotal players in an organization's sourcing system. This system will be only as good as the service purchasers render to their customers. Rather than being reactive and passive conduits, purchasers are and should be proactive participants in the sourcing system. How well the organization as a whole performs hinges on how well they perform in meeting their customers' requirements. They are responsible for their own performance as well as the performance of the suppliers they manage.

Enlightened purchasers thus apply the same quality principles that they use with external suppliers to their own work. They ask their customers what their requirements are and ask them for performance ratings and improvement suggestions. They are not afraid of learning about their weaknesses because they are professionals who cherish the opportunity to improve. Being human, they delight in praise. They also appreciate the fact that only a learning, improving organization will survive and prosper in a turbulent environment, and that improvement means "us," not "them."

Since meeting customer requirements means not only understanding them but also being able to meet them, quality purchasers continually build their professionalism. They read the professional literature; attend lectures, workshops, seminars, and conferences; and pursue professional certification as C.P.M.s, a competence designation awarded by the National Association of Purchasing Management in a rigorous program. More than that, they make a strong commitment to and partner with their internal customers, who ultimately serve external customers, the lifeblood of the organization.

World-class purchasers benchmark their practices by comparing them with the best in the world. They study other organizations' purchasing systems and processes to obtain ideas on how they can improve theirs, and they are willing to reciprocate by sharing information freely. They look to improve productivity and eliminate waste in purchasing by using annual blanket orders and systems contracts to secure their organizations' needs from selected sources without having to issue a torrent of paperwork. They avail themselves of artificial intelligence and expert systems in managing their sourcing responsibilities, and they rely on electronic linkages to their external suppliers for quick, low-cost, accurate information exchanges. Where possible, they employ computerized inventory models and electronic data interchange (EDI) in the standard ANSI X.12 format to minimize inventory-related costs. Electronic transmission of purchase orders, invoices, and other documents reduces lead times, required inventory levels, and investment, and consequently reduces cost.

To achieve and maintain service quality in their own endeavors, purchasing professionals keep in touch with their customers. They inform them of new products and services, new sources, savings and performance improvement opportunities, delivery schedules, price changes, and other matters of interest. They issue correct purchase orders and carefully crafted contracts to avoid subsequent adjustments; they select well-qualified suppliers and audit, monitor, and manage the quality of their output; and they ensure on-time, if not just-in-time (JIT), delivery or performance. They negotiate favorable terms and conditions and make sure that invoices are accurate. In short, they provide their customers with peace of mind through mutually beneficial relationships.

Unfortunately, in most organizations, purchasing toils in relative obscurity and does not really get to enjoy the fruits of its labors. Its customers tend to be quick to complain about any shortcomings and slow with their praise. They may even bypass purchasing partially or completely and deal directly with external suppliers, often in violation of written policy. Conversely, most purchasers do not enjoy pay-for-performance arrangements that allow them to share in the savings they help generate for their organizations. Their "reward" for exceptional performance is typically a pat on the shoulder and continued employment. Even recognition is usually lacking. Although many organizations recognize outstanding suppliers with plaques and ceremonies, outstanding purchasers do not enjoy such moments of glory. Yet the same organizations will celebrate their outstanding sales achievers in elaborate ceremonies, followed by material rewards. They do this in spite of the fact that a dollar saved in purchasing adds a dollar to the bottom line, whereas a dollar in sales revenues adds only pennies of profit.

World-class purchasers deserve the same kind of reward, recognition, and celebration for their contributions to their organizations' performance. Service quality is not, cannot be, and should not have to be its own reward. Research has amply demonstrated that behavior that goes unrewarded will cease. Enthusiasm and professionalism in purchasing are highly desirable and beneficial. But they need to be appreciated, supported, and reinforced. It is prudent to give purchasers respect and appropriate rewards.

Managing Supplier Service Quality

Service quality means understanding and meeting customer requirements. Consequently, it needs to be practiced by all suppliers, regardless of whether they supply goods or services, tangibles or intangibles. To ensure that all of an organization's external suppliers adhere to this philosophy, purchasing must begin by selecting them well. Supplier selection is both a privilege and a key responsibility of purchasing, since it affects the organization's ability to function smoothly, produce quality outputs, and achieve its strategic objectives.

Although other players, particularly internal customers, should be consulted and involved in the process, for ethical and practical reasons purchasers must make the selection decisions. These must be based strictly on the organization's best interests, which are best served by a purchaser who acts in accordance with the code of ethics promulgated by the National Association of Purchasing Management (see Figure 30-1). Potential suppliers can be identified based on inputs from a variety of information sources. Then a set of selection criteria must be drawn up and applied to narrow the field of candidates. Semifinalists should be asked to fill out a questionnaire, supply financial information, and furnish references. A visit to a plant or performance site rounds out the picture and affords the opportunity to conduct a quality audit, usually with the assistance of quality assurance specialists.

It is essential for purchasing to ascertain what efforts the prospective supplier is making toward quality achievement. Does the supplier have a formal quality process? If so, how well is it working? If not, why not, and what steps are being undertaken to initiate one? Does the quality function report to the top of the organization, and does it receive adequate support? Once a new supplier is brought on board, this dialogue is continued to ensure continuous improvement toward the goal of supplier certification. Certified suppliers have demonstrated their service quality over an extended period of time and have thus become preferred suppliers, if not partners, of the buying organization.

A supplier who has been qualified will initially receive only a limited amount of business to allow for an experience curve to build confidence. As the service quality becomes evident, the frequency of interaction will increase, enlarging the supplier's opportunity to serve varied customer requirements. A vital tool in this learning process is the supplier report card. This document contains a list of agreed-upon evaluation criteria, weighted to reflect their relative importance. On each of these criteria, the supplier receives a performance rating for the latest period; this is determined through a joint effort of all interested parties but managed and communicated by the purchaser. This tool provides an extremely

Figure 30-1.   National Association of Purchasing Management code of
ethics.

Principles and Standards
of Purchasing Practice

LOYALTY TO YOUR ORGANIZATION
JUSTICE TO THOSE WITH WHOM
YOU DEAL
FAITH IN YOUR PROFESSION

From these principles are derived the NAPM standards of purchasing practice.
(Domestic and International)

1. Avoid the intent and appearance of unethical or compromising practice in
   relationships, actions, and communications.
2. Demonstrate loyalty to the employer by diligently following the lawful instructions of the employer, using reasonable care and only authority granted.
3. Refrain from any private business or professional activity that would create a
   conflict between personal interests and the interests of the employer.
4. Refrain from soliciting or accepting money, loans, credits, or prejudicial dis-
   counts, and the acceptance of gifts, entertainment, favors, or services from
   present or potential suppliers that might influence, or appear to influence,
   purchasing decisions.
5. Handle confidential or proprietary information belonging to employers or
   suppliers with due care and proper consideration of ethical and legal ramifications and governmental regulations.
6. Promote positive supplier relationships through courtesy and impartiality in all
   phases of the purchasing cycle.
7. Refrain from reciprocal agreements that restrain competition.
8. Know and obey the letter and spirit of laws governing the purchasing function
   and remain alert to the legal ramifications of purchasing decisions.
9. Encourage all segments of society to participate by demonstrating support for
   small, disadvantaged, and minority-owned businesses.
10. Discourage purchasing's involvement in employer-sponsored programs of per-
    sonal purchases that are not business related.
11. Enhance the proficiency and stature of the purchasing profession by acquiring
    and maintaining current technical knowledge and the highest standards of
    ethical behavior.
12. Conduct international purchasing in accordance with the laws, customs, and
    practices of foreign countries, consistent with United States laws, your organi-
    zation policies, and these Ethical Standards and Guidelines.

Source: Reprinted with permission from the publisher, the National Association of Purchasing Management, "Principles and Standards of Purchasing Practice," adopted January 1992.

useful and meaningful means of communication, since it unequivocally highlights supplier achievements and weaknesses. It thus recognizes quality accomplishments and pinpoints opportunities for further improvements. By closing the feedback loop with the supplier, the report card enables the purchaser to both monitor and manage supplier service quality on an ongoing basis.

Another powerful tool in managing supplier service quality is measuring and reducing the cost of quality. Xerox divides such costs into three categories: costs of conformance, costs of nonconformance, and lost opportunities. Contrary to the title of Phil Crosby's book, quality is not free—achieving and maintaining it will always entail costs of conformance. These include the cost of continuing quality education and training and the cost of supplier quality management. In contrast, inadequate or excessive quality and its consequences produce inappropriate costs that must be eliminated. These costs of nonconformance and lost opportunities are due to either poor communications or sloppy execution. Enlightened purchasers measure the cost of service quality for every supplier and assist valued suppliers in reducing the cost of "unquality." They offer suggestions and even training or hands-on consulting assistance to help suppliers overcome wasteful habits and instill a passion for quality in their people.

Benefits of Service Quality in Purchasing

Understanding and meeting customer requirements produces solid, lasting customer relationships based on loyalty and trust. It eliminates waste of time and money and generates a dynamic momentum for change. The spirit of continuous improvement requires ongoing dialogue to communicate evolving changes in requirements and capabilities, continued updating and upgrading of skills in ways of doing business, and feed back loops that provide performance evaluation. Not only are opportunities for improvement identified but means for effecting this improvement are offered, supported by appropriate assistance and guidance.

World-class purchasers are professionals who help their organizations gain and sustain competitive advantage in a turbulent world by selecting quality suppliers and continually nudging them toward greater achievement. They are committed to continuing professional development to improve service to their customers through enhanced productivity. Their organizations benefit from this professionalism by squeezing out unnecessary costs, dramatically reducing cycle time, and streamlining processes and inventories. Their suppliers benefit by obtaining guidance and support in improving both their performance and their competitiveness.

Service quality in purchasing means that contemporary purchasers render quality service to their customers to enable them to perform their tasks well. It also means that they select suppliers who provide quality service and challenge them to continuously improve their quality achievements. And they thrive on feedback that helps them to perform their jobs even better.

PART VIII

MEASURING SERVICE QUALITY

31

Benchmarking Practices and Processes

Robert C. Camp and John E. Kelsch, Xerox Corporation

Benchmarking, a method of establishing performance goals and quality improvement projects based on the best industry practices, is one of the most exciting new tools in the quality field. Searching out and emulating the best can fuel the motivation of everyone involved, often producing breakthrough results.

Although companies have studied their competitors for years, Xerox developed a disciplined approach to the study of its competitors beginning in late 1979 by demonstrating the power of benchmarking in its manufacturing operations. The company wanted to compare its U.S. manufacturing performance with the performance of its foreign and domestic competitors. One finding was that competitors were selling products at Xerox's cost of producing them. As a result, Xerox quickly shifted to adopt externally-set benchmark targets to drive its business plans.

The experience so dramatically turned the manufacturing operation around that Xerox adopted benchmarking as a corporatewide effort in late 1981. It expanded the use of the benchmarking process to the more than 70,000 Xerox people involved in delivering services to customers—sales, order entry–distribution–billing, equipment service, software, and other after-sale support activities. Today, the company uses benchmarking as a key component of its total quality effort and has broadened its benchmarking activities to include the identification and adaptation of best practices from any industry.

The Japanese word *dantotsu*—striving to be the *best of the best*—captures the essence of benchmarking. Benchmarking is a positive, proactive process to change operations in a structured fashion to achieve superior performance. The purpose of benchmarking is to gain a competitive advantage.

Benchmarking Defined

The formal definition of benchmarking is *the continuous process of measuring products, services, and practices against those of the company's toughest competitors or companies renowned as industry leaders.*

To achieve a leadership position in service delivery, it is essential to learn *how* leading companies achieve their performance levels and then to adapt these best practices to fit your industry.

Objectives of Benchmarking

The purpose of benchmarking is to establish more credible goals and pursue continuous improvement. It is first a direction-setting process, but, more important, it is a means by which the practices needed to reach new goals are discovered and understood.

Benchmarking legitimizes goals and direction based on external orientation instead of extrapolating from internal practices and past trends. Because the external environment changes so rapidly, goal setting that is internally focused often fails to provide what customers expect from their suppliers.

Customer expectations are driven by the standards set by the best suppliers in the industry and by experiences with suppliers in other industries. Thus, the ultimate benefit of benchmarking is to help achieve the leadership performance levels that fully satisfy these ever-increasing customer expectations.

Strategic vs. Operational Benchmarking

Benchmarking is an important ingredient in strategic planning as well as in operational improvement. Longer-range strategies require organizations to continuously change and adapt to the marketplace of today and tomorrow to remain competitive. To energize and motivate its people, an organization must:

- Believe that there is a need for change
- Determine what it wants to change
- Create a picture of how it wants to look after the change

Benchmarking achieves all three. By identifying gaps between your organization and the competition, it creates a need. By helping you understand how industry leaders do things, it helps you identify what you have to change. And by showing you what is possible and what other companies have done, it motivates your people with achievable goals and strategies that drive their efforts.

Benchmarking Fundamentals

Embarking on a benchmarking activity requires acceptance of the following fundamentals:

- ▲ Know your operation. Assess its strengths and weaknesses. This should involve documentation of work process steps and practices as well as definition of critical performance measurements used.
- ▲ Know industry leaders and competitors. You can differentiate capabilities only by knowing the strengths and weaknesses of the leaders.
- ▲ Incorporate the best and gain superiority. Adapt and integrate these best practices to achieve a leadership position.

Practices and Performance Levels

Benchmarking can be divided into two parts: practices and performance levels. Based on experience, most Xerox managers now understand that benchmarking should first focus on industry best practices. The performance levels that result from these practices can be analyzed and synthesized later. Once you have identified the best practices of several companies, you can integrate the lessons learned to create world-class work processes. At that stage, the expected performance from these work processes can be determined so that you can deliver service levels that are superior to those of the best of your competitors.

When preparing for benchmarking, it is equally important to engage line management so that the findings are understood and accepted and result in a commitment to take action. This requires concerted management involvement and carefully designed communications to the organization units that must implement the action plans.

Getting Started

Experience with benchmarking has resulted in a ten-step process for conducting a benchmarking investigation (see Figure 31-1). The process consists of five essential phases:

Figure 31-1. Benchmarking process.

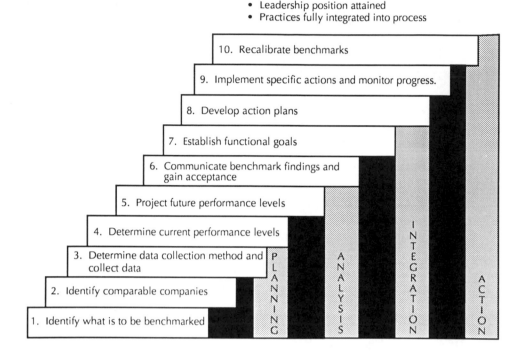

1. Planning
   - What to benchmark. Every function has a product or output. These are priority candidates to benchmark in order to improve performance.
   - Whom to benchmark against. World-class leadership companies or functions with superior work practices, wherever they exist, are the appropriate comparisons.
   - Data sources and data collection. A wide array of sources exists, and a good starting point is a business library. An electronic search of recently published information on an area of interest can be requested.
2. Analysis
   - Measuring the gap. It is important that you have a full understanding of your internal business processes before you compare them with those of external organizations as the baseline for analyzing best practices.
   - Projecting the gap. Comparing performance levels provides an objective basis on which to act and to determine how to achieve a performance edge.
   - However, the competition will not stand still while you improve. Thus, goals must reflect projected competitive improvement.

3. Integration
   - Based on the benchmarking findings, the targets and strategies should be integrated into business plans and operational reviews, updating as needed.
   - Progress should be reported to all employees.
4. Action
   - Specific implementation actions, milestones, and assessments of progress should be put in place.
   - People who actually perform the work should be responsible for implementation.
   - Stay current with ongoing industry changes by continuously benchmarking and updating work processes.
5. Maturity
   - Maturity is achieved when best practices are incorporated in all business processes, benchmarking becomes a standard way of doing work, and performance levels are continually improving toward a leadership position.

What to Benchmark

The first step in determining what should be benchmarked is identifying the product or output of the business process or function. Fundamental to this is the development of a clear mission statement detailing the reason for the organization's existence, including key outputs expected by its customers that are critical to successfully fulfilling the mission. Next, each function's broad purposes should be broken down into specific outputs to be benchmarked. Outputs should be documented to a level of detail necessary for quality, cost, and delivery analyses; analyses of key tasks; hand-offs; and both in-process and end results measurements.

One good way to determine which outputs are most in need of benchmarking is to pose a set of questions that might reveal current issues facing the function. Questions might focus on customer care, including service, cost, or perception of product offerings. Another way to identify key outputs is to convert the problems, issues, and challenges faced by the function into problem statements and then develop these into a cause-and-effect Ishikawa diagram (Figure 31-2). The causals in the diagram are candidates for benchmarking.

An early classic example of successful benchmarking by Xerox focused on L.L. Bean, the outdoor specialties mail order firm recognized for its superiority in warehousing and materials handling. Its warehouse operations were of great interest because, like Xerox, L.L. Bean handles products that are diverse in size, shape, and handling characteristics. As

Figure 31-2.   Ishikawa cause and effect diagram.

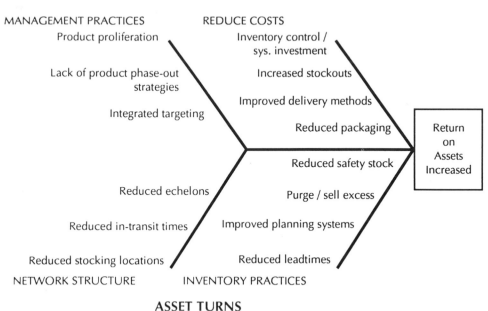

PROFIT MARGIN

MANAGEMENT PRACTICES   REDUCE COSTS

Product proliferation   Inventory control /
                                                      sys. investment

Lack of product phase-out   Increased stockouts
strategies
                                                  Improved delivery methods

Integrated targeting
                                                        Reduced packaging

                                                                                    Return
                                                                                    on
                                                                                    Assets
                                                    Reduced safety stock   Increased

Reduced echelons   Purge / sell excess

Reduced in-transit times   Improved planning systems

Reduced stocking locations   Reduced leadtimes

NETWORK STRUCTURE   INVENTORY PRACTICES

ASSET TURNS

a result of the benchmarking visit, Xerox incorporated several of L.L. Bean's practices in a logistics program to modernize its warehouse operations. Of the 8 to 10 percent productivity gains subsequently realized, 3 to 5 percent were a direct result of successful benchmarking activities. The range of practices benchmarked at L.L. Bean included bar coding materials for stock tracking, management of inventories, office supply product distribution, and quality assurance processes.

Whom to Benchmark Against

The difficulty is in identifying which leading-edge companies possess functions that truly are best industry practices. Determining whom to benchmark against is a search process that starts with consideration of, in broad terms, an operation's primary competitors and then extends to leading companies that are not competitors. Although the process is one of comparison, the goal is to identify and understand where doing things differently can produce breakthrough results.

A successful approach encompasses internal, competitive, and functional benchmarking. *Internal* benchmarking is the comparison of practices among similar operations within a firm. One distinct benefit of this type of benchmarking is that it forces documentation and allows easy comparison of the work process to uncover best practices. *Competitive* benchmarking is the comparison with face-off competitors, and the results are quite obvious. However, *functional* benchmarking, the comparison of functional activities, even in dissimilar industries, holds the most potential for uncovering innovative practices.

Over the past decade, the list of companies Xerox has benchmarked against has grown. It includes some of America's largest corporations: American Express (billing and collection); American Hospital Supply (automated inventory control); Ford (manufacturing floor layout); IBM and General Electric (customer service support centers); L.L. Bean, Hershey Foods, and Mary Kay Cosmetics (warehousing and distribution); Westinghouse (National Quality Award application process, warehouse controls, bar coding); and Florida Power and Light (quality process).

As a multinational corporation, Xerox operates in more than 100 countries and conducts benchmarking worldwide. Xerox regularly benchmarks against Fuji Xerox, the company's affiliate in Japan and a 1980 winner of the Deming Award. As a result of its own benchmarking activities, Fuji Xerox has instituted many practices to enable it to meet and exceed the performance of various Japanese companies and others in the Pacific Rim.

Behavioral Benefits

Benchmarking is essentially a learning experience. It helps an organization focus and drive for consensus on what needs to be done and how to achieve it, not argue over what should be done. It can provide the stimulus for improvement by people at all levels through an externally focused, competitive effort to achieve world-class performance with increased customer satisfaction. Very few people are willing to settle for second place once they are aware of what needs to be done and know how to do it.

Competitiveness

The bottom-line benefit of benchmarking is improved competitiveness and increased value in the eyes of your customers. Effective use of benchmarking to develop and implement improvement actions can help organizations achieve a superior level of customer service. This, in turn, will lead to increased market share and improved financial results.

References

Biesada, Alexandra. "Benchmarking." *Financial World* 169, no. 9 (September 1991), pp. 28–54.

Camp, Robert C. *Benchmarking: The Search for Industry Best Practices That Lead to Superior Performance*. Milwaukee, Wis.: American Society for Quality Control, Quality Press, 1989.

Garvin, David A. "Quality and the Competition." *Competing Through Quality*. Segment 3 of interview, Harvard Business School Video Series, 1990.

Kelsch, John E. "Benchmarking: Shrewd Way to Keep Your Company Ahead of Its Competition." *Boardroom Reports* (December 1982), pp. 3–5.

Tucker, Francis G., Seymour M. Zivan, and Robert C. Camp. "How to Measure Yourself Against the Best." *Harvard Business Review* 87, no. 1 (January–February 1987), pp. 8–10.

"World Class Organizations: Xerox." *Industry Week* (March 9, 1990), pp. 14, 16.

32

Measuring Customer Satisfaction

Lawrence A. Crosby, Arizona State University

Organizations throughout the world are beginning to recognize that measuring customer satisfaction is no longer an option but an essential part of their management systems—perhaps on a par with strategic planning or even accounting. This is especially true for companies operating in competitive markets where customers have numerous options should they become dissatisfied. But concern about customer satisfaction has also begun to permeate organizations operating in protected markets and even government because of such factors as trade unification, privatization, deregulation, and intraform competition. Such factors have conspired to loosen the hold that these organizations previously had on their customers.

It makes good managerial sense to have an organizational focus on customer satisfaction for the following three reasons:

1. Satisfied customers are more likely to recommend the organization to others, which is the cheapest and most effective form of promotion.[1]
2. Satisfied customers are loyal customers. It is estimated to be five to seven times more expensive to attract a new customer than to keep an old one.[2]
3. Satisfied customers are better customers. They buy more, more often and are willing to pay higher prices.[3]

It can be said that customer satisfaction is the objective and end result of effective relationship management. The goals of relationship marketing/management are to attract, retain, and enhance customer relationships.[4]

Parts of this chapter are adapted from Lawrence A. Crosby, "An Assessment of the State of Customer Satisfaction Measurement Research: Total and Global," *Proceedings*, 44th ESOMAR Congress, Amsterdam, The Netherlands: ESOMAR, 1991, pp. 37–48 (special issue supplement).

Evolution of Customer Satisfaction Measurement

Without question, the interrelated issues of customer satisfaction measurement and management are receiving considerable attention by business today. Yet, these topics also have a long history that can be traced back thirty years or more. During this period, the concept of customer satisfaction measurement has evolved through several phases, which are described briefly below.

Corporate Image Studies

The early roots of customer satisfaction measurement can be found in the corporate image studies of the 1960s. Measures of satisfaction and perceived quality were often buried in the image batteries of customer surveys along with such items as the company's "progressiveness" or its "involvement in community affairs." The presumption was, in many companies, that quality deficiencies detected in these surveys could be viewed as "marketing problems" to be corrected through more skillful use of advertising.

Product Quality Studies

Popularization of the "marketing concept" in the late 1960s, as a philosophy of conducting business, caused some businesses to rethink the importance of customer satisfaction.[5] The obvious connection between "meeting customer needs" and "customer satisfaction" was properly noted. However, a limiting factor was the tendency to conceptualize satisfaction strictly in terms of the quality of tangible product features. Here, the adequacy-importance model was the main measurement tool.[6] This model involved creating an index by summing (across attributes) measures of satisfaction with product performance multiplied by measures of feature importance. The index, in turn, was used to explain customer attitudes and behavior.

It is worthwhile to note parallel academic developments during this period that set the stage for the expectation confirmation/disconfirmation paradigm of customer satisfaction.[7] Like practitioners, however, the academics concerned themselves mainly with tangible product quality.

Early Satisfaction Studies in the Utility Industries

Regulated monopolies in the utility industries of North America and Europe were among the first *service* companies to concern themselves with the question of customer satisfaction. Notable in this regard were the large TELSAM programs (*te*lephone *s*ervice *a*ttitude *m*easurement) undertaken by AT&T in the United States during the 1970s. These programs involved the ongoing tracking of customer service satisfaction, with the results made regularly available to various operating units. The electric power companies were quick to follow suit. The early interest of utilities in customer satisfaction measurement can be traced, in part, to their monopoly status. Lacking a market test of their performance in meeting customer needs, they hoped to obtain favorable customer satisfaction measurement results to justify rate increases to their regulatory agencies.

Syndicated Auto Studies

Perhaps the next major development in the evolution of (applied) customer satisfaction measurement was the advent of syndicated automotive studies, spearheaded by J. D. Powers and Associates of Los Angeles. This company correctly noted the increased competitiveness of the world car market and the obvious challenge to the market share positions of automotive manufacturers (especially in the United States). Beginning in the early 1980s, information from these studies was widely used by manufacturers to discipline dealers and zone/district personnel, and to set the agenda for new product development efforts. Still, customer satisfaction measurement continued to be viewed mainly as a marketing tool. By the end of the 1980s, results from these syndicated studies were also being used in advertising to support the manufacturers' claims of product superiority.

Era of Services Enlightenment

By the mid-1980s, business and academia began to wake up to the fundamental shifts taking place in Western economies. Almost overnight, it seemed, the economies had come to be dominated by service industries, measured in terms of both GNP and work force employment. In reality, the growth in services was due less to a decline in manufacturing and more to a shift away from mining and agriculture. Nevertheless, business immediately found itself lacking in appropriate principles, methods, and tools for managing these intangible, labor-intensive services, characterized by customer participation (simultaneous production and consumption) and highly variable outputs.[8]

Since there was no "product" to inspect, service companies had no choice but to look for other measures of quality. Thanks in part to the pioneering work of a handful of academics, service practitioners were persuaded to look to the customer for a definition of quality. Customer-perceived quality was once again defined as "meeting or exceeding customers' expectations."[9] Many service firms in North America and

Scandinavia were quick to adopt this conceptualization of quality, the "gap model," and certain elements of the SERVQUAL instrument.[10]

Era of Business-to-Business Enlightenment

Following closely on the heels of the service industries, a number of industrial companies began to espouse the belief that their competitiveness had been hurt by a product manufacturing mentality when, in fact, some of the most important opportunities for differentiation rested in the company's service and administrative processes. Again, the quality of these processes could be gauged (accurately) only by measuring customer satisfaction.

The Dawn of Total Quality

Despite these favorable evolutionary trends, the current popularity of customer satisfaction measurement and management is largely attributable to the quality movement in business. By the late 1980s, management thinking in both North America and Europe was becoming fixated on the quality issue (which had taken root in Japan over forty years before). The emphasis on quality was a natural outgrowth of intensified global competition, a response to the strong value ethic of today's customer, and a reaction to PIMS results (*profit impact of marketing strategy*) that indicated that customer-perceived quality influences profitability directly as well as indirectly through market share.[11]

The heightened attention to quality can also be traced to what has been called an industrial paradigm shift to the philosophy of total quality management.[12] Total quality management (TQM) means that all functions within the company are blended into a holistic, integrated philosophy built around the concepts of quality, teamwork, productivity, and customer understanding and satisfaction.[13] A key premise of TQM is that "the customer is the final judge of quality." Consequently, the TQM process begins with an effort to identify customer requirements. These requirements, in turn, are translated into internal standards and specifications. Finally, the entire organization is realigned to ensure both conformance quality (adherence to standards and specifications) and perceived quality (meeting or exceeding customer expectations). Clearly, there is a potentially large role for customer satisfaction measurement in facilitating the TQM process.[14] Customer satisfaction measurement is instrumental in identifying customer requirements. Also, low customer satisfaction measurement scores signify a breakdown in the TQM process and help provide direction to the company's quality improvement efforts.

How Customer Satisfaction Measurement Differs From Traditional Marketing Research

Despite its having roots in the marketing research area, it is apparent that customer satisfaction measurement has evolved into something quite different. It is true that many of the same basic methods are involved (e.g., survey research, multivariate data analysis) and that the majority of the outside suppliers of customer satisfaction measurement services are marketing research firms. However, there are fundamental differences in the way these programs are organized, conducted, and utilized. Also, the personnel involved in managing these programs need broader skills.

Utilization of Results

Compared to the typical marketing research study, the use of customer satisfaction measurement information is much more widespread in the organization and much more closely linked to the management of overall operations. In some highly customer-driven firms, customer satisfaction measurement serves as the primary means for aligning the entire organization (mission/vision, strategies, culture, structure, systems, management approaches, etc.) with the customer's total needs. Thus, in theory and in practice, customer satisfaction measurement is not so much a research activity as it is a management tool. It is:

- A strategic tool for determining how to allocate the company's resources to obtain a competitive advantage
- An operations tool for determining how to improve the company's business processes
- A public relations tool for communicating the company's commitment to quality
- A motivation/leadership tool for giving energy and direction to the efforts of employees
- An auditing tool for assessing the company's performance on customer-oriented variables that ultimately determine its financial standing and market position

Ownership of the Customer Satisfaction Measurement Program

Tied to this notion that customer satisfaction measurement is used more for general management purposes, it is often the case that "ownership" of the customer satisfaction measurement program resides somewhere other than the marketing research department. Responsibility for conducting the customer satisfaction measurement program may rest with a multifunctional team that reports directly to upper management or even the chief executive officer. The day-to-day management of the program is often outside marketing or marketing research, and may rest with the staff of the director or vice-president of quality. A few companies (Xerox, for example) have even created a new position called manager or director of customer satisfaction.

It seems wise to have the departments that will ultimately act on the customer satisfaction measurement information also involved in directing its collection and deployment (e.g., operations/manufacturing, human resources, accounting/finance, etc.). Yet it is clearly a mistake to exclude the marketing and/or marketing research departments from this coordinating group. For one thing, marketing controls many (although certainly not all) of the processes that directly impinge on customers. Marketing also has a major influence on setting customers' expectations. Personnel from marketing research can make a significant contribution to the design of the program, *provided* they realize the broad context in which the information will be applied.

Continuous Nature

The term customer satisfaction measurement *program*, as opposed to customer satisfaction measurement *study*, has been carefully used above to denote the continuous nature of these tracking programs. In fact, some customer satisfaction measurement programs are virtually always in the field. Regardless of whether the data are obtained continuously or at regular intervals, the point is to establish an ongoing performance monitoring system that can detect quality improvement from baseline levels. In this way, customer satisfaction measurement scores can serve as the dependent variables in quality improvement experiments and quasi-experiments.[15]

The influence of customer satisfaction measurement is greatly enhanced when these programs are integrated into the strategic and operating control systems of the organization and, possibly, the evaluation and compensation systems. When this is true, there is a demand not only for continuous measurement but also for a high level of consistency in those measurements. One can easily imagine the internal forces to resist change when the top executives of the company have 25–50 percent of their bonuses tied to the customer satisfaction measurement results! An implication is that the customer satisfaction measurement program that the company installs in the beginning should be one it can live with for a long time.

Skill Sets

The fact that customer satisfaction measurement is different from traditional marketing research has implications for the qualifications and training of the internal and external consultants responsible for these programs. Most marketing researchers received their education in either marketing or one of the social science disciplines. This background is very useful in conducting customer satisfaction measurement programs, but it is not sufficient.

Complete knowledge of the *survey research process* provides the foundation for conducting customer satisfaction measurement. However, in addition to these basic research capabilities, the customer satisfaction measurement practitioner should also have knowledge of *advanced research methods* that have proved instrumental in assessing and improving a company's market perceived quality:

- Sophisticated data analysis techniques, such as causal models of customer satisfaction
- Methods for linking customer satisfaction measurement data to financial performance data, such as time series analysis
- Employee survey methods for identifying quality obstacles and barriers, such as psychometric scale development or internal dissemination of results
- Methods for identifying specific customer expectations in business process areas, such as critical incident technique or problem detection
- Methods for quantifying the importance of specific customer expectations in business process areas, such as conjoint measurement
- Database techniques for linking external performance information to internal quality indicators for statistical process control

As if research expertise were not enough, those in charge of coordinating or providing customer satisfaction measurement should also have demonstrated capability in the *management consulting* area. The ideal candidate for this type of work not only scores high on research competence but also has significant expertise and experience advising top management on issues of strategic importance. Specifically, the customer satisfaction measurement practitioner should be able to speak intelligently to management on the following quality-related topics:

- Culture change and organizational development
- Customer relationship management

- Linking executive compensation to customer satisfaction measurement
- Employee recognition and empowerment
- Formulating world-class quality strategies
- Competing for national and international quality awards
- Organizational design and teamwork
- Information systems and quality
- Hiring service-oriented employees
- Business process blueprinting
- Diagnosing fail points and design problems in business processes

Last, the fully qualified customer satisfaction measurement practitioner needs more than just a passing familiarity with an entirely different set of methods and tools that have nothing to do with marketing research at all. These are the *methods and tools of total quality management*, which come from the industrial management and manufacturing disciplines. Many of these tools have been invented or refined by the Japanese since the end of World War II, and are only now coming into general use in most major world corporations.[16] Examples include concepts and techniques like policy deployment (PD), the PDCA cycle for quality improvement, quality function deployment (QFD), House of Quality, competitive benchmarking, control charts, statistical process control (SPC), cause-and-effect diagrams, and Pareto analysis.

Clearly, these lists of desirable skills represent a formidable challenge when recruiting staff or suppliers to participate in a company's customer satisfaction measurement program. Yet, all of these capabilities must exist if the company is to realize the full integrative potential of customer satisfaction measurement. One obvious solution is to form a customer satisfaction measurement team composed of persons with diverse backgrounds. Outside consultants can establish strategic alliances with marketing researchers, management consultants, and quality experts. Still, there is a need for the customer satisfaction measurement "generalist" with broad training and experience who can pull the entire program together. Such individuals are in short supply, since few universities in North America or Europe are currently geared to produce graduates who can fill the customer satisfaction measurement generalist role.

General Methodologies of Customer Satisfaction Measurement

Although there seems to be a growing consensus among companies that customer satisfaction measurement (CSM) is a necessity, there is a lot of variation in what firms mean by CSM. To some companies, CSM simply implies talking to customers during the normal course of doing business and attempting to assess whether they are pleased or displeased with the company. Special visits to the customer's premises for this purpose might also be arranged. Although this form of direct communication with customers is to be encouraged as one source of customer insight, other approaches for bringing the voice of the customer into the organization may be less biased, more thorough, and more systematic.

In fact, there is quite a variety of data collection and research methodologies that can be employed to determine customer requirements and to gauge the firm's performance in meeting customer expectations. Although most managers tend to think primarily in terms of survey methodology, which is certainly the mainstay of CSM today, other methods may be appropriate in certain instances or phases of getting to know the customer. Some of these general methodologies are reviewed briefly below.

Customer Satisfaction Surveys*

The survey is known for its flexibility and the wide variety of uses to which it may be applied. These range from identifying quality strengths and weaknesses to tracking the results of organizational changes on customer perceptions. However, surveys are not without their limitations. Principal among these are difficulties in inferring causality based on correlational data, the lack of perfect correspondence between customer attitudes and behavior, and the need to control a variety of sampling and nonsampling errors that could render the survey invalid. Fortunately, it is possible to deal effectively with most of these problems by following well-established, sound survey research procedures.[17]

In designing a customer satisfaction survey, it is necessary to answer Rudyard Kipling's six questions: who? what? where? when? how? and why? Some of the issues underlying these questions are as follows.

1. *Why interview?* This question concerns, of course, the reasons for doing the CSM survey in the first place. Some of the more important research objectives are likely to be:

- ▲ To determine customer expectations
- ▲ To measure the company's performance in satisfying customer expectations
- ▲ To benchmark the company's performance relative to the competition

*Parts of this section are adapted from Lawrence A. Crosby, "Expanding the Role of CSM in Total Quality," *International Journal of Services Industries Management,* 2 (1991): 5–19.

▴ To "explain" customer satisfaction based on the company's perceived performance in key areas of customer interaction
▴ To prioritize performance areas for quality improvement and additional resource allocation

2. *Who to interview?* This question is related to the question "who is the customer?" The answer may involve selecting one or more levels of the channel of distribution to study. It may require distinguishing among new customers, continuing customers, and former customers. It may suggest interviewing more than one person in the buying center of the customer organization.

3. *What to ask?* The obvious answer is to ask "are you satisfied?" but this may not be sufficient. Satisfying customers might imply simply meeting their minimum requirements, which does not give them a compelling reason to buy. Concepts of relative quality and relative value have more to do with delighting customers and establishing an image of excellence. Regardless of the measurement concept, however, the assessment must be across all the key areas of customer contact (e.g., core product/service, sales/marketing, order processing, delivery, billing, etc.). The company's relationship with its customers is only as strong as its weakest link.

4. *Where to interview?* Typically, customers are interviewed at their own homes or places of business. On occasion, an "intercept" approach is used to capture customers at retail sites immediately after they have purchased or used the product or service. This has the advantage of obtaining the customer's evaluation while the experience is still fresh, but subtle biases such as selection can arise.

5. *When to interview?* This question has mainly to do with the frequency of interviewing. Some issues involve the degree to which the market is dynamic and the degree to which the organization can absorb and act upon the information. Especially in finite customer populations (e.g., business-to-business), attention must also be given to the possibility of respondent burnout as a result of repetitive interviewing.

6. *How to interview?* The modes of interviewing are personal (face-to-face), telephone, and mail. Each form has its pros and cons, although mail surveys are generally considered the weakest approach from a scientific standpoint (although they tend to be the most economical). The trend for many years has been toward computer-assisted telephone interviewing (CATI), but personal interviewing is still required in some places outside of North America.

Once the survey data have been obtained, they are subjected to a series of statistical procedures designed to provide management with both scorecard and diagnostic information. Much like periodic reports of net profit, earnings, or ROI, scorecard CSM results are used to audit the company's performance in meeting or exceeding customer expectations. Comparisons are made across product/service lines, customer segments, and organizational units; against the competition; and over time (trend analysis). From a descriptive standpoint, a challenging problem for multinational companies is determining how to best "roll up" international results (the "apples and oranges" problem).

The other type of information is more diagnostic and focuses on the "why" questions. Diagnostic information is needed to explain the antecedents and consequences of the customers' satisfaction/quality evaluations. Diagnostic information is also needed to predict the gains in customer satisfaction likely to result from making certain quality improvements. Analysis of the customer survey data involves the application of bivariate and multivariate statistical procedures to determine:

- ▴ The effects of overall satisfaction/perceived quality on customer behavior
- ▴ The relative impact of the company's perceived performance in major (customer impinging) processes on overall satisfaction/perceived quality
- ▴ The relative impact of secondary attributes (reflecting customer expectations) on the perceived quality of the company's major processes

With respect to the core CSM objective of "prioritizing performance areas for quality improvement and additional resource allocation," the strategic improvement matrix has proved to be a useful communications device.[18] As shown in Figure 32-1, this 2 × 3 matrix cross-classifies performance areas according to their impact on satisfaction/perceived

Figure 32-1. Strategic improvement matrix (hypothetical bank example).

High Impact on Customer Satisfaction	• ATM machines • Loans	• Rates on savings	• Tellers
Low Impact on Customer Satisfaction	• Rates on checking	• Account features	• Non-teller staff • Ease of opening accounts
	Better than the Competition	Same as the Competition	Worse than the Competition

quality (high or low) and according to the company's relative level of performance (better than, the same as, or worse than the competition).

The combination of high impact and low relative performance is a "critical improvement area" needing additional resources (e.g., tellers).

Quality Improvement Experiments

Perhaps the strongest but least used design is the quality improvement experiment. As in the cross-sectional survey, customer satisfaction or perceived quality typically serves as the outcome measure. The experiment is unlike the survey, however, in that it is possible to make fairly strong causal inferences if the experiment is properly conducted.

Experiments are made to order for testing and evaluating quality improvement programs on a limited basis prior to systemwide rollout. For example, employees at selected bank branches might be trained in a new approach to customer service. At a later date, the satisfaction of their customers might be compared with the satisfaction of customers serviced by branches that did not receive the training. If the two groups of branches differ only with respect to the training, then observed differences in customer satisfaction are probably attributable to the training.

Critical Incident Technique

Another design alternative is the critical incident technique (CIT), which has recently been applied to the evaluation of services from the customer's point of view.[19] Again based on surveys, respondents are asked to describe in storylike fashion memorable service and sales encounters that materially affected their satisfaction. The CIT method can be used for exploratory purposes such as identifying expectations or after a customer satisfaction survey to get behind the quantitative ratings.

Below are two critical incident examples taken from Bitner's study of customer satisfaction with hotels. The category is employee response to unavailable service. In the satisfactory incident, the customer reports:

> "They lost my room reservation but the manager gave me the V.I.P. suite for the same price."

Reflecting upon a dissatisfactory incident, another customer responds:

> "Although we made advance reservations, when we arrived we had no room—no explanation, no apologies, no assistance in finding another hotel."

CIT information can be very helpful in attempting to understand customer expectations in a qualitative way. When combined with quantitative survey information, the rich nature of the CIT data can put "flesh on the bones" of otherwise sterile statistics and bring them to life for managers and employees.

Problem Analysis

A related set of methods falls into the general category of problem analysis.[20] What they have in common is, first of all, an effort to develop, via exploratory methods, a list of problems. The second phase involves an effort to evaluate the impact of the problems on customer satisfaction. The most common procedure is to assess problem impact via statistical analysis such as multiple regression. In that case, the dependent variable is usually satisfaction or perceived quality, and the independent variables represent the reported frequency of various types of problems and, in some applications, whether they were effectively resolved or not.

Limitations of problem analysis may include unreliable frequency estimates by customers and a tendency for the statistics to underestimate the importance of low-incidence events. The method also gives very little attention to the company's leverageable strengths.

Conjoint Measurement

Conjoint measurement is a technique borrowed from new products research[21] that can be used to help align performance standards with customer expectations and to evaluate quality improvement concepts with customers before introducing them. It involves asking customers to make tradeoff decisions among levels of product or service attributes. For example, as shown in Figure 32-2, customers might be asked to rank-order their preference for nine customer service configurations that cross three different methods of telephone answering with three levels of responsiveness based on the number of rings. Note that some or all of these choice alternatives may not be currently available or even feasible.

From a customer's rank-ordered preferences for the alternatives, it is possible to deduce the implicit utility weight for each level of "method" and each level of "number of rings" (see numbers in parentheses). When this information is aggregated over a representative sample of customers, useful insight is gained regarding the relative importance of the service components, customer expectations, and optimum service levels.

Conjoint measurement is probably best suited to finding solutions to quality problems that have already been identified and prioritized. It has limited use as a tracking device because it is focused more on customer *needs* than on *perceptions* and because it requires an hour-long,

Figure 32-2.   Conjoint measurement tradeoff matrix (telephone customer
service example).

METHOD	NUMBER OF RINGS		
	Answered in 2 rings or less (+4)	Answered in 3–4 rings (+3)	Answered in 5–6 rings (+.5)
Always answered by a person (+6)	Rank =1	Rank = 2	Rank = 5
Answered by a recording "Please hold for the next available..." (+4)	Rank =3	Rank = 4	Rank = 6
Answered by voice mail (+0)	Rank =7	Rank = 8	Rank = 9

face-to-face interview with the customer. Finally, the results are derived
from a hypothetical choice situation that raises questions about their
"real-world" validity.

Mystery Shopper Studies

Another method that has been around for a long time but is greatly
misunderstood and abused is the mystery shopper study. This is where
people posing as customers or prospects visit retailers, dealers, or service
outlets in an effort to gauge the performance of contact employees. Done
properly, the mystery shopper study is a valid observational research
technique. However, the limitations of the methodology are numerous.
After a period of time, managers begin to think of the mystery shoppers
as real people who perceive reality the same way as normal customers.
This is very doubtful, especially as the shopper gains experience and
expertise with the product or service. Also, the mystery shopper evaluation must be built around prior knowledge of the performances that
influence customer satisfaction. Perhaps the biggest drawback is that
employees may perceive that they are being spied upon, which may add
to their mistrust of management.

Complaint Analysis

Perhaps the oldest form of customer satisfaction measurement involves
efforts to record, categorize, analyze/track, act upon, and—more recently—solicit customer complaints. Handling complaints is an impor-

tant part of any quality program.[22] Successful recovery can often lead to a customer who is very satisfied. Also, since most unhappy customers don't complain but walk, an assertive program of customer complaint management is probably in order.[23] However, as a customer satisfaction measurement tool, complaint analysis suffers from some severe limitations regarding the representativeness of the problems reported and the customers who complain.[24]

Comment Cards

And then there are comment cards. Obvious limitations are low response rates, a tendency toward extremes (meaning that comment cards are more likely to be completed by customers who are exceptionally pleased or displeased), and lack of control over who in the customer company or household actually fills them out.

Integration of the Information

Now that these various methodologies and approaches have been reviewed, a key point to remember is that CSM should be viewed not simply as a research project or activity, but as a management tool. It is too easy to get lost in a technical debate as to whether one method is better than another. Actually, each has a potential role to play in helping management better understand the customer. Returning to the notion of customer insight, each of the approaches provides a unique perspective on the customer that can be integrated into a systematic and continuous CSM research process. The ultimate aim of this process is to better align the organization with the markets it serves.

A framework for integrating different types of external and internal customer satisfaction measurement information has been described elsewhere.[25] The integration process may take 3 to 5 years to become fully operational. The measurements may include (1) qualitative research with customers, employees, and managers, (2) quantitative tracking of customer relationships, (3) quantitative quality assessments conducted among employees, (4) various types of ad hoc research studies to get a better handle on customers' expectations and requirements, (5) quantitative tracking of customer "transactions" in critical improvement areas, and (6) postmeasurement work to deploy the information and use it as a guide for quality improvement. In some of the most advanced applications, customer satisfaction measurement data are linked with internal process, market, and financial data in a knowledge-based system resident on the company's EIS.[26]

Globalization of CSM

As the interest in total quality management (TQM) spreads throughout the world, so does the interest in CSM. This is especially true in Western Europe, where quality award programs similar to the U.S. Malcolm Baldrige Award have recently been introduced (e.g., by the European Federation for Quality Management). Virtually all of these programs place a strong emphasis on customer satisfaction measurement and management. CSM is also making major inroads in places such as Australia, Southeast Asia, and Japan. Despite the fact that Japanese companies already do an excellent job of listening to customers, many are seeing the merits of the systematic, objective, third-party information that CSM can provide.

The second major globalization development is the growth of multi-country CSM. Five years ago, the topic of multicountry CSM was virtually a nonissue. Except in some forward-looking firms like IBM and Xerox, the vast majority of CSM work was domestic in nature and confined to North America. That situation is rapidly changing, however. Some of the most enthusiastic proponents of CSM today are multinational firms with worldwide operations.[27] These companies recognize that only a portion of their sales and profits are generated in the countries where they are headquartered. As global competition becomes more intense, and as CSM gains acceptance as a leading indicator of the company's performance, there is pressure on these firms to implement CSM throughout all of their operations.

Effective management of a CSM program can be a challenging task under any circumstances. But challenging as it is to conduct CSM in a single country, the task becomes many times more complicated when the program is conducted internationally. The complexity arises from the fact that data are being collected, analyzed, interpreted, and acted upon in a multicultural context.

Beyond the basic questions of research methodology, the design of multicountry CSM also requires that decisions be made with respect to what might be called "program architecture." The crucial decisions concern the degree of standardization versus local customization of the research and the degree of centralized versus decentralized control. The standardization issue concerns the possible tradeoff between obtaining highly comparable CSM information from each country and taking into account the unique characteristics of each market (and possible restrictions on research procedures). It has been argued that *100 percent standardization may be neither possible, necessary, nor desirable.*[28]

The centralization decision is strategic in nature and has fundamentally to do with the ownership of the program within the multinational organization. In a multinational firm, the locus of control of a CSM program can be at the corporate, regional, or local level. It has been argued that a multicountry CSM program should be *decentralized to the lowest feasible level of the organization.*[29]

Even if the company is successful in finding the proper levels of standardization and centralization, there is yet another challenge to the valid interpretation of multicountry CSM information. This involves international scale comparability. In general, the customer's reaction to a scale is affected not only by the customer's true underlying disposition but also by a variety of cultural and market factors. Consequently, the scores obtained from different countries may differ by a response bias of unknown magnitude and direction. The logic for calibrating the magnitude of the response bias and making corrections is provided elsewhere.[30]

Conclusion

As customer satisfaction measurement programs become more widespread and mature, there is increasing demand for practical findings and recommendations rather than just sterile statistics. Whether it is conducted on a national, international, or global basis, managers expect that the company's customer satisfaction measurement program will (1) provide direction to the company's quality improvement efforts and (2) be able to detect modest changes when they occur. Too often, though, companies adopt unsound customer satisfaction measurement methodologies that result in:

- A lack of discrimination in customer responses
- Highly skewed results
- Unstable findings that vary randomly between reporting periods
- An inability to determine the factors driving customer satisfaction/perceived quality
- A lot of missing data
- Meaningless conclusions (e.g., "employees should smile more")
- Interpretational problems
- Lack of organizational buy-in
- Disuse of study results

In building a global customer satisfaction measurement capability, therefore, it is essential to adopt a core of proven procedures that are both scientifically valid and capable of providing management information that will lead to quality improvement. Hopefully, this chapter has provided some suggestions in that regard.

Notes

1. J. A. Goodman, A. R. Malech, G. F. Bargatze, and C. Ledbetter, "Converting a Desire for Quality Service Into Actions With Measurable Impact," *Journal of Retail Banking* 10, no. 4 (1988), pp. 14–22.
2. L. J. Rosenberg and J. A. Czepiel, "A Marketing Approach for Customer Retention," *Journal of Consumer Marketing* 1, no. 2 (1983), pp. 45–51.
3. M. M. Lele and J. Sheth, *The Customer Is Key* (New York: Wiley, 1987).
4. L. L. Berry, "Relationship Marketing," in *Emerging Perspectives on Services Marketing*, L. L. Berry, G. L. Shostack, and G. D. Upah, eds. (Chicago: American Marketing Association, 1985), pp. 25–28.
5. J. B. McKitterick, "What Is the Marketing Management Concept?" in *Frontiers of Marketing Thought and Action* (Chicago: American Marketing Association, 1957), pp. 71–82.
6. J. B. Cohen, M. Fishbein, and O. T. Athola, "The Nature and Uses of Expectancy-Value Models in Consumer Attitude Research," *Journal of Marketing Research* 9 (November 1972), pp. 456–460.
7. R. Cardozo, "An Experimental Study of Consumer Effort, Expectations, and Satisfaction," *Journal of Marketing Research* 2 (August 1965), pp. 244–249; R. B. Woodruff, E. R. Cadotte, and R. L. Jenkins, "Modeling Consumer Satisfaction Processes Using Experience-Based Norms," *Journal of Marketing Research* 20 (August 1983), pp. 296–304.
8. C. H. Lovelock, "Classifying Services to Gain Strategic Marketing Insights," *Journal of Marketing* 47 (Summer 1983), pp. 9–20.
9. J. R. Lehtinen, *Quality Oriented Services Marketing* (Helsinki, Finland: Service Management Institute, 1985); C. Grönroos and E. Gummesson, *Service Marketing—Nordic School Perspectives* (Stockholm: Department of Business Administration, University of Stockholm, 1985); A. Parasuraman, V. A. Zeithaml, and L. L. Berry, "A Conceptual Model of Service Quality and Its Implications for Future Research," *Journal of Marketing* 49 (Fall 1985), pp. 41–50.
10. A. Parasuraman, V. A. Zeithaml, and L. L. Berry, "SERVQUAL: A Multiple-Item Scale for Measuring Consumer Perceptions of Service Quality," *Journal of Retailing* 64 (Spring 1988), pp. 12–40.
11. B. T. Gale and R. D. Buzzell, "Market Perceived Quality: Key Strategic Concept," *Planning Review* (March–April 1989), pp. 6–48.
12. W. Locander, "Total Quality Management Systems and Customer Measurement." Paper presented at the Customer Satisfaction Measurement Conference, American Marketing Association, Atlanta, Georgia, 1989.
13. K. Ishikawa, *What Is Total Quality Control?* (Milwaukee, Wis.: Quality Press, 1985).
14. L. A. Crosby, "Integrating Customer Satisfaction Measurement (CSM) With Total Quality Management (TQM)," *Managing Service Quality* 1, no. 3 (March 1991), pp. 137–140.
15. J. A. Caporaso and L. L. Ross, Jr., *Quasi-Experimental Approaches: Testing and Evaluating Policy* (Evanston, Ill.: Northwestern University Press, 1973).

16. E. C. Huge, *Total Quality: An Executive's Guide for the 1990's* (Homewood, Ill.: Dow Jones-Irwin, 1990).
17. C. Selltiz, L. S. Wrightsman, and S. W. Cook, *Research Methods in Social Relations* (New York: Holt, Rinehart and Winston, 1976).
18. J. A. Martilla and J. C. James, "Importance-Performance Analysis," *Journal of Marketing* (1977), pp. 77–79.
19. M. J. Bitner, B. M. Booms, and M. S. Tetreault, "The Service Encounter: Diagnosing Favorable and Unfavorable Incidents," *Journal of Marketing* 54, no. 1 (January 1990); pp. 71–84.
20. K. Berwitz, "The Problem Research Method," *Marketing Review* (Fall 1979), pp. 19–23; D. D. Brandt and K. L. Reffett, "Focusing on Customer Problems to Improve Service Quality," *Journal of Services Marketing* 3, no. 4 (Fall 1989), pp. 5–14.
21. P. E. Green and V. Srinivasan, "Conjoint Analysis in Marketing Research: New Development and Directions," *Journal of Marketing* 5, no. 4 (October 1990), pp. 3–19.
22. M. C. Gilly and R. W. Hansen, "Consumer Complaint Handling as a Strategic Marketing Tool," *Journal of Consumer Marketing* 2 (Fall 1985), pp. 5–16.
23. J. A. Czepiel, *Managing Customer Satisfaction in Consumer Service Businesses,* Report No. 80-109 (Cambridge, Mass.: Marketing Science Institute, 1980).
24. Brandt and Reffett, "Focusing on Customer Problems."
25. L. A. Crosby, "Expanding the Role of CSM in Total Quality," *International Journal of Service Industry Management* 2, no. 2 (1991), pp. 5–19.
26. L. A. Crosby, "A Sequential Procedure for Driving Customer Satisfaction Measurement Results Back Into the Organization," in *New Ways in Marketing and Marketing Research* (Amsterdam: ESOMAR, 1990), pp. 247–256.
27. L. A. Crosby, "Some Factors Affecting the Comparability of Multicountry CSM Information," *Proceedings* of the Quality in Service (QIS 3) Conference, University of Karlstad, Sweden, 1992.
28. Ibid.
29. Ibid.
30. L. A. Crosby, "Toward a Common Verbal Scale of Perceived Quality," *Proceedings* of the 45th ESOMAR Congress, Amsterdam, The Netherlands, 1992.

33

Using the Critical Incident Technique in Measuring and Managing Service Quality

Bernd Stauss, Katholische Universität, Eichstätt, Germany

The Attribute-Based Measurement of Service Quality and Its Limitations

Scientific and practical discussion has resulted in a broad consensus of opinion that service quality has to be understood in terms of customer-perceived quality. The best-known and most widely used methods for measuring perceived quality involve quantitative multiattribute measurements. Within this approach, there are a great number of variants, which can be classified according to either the tradition of attitude research or satisfaction research. Among these variants, the SERVQUAL instrument has attracted the greatest attention in recent years because of its claim to be able to measure the relevant dimensions of the perceived quality, regardless of which service industry is being considered.

Even if the methodological variants differ substantially, all of them share the common notion that a customer's global quality judgment is the result of the evaluation of the different quality attributes. Therefore, within the multiattribute approach, lists of relevant quality attributes are always established, and respondents are asked in interviews to evaluate and weight the attributes of a particular service.

Multiattribute methods give differentiated information on the desired quality level and the perceived deviations from this ideal in the service consumption process. The survey results highlight quality strengths and weaknesses, particularly when they are compared with results of the previous period or with data on the perceived quality of competitors. In view of the insight that management derives from multiattribute methods within a continuously executed monitoring program, these measurements normally form the key element of service quality information systems.

However, a closer look reveals some deficiencies in the multiattribute measurement. First, it is quite possible that the quality attributes of the questionnaire reflect much more the company's perspective than the customer's view. Second, the data collected by these methods cannot grasp the customer's quality perception completely. A comprehensive listing of all quality aspects would result in a questionnaire that would exceed by far the normal customer's willingness to answer. So it is highly likely that a multitude of problems and positive service contact experiences will not be listed at all, particularly those that do not address the core service and that management deems to be of secondary importance.

This defect becomes even worse because multiattribute methods are not able to take the episodic nature of service experiences into consideration. Services require the participation of customers in the service production process. That is why services are perceived as processes and are kept in mind, to a large extent, as episodes, too. Multiattribute methods can record only to what extent these episodes are translated into attitude or satisfaction scores, not the stored episodes themselves. Third, as the quality items are necessarily formulated in an abstract manner, survey results are not particularly concrete. For example, a considerable discrepancy between expectations and the perception of the attribute "friendliness of the staff" would seem to point to a deficiency in quality, yet it doesn't at all indicate which specific behavior customers perceive as unfriendly and what concrete quality improvement measures should be taken to overcome this deficiency.

In other words, the traditional, standardized, and attribute-based quality and satisfaction surveys seem to be incomplete and not sufficiently differentiated with respect to the information needs of quality management. Therefore, and because of the episodic character of service encounters, it is advisable for companies to improve their knowledge by collecting "stories" about experiences their customers had with them. For this task, the application of the Critical Incident Technique can be considered.

Measuring Service Quality by Applying the Critical Incident Technique (CIT)

The Critical Incident Technique (CIT) is essentially a means of collecting and classifying stories or "critical incidents" by employing content analysis. Flanagan, who originally developed this method to identify requirements for effective job performance, defines an incident as "any observable human activity that is sufficiently complete in itself to permit inferences and predictions to be made about the person performing the act." An incident is called critical "if it makes a 'significant' contribution, either positively or negatively, to the general aim of the activity."[1] In this context, the Critical Incident Technique focuses on events that have been seen to lead to success or failure in accomplishing a task. The method has been used extensively in diverse disciplines, including education, human resource management, and work satisfaction research. But only in the most recent years has the Critical Incident Technique been applied as a quality measurement tool, too.

The credit for recognizing and further developing the Critical Incident Technique as an instrument for measuring perceived service quality goes to Bitner, Nyquist, Booms, and Tetreault. In numerous publications, they report on the application of CIT to service industries, concentrating their analyses on communication problems between frontline personnel and customers.

Bitner, Nyquist, and Booms report on the application of CIT to identify critical communication incidents that service industry employees in hotels, restaurants, and airlines find difficult to handle while interacting face to face with customers. Nyquist and Booms illustrate the advantages of CIT by presenting an application to the service of nursing homes. In two publications, Bitner, Booms, and Tetreault describe a CIT study in which respondents were asked to recall a time when, as customers, they had a particularly satisfying or dissatisfying interaction with an airline, hotel, or restaurant employee.

Stimulated by these findings, researchers in numerous countries have been conducting more CIT measurements of the quality of various service industries. Edvardsson describes and analyzes service-related critical incidents in the selling process between Swedish mechanical engineering companies and their customers. Olsen reports on Swedish CIT research analyzing the customers' experiences of problems with banking services. Stauss and Henschel classify and interpret critical incidents experienced by customers of a German car maintenance and repair service company and compare the outcome with the results of a simultaneously conducted multiattribute measurement. Figure 33-1 summarizes important characteristics of the above-mentioned studies.

Methodology

The methodology involves the usual research tasks of collecting, interpreting, and classifying data; conducting reliability and validity tests; and reporting data.

DATA COLLECTION

Originally, the Critical Incident Technique was created as a means of direct observation, but in its application to the measurement of the perceived service quality, observations are practicable only in the most

Figure 33-1. Critical incident studies on service quality.

Authors	Bitner / Nyquist / Booms	Nyquist / Booms	Edvardsson	Bitner / Booms / Tetreault	Olsen	Stauss / Hentschel
Publication year	1985	1987	1988	1989 / 1990	1991 / 1992	1992
Industry	hotels, airlines, restaurants	nursing homes	mechanical engineering firm	hotels, airlines, restaurants	bank	car repair service
Respondents	employees	customers	representatives of selling firm	customers	customers	customers
Valence of incidents	negative	positive and negative	negative	positive and negative	negative	positive and negative
Usable critical incidents	355	?	205	699	272	599
Main classification categories	1. difficult interactions due to customer expectations that exceed the capacity of the service delivery system to perform 2. difficult interactions due to firm or employee performance that does not match the capacity of the service delivery system	?	1. cause 2. course 3. result	1. Employee response to service delivery system failures 2. Employee response to customer needs and requests 3. Unprompted and unsolicited employee actions	1. design quality 2. service production quality 3. process quality	1. tangibles 2. reliability 3. responsiveness 4. assurance 5. empathy

exceptional cases. Observations can measure only limited parts of the aggregate volume of critical incidents. They are unable to determine the intensity of the emotion experienced during the critical incident, and an appropriate method of application is both difficult and expensive. Thus, as a substitute for direct observations, critical incidents are normally collected by direct, open-ended interviews, either face to face or by telephone. During the interviews, respondents are asked to recall a contact situation with the service provider where the experience was either especially satisfying or especially dissatisfying. This approach is suitable because it is likely that customers will keep in mind (as stories) those events they perceive as being extremely positive or negative.

In the data collection process, it is important that the interviewer clarify how the incident happened, which of the involved persons acted in which ways, and which circumstances were decisive for the customer's evaluation.

Usually, a two-step questioning process is followed. The first question contains the request for a comprehensive description of the incident in the customer's own words, e.g., "Think of a time when you gained a particularly satisfying or dissatisfying impression of the service at restaurant X. Please describe in detail the circumstances of the incident." Through follow-up questions, it has to be ensured that the description is as detailed as possible. So the interviewer has to examine whether the stories told contain the most important components of episodic information. Depending on the comprehensiveness of the initial description, several or all of the following questions may have to be asked:

- Exactly *what* happened (action)
- Exactly *who* did what? (actor)
- *Who or what* was the subject of the incident? (object)
- *Where* did the incident take place? (place)
- *When* did the incident take place? (time)
- *How* do you evaluate the incident? (evaluation)
- *What* exactly made you feel the situation was satisfying (dissatisfying)? (cause of evaluation)
- *How* did you or how do you intend to respond to the incident? (consequence).

The customer reports are either written down verbatim or recorded on tape and transcribed.

DATA INTERPRETATION AND CLASSIFICATION

Once the data collection has been completed, the process of interpreting and understanding the service-related incidents commences.

This evaluation of the stories occurs in various steps. First of all, reported incidents that do not meet minimal criteria are eliminated. Bitner, Booms, and Tetreault suggest accepting for further analysis only those incidents that meet the following four criteria: The incident has to (1) include a direct contact between service provider and customer, (2) be very satisfying or dissatisfying from the customer's point of view, (3) be a discrete episode, and (4) have sufficient detail to be fully understood by the interviewer.

The second step involves the systematic coding and classification of the remaining incidents. The main categories of classification can be deduced from theoretical service quality models or formed on the basis of inductive interpretation. Examples of the deductive approach are provided by Olsen and Stauss and Hentschel. Olsen bases his approach on the Gummesson service quality model, and the problematic incidents collected are divided into three model categories: design quality, service production quality, and process quality. Stauss and Hentschel employ the five dimensions of the SERVQUAL model for the classification of critical incidents: tangibles, reliability, responsiveness, assurance, and empathy.

Edvardsson and Bitner, Booms, and Tetreault are among those authors who do not use a theoretically based classification scheme at the beginning but develop a new classification system through the process of interpreting critical incidents. By proceeding this way, they hope to gain new insight into the structure of perceived service quality. Edvardsson's approach results in an analytical structure that enables each incident to be described according to three main criteria and six subcriteria: "Cause" (source, type), "Course" (activities of the selling and the purchasing companies to solve the problems), and "Results" (business results, effect on relationship with customer). Of the different classification systems developed by Bitner et al., the one published in 1990 has proved particularly beneficial for scientific and practical purposes. As a result of an interpretive sorting process, the authors identified three major groups of incidents, namely Group 1, employee response to service delivery system failures; Group 2, employee response to customer needs and requests; and Group 3, unprompted and unsolicited employee actions. Within these major groups, a total of twelve categories emerged (see Figure 33-2).

Regardless of the way the main categories are determined, the single incidents have to be classified via a multistep inductive and iterative process consisting of repeated, careful readings and the sorting of the incidents into groups according to similarities in the reported experiences.

Figure 33-2.   Group and category classification of critical incidents.

Group 1.
Employee Response to Service Delivery System Failures
  A: Response to unavailable service
  B: Response to unreasonably slow service
  C: Response to other core service failures

Group 2.
Employee Response to Customer Needs and Requests
  A: Response to "special needs" customers
  B: Response to customer preferences
  C: Response to admitted customer error
  D: Response to potentially disruptive others

Group 3.
Unprompted and Unsolicited Employee Actions
  A: Attention paid to customer
  B: Truly out-of-the-ordinary employee behavior
  C: Employee behaviors in the context of cultural norms
  D: Gestalt evaluation
  E: Performance under adverse circumstances

Source: Bitner/Booms/Tetreault, 1990.

RELIABILITY AND VALIDITY TESTS

The process of classifying critical incidents can be verified by various reliability and validity tests. The following approaches are particularly useful:

  ▲ Conducting the categorization process several times by employing different coders and examining the intercoder reliability
  ▲ Dividing the total set of incidents into two halves, using one half to create categories and the other half to test whether all of the incidents can be classified within the category scheme
  ▲ Analyzing whether critical stories known from the literature or other sources, such as the company's collection of customer complaints, can be categorized within the developed classification system

REPORTING DATA

During the last phase of the process, the most appropriate level of specificity for reporting the data has to be determined. Then the advantages of a clear arrangement of data in a small number of main categories on the one hand have to be weighed against the completeness and exactness expressed in a wealth of subcategories on the other. In any case, each report should contain an illustration of all categories by exemplary critical incidents. In addition to the specific data presentation of each CIT inquiry, all critical incidents should be stored in a database to ensure easy access for quality management purposes.

The Information Value of Quality Measurement by Means of the Critical Incident Technique

Applications of the Critical Incident Technique in different service industries have consistently demonstrated the following advantages of this technique as a means of measuring perceived service quality:

1. *The Critical Incident Technique is particularly well suited to measuring perceived service quality.* It is especially qualified to measure service quality because of the characteristics common to all services. First, services can be understood as processes. The dominating mode of experience within processes, however, is "episodic" and not attribute-based, and that is why service contact situations are remembered as episodes with references to specific places and times. Second, services are basically intangible. Therefore, the transformation of concrete incident-based experiences into abstract attribute-based evaluations is more difficult with services than for goods. This, in turn, leads to the fact that more incidents as such are remembered. Third, the customers are at least partially involved in the production of services. It is evident that they will experience their participation essentially as a sequence of incidents and not as a sum of attributes. Fourth, customers intending to buy services perceive high risk according to the degree of intangibility and customer participation in the service production and delivery process. Therefore, they tend to reduce the perceived risk by personal word-of-mouth communications. It is not abstract discussions of service attributes that are the subject of these personal face-to-face communications, but special incidents, since these little stories are easy to talk about and attractive because of their authenticity.

2. *The Critical Incident Technique reflects the normal way service customers think.* The Critical Incident Technique allows customers to think about services the way they normally do. During an interview, customers are not forced into any given framework, they are simply asked to recall specific events. The respondents can use their own terms and familiar language. "The result is 'pure' consumer data. CIT allows marketers to see how customers think."[2]

3. *The Critical Incident Technique produces information on service quality experiences that guide consumer behavior.* The subjective relevance of the stories collected by CIT becomes obvious in various respects. It is highlighted by the fact that the customer remembers these reported cases as being particularly satisfying or annoying. Critical incidents seem to be "the moments of truth that, in a special way, remain in the long-term memory of the customer."[3] This is supported by the results of the CIT study conducted by Stauss and Hentschel, which shows, for example, that 19.4 percent of the (predominantly negative) incidents referring to a *previous* car dealer dated back more than 10 years.

Critical incidents determine not only the customer's evaluation of service quality but also the customer's behavior. This includes both the company-directed behavior (for example, praising or complaining, repeat purchasing) and third-party-directed behavior (recommending, warning in personal communication). Edvardsson's empirical study reveals the behavior-influencing effect of negative incidents that in 23 percent of the incidents studied led to the loss of a deal while in 19 percent of the cases the relationship with the customer was impaired, and in 6 percent of the cases the relationship with the customer ended as a result of a critical incident.

The car service study demonstrates the relevance of perceived incidents for consumer behavior, too. About three quarters of the respondents claimed that they gave the service company immediate feedback (79 percent complained about negative incidents, 73 percent offered praise in the case of positive incidents). The amount of word-of-mouth communication is tremendous. The respondents tell an average of ten people about a critical incident, regardless of whether it is a positive or a negative one. The switching behavior caused by negative incidents is also considerable. Four to seven percent of the incidents were evaluated as being important enough to "definitely change the car dealer."

4. *The Critical Incident Technique produces unequivocal and very concrete information.* Since the customers in CIT interviews have the opportunity to give a detailed account of their own experiences, a wealth of unambiguous and very concrete information becomes available that can be translated into specific measures for operational and strategic modifications of the services provided.

5. *The Critical Incident Technique is a useful instrument for identifying minimum requirements and value-enhancing service components.* In applying the Critical Incident Technique, it is possible to differentiate between quality aspects relating to minimum service requirements and value-enhancing service aspects. The distinction between minimum requirements and value-enhancing quality elements is rooted in labor satisfaction research and has been applied to service quality by Brandt and

Cina. Value-enhancing elements include all service elements that have the potential to increase customer satisfaction and perceived value by exceeding expectations. In contrast to this, minimum requirements address those service elements that are expected as a minimum by the customer. "A service provider gets no 'bonus points' for meeting minimum requirements—only 'demerits' for failing to do so."[4]

Respondents who are asked for critical incidents search in their minds for situations in which their expectations clearly were not met, either in a positive or negative sense. Thus, the questioning triggers a thought process that makes the customer identify minimum requirement elements in negative incidents and value-enhancing elements in positive incidents. This conclusion is supported by the results of empirical CIT studies.

The research of Bitner, Booms, and Tetreault produced the following distribution of negative incidents: The biggest share (42.9 percent) falls into category 1, which reflects employee responses to core service delivery system failures, such as unavailable or unreasonably slow service. An almost equally large percentage (41.5 percent) falls into category 3, "unprompted and unsolicited employee actions," where behavior such as rude outbursts to customers or discrimination against female or black customers are classified. In both of these categories, minimum customer requirements of employee behavior were not fulfilled by the employees. The basic expectations of each service—the adequate handling of core service failures and absence of unprovoked negative treatment—were not met. By far the smallest share of negative incidents (15.6 percent) is found in category 2, "employee response to customer needs and requests." In fact, customers could not really expect the staff to alter the systems and procedures to accommodate their special requirements or to strive for a solution to a problem caused by the customers themselves.

The distribution of the positive incidents over the same categories provides a totally different picture: Group 3, 43.8 percent; Group 2, 32.9 percent; Group 1, 23.3 percent. Irrespective of the category into which the positive incidents are classified, these incidents are perceived as being extremely positive because the customers got something they could not have expected to get. They experienced extraordinary actions or expressions of courtesy (Group 3) or an unusual customization of the service in line with their special requests (Group 2). The fact that even employee responses to service delivery system failures (Group 1) are perceived at such a high rate as being *positive* can also be explained by the surpassing of expectations: The customers experienced an unexpectedly positive response, such as full acknowledgment of the problem, a comprehensive explanation, a sincere apology, or generous compensation.

The ability of the Critical Incident Technique to identify minimum requirements and value-adding quality components is particularly important for quality management. On the one hand, the service provider learns which grave deviations from their minimum expectations customers experience and can direct quality management measures towards avoiding incidents that cause considerable dissatisfaction. On the other hand, management finds out which components the customers perceive as being valuable additions to the basic service offered. Thus, the service provider can concentrate further quality efforts on enhancing those aspects that lend themselves particularly well to differentiating service from those of competitors.

Critical Incident-Oriented Service Quality Management

One of the conclusions that can be drawn from the critical incident approach is that service management should view service quality in terms of incidents. By accepting that customers perceive service quality contacts as episodes, the service provider has to direct quality management activities at these perceived events or practice incident-oriented service quality management. Among the main tasks of incident-oriented management are the establishing of a critical incident database, incident-oriented quality planning, external communication, and internal marketing.

Establishing a Critical Incident Database

For the practical purposes of service quality management, it is necessary not only to interpret and classify the single incidents but to make them immediately accessible for differentiated analyses and quality improvement measures. This requires the establishment of a critical incident database within a service quality information system.

The incidents should be stored in the database as stories, perhaps slightly modified by deleting superfluous information and adding customer answers to the additional questions. By means of adequate coding, it is possible not only to analyze the incidents quantitatively with respect to different categories but also to recall single stories.

The coding of the incidents has to consider all criteria mentioned in the description of the data collection process. This means:

Action:	Exact description of the incident.
Actor:	The company (airline x), employee category (steward), a special member of staff (Mr. Smith) . . .

Object:	Respondent, member of the family, other persons, own possession, other peoples' possessions . . .
Place:	On the phone, in the building, at the counter . . .
Time:	Year, month, day, time of day . . .
Evaluation:	Positive/negative, precise formulation of the evaluation ("very annoyed . . .")
Cause of evaluation:	"Employee's response to unreasonably slow service" . . .
Consequence:	Praise, complaint, word-of-mouth, switch to the competitor . . .

When critical incidents are coded in such a way, a lot of different analyses are possible. For example, the occurrence of negative or positive incidents can be appraised with respect to the following questions:

- How is the distribution in relation to the causes of evaluation?
- In which order of magnitude do they appear in the different subsidiary companies, departments, staff member groups, or individual persons?
- At what times do they happen particularly frequently?
- Which negative or positive consequences do they lead to?

The answers to these questions provide management with details on the role that the company, internal staff groups, or individual employees play in the customer's quality experience, which places and contact situations systematically produce customer problems, and whether some quality-related activities are perceived more sensitively than others. More complex analyses are also possible that cast light on the pattern of quality experiences—whether specific actors tend to perform specific actions or whether there is a clear relationship between actions and the resulting customer behavior.

In addition to recording the stories customers tell about their experiences with the services offered, it is helpful to integrate other kinds of critical incidents into the database:

- Customer experiences that have not been perceived by the respondents themselves but have been told to them by others. By means of these stories, the company gains an insight into the type of comments and opinions currently circulating with reference to its service quality.
- Customer experiences with the services of competing companies. They show which aspects of the competitors' services are perceived as being particularly positive or negative.

▴ Past experiences the customers had with other service providers that caused the customers to break off the relationship with these service companies. From these stories, the company can learn a lot about customer-specific sensitivities toward service quality components.

▴ Critical incidents experienced by managers and contact employees. The analysis of these stories gives a clear picture of the staff's service contact perception and of the discrepancies in the way in which customers and employees perceive the entire service delivery process and its outcome.

Incident-Oriented Quality Planning

Essential starting points for incident-oriented service quality planning are provided by the classification scheme presented by Bitner, Booms, and Tetreault (see Figure 33-2). Essentially, negative incidents in terms of deviations from the minimum expectations of the customer are to be avoided and positive service experiences perceived as being of added value should be created.

AVOIDANCE OF DELIVERY SYSTEM FAILURES

The main goal of incident-oriented quality planning has to be the avoidance, or at least the considerable reduction, of service delivery system failures. A consistent zero-defects strategy requires the negative critical incidents experienced with various aspects of the core service to be analyzed carefully with respect to the underlying reasons. To this end, it is advisable to apply total quality management tools such as Failure Mode and Effects Analysis (FMEA) or a variant of Quality Function Deployment (QFD) adjusted for the purpose of directing the process of problem analysis to problem prevention activities.

MEASURES FOR THE RESPONSE TO SERVICE DELIVERY SYSTEM FAILURES

One of the fundamental findings of several CIT studies is that what customers normally perceive as being decisive for their dissatisfaction is not the occurrence of failures but the inappropriate response of the company or the employees to them. Analogous to this is the fact that a company's quick, generous, and nonbureaucratic reaction to service problems is kept in mind for a long time and rewarded by customers. So even service delivery system failures can strengthen the customer relationship if they are handled properly.

Despite all zero-defects efforts, failures in service delivery processes cannot be avoided completely because, quite simply, determinants such as the weather or customer behavior are beyond the company's control. Thus, employees have to be prepared for the occurrence and handling of problems and have to be in a position to deal with annoyed customers. The critical incidents collected and stored in the database show which types of service failures appear and what kind of response is or is not advisable. On the basis of these insights, managers and line employees can jointly define a range of response alternatives and specific actions as part of a consistent service complaint management and recovery policy.

ANTICIPATION OF SPECIAL NEEDS AND REQUESTS

If service companies respond to the specific needs of individual customers and fulfill their special wishes, this personalized treatment will be perceived as value-added service. So service providers have to identify situations in the delivery process that take place repeatedly for the provider but are experienced by the customer as being unusual and rare. The Critical Incident Technique and the classification systems proposed are a good basis for this. The special customer problems documented in the critical incidents can be classified into different groups, such as problems of customers with personal difficulties (linguistic, medical), special preferences with respect to the customization of the core service, or problems caused by the customer's own errors or mistakes (loss of tickets) (see the category system of Bitner, Booms, and Tetreault in Figure 33-2). Consequently, measures have to be planned for the handling of these problem categories by developing standard response alternatives and granting sufficient freedom for flexible responses.

PUTTING PLEASANT SURPRISES ON STAGE

Service quality planning does not only have the task of preparing the company for proper reactions to delivery system failures. Just as important is the proactive planning of value-enhancing quality components. The positive critical incidents give a wealth of stimulating information for the development of service aspects that are perceived by customers as pleasant surprises and rewarded by positive word-of-mouth and provider loyalty.

Incident-Oriented External Communication

The critical incidents collected have a twofold application in the external communication process: They themselves can be used in advertising campaigns, or the contents of the incidents can be used to optimize advertisement design, with the particular aim of influencing customer expectations.

Using Positive Critical Incidents in Advertising

Positive stories about customer experiences with the service provider, which highlight the company's ability to come up with customer-oriented flexible responses, can be put in the center of an advertising message. The demanding quality commitment of the service provider can be illustrated particularly credibly if the customers themselves can tell their service story in the advertisement in their own words. Thus, the story-telling process between customers can be influenced by providing examples in advertisements.

Reducing Customer Expectations

One of the particularly interesting findings of the CIT study conducted by Bitner, Nyquist, and Booms is that only about one-quarter of the negatively perceived incidents were caused by service delivery system failures, whereas nearly three-quarters of the negative contact experiences were the result of customer expectations exceeding the service delivery system's capacity to perform. Incidents in this group suggested that the customers had unrealistic expectations, ranging from the wish to take oversize luggage on board the airplane to requests for much larger hotel rooms for the same price. Thus, the negative critical incidents have to be analyzed with respect to these unrealistic expectations, so that a correction of these expectations using communication measures can be embarked upon.

Incident-Oriented Internal Marketing

Another essential starting point for the use of critical incidents in service quality management is internal marketing, which can be defined as the application of marketing strategies and tools within an organization to gain the cooperation and support of other units and employees. The greatest benefits can be derived in the areas of personnel recruitment, motivation, training, internal interactive communication, and internal mass communication.

Personnel Recruitment

Critical incidents can be used very effectively in personnel selection discussions. Applicants can be confronted with a description of real employee-customer situations and asked for the proper reaction. Their answers give an invaluable indication of the strength of their customer- and service-oriented attitudes and their willingness to react appropriately.

PERSONNEL MOTIVATION

If, in continuously conducted critical incident analyses, employee behavior that is perceived as being extremely positive can be related to individual members of the staff or a specific group of staff, it is advisable to reinforce this behavior by offering material and nonmaterial incentives (bonuses, appreciation).

TRAINING

The appropriate behavior in customer contact situations has to be the most essential element of personnel training programs because this is the basic prerequisite for the avoidance of negative and the stimulation of positive incidents. Difficult situations have to be simulated in group discussions and role plays, a broad repertoire of responses has to be tried out, and the proper utilization of an employee's discretion has to be practiced. Employees must be empowered to respond in the way they deem proper in the given circumstances. The use of critical incidents is particularly well suited for this purpose because they document successful and unsuccessful service transactions from the customer's point of view in a very specific and authentic way.

INTERNAL INTERACTIVE COMMUNICATION

Stories told by customers about their contact experiences with any aspect of the service offered can be used in internal interactive communication to influence employee behavior directly or improve the service delivery process. The incidents give a very detailed indication of the company's quality strengths and weaknesses, which cover, to a certain extent, specific persons or staff groups. This information can be used for quick, individual feedback to reinforce or modify employee behavior. Besides this, incidents can become topics for problem solution teams, quality project teams, or quality circles, which have the task of detecting customer problems, analyzing their root causes, developing improvement proposals, and taking responsibility for the realization of improvement plans.

INTERNAL MASS COMMUNICATION

According to the frequency of occurrence of specific critical incident categories, exemplary positive or negative critical incidents can be selected from the database and communicated in circulars, internal newsletters, videos, and other media. In this way, personnel reactions to negative customer behavior can be demonstrated conclusively and with reference to real cases, as can actions that lead to the desired customer perception of excellent service quality.

Conclusion

The critical incident method has shown itself to be a particularly appropriate tool for measuring perceived service quality. It is well suited to the specific characteristics of services. It considers the normal way service customers think and produces relevant, unequivocal, and very specific information. Moreover, it is possible by means of this method to identify minimum requirements and value-enhancing service components. Because of these informational advantages, critical incidents should be stored in a database and become a key part of any quality information system. This done, incident-oriented quality management can be performed. Its most essential tasks are to ensure that deviations from the customer's minimum expectations are avoided and positive service experiences perceived as being of added value are created. This can be achieved above all by implementing the following measures: (1) Conducting incident-oriented quality planning to avoid delivery system failures, prepare employees and delivery systems for the proper response to failures in the core service, anticipate special customer needs and requests, and develop pleasant surprises for customers; (2) cultivating incident-oriented external communication, either by using positive critical incidents in advertising to stress the company's quality commitment or by correcting unrealistic customer expectations that became apparent through negative critical incident analysis; (3) pursuing incident-oriented internal marketing by applying a differentiated mix of measures (personnel recruitment, motivation, training, internal interactive communication, and internal mass communication) to gain the necessary support of company units and employees for the delivery of excellent service.

The Critical Incident Technique is more than just another means of measuring perceived quality, it is also a powerful management tool. Service providers who take the challenge of Total Quality Management seriously will do well to avail themselves of this tool.

Notes

1. John C. Flanagan, "The Critical Incident Technique," *Psychological Bulletin* 51 (July 1954), pp. 327–358.
2. Jody D. Nyquist and Bernard H. Booms, "Measuring Services Value From the Consumer Perspective," in *Add Value to Your Service*, Carol F. Surprenant, ed. (Chicago: American Marketing Association, 1987), pp. 13–16.

3. Bo Edvardsson, "Service Quality in Customer Relationships: A Study of Critical Incidents in Mechanical Engineering Companies," *The Service Industries Journal* 8, no. 4 (July 1988), pp. 427–445.
4. D. Randall Brandt, "A Procedure for Identifying Value-Enhancing Service Components Using Customer Satisfaction Survey Data," in *Add Value to Your Service*, Carol F. Surprenant, ed. (Chicago: American Marketing Association, 1987), p. 61.

References

Andersson, Bengt-Erik, and Stig Goran Nilsson. "Studies in the Reliability and Validity of the Critical Incident Technique." *Journal of Applied Psychology* 48, no. 5 (1964), pp. 398–403.

Berry, Leonard L. "The Employee as Customer." *Journal of Retail Banking* 3, no. 1 (1981), pp. 33–40.

Berry, Leonard L., and A. Parasuraman. *Marketing Services.* New York: The Free Press, 1991.

Bitner, Mary Jo, Bernard H. Booms, and Mary Stanfield Tetreault. "The Service Encounter: Diagnosing Favorable and Unfavorable Incidents." *Journal of Marketing* 54 (January 1990), pp. 71–84.

———. "Critical Incidents in Service Encounters." In *Designing a Winning Service Strategy*, Mary Jo Bitner and Lawrence A. Crosby, eds. Chicago: American Marketing Association, 1989, pp. 89–99.

Bitner, Mary Jo, Jody D. Nyquist, and Bernard H. Booms. "The Critical Incident as a Technique for Analyzing the Service Encounter." In *Services Marketing in a Changing Environment*, Thomas M. Bloch, Gregory D. Upah, and Valarie A. Zeithaml, eds. Chicago: American Marketing Association, 1985, pp. 48–51.

Brandt, D. Randall. "How Service Marketers Can Identify Value-Enhancing Service Elements." *The Journal of Services Marketing* 2, no. 3 (1988), pp. 35–41.

Brown, Stephen W., and Teresa A. Swartz. "Gap Analysis of Professional Service Quality." *Journal of Marketing* 53 (April 1989), pp. 92–98.

Carman, James. "Consumer Perceptions of Service Quality: An Assessment of the SERVQUAL Dimensions." *Journal of Retailing* 66, no. 1 (1990), pp. 33–55.

Cina, Craig. "Creating an Effective Customer Satisfaction Program." *The Journal of Services Marketing* 3, no. 1 (1989), pp. 5–14.

Freiden, John B., and Ronald E. Goldsmith. "Correlates of Consumer Information Search for Professional Services." *Journal of Professional Services Marketing* 4, no. 1 (1988), pp. 15–29.

George, William R. "Internal Communication Programs as a Mechanism for Doing Internal Marketing." In *Creativity in Services Marketing: What's New, What Works, What's Developing*, M. Ven Venkatesan, Diane M. Schmalensee, and Claudia Marshall, eds. Chicago: American Marketing Association, 1986, pp. 83–84.

Grönroos, Christian. "Internal Marketing—Theory and Practice." In *Services Marketing in a Changing Environment*, Thomas M. Bloch, Gregory D. Upah, and Valarie A. Zeithaml. Chicago: American Marketing Association, 1985, pp. 41–47.

Hart, Christopher W. L., James Heskett, and W. Earl Sasser. "The Profitable Art of Service Recovery." *Harvard Business Review* 68 (July–August 1990), pp. 148–156.

Hentschel, Bert. "Die Messung wahrgenommener Dienstleistungsqualität mit SERVQUAL." *Marketing—Zeitschrift für Forschung und Praxis* 12 (November 1990), pp. 230–240.

———. *Dienstleistungsqualität aus Kundensicht.* Frankfurt: Deutscher UniversitätsVerlag, 1992.

Herzberg, Frederick. *Work and the Nature of Man.* New York: World Publishing, 1966.

Herzberg, Frederick, Bernard Mausner, and Barbara Snydermann. *The Motivation to Work.* New York: Wiley, 1959.

Murray, Keith B. "A Test of Services Marketing Theory: Consumer Information Acquisition Activities." *Journal of Marketing* 55 (January 1991), pp. 10–25.

Nyquist, Jody D., Mary J. Bitner, and Bernard H. Booms. "Identifying Communication Difficulties in the Service Encounter: A Critical Incident Approach." In *The Service Encounter*, John A. Czepiel, Michael R. Solomon, and Carol F. Surprenant, eds. Lexington: Lexington Books, 1985, pp. 195–212.

Olsen, Morten J. S., and Bertil Thomasson. "Qualitative Methods in Service Quality Research: An Illustration of the Critical Incident Technique and Phenomenography." Paper presented at the QUIS 3 Symposium, Karlstad, Sweden, 1992.

Parasuraman, A., Valarie A. Zeithaml, and Leonard L. Berry. "SERVQUAL: A Multiple-Item Scale for Measuring Consumer Perceptions of Service Quality." *Journal of Retailing* 64 (Spring 1988), pp. 12–40.

Parasuraman, A., Leonard L. Berry, and Valarie A. Zeithaml. "Refinement and Reassessment of the SERVQUAL Scale." *Journal of Retailing* 67, no. 4 (1991), pp. 420–450.

Ronan, William W., and Gary P. Latham. "The Reliability and Validity of the Critical Incident Technique: A Closer Look." *Studies in Personnel Psychology* 6, no. 1 (1974), pp. 53–64.

Scheuing, Eberhard E., and George Cirasuolo. "The Risk Manager's Guide to Internal Marketing." *The John Liner Review* 5, no. 1 (1991), pp. 45–50.

Schlissel, Martin R. "The Consumer of Household Services in the Marketplace: An Empirical Study." In *The Service Encounter: Managing Employee/Customer Interaction in Service Businesses*. John A. Czepiel, Michael R. Solomon, and Carol F. Surprenant, eds. Lexington: Lexington Books, 1985, pp. 303–319.

Stauss, Bernd, and Bert Hentschel. "Verfahren der Problementdeckung und -analyse im Qualitätsmanagement von Dienstleistungsunternehmen." *Jahrbuch der Absatz- und Verbrauchsforschung* 36, no. 3 (1990), pp. 232–259.

———. "Attribute-Based versus Incident-Based Measurement of Service Quality: Results of an Empirical Study Within the German Car Service Industry."

In *Quality Management in Service,* Paul Kunst and Jos Lemmink, eds. Assen/
Maastricht: Van Gorcum, 1992, pp. 59–78.

Tulving, E. "How Many Memories Are There?" *American Psychologist* 40 (1985),
pp. 385–398.

Zeithaml, Valarie A. "How Consumer Evaluation Processes Differ Between
Goods and Services." In *Marketing of Services,* James H. Donnelly and
William R. George, eds. Chicago: American Marketing Association, 1981,
pp. 186–190.

Zeithaml, Valarie A., A. Parasuraman, and Leonard L. Berry. *Delivering Quality
Service.* New York: Free Press, 1990.

34

Performance Measurement

Alfred C. Sylvain,
MONY

Creating or changing a performance measurement system is a major undertaking, and, indeed, few companies have done it well. Those who have gone through this experience will tell you that, for the most part, this is so because people naturally resist measuring and being measured. Therefore, how we treat one another is the cause of our success or failure in installing performance measures.

The following three short stories illustrate some of the challenges that one is likely to encounter in introducing performance measures into an organization.

1. *Customer Survey Surprise* (MONY Pension Operations, New York, May 1990). The division announced that it was going to be sending a customer survey to all of its customers. Mary Stevens, Account Manager for the Eastern Region, was visibly upset by the decision. She had developed a routine that gave her a sense of security. She also knew, or thought she knew, what her customers expected and from whom she could expect glowing reports. She managed a large portfolio for John Enterprise Inc., and she believed she had done a good job servicing this customer's account. The relationship was as long-standing as her tenure with the company. Despite all the turnover in the office, the "systems" problems, the delayed production of financial reports, she had been able to get John to laugh about the mistakes and inefficiencies. They were used to problems, and humor was often the best antidote. She had often said to her boss, "If they all were as loyal and easy to please as John, I would be out of a job." So, when the survey results from John said that timeliness, accuracy, and ability to resolve problems averaged 4.6 on a scale of 1 to 10, Mary was dumbfounded, and felt betrayed. There had to be some kind of mistake in the survey calculations, or some administrative way to account for the difference between the survey findings and her perception of how well she had done for John all these years. After a period of denial and deliberation, she finally came to the conclusion that some of the time she spent laughing with John to cajole him out of his

complaints could have been allocated instead to examining and improving the underlying processes.

2. *Measuring Employee Performance* (MONY Pension Operations, New York, July 1991). Joe Johnson, Supervisor of Customer Service, passed out bonus checks today, and as he reflected on those moments with each of the recipients, he was surprised at how good he felt about the whole process. He had originally objected vehemently to the idea of linking recognition to measurable performance results. He had protested that you cannot really measure success quantitatively. It was the intangible, unquantifiable stuff that star performers in customer service were made of—characteristics like courtesy, hard work, energy, and loyalty. While he really believed that what he had said at the time was valid, he had to admit that something did feel better, and more fair, about this new system. It was interesting to discover that as he started to expect measurable results, one of his quieter, seemingly less energetic employees turned out to be a star performer.

3. *Improving the Bottom Line* (MONY Pension Operations, New York, December 1989). When Christian Blain, Assistant Vice-President, first joined the business unit several months ago as its leader, he asked to see the departmental reports used to monitor salary-related and other operating expenses, as well as the documented procedures for paying invoices and rationales for purchasing equipment. What he thought would be delivered to him promptly took a couple of weeks; the directors needed to gather the information from many separate sources. Moreover, the data were not particularly reliable when received. He was starting to understand why the culture seemed so busy and time-pressured, yet so chaotic and disorganized. He decided to request that certain management reports be prepared weekly to track those expenses. Though there was a lot of reluctance to comply with the request, after one month of tracking, the directors produced reports that yielded some interesting results. One vivid example was the reduction in overtime expenses, which dropped by 35 percent with absolutely no change in procedures.

What Is Performance Measurement?

Measurement in its simplest definition has to do with numerically placing value on an object, an event, a condition, a level of performance, etc. It first establishes a point of reference, then provides an evaluation of either progress or deterioration, growth or decline.

A number of authors on performance measurement quote Lord Kelvin, a British physicist who developed a fundamental temperature scale: "When you can measure what you are speaking about, and express it in numbers, you know something about it. But when you cannot measure it, when you cannot express it in numbers, your knowledge is of a meager and unsatisfactory kind."

It has also been said repeatedly that "what gets measured, gets managed." Measures, correctly used, have the power to change behavior and change the way people think. The challenge is to harness the directive power of measures and use it for the good of the company, its customers, and its employees. We are all very familiar with the power of measurement, for good and for bad. We grew up on measurement, on report cards in school and score-keeping in sports. The fact is, however, that we resist measuring and being measured, and we need to factor that resistance into any attempt to install a measurement system in our own organizations.

Because only so many students can be at the top of the class, the majority of the class will feel less than capable. Most people are average! So measures remind most of us of how inadequate we are as compared to the top performers. And measures, such as grades, without comments or tools that direct the correction of the problems can leave us feeling judged—with no recourse! Like a nationally scored exam in which we come out in the 70th percentile, we know we feel inadequate, but we have not been given the tools with which to increase our score.

When we use measures as a point of reference, coupled with an improvement plan that we took part in developing, we tend to compete against ourselves, and we then have a very different experience. In the privacy of our own comfort zone, where we have set our own standards and stretch goals and we know how to correct our own performance, we are self-motivated and self-challenged. This is especially powerful when the climate encourages that kind of behavior. The success of performance measures depends squarely on our willingness to accept them, and their acceptance depends on whether or not the answer to the question "What's in it for me?" is satisfactory. The challenge is to prove that performance measures can be used as a tool to increase our level of job satisfaction and self-esteem.

The MONY Pension Operations Experience

Our experience in quality improvement is just over two years old, and therefore it would be presumptuous to suggest that we have discovered the ultimate formula. However, we are proud of the successes that we have enjoyed in this short period of time and feel that they are worth sharing. In addition, they could serve as a form of benchmarking.

We initiated our Quality Enhancement Process (QEP) at MONY

Pension Operations in mid-1989, during a time when our business was growing rapidly and the external and internal pressures were high.

Market Environment at MONY Pension Operations: External Pressures

Starting in the early 1970s, new legislation and regulations were being introduced to the retirement benefit market at an unprecedented pace. Pension plan sponsors were becoming increasingly dependent on financial institutions to meet their record-keeping and investment needs. Our book of business was growing rapidly, and the types of services required were becoming more diversified and more complex.

This increase in business and complexity of services was occurring at a time when the market continued to be increasingly competitive. A number of new providers and traditional financial institutions were becoming more active in the marketplace because of the rapid growth in pension assets. This set the stage for a highly competitive environment, well into the 1980s.

Given such developments, it was our intuition that our customers' priorities were expanding to include concerns about service quality, in addition to concerns about investment performance and interest guarantees. This was particularly critical to us because with the growth of our book of business (sales volume) came increasing demands on our computer systems, which had to be upgraded, and on our labor force, which had just relocated to Westchester from New York City.

Market Environment at MONY Pension Operations: Internal Pressures

We were an organization that placed great value on its product and technical expertise. It relied heavily on the knowledge and talents of individuals and on its creativity. The organization prided itself on its ability to customize and be flexible. Managers were rewarded for their technical expertise, for responding promptly to changing market demands, for micro-managing every challenge. Managers rated people based on sensible and important subjective criteria. There was a lot of respect for profitability models and achieving desired interest margins and other financial performance measures. In the 1980s, that strategy served us well.

In this high-growth, competitive, continually changing environment, tracking and measuring were critical. It was fertile territory for those who would champion quality and performance measures to establish appropriate systems to monitor the effects of those changes. It was a perfect time to establish a more disciplined predictable environment, for managers to develop interpersonal skills, for preventing rather than reacting, and for using objective, measurable criteria in the performance appraisal process.

In the summer of 1989, we decided to verify whether or not our customers' priorities were shifting and we conducted some market research. We learned from the study that service quality was in fact an overwhelming concern in the marketplace, and so we decided that a Total Quality Management approach was the most viable long-term strategy for our business, even if we were the only line of business in the company to pursue it. I was appointed the Quality Management Officer, reporting directly to the Pension Operations' chief executive. Also, because we intuitively believed that the success of our quality initiative would depend heavily on human resources issues, we merged the human resources management responsibility into the position.

The Role of Measurement

Our Quality Enhancement Process (QEP) is guided by six operating principles: leadership, customer involvement, employee involvement, rewards and recognition, training and communication, and continuous improvement. These principles govern a myriad of initiatives designed to maximize the performance of all *employees* and of the *organization* in its quest toward total *customer* satisfaction. It is our stated vision that total customer satisfaction will provide the added impetus for Pension Operations' continued profitability and the basis for retaining talented employees.

Measures have been critical to the success of the many initiatives that we have undertaken. Our discussion here will be limited to a few, including the following:

Customer Data

- Customer Survey
- Customer Focus Groups

Employee Data

- Employee Survey
- Employee Focus Groups
- Internal Customer Survey
- Performance Objectives
- Recognition Programs
- Quality Training

Organizational Data

- Financial Performance
- Quality Indicators

CUSTOMER DATA

The concept of performance measurement came alive at the onset of the effort. While we did not at first commit ourselves to a long-term vision, we knew that we wanted to serve our customers better, eliminate waste, and increase our book of business. We also knew that we would have to change the way we did business and the way we performed our jobs. However, in the absence of specific knowledge about customer needs and how to serve them better, we felt unable to articulate much more than that intention. So our efforts began with a series of tactical moves, rather than a far-reaching strategy. The customer survey was the first of those moves.

▲ *Customer Survey*: I can vividly recall our first discussions at one of our senior staff meetings, trying to achieve consensus about whether to survey our customers. There was a lot of resistance. The resisters asked why we should venture into unfamiliar territory when we did not have the time and resources to support the additional work that seemingly would result from this. They claimed that they already knew what our customers would tell us, i.e., some form of bad news; that our people would be demoralized and our customers would expect us to fix things we were not sure we could fix. They thought we should instead spend the time fixing those things that we saw as problematic, so that the results would be more favorable.

A few of us who endorsed the survey argued that:

- ▲ In order to satisfy our customers, we needed to define our customers' needs and expectations.
- ▲ Once we knew what was most important to our customers, we could then set our business priorities and allocate resources according to their expectations.
- ▲ We needed to translate their expectations into measurable service standards and to establish a baseline level of performance from which to measure progress at both the individual and organizational levels.
- ▲ We knew that dissatisfied customers would rather "switch than fight," and that if we did not allow them the opportunity to complain, they could easily take their business elsewhere.

The resisters were overruled. Four months later, after a lot of planning and developmental effort, the survey was conducted, and the results were distributed to all employees. Surprisingly, the results were not as dire as predicted. The survey had been carefully designed and administered. The format was short and simple, and both importance

ratings and performance ratings were included. We established a customer satisfaction index of the ten most important items as defined by
our customers. Those issues that people were afraid of became known
facts, so the anxiety disappeared. Managers soon wondered how they
had ever managed before without knowing what our customers expected
or without tracking their performance in a measurable way.

   ▴ *Customer Focus Groups*: We chose to hold focus groups because we
needed to further understand what the tabulated results indicated and
to be able to identify courses of action that would allow us to effectively
improve the results. We invited a group of customers to Westchester,
N.Y., to help us focus on those issues that they told us were important
and to jointly explore ideas for improvement. Those customers were very
enthusiastic about this process; they appreciated being listened to; they
enjoyed contributing their recommendations. An unanticipated result
was the enthusiasm that was generated among our employees by the
mere presence of those customers on our premises.

The results from both the survey and the focus group sessions were
used to develop action items to improve our performance rating and to
set goals for the upcoming year. For example, based on our customers'
recommendations, we modernized our toll-free service, revamped our
informational reports, and tightened our compliance with service standards, all of which were very visible to our customers and thus helped
improve their satisfaction level.

EMPLOYEE DATA

The merging of the Quality Management and Human Resources
organizations highlighted the fact that the technical or process aspects of
quality were incomplete without the interpersonal aspects. We knew we
needed to seek our employees' views on a variety of topics, including
recruitment, training, career development, compensation, service quality, and management style.

   ▴ *Employee Survey*: We again met some resistance as we proposed
surveying all employees. We were advised that employees are never
satisfied, and that given an outlet, they would exaggerate their dissatisfaction. Some questioned whether we would be able to deliver on what
would be identified as problematic, especially once expectations were
raised. Managers were concerned that their authority would be compromised. In fact, they felt that their jobs were to give direction rather than
to solicit feedback.

The arguments that we offered in favor of surveys were as follows:

▴ Employees are closer to the customer and are therefore a source of valuable ideas about how to make the organization better.

▴ Employees are more motivated if they participate in the decision-making process, and if they have a say in how they are managed.

▴ By identifying what people in the organization value, the survey would allow us to better align the individual with the business objectives.

We did conduct the survey, and we presented the tabulated results to all employees. An employee satisfaction index was developed, which covered those issues that were most important to our employees.

▴ *Employee Focus Groups*: After our first survey, we organized employee focus groups across business units, by grade level, to further understand the data and solicit recommendations for improvement. Like the customer focus groups, the employee focus groups led us to develop action items that were intended to improve the survey numbers. For example, a lower than desirable rating in compensation led us to develop a number of initiatives, including a bonus program, a new performance appraisal system, and career advancement criteria. Again, it was a relief to management to know what they were dealing with, and to either correct the problems or manage unrealistic expectations.

▴ *Internal Customer Survey*: By the time we administered this survey, we were so used to surveys that overt resistance was minimal. We decided to survey customers of those centralized functions that support more than one cost/profit center, such as Marketing, Systems, Accounting, and Human Resources. Most of those functions are project-oriented rather than transaction-oriented. We experienced some resistance because processes could not be easily identified. And because those responding were less able to readily identify the underlying processes, they were less able to identify corresponding measures.

We have set higher incremental improvement goals for our internal customer survey than for our external customer survey because of the higher frequency of customer contact, because of the collective commitment to setting higher performance standards, and because of the nature of the relationship, as joint owners of processes used to service the ultimate customer. Again, we used focus groups to further analyze the data, generate recommendations for improvement, integrate those actions into our business plans, and establish measurable goals for improvement.

▴ *Performance Objectives*: Our employees told us via the employee survey that performance appraisals were too subjective, that star performers were not being rewarded, and that favoritism sometimes seemed to be the basis for promotion. By creating a new performance appraisal system that called for supervisors and employees to set mutually agreed upon measurable objectives, we started to reverse these negative perceptions. The performance objectives were structured by what mattered most to us: customers, employees, and the organization (including financials), so that each individual's objectives were aligned with the Pension Operations' vision. Again, we encountered some difficulty.

Educating managers to help their employees set these objectives was a difficult process for all involved. The tendency was to set objectives around what could easily be measured, even if it was not a central piece of the job. It was easier to develop specific measurable objectives for those job families that were more production-oriented rather than project-oriented. What we found was that, once the underlying processes were documented, with specific inputs and outputs clearly identified, performance objectives were more easily developed. The challenge for managers was to define the dimensions of these processes in terms of accuracy, quantity, timeliness, quality, etc., so that employees had a clearer understanding of their accountabilities. The desired dimensions for the processes were then easily translated into individual performance objectives, and merit and bonus compensation were linked to successful attainment of the objectives.

It was also a challenge to find meaningful, measurable objectives that did not require elaborate measuring devices, and to limit those objectives to no more than seven which could define success relative to the critical aspects of the job. The installation of this new appraisal system ultimately changed the way we thought about quality and forced us to think in a more results-oriented rather than activity-oriented manner.

▲ *Recognition Program*: Performance measures have been vital to the success of our recognition efforts. We created a Bonus Program to reward star performers. The bonus pool is based on our financial performance and the customer satisfaction index. Those who are eligible must exceed their measurable performance objectives.

In addition, both individual and team recognition awards recognize those individuals who measurably close the gap between what the customer expects and what the customer is getting. Whereas our former recognition system recognized employees who worked hard or performed above and beyond the call of duty in the eyes of their managers, this new system recognizes people based on their initiatives, suggestions, and ultimately the measurable service quality improvement that they achieved.

ORGANIZATIONAL DATA

Organizational data refers to those measures that we have installed to monitor the success of the Pension Operations organization as a whole. The organization is defined in terms of its management reporting structure, its financial performance, the products and services offered, and the internal processes that have been put in place to deliver those products and services. It is the machine that people use to produce whatever goes to the customer.

▴ *Financial Performance*: This is probably the only type of performance measure that did not require a tremendous amount of discussion. Historically, most companies have been driven by profit motives and thus have always needed to track financial measures. However, as Tom Peters has said, our fixation with financial measures has caused us to ignore less tangible nonfinancial measures, and those other measures are the "real drivers of corporate success."[1]

While we continue to monitor financial performance as we have always done, our management focus has today been expanded to include nonfinancial performance measures. While our business plans used to be developed solely around improving the financials, they are now developed based on a number of other improvement goals.

▴ *Quality Indicators*: At MONY Pension Operations, the terms *quality indicators* and *performance measures* have been used interchangeably. Quality indicators are those measures, either external or internal, that reflect what the customer expects or alert management to potential breakdown points within a given process. Both types of measures must be aligned with the business strategy, which is based on customer expectations, as well as with individual performance objectives. Since we are a financial services organization, in the business of selling information, expertise, and investment performance, our customers are most concerned with such measures as accuracy, responsiveness, and reliability. For a more complete list of measures, see Figure 34-1.

Early in our efforts, we introduced a process review program intended to examine critical processes. The purpose of the process review was to identify redundancies, inefficiencies, and other improvement opportunities. A byproduct of that program was the identification of control points where quality indicators could be installed.

We had a bit of a false start in this effort. Because the management team had not yet developed a full appreciation of the benefit of the process review concept, our ability to offer recommendations was not matched by our ability to implement those recommendations.

We then approached it from a different angle and decided instead to develop quality indicators for each critical process, whether or not a

Figure 34-1.   MONY Pension Operations: Key components of our quality
measurement system.

Focus	Quality Indicator
Customers	• Customer survey participation rate • Customer satisfaction index comprising the following success factors: —responsiveness —reliability (products, services, and people) —thoroughness (tangible outputs) —ease of doing business with us • Investment performance • Number and cause of client inquiries • Number of client visits
Employees	• Employee survey participation rate • Employee satisfaction index comprising the following environmental factors: —training —career development —management style —performance appraisal —recruitment practices • Level of participation on improvement teams • Number of employees recognized for implementing improvement ideas • Number of actionable improvement ideas suggested • Number of improvement ideas accepted • Training hours • Percent of objectives met versus objectives set • Internal customer satisfaction index (same factors as external customer survey)
Organization	• Number of new clients • Number of client references • Number of suspended contracts (terminations) • Compliance with service standards • Compliance with project plans • Turnover • Attainment of financial objectives —earnings —sales —new deposits —withdrawals

Source: A. C. Sylvain.

process review was conducted. There was still a lot of resistance. For example, functional areas that were highly specialized could not relate to the concept of process management. Again, there was a belief that their processes either did not exist or were too variable and qualitative to be quantifiably measured. They found that it was difficult to set measurable targets for improvement and even more difficult to establish reliable tracking devices. Persistence and top management commitment were the reasons for the success of this major effort. Today, every business unit from the Mailroom to Actuarial, from Systems to Customer Service, from Human Resources to Marketing and Sales, has business plans and objectives that are supported by quality indicators. These indicators are reviewed at our monthly Quality Steering Committee meetings. When appropriate, corrective actions are initiated.

While we would be remiss in not discussing benchmarking or cost of quality in any paper on performance measurement, our own experience with these practices to date is in its infancy. Suffice it to say that we are aware that quality is not total without them. With regard to benchmarking, it made sense to us to first establish measures based on our customers' feedback, and only now to benchmark, to make sure our standards are consistent with the best. In terms of cost of quality, we know that organizations that are serious about total quality routinely measure the cost of nonconformance. In our case, because we realized significant efficiencies through our quality efforts, we did not feel pressured to prove ourselves through using cost of quality measures. We are nevertheless interested in pursuing a program in this area because we believe there might still be some hidden opportunities.

Quality Training

More than any other effort, training brought out the value of measurement and the importance of gathering "facts and data" rather than relying solely on hunches. The majority of this first wave of training had to do with how to use measurement tools to make a process more efficient. We started training with the senior management team first, and cascaded the training down throughout the organization. It was preparing for Quality Training that gave us the discipline to structure, organize, and assign accountabilities and thus measures, and ultimately to take the entire quality improvement process more seriously.

The Correct Use of Measures: The Technical Side

We have learned that, to be effective, a measurement system needs to meet both technical and human requirements. On the technical side, the following should be considered:

1. *Develop both internal and external measures.* It is important to have both types of measures and to understand their use. As we have seen earlier, internal measures measure the success of the organizational processes, preventively alert us to potential breakdowns in the process, and identify opportunities for improvement. Of course, internal processes either can be within a department or cross departmental lines. By contrast, external measures measure the level of customer satisfaction, are detective, and alert us to errors that will be visible to our customers. Knowing the difference ensures that we have covered all bases.

2. *Link frequency to customer interactions.* How frequently you measure is a function of how often your customer has an opportunity to interact with you or evaluate your service. As a general rule, the frequency of measures installed must be greater than the number of transactions/interactions with the customer. Using a monthly accounting report as an example, there need to be a number of quality indicators along the process of producing that report to ensure that the data elements reported are complete and accurate. In addition, the cycle time associated with the processing of those transactions must support the ultimate objective of publishing the monthly report by the promised due date. Moreover, frequency of measuring is also dependent on how quickly what you are measuring changes—i.e., what can change considerably during a week should be measured daily.

3. *Align business strategy with customer expectations.* Measuring for the sake of measuring is costly. Management must determine what is important to the customer, then use that information to formulate an overall business strategy, and finally translate that into objectives and performance measures at the individual and organizational levels.

4. *Limit number of measures.* Efforts must be made to use as few measures as possible and to choose those that capture as much as possible. The simpler the system, the better. Measures used must be easily understood by those using them.

5. *Set stretch but realistic goals.* A numerical goal that is too high will demoralize; one that is too low will underchallenge and lead to complacency. Study previous results, and establish targets that are greater than what you have demonstrated you can achieve.

6. *Seek to measure the intangibles.* It is important to account for the success of those activities that appear to be abstract or intangible, such as the recruitment of an employee with certain unique talents, the creation of a new product or service, the application of business philosophies and values, and the response to economic and market trends. If you cannot do this, then it is important to identify those individuals who can best provide feedback on the effectiveness of these intangibles, poll

them, tabulate their responses, and compile the numerical results using a simplified scale. This too will assist greatly in identifying long-term strategic opportunities.

The Correct Use of Measures: The Human Side

No matter how technically successful you are in installing measures, if the human side is ignored, your system is likely to fail. The human side includes the culture or environment in which employees are asked to function. That culture must be quality-focused. A quality culture is one that is dynamic and highly interactive, with feedback and ideas flowing continuously. It is structured so that people are close to their customers. It is one in which management is ready to be accountable. One of the best ways to be accountable is to be willing to be measured. A quality culture is one in which people are not afraid to display the truth, where shortcomings can be exposed without fear, and where all those involved in the process are encouraged to improve it.

What works about the quality philosophy is that companies need exactly what individual employees want for themselves—an environment in which people feel they can grow, prosper, and add value. Companies have been realizing that people do not need to be pushed or "managed" to do good work—given the right culture, you could not stop people from being creative and using all the tools available, including measures, even if you tried.

We have learned that the following are requirements for the effective use of performance measures:

1. *Gain top management endorsement.* If measuring is done as an exercise or drill and not endorsed by top management, efforts will backfire. A culture needs to be created such that people react predictably to numerical measures.

2. *Trust.* Top management further needs to model quality as it relates to measurement. There must not be punishment for poor numbers, only encouragement to find the solution to correct the problem. Management needs to welcome the bad news, or people will distort the data.

3. *Mutually develop measures.* All those accountable for a successful process need to develop the measures together. The best person to do the actual measuring is the one who is doing the job. People who measure themselves are challenged to improve and are also more receptive to correcting problems. The difference between an empowered staff and an unmotivated staff depends on whether measures are mutually set or simply handed down from management. As Jim Clemmer, author

and co-founder of The Achieve Group, said, "Don't confine results to the executive team. If employees are going to help with (or even care about) service/quality improvement, they need to know the score. Besides, *your front-line staff* should be deciding what to measure, how to measure it, how to record and communicate it, and how to use it."[2]

4. *The system must be credible.* The system will not work unless there is an owner, and hence accountability, for each measure. Ultimately, this accountability should be directly tied to this individual's compensation.

5. *Update your system regularly.* It is easy for measures, once set, to take on a life of their own, which is good. It becomes problematic, however, when you do not update or delete measures that are no longer useful. In the spirit of continuous improvement, measures should be reviewed periodically and the system overhauled, if necessary.

6. *Blame the process, not the person.* Fritjof Capra, a renowned physicist and author, talks about the shift from the old to the new paradigm, or the shift from structures to processes. "In business terms, the new paradigm tells us that when there's a problem in an organization, you do not blame people, you do not blame departments . . . but you look instead at the processes." He further states that physics has taught us that structures really have no independent life, that they are literally a reflection of energy, of process.[3] A good system, therefore, allows us to blame the process, not the person—to divorce personalities from the issues. It allows us to avoid subjectivity and bias, to avoid favoritism, and hence to encourage the involvement of all employees, regardless of their differences. Furthermore, the environment that is needed is one in which the culture is flexible enough to embrace those differences and to question the status quo. In fact, David Kearns, former chairman and CEO of Xerox, said that there need not be any compromise in recognizing people of different genders, cultures, and races; "If you give the people the right experiences, the normal measurement system of competence and results will prove itself."[4]

7. *If your organization is not already in crisis, create one.* It is our contention that measures can help most when your company is least likely to remember to use them. When a company is in the type of crisis that constant change brings, taking the time to measure and put in controls, from the customer, employee, and organizational perspective, will reduce panic and stress and increase productivity and morale.

The Power of Performance Measurement

In the minds of our leaders and employees at MONY Pension Operations, performance measurement has shifted the organization very significantly. By surveying our customers and employees, we made a commitment to be held accountable for our service and to manage and exceed their expectations rather than only react to what we thought they wanted. We shifted from being more short-term and reactive to being more goal-oriented and proactive. By setting measurable performance objectives with our employees, we immediately became more results-driven and less activity-driven, more consensus-oriented and less hierarchical. By installing quality indicators for all our key processes, the organization shifted from being more task-oriented to being more process-oriented.

Your Organization's Readiness

As you create or overhaul your organization's performance measurement system, you may want to ask yourself the following questions:

1. Does your top management team endorse the value of a comprehensive performance measurement system?
2. Is your organization willing and able to trust your employees with data that they can use to improve the level of service quality?
3. Is your organization willing to have performance measurements developed jointly by management and employees?
4. Is your organization willing to commit the resources required to train people in the correct use of performance measures?
5. Does your organization appreciate the value of procedures?
6. Are your employees' priorities aligned with the needs of the customers?
7. Do your employees feel that the main way people get ahead in your company is through objective promotional criteria?
8. Do your employees feel that your current measures are user-friendly and effective?
9. Is your organization more interested in preventing mistakes than in blaming the person who made the mistakes?
10. Is your organization aware of your customers' and employees' expectations?
11. Is your organization very proactive in meeting customers' and employees' expectations, e.g., spending less time resolving problems and more time anticipating changing needs?
12. Are your managers able to go on vacation and within a short

period of time understand what has happened while they have been gone?*

13. Would your employees agree that your recognition and compensation systems distinguish good from poor performers?

"No" answers to the above questions suggest that your organization would benefit a great deal from a quality performance measurement system.

Conclusion

The biggest mistake an organization can make is to develop and install a system in isolation, hand down prescribed targets for employees to reach, and then punish them for poor performance. Yet this is what we have experienced since we were in school, and it is one of the reasons why we have instinctively resisted measuring and being measured.

On the other hand, we have also learned that when people have an opportunity to be involved in the development, implementation, maintenance, and continuous improvement of the performance measurement system, they learn that "what is in it for me" can be personally rewarding while supporting business objectives.

Notes

1. Tom Peters, *Thriving on Chaos* (New York: Knopf, 1987), p. 488.
2. Jim Clemmer, *Firing on All Cylinders* (Toronto: Macmillan of Canada, 1990), p. 242.
3. Fritjof Capra, "Interview: Fritjof Capra," *Business Ethics* (January/February 1992), p. 29.
4. From Valuing Diversity Video Part 3, Copeland Griggs Productions, San Francisco, 1987.

---

*Will Kaydos captured this idea well. He said, "If a manager has a good performance measurement system he or she should be able to take a vacation for a few weeks and be able to tell, within thirty minutes of returning: 1) how well the department performed overall 2) where the problems occurred and 3) exactly who needs to be talked to first." Will Kaydos, *Measuring, Managing and Maximizing Performance* (Cambridge, Mass: Productivity Press, 1991), p. 49.

PART IX

REINFORCING SERVICE QUALITY

35

Sunburst Farms: Leaders Through Alignment in Flower Distribution

Paula Anderson-Findley, Abraham Gutman, and Abe Wynperle
Sunburst Farms, Inc.

Venture into any of the high-quality florist shops in the United States and you will find our products. Over the past twenty years, wholesalers have been supplying retail florists with Sunburst fresh-cut flowers. We have built a reputation for quality and service, and are, like most organizations today, undergoing a tremendous shift in alignment. From the recognition of the criticality of partnerships with our distributors to the quality message that must be sent in all our daily activities, from the strong pursuit of continuous improvement on the part of all our managers to the dramatic change in focus and behavior of all our sales representatives, we are working to align our mission, vision, and values.

About $25 billion of fresh-cut flowers are consumed worldwide annually. The European retail flower market comprises approximately $17 billion of this market, with the United States and Japanese markets representing approximately $5 billion and $3 billion, respectively.

Our focus on quality starts with our suppliers' flower production on farms located in Colombia, Ecuador, and Mexico with additional procurement from selected other sources worldwide. The company markets its flowers to the wholesale trade and through upscale supermarket channels. In addition, through a separate division, we also target the final consumer through a mail order operation.

Managing our business used to be simple: high-quality products at fair prices. As a result, we were able to maintain a pricing strategy consistent with pricing expectations for excellent quality flowers. Firmly planted in the high end of the market, we have earned the right to be known as a company with "a growing reputation for quality."

Since our founding, we have sustained substantial growth with new product and variety introductions, innovative floriculture technologies, and leadership in the industry. Through developmental activities in plant breeding and research, we have been recognized over the years several times for our outstanding flower varieties.

Challenges in Alignment

Several years ago, we were confronted with rapid growth in the industry and had to rethink our business strategies. Global flower production was increasing, and demand was not keeping pace. We knew that it would not be enough just to change our market strategies; the company culture needed to be linked to the shifting business environment if we were to remain a leader in the flower industry. We needed internal strategies that would nourish fresh behaviors and move our culture from a quality product orientation to a quality services and quality product orientation.

Flowers suddenly became a commodity. Established organizations decided to aggressively expand production, and new companies entered the market. Many of these companies' flowers were produced in low-cost environments, and investments to guarantee high-quality production and to market products efficiently and profitably were not made. Oversupply was evident, and prices eroded rapidly with the influx of poor-quality products. Soon, producers had a difficult time keeping their heads above water. Wholesalers were buying at low prices, applying normal margins, and generating lower overall profits. The final consumer only experienced a minimal effect on prices, however, since most retailers did not pass on their savings.

At Sunburst, we decided to maintain our focus on quality and value as our competitive strategy. We did not want to become part of the trend toward high volumes, low prices, and marginal levels of service. In order to continue our growth and profitability, we had to find ways to clearly distinguish ourselves from our competition. We did this, and are still doing it, through "Service Quality in Distribution Partnerships."

A Company in Transition: A View From the Top

Partnerships in distribution can be built only if the entire organization truly understands and practices quality customer service. All the elements of quality service, including mission, vision, and values, must be aligned. For most organizations, this translates into massive cultural change. This change must first take place internally before customers can be involved in the process. Once internal building blocks are in place, partnerships can be built with customers.

The most difficult challenges occur at the top of the organization. Our key managers had been promoted because of their commitment and contributions. Suddenly, they were confronted with the fact that a change of focus was required, that things had to be done differently than before. People got confused and traumatized, asking themselves why they had to change. Because of such fears, those in charge of a change process must make absolutely sure that the process is well managed. Once the transformation starts, the leaders of the process are involved for the long haul.

Our customers perceived our service as fair and our products as better than average. Our long-standing commitment to product quality and our basic commitment to our people had developed a solid service quality commitment. Processes and procedures had been developed to get the job done fairly well as long as a particular task did not require something out of the ordinary. Without directed action from the top, our associates took on the responsibility and got the job done. They took care of our customers' basic needs, often bending our policies and procedures to get things done. But the level of service never evolved beyond meeting those basic needs. When things got rough, our people often got stuck and handled our customers' needs in a less than professional manner. It was quite clear as we stepped back and observed our own behaviors that we needed to change our focus to ensure that customer-service-related processes were structured and effective, yet flexible enough to enable our people to improvise whenever appropriate. What we needed was empowerment.

We conducted a survey to learn more about our corporate culture. It showed us through the eyes of our people, and sometimes quite painfully, where our deficiencies were. We looked very hard at the results and decided to accept fully the outcome of the data and build our new organizational culture using this feedback. Department and division managers argued with the results and tried to hold on to the past, but there wasn't any time for looking back.

The survey showed that our people were very committed to the long-term success of the company, but that they felt that communications were far from optimal. Developing our communication and information systems became our focus.

Excellence in customer service can never be achieved without the profound understanding that we all are servicing one another at the intracompany level. When Marketing needs information from Sales, Marketing is the customer. When Finance needs information from Production, Finance is the customer, and when Sales needs action, we must all respond to meet their needs. External customer service can never be achieved unless we are all focused internally on the same target.

When calling for intracompany service, departments need to know and respect one another. We developed training classes that each associate is required to attend. As these classes have evolved, an open forum takes place at the end of each class. Participants have learned that they can talk freely about past problems, swap success stories, or start discussions leading to a better understanding of one another's work environment. In the end, we conclude that we must help and support one another in building the strength of the organization.

Through the various initiatives discussed above, we have been able to plant the seeds for excellent customer service and building real partnerships with one another and with our customers. This internal environment provides the basis for building open relationships with our business partners.

Like relationships within our organizations, global import-export relationships must be open. When this openness can be defined by enhancing each partner's ability to operate, the entire chain benefits. At Sunburst, we committed to open systems to achieve this goal—open computer system architectures, open communication systems, and openness to learning new ways of doing things, therefore, openness to change.

Partnership Building Blocks: Planting the Seeds

Before we could start addressing the issues of building true partnerships with our customers, we had to understand where we stood on service issues both externally and internally. We wanted to base our strategic market decisions on a global perspective. We wanted to begin the process of internal change with a clear understanding of our opportunities and to build on our strengths.

Our first step was to conduct an industrywide market research study. The results provided us with a comprehensive analysis of our current business situation and benchmarking data on consumer satisfaction as well as information about opportunities for alignment throughout our distribution network.

Once we knew strategically where we had to build stronger quality service, we needed to understand how our associates felt about the current state of the organization. A companywide assessment was conducted, using a survey, personal interviews, and observations to determine how our people felt about a variety of issues. These issues included how satisfied and committed they were to Sunburst; how they viewed the interaction within departments among coworkers and management; and how they perceived their job roles and work flow among departments and divisions in the organization. Finally, we needed to know their perspective and ideas on varied issues related to opportunities for improvement.

With a clearer vision of where we stood, we fine-tuned our strategic planning process to better detail those strategies and action plans dealing with achieving excellence and care in customer service and building internal and external partnerships. During the process, we aligned operating committees across the organization with our strategic goals.

The original plan's framework was reviewed by these committees, which then identified key objectives for our strategic goals that would continue to serve as our targets throughout the life of the plan. With a strategic plan involving internal and external alignment, we communicated our commitment through aggressive plans for marketing and training and development. Our approach was to have internal and external needs drive our change effort.

Workshops and team building activities are held periodically throughout the year. In these workshops, skills and competencies to evaluate, monitor, and improve work processes are taught, as well as back-to-basics skills for business. Additionally, every summer, each Sunburst department gives classes conducted by associates who have volunteered to be trainers. During these classes, associates throughout the company are given an overview of the individual department and learn about the type of work that takes place in each function.

Sunburst's team building activities range from organized activities at company functions, such as picnics or celebrations, to experiential-based learning programs designed to challenge individuals and groups in problem-solving scenarios. Activities that have generated the greatest amount of positive feedback and results in motivation and enthusiasm for improvement of work relations and processes are those programs that by design support coworkers in building trust and self-confidence. Two programs in particular, Project Challenge, an outdoor ropes course, and Gold of the Desert Kings, an indoor simulation game of adventure, have been used at Sunburst.

During the ropes course, individuals gain insight and an understanding of themselves and others while engaged in group activities. Areas such as self-esteem, trust, communications, problem solving, decision making, and appropriate risk taking are addressed metaphorically. Weeks later, associates who participated in these activities are still motivated to work more productively, feel more comfortable, and are willing to talk openly with coworkers. A couple of years later, some of these same associates express how a personal experience in the course helped to resolve an internal or external problem at work.

We've used Gold of the Desert Kings for management retreats and sales training. In a desert situation, participants are challenged to manage resources to overcome common obstacles to goal achievement, such as information analysis, decision making, strategic planning, delegation of authority, communications, teamwork, and plan execution.

Once participants in these kinds of activities talk openly, using metaphors to discuss challenges in the workplace, they call upon these experiences again and again to return to a solution process that works.

Partnership Building Blocks: Fostering Customer Relationships

We also needed to reach out to our customers differently than we had in the past. Based on customer and associate feedback, Sunburst marketing associates developed the "Quest for Customer Service" campaign, which asked our customers to tell us what they believed to be an innovative standard of customer service in the fresh-cut flower industry. Backed by personal requests for input as well as other corporate initiatives, "Quest" generated a significant response rate of 46 percent and provided us with at least 500 excellent suggestions. These suggestions for improvement focused on special attention to instant response to special and changing situations involving distribution, delivery, and telephone communications as well as continued educational support for new products and situations in the industry. These suggestions were then grouped into major categories by the Quality Services strategic operating committee and circulated throughout the company.

Once this had been done, departments developed quality standard parameters (QSPs) from our "Quest" suggestions. With service performance goals outlined by our customers, we can address their needs in our daily operations. On a monthly basis, we measure our performance against QSP. These suggestions thus become daily work goals for continuous improvement. QSP results are communicated companywide, and improvements in quality of service are provided to our suppliers, to one another, and to our customers.

Sometimes we up the ante on our QSPs or simply introduce a new meaningful goal when reviewing them monthly. When the entire organization is involved in the process of evaluating standards of service performance, associates become extremely creative and continuously suggest changes to the system.

Each quarter, we survey a representative sample of our customer base to measure their ongoing perception of Sunburst's products and service quality against our internal QSPs.

There are approximately 1,200 wholesale florists currently operating in the United States, and Sunburst conducts business with two-thirds of these wholesalers. We view our relationships with our customers as long-term distributor partnerships. Unlike consumer electronics such as computers and VCRs, flowers can be differentiated by a number of factors; color, size of bloom, freshness, and ability to live in a vase longer than a competitor's product are a few. But the consumer, for the most part, must rely on the florist for honesty and value.

Partnership Building Blocks: Adding Value

Some of the ways in which Sunburst strengthened its relationships with its distributors are identified below:

1. *Service Differentiated Marketing Programs*. Based on the wholesaler's needs, we have developed specialized marketing programs based on customer marketing philosophies that range from very traditional (no risk) to very innovative. In some cases, we have collaborated with our customers to tailor joint marketing programs, leading to mutual success for both companies in revenue and exposure while increasing Sunburst brand recognition. Two examples of these kinds of programs are joint direct mail campaigns designed to promote specific flower varieties, and flower care and handling cards for florists.

2. *Global Partnerships*. Since we operate in markets characterized by vast cultural differences, we recognized the need to conduct detailed assessments of these cultures as we were expanding operations. For example, when building partnerships in Holland and South America, we decided to work closely with distribution companies in these countries to better deal with the existing complex distribution systems. In some countries, there are many more entities involved in the distribution network of imports and exports than in the United States. By working with these distributors, we were able to eliminate some of the links in the distribution chain. When managers were assigned to operations, we made sure that they not only were familiar with a particular culture and the way business is conducted, but also spoke the language fluently.

3. *Training Workshops for Customers*. We invite customers to attend our training and development activities, and sometimes conduct a program with them. Once we determined that our internal development activities were yielding results, we decided to provide these services to our customers. We now, for example, provide workshops on sales techniques and team building. It is our intention to share our organization's values with our distribution customers.

Partnership Building Blocks: Linking the Distribution Chain

Technology will continue to play a central role in maximizing the quality of distributor partnerships. We chose to use technology in two discrete areas, ensuring from the outset that each would integrate seamlessly with the other. The first area was partnership systems, and the second was the link to our customers.

Partnership Systems

The most successful relationships between individuals are those characterized by openness. An adequate flow of information and a sensitivity
toward the requirements of others can greatly improve the effectiveness
of any alliance. We believe that this applies equally to business partners
and should be facilitated through information and telecommunications
systems. For this reason, Sunburst and its suppliers decided three years
ago to develop their systems strategies using three simple maxims:

1. The data flow between the partners is the minimum required by
   each to operate its business independently. This ensures that no
   one party will be performing the work of another, while enabling
   databases to be cross-indexed.
2. The operational and system requirements of one company will
   not be allowed to "contaminate" the design of the partners'
   systems. This is ensured by point one above and paves the way
   to a well-defined list of roles and requirements for each partner.
3. Data entered into the system of any company should never have
   to be reentered into the system of any other. This ensures that
   responsibility and accountability for action is always crisp and
   obvious.

With these maxims in place, Sunburst and its primary suppliers
have defined for themselves a very flexible technological environment
that allows them to develop systems without regard to any kind of rigid
hardware or software standardization. At the same time, it defines in
clear terms the ultimate point of contact or "interface" between their
systems. This interface is analogous to Henry Ford's idea of black cars:
"It doesn't matter what data is processed or how, as long as the customer
gets only the data needed and does not have to enter it again."

Sunburst and its suppliers chose to develop systems using open
standards, UNIX, relational databases, client-server architectures, and
public electronic mail carriers directly accessed by local computers.
Furthermore, in order to maintain the focus on the production and
distribution of high-quality fresh-cut flowers, the companies made the
explicit decision to acquire, whenever possible, off-the-shelf software
instead of developing systems in-house. This was a major achievement
in light of our cultural differences. Our eclectic partnerships include
companies worldwide. Needless to say, the phrase "open standards"
means different things in almost every location. It was through negotiation, and sometimes not-so-gentle persuasion, that we ultimately
achieved a solid consensus.

These achievements have had a tremendous impact on our supplier relationships. The quality of our interactions has increased because we all know what to expect and realize one another's capabilities. The speed and accuracy with which we communicate has allowed us to bring product to the market faster and better than any other such alliances in the world. This in turn translates into substantially better service to our customers, who now have access to a window overlooking purchases from product planning at the farm to delivery at the dock.

Information Links to the Customer

Our partnership systems would be futile if they were not accessible to our customers. After all, we not only sell fresh-cut flowers, we supply our customers with the strength of our supplier-distributor relationships, total information about the product they buy, and information about market conditions that may affect their current and future purchases.

In order to provide our customers with this advantage, we created three points of entry to the distribution chain, namely the Quality Assurance Information System, Suntrends, and Flowernet.

THE QUALITY ASSURANCE SYSTEM

This system is initially fed by the growers, who cross-reference an electronic mail transmission containing expected product shipments with the output of a laser scanner that scans all incoming product and confirms the integrity of the shipment. The list of products and codes contained in the final confirmation represents the link between the complete life of the product in the field and the new life that starts at our distribution center in the United States. The shipment-specific data grow day by day through quality assurance procedures and inventory movements. When the product leaves for a customer site, a full history of any specific box can be traced back to its point of origin. This information is accessible to our Quality Assurance group for answering customer questions and quick resolution of customer concerns.

SUNTRENDS

Suntrends is a weekly report published by Sunburst on the state of the market. The information contained in this electronic newsletter is compiled from multiple sources, including historical, government, and grower data and production forecasts. It also keeps the reader informed on weather conditions in the main growing regions worldwide and market conditions at auctions around the world. This information is transmitted to our customers weekly, providing them the capability to plan their strategies based on the same types of information that global importers and exporters are using.

FLOWERNET

Flowernet is a unique implementation of a computer information system. The goal of this system is to provide customers with daily access to inventory at our distribution center and enable them to make purchases without human intervention. Data on Flowernet include a complete view of all available products, prices, available quantities, and packing information. Users can look at the inventory in multiple ways, including by variety and color. Once the customer makes a choice, the order can be processed electronically. The customer's credit status is checked, and the order is automatically forwarded to the distribution center for air or ground delivery. The customer's invoice for the transaction is also confirmed electronically on the system. At any time, the user can check the status of orders, invoices, and total amount of purchases to date and can communicate with our sales representatives or our Flowernet user support group via the system's electronic mail feature.

Flowernet is the first successful EDI (electronic data interchange) implementation in the fresh-cut flower industry. It gives our customers the ability to minimize the amount of time and expense required for purchasing activities, while maximizing their ability to dedicate more time to their customers. This newly found time allows Sunburst's customers to nurture supplier-customer relationships, creating a synergy that is beneficial to the entire chain, from the grower to the final consumer.

Conclusion

Our success in improving the quality of the relationship with our suppliers and the benefit that this relationship brings to our customers tells us that we are on the right technological and market path. The drive toward service excellence and partnership building in distributor relationships will not progress unless those who are responsible for putting the process together become the architects of the process. As we continue to adjust our action plans because we are in a dynamic environment, we will always involve our associates. They know best where we can excel and where we can have the greatest competitive impact.

References

Bagley, D. and E. Reese. *Beyond Selling: How to Maximize Your Personal Influence.* California: Meta Publications, 1987.

Heil, G. M. and R. W. Tate. "Legendary Customer Service and the HRD Professional's Role." *Developing Human Resources*, the 1990 Annual (1990).

LaBorde, G. *Influencing with Integrity: Management Skills for Communication and Negotiating*. California: Syntony Publishing, 1987.

Lewin, K. *Field Theory in Social Science: Selected Theoretical Papers*. New York: Harper & Brothers, 1951.

Peters, Tom. *Thriving on Chaos: A Handbook for a Management Revolution*. New York: Harper & Row Publications, 1987.

Reichheld, F. F. and W. E. Sasser Jr. "Zero Defections: Quality Comes to Services." *Harvard Business Review* (September–October 1990).

Simmerman, Scott J. "Power-Up Your Organization for Maximum Retention." *International Customer Service Association Journal* (Spring 1991).

36

Customer Service and Service Quality

George L. Mueller and Don E. Bedwell, American Airlines

Every service company faces the challenge of training and motivating employees to deliver quality customer service. The willingness of a company to set service goals that match or exceed customers' expectations, and to treat employees as partners in accomplishing those goals, will determine its success or failure.

In delivering quality service, American Airlines faces a unique challenge. An American Airlines/American Eagle aircraft departs every 20 seconds—24 hours a day, 365 days a year. Our success is contingent upon doing things right the first time. Dissatisfied customers may not give us a second chance if we don't meet their expectations of good service.

This is not an easy task, but the challenge of delivering a quality product is a universal one that is real for *any* business that earns a profit by serving customers. It is especially important to companies involved in travel and tourism, an industry that—by some estimates—has become the largest. Around the globe, travelers spend an estimated $3 trillion annually.

This is an impressive number, but the question remains whether it is as good as it could be. When we consider the hundreds of millions of dollars being spent on travel advertising, we may even start asking ourselves: Why isn't tourism growing even faster? Why aren't planes full?

The Quality Imperative in Air Travel

One reason, we suspect, is that too many potential travelers feel that they don't receive real value for their dollars or have been turned off by past experiences—by rude employees, late flights, slow service, and the like. Careless service can erode any industry's future opportunities— just as excellent service can enhance them.

People don't automatically think of an airline as being in the service business. They figure airlines are simply transportation companies, interested only in hauling people and goods—by air—from point A to point B.

Unfortunately, some airlines came to think of themselves that way, and forgot that they were in the business of serving people. Today, a few of those airlines aren't in business any more.

To be successful, an airline *must* think of itself as being a service company that happens to fly airplanes.

Good service, consistently delivered, is a competitive advantage for any business. Conversely, the breakdown of good service can have damaging results. Comedian Mark Russell poked fun at the airline industry when he revealed his theory that the rings of Saturn are comprised of lost luggage.

Striving for Service Excellence

To be a leader in service is a formidable task. Our managers' perceptions don't always match our customers' expectations. Our budgets don't always allow the luxury our customers want at a price they are willing to pay.

Therefore, American measures service excellence in several different ways:

- Setting the industry standard for safety and security
- Providing world-class customer service
- Creating an open and participative work environment that encourages positive change, rewards innovation, and provides growth and opportunity to all employees
- Producing superior financial returns for investors

That's a different approach from the one taken by several of our competitors. Frankly, since deregulation, a lot of carriers became so obsessed with lowering fares that they forgot that the airline industry was built on service. Some air carriers grew so quickly through mergers and acquisitions that they found it easier to promote price rather than motivate their employees to provide service.

The result? Airline consumers wound up with a distinctly bitter taste in their mouths as they learned that some airfare "bargains" weren't bargains at any price. They began to complain. The media magnified their cries. Meanwhile, American Airlines welcomed the opportunity to show we could compete against any airline when it comes to delivering first-rate quality service.

To accomplish this, we needed to set appropriate objectives. Once those objectives were set, we needed a framework that would allow us to meet our objectives. Last, we needed to measure customer satisfaction with our service and product.

None of this is achieved by adopting catchy slogans. It takes the commitment of top management to be the best. It takes the conviction of an entire work force that delivering quality to customers is what really matters. It takes the dedication of every employee to succeed in delivering quality.

To achieve consistent quality, every individual in a service organization must believe that success depends on how well he or she serves the customer. Managers must be attuned to the needs of customers and to how attentive employees are to these needs. Often, delivering customer service means anticipating and averting problems before they inconvenience customers. At American, it also means the widespread use of technology to schedule aircraft maintenance, board customers smoothly, and ensure that our aircraft take off and arrive according to schedule.

Quality Makes the Difference

In a service business, the product is quality. Our competitors operate the same airplanes we do, charge the same prices, and have roughly the same costs. If we want to distinguish ourselves, we have to do it through the quality of our service.

Aristotle recognized the importance of consistency when he said, "Quality is not an act . . . it is a habit." Quality doesn't just happen. You can't buy it. And no amount of advertising can transform a turkey into an eagle. Let us emphasize that quality is different things at different times to different people—and we are not going to denigrate the importance of any of them. But we think it's important to avoid confusing "quality" with "luxury."

You can bet that not everyone is willing to pay for luxury, but every customer wants quality—whether flying first class or riding on a bargain-basement ticket back in the main cabin. Luxury is great—but all the champagne and caviar in the world won't compensate for rude employees, long lines, or late baggage.

In our view, quality means giving our customers exactly *what* we promise, *when* we say we will deliver it.

From the customers' point of view, quality happens—or doesn't happen—at the point where they meet our people face to face. At American, as in any service business, we have many people in frontline positions we rely on to represent us every day, virtually without supervision, and who spend more time with our passengers than any of us in management. So for all intents and purposes, they—not the folks in the ivory tower—determine how customers feel about our company.

Achieving Employee Participation

Quality service also stems from employee participation. To encourage that, we treat our employees the way we want them to treat our customers—with care and respect.

Our task in management is to make sure our frontline employees are trained and motivated to deal with customers in a professional, efficient manner that will make us proud and give our customers what they expect.

It makes sense to give our employees the best training, efficient facilities, and logical procedures that enable them to do their jobs and do not get in their way.

The rewards of this investment are satisfied, loyal customers. A true service company must abandon the concept of "processing" customers and develop a total service orientation. Managers who provide the tools that employees need to accomplish those goals will find that:

- The better employees feel about themselves
- The better they feel about their company
- The more they know about their business
- The more they believe they have a stake in the company's success
- Then the better the product they deliver will be

To give our customers better service, we revised many of our procedures to give employees greater freedom to service customers. We've given employees more opportunity to solve problems themselves on the spot rather than forcing them to go up a chain of command.

Our customers like this because we usually solve their problems quickly. But it has meant as much to our front-line employees. We have shown them that we trust them enough to give them the responsibility—and the authority—to take whatever action is necessary to solve a customer's problem. It's our way of saying, "Do what you think is right; we trust your judgment."

We have also solicited the help of employees in writing new policies or procedures. After all, they are on the front lines, accommodating the customers.

So many good ideas come from employees. In 1991, American Airlines realized more than $58 million in savings from employee ideas. Those 1991 savings paid for a new Boeing 757 aircraft, which employees name "Pride of American."

Quality Requires Leadership

Communication is the key to any company's success. Managers must be leaders. They must teach, coach, counsel, excite, and motivate. At the same time, they must inspire participation and dedication to excellence among their coworkers.

In our view, many traditional management concepts just aren't relevant in a modern service economy. Managing is often taken to mean *coping*, and that's just not good enough. We need leaders—men and women who can, and will, mobilize the enthusiasm of everyone involved. We need leaders who recognize that maintaining the division between superiors and subordinates isn't nearly as important as getting everyone working together as teammates.

Of course, it's tough to get everyone in sync with the concept of participative management. One big obstacle is persuading veteran managers to change the way they've dealt with people all their working lives. To help them make the adjustment, we are investing heavily in training to turn bosses into leaders. There's a big difference! Bosses merely give orders. Leaders maximize performance by teaching, coaching, counseling, exciting, and motivating their people to work, in cooperation, toward the goal of satisfying every customer, every time.

Producing quality doesn't mean throwing money at things. Quite the opposite: Quality is a great money saver. It's inadequate quality that costs. Every time a flight is late or a bag is mishandled, it costs—in terms of both money and lost customers! Every time one of our people makes a mistake that antagonizes a customer, it costs.

Quality is also a powerful revenue generator. Better service brings in more business. And better service helps us keep the business we already have. That may be even more important. Studies in various industries show that it costs five times more to sign up a new customer than to generate repeat business from one you already have. Other research shows that it takes roughly a dozen positive experiences to override a single negative one.

Quality offers a third reward: It's the most powerful motivator around. When people produce a quality product, they are proud of what they do, they are proud of themselves, and they are motivated to do even better tomorrow!

Quality and profitability should be common goals for management and labor. For in the global world of competition, quality, customer service, and value determine who wins. When a company's product is service, well-trained employees, supported by efficient procedures and motivated by a strong corporate commitment to participative management, will translate into service excellence.

37

The Art of Service Recovery: Fixing Broken Customers—And Keeping Them on Your Side

Ron Zemke, Performance Research Associates

In a perfect world of perfect products and perfect performances, the idea of service recovery would be nonsensical. But ours is not a perfect world, it is a world filled with Murphy's gremlins. And when things go wrong, the customer expects and demands redress. The true test of an organization's commitment to service quality isn't the stylishness of the pledge it makes in its marketing literature, it is the way the organization responds when things go wrong for the customer.

It makes perfect sense, then, to investigate the difference between organizations that routinely succeed in surmounting the challenge of day-to-day catastrophes and foul-ups and those in which people always seem caught flat-footed. Our research, and that of others, confirms that the difference lies in forethought or "planned service recovery": a thought-out, preplanned process for returning aggrieved customers to a state of satisfaction with the company or institution after a service or product has failed to live up to expectations or promised performance.

Bottom-Line Impact of Service Recovery

There is a growing body of data suggesting that companies performing high-quality service recovery for customers can realize substantial economic payoffs. According to John Goodman, president of Technical Assistance Research Programs, Inc. (TARP), a Washington, D.C., research and consulting organization specializing in customer service research, studies conducted across numerous industries over the last five years all find that the loyalty and repurchase intentions of customers whose problems were satisfactorily handled and resolved are "within a few percentage points" of the same indices for customers who had experienced no product or service failure.[1] See Figure 37-1.

Figure 37-1. Customer's repurchase intentions.

How Many of Your Unhappy Customers Will Buy From You Again?

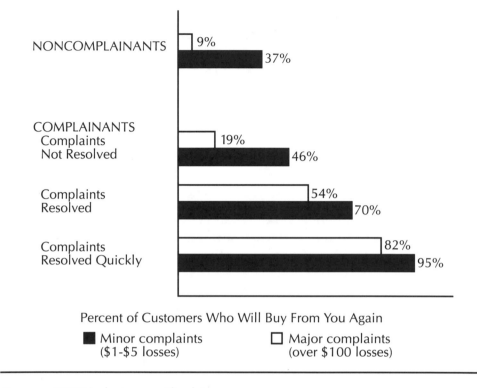

Percent of Customers Who Will Buy From You Again

■ Minor complaints   □ Major complaints
  ($1–$5 losses)   (over $100 losses)

Source: TARP industry specific data.

Even more intriguing are three more TARP studies—one of industrial customers of a Canadian chemical company, one of high-value customers of an American bank, and the other of professional photographers, customers of a European photographic supply company—which found that customers who complain and have their complaints satisfied are more likely to purchase additional products from these companies than are customers who experienced no problems with the organization or with its products. In the United States, a study for Polaroid found that customers who telephone to ask questions about, or report problems with, camera gear "can be sold additional photographic equipment—once the subject of the call has been handled to the customer's satisfaction."[2]

In other words, TARP's research strongly suggests that swift and effective service recovery enhances customers' perception of the quality of the products and services they have already purchased, as well as their perception of the competence of the organization. As a result, the perceived quality and value of other products and services offered by the organization is also enhanced.

Leonard L. Berry, JC Penney Chair of Retailing Studies, professor of marketing, and director, Center of Retailing Studies at Texas A&M University, and one of the United States' leading service quality researchers, is equally adamant about the importance of good service recovery: "The acid test of service quality is how you solve customer problems."[3] And though he is cautious about Goodman's assertion that good recovery can lead to better than average customer loyalty, he is very sure that the quality of recovery the customer experiences when things go wrong has a strong impact on overall customer satisfaction.

Berry explains that in a series of studies he and colleagues Valarie A. Zeithaml and A. Parasuraman conducted over the past ten years, they consistently found that "the best satisfaction scores come from customers who have experienced no problems, the second best from those who have had problems resolved satisfactorily, and the worst from customers whose problems go unsolved. Those differences are statistically and practically significant. The message from our research is pretty clear: Do it right the first time. If you don't, you'd better be darned sure you do it right the second time. If you fail, you've not met the customer's expectations twice—that's about all the room he'll give you."[4]

Using research models similar to those employed by TARP and by Len Berry and his colleagues, individual businesses are learning about the impact effective service recovery can have on their customers. Research at National Car Rental found that while a satisfied customer is 85 percent likely to rent from National again, disappointed customers who experience outstanding service recovery become 90 percent likely to choose National for their future car rental needs.[5]

One of the United States' largest hotel corporations has also studied the lost dollar value of unhappy and unrecovered hotel guests. Researchers took into account the average number of room nights per year per business travel customer (the largest segment of its business), the number of other travelers that guest will influence to stay at (or avoid) its properties, the marketing acquisition cost for that original traveler, and the marketing cost involved in replacing that traveler if he or she decides never to return. While the exact calculations are proprietary, this corporation believes that the net loss value of one business traveler guest is equivalent to 81 room nights, or $6,480.*

The impact of poor recovery goes beyond the disappointment and

---

*This research was initiated by an executive of the hotel corporation as part of a Service Management Operations course at a local university. The corporation now uses these data to justify making the bottom 5 percent of its franchisees (as determined by CSI) "available to the industry." They simply can't afford to keep properties that drive away customers.

loss of a single customer. The salesperson or customer service rep who dismisses an unhappy or complaining customer with a perfunctory, almost parental, "I can't help you, that's our policy," positions the company to lose dozens if not hundreds of current and potential customers. The problem, as Radisson found so clearly, is that the summarily dismissed customer doesn't simply go away. He or she goes away and doesn't come back. Worse yet, that customer takes every opportunity possible to tell anyone who will listen what rotten treatment he or she was made to endure at the hands of your company.

Data from TARP's research confirm that while as many as 96 percent of unhappy customers won't complain to the offending business, they *will* tell, on average, nine to ten friends, acquaintances, and colleagues how bad your service is.[6] One study conducted by Performance Research Associates found that 18 percent of customers were upset with the treatment they received at the hands of a Midwestern phone company. These upset customers reported they had each told twenty or more people of their plight.[7] And according to a study conducted by General Electric, there is a significant impact on sales as well. The GE study found that "the impact of word of mouth [recommendations from friends and acquaintances] on a customer's repurchase decision is twice as important as corporate advertising."[8]

What the Customer Expects

Given that service recovery can have such impact on the corporate bottomline, it is important to ask: "Just what do these unhappy customers want from us?" Most research into what customers require when their initial expectations have not been met or the company's promises to them have been broken suggests that they simply want what they were promised, some personal attention, and a decent apology. What they don't want is to be made to feel that *they* are the cause of the problem or that they are stupid for making a mistake—according to TARP, customers themselves cause on average 30 percent of the product or service problems they report to companies[9]—or to be treated as an imposition or nuisance.

We recently conducted a series of focus group sessions and telephone interviews to find out exactly what customers expect from an organization when things go amiss. While there are "by-industry" variations in the details of specific solutions, there are basic similarities of customers' recovery expectations. In all types of service transactions—from business-to-business, to traditional consumer services, to professional services—when something goes wrong with the service encounter, customers express the same core expectations of, and shared stories of similarly disappointing responses from, the organizations with which they do business. Figure 37-2 summarizes the service recovery expectations voiced by our group participants. Expectations are reported by the percentage of groups ($N = 81$ sessions) in which this expectation was shared.

An Approach for Meeting Service Recovery Expectations

During 1991 and 1992, Performance Research Associates Inc. staff members conducted 81 focus group and discussion sessions asking customers what they expected, and what they had experienced as positive, from companies when they experienced a "service breakdown." The average group size was 12 discussants, with individual groups ranging from 8 to 20 participants.

Figure 37-2. Core customer expectations for effective service recovery.

What was remembered and *found impressive by focus group members.*	*Percentage of groups who commented on or were impressed by this action.*
1. CSR dealt with customer upset, and was *not* patronizing.	79.0
2. CSR apologized.	69.1
3. CSR didn't become defensive, showed humility and poise.	62.9
4. CSR followed up after the complaint transaction.	56.8
5. CSR showed skill at problem solving.	53.0
6. CSR, when appropriate, was proactive in admitting organizational error, didn't try to shift blame.	44.4
7. CSR acted in a fully responsible/empowered fashion on the customer's behalf.	40.7
8. CSR showed good interpersonal skills, particularly listening.	40.7
9. CSR showed empathy for the customer's plight and/or upset.	38.3
10. CSR acted quickly to solve the problem, showed urgency.	35.8
11. CSR created added value for the customer.	32.1
12. CSR believed the customer, valued the customer's perception.	24.7

CSR = Customer Service Representative

Clearly, customers have defined expectations for what ought to happen when service goes wrong. Since those expectations are knowable, why do we still hear so many stories of poorly handled service breakdowns? What is needed to make planned service recovery an effective practice for more businesses?

Based on our research, we suggest that organizations need to establish a consistently applied process for the handling of disappointed customers. A six-step process can be employed to meet customer expectations.

STEP 1. APOLOGIZE FOR, OR ACKNOWLEDGE, THE FACT THAT THE CUSTOMER IS EXPERIENCING AN INCONVENIENCE

As can be seen in Figure 37-2, apologizing without becoming defensive or shifting the blame to the customer is a key expectation (points 2, 3, and 6). Although a simple apology costs nothing to deliver, we find it forthcoming in fewer than 48 percent of the cases in which a customer contacts a company to report a problem with a product or service.

Apology is most powerful when delivered first person. Group members confirmed that the corporate "We're sorry" form letter lacks the sincerity and authenticity of a personal, verbal acknowledgment delivered on behalf of the organization. A sincere, nonrobotic-sounding, "I'm sorry for any inconvenience this late arrival may have caused you" suggests that the pilot, cabin lead, or whoever is making the apology is taking a personal, professional interest in the situation.

STEP 2. LISTEN, EMPHATHIZE, AND ASK OPEN QUESTIONS

Focus group participants made a clear distinction between empathy—acknowledging and understanding the customer's emotional upset—and sympathy—sharing that upset, getting angry for the customer. Customers do not want service professionals to join them in a "those guys in shipping should be shot" tirade. Rather, customers are looking for a good listener who allows them to vent their frustrations (point 8), shows understanding of their upset (points 1 and 9), and, by listening, offers tacit evidence of believing the customer's report of the incident or error (point 12).

STEP 3. OFFER A FAIR FIX TO THE PROBLEM

After the emotional side of the service breakdown has been acknowledged, customers want what went wrong to be made right. It is important that customers perceive the individual service provider as skilled, empowered, and interested in a timely resolution (points 5, 7, and 10).

In return, customers typically bring a sense of fair play to the table when service breakdowns occur. If the service provider offers a rational explanation and demonstrates sensitivity and concern, the customer will respond with like respect.

Asking customers what the fair fix for a problem might be is quite revealing. Once, when asking telephone subscribers what they expected from the company when service failures occurred, we found that they made a clear distinction between a service failure that happened on a weekend and one that happened on a weekday. They told us, in effect, that it was OK for the phone company to be more sluggish in its response on a weekend because, after all, "Sunday is a weekend, and most of them like to be home with their families just like the rest of us."[10]

STEP 4. OFFER SOME VALUE-ADDED ATONEMENT FOR THE INCONVENIENCE OR INJURY

We refer to this step as symbolic atonement. While it was remembered and found impressive by 32.1 percent of our groups (point 11), it doesn't appear to be a requirement for recovery from *every* service or product breakdown. Rather, atonement is critical to satisfaction when the customer has been "injured" in the service delivery process—when the customer feels victimized, greatly inconvenienced, or somehow damaged by the problem.

At the most basic level, atonement is a gesture that clearly says, "We want to make it up to you." Atonement is the "it's on us," "free drink," "no charge," demonstration of goodwill. The word "symbolic" is carefully chosen. It suggests (and the examples offered by our group participants support) that little things, when sincerely done, mean a lot to the customer. Customers do *not* expect we will offer to shoot the branch manager or give the customer a trip to Disney World for keeping him or her waiting in the reception area an extra ten minutes.

There is an easy way to confirm this for your own customers. Create ten to twenty typical service breakdown scenarios, each ending with the question, "What do we need to do to make things right for this customer and win back his or her loyalty?" Then give the scenarios to ten customers and to ten customer service representatives. You will find that in the majority of cases, what customers ask for by way of atonement will cost less and be easier to deliver than what your service representatives will suggest.

There are times, however, when a custom-tailored or highly aggressive act of atonement may be necessary to keep the customer. And there are times when a determined, proactive effort can both impress the customer and give your organization that extra satisfaction "bump" TARP's Goodman talks about. When L.L. Bean management learned that a sport shirt it was selling had a tendency to fray at the collar after only a few washings, the Freeport, Maine, catalogue retailer took the initiative. Every customer who had purchased the shirt received a letter informing him or her of the problem and encouraging return of the shirt. The letter further instructed that should return of the shirt be inconvenient, the Bean customer service unit would be pleased to arrange a pickup for the customer.

STEP 5. KEEP YOUR PROMISES

Focus group participants were skeptical that what was promised by service representatives would actually be done. Customers would rather be given bad news than be lied to, or even slightly misled. For example, customers would rather be informed that their flight may be up to ninety minutes late than be told of a fifteen-minute delay—six different times. Group participants valued CSRs who displayed a "can do" attitude and ability (points 5, 7, and 10) and shared horror stories of promises made but broken.

STEP 6. FOLLOW UP

Participants were favorably impressed when either the individual with whom they worked or another person representing the company followed up with them after the initial service recovery episode to make sure that the implemented solution was still satisfactory (point 4).

This "after the fact" service assessment is particularly important in breakdown situations where customers perceive that they may be "at risk" if they voice their anger or upset. For example, research conducted by Philip A. Newbold and Diane Serbin Stover at Memorial Hospital in South Bend, Indiana, found that "because of fear of retaliation, some patients kept quiet (about service disappointments) until after discharge, particularly regarding nursing issues."[11]

This step also implies an internal follow-up. Service representatives should be able to communicate inside their organizations to ensure that the solutions they put in motion are actually executed (the package was shipped, the account credited) and to allow recurring problems to be tracked and removed from the delivery system. Without internal follow-up, service recovery is a one-shot, spray-and-pray approach, not part of a planned system of problem solving and problem elimination.

The Axioms of Service Recovery

What we know about good service recovery can be summed up in six axioms. First, customers have definable and understandable service recovery expectations. We've only to ask to learn what they are. Second, the most important expectations can be summarized by saying, "Customers expect you to care"—to care about them, about fixing their problems, and about rebuilding their trust. Third, service recovery is both a psychological and a physical endeavor. Empathy without action is as dissatisfying to customers as the reverse. Fourth, we know that in enacting effective service recovery, fixing the customer (the empathy part) must precede fixing the problem. Fifth, recovery works best in a spirit of partnership. Customers want to be part of their own solutions, to have their opinions about what should or must be done valued. Finally, service recovery must be a planned process. The stakes are too high—in terms of bottom-line impact and future customer loyalty—to leave it to chance.

It Starts Inside

World-class, knock-their-socks-off problem fixing doesn't happen by accident—not when it is (or is to be) a consistent, distinctive feature of an organization's image and reputation in the marketplace. Creating a strong service recovery effort requires careful training of those who will deal with aggrieved customers, a detailed analysis of the most common problems customers encounter and bring to the company for resolution, and an intimate understanding of the "solution space" from which acceptable solutions can be drawn.

Unfortunately, many organizations inadvertently create conditions that make enacting the seemingly simple steps to effective service recovery a Herculean task. Most companies have neither empowered and trained their employees to meet customers' service recovery expectations nor built reliable support systems so that these expectations can be met. And most companies certainly have not taken the time to think through the range of acceptable solutions that need to be offered to return the customer to a state of satisfaction.

Service recovery must be a broad, organization-wide, planned, mapped-out, focused-on, refined, and consistently worked-upon set of systems, operations, and actions. The great customer service representative at L.L. Bean, or GE, or Federal Express is certainly the point person, but the customer service person is only the most visible part of a much larger effort. Human performance expert Geary Rummler's classic admonition is as true for a service recovery system as it is for a loading dock: "Put the best trained, most highly motivated person in a bad system—and the system wins every time."

Recovery-Savvy Organizations

Performance Research Associates, in conjunction with Questar Data Systems, Eagan, Minnesota, has surveyed 40,000 managers, staff support, and customer contact employees in over 200 organizations looking for the elements of organizational culture that contribute to exceptional customer service. We also looked closely at conditions within an organization that lead to and support first-rate service recovery. We found that four subfactors from our surveys of organizational structure, policies and procedures, management behavior, and the like correlate highly with good service recovery, and cover 38.7 percent of the difference between good and bad recovery results. In order of their impact, the subfactors are:

1. Employees are trained in the fine points of handling customer problems, know the most common kinds of problems customers experience, and are skilled at enlisting the customer in generating an acceptable solution to the problem.
2. There are formal standards and informal norms that reinforce the message that solving customer problems quickly and with a minimum of inconvenience for the customer is a top priority, and that encourage employees to go "above and beyond" for the customer.
3. There are systems, policies, and procedures that are focused on making it easy for customers to report problems and complain, and for employees to respond positively to these problems and complaints.
4. Frontline employees are confident that problems will stay solved *and* that others in the organization will work as hard on the customers' problems as they do.

Creating the Culture

From Berry to Goodman, there seems to be significant consensus: solving customer problems well and providing exceptional service is more than just a strategy and a set of skills, it is a way of life. It is part of the culture of those organizations that do it well. We can see it, feel it, describe it, and measure its bottom-line impact. We can identify individuals who are likely to perform well in such a culture and those whose talents might be best utilized elsewhere. And we can begin to design and implement systems to support it.

Our experience suggests an eight-step process for making service recovery a functional attribute of a corporate culture.

1. Work at a Functional Unit Level Rather Than at the Corporate Level

This is not to imply that top-down commitment to service recovery is optional—it's not. Rather, we find that specific service recovery solution spaces (predetermined fixes for typical service breakdowns) vary from area to area. Therefore, it makes sense to work on implementation at the unit level.

2. Gather a Broad Sample of Customer Problems, Questions, and Complaints to Analyze, Categorize, and Create Solutions For

While many organizations already have some mechanism in place for tracking customer satisfaction, a detailed understanding of what upsets customers and how those upsets are resolved, and a philosophy and lore of the importance of recovery is needed before service recovery can become part of a service-centered culture. In this stage, representatives gather data on all possible breakdown transactions—what the customer wanted, what the customer actually got, and what was done to correct the problem.

This stage allows the organization to accomplish two things. First, the organization is able to learn how problems and potential problems are currently being handled. Our experience has been that organizations are surprised and often alarmed to learn how right-intended service representatives currently bend and break bad systems in order to meet customers' needs. Second, the organization has an opportunity to review and change existing systems where appropriate, and to create consistent and reasonable responses to breakdowns that cannot or will not be removed from the system (airline overbooking is an example of a "breakdown" that airlines choose to keep in their system).

3. Create Solution Spaces

Solution spaces in this context are descriptions of classes of service breakdowns, the goals and tactics service professionals should keep in mind when confronted with such breakdowns, and examples of effective responses to customers experiencing these types of breakdowns.

The solution space becomes a tool in training and evaluating employee problem-solving performance. It is used quite effectively by Hardee's Restaurants as part of their "Don't Fight, Make It Right" program. In the breakdown called "customer waits for food item," for example, service representatives know that their goals are to assure the customer that waiting is not normal or acceptable and to encourage the customer to visit again to experience better service. Tactics available include upgrading the customer's order (i.e., offering large fries in place of small fries) and coupons for future visits.

4. REVIEW THE SERVICE FOCUS OR STRATEGY OF THE ORGANIZATION TO ENSURE ALIGNMENT

Each solution space, as well as general training on the basic steps for managing the recovery interaction, must be consistent with the organization's overall strategy for service excellence. Ideally, this step is where organizations will address cultural barriers to empowered recovery action. For example, one department store we worked with wanted every employee to willingly accept returns without a sales receipt. Unfortunately, if the customer did not have the receipt, the dollar amount of the return was charged against the weekly sales of the employee who processed it. Once it was identified as a performance barrier, this policy was changed.

5. VERIFY WITH MANAGEMENT AND IMPORTANT THIRD PARTIES

Since service recovery is best created at the functional unit level, periodic review with upper management and with other units affected by the breakdown or recovery actions is important for organizational consistency.

6. TRAIN SERVICE PEOPLE ON SOLUTION SPACE MODELS, TECHNICAL SKILLS, AND TRANSACTIONAL SKILLS

A pleasant, well-intentioned employee with limited skills and authority cannot create effective service recovery. Likewise, customers report that *what* the employee actually does (full refund, replacement, or discount) is often less important than *how* the employee does it—the employee's skill at managing the transaction. Therefore, it is important that employees have specific technical tools and techniques, as well as strong interpersonal skills.

7. KEEP THE PROCESS BOTH INTERACTIVE AND ONGOING; FEED ERROR INFORMATION INTO THE SYSTEM

For each breakdown that is permanently removed from a service delivery system, a new one will appear. Additionally, customer expectations of how specific problems ought to be solved are continually changing and vary from customer to customer. A service recovery program that is established and then left static will soon fall behind and lose its effectiveness.

8. REPEAT IN OTHER UNITS AND COMMUNICATE RECURRING PROBLEMS

Practicing effective service recovery in one unit of an organization will raise the stakes as customers interact with other units. Customers reason, and rightly so, that if one area or service representative can serve them well, then all areas and individuals in the organization should be able to do the same.

Summary

Zero defects thinking may tempt some to view service recovery as a "way to excuse errors." It is not. Rather, recovery is a way to use errors— defects that cannot be prevented or even anticipated—to actually improve customer loyalty. Organizations that practice planned service recovery ensure that each breakdown will be handled in a creative way that will satisfy both customer and organizational needs. Such organizations realize that planned recovery encourages the identification of recurring problems so that changes and corrections can be made in service delivery systems.

Because only a customer can tell how annoying or victimizing a particular breakdown has been, only the customer can determine when appropriate recovery has occurred. Fortunately, customer expectations of effective service recovery are knowable. Wise service providers understand that falling short of a customer's recovery expectations is like injuring the customer twice. Therefore, they continually seek to understand their customers' recovery expectations and to find ways to ensure that both the process and the outcome of every service encounter build their customers' trust.

Notes

1. C. R. Bell and R. Zemke, "Service Breakdown: The Road to Recovery," *Management Review* (October 1987), p. 33.
2. Ibid.
3. Ibid.
4. Ibid.
5. Jean M. Otte, Corporate Vice President, Quality Management, National Car Rental System, Inc., presentation to Minnesota Chapter, Society of Consumer Affairs Professionals in Business, June 8, 1992.
6. *Consumer Complaint Handling in America: An Update Study, Part II*, conducted by Technical Assistance Research Programs Institute for the U.S. Office of Consumer Affairs, March 31, 1986, p. 50.
7. Unpublished study conducted by Performance Research Associates, Inc.

8. J. Goodman et al., "Setting Priorities for Satisfaction Improvement," *The Quality Review* (Winter 1987); reprinted in *Service Wisdom: Creating and Maintaining The Customer Service Edge*, R. Zemke and C. R. Bell, eds. (Minneapolis: Lakewood Books, 1989), p. 292.
9. Bell and Zemke, "Service Breakdown" p. 34.
10. Unpublished study conducted by Performance Research Associates, Inc.
11. P. A. Newbold and D. S. Stover, "Patient Satisfaction Pilot Reveals Gains and Limits," *Healthcare Forum Journal* (November/December 1991), p. 51.

References

Anderson, K., and R. Zemke. *Delivering Knock Your Socks Off Service*. New York: AMACOM Books, 1991.

Bell, C. R., and R. Zemke. *Managing Knock Your Socks Off Service*. New York: AMACOM Books, 1992.

———. "Service Breakdown: The Road to Recovery." *Management Review* (October 1987), pp. 32–35.

Berry, L. L., and A. Parasuraman. *Marketing Services: Competing Through Quality*. New York: The Free Press, 1991.

Berry, L. L., et al. *Service Quality: A Profit Strategy for Financial Institutions*. Homewood, Ill.: Dow Jones-Irwin, 1988.

Consumer Complaint Handling in America: An Update Study, Part II, conducted by Technical Assistance Research Programs Institute for the U.S. Office of Consumer Affairs, Mar. 31, 1986.

Goodman, J., et al. "Don't Fix the Product, Fix the Customer." *The Quality Review* 2, no. 3, pp. 6–11.

Hart, C. W. L., et al. "The Profitable Art of Service Recovery." *Harvard Business Review* (July–August 1990), pp. 148–156.

Increasing Customer Satisfaction Through Effective Corporate Complaint Handling, U.S. Office of Consumer Affairs and Technical Assistance Research Programs Institute, 1986.

Newbold, P. A. and D. S. Stover. "Patient Satisfaction Pilot Reveals Gains and Limits." *Healthcare Forum Journal* (November/December 1991), pp. 48–51.

Zemke, R., and C. R. Bell. *Service Wisdom: Creating and Maintaining the Customer Service Edge*. Minneapolis: Lakewood Books, 1989.

———. "Service Recovery: Doing It Right the Second Time." *Training* (June 1990), pp. 42–48.

Zemke, R., and D. Schaaf. *The Service Edge: 101 Companies That Profit from Customer Care*. New York: New American Library, 1989.

38

Using Service Guarantees

Christopher W. L. Hart, The TQM Group, Ltd.

The Bible describes the word of God as "quick and powerful, and sharper than any two-edged sword, piercing even to the dividing asunder of soul and spirit . . . and a discerner of the thoughts and intents of the heart."

That applies to the word of business gods too.

When a company commits to perfect service—when the head of a business sends down word that the firm is making an iron-clad bond to serve customers or pay a price—it sends a message. Customers hear that and, in an instant, understand "the thoughts and intents" of an entire company.

It may sound like hyperbole, but that's what service guarantees deliver. And service guarantees are based on stunningly simple principles dating back ages:

Find out what customers want and promise to deliver it. If you can't, find a way to make the customers happy so that they will come back. And be sure, the next time, to deliver quality service as promised.

That's how service companies are made.

And service guarantees can, indeed, make a company.

Otherwise, you wouldn't recognize phrases like "absolutely, positively overnight," or "30 minutes or less" and immediately identify them with companies where strong leadership built the business around a service guarantee.

It's not a slogan, or even the implementation of a perfect-service promise, that delivers results for a business; instead, a company must develop a method to efficiently deliver service the customer wants and can't be sure to get anywhere else.

Customers order from Domino's Pizza because they know their order will arrive within a half hour; they use Federal Express because they are assured of next-day delivery. Despite all of the imitators, these companies—and many others like them, both large and small—have been able to achieve breakthrough levels of service through the successful use of a service guarantee.

How Not to Lose Business

You've taken your date to a fancy restaurant. The food is supposed to be great, the service impeccable, the wine list outstanding, and the strolling violinists of concert quality.

But when dinner arrives cold, the waiter gets surly about taking it back to the kitchen; the wine you order has been improperly stored and is best suited for salad dressing; the violinists play the favorite song of your date's recently deceased mother.

Any one of those reasons is enough to make you cross the restaurant off your list.

And that's exactly what you would do, until the maitre d' hands you a note saying that there's no charge for the wine or dessert and that management would like you to come back . . . as their guest.

If you're like most people, you'll go back—although you might take a different date. And if the service, wine, food, and music all surpass your original expectations and you have a wonderful evening, the restaurant has saved itself a customer.

It works in the real world, not just hypothetically.

Hampton Inns, for example, developed a 100 percent customer satisfaction guarantee, one you might have heard about in television ads.

No matter what is wrong with their service—if the room is uncomfortable because there is too much noise from the nearby highway, for example—the customer who complains gets the room for free.

The company's initial benchmark study proved that the guarantee strongly influenced customers' intent to return. Of the people who had invoked the guarantee, 74 percent said they were more likely to return to Hampton Inns as a result of being compensated for the hotel's service being below their expectations. (See Figures 38-1 and 38-2.)

Nearly 40 percent of the people using the guarantee during the study period—the fourth quarter of 1989 and the first quarter of 1990— had stayed at Hampton Inns since the incident that initiated their claim on the guarantee; 70 percent of those returning guests said the guarantee influenced their decision to come back.

And one-third of the people who invoked the guarantee said they most likely would not have stayed again had the company not made good on its service promise. (See Figure 38-3.)

Customers want the service they expect, not the payout on a guarantee. But when service does not meet expectations, a guarantee keeps the company from losing business.

It's a truism in business that it's more difficult to retain customers than it is to get new ones; a guarantee does both.

Figure 38-1. Guarantee impact on return intent.

Over seven in ten (74%) guests are "more likely" to return . . . 32 percentage points higher than those who had <u>not</u> actioned our guarantee. Clearly, once a guest has "seen the guarantee process in action," it becomes more important.

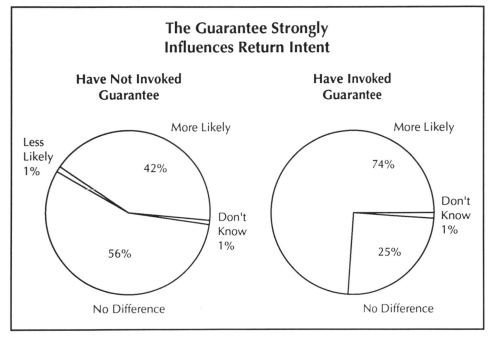

Source: Hampton Inns.

Training Employees and Customers

It's easy to provide training. But even if a worker has been taught to answer the phone properly, to prepare and serve a meal in a few minutes, or to fix a car correctly, there is no certainty that the customer will be satisfied.

In an age where quality is defined as "meeting customer expectations," exceptional service is best accomplished by training the customer.

While this thought evokes a little chuckle—customers going through a conditioning regimen just to be happy with your service—training customers on what to expect and living up to promised standards affects all aspects of a company's performance.

A well-written service guarantee (a simple vow to deliver error-free service or provide adequate compensation for falling short) focuses a customer's expectations. He or she wants a clean, comfortable hotel room with no hassles, wants to be waited on in five minutes, or wants to have a product delivered, come hell or high water.

A service guarantee not only sets this type of criteria for customers,

Figure 38-2.   Why return intent is higher among those who have activated a guarantee.

**Reasons Why Return
Intent Is Higher**

- Higher—and Unique—Customer Service
  Orientation. They Perceive That
  Hampton Inn . . .
    –Wants Satisfied Customers
    –Stands Behind What They Sell
    –Cares About Customers
    –Tries Harder Than Competitors
    –Is the Only Hotel That Offers This
      Type of Guarantee

- Higher Perceived Price/Value at
  Hampton Inn Compared to Similarly Priced
  Hotel Chains

Source: Hampton Inns.

it creates a standard to which workers can be trained, thereby ensuring delivery of the promised, premium-quality service.

Training customer and employee expectations allows a company to pinpoint its failure rate; unlike manufacturers, who can calculate failure based on warranty claims, service providers have never had an easy time measuring the quality of their service delivery systems.

Knowing how many failures occur, and where the company falls short, becomes a catalyst for improvement. This is particularly important because services are usually consumed as they are provided; since you can't preinspect an employee's attitude or send a bad haircut back for repair, the implementation of standards that both customers and employees understand is key to providing quality service.

For example, the president of JWS Technologies Inc., a Piscataway, New Jersey industrial gas distribution company, decided in 1988 that he wanted to implement a guarantee; if his company missed a promised delivery time, the customer's entire order would be free, regardless of the dollar amount involved.

It sounded simple enough, with easy criteria to meet. In September 1988, according to company records, JWS Technologies would have given

Figure 38-3. Effect of guarantee on retention of guests.

One-third were "unlikely" to stay again had it not been for our guarantee and the way it was handled.

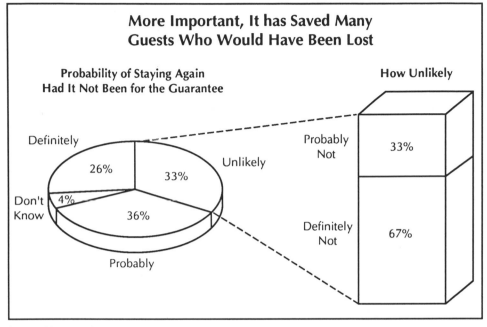

Source: Hampton Inns.

away 311 cylinders of gas had the guarantee been in place. At the time, the company was delivering about 7,500 cylinders per month.

So JWS officials talked to employees, even adding incentive bonuses to the guarantee program; every worker would get a bonus for each day the entire company made all of its deliveries.

JWS had developed a standard none of its competitors offered and had shown workers the depth of its commitment.

But there were problems.

Customers wanted to invoke the guarantee when JWS delivered a cylinder with a leaking valve, even if it was the fault of JWS's supplier. Other troubles—not caused by JWS's delivery system—also challenged the guarantee.

JWS officials paid off on all claims, regardless of who was at fault; a faulty valve, for example, made delivery worthless, on time or otherwise. (See Figure 38-4.) To meet the increased expectations of customers and this even more stringent standard, JWS officials instituted measures to ensure that valves were checked when cylinders were received from suppliers. It was one of several operational changes made to accommodate the guarantee and make the company more efficient.

In September of 1989, JWS gave away just 17 cylinders, and that was

Figure 38-4.   Sample guarantee.

Source: JWS Technologies and Blue Valley Welding Supply.

on the stiffer criteria developed after the guarantee was in place. JWS customers have come to expect on-time delivery, and with good reason—the company now delivers more than 99.75 percent of its orders on time, up from about a 95 percent success rate before the guarantee.

Frequently, a guarantee becomes a self-fulfilling prophecy. Promising perfect service forces a company to do it, setting a high performance standard that not only attracts customers but that employees are proud to achieve, thereby improving morale and developing an esprit de corps.

The Elements of a Guarantee

Developing a guarantee is a bit like baking a pie: It doesn't work if some of the ingredients are missing, and it leaves a bad taste in your mouth if the ingredients are of poor quality.

There are two basic ways to make a guarantee, and while both include many of the same elements, the difference is akin to using a store-bought pie shell versus making the crust from scratch.

Companies that build from scratch have implicit guarantees, where perfect service is not a written promise, but a fact of life—an integral part of the company's operating procedures that exists without question and above reproach.

Most people might recognize this kind of service from a place like Nordstrom's Department Stores, which have long had a reputation for doing anything possible to please a customer. For Nordstrom's, having a public proclamation that customers get, say, free shoelaces when service is slow would demean the service quality currently offered.

Implicit service guarantees are woven into the fabric of a company. Avian Flyaway, for example, is a four-person Dallas-area company that "relocates" birds, installing a wire system that discourages pigeons from nesting and roosting. To combat the fact that he is sometimes greeted as if he's the Pied Piper, company president Richard M. Selzer won't invoice a customer until weeks after a job is completed, when he is sure that the birds are gone and the customer, sometimes stunned that Avian Flyaway's methods have worked, is satisfied.

"It's not in our literature, but it's clear by what we do when it comes to billing," Selzer explains, "that if you're not satisfied with my work, don't pay me."

But most companies are in business (filling the pie shell instead of starting from scratch) when management decides to take the plunge into promising perfect service.

In such cases, explicit guarantees are built on a company's existing operational framework; over time, the explicit guarantees eventually become ingrained behaviors, with the customers and workers so aware of the service promise—"absolutely, positively overnight," for example—that it allows a company to develop the kind of reputation normally reserved for those few firms with implicit guarantees.

Of course, not every company is ready to offer perfect service. The best way for an executive or entrepreneur to determine a company's ability to deliver is to write a simple guarantee, something like "If you're not satisfied with our service for any reason, pay us nothing." If that creates the specter of huge losses, the company may need to step up its service efforts before putting a guarantee in place.

But for a company's word to become a value-added part of the business, it must develop a service guarantee that is:

- Unconditional
- Easy to understand and communicate
- Meaningful
- Easy to invoke
- Quick and easy to collect

Unconditional

Restrictions are preapproved excuses. Once you've promised it, your customers expect perfect service; when you don't deliver, they should get the proper reward, not alibis.

Hampton Inns, for example, promises "high-quality accommodations, friendly and efficient service, and clean, comfortable surroundings" and tells customers that if they are not satisfied, "we don't expect you to pay."

That leaves plenty of room for alibis, such as boisterous neighbors who keep you up all night.

But for the exhausted, sleep-deprived traveler, a deskperson's "I'm sorry, we can't control our guests" is a lame excuse.

Weeks after instituting a comprehensive set of service promises, including error-free bank statements or $5, First Interstate of California mailed about 40,000 monthly statements that contained an error. The bank could have tried to make excuses to nullify the guarantee on a computer error like this one; instead, it took the opportunity to show customers the kind of service it intended to provide.

First Interstate notified customers affected by the problem, and reminded them about the guarantee; while liability amounted to $200,000, bank officials say the actual payout was small.

If a guarantee must be restricted, it should be for elements beyond the control of the company; for example, a florist can guarantee on-time delivery, except in blizzards.

Beyond that, conditions only make the customer think you're trying to weasel out of your promise.

Easy to Understand and Communicate

Well-written guarantees are specific and clear, so that everyone from the worker to the customer knows exactly what's involved.

"Delivery by 10:30 a.m." or "no more than five minutes waiting in line" leaves no room for misunderstanding. A promise of "prompt service" is open to interpretation.

Meaningful

Assuming the buyer values the service, give something significant when you don't deliver.

Using a guarantee to improve service delivery means taking a risk; companies that use a guarantee as a schlocky advertising gimmick and that offer "status quo or your money back" do not realize service quality improvements.

There was, for example, an airline that guaranteed that first-class travelers would receive "first-class service, or your money back." Had the company really wanted to take a risk, it might have also guaranteed coach service for coach passengers; that would have had as much meaning as the program it created.

That kind of guarantee tells customers a lot about the "thoughts and intents of the heart" of company executives.

Almost without exception, customers want the promised service, not the payout. Offering, say, a free coffee mug is insulting when your mistake costs a customer time, money, and aggravation, although it might be appropriate for a guarantee that service representatives will greet all customers with a smile.

Maryland National Bank's "Performance Guarantee," for example, stipulates that if the bank makes a mistake on an account, it will give the customer $10, absorb any overdraft charges, and write a letter of apology to the customer and to any third party affected by the mistake.

Ideally—for both the bank and the customer—none of this is necessary. But when mistakes are made, the guarantee is meaningful because it clears the customer's name, handles all charges, and kicks out $10 to cover the "hassle factor."

The payout for a guarantee is a function of how much "pain" a company is willing to absorb in the event of a service failure. Ideally, all of a customer's "costs"—time, money, and aggravation—are tallied up and given back to the customer in an appropriate form.

Easy to Invoke

The customer is already aggravated that your promise was not kept; barriers to making a claim exacerbate that frustration.

If your employees are trained to deliver the service, they should also know what to do when they fall short, namely, help the customer get his or her reward.

At JWS Technologies, for example, customers don't have to ask to claim the guarantee; as soon as JWS officials know they have a problem, they notify the customer that the order is free.

Bank of America, by comparison, once offered a guarantee on checking account service that could be invoked only if the customer closed his or her account. Not only does this require effort on the customer's part (someone has to be pretty disgusted with service to close an account), it also meant that the bank lost every customer served by the guarantee.

Similarly, Pan American World Airways once had a guarantee program for certain first-class, cross-country travelers that had to be claimed in writing, attached to paperwork from the trip and with suggestions for improvement; even then, the company only promised to pay out after several weeks, during which time the customer, probably still upset at shoddy service, was resolving to use other airlines.

For the guarantee process to work, the program *must* pay out; if the object is to train employees to meet customer expectations, then the workers must be able to deliver the service or the payout.

Forcing customers to go through a maze of people and paperwork wipes out the goodwill that service promises normally deliver.

Quick and Easy to Collect

If possible, payout should be immediate; the customers will remember being treated well, not the service mistake, and that's what brings them back.

Making It Work

When word of a guarantee comes down from on high, it will have a tremendous impact on a company, but it won't make the firm more efficient.

Creating a service guarantee requires a leap of faith; company officials need to believe that the program they are setting up will not become a financial drain.

Most companies that offer a financial reward when service falls short do not seem to be too hard hit by payouts and have reaped significant benefits in worker efficiency, morale, customer retention, and marketing.

Minnesota-based Marquette Banks, for example, budgeted about $20,000 for the first year of its guarantee, a promise of $5 for any type of mistake on checking and savings accounts and certificates of deposit. According to a company spokeswoman, the bank had paid out about $5,000—25 percent of what it had expected to spend—by the time the first year ended in early 1989; the payout for the program's second year was even less.

Developing a properly designed guarantee challenges workers to eliminate problems that currently keep the company from delivering quality service and dares the competition to do the same thing. It separates advertising hype from real performance.

When Wells Fargo Bank wanted to institute a guarantee that customers would wait no more than five minutes on line before seeing a teller or the bank would pay them $5, bank officials studied operations at every branch. By analyzing the traffic flow, the company was better able to determine when they should staff up to handle peak loads. The staffing changes needed to serve customers more efficiently were made *before* the guarantee was put in place.

The bank even told several large companies with factories near branches that they might consider switching payday to a different day of the week than other big employers; not only would this allow the bank to serve customers better, but living up to the five-minutes-or-less deal ensured that the company would get its workers back in the plant on time. Several companies made the switch.

Whether it is a better delivery route, different staffing, or improved supply intake procedures like those of JWS Technologies, a service guarantee will be an impetus for improvement. These added efficiencies, which can arise out of incidents in which the guarantee is invoked, allow a company to take the financial risk of a guarantee with an assurance that the program will pay off.

Service Guaranteed—For Life

For companies that want a service guarantee to deliver quality improvements, a better reputation, and a competitive edge, promises are forever.

Short-term guarantee programs are good at getting people through the door, but they also leave a bad smell with those new clients: Think of Bank of America customers, for example, enticed by the promise of error-free checking service, only to find out that the program was first difficult to use and later cancelled.

Guarantees may change—Domino's originally offered free pizzas, rather than $3 off, if delivery required more than 30 minutes—but the best ones become a permanent part of operations; the payout is a budget item, on the income statement forever.

Once a company has built a reputation and a service-delivery system around providing error-free service, reneging on the promise could have damaging after-effects. The guarantee can be built into corporate culture over time, becoming more implicit than explicit, and may not stay in the advertising focus of the company, but the gains created by delivering quality service will remain. Federal Express, for example, advertises a lot of aspects of its service beyond the guarantee; still, imagine the hue and cry from customers if the company suddenly changed that crucial element of its service.

Guarantees provide a straightforward way for a company to deliver quality service to customers and a message to the world.

Once a company sends that message that lets the world discern the thoughts and intents its managers have at heart, there is no turning back. For companies that use a service guarantee, there is no reason to want to.

39

Recognition, Gratitude, and Celebration

Patrick L. Townsend and Joan E. Gebhardt, Townsend & Gebhardt

Recognition. Gratitude. Celebration. These three building blocks of morale and commitment bridge the gap between the rational and the emotional aspects of quality. Precisely because they evoke emotion, however, all have been viewed by "hard-headed" business people as secondary quality issues. They are not. Recognition of employees as individuals, gratitude for a job well done, and celebration of a common goal are the foundation of a quality process. They bind a company together into the kind of effective team that makes quality a way of life.

Recognition and Leadership

Recognition of employees is directly linked to effective leadership practices. One definition of the difference between a leader and a manager puts it succinctly: A manager cares that the job gets done; a leader cares not only that the job gets done, but *also about the people doing the job*. It truly is that simple: A leader cares about people. He or she sees employees as individuals, values their contributions, and meets their basic needs for self-esteem and growth. The result is a strong emotional bond based on mutual trust.

Employees know the difference between a manager and a leader. So does the United States Marine Corps. Its quality efforts are identified as "Total Quality Leadership," acknowledging that the term "Total Quality Management" falls considerably short. Since the military has made a study of leadership theory over the last 2,500 years, routinely teaching leadership basics to eighteen-year-olds, this emphasis on leadership is not surprising.

Military leadership theory identifies three leadership styles: authoritarian, participative, and delegative. Authoritarian leadership is tolerated only when three conditions apply: the leader is making a decision in a situation where time is of the essence, the leader has all the necessary information, and *the subordinates have high morale*. It may unnerve some business executives to find their own beliefs echoed by the armed forces, but the universal truth—civilian and military—is that morale can remain high only when the predominant leadership styles of an organization are participative and delegative.

It is easy to see why participative and delegative styles are most effective. People are not at their best when they are compelled to do a task without bringing their own talents to bear. Participative and delegative leaders take into account the worth, knowledge, and dignity of the individual workers. Whether implicitly or explicitly, such leaders invite everyone to contribute to the full extent of their capabilities. It is also easy to see why the delegative style brings greater rewards than the participative style in terms of morale. The degree of trust exhibited by a delegative leader is enormous.

On those rare occasions when authoritarian leadership is appropriate, common courtesy (a shorthand for recognizing the worth of individuals) can work wonders. It was no fluke that your mother identified "please" as the magic word. Nor is it a fluke that concomitant with the word please, "thank you" plays a powerful role in relationships.

Gratitude

There are presidents of companies who (even today) will look you in the eye and say with a straight face, "Saying thank you is not my job." Their view of the workplace is a rational one, based solely on work and wages as a quid pro quo contract. These executives are perfectly comfortable with the most common excuse for a paucity of recognition and gratitude in their organizations: doing a good job is what "they" are paid for.

Even rationally, that statement is suspect. What they (be they management or nonmanagement personnel) are paid to do is what they did in the last pay period before they received their last pay. The company proved that beyond all argument by handing them a check that validated those efforts. If employees or managers (at any level) make improvements in their performance, they deserve to be thanked. The "rational" reason for doing so is that saying thank you helps to redefine this new, higher level of performance as the norm. The "irrational" reason is that thanking someone is the right, the moral thing to do. The person took a chance, he or she put his or her ego on the line, and the company benefited as a result. Then, too, the act resonates emotionally. It feels good to say thank you, and it feels good to be the recipient of gratitude.

There is another reason for a concerted effort to thank employees. If employees hear the organization say thank you, the odds are that they will continue their efforts. When continuous improvement is the goal, this may be the most compelling reason of all.

To illustrate the point, picture this scene: A twelve-year-old is seated at a kitchen table on December 26. There is a stack of stationery on the table, and the child's mother is standing in the kitchen, list in hand. Today's chore before the youngster can go out and play is to write thank you notes. The mother, of course, has already explained, perhaps several times, various reasons why the youth is writing to thank Aunt Hazel for the gawdawful paisley pajamas. Not only is Aunt Hazel a wonderful, sweet lady who went to all the effort to buy those pajamas, but she also sends a present every year—or has to date. "Do you want anything next year?" This mixture of the rational and the emotional is generally potent enough to produce at least a short note.

Even when executives pay lip service to employees deserving the company's gratitude, many still fight a rear-guard action to keep the transaction strictly rational. Incentive programs fall into this category. Here, again, the employee is offered a quid pro quo, usually in the form of a percentage of savings, a promotion, or a bonus. What is wrong with these schemes is that they breed competition and cynicism. Employees vie for credit and expect to be paid what they perceive as a fair market value for every action on their part. Since the regular promotion system and salaries are already designed to meet those needs, the extra effort, the identification with the good of the organization, and the joy of a job well done—the intangibles—get short shrift.

In organizations where employees' current efforts are routinely ignored, soliciting ideas for improvement may initially be met with indifference, if not outright hostility. When morale is low, it takes time to establish the kind of give and take that makes an organization's program of recognition, gratitude, and celebration credible. When morale is high, the success of a program of saying thank you still depends on keeping two things firmly in mind: (1) a thank you must be extended to all deserving people, and (2) different people hear thank you in different ways.

This may mean giving up cherished preconceptions. Some organizations, for example, prefer to recognize teams, while others are more comfortable recognizing individuals. Neither is right or wrong, but a mixture is likely to be more effective. Some people feel safer being recognized in groups; others crave individual acclaim. Both needs must be met. Equally unproductive are attempts to appear scrupulously fair by giving every deserving individual the same thing—perhaps an engraved plaque presented to every worthy employee in a small, informal ceremony. Employee A may spend the entire evening polishing the plaque preparatory to hanging it above the fireplace, while Employee B puts the plaque directly into the fireplace (although if morale in the organization is high, Employee B may settle for putting the plaque in the back of a closet with a rueful shake of the head).

Individuals, particularly in a country like the United States where cultural diversity is the norm, respond in different ways to different forms of recognition and gratitude. It bears repeating: Different people hear thank you in different ways. It is the responsibility of the organization to find a way to thank everyone; it is not the responsibility of the individuals to be pleased with half-measures. The key words are flexibility and common sense.

A Button-Down Model

Both the Paul Revere Insurance Group, Worcester, Massachusetts, and Froedtert Memorial Lutheran Hospital, Milwaukee, Wisconsin, have designed recognition programs that employ every tool at their disposal: team and individual recognition; tangible and intangible awards; long-term and short-term approaches. The Paul Revere Quality Has Value (QHV) process is now in its eighth year; the Froedtert Quality Underscores Every Single Task (QUEST) is completing its first.

Although QHV has modified its team recognition program several times to keep it fresh, it began with an approach quite similar to that of QUEST. During the first and second years of QHV, the standards for receiving team recognition (every employee in both organizations was, and is, on a quality team) reflected the knowledge that some teams could effect savings in money and others were more likely to effect savings in time. The various levels of recognition included Bronze, Silver, and Gold: 10 implemented ideas or $10,000 saved (on an annualized basis) = Bronze; 25 implemented ideas or $25,000 saved = Silver; and 50 implemented ideas or $50,000 dollars = Gold. After a team achieved Gold, the progression continued in units of fifty (e.g., fifty more implemented ideas or $50,000 more in savings made a team Double Gold, etc.).

Thank you was expressed in a number of different ways. When a quality team made it to any level of recognition, the team leader was contacted by the director of the quality process, and a time was agreed upon that was mutually convenient for the team and one of the top three executives of the company. At the agreed-upon time, the company president or one of the two co-chairmen of the QHV Steering Committee arrived at the team's work area.

The members of top management (a precious few by definition) must be involved in the effort to extend recognition and gratitude to deserving employees at all levels. Peer recognition, the fallback position taken by an increasing number of lazy management teams, is certainly nice, but it is the personal touch by the president or a very senior vice president that makes an occasion truly memorable. During the first two years of QHV, the president and two senior vice presidents took part in 725 team recognition ceremonies.

The first thing that happened was that the executive would ask the team members what they had done to earn the recognition. In short, the team members were given a chance to brag about themselves and their accomplishments. Two things occurred as a result. The top executives put into practice one of the basic tenets of good leadership: know your people. This continuing education of the top executives as to who did what inside their company yielded long-term benefits for both the individuals and the company as a whole. At the same time, some of the team members felt thanked right then; for them, sufficient recognition had already been extended. For the majority of team members, the conversation was pleasant enough, but it was just the beginning.

The executive then gave each member of the team $10 Paul Revere gift certificates, redeemable in over fifty stores and restaurants in the community. Bronze team members earned one certificate each; silver, two; and gold, four. Certificates were given instead of cash for a very good reason: small amounts of cash are anonymous. A ten-dollar bill may be enjoyed for about 15 seconds, but it is subsequently put into a pocket or purse, used for gas or groceries, and never thought of again. Certificates have a longer life. They are shown to family and friends. When someone asks, "Gosh, why did you get those?" the answer is obvious: "Because I am a valuable person, I work with a good bunch of people, and we work for a great company." It is to the company's benefit to have the employee say and feel (even approximately) such sentiments.

For some employees, this tangible award meant "thank you." The feeling in those cases was, "If you give me money, I understand that you are grateful." Others greeted the certificates with a quiet and nonchalant, "Well, of course you should give me money—I'm underpaid. Now, how are you going to say thank you?" So the ceremony continued.

Next, each person received either a lapel pin or a charm with the Paul Revere Quality logo on it. The pins and charms were symbolic, as are desk items or the like that are used by other organizations. While not worth a great deal on the open market, they do serve as a statement to everyone who sees them (including the recipient) that the company is aware of the contribution that has been made, and is grateful for it.

In the first year of the QHV, only lapel pins were distributed. Few women wore their pins. Questioning by the men whose responsibility it was to define the recognition program uncovered the fact that women's clothing is far more delicate than men's. For a woman to wear a lapel pin on a blouse was to risk ruining the blouse. The second year, charms were offered.

For some people, this symbolic recognition was the important thing. Long after the gift certificate was spent, long after the executive had left the area, the pin or charm or desk plaque was a reminder of a significant moment. For others, the symbolic gesture had little or no value, and the item in question quickly took up residence deep inside a desk drawer.

An additional thank you was extended every time a team reached a new level of recognition at Paul Revere. The team's name and the names of the members made it into print, either in the *Quality News* (the monthly bulletin devoted entirely to the QHV process) or in the *Landmark* (the regular company publication). Some employees were most excited about this aspect of recognition, since they could then highlight their name and send the publication home to their mother with a note, "See, Mom, the rumors you heard aren't true! Check out my name!"

When an employee hears "thank you" is irrelevant. While some employees might take part in the initial brag session, spend the money, wear the pin, and skim the article about their team, what really got the company's gratitude across was having the president of the company shake their hand, look them in the eye, and say those two words, "Thank you."

The managers of a quality process cannot predict with any certainty which method of recognition and gratitude will be meaningful to a particular individual. Often, even the individual cannot pinpoint it. The only choice, then, is to say thank you to each deserving person in three or four ways. Let each person hear the one he or she wants to; it is important only that each of them hears it.

In addition to the core system of recognition, gratitude, and celebration (the ten-minute meetings being mini-celebrations) described above, both Paul Revere and Froedtert looked for a way to implement spontaneous, timely recognition for specific deeds by individuals. Enter the quality coin. At both Paul Revere and Froedtert, top executives always carry quality coins (even spontaneity takes a degree of planning).

Froedtert's coins are copper-colored, slightly bigger than the old silver dollars, and engraved on one side with the legend, "In RECOGNITION of exhibiting excellence in your job." Employees receive them when an executive learns of (or discovers on his or her own) any act that merits a thank you. The coins can be traded in for $10 in cash. After the first several hundred coins had been awarded during the first year of the process, Froedtert was delighted to note that barely half of the coins had been "cashed in." For the majority of employees, the memory of being thanked was too precious to surrender—at least until the occasion was repeated. Second and third coins tended to be cashed more regularly.

An informal measure of the involvement of the executives in saying thank you (and of the health of the entire quality process) is the number of quality coins distributed in a month. Executives who are actively looking for things to praise have a positive impact on morale.

Teams and individuals, tangible and intangible awards, long-term and short-term approaches create opportunities to mix and match to suit any occasion. Froedtert recognizes team leaders during National Quality Month in October by offering $20 gift certificates. Team leaders choose one of five types: sport, restaurant, movies, cultural event, shopping mall. Paul Revere generated enthusiasm with a month-long campaign that was downright frivolous. Any written thank you from a customer—For One Month Only!—could be traded in for a cactus. Why a cactus? First, it lent itself to a sticker on the green plastic pot with the terrible pun, "I'm stuck on Quality." Second, in February in Massachusetts, cactus plants are delightfully incongruous. Third, it is extremely difficult to kill a cactus plant. Some survived in the office for years.

The cactus campaign was not without its hazards. A quality purist approached the director of the quality process with the news that two individuals had arranged to write thank you notes to each other so that they could each get a cactus. (It was true that by the second week, having a cactus plant on your desk was seen as a status symbol of sorts—after all, the occupant of the desk had done something so well that someone else had taken time to write down their appreciation.) The director was delighted. "Look," he said, "first Fred had to sit down at his PC and actually write a note to Mary. He had to actually think of something that Mary and/or her people had done for him and/or his folks. In doing so, he was reminded how valuable Mary and her people are to his operation—and Mary found out that she was appreciated. Then the same thing happened in reverse when Mary wrote to Fred. What we end up with are two employees who understand and appreciate each other's contributions more, and all it cost the company was two $1.75 cactus plants. Looks like a good deal to me." The key words are still flexibility and common sense.

Celebration

Celebration is a vital part of a quality process. Once a year, Paul Revere gathers all of its employees at Mechanics Hall for the Quality Celebration, a chance to review the year and congratulate all the employees for a job well done. It works because the Quality Celebration is the culmination of a year of recognition of employees, of thousands of expressions of gratitude and hundreds of mini-celebrations. In 1991, there were ten awards in two categories (individual customer service and team leader excellence) and five team awards for service excellence, and each division highlighted its honor team; in a larger sense, everyone walked away a winner.

In too many organizations, the entire recognition effort is centered on one annual event at which the best person or team is called out for special awards and emphasis—without any other activities throughout the year. The result is one winner and a many-way tie for last. The focus of such a gathering can easily change from celebration to resentment—no matter how much better the winner's performance has been by any objective measure.

Taking time to celebrate quality throughout the year supports both recognition and gratitude. Froedtert launched its QUEST process with a celebration in March 1991. At one of the tables, there was a pad of QUEST-O-GRAMS, a simple form asking for the following information: To, Dept, Thanks for, From, Dept. Merely by filling out the form, any employee could arrange for an executive to hand deliver a message of thanks to another employee. Over 2,000 QUEST-O-GRAMS (along with bags of mints) were delivered. The program proved so popular that executives were asked to repeat their performance during National Quality Month. Team leaders and department managers have QUEST-O-GRAM forms available on a day-to-day basis for one employee to deliver to another.

While National Quality Month in October provides a natural occasion to celebrate, there is no reason to wait. In 1991, Paul Revere shifted its fifth Qualifest to June. During this week-long annual celebration, all the quality teams are invited to put together displays that inform other teams about their best ideas. First-, second-, and third-place exhibits are awarded trophies. That year, the first-place team was also given a gift certificate for lunch at a local restaurant; second-place team members won tee-shirts with the Qualifest logo; and the third-place team was served coffee and pastries at their next team meeting by a "mystery guest"—who turned out to be the company president Chuck Soule, complete with apron and bell to announce the snack cart. His informal, hour-long visit was the team's greatest award.

There are other ways to celebrate. Paul Revere has had executives serve ice cream sundaes to employees to thank them; lunches (and breakfasts) with both executives and employees have been arranged either for new employees or to acknowledge the contribution of a group of employees. Celebration does not have to be big nor does it have to be expensive. It does have to be fun.

The Challenge

As with all aspects of a quality process, just saying it does not make it so. In 1992, Lakewood Research published a poll in which both executives and employees were asked if they agreed or disagreed with this statement: "This company genuinely cares about the well-being and morale of the employees and takes actions to help people feel good about working here." Among the executives, 67 percent agreed with the statement; 18 percent of their employees agreed.

Conveying recognition and constructing procedures to express gratitude and celebration that acknowledge the dignity and the individuality of every employee is the challenge. Much of what is now called a quality process amounts to ways in which to say "please, we acknowledge your value and your ability—we need your ideas," and "thank you, we appreciate your efforts."

PART X

MANAGING QUALITY IN GOVERNMENT SERVICES

40 ──────────────────

TQM: An Integrative Methodology for Doing "More With Less" in Public Service

B. Terence Harwick and Marty Russell, Total Quality Performance Research Institute

Introduction

If Total Quality Management (TQM) has a distinctive strength, it is its capability of providing an integrative methodology for accomplishing "more with less" through complex organizational action. TQM as a cohesive frame of reference for management is indebted to the splendid contributions of Deming, Feigenbaum, Juran, and others. Its unacknowledged roots are older, however, and important parallel contributions can enrich the methodology of a total quality approach to performance. Indeed, nothing is more central to the development of TQM as a management approach than clearly articulating and continuously improving its application as an action methodology.

Under other names, we have been experimenting with quality management since the beginning of the century. It may be precisely because of the intensity of the fiscal and performance dilemmas increasingly faced in the 1990s by managers and employees, agencies and enterprises, in the private and public sectors that we may be in a position to reap the benefits of this accumulating knowledge, including what has become known as TQM.

The term TQM was coined by the Naval Research Center in San Diego, California. Interestingly enough, the Navy has since replaced the term by TQL (Total Quality Leadership). A number of different acronyms have been coined, each of which tends to express different aspects of the process. One difficulty with the term TQM voiced by some labor groups, especially those with traditionally antagonistic relations with management, is that they, very sensibly, are not interested in having another management technique imposed upon them. If they are going to have anything to do with this process, some of these groups would prefer, for example, the term TQI and actions that emphasize a "Total Quality Involvement." We have nothing against any of these terms; we only point out that to the extent they are adhered to by one "side" or another on the basis of a rationale such as the above, they ironically represent the old way of thinking and acting that this new way of thinking, by whatever name, understood as an integrative action methodology in the sense that will be discussed in this chapter, is intended to supplant. Our preference would be for a term like "Total Quality Performance," which presumably it is the joint objective of both "sides" to achieve; we think it expresses the ultimate concern of an organization's mission, which can provide a context of shared meanings for management and labor. However, since TQM has been conventionally accepted in the United States, we defer to conventional usage.

A focus today on total quality performance in public service holds the promise of providing an integrative methodology for drawing together a good deal of this *accumulated* knowledge, furthering it through action research, and focusing it in an accessible way for practicing managers.

It is clear that Total Quality Management is not receiving attention by governments or businesses today simply for theoretical reasons. If this were the case, we could have begun attending to its central tenets a long time ago.* Yet, if quality management is to have a more systematic impact and be skillfully applied, greater theoretical clarification is necessary to continue to improve its methodologies.

Even though government agencies often have monopolies on the delivery of public services, many now face unprecedented fiscal crises. Their problems have important political and public administration consequences. American governments are increasingly characterized by relatively flat or decreasing revenues, and at the same time elected officials are facing political pressures to provide more and better government services. This political pressure is translating into unprecedented administrative pressures on public managers to employ initiative and creativity to deliver more services for the same tax dollar, or "more with less."

---

*Even before the work of Deming, Juran, and Feigenbaum, the philosophy, action, and analytic principles today recognized as Total Quality Management in its methodological sense were articulated by Mary Parker Follett and may be found in her book *Creative Experience* (New York: Longmans, Green and Co., 1924) and a set of speeches edited posthumously. These speeches were more recently published with Elliot M. Fox and L. Urwick as editors in *Dynamic Administration: Collected Papers of Mary Parker Follett*, 2d ed. (London: Pitman Publishing, 1973). For a more recent analysis of her contribution, see B. Terence Harwick, *Integrative Administration: The Contribution of Mary Parker Follett* (Los Angeles: Ph.D. Dissertation, University of Southern California, 1985).

Dilemmas of Governance in the United States: Fiscal Crises and Increased Demand for Public Services

In the late 1970s, a series of tax revolts were initiated throughout the country, fueled by high inflation and dissatisfaction with public services. By 1982, state and local governments had lost one out of every four federal dollars received in 1978. Yet in 1990, federal legislators passed laws that will cost states more than $15 billion over the next five years. By the late 1980s, approximately three out of every four Americans said that they felt the federal government delivered less value for the dollar than it had ten years earlier.

A 1989 survey of seventy major U.S. cities (with twenty-one responding) revealed the following demand for services:

Demand	Number of Cities	Percent Demand
More government services even with higher taxes	3	14
More government services but with lower taxes	15	71
Less government services but with lower taxes	0	0
Redefine and eliminate services	2	10
Redefine and eliminate services but with lower taxes	1	5
N =	21	100

By 1990, the actual deficits of many large cities and states had jumped into the billions, despite limitations on indebtedness. At that time, the National League of Cities reported that 85 percent of all U.S. municipalities said they did not have enough money to pay their bills. Several cities were on the verge of bankruptcy.

"More With More" or "Less With Less"?

In the past, government leaders were expected to respond to financial crises in one of two ways: they either raised taxes or cut services. Public administrators, under political pressure to eliminate waste as well as follow traditionally accepted professional norms, have generally responded by centralizing control bureaucratically or by looking for alternative ways of delivering public services. The search for alternatives has introduced new challenges in areas such as contract writing and performance monitoring. Attempts to impose control have generally failed to alter those political-bureaucratic incentives. Indeed, they have had the predictable effect, albeit unintentionally, of producing systemic waste. Today, "business as usual" in government is less acceptable than ever, both politically and administratively.

Politically, raising taxes is less and less tenable. Few cities seem inclined to provide more or better services at the cost of higher taxes. Voters seem inclined to support or approve additional taxes primarily in those limited cases where they can see a direct link between particular costs and their consequences. Even so, this tolerant attitude toward increased taxation remains the exception.

Administrative interventions that have sought to impose control bureaucratically (or that have overestimated the automatic character of voluntary or market dynamics in areas of public service) have often cost as much as they were expected to save. We will review below these earlier and ongoing attempts to impose control bureaucratically or to depend on market dynamics to resolve problems of inefficiency and ineffectiveness in the provision of public services. To the extent that these intervention techniques are imposed politically or administratively, they lock those involved into a vicious circle in which good intentions of good individuals are doomed from the outset.

In Search of a "Third Alternative"

In terms of government service delivery and service provision, is there a third alternative? Does a leadership or management approach exist that can facilitate accomplishing "more with less" on a sustained, institutionalized basis? If so, how would we recognize it?

Let's take a look at the promise of a Total Quality Management approach to consider whether and how it may provide a "third alternative." *What* we understand TQM to be and *why* we may understand it to work will directly affect *how* we go about its implementation. As the term has gained in notoriety, many consultants have simply recast what they were previously doing under this acronym. We are clearly not considering this broad range of intervention techniques. Instead, we address the question of whether the methodology of TQM can focus attention on neglected systems, dimensions, or realities of organizational life in ways that can help governments get out of the vicious circle of conducting "business as usual." If so, how?

TQM as Action Methodology for Generating Self-Control and Achieving "More With Less": Control as Consequence

The distinctive contribution of TQM is to be found precisely in its leadership and management methodology. Management methodology here means a systematic approach to practical problems that has a theoretically specifiable foundation, corresponding analytic tools, and action skills that are themselves subject to systematic inquiry and improvement. In the dynamic world in which we live, it is crucial to distinguish management *methodologies* from management *techniques*. A technique represents past knowledge generated under specific conditions and is thus suitable for mechanical application under recurring conditions. In short, a technique is appropriate where problems may be validly and reliably routinized. A methodology generates working models that can be adapted to varying circumstances. Methodology incorporates a self-correcting character into its approach that makes it more suitable for practical application in a changing and uncertain world.

To employ TQM reliably from an action perspective, we must understand that it must be differently applied with respect to different customer bases and dynamics. Unless we comprehend techniques in terms of an informing methodology, to the extent that we are working in complex and turbulent environments, we may employ them in proper contexts only by hunch, chance, and good fortune. It is thus vitally important to understand *TQM as an action methodology*. Moreover, on such grounds, it becomes possible to think of the quality movement not only in terms of schools of thought, but as a contemporary contribution with an older heritage that can continue to build in the future an *integrative* and *service-oriented* policy-administrative discipline.

CONTROL AS CAUSE VS. CONTROL AS CONSEQUENCE

TQM as an action methodology reverses "business as usual" by treating *control* not as the *cause* of requisite organizational behavior but as a *consequence* of an institutionalized capacity to meet and exceed the expectations of one's customers. Control may be understood less as something that emerges through the imposition of *techniques* upon human behavior and more as something that emerges as a consequence of *methodologies* capable of meeting the circumstance. Control occurs in the interaction and is not something we impose on top of it. This methodological distinction is especially relevant under circumstances characterized by complexity and rapid change. It becomes crucial if we want to institutionalize the capacity to accomplish "more with less."

TQM AS AN INVESTMENT STRATEGY

How then may the methodology of TQM be best understood? In terms of time frame and scope, it is important to note that Total Quality Management represents a long-range *investment strategy aimed at reversing systemic dysfunctions* rather than a short-term "fix" to extinguish fires.

The logic of TQM clearly suggests that performance results do not have a simple linear relationship with inputs or resources but critically depend on the *way* public service is organized, institutionalized, and goes about its business. It emphatically should not be understood as a technical intervention for next year, though it may, of course, be undertaken in phases beginning immediately and produce short-term tactical gains. TQM may be understood and tested as a methodology to institutionalize a sustained capacity for escaping the traditional either-or alternatives of achieving "more with more" or "less with less."

TQM as *customer-leadership methodology* should be understood as a strategy for the 1990s and beyond, involving long-term *changes in institutional culture* and *institutional structure* that begin and work through change in institutional *process*.*

Methodologically undertaken, the institutionalization of TQM in public service should help state and local governments accomplish "more with less" systemically in three areas: (1) eliminate waste, (2) increase productivity, and (3) leverage nongovernmental resources in the provision of public service.

TQM AS ACTION METHODOLOGY

TQM, properly understood, constitutes an *action* methodology (which is to say, an ethics and philosophy of action, analytic tools suitable for action in real time, and principles of skillful action suitable for learning as one acts). As methodology, TQM reorients joint action from an emphasis on a command orientation and corresponding control techniques to an emphasis on leadership, teamwork, and continuous learning throughout the organization in the articulation, development, and achievement of shared purposes.

TQM does not negate the validity of command and the appeal to authority. Rather, it conceives of this authority more broadly and in task-related terms, so that the organizational hierarchy constitutes only one of its dimensions. A TQM methodology points out that relying on hierarchical dynamics to control the work that gets done is an extraordinarily unintelligent way of managing the public's business, especially in contexts of complexity and uncertainty. This control orientation absorbs scarce executive energy and distracts from strategically important hierarchical functions that bear decisively on performance.

TQM as management methodology seeks rather to focus executives on their key tasks, such as leadership (articulating mission and role, embodying institutional purposes and values, and maintaining institutional integrity) and maintaining accountability (carefully monitoring

---

*For a well-written text with an action perspective on constructive processes for building a strong corporate service culture, see Charles Hampden-Turner, *Creating Corporate Culture: From Discord to Harmony* (Reading, Mass.: Addison-Wesley Publishing Co., 1992).

performance or what actually gets done), in ways conducive to continuous quality improvement. It serves to refocus executive attention upon closing the gap between promise and performance in the delivery of public services.

MANAGEMENT AS CONTEXT SETTING AND FOLLOWING THE "LAW OF THE SITUATION"

Seventy years ago, Mary Parker Follett addressed and furthered these immediately recognizable aspects of a total quality management method by redefining effective management. For Follett, the task of management is inseparable from the leadership challenge: to *set a context or field of action* through which effective control can emerge as a *consequence* of taking one's orders from the "law of the situation" (or, in the language of TQM, by meeting and exceeding the needs of one's internal and external "customers").

Discovering the "law of the situation" through identifying, meeting, and exceeding the needs of one's customers requires that managers attend to the evolving relationship between purposes and instrumentalities, ends and means, objectives and resources. This is done through institutionalizing employee involvement, rather than treating such complexity as an obstacle and settling for techniques of simplifying decision making from the perspective of managers at the top.

MANAGEMENT BY JOINTLY DETERMINED FACT

Properly applied, TQM generates indicators and measures *jointly* with employees and places them *at the service* of organizational members to better meet the needs and expectations of "customers." TQM as action methodology requires that throughout the organization, requisite accountability and incentives be structured so that employees are encouraged to learn continuously to meet the needs and expectations of their internal and external customers. Within the bounds of clearly understood and hierarchically validated institutional purposes, employees are given discretion to act to fully engage the "law of the situation." One might say that TQM as methodology helps build reliable mission-driven organizations focused on accomplishing purposes rather than rule-driven organizations preoccupied with technicalities.

MANAGEMENT THROUGH EMPLOYEE INVOLVEMENT

Within the TQM methodology, there is no substitute in the pursuit of shared purposes for a spirit of initiative and sense of entrepreneurship by individuals, or an embracing spirit of community and sense of teamwork by groups and networks of groups. Indeed, TQM is well understood as a methodology for evoking just such human qualities, disciplined by the tasks at hand, and channeling them creatively and constructively within the confines of accomplishing an organization's mission.

CONTROL AS CONSEQUENCE OF CUSTOMER SATISFACTION

From the standpoint of management as a "command-obedience" dynamic, techniques or instrumentalities of control are assumed to function as the operative *cause* of human behavior. From the standpoint of the "leadership-customer" dynamic, control emerges as a *consequence* of situational leaders throughout the organization attending closely to the needs and expectations of their "customers."

RECOVERY OF PUBLIC ADMINISTRATION AS CREATIVE EXPERIENCE

The 1990s may be a timely decade for public administration to reexamine its foundations, parameters, and working tools. In so doing, it might build upon the contribution of TQM and its heritage. It would be appropriate for public administration to both build upon new knowledge and return to its neglected heritage in learning how to better serve its publics. The field could benefit from action research by scholars and practitioners concerned with further developing methodologies for meeting the needs and expectations of public service customers. Indeed, the moment may be ripe for public administration to become what Mary Parker Follett had hoped for it, *an arena of creative experience*.

It is no accident that Mary Parker Follett—who deserves to be considered the Godmother of TQM as action methodology—worked and wrote in the areas of both business administration and public administration. For her, the proper ground of each arena of activity was nothing less than creative experience, for which she pioneered a methodology in her book and in her subsequent administrative presentations and applications.

QUALITY AS COMMON CHALLENGE OF PUBLIC ADMINISTRATION AND BUSINESS ADMINISTRATION

Mary Parker Follett would instantly recognize and be greatly encouraged by TQM as an applied and developing methodology. Yet, she would no doubt issue a cautionary note about potential pitfalls in construction and application, which is what we have tried to do here. She would immediately recognize that the record of the 1980s in America has shown that the challenge of quality management is no less real for the private sector than for public service. She would recognize that administrative problems are not automatically solved and may in some circumstances be exacerbated by transferring them to the private sector. In particular, she would appreciate the relevance and applicability of TQM as a methodology for reducing systemic bureaucratic dysfunctions in both business and government.

THE TQM CUSTOMER-LEADERSHIP DYNAMIC: METHODOLOGY FOR DISCOVERING THE "LAW OF THE SITUATION"

In sum, the strength of TQM, properly applied to business or public administration, may be seen as reversing the primacy of the "command-obedience" organizational dynamic and supplanting it with the primacy of a *"leadership-customer" dynamic*, which Senge prefers to call the *"learning organization."*[1] In Mary Parker Follett's terms, the strength of such complementary approaches is in their contribution to an action methodology for *discovering the "law of the situation."*

Tried Government Methods of Imposing Control Upon Bureaucratic Waste: Control as Cause

Earlier attempts to eliminate waste or increase productivity in government service delivery have relied primarily on instrumental means to impose control. From the vantage point of total quality management, *to rely primarily on such dynamics is to approach the problem backwards* because it systematically suppresses motivation and neglects intelligence otherwise available for problem solving. Rather, in the political context of fiscal stress combined with increased demand for services, the problem of low utilization of resources has become a leadership challenge that requires active two-way cooperation between elected officials and public managers.

To put this challenge in context, let us briefly highlight and contrast other principal forms of political-administrative intervention that have sought to eliminate bureaucratic waste.

LINE ITEM BUDGET CONTROL AS SOLUTION

Getting at waste through line items in public budgets has not proved especially effective. It offers political-administrative power to those with decision-making authority, but it is probably better understood as a means of addressing political/organizational dissension than of getting at waste. The waste is usually more subtly interwoven into the standard operating procedures of bureaucratic organizations. These procedures include (1) the bureaucratic disposition to produce standardized outcomes irrespective of varying needs, (2) budgetary incentives conducive to spending, irrespective of performance results, and (3) personnel policies circumscribed by limitations irrespective of individual and group incentives for performance. These commonplace bureaucratic incentives result in expending resources irrespective of performance, yet they are inaccessible to control through budgetary line items. *The problem is institutionalized waste,* and TQM offers a methodology for its resolution.

STRUCTURAL REFORM AS SOLUTION

As the complexities of government have grown in this century, repeated efforts have been made to address the problem of waste through organizational reform efforts. At the federal level, virtually every presidential administration since that of Theodore Roosevelt has offered proposals to get at problems of ineffectiveness, inefficiency, and waste through structural reorganization. Such efforts have met with only limited success. After all, when dealing with human problems, unless one constructively alters the incentives for individual initiative and teamwork among functionally related groups through such reorganization, moving the organizational-chart boxes in narrow ways is not likely to improve the quality of human performance or service to the customer. Instead, governmental reorganizations have had the principal long-term effect of imposing or rearranging political power rather than meeting their espoused aims of achieving sustainable gains in efficiency or productivity. This is not to say that organizational restructuring is irrelevant to performance. But when it is undertaken apart from a *total* quality management approach, it is unlikely to achieve its intended result.

CONTROL THROUGH MICROMANAGEMENT

When resources are tight and levels of trust are low between politicians and administrators or executives and employees, there is a tendency for political or executive leaders to micromanage affairs as a way of gaining or retaining control. Micromanagement generally focuses on control over "inputs" and "processes," since these are the easiest and most readily accessible forms of intervention.

When the micromanagement tactic is adopted, it virtually assures that productivity declines, as this intervention drains enormous organizational energy, channeling it into extraordinary documentation exercises and grinding the organizational machinery to a virtual halt.

CONTROL THROUGH TECHNICAL SOLUTIONS

A fourth mode of attempting to impose control on administrative situations relies less on overt political or executive power and more on an appeal to technical expertise. Widely publicized attempts over the last couple of decades include efforts to impose control through management information systems (MIS) or efforts to rationalize the politics of budgetary systems through devices such as zero-based budgeting. Their common shortcomings are the administrative reliance on technique and the attempt to impose such measurement devices as control mechanisms.

Governments need the capacity to impose control on bureaucratic waste. However, undue reliance upon these enforcement mechanisms has often only compounded the problem of high waste and low productivity.

The dilemma with all these strategies may be stated as follows. Systemic attempts to impose control depend upon some form of measurement in order to monitor and enforce that "control." But the imposition of technical control systems fails to take into account human response. When measures to control human behavior are identified, we discover that the measures do not simply drive behavior. A reciprocal process is generated through which adaptive human behavior drives the measures—irrespective of the performance the indicators were originally intended to measure. The "learning organization" builds on this insight and deserves considerable attention from the standpoint of further developing TQM's continuous learning methodology.

The design flaw in these types of control-system interventions, of course, is not in their attempt to correlate resources with objectives or measure performance. To the contrary, more capacity to measure public service performance is needed, not less. The shortcoming of control systems is the presumption that they cause human behavior and the failure to recognize that human behavior will adapt reciprocally, driving instead the indicators of control or measurements. When measures become standards of evaluation and mechanisms for imposing control, not surprisingly, people have a way of adapting to and meeting those measures, at least on paper, irrespective of the actual services rendered to customers.

THE VICIOUS CIRCLE

From the standpoint of the traditional control orientation to political and public administrative management, then, this represents a double-bind dilemma. It has the effect of locking politicians and administrators alike into a vicious circle. The reciprocal character of human behavior reliably undermines attempts to eliminate waste and increase productivity through the imposition of bureaucratic control from above.

The command-obedience construct of management distracts time and attention from eliminating *systemic* incentives for low productivity and waste in the first place. All the while, this control-imposition orientation justifies itself in terms of the waste that it reliably and systemically produces. As public managers find their energies sucked into continuous firefighting, they "need" to focus their attention on control techniques, which in turn, further exacerbates performance problems. This approach to public service management then becomes a vicious circle.

In sum, primary reliance on a control orientation to management reflects not only a failure to appreciate the reciprocal character of human behavior, but also a failure to address built-in structural incentives in typical political-administrative arrangements whose organizational consequences effortlessly produce waste in the use of resources.

In Search of Alternatives: Experimentation With Privatization and Other "Third-Party" Modes of Service Delivery

For political and economic reasons, governments have experimented with alternatives to bureaucratic service delivery, ranging from privatization to other "third-party" modes of delivering public services. From the standpoint of improving administrative efficiency and effectiveness, they have produced some notable successes, some notable failures, and generally mixed results. For example, the relative success or failure of privatization of public services may depend as much on how well or poorly a particular public program was previously managed as on how carefully contracts are specified, a privatization option is implemented with respect to existing resources, or performance is monitored.

It should be recognized that alternative forms of policy administrative action no more represent a solution set for what has become a political problem of waste or low productivity in bureaucratic settings than do the variety of control techniques with which governments have experimented more widely for an even longer period of time. That is, experimentation with alternative forms of public service provision may represent a necessary and yet insufficient attempt to deal with the problem of increased demand for services under conditions of fiscal stress.

The public service challenge that remains may well be understood as one of increasing the quality of public service provision, whether the policy-administrative instruments upon which one relies in service delivery are primarily those of the market, nonprofit, or direct governmental action. Indeed, it would seem that regardless of the policy dynamics employed, to the extent that government retains oversight responsibilities with respect to service provision, the quality challenge emerges as central to public service and its political-administrative leadership.

Public Service Through Bureaucracy or Alternatives to Bureaucracy: The Need for Quality as the Common Denominator

However advisable alternative service arrangements may be under some circumstances, the issue of quality management is hardly automatically solved by transferring the delivery of services to the private sector. From the standpoint of formal organizations, the challenge of quality management and achieving quality performance remains constant; that is, whatever policy dynamic or administrative modality may be proposed as solution set in a particular circumstance, one common implementation problem is clear. *We are still left with the practical administrative challenge of achieving quality performance through that modality of governance.*

Across the United States, creative political-administrative leaders at all levels of government are looking at innovative ways of resolving performance and financial problems instead of conducting business as usual by choosing between "more with more" and "less with less." Rather than passively reacting to the traditional vicious circle of established politico-administrative norms that reliably produces systemic inefficiencies and shortfalls in effective public services delivery, cities, counties, regional governments, and states, impelled by circumstances largely not of their making, are seriously and creatively experimenting with alternative forms and with revitalizing bureaucratic modalities of public service provision.

COMMON DENOMINATOR OF SUCCESS

One common denominator of the success stories seems to be that they most often provide or work within *a mission-oriented political-administrative context conducive to the emergence of situational leadership.* Such leadership is noteworthy in *giving expression and place to a spirit of individuality and community in addressing practical problems at hand.* TQM, skillfully applied as action methodology, evokes just these qualities of the human spirit, within the bounds of the development and achievement of the institutional mission. Successful executive leadership provides an institutional context and sense of direction within which entrepreneurial adventure and teamwork can thrive. Leadership in administration builds also the technical competencies and measurement capacities that facilitate the accomplishment of purpose. Quality Management, where understood and skillfully implemented as action methodology, *systemically builds institutional capacity to provide "more with less."*

"TQM" AS AN INTEGRATIVE MANAGEMENT DISCIPLINE?

While public service application of TQM is still in its early stages and, on its own, does not constitute a complete solution, the methodology may be able to offer an integrative discipline for tackling long-standing problems of eliminating waste in government, increasing productivity, and leveraging nongovernmental resources for the provision of public services. As an action methodology, it corresponds with the methodological development of managerial leadership that Mary Parker Follett pioneered seventy years ago. Follett observed closely the high-quality organizations of her day in business, government, and community affairs. It may be that by studying excellent public service organizations, a more adequate theory of organization can be built for guiding management practice.

As *action methodology*, TQM has a continuity stretching from the formation of the management discipline through other parallel powerful contributions. One may hope that bodies of knowledge such as these can mutually enrich one another and contribute to the development of a leadership and management methodology for formal organizations that is capable of achieving a genuine total quality performance in public services.

Conclusion

TQM has produced remarkable results. It is, however, not a technique that runs on automatic pilot. TQM is properly applied as action methodology when it focuses attention and directs energies where they need to be from the standpoint of managerial leadership. The strength of TQM is precisely that it offers an *integrative* approach for focusing attention *in real time* and in *actionable and accountable ways* upon the *complexity* of an organization's *evolving context* (through attending to one's external customers), *constituent parts* (through attending to dynamics among one's internal customers), and *performance* (whereby actual service rendered is attended to and constitutes the central criterion of evaluation).

While the language of TQM may be remarkably simple, it also entails a different way of seeing organizational life by inverting fundamental incentives and relationships through placing actual *service to the "customer"* at the center of its methodology. While its approach is not unique in the annals of management thought, rather than sanctioning "business as usual," TQM suggests and continues to develop a methodology remarkably different from the ways of organizing public service that have dominated public service provision for most of this century.

TQM, as an action methodology, is predicated on the underlying *value and ethics of service*. As such, it may help an institution in evolving its *purposes* along with and in dynamic relation to its *modalities*. To the extent that an institution is faithful to its core value of service and otherwise increases its capacity for *reliably and responsively* meeting its *shared and differentiated* customer expectations, the administrative consequences of TQM could go beyond improving organizational efficiency and effectiveness. TQM may then also prove helpful in addressing problems of institutional legitimacy within public service.

Notes

1. Peter M. Senge, *The Fifth Discipline: The Art and Practice of the Learning Organization* (New York: Doubleday, 1990).

The authors would like to express their appreciation to Professor Chester A. Newland of the School of Public Administration at the University of Southern California for his review of the original manuscript.

41

Quality in Public Services: The IRS Quality Journey

Joel Parfitt, Internal Revenue Service

If you had observed a high-level management meeting in the Internal Revenue Service in the mid 1980s, the topics and concerns would most likely have been program delivery, "filing season" processing, legislation, automation, budget restrictions, union/employee relations, staffing, problem solving, and functional management. A similar meeting in 1993 would have many of the same components, but with several additions: customer satisfaction, product cycle time, product quality, continuous improvement, upgrading measurement systems, and managing cross-functional work systems. The inclusion of these key topics represents a vast realignment of the agency's management philosophy and a significant upgrading of its management skills.

Historical and Cultural Perspective

To understand how profound a change this is, it is helpful to learn some of the background of this large and powerful agency.

In the 1950s and 1960s, the IRS reinvented itself. In the early 1950s, it dealt with real and potential corruption problems by reorganizing and establishing an elite Inspection Service to prevent the recurrence of integrity abuses by rigorously policing itself. Internally, it entrenched the principle that a voluntary assessment system absolutely requires popular confidence in the integrity of the taxing authority. In the early 1960s, it established as its mission "to encourage and achieve the highest possible degree of voluntary compliance with the tax laws and regulations and to maintain the highest degree of public confidence in the integrity and efficiency of the Service." During this time, the service also became a forerunner in automating work systems to meet standards of modern management and the demands of a growing workload.

These and other management actions established the IRS as a "blue ribbon agency" with a reputation as one of the best run of all federal bureaucracies. It was consistently successful in meeting critical program goals, such as timely completion of tax form processing in the January–April "filing season."

Several cultural themes have long dominated the IRS landscape. One of the most powerful is a "can do" attitude—the organization demands that its managers and employees accomplish tasks set for them. Problems will be solved, and quickly, and program goals will be met. Accomplishment, much more than education or any other factor, leads to advancement. People work hard, and rewards tend to come not in monetary terms, but in the form of step-by-step advancement, respect, self-satisfaction, and often more work.

Service employees tend to stay with the agency for their entire career. This is especially true of managers. Most current top and middle managers started their careers with the service in the 1960s or early 1970s, and have worked their way up with little non-IRS career experience. Many are accountants; most started their career in direct tax enforcement jobs. Managers and employees tend to be pragmatic and at ease with rules and directives. Many more are action- or procedure-oriented than conceptually or philosophically oriented. Historically, the service's leadership model was "top-down" and directive.

Labor relations are, in general, good. Most employees are members of the National Treasury Employees' Union. The agency is tough on bad conduct. On the other hand, it has maintained a "no layoff" policy even during major restructurings, such as the conversion from manual to computer processing. This policy goes a long way toward maintaining solid labor relations.

All employees and managers, except the commissioner, are career civil servants. The training infrastructure is strong, and a high percentage of employees are professional level and well educated. The IRS is successful and enjoys a good reputation, despite a somewhat unpopular mission.

Forces of Change

As in most private-sector organizations that have undertaken a change to quality management, the IRS change was assisted by a crisis. In 1985, the agency and its leaders suffered a profound shock. Because of a troubled computer replacement and a well-intended but overzealous drive for "efficiency," the filing season processing cycle faltered. The integrity of the tax system was maintained and the processing was completed, but there were significant delays, errors, and negative publicity. IRS leaders saw, dramatically and perhaps for the first time, that success was not assured, despite their hard work, excellent record, and strong management systems. It is not too dramatic to say that in 1985 they glimpsed the unthinkable.

It would be a mistake, however, to say that the 1985 filing season problems were the only reason IRS adopted quality management. Prior to 1985, Commissioner Roscoe Eggar and other key managers were exploring "quality," ways to change the service's culture, balancing efficiency with effectiveness, quality circles, and other improvement strategies. The need for change was made evident by several factors:

- Constant law changes (twenty-three in twenty-five years)
- Changing public expectations
- Increased congressional oversight
- The prospect of flat budgets and rising workloads, necessitating doing more with less.

Many of these issues were being explored formally through the service's Strategic Initiative processes, in which key executives are charged with studying and proposing solutions to potential problems. A prime example was the ground-breaking study by which the IRS explored the widely accepted principle that in-process review has advantages over traditional post review.

Initial Quality Efforts

At the end of 1985, the commissioner created the Commissioner's Quality Council and formally began the pursuit of "quality" as an improvement strategy. During early 1986, the council considered several possible quality consultants, and selected the philosophy of Dr. Joseph Juran as the most compatible with the IRS culture. Dr. Juran thus became the service's first major advisor in quality management. During 1986, he trained the top staff and all executives in his philosophy and practices. He defined quality as "fitness for use" and advised the service to begin its quality efforts by concentrating on the Quality Improvement aspect of his Quality Trilogy.

To support the new quality process, a top executive assumed an informal, part-time role as its champion, using his key position and personal commitment to create improvement. He called on several progressive staff members with backgrounds in training and planning to serve as the nucleus and knowledge resource for the quality change process. He also played a major role in the development of five strategic initiatives to explore quality management issues and initiate change. The initiatives, which were proposed by the Commissioner's Quality Council in 1986 and approved by the Commissioner in July 1987, addressed the following issues:

1. Developing program effectiveness measures
2. Developing a greater concern for the customer
3. Identifying and removing barriers to quality
4. Instilling a commitment to quality
5. Adapting management information systems to a quality management environment

Quality Improvement Projects (QIPs) were chartered to bring about improvement and test the applicability of Juran's techniques in the service. One of the most notable tests was to improve the federal tax deposit system, which is the process used by businesses to deposit money withheld for employees' income tax and Social Security contributions. This is a high-volume (72 million deposits made by 5 million businesses), complex, cross-functional system with great impact on business taxpayers. Because of these factors, there is a vast potential for errors and resulting rework. A team applied the analytic techniques used in the Juran Quality Improvement Process to solve several chronic problems that had previously defied typical IRS problem-solving approaches. The benefits of quantitative analysis, determination of root cause, and cross-functional problem solving were demonstrated. The test was a success—benefits to the service and its customers were very large, including the reduction of errors of untimeliness from 3.1 percent to 0.2 percent. The success of this and other projects in major IRS work systems proved the value of Dr. Juran's teachings and gave impetus and credibility to the QIP process.

QIP Mobilization—Successes, Problems, and Continuing Commitment

The Commissioner's Quality Council continued to serve as a policy body for the Quality Improvement Process. The agency geared up for implementation in typical fashion: directive and fully mobilized for accomplishment.

Key staff members learned and adapted the analytic, team-oriented, rational problem-solving process that Juran calls Quality Improvement. These staff members developed internal training programs for QIP team leaders, facilitators, and members. All major field offices were directed to form Quality Councils consisting of executives and senior staff members to select QIPs and project teams. Each office appointed Quality

Improvement Coordinators as local experts and focal points for the effort. Usually, the individuals who gravitated to these jobs were intellectually curious and disposed to promote organizational change and improvement.

Coordinators and top managers were trained and required to teach a centrally developed three-day management orientation class, called Quality Leadership Training, to all 10,000 managers servicewide. This course introduced many key concepts of quality management: customer satisfaction, analytic tools supporting data-based decision making, variability, team problem solving, and root cause analysis.

It was at this time that classic change resistance effects began to surface. The most notable ones were outspokenly stated by some managers attending the classes: skepticism, disbelief in the permanence of the change effort, the tendency of those being affected by the change to minimize the potential benefits and maximize the problems, doubt that an authoritarian bureau would be able to change fundamentally, a belief that quality and productivity were in competition, and for enforcement-oriented personnel, a real difficulty in reconceptualizing "taxpayers" as "customers."

Proponents argued that Juran's methods were proved in Japan, in American industry, and in IRS tests. These arguments swayed some but not all of the skeptics. The bottom line, of course, was that quality procedures were mandated. This top-down insistence ensured that quality had a chance to prove itself and become ingrained in the agency, but did little to deal with the essential skepticism felt by some.

Each Quality Council began to meet and chartered QIP teams staffed by managers to solve locally selected problems, working one to two hours per week on the project. Members and leaders were trained in the problem-solving process and group dynamics. Each team also had a trained facilitator to assist them. Some successes rolled in, but many teams just rolled on. Progress on many problems was slow, and some teams struggled along applying individual techniques without a coherent vision of the overall problem-solving process. In hindsight, it should not have been surprising that the massive mobilization effort would start to show problems at this point. These problems were caused by several conditions:

▲ Some important initial QIPs were done on major, national, cross-functional systems. When the process was rolled out servicewide, however, the local councils necessarily selected local problems. Potential benefits were smaller, and the priority was less in some cases.

▲ Teams were deliberately not given a deadline for completing their work. This was designed to ensure that full root cause analysis was done and eliminate the possibility that teams would deliver an inferior product just to meet a deadline. This decision had some merit and was made carefully by people who understood the IRS' "can do" culture. Unfortunately, the unintended side effect of this was to severely reduce the priority of the QIP. Managers working on teams were already working very hard, and tasks without deadlines had overwhelming competition from those with them.

▲ Mid management was unintentionally disenfranchised. Top managers chartered the QIPs, and first-line managers usually staffed the teams. Managers in the middle still faced the same expectations from above and tended to expect the same behavior from their subordinates. QIPs were often not a priority for them.

▲ Many councils were not adequately prepared for their role. Although councils were trained initially and later received advanced training, most did not take on a QIP project themselves, and therefore lacked direct personal knowledge of the process.

▲ The slowness with which many teams progressed caused some managers to lack confidence in the process, and this caused issues of lesser priority to be chosen for QIPs

▲ Too much was started too soon

▲ Training was done broadcast fashion, instead of just-in-time

Managers and Quality Improvement Coordinators attacked these problems individually, as they diagnosed them, with some success. They shared their diagnoses and successful interventions at a series of Coordinators' Conferences, and some improvements were made.

Despite these start-up problems, the QIP process continued to enjoy full support from the top of the organization. The process and its potential were simply too attractive to abandon, regardless of implementation problems. Additionally, a lot of QIP successes were occurring despite the problems encountered, and this continued to prove the worth of quality management. Juran had told service executives that the change to quality management was a multiyear process, and they believed him. There was also a governmentwide emphasis on quality that further encouraged continued efforts in this direction.

Establishment of the "Principles of Quality"

In 1987, the Commissioner established the "Principles of Quality" as operating guidelines and a philosophic basis for the quality process. These principles are:

‣ Establish a quality climate where quality is first among equals with schedule and cost
‣ Emphasize product and service quality by eliminating systemic flaws during the planning, implementation, and operational processes
‣ Improve responsiveness to the public and other service components
‣ Install a quality improvement process in every field and National Office organization
‣ Develop evaluating systems consistent with and reflective of the quality principles

Establishing a set of guidelines is, of course, far different from enacting lasting change. However, the adoption of these principles did help focus agency commitment to the effort and provided a touchstone for those actively trying to further the process. Large-scale change was implied and predicted by these principles, but was far from achieved.

Employee and Union Involvement

In recognition of the knowledge and potential contribution of the service's 100,000-plus individual contributors, steps were taken to bring them into the QIP process. Doing this required reaching an agreement with their representative, the National Treasury Employees Union (NTEU). In October 1987, the IRS and NTEU signed an historic agreement arrived at through a cooperative process, not collective bargaining. The Cooperative Agreement assured the union of membership on all of the renamed "Joint Quality Councils" and a full voice in consensus decision making on all Council decisions. It also brought bargaining unit employees into Joint QIP Teams (JQIPs) on a large scale without the need for negotiation. There were many effects of this agreement, but one of the most important was that it contributed to the continuation of the JQIP process by creating an official commitment to the union. Of course, the addition of bargaining unit employees to JQIP teams vastly increased the resources of the teams, and thousands of employees have contributed to teams servicewide.

The Assistant to the Commissioner (Quality)

Also in 1987, the service invited the Juran Institute to review its progress. Of the many recommendations made by Juran, the most far-reaching one was the suggestion to establish a position with full-time responsibility for quality. After experimenting with an interim appointee, in early 1989, the position of assistant to the commissioner (quality) was permanently established on the Commissioner's immediate staff. The individual selected had ideal personal characteristics for the job—the ability to think conceptually, a career history that endowed him with total credibility, practical quality experience, the attitude of a lifelong learner, and a true belief in quality as a tool for organizational improvement. It is impossible to detail all of the effective and persistent interventions made by this appointee on behalf of the quality process. To summarize, however, he is the bureau's top quality advocate, he has used his access to the top of the management structure to sustain and develop quality management in the IRS, and he has personally brought about the next major phase in the IRS's quality development, the movement toward total quality management described below.

Organic Influences

Above and beyond the discrete and deliberate factors encouraging continuation of quality management in the IRS, there were two more subtle and powerful influences that occurred "organically" as a result of quality efforts. The first was a learning explosion and the second a greater freedom to experiment with improvement efforts.

The educational explosion was a major side effect of educational processes surrounding QIPs. Knowledge about quality management simply began to go beyond what was being officially taught in mandatory classroom training. Curious and progressive individuals began to explore other sources of quality training. Most offices actively supported these activities. Others tolerated them, even though they weren't sure what the outcome would be.

It is an axiom in the social sciences that a liberating educational process is sometimes able to take on a life of its own—early learning stimulates curiosity, encourages more learning, and empowers individuals to push the limits of knowledge. In this case, the promise of the quality technology and its proven successes in the IRS and the business world created a true fascination for progressive individuals servicewide. Many sought out additional training from universities, corporations, associations, and consultants.

The second phenomenon was an increased openness to change and experimentation. The quality process demonstrated that the service was rethinking many of its traditional precepts, especially its view of its customers and the use of measures. This convinced many that the service had entered an era of greater willingness to change. Managers who previously had felt constrained by what is, after all, a massive bureaucracy saw increasing opportunities to change for the better. This belief further pushed quality management changes. Another result was that on some issues, the offices outside of the Washington, D.C., headquarters took over the leading edge of quality in the IRS.

Because of these two factors, the service began to experiment with quality technologies such as process analysis, self-managing work groups, and variants of problem-solving processes that were better adapted than QIPs to solving certain types of problems.

The Drive Toward Total Quality

During 1988 and 1989, those who worked full time in quality and several senior managers, including the assistant to the commissioner (quality), crystallized their feelings that the JQIP process was far from all there was to quality. There were several major influences that accounted for this feeling, although these are probably clearer in hindsight than they were at the time:

- ▲ An increasing understanding of quality management
- ▲ Some dissatisfaction with progress to date
- ▲ A realization that, although thought leaders such as Juran and Deming taught that system problems account for a huge proportion of an organization's problems, the IRS was spending little time on improvement of major systems

In 1989, the assistant to the commissioner (quality) proposed a major expansion of the IRS drive toward quality management. He suggested to the senior management staff that the service needed to set the goal of becoming a "Total Quality Organization." Clearly, few in the service understood at first the implications of this suggestion—for many, "quality" had become synonymous with QIPs. After much work on the part of the assistant to the commissioner (quality), however, understanding increased, and the suggestion was adopted. An early action in this effort was to charter a group to formulate a long-range plan for quality in the IRS. It was around this time that the IRS mission statement was revised to reflect the growing importance of continuous quality improvement:

> The purpose of the Internal Revenue Service is to collect the proper amount of tax revenue at the least cost; serve the public by continually improving the quality of our products and services; and perform in a manner warranting the highest degree of public confidence in our integrity, efficiency, and fairness.

A Long-Range Plan for Quality

In its early stages, the group saw its mission as codifying and scheduling the accomplishment of scores of existing recommendations for improving quality and productivity. These recommendations had been developed by the Juran Institute, IRS Strategic Initiative Teams, the Government Accounting Office, and others. The team started by classifying all of the recommendations according to the criteria in the guidelines for the President's Award for Quality and Productivity and deciding the order in which they needed to be accomplished. Up to this point, they had operated in a fashion typical of many government task groups: list, prioritize, do (or recommend). Fortunately, however, this group was composed of deep thinkers, and they became dissatisfied with such a simplistic approach. They decided to perform a critical analysis of the recommendations to determine if accomplishing all of them would actually create a "Total Quality Organization." They concluded that the recommendations, worthwhile as they might be, were not sufficient to create total quality in the IRS.

This began a journey of exploration that led in 1991 to the realization that the agency could achieve total quality only by adopting a true "systems approach" to managing. The long-range planning group proposed a plan, significantly influenced by the Management Development Center at the University of Tennessee, that called for a top-down approach in which all major, cross-functional work processes of the service would be mapped, analyzed, and improved. The conceptual framework of this approach has eight parts:

1. Create unity of purpose by reassessing, clarifying, and communicating service objectives: increase voluntary compliance, reduce taxpayer burden, and improve quality-driven productivity and customer satisfaction.
2. Clarify management's responsibilities and accountability for improved organizational performance. This is achieved by actively managing and improving IRS work systems and paying constant attention to taxpayer and employee needs.
3. Revamp measurement systems.
4. Establish and accomplish ambitious annual and multiyear improvement goals.
5. Revise systems for reward and recognition.
6. Increase the ability of all employees to be successful and to contribute to improved performance of the service and increased customer satisfaction.
7. Thoroughly engage customers in the design of products and systems.

8. Reexamine the structure of the organization as our understanding of products and system performance increases.

The plan was shared with top executives and modified based on their input, and in the spring of 1992, implementation of the "Internal Revenue Service Plan for Improving Customer Service and Organizational Performance" was accepted by the Commissioner and top executives. The major operational concept in the plan is the need to manage the major business systems of the IRS that cut across functional lines in producing products. The initial step of identifying the "core business systems" and appointing executive systems owners was done at the same time the plan was adopted. The systems that define the basic business of the IRS are:

▲ Informing, educating, and assisting taxpayers
▲ Ensuring compliance
▲ Managing accounts
▲ Resourcing
▲ Value tracking

All of the systems already existed in some form in the service, but generally parts of each system inhabited different functional "stovepipes." This situation prevented both integration and optimization. Conversely, improving the management of this situation offers major opportunities.

Each core business system owner has assembled a team to assist with initial steps: mapping the system, identifying subsystems, and upgrading measurement systems by making them more reflective of customers' needs and eliminating dysfunctional measures. Future activities will include detailed analysis and (as the ultimate objective) redesign of actions at the system and process level to ensure continued improvement in both the quality of products delivered to IRS customers and the productivity of service operations.

Value Tracking

The greatest departure from traditional IRS practice was the establishment of the Value Tracking Core Business System. Its purpose is to determine "net customer value" calculated by finding out what customers receive, or "realize," from the service, less the costs (sacrifices) they encounter. The establishment of this system focuses and integrates numerous customer need/satisfaction research efforts implemented over the past several years. As a coherent strategy, it will allow the service to greatly improve its knowledge of how well it serves its customers. By managing toward increases in net customer value, it will be able to make much better decisions aimed at satisfying customer needs. By operating on a permanent basis, the Value Tracking System will also be able to provide this type of information over time and keep the service in tune with customer needs and satisfaction as conditions and expectations change.

Benefits

The benefits derived to date from quality management are considerable:

- ▲ The JQIP process has yielded approximately $100 million in direct cost savings, the equivalent of a $300 million reduction in "taxpayer burden" (time, money, and frustration customers experience in complying with tax laws), and hundreds of millions of dollars in "opportunity benefits" and additional tax dollars collected.
- ▲ JQIPs have also greatly increased employee participation, resulting in decreased grievances, better labor relations, higher morale, and an improved quality of work life.
- ▲ Quantum increases in the correctness and completeness of answers given over the toll-free tax inquiry system have occurred.
- ▲ The process has produced large decreases in untimely processing of refund returns, major decreases in rework, and an increase in productivity in the processing function.
- ▲ Quality management has increased assessments, increased productivity, decreased inventories, and decreased cycle time in several functions.

One IRS installation, the Ogden (Utah) Service Center, has won the 1992 President's Award for Quality and Productivity Improvement. The President's Award is the federal version of the Malcolm Baldrige National Quality Award. This was the first non-Defense office to ever win this award, and only this award was given in 1992. The only other finalist in the competition was the IRS's Fresno Service Center.

The service is pleased with its accomplishments to date but believes that much more will be realized when the Core Business System/Total Quality Organization concepts have been fully implemented.

Lessons Learned and Critical Success Factors

Along its quality journey, the IRS has grown through a learning process that has brought it to several critical realizations. Amazingly, these realizations are the kinds of things any good quality consultant can tell any executive in the first hour after they meet. They are also the kinds of things that an organization comes to believe or "own" only after years of struggle, trial, defeat, success, and reevaluation. This is the meaning of "cultural change," and, as in the process of growing up, these lessons are never internalized until they are learned through direct experience. The major ones are:

- The IRS has products, not just programs.
- Those products are the goods and services that are delivered to customers, who (along with the nation's statutes) are the arbiters of quality.
- Changing to a customer/product-focused view mandates a major change in measurement systems.
- Teams of employees and managers have vastly more problem-solving power than individuals in either category; training mobilizes that power.
- Addressing the root cause of problems will create lasting solutions, and even though the cost of real solutions can *look* higher than the cost of quick fixes, the cost/benefit ratio is much greater because solutions to the root cause really work and tend to be permanent.
- A structured analytical process and an understanding of statistical concepts such as variation are necessary to solving many kinds of problems.
- Work often flows across functions, and profound improvement comes only from reconsidering major systems that flow across traditional functional boundaries.
- Training needs to be upgraded as understanding increases, and new tools need to be added to the quality tool kit along the way.
- Quality management can and must be integrated with other major change efforts; in the case of the IRS, these included improvement of the Strategic Planning System, complete reengineering of information systems, a modernized view of ways to ensure compliance with tax law, and major emphases on ethical behavior and the organizational benefits of human diversity.

An organization can reach this stage of cultural change only if it is fortunate enough to sustain its change effort. In the IRS's case, the factors that helped sustain the effort were these:

- Motivation born of a deeply felt desire to improve
- The knowledge that change was absolutely necessary
- A strong top-down mandate and a culture that accepts such direction

- A world-class consultant to set the course and begin the training
- Strategies for learning—a formal method of expanding the organization's knowledge base; the search for more knowledge from more than one consultant; the ability to get generous help from universities and private sector companies; a willingness to expend resources to enhance learning
- A training infrastructure capable of supporting the necessary skill development
- A long-term view—the understanding that the change to quality management will neither truly succeed nor truly fail in a couple of years, and that abandoning the quality course will destroy any chance of starting over for at least a generation
- Four consecutive commissioners who initiated, accepted, supported, and advanced the quality process
- Empowering an infrastructure that is intellectually curious and disposed to change
- Establishing a full-time, top-level policy executive for quality, and filling that job with the right person
- The realization that approaches to major change will develop and mature over time; persistence; some willingness to accept experimentation;
- Seeing results
- Applying for quality awards; accepting the encouragement that winning brings while truly holding the view that the organization learns more from losing than winning in an award competition.

Summary

The IRS has come a long way toward quality management. The commitment to the Core Business System approach was a huge accomplishment that came about as the result of major efforts and a great amount of learning. But, as has been said at countless high school commencement ceremonies, this accomplishment is a beginning. It is well intended and well founded, but it is just the first step in the second phase of a life-long journey. The payoff will be breakthrough improvements in customer satisfaction and tax administration. The service is confident that the ultimate beneficiaries will be the individual customers it serves and the nation as a whole. And those of us who are players in the change effort look forward to continuing satisfaction and more than a little fun along the way.

Index

[Page numbers in *italics* refer to illustrations.]

ACCESS program, 107–108
alignment, *see* system alignment
Amalgamated Clothing and Textile Workers Union (ACTWU), 89–94
American Airlines, 458–462
American Society for Quality Control (ASQC), 45–46
apologies to customers, 468
AT&T, 11, 391
    Universal Card Service program at, 55–68, 251, 255
Au Bon Pain, 209
Automotive and Miniature Lighting, 288–292

Baldrige Award, *see* Malcolm Baldrige National Quality Award
Baxter Healthcare Corporation, 95–108
benchmarking, 32–33, 381–388
    benefits of, 387
    defined, 382
    fundamentals of, 383
    at GTE Corporation, 69
    identifying subject of, 385–387
    internal, competitive, and functional forms of, 386–387
    objectives of, 382
    practices and performance levels of, 383
    for purchasing function, 373–374
    strategic vs. operational, 382–383
    ten-step process of, 383–385
    at Xerox Corporation, 92, 381, 385–387
business reengineering and performance improvement, 223, 224 226

Carlzon, Jan, and the inverted pyramid, 9, 279–281
celebrations, for employees, 488, 494–495
change
    in corporate culture, 134–147, 283, 448–450, 471–475
    management of, 223, 224, 226–227
comment cards, 403
communication(s)
    critical-incident oriented, 421–424
    of customer feedback, 201–202
    with customers, 74–75, 455–456
    with employees, 74, 114–120, 423
    on internal service, 81
    with organized labor, 89–90
    personal quality in, 298
    quality improvement and, 100–101
    with suppliers, 75, 100–101
    technology for, 47
    three audiences for, 74–75
competitors, analysis of, 342–343
    see also benchmarking

complaints, 195–196, 198–200
    analysis of, 402–403
    at Japan's Imperial Hotel, 322–324
confirmation/disconfirmation concept, 20, 21, 22–23
conjoint measurement, 401–402
constant values methods of error detection, 351, 352–353
contact methods of error detection, 351–352
context setting, management as, 505
control as cause, vs. as consequence, 502, 503, 506
core business, protecting, 56
Corning Inc., 302–311
corporate culture, 111–123, 339
    employee enablement and service-oriented, 114–115
    employee involvement and service-oriented, 115–116
    feedback devices for, 116–120
    industry maturation and service-orientation in, 120–122
    leadership and, 112–114
    management's role in changing, 136, 144, 145, 147, 283
    personnel creed at USAA and, 234, *235*
    pilot programs for creating change in, 134, 138–147
    service recovery and, 471–475
    system alignment and, 448–450
    Total Quality Management concept and, 111–112, 134, 136, 147
    see also organizational climate
corporate image, 22, 339, 390
cost reduction, 222
creativity and innovation
    Baldrige Award and, 34–35
    in public administration, 506–507, 521–522
credit bureau reporting, 59
Critical Incident Technique (CIT), 400–401, 408–427
    information value of quality measurement by, 415–418
    limitations of attribute-based measurements, 408–409
    methodology of, 410–415
    service quality management oriented to, 418–424
    studies based on, 410, *411*
culture, *see* corporate culture
customer(s)
    analysis of, for design of services, 342–343
    communicating with, 74–75, 455–456
    empowerment of, 103
    handling problems of (*see* service recovery)
    ideas of, 197–198
    internal, 79–81, 140, 260, 435
    point-of-view of, 158, 160

customer(s) (*continued*)
    repurchase intentions of, 463, *464*
    strategic alliances with, 95–108
    training workshops for, 453
customer-driven quality concept, 36–38
customer expectations, 19–21, 149, 151–153, 165, 332–333
    aligning strategy with, 440
    critical-incident communications and, 421–422
    Gaps model of, 177–179, 185
    needs and wishes vs., 336
    new model of, 179–180, 185–186
    personal quality and, 294, 295–296, 298
    process generating, 180–182
    service guarantees and, 478–479
    service recovery and, 466–470
    should and *will*, 180–186
customer experiences, 19–21, 151–153, 416
customer feedback, 195–204
    communicating, 201–202
    complaints as, 195, 198–200
    focus groups, 200–201, 434
    at Japan's Imperial Hotel, 322–324
    learning from, 201
    service quality and, 202–203
    suggestion box for, 196–197
    suppliers and, 203–204
    surveys, 397–400, 428–429, 433–434
    system for continuous, 82
    using ideas from, 197–198
customer focus, 8, *11*
    at AT&T, 58, 65
    total quality system and, 221
Customer Focus Framework, *228*, 229
customer needs and requirements, 168
    anticipating, 421
    expectations/wishes vs., 336
    primary/secondary, 335–336
    purchasing function and, 371–372
    quality education and, 281, 287
    service profit chain and focus on, 209–210
customer perception of quality, 11, 19–23, 73, 127, 177–194, 260, 333, 391–392
    critical-incident technique and, 415
    Gaps model of, 177–179, 185, 392
    new model of, 179–180, 185–186
    Perceived Service Quality model for, 19–22
    process generating, 183–185
    service recovery and, 464–465
customer relationships, 8, *10*
    management of, *37*, 38
    with marginal customers, 65
    service construct and, 125–127
    strategic alliances for improved service, 95–108
    system alignment by fostering, 452–453
customer retention, 98, 150
    customer satisfaction link to, 206–207
    profit link to, 205–206
customer satisfaction, 177
    control as consequence of, 506
    customer retention link to, 206–207
    employee satisfaction link to, 249
    principle of, 165
    reasons for focus on, 389
    service quality/delivery strategy link to, 207
customer satisfaction measurements, 389–407
    evolution of, 390–392
    globalization of, 404–405
    marketing research vs., 393–396
    methodologies of, 396–403
    unsound, 405

customer service, 458–462
    employee participation in creating quality, 461
    leadership required for quality, 462
    objectives and measurements of, 459–460
    quality as imperative, 458–459
    quality as product, 460–461
Cycle of Failure, 207, *208*

database
    of critical incidents, 410–415, 418–420
    electronic, 47, 62, 456
decision making, employee involvement in, 130–131, 145
Deming, W. Edwards, 101–102
Deming Prize, 164, 165, 267, 275, 387
design for quality, *9*, 331–346
    definition/model of service construct, 333–341
    fail-safing services by, 347–357
    four-phase model for quality service design, 341–343
    implications of service and quality characteristics for, 332–333
    service mapping for, 148–163
distributors, partnerships with, 453–456
dynamic complexity, 150, 153

earned authority, 83–84
education and training for quality, 8, *10*, 279–293
    in AT&T, 62–63, *64*
    case study on, at GTE, 288–292
    on critical-incident technique, 423
    curriculum for, 287, *288*
    of customers, 453
    employee involvement in, 292–293
    employee motivation and, 252–254
    enabling employees with, 114–115
    for executives, 281–283
    for frontline employees, 286–288
    at Japan's Imperial Hotel, 312–328
    management's commitment to, 292–293
    for management employees, 284–286
    organizational structure and, 279–281
    performance measurement program and, 139
    service climate and, 129–130
    on service guarantees, 479–482
    service profit chain and employee, 212–215
    as service quality principle, 71–72
    for service recovery, 471, 474
    at USAA corporation, 241–243
efficiency, 64–65, 168
electronic databases, 47, 62, 456
electronic newsletter, 455
Employability Index (EI) program, 238–239
employee(s)
    boundary-spanning, 126
    communicating with, 74, 114–120, 423
    defining quality in, 235–236
    as evidence of service, *359*-360, 365, 366–367
    fair treatment of, 249–252
    front-line (*see* front-line employees)
    key to quality, 338–339
    orientation of, 241
    respect for, 165–166, 249–252
    socialization of, 129
    training (*see* education and training for quality)
employee compensation, 59
    corporate culture and, 119
    empowerment and, 211
    motivation and, 254–255
    service climate and, 130–131
employee development, 86, 212–215, 241–243, 252–254

employee empowerment, 6–7, 114–115, 210–211, 259–266
  benefits of, 262–264
  implementation of, 264–265
  nature of, 260–262
  service business and, 259–260
employee feedback
  focus groups, *115*, 116, 435
  surveys, *115*, 116, 434–435
employee involvement, 115–116
  at AT&T, 59, *60*
  in decision making, 130–131
  management through, 505–506
  motivation and, 256–257
  in quality customer service programs, 461
  in quality education, 292–293
  at Xerox Corporation, 89–90
employee motivation, 248–258
  compensation for, 254–255
  critical-incident technique and, 423
  fair treatment for, 249–252
  involvement for, 256–257
  opportunity for, 257–258
  recognition for, 255–256
  training for, 252–254
employee promotions, 119–120, 257–258
employee recognition, 488–489
  at AT&T, 61–62, 64–65
  celebrations as, 488, 494–495
  customer feedback and, 198
  gratitude expressed to, 488, 489–491
  model program for, 491–494
  motivation and, 255–256
  performance measurements and, 436
  servant leadership and, 86–87
  service climate and, 130
  service-oriented corporate culture and, 116–119, *120*
  as service quality principle, 75–76
employee recruitment, 212, 422
  at USAA, 236–41, 242
employee retention, 67–68
  employee satisfaction link to, 207
  external service quality link to, 207, *208*
employee satisfaction, 67–68
  customer satisfaction link to, 249
  employee retention link to, 207
employee selection, 129, 212, 236–241, 422
employee suggestion program
  Bright Ideas system as, 270–272
  changes and need for, 267
  effects/benefits of, 274–275
  results of, 272–274
  original design of, 268–270
employment security, 92–94
employment testing, 237–238
EQUIPE concept, 139–143
error detection, *see* fail-safing
ethics, 375, *376*
evidence of service, 358–370
  categories of, *359*–362
  guidelines for, 367–369
  identifying, 362–367
  intangibility and, 358–359
express mail delivery
  service evidence opportunities for, 366
  service map of, 362, *363*

fail-safing, 347–357
  applying, to services, 349–350
  implementing, for services, 354–356
  primer on technical elements of, 348–349
  service fail-safe classification, 350–354
Fairfield Inn, 209, 211
feedback, 150–153
  see also customer feedback; employee feedback
financial performance
  Baldrige Award and, 33–34
  as performance measure, 429, 437
  service recovery and, 463–466
financial service companies, service quality in, 116, 121–122, 336, 337
flag system, 169, *171*
Florida Power and Light (FPL), 164–174, 267–275
focus groups
  customer, 200–201
  employee, *115*, 116, 434
Follett, Mary Parker, on Total Quality Management method, 500 *n*, 505, 506, 507
forcefield diagram, 103, *104*
formal authority, 83
Froedtert Memorial Lutheran Hospital, 491, 492–495
front-line employees, 212, 260, 461
  personal quality in, 294–301
  quality education for, 286–288

Gaps Analysis model, 177–179, 185–186, 392
government administration
  finances and increased demand as problems of, 501–502
  performance reviews in, 47–48
  quality awards for, 44–45, 525
  quality management as task of, 511–512
  Total Quality Management as action methodology for, 499–500, 502–507, 511–513
  tried methods of controlling waste in, 507–510
  see also Internal Revenue Service, quality management at
gratitude, expressing, to employees, 488, 489–491
GTE Corporation
  quality education at, 288–292
  service quality principles at, 69–76
guarantees, *see* service guarantees
Guidelines for Quality Management and Quality Systems, *see* ISO Standard 9004

health care, 46, 95–108
hotel stay
  service evidence opportunities for, 365, 366–367
  service map of, 362, *364*
human resources
  service climate and, 126, 128–131
  service profit chain and strategies of, 207, 209–217
  see also employee(s)

image, corporate, 22, 339, 390
IMPACT program, 138
Imperial Hotel, Japan, 312–328
  employee case history, 326–328
  guest critiques and, 322–324
  patron increase at, 324–325
  service improvement committee at, 324
  staff capability development, 314–321
  staff occupation training, 322
  staff personnel development, 312–314
  zero complaints movement, 324
improvement, continuous, 166, 223, *226*, 262, 282
  see also performance improvement; quality improvement
information systems, 8, *10*, 47, 62
inspection, fail-safing and methods of, 348, 349
interactive marketing, 19

internal marketing, critical-incident oriented, 422–424
Internal Revenue Service, quality management at, 514–527
  benefits of, 525
  education and innovation for, 521–522
  employee and union involvement in, 520
  expansion of, 522
  initial efforts toward, 516–517
  lessons/critical success factors of, 525–526
  long-range plan, 523–524
  organizational history and culture, 514–515
  Principles of Quality for, 519–520
  processing failure as impetus for, 515–516
  Quality Improvement Projects (QIPs) program introduced for, 517–519
  quality management position established for, 520–521
  value tracking as, 524–525
internal service, 260
  applying model of, 82–87
  assuring employee hiring quality as, 243–246
  concept of, 77–78, 87
  five-step model for leadership in, 79–82
  seven sins of, 79–81
internationalization of consumer satisfaction measurements, 404–405
Ishikawa diagram, 385, 386
ISO Standard 9004, 7–8, 164, 333–334

Japan, 166, 168
  Imperial Hotel staff training, 312–328
  suggestion program in, 268, 270
job security, 92–94
Johnsonville Foods, 263, 264
Juran, Joseph, on quality defects, 331, 356, 516
Juran Institute, 7

labor, see organized labor
law of the situation, 505, 507
leadership, 8, 11
  concept of servant, 84–87
  corporate culture and, 112–114, 147, 283
  employee recognition and effective, 488–489
  formal vs. earned authority and, 83–84
  management vs., 488
  in middle managers, 77–87
  for quality customer service, 462
  quality education and, 281–282
  as service quality principle, 70–71
line item budgets, 507–508
L. L. Bean, 385–387

McDermott, Robert E., and quality leadership, 233
Malcolm Baldrige National Quality Award, 16, 25–52, 164, 251
  applicants for, 42–43
  criteria of, 25–26, 27, 30–32
  criteria distribution of, 41–42
  extended impact of, 43–47
  international impact of, 50
  performance reviews and, 47–49
  purposes of, 39–41
  quality and operational results category of, 27–32
  quality-related corporate issues and, 32–35
  service quality aspects of, 35–38
management
  education of, 71–72
  as leaders, 462 (see also leadership)
  participatory (see participatory management)
  performance expectations of, 287
  placing, at USAA, 242

relations between labor and, 88–89, 90–92
  as role model, 283
  service recovery and, 474
  see also middle management; top management
management by fact, 166, 282, 505
manufacturing quality vs. service quality, 261
  Baldrige Award and, 35–38
  maturation of quality process link to, 120–122
  myths about, 3, 4–9
marketing
  perceived service quality and model of, 17, 19–22
  service differentiated, 453
  of services, 17, 18, 19
marketing research vs. customer satisfaction measurements, 393–396
  continuous nature of, 394
  responsibility for, 393–394
  results utilization, 393
  skills sets of, 395–396
Marriott Corporation, 248–258, 337
measurements of quality, 8, 10
  customer perceptions and, 177–179
  group performance index for, 140, 141
  informing employees of, 59, 61
  for internal service, 82
  in services vs. in manufacturing, 12–14
  see also Critical Incident Technique (CIT); customer satisfaction measurements; performance measurement
Merrill Lynch, 336, 337
Metropolitan Life Insurance Company, 294–301
micromanagement, 508
middle management
  integration of human resources and service delivery by, 217
  internal service and leadership of, 77–87
  pilot programs and, 146
  quality education and, 284–286
mission statements, 70, 81, 168, 385, 514, 522
MONY Pension Operations, performance measurement at, 428–444
motion step methods of error detection, 351, 353–354
mystery shopper studies, 402
myths about service quality
  manufacturing quality as different from service quality, 3, 4–9
  service companies as all alike, 15
  service quality as determined in real-time, 14–15
  service quality as harder to measure, 12–14
  service quality as solely personal contacts, 9–12

National Association of Purchasing Management, 375, 376
National Demonstration Project in Health Care Quality Improvement, 16
National Institute of Standards and Technology (NIST), 41
National Treasury Employees Union (NTEU), 520
newsletter, customer, 455
Nordstrom Corporation, 209, 210, 211

Ontario Training Corporation (OTC), SkillsLink service maps of, 156–162
open systems, organizations as, 127–128
organizational climate
  defined, 124–125
  human resources subsystem and, 128–131
  open systems concept and, 127–128
  service construct and, 125–127
  see also corporate culture
organizational involvement in quality, total, 8, 10

organizational restructuring, 223, 508
organized labor, 88–94
    building partnership with, 90–92
    culture change and, 146
    at Internal Revenue Service, 520
    introducing total quality program to, 89–90
    meeting concerns of, 92–94
    trust between management and, 88–89

participatory management, 130–131, 145, 462
    total quality system and, 221
partnership process for self-managed teams, 303–305
    characteristics of, 304–305
    seven-step model for, 305–309
partnerships with customers, 452–456
Paul Revere Insurance Group, 491–495
people as evidence of service, *359*-360, 365, 366–367
perceived quality, *see* customer perception of quality
performance goals and objectives
    benchmarking for, 381, 382, 383
    set by employees and managers, 435–436
performance improvement, 219–229
    building culture of, 220
    evolution of total quality system for, 220–222
    holistic approaches to, 223–227
    implementation, 227–229
    typical approaches to, 222–223
    see also personal quality
performance measurement, 428–444
    defining, 429–430
    experience of, at MONY Pension Operations, 430–439
    human aspects of, 441–442
    organizational readiness for, 443–444
    power/benefits of, 442–443
    six principles of, 432–439
    technical aspects of, 439–441
    see also measurements of quality
performance reviews
    in AT&T's Universal Card program, 59–62
    Baldrige Awards and, 47–49
    EQUIPE program and, 140–141
    service climate and, 130
    service-oriented corporate culture and, 119–120, *121*
personal contacts, myth of service quality as solely, 9–12
personal quality, 294–301
    characteristics of, 295–298
    program elements for, 300
    self-mastery and, 299–300
    service quality basics and, 294–295
    see also performance improvement
physical evidence of service, *359*, 361–362, 365, 366–367
pilot projects
    failures of, 143–146
    pilot districts and EQUIPE concept, 138–143
    productivity council's efforts, 135–138
    role of top management in, 136, 144–45, 147
planning for quality, 7, *9*
    critical-incident technique and, 420–421
    at Internal Revenue Service, 523–524
    as service quality principle, 72–73
poka-yoke devices, 349
    error-detection by, 351–354
policy management, 167, 168–169, *170*, *171*
prioritization principle, 166
privatization of government services, 510
problem analysis of customer satisfaction, 401
process as evidence of service, *359*, 360–361, 365, 366–367

process flow diagramming, 103, *104*
process management, 167, 172, 283
    performance improvement and, 223, *224-226*
    total quality system and, 221, *222*
productivity council, culture change and, 135–138
product quality studies, 390
professional associations, 45–46
profit link to customer retention, 205–206
public administration, *see* government administration
purchasing function, 371–378
    benefits of service quality in, 377–378
    managing supplier service quality through, 375–377
    principles/standards of, *376*
    purchasing quality vs. quality of purchasing, 373–374
    role of, in quality management, 371–372

quality
    as common challenge of government and business, 506–507
    customer perception of (*see* customer perception of quality)
    defined, 332–333
quality assurance system, 8, *10*
quality awards
    employee recognition using, 117, *118*, *119*
    federal and state government, 44, *45*
    international, 50
    see also Deming Prize; Malcolm Baldrige National Quality Award
quality control, 7, *9*
Quality Enhancement Process (QEP) at MONY, 430–439
quality improvement, 7, *9*, 101–108
    continous, 166
    creating/adding value for, 103–108
    methodology of, 102, 103, *104*
    processes of, 15
    strategic alliances with customers for, 95–108
    transformation principle and, 101–102
quality improvement experiments, 400
quality indicators, 437–439
    see also measurements of quality
Quality Leadership Process (QLP), 99–101, 107
quality management
    basic elements of, 7, *8–11*
    creating system of service, 164–174
    at Internal Revenue Service, 514–527
    oriented toward critical incidents, 418–424
    purchasing's role in, 371–372
    roles of, 10, *12*
    service quality management system, 164–174, 339–340
    strategic alliances for, 101–108
    see also strategic quality management; Total Quality Management (TQM)
quality-of-work-life (QWL), 90
quality planning
    see planning for quality

Ramada Hotels, 337
review as service quality principle, 73–74
    see also performance reviews
rewards
    see employee compensation; employee recognition

Scandinavian Airlines (SAS), 279–281
self-managed teams, 302–311
    benefits of, 302–303
    partnership process for, 303–309
    tips on coaching, 309–310

Semco Corporation, 263, 264
servant leadership, 84, *85-87*
service(s)
    defined, 332–333
    fail-safing, 347–357
    managing evidence of, 358–370
    marketing of, 17–19
service chain, 340–341
service concept, 342
    model of, 334–337
service construct, 333–341
service delivery
    customer satisfaction link to strategies of, 207
    systems redesign of, 215–217
service guarantees, 477–487
    added efficiencies from, 486–487
    customer expectations and, 478–479
    elements of, 482–486
    training employees and customers on, 479–482
service mapping, 148–163
    as evidence of service, 362–365, 367–368
    origins of, 149–155
    SkillsLink as, 156–162
    system design and, 148–149
ServiceMaster, 209, 210, 214
service profit chain, 205–218
    leverage points in, 208–217
    links in, 205–208
    middle management in, 217
service quality
    Baldrige Award and, 35–38
    customer feedback and, 202–203 (*see also* customer
        feedback)
    in customer service programs, 458–462
    defined, 332–333
    empowerment and, 259–260
    EQUIPE concept for, 139–143
    external, link to customer satisfaction, 207
    external, link to employee retention, 207
    internal, link to employee satisfaction, 208
    internal, model of (*see* internal service)
    manufacturing quality vs., 3, 4–9, 120–122, 125–127,
        261
    marketing and, 17, 19–22
    measurement of, 12–14, (*see also* Critical Incident
        Technique (CIT); customer satisfaction measure-
        ments; measurements of quality; performance
        measurement)
    myths about, 3–9
    personal aspects of, 294–301
    purchasing and, 371–378
    real-time interactions and, 14–15
    SERVQUAL factors, 155, 160
    six principles of, 69–76
    strategic aspects of (*see* strategic quality manage-
        ment)
service quality assessment
    conclusions on, 190–192
    customer expectations and, 180–182
    customer perceptions and, 183–185
    Gaps model of, 177–179
    new model of, 179–180
    new model vs. Gaps model, 185–186
    studies on, 186–190
    see also measurement of quality
service quality management system, 164–174
    design of, 339, *340*
    framework of, 167–172
    integration and implementation of, 172–173
    Total Quality Management applied to, 165–166

service recovery, 463–476
    changing corporate culture to foster, 471–475
    customer expectations and, 466–470
    financial impact of, 463–466
    six axioms of, 470–471
servicescape, 361–362, 367, 368
service systems
    feedback in, 150–153
    structure of, 153–155
SERVQUAL factors, 408
    service mapping and, 149, 155, 160
servuction (service and production), 337–341
    process, 340–341, 343
    system, 337–340, 343
Shingo, Shigeo, on fail-safing, 347–349
SkillsLink maps, 156–162
solution spaces, 473–474
Stew Leonard's, 195–204
strategic alliances for improved service, 95–108
    Baxter Corporate Program for, 95, 96–99
    concept and methodology of, 101–108
    Quality Leadership Process in, 99–101
strategic quality management, 8, *11*, 55–68
    Baldrige Award guidelines in, 57–58
    as consumer advocacy, 58
    coping with success in, 66–67
    customer service as, 65
    beyond efficiency in, 64–65
    employee motivation and, 67–68
    employee recognition and, 59–62, 64–65
    employee training and, 62–64
    information systems for, 62
    protecting core, 56
    responding to opportunity, 56–57
    suppliers and, 59 (*see also* supplier relationships)
success, coping with, 66–67
suggestion box, 196–197
Sunburst Farms, 447–457
supplier relationships, 8, *10*
    communication and, 75, 100–101
    customer alliances and, 100–103
    customer feedback and, 203
    purchasing function and, 371, 372, 375–377
    strategic management of, 59
surveys
    of customers, 428–429, 433–434
    of customer satisfaction, 397–400
    of employees, *115*, 116, 434–435
Swedish Telecom, 332, 334
syndicated auto studies, 391
system alignment, 286–287, 447–457
    Baldrige Award and, 31–32
    challenges in, 448
    changes in corporate culture and, 448–450
    customer expectation and, 440
    customer relations and, 452–453
    distribution chain and, 453–456
    for internal service, 81–82
    organizational assessment for, 450–452
    service recovery and, 474
systems thinking, 150

Taco Bell, 209, 210, 212, 213, 215–217
Tarkenton methods, 138–139
Taylor's scientific method, 137
team-building, 451
teams, service quality, 167, 170–172
    as implementation tool, 115–116, 121
    self-managed, 302–311
technical solutions for government administration
    problems, 508–509

tools, 287
  service profit chain and successful, 211–212
  teams as, 115–116, 121
top management
  commitment of, 173, 280, 292–293, 441
  corporate culture change and role of, 136, 144, 145, 147, 283, 448–449
  employee recognition from, 117
  leadership from, 70–71, 462 (*see also* leadership)
  quality education for, 281–283
Total Quality Management (TQM)
  corporate culture and, 111–112, 134, 136, 147
  in education, 46–47
  empowered employees and, 6–7, 259 (*see also* employee empowerment)
  era of, 392
  foundations of, 7, *8, 11*
  goals and results of, in both manufacturing and services, 4, *5,* 6
  infrastructure of, 7, *8, 10*
  as methodology for quality management in government, 499–500, 502–507, 511–513
  performance reviews and, 47–49
  principles of, 165–166

  processes of, 7–8, *9*
  strategic alliances with customers as form of, 99–101
training, *see* education and training for quality

Union of Japanese Scientists and Engineers (JUSE), 164
unions, *see* organized labor
United Services Automobile Association, 233–247
utility industries, 390–391

ValueLink, 106
values, of company
  creating/adding for improved service, 103–108
  front-line employees' representation of, 286
  tracking, 524–525
variation principle, 166
vision, 85, 168
voice of the business, 169
voice of the customer, 168, 177

Xerox Corporation
  benchmarking at, 92, 381, 385–387
  service quality program and labor relations at, 88–94

About the Editors

Dr. Eberhard E. Scheuing was born and educated in Stuttgart, Germany. Working for Deutsche Bank, he acquired a professional license as a commercial banker. In 1964, he received an M.B.A. degree in management from the University of Munich. He joined Eva Corsetfabrik in Stuttgart, rising to the rank of vice president, operations. In 1966, he earned a Ph.D. degree in marketing summa cum laude from the University of Munich. Having published his first article in 1963, he continued to contribute prolifically to a variety of business periodicals on a wide range of subjects. He also acted as a frequent speaker at executive seminars and as a consultant to business firms in several European countries.

Upon coming to the United States in 1967, Dr. Scheuing served as a consultant to the Marketing Science Institute before joining the faculty of St. John's University in New York, where he rose to the rank of professor of marketing. In 1981, he was named Director of Continuing Management Education. In 1990, he also assumed the duties of director of the Business Research Institute.

Since 1975, Dr. Scheuing has also been strongly involved in purchasing research and education. He is an academic member of the National Association of Purchasing Management (NAPM) in New York and of NAPM Seven Counties, as well as an honorary member and honorary board member of NAPM Long Island. He earned the designation Certified Purchasing Manager (C.P.M.) in 1982 and was recertified in 1987 and 1992. His book *Purchasing Management* was published by Prentice Hall in 1989. In the same year, NAPM New York honored him with its Outstanding Educator's Award, only the second such award in its 75-year history. He regularly conducts executive development programs in purchasing and quality management for professional associations and business firms, serves as a consultant, and gives presentations at national and international conferences. In 1991, he went on an invited two-week lecture tour to universities and companies in Finland, Sweden, and Norway.

To date, Dr. Scheuing's extensive publication record consists of nineteen books and more than five hundred articles. His most recent books include *Profitable Service Marketing* (Dow Jones-Irwin, 1986), *New*

Product Management (Merrill, 1989), and *Customer Service as Essential Corporate Strategy* (Planning Forum, 1991). Long interested in the management of service enterprises, Dr. Scheuing designed, moderated, and edited the prestigious ITT Key Issues Lecture Series on "The Service Economy." In 1990, he organized and chaired the Second International Conference on Quality in Services (QUIS 2). In 1991, he founded and was elected president of the International Service Quality Association (ISQA).

William F. Christopher is president of The Management Innovations Group. The Group is a consortium of consulting firms providing services in productivity and quality measurement and improvement; marketing and sales; new products and new ventures; cost management and profit improvement; information systems; and planning, budgeting, and control. Previously, he served in sales, marketing, executive, and consulting positions in General Electric, Hooker Chemical, and Occidental Chemical.

Mr. Christopher's work in productivity measurement and improvement began in the 1960s while he was corporate director of marketing for Hooker Chemical. Productivity improvement was part of the company strategy for competitive advantage. Measures were developed in plant operations and in staff departments, with action programs for improvement. Company mission/vision, goals, and measures, and staff department measures and improvement in manufacturing, engineering, R&D, sales, marketing, and new product commercialization were all part of this strategy. Work in productivity/quality measurement and improvement continued in his corporate assignments, and in recent years in his work with clients. Mr. Christopher has now developed and worked with these methods with more than a hundred businesses in seventeen countries.

He is the author of three books. His book *The Achieving Enterprise* won the James A. Hamilton Book Award for the best book of the year on business management. His second book on business management, *Management for the 1980s*, was published in both hard cover and soft cover editions. Both books describe concepts and methods for improving performance in key areas of business operations; among these the key performance area of productivity measurement and improvement. Many Total Quality concepts and methods were described in these books.

Mr. Christopher has edited the Productivity Press *Productivity Measurement Handbook* since 1980 and is now co-editor with Carl G. Thor of the all-new *Handbook for Productivity Measurement and Improvement*. His education includes a B.A. from DePauw University, an M.S. from Columbia University, and five years in the U.S. Army Air Force.

About the Contributors

Karl Albrecht is a management consultant, seminar presenter, speaker, and author. He has worked with many different kinds of organizations, large and small. Dr. Albrecht concentrates almost exclusively on pioneering new concepts that show promise for increasing individual or organizational effectiveness. He is also actively working in the area of Service Management, a concept which deals with the management of companies in service industries. He is the author of many books, including *Stress & the Manager*, *The Service Advantage*, and *Service America!* His company, Karl Albrecht & Associates, is located in San Diego, California.

Paul A. Allaire is chairman of the board of directors, chief executive officer and chairman of the executive committee of Xerox Corporation, Stamford, Connecticut. He has served as director of financial planning and control, chief staff officer and executive director, and managing director at Rank Xerox in London, England. He later served as corporate senior vice president and chief staff officer; and president and chief executive officer at Xerox headquarters in Stamford. Mr. Allaire has a B.S. in electrical engineering from Worcester Polytechnic Institute and an M.S. in industrial administration from Carnegie-Mellon. He lives with his wife and two children in Fairfield County, Connecticut.

Paula Anderson-Findley is the manager of training and development for Sunburst Farms, Inc. She has played an instrumental role in the company's strategic initiatives in quality improvement process and customer service. She has conducted training workshops for clients and conference seminars in sales and customer service. Prior to joining Sunburst, Ms. Anderson-Findley was the marketing development officer for ERM-South, Inc., in Florida. She earned her B.B.A. and M.B.A. in organizational design and development from the University of Miami.

David D. Auld is the vice president of the Quality Leadership Process Group for Baxter Healthcare Corporation, headquartered in Deerfield, Illinois. He also served as director of program management and director of technical operations in Baxter's R&D operations. Mr. Auld has been responsible for founding the Quality Leadership Process and directing its development. He graduated with an engineering degree from the U.S. Naval Academy and was commissioned in the U.S. Marine Corps. Mr. Auld received an M.B.A. from Eastern Michigan University.

Don Bedwell, the editor of American Airlines' employee newspaper *Flagship News*, joined American after a long career in journalism. Mr. Bedwell was with the Miami Herald for 15 years, many as aviation editor and columnist, covering Miami's aviation and tourism industry. After moving to North Carolina, he covered business news for the Charlotte Observer, a newspaper in the Knight-Ridder organization. Through the years Mr. Bedwell has also contributed to other national and international publications, including *American Way* inflight magazine, *USA Weekend, Touring America,* and *Vista USA.* He did his graduate study at the University of Missouri School of Journalism.

Mary Jo Bitner, Ph.D., is associate professor of marketing at Arizona State University. Dr. Bitner has taught courses in service marketing at both the undergraduate and M.B.A. level and has served as program director of the annual Services Marketing Institute. Her research on customer evaluation of service encounters has appeared in the *Journal of Marketing, Journal of Retailing,* and *Cornell Hotel and Restaurant Quarterly.* She received her Ph.D. in marketing from the University of Washington in Seattle.

William Boulding, Ph.D., is associate professor of business administration at The Fuqua School of Business at Duke University. He has also been involved in either sponsored research or consulting with a number of companies, including IBM, AT&T, Bank of America, Sears, and Leo Burnett. His general research interest is in the area of competitive marketing strategy, particularly how managers and consumers "think" about quality. Dr. Boulding received his B.A. in economics from Swarthmore College and his Ph.D. in marketing from the Wharton School, University of Pennsylvania.

Kateri T. Brunell is a consultant with Qualtec Quality Services, Inc., an FPL Group company that specializes in TQM training and consulting. In addition, Ms. Brunell is a faculty member of the Qualtec Institute for Competitive Advantage. Before joining QQS, she was a director at a consulting firm that provided marketing planning and research services to numerous service industry clients. Ms. Brunell holds a B.A. in mass communications from the University of South Florida and an M.B.A. from Florida Atlantic University. She is the author of *Seven New QC Tools,* a course manual.

Douglas P. Brusa is purchasing supervisor of the Lamont-Doherty Geological Observatory of Columbia University and a Certified Purchasing Manager. Prior to joining Columbia, he worked for group-purchasing organizations serving healthcare and educational institutions and for the National Park Service. He has written articles on purchasing for *The NonProfit Times* and for the *Bulletin of the National Association of Educational*

Buyers. Mr. Brusa holds a B.S. from Adelphi University and an M.P.A. from Columbia's School of International and Public Affairs.

Nancy J. Burzon is the director of quality education at GTE Corporation. She is responsible for the corporate-wide direction of GTE's total quality education activity for management employees as well as for assuming a leadership and direction-setting role for quality throughout GTE. Previously, she was manager-strategic plan development for GTE Telephone Operations in Stamford, Connecticut. Ms. Burzon graduated from the University of Tennesee with a B.A. in psychology and has completed graduate courses in marketing at Butler University in Indianapolis, Indiana.

Robert C. Camp, Ph.D., is manager, benchmarking competency, Quality Office for Xerox Corporation's U.S. Marketing Group (USMG). He has held various managerial positions with Xerox, including manager, planning, logistics and distribution department; manager, business planning, USMG; and manager, business analysis, Xerox Business Services. Dr. Camp is the author of *Benchmarking: The Search for Industry Best Practices That Lead to Superior Performance*. He has a bachelor's degree in civil engineering from Cornell University and an M.B.A. from Cornell University's Johnson School of Management. He earned a Ph.D. from Pennsylvania State University. Dr. Camp lives in Brighton, N.Y. with his wife.

Richard B. Chase, Ph.D., is the director of the Center for Operations Management Education and Research at the School of Business Administration at the University of Southern California and also the Justin B. Dart Term Professor of Operations Management. He has taught at the Harvard Business School, IMD, and the University of Arizona. His research examines service strategy, service quality, and value added service in manufacturing. He has published articles on service systems in such journals as *Harvard Business Review, Management Science, Decision Sciences,* and *Operations Research*. Dr. Chase received his Ph.D., M.B.A. and B.S. from UCLA.

Beth Chung received her B.A. from the University of California, Berkeley, and is presently a Ph.D. candidate in industrial/organizational psychology at the University of Maryland, College Park. Her research includes work on entry-level and international selection, promotion tests, assessment centers, work-family issues, and employee commitment. Her masters thesis deals with the effects of service orientation discrepancy on role stress, job satisfaction and employee outcomes.

Betty A. Conway is a field director in the Quality Leadership Process Group for Baxter Healthcare Corporation. She joined Baxter as a quality control laboratory supervisor and has assumed managerial positions in the areas of quality control, regulatory compliance, product complaint handling, manufacturing operations, and production scheduling and inventory control. Ms. Conway holds a B.S. in medical technology from Eastern Michigan University, an M.S. in microbiology and public health from Michigan State University, and an M.B.A. from Lake Forest School of Management.

M. Ignatius Cronin III is owner of his own public relations and marketing communications firm, Naçio Cronin, Inc. in Tokyo, and specializes in the hotel, travel, and restaurant industries. Previously, he worked for an American public relations firm in Tokyo, where he organized trade shows for the United States Department of Commerce and the Department of Agriculture. He studied at the University of Hawaii, Sophia University in Tokyo, and the International Christian University in Tokyo, where he received the equivalent of a B.A. in Japanese studies.

Lawrence A. Crosby, Ph.D., is the president and managing director of CSM Worldwide, an international network of research and consulting companies. Dr. Crosby is also professor of marketing in the College of Business at Arizona State University (ASU) where he teaches courses on marketing management and marketing research. Previously he was the research director of the First Interstate Center for Services Marketing at ASU, served on the faculty of the University of Nebraska, and was a senior project director for Nordhaus Associates, a marketing research and consulting company. Dr. Crosby received all of his degrees from the University of Michigan and works out of Phoenix, Arizona.

Roger J. Dow is vice president and general sales manager for Marriott Hotels, Resorts, and Suites. During his 20 years with Marriott, he has directed every aspect of sales and marketing, including advertising, public relations, promotion, sales training, compensation, and succession planning. Mr. Dow has worked with the Tom Peters Group as an executive consultant. He holds a B.S. in psychology from Seton Hall University. He resides in Bethesda, Maryland with his wife and two children.

Dale C. Durkee is a consultant for quality and training working with Southern Pacific Transportation Company in San Francisco. He is assisting in training needs identification and development of training delivery systems. Mr. Durkee assisted in the Ernst & Young–directed quality process implementation at Blue Cross and Blue Shield of Ohio. He was manager, organization development and training at Florida Power and Light Company. Mr. Durkee earned a B.B.A. in business management from Baldwin-Wallace College and an M.B.A. in banking and finance from Case-Western Reserve University.

Bo Edvardsson, Ph.D., is associate professor of business administration and director of the Service Research Center (CTF) at the University of Karlstad, Sweden. He is also involved with management consulting in leading Swedish service companies and in executive development programs. Dr. Edvardsson has held various administrative positions, such as the chairmanship of the department of business studies. He is the author or co-author of six books, most recently co-authoring with Bertil Thomasson a book in Swedish, *Quality Improvement: A Management Perspective*. He graduated from Uppsala University in business studies and obtained his doctorate from the same university.

Michael T. Fraga is vice president of quality services at Florida Power & Light Company. He helped develop the implementation plan for quality improvement and participated in the Deming Prize preparation and examination. Mr. Fraga began his career at FPL in a local district office where he learned the business office operations. He served as division manager of governmental services, division manager of the Hollywood district office, division commercial manager, and district general manager for Ft. Lauderdale. Mr. Fraga served in the United States Air Force and graduated from the University of Miami with an M.B.A.

Joan E. Gebhardt is a partner in the firm Townsend & Gebhardt—Advisors on Quality. She collaborated with Patrick Townsend on *Commit to Quality* and co-authored *Quality in Action: 93 Lessons in Leadership, Participation, and Measurement*. She honed her opinions on quality in a number of settings, including elementary school teaching, public relations, electric motor sales, administrative assistant, dorm mother, and professional entertainer.

A. Blanton Godfrey, Ph.D., is chairman and chief executive officer of Juran Institute, Inc., which is respected worldwide for its leadership in managing for quality. Prior to joining Juran Institute, Dr. Godfrey headed the quality theory and technology department at AT&T Bell Laboratories. He is a co-author of *Modern Methods for Quality Control and Improvement* (Wiley, 1986) and a co-author of *Curing Health Care: New Strategies for Quality Improvement* (Jossey-Bass, 1990). Dr. Godfrey holds an M.S. and a Ph.D. in statistics from Florida State University, and a B.S. in physics from Virginia Tech.

Christian Grönroos, Ph.D., a past visiting professor at Arizona State University and a research fellow of First Interstate Center for Services Marketing, is currently professor of international marketing at the Swedish School of Economics and Business Administration in Helsinki, Finland. He is chairman of the marketing department and of the Management Education Center of the school. He has written numerous articles and written or co-authored eight books, including *Service Management and Marketing: Managing the Moments of Truth in Service Competition* (Free Press, 1990).

Abraham Gutman is Sunburst Farm's chief information officer. Previously, Mr. Gutman was director of knowledge engineering for Inference Corporation in Los Angeles. Among his most notable achievements were the creation of the Ford Motor Company Center of Excellence in Dearborn, Michigan, and the development of a technology transfer team assigned to the information systems group managing the operational requirements of the office of the Secretary of Defense and the Air Staff at the Pentagon. Mr. Gutman holds a bachelor's degree in computer science from Cornell University and a master's degree in computer science from Yale University.

Roger H. Hallowell is research associate to the Service Management Interest Group at Harvard Business School. He has served as both an operating manager and a consultant for service organizations. He has written case studies and teaching notes based on research performed at service organizations. Mr. Hallowell has an A.B. from Harvard College and an M.B.A. from Harvard Business School.

Christopher W. L. Hart, Ph.D., is president of the TQM Group, Ltd., a consulting firm specializing in Total Quality Management. He has served as an examiner for the Malcolm Baldrige National Quality Awards and as an assistant professor at the Harvard Business School, where he taught operations management and service management. One of his most recent books is *The Baldrige: What It Is, How It's Won, How to Use It to Improve Quality in Your Company*. Dr. Hart received his bachelor's degree from Cornell University, his M.B.A. from Harvard, and his Ph.D. from Cornell.

B. Terence Harwick, Ph.D., is the director of the Total Quality Performance Research Institute and is currently serving as visiting professor and advisor at the National School of Public Administration in Warsaw, Poland. He has served as a visiting scholar at the University of California at Berkeley and a scholar-in-residence at the University of Virginia's Center for Public Service. Dr. Harwick was an international business manager and served in advisory capacities for business and governments in the United States, Latin America, and Europe. He graduated from the University of California at Berkeley and completed his graduate studies at the University of Southern California.

William Hensler is vice president of quality services for Qualtec Quality Services, Inc., an FPL Group company. During his 17-year career with Florida Power & Light, Mr. Hensler held various positions, including director of quality improvement at the time FPL was awarded the Deming Prize. He participated in the pilot program to institute quality improvement teams in the company. He implemented TQM as the management system for the Martin Power Plant. Mr. Hensler holds a bachelor of science degree in mechanical engineering from the University of Illinois.

Paul G. Kahn is president and chief executive officer of AT&T Universal Card Services Corp. He led the effort to bring the AT&T Universal Card to the marketplace. He is also a member of the board of directors of the U.S. region of MasterCard International. Before joining

AT&T, Mr. Kahn spent 10 years in executive positions with Wells Fargo Bank, First National Bank of Chicago, and Mellon Bank. He holds a B.B.A. from Antioch College. Mr. Kahn and his wife, Cathleen, live in Jacksonville, Florida, with their three children.

Edward J. Kane is vice president, quality and management systems for Dun & Bradstreet Software Services. Formerly, Mr. Kane worked for the IBM Corporation. He joined IBM as a marketing representative and held several sales and marketing management positions. Later he became corporate director of marketing planning, DPD director of industry relations, director of market development strategy, and the director of quality. Mr. Kane is a graduate of the University of Connecticut and served as an officer in the U.S. Navy. He and his wife live in Waccabuc, New York.

John E. Kelsch is director, quality of Xerox Corporation. He has been a member of the corporate quality office involved in the initiation, development, and implementation of a corporate-wide Total Quality Control Strategy. Mr. Kelsch has held various financial positions with Xerox, including chief financial officer of the Latin American Group, controller of Xerox Data Systems, and manager of corporate accounting. He also worked with the Mayor's Office of Operations in New York City to develop a productivity program with various municipal agencies. He graduated from the University of Notre Dame with a B.S.C. in accounting.

Jane Kingman-Brundage is president and founder of Kingman-Brundage, Inc. She incorporated the firm in 1978 and in 1982 pioneered the practice of service mapping, the blueprinting technique that is the cornerstone of Strategic Service System Analysis. She introduced her ImpleMentor Service Mapping Workshop at the International Quality & Service Forum held at EuroDisney outside Paris, France. Jane Brundage holds M.A.'s from Columbia University in personnel psychology and from The New School for Social Research in sociology.

Stephen G. Leahey established and is president of the Canadian Quality Management Centre (CQMC). He does research with the University of Montreal, teaches at McGill University, and has held senior postings in Toronto and Montreal, where he started and headed the economics, quality, and strategic planning departments of Canada's largest private corporation. Mr. Leahey graduated with an M.B.A. (honours finance) from Queens University in 1966 and is also a professional engineer, graduating from the Technical University of Nova Scotia in 1964.

Stew Leonard, Jr., is president of Stew Leonard's, the world's largest dairy store. The store was started in 1923 by Mr. Leonard's grandfather as a home delivery milk business. Today Stew Leonard's has annual sales in excess of $100 million at its original location in Norwalk, Connecticut.

Mr. Leonard grew up in the family business. He started at his father's side and has worked in every job. This includes cleaning milk cans, stocking shelves, managing the store, and even filling in for the costumed character Wow the Cow. Mr. Leonard received an M.B.A. from UCLA in 1982.

George L. Mueller is vice president-customer services for American Airlines. He is responsible for American's worldwide inflight product from flight services, duty free sales, inflight entertainment, and aircraft interior design to food and beverage services. He previously held a number of management positions at American, including manager-ramp services in Chicago, manager-services at JFK Airport in New York, senior director-freight sales and advertising, senior director-new product development, assistant vice president and general sales manager, and vice president-passenger sales. Mr. Mueller graduated from Northwestern University with a B.S. in marketing.

Joel Parfitt is a quality analyst on the staff of the Commissioner of the IRS. His work focuses primarily on quality measurements, customer value tracking, customer satisfaction surveys, cost of poor quality analysis, and benchmarking. Previously, Mr. Parfitt was a quality coordinator in an IRS district office. His experience also includes several years as a training manager in IRS field offices. Mr. Parfitt graduated from St. Francis College and has done graduate work at George Washington University and Central Michigan University.

Curt W. Reimann, Ph.D., is director of the Malcolm Baldrige National Quality Award and director for quality programs at the National Institute of Standards and Technology (NIST). Dr. Reimann has served as deputy director of the National Measurement Laboratory and as director of the NIST Center for Analytical Chemistry. He received his B.A. in chemistry from Drew University and a Ph.D. from the University of Michigan.

Robert S. Rider is division vice president and business manager for Lighting Products of Corning Incorporated. He joined the company in a product engineering capacity and served in various production and engineering positions in four different manufacturing locations. He has served as sales manager-automotive, lighting products sales and marketing manager, sales manager and business manager in electrical products, and quality manager. Mr. Rider was also a member of Corning's Corporate Quality Council. He has a B.S. in mechanical engineering and a B.A. in mathematics from Bucknell University. He received his M.B.A. from Syracuse University.

Antonio T. Rivera is vice-president, personnel operations, at USAA. He also served the company as director of human resources support and assistant vice-president, personnel operations. Prior to coming to USAA, he held numerous personnel positions with the Department of the Air

Force. Tony serves on the Society for Human Resource Management's National Committee for Human Resource Information Systems and its Education Task Force. Mr. Rivera received a B.A. from the University of Arizona in Latin American Studies.

Norma M. Rossi is a senior program consultant on the corporate quality staff of the Metropolitan Life Insurance Company. Ms. Rossi served as an examiner for the Federal Quality Institute for both the prototype Quality Award and the Presidential Quality Award. In 1992, she was appointed to the board of examiners for the Malcolm Baldrige National Quality Award. She has co-authored a book on service quality with Mary Lo Sardo titled *On the Service Quality Frontier*. Ms. Rossi holds a B.A. from the City College of New York and an M.A. in human resource planning and development from the New School for Social Research.

Marty Russell is the director of the Total Quality Performance Consortium and a consultant for Los Angeles County. She specializes in consulting for the service industry and governmental institutions. Ms. Russell has worked in the service industry as an internal and external consultant in quality improvement initiatives. She also served as convener of meetings that over a two-year period formulated the criteria for the Malcolm Baldrige National Quality Award. She graduated with a degree in human resources management from the University of Texas at Houston.

Lawrence Schein, Ph.D., is program director, quality research, of The Conference Board. Prior to joining The Conference Board in 1982, Dr. Schein was research group manager at Audits & Surveys, a national marketing research firm. Previously, he has held the posts of assistant research professor at the University of Pennsylvania School of Medicine and chief of evaluation and survey research at the West Philadelphia Community Mental Health Consortium. He serves as staff representative to the Board's U.S. Quality Council and is currently involved in developing a center for total quality management.

Leonard A. Schlesinger, Ph.D., is professor of business administration and Berol Foundation Faculty Research Fellow at the Harvard Business School, where his teaching and research focus on the management of service organizations. Previously, he served as executive vice president and chief operating officer of Au Bon Pain Co. Working with James L. Heskett and W. Earl Sasser he has recently completed a videotape series called *Achieving Breakthrough Service* for Harvard Business School Publishing Division. Professor Schlesinger holds an M.B.A. in corporate and labor relations from Columbia University and a doctorate in organizational behavior from Harvard University.

Benjamin Schneider, Ph.D., is currently professor of psychology and of business management at the University of Maryland, College

Park. Dr. Schneider's academic experience includes a position at Yale University, a Fulbright to Israel, and a chaired professorship at Michigan State University. He has published more than 70 articles and book chapters as well as five books. Dr. Schneider has a B.A. from Alfred University and an M.B.A. from the University of the City of New York (Baruch School). He received his Ph.D. in industrial and social psychology from the University of Maryland, College Park.

Richard Staelin, Ph.D., is the Edward and Rose Donnell Professor of business administration at the Fuqua School of Business at Duke University. He served as associate dean for faculty affairs at the Fuqua School and then accepted an appointment as executive director of the Marketing Science Institute in Cambridge, Mass. Dr. Staelin has published over 50 articles in reference journals and co-authored a book entitled *Consumer Protection Legislation and the U.S. Food Industry*. He holds two bachelor degrees in engineering and mathematics, an M.B.A. and a Ph.D. from the University of Michigan.

Bernd Stauss, Ph.D., is head of the Chair of Business Administration and Marketing at the Catholic University of Eichstätt, faculty of business administration, in Ingolstadt, Germany. He has served as visiting professor at the marketing department of the University of Innsbruck, Austria, and as a research assistant for the marketing department of the University of Hannover, Germany. Dr. Stauss has written a number of books and articles, including "Attribute-Based versus Incident-Based Measurement of Service Quality" in *Quality Management and Services* with B. Hentschel. He received his degrees from the University of Hamburg, Germany, and the University of Hannover, Germany.

W. Kent Sterett is executive vice president, quality, at Southern Pacific Transportation Company in San Francisco. He created Southern Pacific's quality improvement program. Mr. Sterett was assistant vice president, quality, with Union Pacific and director of the quality improvement department with Florida Power and Light. He has served as a judge for the Malcolm Baldrige National Quality Award. Mr. Sterett is a registered professional engineer and has a B.S. in mechanical engineering from the University of Missouri. He holds an M.B.A. from Florida International University.

Douglas M. Stewart is a doctoral student at the School of Business Administration at the University of Southern California. His research interests are in the areas of service quality and Total Quality Management. Mr. Stewart received a B.S. in engineering and an M.S. in management with the technical option of quality management from North Carolina State University.

Alfred C. Sylvain is vice president of quality management and staff services for the Pension Operations Sector of Mutual of New York (MONY) and is responsible for quality management, human resources, corporate relations, accounting, and staff services for MONY's Westchester Operations Center. Previously, Mr. Sylvain was assistant vice president of MONY's investment services division and assistant vice president of quality management/staff operations. He also worked for Citibank in a variety of positions. Mr. Sylvain has a bachelor's degree in economics from Hofstra University.

Patrick L. Townsend is president of Townsend & Gebhardt—Advisors on Quality. He is a noted speaker and consultant on quality. Mr. Townsend directed and coordinated the employee participation quality process at the Paul Revere Insurance Group. He is the author of *Commit to Quality* and co-author (with Joan Gebhardt) of *Quality in Action: 93 Lessons in Leadership, Participation, and Measurement.* He received a B.S. in mathematics from Marquette University and an M.S. in computer science from the U.S. Naval Postgraduate School.

Kathryn Troy is a senior research associate in the quality and productivity program of The Conference Board. She is also responsible for the Board's corporate communications research and is staff representative to its Council of Corporate Communications Executives. Prior to joining the Board, Ms. Troy was employed for 13 years as a business planner and research manager at major divisions of Time and CBS. She is the author of 17 Conference Board Reports, including *Recognizing Quality Achievement: Noncash Award Programs; Employee Buy-In to Total Quality;* and *Quality Training: What Top Companies Have Learned.*

M. Ven Venkatesan, Ph.D., is professor of marketing at the College of Business Administration at the University of Rhode Island. He was chairman of the department of marketing at the University of Rhode Island. Previously, he was the David L. Rike Professor of Marketing at Wright State University. He has also been associated with the University of Massachusetts, the University of Iowa, and the University of Oregon. Professor Venkatesan obtained his Ph.D. in business administration and his M.S. in industrial administration from the University of Minnesota.

D. Otis Wolkins is vice president—quality services/marketing administration of GTE Corporation. Previously, he served as vice president/quality services. Mr. Wolkins also served as president of GTE Microcircuits, held various positions in engineering and manufacturing with Motorola, and was vice president and general manager of the semiconductor division of General Instrument Corporation. Mr. Wolkins received a bachelor's degree in physics from Greenville College in Greenville, Illinois, and did graduate studies at Arizona State University.

Abe J. Wynperle is president of Sunburst Farms, Inc., in Miami, Florida. Sunburst Farms is the leading importer of fresh-cut flowers, distributing to wholesalers in the United States and Canada. Sunpetals, Inc., a wholly owned subsidiary, is a floral bouquet manufacturing company. Prior to joining Sunburst Farms, Mr. Wynperle was managing director of Sunburst Farms Holland B.V. He is a graduate of the Netherlands School of Business (Nyenrode). He obtained a B.B.A. from Temple University and an M.B.A. from the University of Washington.

Ron Zemke is president of Performance Research Associates Inc. Mr. Zemke founded the company to conduct organizational effectiveness and productivity improvement studies for business and industry. His clients have included Citibank, Wells Fargo Bank, GTE-MTO, 3M Company, Ford Motor Co., and Air Canada. He is also the senior editor of *Training* magazine and editor of *The Service Edge*. He is the author or co-author of eleven books, including *Delivering Knock Your Socks Off Service* (with Kristin Anderson) and *The Service Edge: 101 Companies That Profit From Customer Care* (with Dick Schaaf).